Monty Python's Flying Circus

Monty Python's Flying Circus

An Utterly Complete, Thoroughly Unillustrated, Absolutely Unauthorized Guide to Possibly All the References

From Arthur "Two Sheds" Jackson to Zambesi

Volume 2
Episodes 27–45

Darl Larsen

TAYLOR TRADE PUBLISHING
Lanham • New York • Boulder • Toronto • Plymouth, UK

Published by Taylor Trade Publishing
An imprint of The Rowman & Littlefield Publishing Group, Inc.
4501 Forbes Boulevard, Suite 200, Lanham, Maryland 20706
www.rowman.com

10 Thornbury Road, Plymouth PL6 7PP, United Kingdom

Distributed by National Book Network

Copyright © 2008 by Darl Larsen
First Taylor Trade Edition 2013

British Library Cataloguing in Publication Information Available

Library of Congress Cataloging-in-Publication Data

Larsen, Darl, 1963–
    Monty Python's flying circus : an utterly complete, thoroughly unillustrated, absolutely unauthorized guide to possibly all the references from Arthur "Two Sheds" Jackson to Zambesi / Darl Larsen. — First Taylor trade edition.
        volumes cm
    Includes bibliographical references and index.
    ISBN 978-1-58979-712-3 (pbk. : alk. paper)
    1. Monty Python's flying circus (Television program)—Dictionaries. I. Title.
    PN1992.77.M583L37 2013
    791.45'72—dc23
                                                                2012050135

♾™ The paper used in this publication meets the minimum requirements of American National Standard for Information Sciences—Permanence of Paper for Printed Library Materials, ANSI/NISO Z39.48-1992.

Printed in the United States of America

For Nycole, Keir, Emrys, Brynmor,
Eamonn, Dathyl, Ransom, and Culainn,

and

WPW

Contents

Acknowledgments   ix

Introduction or "Notes on a Dead Parrot"   xi

SEASON THREE

Episode 27: *"Whicker's World"*   3

Episode 28: "Trim-Jeans Theatre"   20

Episode 29: *"The Money Programme"*   40

Episode 30: *"Blood, Devastation, Death, War and Horror"*   50

Episode 31: "The All-England *Summarize Proust Competition*"   61

Episode 32: "Expedition to Lake Pahoe"   77

Episode 33: *"Salad Days"*   91

Episode 34: "The Cycling Tour"   101

Episode 35: "The Olympic Hide-and-Seek Final"   110

Episode 36: *"The Life of Sir Phillip Sidney"*   121

Episode 37: "Dennis Moore"   130

Episode 38: "BBC Programme Planners"   140

Episode 39: "Grandstand"   150

SEASON FOUR

Episode 40: "The Golden Age of Ballooning"   161

Episode 41: "Michael Ellis"   170

Episode 42: "Light Entertainment War"   177

Episode 43: "Hamlet"   187

Episode 44: "Mr. Neutron"   195

Episode 45: "Party Political Broadcast"   202

Appendix A: Stock Film Clips and Still Images   211

Appendix B: Recorded and Live Music Cues   215

Appendix C: Sketch, Animation, and Link Listing   221

Bibliography   231

Index   241

About the Author   293

Acknowledgments

Dr. William P. Williams, University of Akron, continues to be a tireless supporter since our days together at Northern Illinois University, and I thank him again and again for his assistance and friendship.

Thanks are also extended to these Brigham Young University entities: the Center for the Study of Western Europe, the Kennedy Center for International Studies, the College of Fine Arts and Communications, and the Theatre & Media Arts Department—providing generous research and travel grants, research sabbaticals and assistants, and wholehearted support for the completion of this project. The wonderful Harold B. Lee Library offered access to databases; their Interlibrary Loan department found every book or recording I requested, no matter how obscure; and this library thankfully maintains a collection that made research for this edition achievable.

The good folks at the BBC's Written Archives Collection in Caversham Park were both gracious and helpful, allowing unfettered access to production files for the *Flying Circus* episodes for the original edition of this work, upon which this edition builds. My own research assistants included Emma Hoskisson, Jason Hagey, Chelsea Gibbs, and Brett Stifflemire; this edition simply could not have been accomplished without their hard work.

Fellow BYU professor Daryl Lee contributed translations to unpack the Pythons' Jabberwock French. I'd also like to thank my colleagues here in the BYU Theatre & Media Arts department who acted as supporters from the first edition to this project, including Amy Jensen, Tom Lefler, Rodger Sorensen, Kelly Loosli, Sharon Swenson, Dean Duncan, Tom and Courtney Russell, Jeff Parkin, Eric Samuelsen, Brad Barber, and Megan Sanborn Jones. Thanks also to Mark Ellsworth, as well as Tomasz Dobrogoszcz, Miguel Angel Gonzalez Campos, Kevin Kern, and all the faculty and student participants at the 2010 Monty Python Conference at the University of Łódź, Poland; their combined support pushed this book to completion. And a special thanks to Randy Malamud, whose collegiality and friendship I treasure.

Also, warm thanks to my parents Norbert and Patricia Larsen, and editors Stephen Ryan at Scarecrow Press and Rick Rinehart at Taylor Trade.

And lastly, a thanks to my family including my wife, Nycole, and our wonderful children—Keir (and Misti), Emrys, Brynmor, Eamonn, Dathyl, Ransom, and Culainn. They gave me all the time and support I needed, and I'm grateful.

Introduction or
"Notes on a Dead Parrot"

The above was a subtitle for a lecture I was asked to give ostensibly to try and explain my area of scholarship to a roomful of English majors and professors. The title more completely read "Notes on a Dead Parrot: Monty Python and/as Scholarship." (The lecture went pretty well—I showed clips.) It seems incongruous from the start—Monty Python and scholarship. Also, the "and/as" isn't an academic handstand but an acknowledgment of the necessary but slippery relationship between the terms. Monty Python isn't Shakespeare or Milton, it's not occasional poetry or courtly revels, and it isn't your standard, sober subject matter for academic study. After all, the Pythons imprecate and deflate all manner of stuffed-shirt-types in their work, from Cambridge dons to monarchs and popes to bowlered representatives of "The City." In one of their feature films they even kill a "Very Famous Historian" as he attempts to apply historical, narrative order to the medieval farrago of uppity peasants and foul-tempered rabbits.

But in the process of determining a thesis subject with the eminent Dr. William Proctor Williams at Northern Illinois University, we were led to another acknowledgment—that the Pythons owe an atavistic debt to the "University Wits" and to Shakespeare of the English Renaissance stage. This led to a successful dissertation in 2000 and then a book, *Monty Python, Shakespeare and English Renaissance Drama* (2003). The challenges encountered when I studied the sixteenth-through eighteenth-century English works of the stage and page (Spenser, Skelton, Dekker, Dryden, et al.) prompted another book project, this one a unique annotation. *Monty Python's Flying Circus: An Utterly Complete, Thoroughly Unillustrated, Absolutely Unauthorized Guide to Possibly All the References from Arthur "Two Sheds" Jackson to Zambesi* (2008) was meant to first dissect the layers and clusters of references and

meanings, and then lay bare the interconnectedness between the Pythons' comedy and the world of history, culture, and literature. That hardcover edition serves as the foundation and jumping-off point for this new work.

And so this project continues to be of two minds, at least. One goal was to perform a simple identification of names, faces, places, musical cues, uncredited actors, slang terms, colloquial expressions, etc., with the hope being that the interested reader and viewer could better appreciate the fractured, polyglot, multilevel nature of the Pythonesque world. More significantly, though, are the deeper dives into that created world, where mini-essays provide explications that surface glossings can't fathom. It was this second thread that wove itself throughout not only the late 1960s and 1970s London, but back through the tapestry of English history and mythology, into Number 10 Downing Street and Westminster and Her Majesty's courts system, into the living rooms and ducks-on-the-wall kitchens of Hull and Bristol, across the green belts of Bucks and Berks and the beaches of Oban and Paignton, and onto the brightly lit stages of recent British television history.

It then becomes possible to go deep *and* far, making connections between the world of the 1960s and classical or existentialist philosophy, for example, and consistently identifying allusions, intertextualities, references, classical and modern parodies and imitations, etc. In this way I will satisfy the demands of myriad reader/viewers, demonstrating the cultural significance of these constructions that become Monty Python's social history.

And now the nuts and bolts. This new project is divided into two volumes—episodes 1–26 and 27–45, respectively, meaning Seasons 1 and 2, then Seasons 3 and 4. The glossings for the episodes in both volumes are provided alphabetically in an encyclopedic format. A reader or viewer interested in finding a particular reference (e.g., "Crunchy Frog" or "Scott of the Sahara") can access the index, of course, but can also turn directly to the particular episode and look up the term, spoken phrase, or name in its alphabetic order. Each episode is also headed with a thumbnail list of every significant scene, animation, and link (transition), all in the order they appear in that particular episode. A quick scan of the thumbnail listing at the beginning of Episode 15 will confirm that both "The Spanish Inquisition" and "The Semaphore Version of *Wuthering Heights*" are indeed part of that second season episode. This will help the viewer as well as the reader, of course. A reader wondering where the "Icelandic Honey Week" sketch is found in Episode 45 can quickly see that it's sandwiched between "The Most Awful Family in Britain" and the opening titles. If you know the sketch but not its episode, the same sketch title (or animation or link) can also be looked up directly in the new "Sketch, Animation, and Link Listing." This list identifies in alphabetical order every different or new section, large and small, in the broadcast episodes, down to the knight-and-chicken links and animated tidbits. The multiple appendices for this edition are made to be as focused and helpful as possible, and include complete listings, by episode, of all stock film and music sources included in the archived records. The index is meant to be as comprehensive as possible. *All* the names, places, dates, and references cited by the Pythons, visible in the images or mentioned in the printed script are indexed. Also, the inferences and references produced by textual analyses are indexed and cross-referenced to other Python work, and to history, literature, and culture. It's a giant, marvelous index. Entries are also cross-referenced to other episodes wherever necessary. Quotations from characters are cited using quotation marks, while stage directions, scene descriptions, and many titles are indicated by the use of italics.

Factual, production information culled from the BBC's Written Archives Collection is cited by folder number (e.g., T12/1,084). Neither the printed *Flying Circus* scripts nor the taped episodes comprise a *locus classicus* for our purposes—both are referenced as needed. Finally, the abbreviation "PSC" (Printed Script Commentary) at the beginning of an annotation means the word or phrase being referenced comes directly from the printed script itself and would not be available to the viewer, just the reader. These strange, "in-house joke" phenomena will be discussed in several annotations.

This new edition has an awful lot of "new" about it. From the day I submitted the first edition in late 2007, I've thought about all the things I should have

included, of course, and this new edition couldn't come fast enough. The identification and analysis of the many animated sequences was a major goal for this new work. The printed versions of the *Flying Circus* scripts generally avoid describing the animated sequences at all—the cartoons tend to be fluid, full of unattributed and undocumented material, and are a stream-of-consciousness labyrinth. Animator Terry Gilliam borrowed characters and backgrounds from newspapers, magazines, period catalogs, and advertisements as well as art, architecture, and history books; he used Edwardian-era photos and postcards; he shot or borrowed London-area photographs, which he then colored and manipulated to create worlds that did not exist. Dozens of these images and references have been identified and discussed in this edition, and many aren't as random as they may first appear. There are also many new cross-references from the *Flying Circus* episodes to other works the Pythons completed during this period—including a special May Day celebration mini-episode produced for European television, two *Fliegender Zirkus* German-language episodes made for Bavarian television, and *Monty Python's Big Red Book*, all produced in 1971. There are also dozens of new or edited entries made possible thanks to ongoing, evolving research. For example, more specific connections are made between a rambling, recognizably canted speech in a courtroom setting in Episode 3 and T.S. Eliot's *The Waste Land*. There are also many more references to contemporary persons, activities, and the zeitgeist of the period from contemporary newspaper pages (the Pythons' response to Enoch Powell's racially charged speech in 1968 mirrored op-ed page anger during the same period); more moments of art imitating life, including parliamentary discussion of slippery door-to-door salesmen and their code of conduct (Ep. 5); many more identifications of film shooting (and photo) locations—alien blancmanges change men into Scotsmen at 19 Southmere Terrace, Bradford (Ep. 7), funeral workers struggle up Harrogate Street, also in Bradford (Ep. 11), Erik Njorl rides through downtown Twickenham (Ep. 27), the Tudor Job Agency can be found at 280 Uxbridge Road (Ep. 36), the lovable losers in *Up Your Pavement* amble up Cowick Street in Exeter (Ep. 42); and more identifications of not only Gilliam's artwork materials (including each Civil War figure and photo employed), but identification of, often, a copy of the actual source titles Gilliam borrowed from his local library for photocopy purposes. Lastly, glaring mistakes have been corrected where necessary, including Bradford Stadium being called Brentford Stadium, *sorry*, and the correct spelling of "Leibniz," among others.

All this in mind, this edition is a far more complete, correct, and readable experience. It's hoped that this venture into an admittedly popular-culture-meets-academia world will be appreciated for what it is—a close, rigorous but still friendly reading of a cultural phenomenon. Shakespeare was the talented, ambitious "upstart Crow" in 1592, and Hitchcock was for many years simply a competent director of pulpy genre films—both have transcended those early straits to become the respected, acculturating institutions they are today. Whither Monty Python? The *OED* accepted "Pythonesque" into its 1989 edition, after all. There were dozens of funny and influential shows on British television, but *Flying Circus* managed to live well beyond not only its natural lifespan and other shows' popularity—but its "Englishness" has ingrained itself into our cultural lexicon along the way. The following pages explore *Monty Python's Flying Circus*'s longevity, complexity, and reflexivity, and promise an illuminating read.

SEASON THREE

Episode 27: *"Whicker's World"*

"Njorl's Saga" (Iceland 1126), interrupted; Nude organist, "And now . . ." Man, and "It's" Man; (New) *Animation: Titles* (silly Palin v/o); Court scene—"Multiple murderer"; *Animation: Into the criminal body*; Icelandic Saga—"Njorl's Saga, Part II," delayed by narration; "We apologize for an error in the saga . . ."; Narrator asks for help getting the exciting Icelandic saga started; BBC Head of Drama office; The North Malden Icelandic Saga Society version; "Welcome to North Malden"; "Njorl's Saga" starts again; North Malden advertisements: "Invest in Malden"; "Njorl's Saga, Part III": Court scene (BBC on trial; Erik Njorl in the dock); Police Constable Pan Am; *Animation: Davis and the Inspector in the criminal body*; Stock exchange report; *Animation: Teleporting Mrs. Cut-out*; **Mrs. Premise and Mrs. Conclusion visit Jean-Paul Sartre**; **Whicker Island**; BBC Head of Drama office; "Njorl's Saga, Part IV" (interrupted by Mrs. Premise and Mrs. Conclusion); At the Sartres'; *Whicker's World*; Closing credits

• A •

"Alitalia" — ("Court Scene [Viking]") Italian airline company, founded in 1947. Perhaps there is a focus on airlines here (and "Cut-Price Airline" in Ep. 22, and the "Bomb on Plane" sketch in Ep. 35) thanks to the dramatic increase in airliner hijackings between 1967 and 1976, with the 1968–1969 period being the worst years.

"And now for something completely trivial" — (PSC; link into "Court Scene—Multiple Murderer") This is one of the handful of asides offered directly to the reader, interestingly, as if the Pythons were considering the script as something that might be studied, as well as something that would be eventually performed (not unlike Ben Jonson, the Elizabethan-Jacobean dramatist—see *MPSERD*). This also may signal the waning interest that the Pythons (and especially Cleese) had begun to experience as the show continued into its third season, and with the standard (now-Pythonesque) openings, transitions, endings, and narrative structures, etc.

See the entry for "he looks identical" below for more on the Pythons' seeming collective disenchantment with the series.

Animated titles — (PSC; ("[New] *Animation: Titles* [silly Palin v/o]") The third season features a new set of animated titles, including a large image of the head and face of an old time cricketer. (A hand pulls the head upwards, revealing lengthening teeth.) This image comes from a complete team photo that Gilliam has used before, in the *Purchase a Past* animated sequence (Ep. 3).

Animation: Manhunt . . . — ("*Animation: Into the Criminal Body*") The fleeing felon is tracked through a number of inverted structures, including a Greek temple and what looks to be the main room of the Panthéon in Paris. The Inspector slides down into one of the domes in this former chapel interior.

"Assaulting a police officer!" — ("Court Scene [Viking]") This may be a reference to a much-publicized case of alleged police brutality going through Criminal Court in Croydon in 1971 and 1972, involving a man who says he was brought in for questioning, then assaulted by police officers before being charged with a crime (see *R v. Inwood*, 23 Feb. 1973). The increasing use of police force since the student riots of 1968, then through and including the abolishment of the Irish Parliament in 1972 and the implementation of emergency powers in Ireland must also be considered.

In the late 1960s the Notting Hill and North Kensington areas (and establishments like the Mangrove and the Metro) endured literally hundreds of race-instigated arrests, harassments, and incidents as the hippie culture and the burgeoning civil rights movement (and immigrant unrest) attracted constant police attention (Vague, chapter four). Police blotters and newspapers of the period are full of these events, with "assaulting a police officer" becoming the sort of catch-all justification for arrest and detention in myriad cases, and thus could be chorused by the jury in this courtroom setting. The fact that the police (Chapman and Palin) are able to enter into evidence "the big brown table down at the police station" and "bouncing around in his cell" indicate trumped-up charges, or at least less-than-reliable probable cause.

Private Eye had covered the allegations of brutal, lying policemen in its 1 November 1963 issue, remarking that since there is no racial discrimination in Britain, everyone "stands an equal chance of being beaten up by bent coppers who later give perjured evidence . . . and are subsequently, having for once been very properly sacked, reinstated in the police force" (Ingrams, 96). Just eight days after this episode first aired, however, (22 December 1970), twenty-four policemen were injured at a Black Power demonstration at the Mangrove Restaurant.

• B •

"BEA" — ("Mrs. Premise and Mrs. Conclusion Visit Jean-Paul Sartre") British European Airways, founded in August 1946, was in operation under this name until 1974.

Birchenhall, Mr. — (PSC; "Court Scene [Viking]") This BBC executive will be sentenced to five years, while the mass murderer was released without punishment earlier, from this same court. In the printed script, Birchenhall (Chapman) is only named in the description of the scene; after the scene begins, he is simply "Man."

"Bjornsstrand" — ("Icelandic Saga") Perhaps a reference to one of Ingmar Bergman's favorites from his stable of actors, Gunnar Bjornstrand (*The Seventh Seal*, 1957). Bergman's film was previously mentioned in the script for Ep. 7.

"bland garbage" — ("Court Scene [Viking]") Available shows on British TV in 1972 included such diverse entertainments as *Clochmerle* (BBC2; lavatorial humor), *Crown Court* (Granada; dramatic serial), *The Frighteners* (LWT; suspense), *Lord Peter Whimsey* (BBC1; sleuthing miniseries), and *Love Thy Neighbour* (Thames TV; crude comedy). Very vocal supporters of the BBC during this period (including Mary Whitehouse's NVLA organization) were adamant that Auntie Beeb not lower herself to the level of established and emerging commercial TV in Britain.

"bonus incentive schemes for industrial development" — ("Icelandic Saga") These are tax and even environmental regulation breaks of many kinds that invite larger businesses to relocate to business-friendlier climes, especially near smaller towns in less-developed areas.

"breed in the sewers" — ("Mrs. Premise and Mrs. Conclusion Visit Jean-Paul Sartre") Fashionable and long-lived urban legend that flushed pets somehow manage to live and thrive underneath major cities. In London, there are significant sightings and even photographic documentation of pigeons riding the underground, getting on at one stop, and getting off at another. There have also been reports of snakes and rats using plumbing fixtures and pipes for transport, but not budgies.

In Thomas Pynchon's *V.* (1963), Benny hunts alligators in the sewers of Manhattan, this based on the report of an eight-foot alligator found in these same sewers in 1935.

bucketful of water — ("Stock Exchange Report") This is a tried-and-true TV variety show or, earlier, music hall (vaudeville) gag, usually to "cool off" an overheating (sometimes sexual, sometimes bombastic) character, or to end a sketch without the traditional spoken punchline. The Pythons usually employ such gags quite self-consciously, like the knight carrying the rubber chicken, and the hammer or sixteen-ton weight on the head, though here the drenching water seems to be used quite traditionally.

The animated character that appears immediately following this scene is actually the one who dumps the water, giving some narrative control to an animated figure, Mrs. Cut-out, which is unusual.

"Budapest" — ("Mrs. Premise and Mrs. Conclusion Visit Jean-Paul Sartre") This grubby laundromat seems an incongruous place for international phone directories (Paris and Budapest), but so is the discussion about the real meanings of Sartre's masterworks carried on by its denizens. Again, these are common folk who, in the Python world, often hold the store of cultural knowledge not given to the upper class.

"budgie" — ("Mrs. Premise and Mrs. Conclusion Visit Jean-Paul Sartre") This is a colloquial abbreviation of "budgerigar," a small Australian parrot or parakeet, and a very popular cage animal in the UK.

• C •

"cheesed off" — ("Court Scene [Viking]") Even the *OED* is unclear as to the etymology of this phrase, though it has been in use since at least the 1940s, and means "to be upset."

chuffed — (PSC; "Court Scene—Multiple Murderer") Counsel (Cleese) is embarrassed, pleased, and even blushing with the defendant's praise.

crashing chord — (PSC; "Icelandic Saga") The stirring music here is from Quatorze Esquisses Pittoresques pour Orchestra, "Au fil de l'eau" (side 2, track 1), by Edward Michael (WAC T12/1,426).

Cut to a courtroom. Severe atmosphere — (PSC; "Court Scene—Multiple Murderer") This set-up is very much modeled after the courtroom setting in the 1957 film *Witness for the Prosecution*, directed by Billy Wilder and starring Charles Laughton, Marlene Dietrich, and Tyrone Power. Even the repeated "calling off" for a new witness (here rendered "Call Erik Njorl!") is heard often in the earlier feature film.

• D •

does a Dickie Attenborough — (PSC; "Court Scene—Multiple Murderer") A reference to Sir Richard Attenborough (b. 1923), now President of the Royal Academy of Dramatic Art, who will appear in an extended, weeping performance (by Idle) in Ep. 39, "Grandstand," as the host of a British film awards show. These moments harken back to both Attenborough's emotional appearance as the host for the 1971 "British Screen Awards: A Gala Night for Television and Film," as well as his turn as the mass murderer John Christie in the 1971 film *10 Rillington Place*. So Idle is not so much caricaturing Christie as he is the later performance(s) of Attenborough, pointing up the somewhat chilling similarities between the depictions. See the Attenborough entries in Ep. 39 for more.

• E •

"elfin glades" — ("Icelandic Saga") Elves (and other supernatural beings) are part of some of the Icelandic sagas, but secondary to the family histories and noble deeds of valorous men and women. Runic inscriptions in Iceland (of the medieval period) tend to mention elves and trolls and the like more often, which just indicates that the influence of the Norse gods and beliefs continued even after the introduction of Christianity. The Pythons, then, are mixing runes and saga literature, and may well be mixing in the more recent and popular J.R.R. Tolkien creations (which make significant use of the Icelandic sagas).

Episode 27 — Recorded 14 January 1972, and broadcast 19 October 1972. This represents almost fifteen months between recording sessions for the season, with Ep. 26 being completed back in October 1970. (In the interim, two *Monty Python's Fliegender Zirkus* episodes for Bavarian TV were written and recorded in Germany.)

Also appearing in this episode, according to WAC records: (in-studio) Rita Davies, Connie Booth, and Lyn Ashley (see "First Juryman" note below). The Clerk "Maurice" is played by the recognizable Frank Williams (*Z Cars*; *Dad's Army*). Nigel Jones (Terry Jones's brother) plays one of the Constables in the scene, and doubles for Njorl.

Extras in this episode: Maureen Nelson (*Softly Softly*), Margo Henson, Pat Quayle (*Bedtime Stories*), Gary Dean (*Doctor Who*), Donald Campbell, Michael Hamilton, Tony Hamilton, Tony Allen (*Rossiter Case*), Michael Buck (*Doctor Who*), Terence Conoley (*Fawlty Towers*), Julia Breck (Ep. 28; *Q5*); (and appearing on film) Peter Kodak, Tony Christopher, Jonas Carr, Jay Neil, Roy Brent, Graham Skidmore, Julie Desmond, Arthur Brooks, David Ewing, Fred Wilkinson, George Wade, John Brunton; and David Stevenson, Neill Bolland, Les King, and P.R. Monument (these last four are locals cast in Norwich) (WAC T12/1,426). Many of these London-area actors will appear as walk-ons in multiple episodes in the third season. See *"Episode"* entries in eps. 36, 37, and 38 for more.

Erik comes into the dock — (PSC; "Court Scene [Viking]") This idea will be revisited in the feature film *Holy Grail*, where the star(s) of a medieval epic (King Arthur, Bedivere, Lancelot) are chased and then arrested for crimes committed in the here and now—namely, the killing of the Learned Historian. In Ep. 3, Cardinal Richelieu (Palin) appears as a character witness in another modern-day trial. Throughout their work, the Pythons manage to tear down the barriers that separate time and place, allowing for historical and ahistorical characters to interact, and for anachronisms like a Viking warrior wandering the streets of a Greater London town. See the discussion of Shakespeare's Falstaff and the Pythons' historical imprecisions in Larsen's *MPSERD*.

"Erik Njorl . . . Hangbard the Fierce" — ("Icelandic Saga") Annotations for this entire naming recitation follow:

"Frothgar"—Probably a play on the name "Hrothgar," the legendary king of the Danes (found in *Beowulf*), whom Beowulf saved from the fiend Grendel and his mother.

"Hangar"—Scandinavian and Anglo-Saxon personal names were primarily formed by combining two common words, e.g., Hrothgar (which became Roger), meaning "fame-spear." In *The Tale of Ragnar's Son*, one of the principal characters is named "Agnar," while his brother's name is "Eirek."

"Thorvald"—Fairly common name, though perhaps here in reference to Eirik the Red's father, Thorvald (son of Asvald) (see *Erik the Red's Saga*). The name Thorvaldr also appears twenty-eight times in the annals of the *Landnámabók* (c. twelfth century).

"Gudleif"—Gudleifr appears just a handful of times in the *Landnámabók*, though spelled not with a medial [d] but with a [ð] (called "edh" and pronounced like the "th" in "this"). Changing it to a [d] is a common typographical mistake.

"Thorgier"—Spelled "Thorgeir," he is a character in *Njal's Saga*, and found in section 146, "The Award of Atonement with Thorgeir Craggier."

"Ljosa water"—See "Ljosa" entry below.

"took to wife Thurunn"—This name (Thórunn) also appears in the *Landnámabók* a total of thirty-four times, and is a feminine name. This name begins, actually, with a þ, called a "thorn," and not with a "Th," which has become customary.

This genealogical recitation can also be found in actual Icelandic epics (see note below), but also in better-known works like the Bible. The book of Samuel begins with this recitation: "Now there was a certain man of Ramathaim-zophim, of mount Ephraim, and his name was Elkanah, the son of Jeroham, the son of Elihu, the son of Tohu, the son of Zuph, an Ephrathite:/ And he had two wives; the name of the one was Hannah, and the name of the other Peninnah: and Peninnah had children, but Hannah had no children" (verses 1–2).

Other portions of the Old Testament also offer such litanies (see Numbers et al.), which the Pythons will further satirize in *Holy Grail*, when portions of the Book of Armaments are read aloud.

"Thorkel Braggart"—"Thorkell" appears a total of fifty-eight times in the *Landnámabók*, and appears to have been a fairly common name. The Thorkell Eyolfson mentioned in *The Laxdaela Saga* is reported drowned at the age of eighty-four, in AD 1026, and a Thorkel is also noteworthy in *Erik the Red's Saga*. Attesting perhaps to its common nature, "Thorkel" is spoken again in this recitation, just below.

A "braggart" is one who brags, and is not necessarily an Icelandic or Scandinavian name. Here "braggart" is used adjectivally, like the following "powerful," "brave," and "fierce." The Pythons will revisit this nominal fun in *HG*, with Lancelot the Brave, Galahad the Pure, Sir Robin the Not-So-Brave-as-Sir-Galahad, etc. In the *Laxdaela Saga*, Thorkell Braggart may be, however, one Thorkell Goat-Peaks, who allowed an ambush to occur without interference, and was later described this way:

> Thorkell has behaved evilly in every way in this matter, for he knew of the ambush the men of Laugar laid for Kjartan, and would not warn him, but made fun and sport of their dealings together, and has since said many unfriendly things about the matter; but it seems a matter far beyond you brothers ever to seek revenge where odds are against you, now that you cannot pay out for their doings such scoundrels as Thorkell is. (chapter 52, *Laxdaela Saga*)

This Thorkell was then led out of his house and killed most unceremoniously.

"slayer"—According to *Njal's Saga*, section 145, Gudmund survived the great battle at the Thing, brokered a peace, exiled various combatants, and returned home laden with rewards.

"Howal"—An uncommon first name, but also the name of an industrial concern founded in 1969, Howal GmbH, in Karlsruhe. The Pythons spent a good deal of time in 1971 in neighboring Bavaria, shooting two *Fliegender Zirkus* episodes, and may have found the name there.

"Arval"—There is a very interesting note in the text of the *Landnámabók*, where the nineteenth-century translator, Loptsson, discusses Arval not as a name, but as part of the ceremony surrounding funereal practices in Nordic lands anciently:

> I may here add the following note on Arvals and Arval in their Cumberland acceptation (Ice erfi). It is given also in my volume on *Lakeland and Iceland*, published by the English Dialect Society. "Arvals is used of meat and drink supplied at funerals. Arval is anything connected with heirship or inheritance; used chiefly in reference to funerals. The friends and neighbours of the family of deceased were invited to dinner on the day of the interment, and this was called the Arval dinner, a solemn festival to exculpate the heir and those entitled to the possessions of deceased from the mulets or fines to the lord of the manor, and from all accusation of having used violence. In later times the word acquired a wider application, and was used to designate the meals provided at funerals generally." (Part 2, page 4)

See the *OED*, as well, for more on this entry.

"Sochnadale"—An Anglicized version of "Soknad-ale" or "Sunnudal," the birthplace of Thorstein Staff-Struck, found in the saga *Thorstein Staff-Struck*. Today spelled "Sokndal," the city is located in Rogaland County in southern Norway.

"Norway"—There is a significant Norwegian and Scandinavian presence in Iceland during this period, with the language being primarily Nordic. These Northerners had come to Iceland about AD 900 looking for more and better farmland than they had in Norway, and by the fourteenth century, Norway would come to rule the island.

"Gudreed"—Gudrid Thorbjarndottir was a world traveler c. AD 1000, making the voyage to Greenland, the New World, even Rome. Several Gudrid characters are mentioned in *Erik the Red's Saga*, as well, including the well-known traveler. In fact, many believe the tale could be more accurately called *Gudrid's Saga*, since she figures so prominently.

"Kettle-Trout"—Made-up name, but there is the name Ketilbjörn which appears in the *Landnámabók* a few times. There is also a male nickname used in the *Landnámabók* of "aurridi" (with medial [ð], not [d]) which means "salmon-trout."

"Half-troll"—An actual nickname also from the *Landnámabók*, and spelled very similarly: hálftröll. It actually means "half-troll."

"Ingbare"—There are a number of period names that begin with "Ing-," including Ingjaldr, Ingolfr, Ingileif, Ingvöldr, etc. These can often be references to Englanders, England, etc.

"Ingbare the Brave"—Compare this to characters in *Njal's Saga*, including Wolf the Unwashed, Harold Greyfell, Harold Fair-hair, Eric Bloodaxe, Gizur the White, Thorolf Bladder-skull (from *The Laxdaela Saga*), and Valgard the Guileful.

"Isenbert"—It's recorded that one Isenbert, a master of schools for the town of Saintes, was recommended by King John in AD 1201 to build a stone bridge across the Thames, and that any edifices erected on the bridge would be taxed for bridge maintenance.

"Gottenberg"—Göteborg is in Sweden, on the Göta Älv.

"Hangbard the Fierce"—Inspired by well-known Northern European and Norse epics like *Beowulf* (c. eighth century) and histories/travel accounts like *Book of the Icelanders* (c. AD 1122–1133) and the *Book of Settlements* (c. twelfth-thirteenth century), but more specifically by other Icelandic sagas, including *Njal's Saga* (aka *Burnt Njal*), the titular character himself being a lawyer. Other significant period sagas include *Egil's Saga* (a Viking warrior-poet), *Laxdaela Saga* (starring contentious foster brothers), and the fantastical *Eyrbyggja Saga*. Most Icelandic sagas were written between the twelfth and thirteenth centuries, and most

were written anonymously, documenting either "the lives of specific people or whole communities" ("Icelandic Sagas," phwibbles.com/sagas/).

A passage from *Njal's Saga* (section 20) will illustrate the structure of the Icelandic writing, and why the Pythons might have enjoyed the prolix style:

> There was a man whose name was Njal. He was the son of Thorgeir Gelling, the son of Thorolf. Njal's mother's name was Asgerda. Njal dwelt at Bergthorsknoll in the land-isles; he had another homestead on Thorolfsfell. Njal was wealthy in goods, and handsome of face; no beard grew on his chin. He was so great a lawyer, that his match was not to be found. Wise too he was, and foreknowing and foresighted. Of good counsel, and ready to give it, and all that he advised men was sure to be the best for them to do. Gentle and generous, he unravelled every man's knotty points who came to see him about them. Bergthora was his wife's name; she was Skarphedinn's daughter, a very high-spirited, brave-hearted woman, but somewhat hard-tempered. They had six children, three daughters and three sons, and they all come afterwards into this story. She was the daughter of Lord Ar the Silent. She had come out hither to Iceland from Norway, and taken land to the west of Markfleet, between Auldastone and Selial-andsmull. Her son was Holt-Thorir, the father of Thorleif Crow, from whom the Wood-dwellers are sprung, and of Thorgrim the Tall, and Skorargeir. (Sunsite.berkeley.edu)

And from the opening paragraph of "Hrafnkel the Priest of Frey":

> It was in the days of King Harald Fairhair, son of Halfdan the Black, son of Gudrod the Hunting King, son of Halfdan the Freehanded but Foodstingy, son of Eystein Fret, son of Olaf Woodcutter the Swedish king. (from *Eirik the Red and Other Icelandic Sagas*, 88)

What's more, even the critical writing *about* the sagas sounds Pythonesque, as displayed by this passage from *The Cambridge History of English and American Literature* (1907–1921):

> Many of the persons and events mentioned in *Beowulf* are known to us also from various Scandinavian records, especially Saxo's *Danish History*, Hrólfs *Saga Kraka*, *Ynglinga Saga* (with the poem *Ynglingatal*) and the fragments of the lost *Skiöldunga Saga*. Scyld, the ancestor of the Scyldungas (the Danish royal family), clearly corresponds to Skiöldr, the ancestor of the Skiöldungar, though the story told of him in *Beowulf* does not occur in Scandinavian literature. Healfdene and his sons Hrothgar and Halga are certainly identical with the Danish king Hafdan and his sons Hróarr (Roe) and Helgi; and there can be no doubt that Hrothwulf, Hrothgar's nephew and colleague, is the famous Hrólfr Kraki, the son of Helgi. Hrothgar's elder brother

Heorogar is unknown, but his son Heoroweard may be identical with Hiörvar[char]r, the brother-in-law of Hròlfr. (Volume I: "From the Beginnings to the Cycles of Romance"; Section III: "Early National Poetry"; §3. "Beowulf: Scandinavian Traditions; Personality of the Hero; Origin and Antiquity of the Poem; the Religious Element")

Finally, the look and presentation of this type of sketch/saga must have been inspired by the many period dramas on British television and available to the young Pythons. These include: *The Black Arrow* (BBC, 1950–1951); *Robin Hood* (BBC, 1953); *The Three Musketeers* (BBC, 1954); *The Adventures of Robin Hood* (ABC, 1955); *The Adventures of the Scarlet Pimpernel* (Towers of London Prod/ITP, 1955); *The Children of the New Forest* (BBC, 1955); *The Adventures of Sir Lancelot* (Sapphire Films, 1956); *The Buccaneers* (Sapphire Films, 1956–1957); *The Count of Monte Cristo* (Vision Prod/ TPA, 1956); *The Adventures of Long John Silver* (ITV, 1957), and many, many more.

Erik riding through a bleak landscape — (PSC; "Icelandic Saga") The music has changed here, from the Edward Michael (Njorl's signature tune) piece to "Monegasque" by Primo di Luca. When Erik reaches North Malden, the tune changes distinctly to the well-known light music composer Wally Stott (now Angela Morley; 1924–2009), formerly of *The Goon Show*, and his composition "Rotten Row" from *London Souvenir*. The International Studio Orchestra's "New World— Man of Destiny" by Sam Fonteyn will also be heard (WAC T12/1,426).

"Essence" — ("Mrs. Premise and Mrs. Conclusion Visit Jean-Paul Sartre") The characters here seem to be named after literary and even philosophical terms. In Sartre's *Being and Nothingness* (1943), he discusses the basics of his philosophical system, where "existence is prior to essence." Mrs. Essence does turn out to be practically useful, though, as she somehow knows Sartre's Paris phone number by heart.

"Exchange Telegraph" — ("Stock Market Report") Prominent UK company that introduced the ticker tape in 1872.

• F •

"Faversham" — ("Icelandic Saga") Faversham is located northwest of Canterbury in Kent. There is a Westbrook Avenue found in Kent, but it is quite a ways from Faversham.

film of Whicker plane — (PSC; "Whicker Island") This stock footage is *"Whickers World"* (K1418) and "Coral Islands" (SKRP65) (WAC T12/1,426).

First Juryman — (PSC; "Court Scene—Multiple Murderer") These three jurists are all women wearing mustaches, suits, and men's wigs. None of the three is credited in the original scripts. The First Juryman is Lyn Ashley, Australian-born actress, usually credited as "Mrs. Idle" (in the closing credits), who was married to Eric Idle from 1969 to 1979; the Second Juryman is Connie Booth (b. 1944), who was married to John Cleese at this time, and would later co-write/ co-star with Cleese on/in *Fawlty Towers* (1975–1979); and the Third Juryman is Rita Davies. Ashley also appears in episodes 18, 23, 32, and 35; Connie Booth also appears in episodes 9, 12, and 18, as well as *FZ* (1972), *Holy Grail* (as The Witch), and *And Now for Something Completely Different* (1971); Rita Davies also appears in episodes 8, 19, and 29, as well as in *HG* as the Historian's Wife.

"fortnight" — ("Mrs. Premise and Mrs. Conclusion Visit Jean-Paul Sartre") Two weeks, or "fourteen nights."

"freedom" — ("Mrs. Premise and Mrs. Conclusion Visit Jean-Paul Sartre") Typically incongruous and deflating transition here, from small animals interrupting excretory performance to the freedom of the individual in a modernist (and approaching postmodern) world. What less auspicious way to introduce the man considered to be the father of modern existentialist thought, Jean-Paul Sartre, then via talk of bowel movements and pet euthanasia?

"Frelimo" — ("Mrs. Premise and Mrs. Conclusion Visit Jean-Paul Sartre") Acronym for the "Front for the Liberation of Mozambique," begun in 1961 with guerrilla activity against the Portuguese colonial rulers in Mozambique. By 1964, the group controlled much of northern Mozambique. In 1974, Portugal would grant independence to the country.

And while Sartre may not have been directly associated with this cause, he was known for his support of the cause of Algerian freedom from France, supporting this "War of Independence" by signing the "Manifesto of the 121," for instance.

French accordion music — (PSC; "Mrs. Premise and Mrs. Conclusion Visit Jean-Paul Sartre") This is Georgia Brown's version of the "Theme from *Roads to Freedom*" by James Cellan-Jones and Herbert Kretzmer. *Roads to Freedom* was a 1970 television adaptation of the Sartre masterwork.

front door of an apartment block — (PSC; "Mrs. Premise and Mrs. Conclusion Visit Jean-Paul Sartre") This was also shot at Elm Hill, Norwich, with the extras being predominantly from local casting calls (WAC T12/1,426). This location was earlier used in the "Colin Mozart (Ratcatcher)" sketch in Ep. 21, as well as some of the "Idiot in Society" and "Hospital Run by RSM" scenes.

"full penalty of the law is hardly sufficient" — ("Court Scene—Multiple Murderer") Probably a comment on Britain's lack of capital punishment, meaning life in prison was the most any criminal could expect in 1971. As early as Ep. 15 a Judge (Chapman) is lamenting the few punitive resources available to him, and announces he's off to South Africa where real justice (executions, whippings, canings, etc.) can still be judiciously meted out. Capital punishment had been abolished in the UK in 1965. The mass murderer that this character is meant to represent, John Christie, was hanged in 1953.

• **G** •

"Gay Lib" — ("Court Scene [Viking]") Gay Liberation is a movement spawned in the 1960s to bring awareness to issues of homosexuality and to give a voice to the gay community. The Gay Liberation Front was officially founded in July 1969 in New York City. The first official Gay Lib Front meeting in the UK took place at the London School of Economics (LSE) in October 1970 (*Eyewitness 1970–1979*, "The Gay Liberation Front"). That the Pythons would attach the judge—an authority figure representing the legal establishment and by association the government—to such a fringe organization is right in line with their "Poofy Judges," gay policemen, and sexually/mentally challenged Upperclass Twits.

"Genet, Mr. and Mr." — ("Mrs. Premise and Mrs. Conclusion Visit Jean-Paul Sartre") Jean Genet (1910–1986) was a homosexual French novelist, playwright, and poet who would have spent his life in prison for theft but was released thanks to the efforts of Sartre and others. Genet supported himself in the 1930s as a male prostitute and thief. Genet's works are peopled by homosexuals, prostitutes, thieves, and outcasts doing self-destructive things, often in confined locations. See Drabble (1985).

"Gildor" — ("Icelandic Saga") Character in J.R.R. Tolkien's *Lord of the Rings* fantasy/adventure series (*The Hobbit* was published in 1937; the *Lord of the Rings* trilogy in 1954–1955). In Tolkien's world, Gildor Inglorion is an elf of the House of Finrod.

Here we see the casual historical mixing that the Pythons so often employ, writing not from a single source, but from a combined (and probably memorial) handful of heteroglossic chains reaching back across history, fantasy, literature, etc. Shakespeare, of course,

would feel the same liberty in his deployment of the ahistorical Falstaff amid the very real characters of English history. See Bergeron and Larsen for more.

"Girl from Ipanema, The" — ("Mrs. Premise and Mrs. Conclusion Visit Jean-Paul Sartre") Ubiquitous "waiting" song heard in elevators and outer rooms around the world, this bossa nova classic was written in 1962, won a Grammy in 1965, and had obviously already reached iconic status less than a decade later.

Glencoe — (PSC; "Icelandic Saga") In central Scotland, on Loch Leven. Parts of the feature film *Holy Grail* would later be filmed here, as well. The Pythons were shooting location footage and insert material for the third season in the Glencoe area in October 1971. These particular shots were made very near the Kings House Hotel in the Glencoe, Ballachulish, Argyll area.

"Gudmund" — ("Icelandic Saga") Spelled often as Gudmundr, but again with the medial [d] (actually [∂]). Here the Pythons are fixing their own error with yet another error. Gudmund the Powerful appears in section 139 of *Burnt Njal*. The "Pedigree of Gudmund the Powerful" is set out in section 112 of *Burnt Njal*, and reads very much like the episode being considered here:

> Einar was the son of Audun the Bald, the son of Thorolf Butter, the son of Thorstein the Unstable, the son of Grim with the Tuft. The mother of Gudmund was Hallberg, the daughter of Thorodd Helm, but the mother of Hallbera was Reginleifa, daughter of Saemund the South-islander; after him is named Saemundslithe in Skagafirth. The mother of Eyjolf, Gudmund's father, was Valgerda Runolf's daughter; the mother of Valgerda was Valbjorg, her mother was Joruna the Disowned, a daughter of King Oswald the Saint. The mother of Einar, the father of Eyjolf, was Helga, a daughter of Helgi the Lean, who took Eyjafirth as the first settler. Helgi was the son of Eyvind the Easterling. The mother of Helgi was Raforta, the daughter of Kjarval, the Erse King. The mother of Helga Helgi's daughter, was Thoruna the Horned, daughter of Kettle Flatnose, the son of Bjorn the Rough-footed, the son of Grim, Lord of Sogn. The mother of Grim was Hervora, but the mother of Hervora was Thorgerda, daughter of King Haleyg of Helgeland. Thorlauga was the name of Gudmund the Powerful's wife, she was a daughter of Atli the Strong, the son of Eilif the Eagle, the son of Bard, the son of Jalkettle, the son of Ref, the son of Skidi the Old. Herdisa was the name of Thorlauga's mother, a daughter of Thord of the Head, the son of Bjorn Butter-carrier, the son of Hroald the son of Hrodlaug the Sad, the son of Bjorn Ironside, the son of Ragnar Hairybreeks, the son of Sigurd Ring, the son of Randver, the son of Radbard. The mother of Herdisa Thord's daughter was Thorgerda Skidi's daughter, her mother was Fridgerda, a daughter of Kjarval, the Erse King. (Section 112, *Burnt Njal*)

• H •

". . . harsh uneconomic realities of life in the land of Ljosa . . ." — (link out of "Court Scene [Viking]") This harks back to the complaint voiced earlier about what viewers really want. The not-so-subtle invasion of commercialism into a BBC program—as North Malden promotes itself in an Icelandic saga—was the very fear of many viewers, politicians, and social welfare types in the decade following the introduction of commercial television in the UK in 1955. By 1956, the regional broadcasters including Granada, Associated Rediffusion, ATV, and others, were also up and running, bringing commercial television to the entire country.

". . . he looks identical to the way he did in that deceased classic of our time 'And now for something completely trivial'" — (PSC; opening credits) This comment is for readers of the scripts only, and further indicates the tiredness with which the Pythons must have been approaching this new season, and especially some of the hoary visual chestnuts from the first season. Cleese indicated early that he was less than excited about another go, and the entire troupe took more than one year off from the BBC version of the series. In 1971 they completed the Bavarian *Fliegender Zirkus* episodes, as well as the feature film (reprising highlights of the first two seasons) *And Now for Something Completely Different*.

Each of the Pythons also worked on individual projects in this 1970–1971 period, including *The Ronnie Barker Yearbook* (Cleese and Chapman), *The Magnificent Seven Deadly Sins* (Chapman), *The Two Ronnies* (Palin), *Ronnie Corbett in Bed* (Idle), *Marty Amok* (Jones), and *The Marty Feldman Comedy Machine* (Gilliam).

"He wants to sit down and he wants to be entertained" — ("Court Scene [Viking]") This idea of TV as entertainment is especially pertinent in this era when commercial television was gaining a strong foothold in Britain. Many viewers felt that the BBC should maintain some sort of high ground in this entertainment-versus-education/culture debate, and not go the way of all commercial television.

The idea of TV entertainment coupled with education is again broached in the "Mollusc Documentary" sketch in Ep. 32, where a documentary program comes into a couple's home, but has to be "sexed up" to be of any interest.

horse — (PSC; "Icelandic Saga") Horses (and not necessarily banners/posters) *had* been a significant part of Iceland's culture since Vikings brought sturdy Nordic horses to Iceland between AD 874–930.

"Hotel Miramar" — ("Mrs. Premise and Mrs. Conclusion Visit Jean-Paul Sartre") Cf. Idle's loudmouthed

tourist (Mr. Smoke-too-Much) in Ep. 31, who bemoans the hopelessly vanilla and ubiquitous hotels of this type catering to penny-pinching British tourists ("Hotel Miramars and Bellevueses and Bontinentals").

"Huddinut" — ("Icelandic Saga") A nonce name, probably meant to sound Icelandic, but actually can mean the husk ("hud" or "hood") of a nut. The fact that Huddinut (Palin) is a local solicitor—an attorney—is significant in that it directly connects him to the actual titular character from *Njal's Saga*, himself a skilled lawyer.

"Humber . . . Mersey" — ("Court Scene [Viking]") The line that historically has divided the north of England from the south.

• I •

"Ibeezer" — ("Mrs. Premise and Mrs. Conclusion Visit Jean-Paul Sartre") Colloquial mispronunciation and misspelling of "Ibiza," another popular British tourist destination off the eastern Spanish coast in the Mediterranean. Mallorca and Manorca are nearby. Biggles (Chapman) will have recently visited "Ibitha" (closer to the Castilian pronunciation) as mentioned by his secretary (Nicki Howorth) in Ep. 33.

"Iceland 1126" — ("Icelandic Saga") Iceland circa 1126 had been settled by Vikings, Celts, and a significant mixture (as the mitochondrial DNA of modern Icelanders would later attest) of Northern and Southern Europeans. This was an active period in early self-governance (without a monarchy) and Icelandic literature, as other annotations will explain.

There is also a more contemporary reason that the Pythons might venture into Icelandic sagas. In 1971, just months prior to this episode's creation, Denmark began a much-celebrated giving-back of Icelandic literature to Iceland, specifically to the Arni Magnusson Institute.

"Icelandic Saga Society" — ("Icelandic Saga") There were all sorts of literary/historical societies in the UK at this time, including: The Society for the Promotion of Roman Studies (1910–); the Society for the Promotion of Hellenic Studies (1910–); The (Samuel) Johnson Society of London (1928–); the Viking Society for Northern Research (1892–), and so on. Perhaps most significantly to this sketch was one of the newer societies—the Tolkien Society was founded in 1969.

Icelandic seashore — (PSC; ("Mrs. Premise and Mrs. Conclusion Visit Jean-Paul Sartre") Chosen as a location due to the rocky beach and visible cliffs, probably, this scene was actually shot on the beaches of Oban Bay (WAC T12/1,428).

Many of the beaches around the UK are so-called shingle beaches, meaning the grain size is between 1 and 200 millimeters (up to about 7.8 inches), so the rocks that are evident in the shot qualify. Icelandic beaches would tend to be volcanic in origin, so often black, and fairly fine-grained.

"ICI" — (PSC; "Icelandic Saga") Imperial Chemical Industries is a British chemical conglomerate formed in 1926, and has large paint plants near a number of rural towns like Stoke Poges and Stowmarket. ICI has already been mentioned as a promising investment by the Village Idiots, in Ep. 20, "The Idiot in Society."

"If any of you at home have any ideas . . ." — ("Icelandic Saga") Coincidentally, when in July 1970 Reginald Maudling was asked for his ideas to bring the "Irish situation" to a successful conclusion, he replied that he had none: "No, not really. If anyone's got any ideas, perhaps they will let me know." *Private Eye* included Maudling's name and direct address for postcards from readers willing to offer solutions (17 July 1970, 5).

"I meant" — ("Icelandic Saga") This is the second time this motif has appeared in this episode. Another miscommunication, this time based on the varying meanings of a single word, "terrible," in various contexts. Later, in the feature film *Life of Brian* (1979), the Jewish Official (Cleese) and an onlooker (Palin) will be stoned to death for committing blasphemy by uttering "Jehovah," but in the context of a court proceeding, where they should be safe.

interior of a laundromat — (PSC; "Mrs. Premise and Mrs. Conclusion Visit Jean-Paul Sartre") Through the back door of the laundromat (over the shoulder of Mrs. Premise and Mrs. Conclusion) a painted set flat can be seen. On the flat is a photograph of a typical building in a typical Greater London high street. In this case, the delicatessen and grocer Sheridan's is visible, meaning the photo was taken at 82 St. Marys Road, Ealing, W5. This was just down the street from Ealing Studios, Pitzhanger Manor (Ep. 15), and Walpole Park (Eps. 8 and 15), all locations for the Pythons.

• J •

"Joe Public doesn't want . . ." — ("Court Scene [Viking]") "Joe Public" is an American vernacularism, originally describing theatrical viewing audiences, and here indicating that the long-term presence and influence of American commercial television (active since at least 1940) on the BBC is being keenly felt in the early 1970s. The advent of British commercial TV in 1954–1955—closer to the American version, but

perhaps a bit more refined—must also have caused a stir at Auntie Beeb, where it didn't used to matter how many households were tuned in—she was the only game in town.

Jones, Nigel — (PSC; end credits) Nigel (b. 1940) is Terry Jones's older brother, and appears in the courtroom scene, as well as doubling for Njorl.

• K •

"kicked" — ("Court Scene [Vikings]") Perhaps no coincidence that police brutality is treated here, as 1972 was the bloodiest year in Northern Ireland to date. The Public Record Office attributes 500 dead, 5,000 injured, 2,000 explosions, and more than 10,000 shootings in 1972 alone to the "Troubles." And though the Irish question is almost never directly addressed in *FC* (notably excepting Ep. 31, in the "Our Eamonn" sketch), the accounts of police beatings, deaths of demonstrators, mysterious abuses/deaths of Irish prisoners in British custody, and the ultimate approval of arrest and internment without trial (introduced in 1971) filled newspapers across the UK, and must have been in the Pythons' minds as they worked. This was also the year that rule of Ireland from Westminster began.

"King" — ("Icelandic Saga") Presumably Njorl's still in Iceland (though he could be in the Faroe Islands, or he crossed into the realm of the fantastic altogether), and one of the peculiarities of medieval Iceland was its lack of a centralized monarchy. Farmers tended to hold most of the power, with many having left Scandinavia to escape oppressive monarchs, a defined aristocracy, and taxation. So, there would have been no King Gildor type in Iceland, but perhaps a wealthy landowner. This may also be the intrusion of the Tolkien-like fantasy involving the sagas, not unlike North Malden will continue to keep its "investment" foot in the BBC's door as the saga moves on.

"dukes"—The aristocracy, as such, was less developed in Iceland of this period, with the powerful men being those not necessarily with titles (as there was no monarch), but with lands.

armoured knights — (PSC) A mixed bag of costuming and prop choices. The Viking-era shield would have been made of wood, not metal, while the helmets the Pythons chose here appear accurate, as do the swords.

"chest . . . letters"—Instead of letters, such warriors would, if they were wearing any insignia or uniforms at all, wear heraldic emblems (dragon, lion, family crest, etc.) on their chests, shields, banners, etc.

The small lake Erik pauses at when the dukes attack is "Hospital Loch" above Glencoe Hospital, and the Forestry Commission had to give approval for the BBC film crew to set up there (WAC T12/1,428).

• L •

"Larches, The" — ("Icelandic Saga") Regional pet name for bed and breakfast–type establishments, housing developments, even country homes in the UK, especially the counties around Greater London. There is a "The Larches" in West Sussex, and also in Bromley.

"Le . . . chose" — (Mrs. Premise and Mrs. Conclusion Visit Jean-Paul Sartre") "Capitalism and the Bourgeoisie are the same thing."

"letters of their dread name" — ("Icelandic Saga") The men playing these roles are: Peter Kodak (*Doctor Who*), Tony Christopher (*Some Mothers Do 'Ave 'Em*), Jonas Card, Jay Neil (*Some Mothers Do 'Ave 'Em*), Graham Skidmore (*Dixon of Dock Green*), and Roy Brent (*Some Mothers Do 'Ave 'Em*) (WAC T12/1,428). They will also play background Pepperpots in the Mrs. Entity and Mrs. Conclusion "Laundromat" scene.

"Ljosa waters" — ("Icelandic Saga") Literally, "good waters," or light waters, etc. (see *Grimm's Teutonic Mythology*). The Old Norse word for light is "ljós." Ljosa is also part of the nearby (to Iceland) Faroe Islands.

"London Borough" — ("Court Scene [Viking]") The London boroughs (areas of London surrounding the oldest part of the city) include: (north of the Thames) The City, Hounslow, Ealing, Brent, Hillingdon, Harrow, Barnet, Hammersmith, Kensington and Chelsea, Westminster, Camden, Haringey, Enfield, Islington, Hackney, Tower Hamlets, Waltham Forest, Newham, Redbridge, Barking, and Havering; and (south of the Thames) Richmond, Kingston, Wandsworth, Merton, Sutton, Lambeth, Croydon, Southwark, Lewisham, Bromley, Greenwich, and Bexley. Most of these boroughs are mentioned at least once in *Flying Circus*.

Counties surrounding the boroughs are Berkshire, Buckinghamshire, Hertfordshire, Essex, Kent, and Surrey. The Maldens are actually in the county of Surrey, and not part of the London Boroughs at all.

"loo" — ("Mrs. Premise and Mrs. Conclusion Visit Jean-Paul Sartre") Toilet. The term perhaps is derived from a collation of "Waterloo" and water closet, perhaps as they are put together by Joyce in *Ulysses*, page 556 (1922).

"Lufthansa" — ("Court Scene [Viking]") German airline company, originally (1926) "Deutsche Luft Hansa Aktiengesellschaft" (and renamed "Lufthansa" in 1933). Chapman played Constable Pan Am in Ep. 17.

• M •

Marty Feldman's Comedy Machine — (PSC; animated link out of "Court Scene [Viking]") A fourteen-episode ATV comedy show starring and written by Marty Feldman, with whom the Pythons had worked (severally) in the past. Gilliam contributed animated sequences to Feldman's show during the Python hiatus in 1971, so this is a very topical reference.

"Marxist" — ("Mrs. Premise and Mrs. Conclusion Visit Jean-Paul Sartre") One who supports the views/writings of Karl Marx in relation to economic systems and their political attributes. Marx himself has appeared on a *University Challenge*–type quiz show in Ep. 25.

Sartre explored his view of Marxist thought and commitment (what some called his "Sartrian Socialism") in *Critique of Dialectical Reason* (1960), and found that a lack of personal freedom (in the Soviet Union, for example) precluded a true Marxist dialectic, and that forcing an individual into a political system would never work to achieve freedom.

"Match of the Day" — ("Icelandic Saga") Originally, the show offered scheduled portions of a football match recorded by BBC cameras and run the same day on BBC2 (1964–1966). When it moved to BBC1, the televising of football was legitimized, and it has been a staple since.

"merde" — ("Mrs. Premise and Mrs. Conclusion Visit Jean-Paul Sartre") Literally, "shit." Often used just as an expression of annoyance or exasperation (*OED*). For the Pythons, though, this was most likely an opportunity to swear without the BBC higher-ups forcing a change.

"Mills, Mr." — ("Icelandic Saga") This is a reference to Michael Mills, Head of Comedy, Light Entertainment at BBC in the early years of the show.

"modern suburban shopping street" — ("Icelandic Saga") There are a handful of hints as to the location of this shot—where Erik Njorl rides, amazed, through a modern high street area. A Milletts outdoor wear shop can be seen, and a "Margaret's Post Office" sign can just be discerned. Taken together, it becomes clear that North Malden is actually Twickenham, the buildings just before Erik comprise The Broadway, and he rides on St. Margaret's Road. The area hasn't changed much since this scene was filmed.

Much of the wilder, highland-looking exterior work for "Icelandic Saga" was filmed in and around Glencoe, Oban, and Duror, all in western Scotland.

"Mrs. Conclusion" — ("Mrs. Premise and Mrs. Conclusion Visit Jean-Paul Sartre") Mrs. Premise and Mrs.

Conclusion are aptly named here, as they both begin and end this entire narrative thread, and even have the ability to overcome the narrative tyrannies that have been and will continue to plague this episode.

"Mrs. Cut-out" — ("Mrs. Premise and Mrs. Conclusion Visit Jean-Paul Sartre") Further proof that the boundaries between sketches and storylines aren't sacred in this episode, or almost anywhere in the Python oeuvre, as an animated character from the animated world can take solid form and "walk" through the live-action world.

In the preceding animated sequence that brings Mrs. Cut-out to the launderette, Gilliam has used a doctored photo of 347-351 High Street North in Newham, Greater London, which is northeast of the City of London. These three buildings are at the middle of the block, and Gilliam has removed the alley and the balance of the city block. The buildings are now a pharmacy, a mobile phone store, and a hairdresser.

"music of repeat fees" — ("Whicker Island") As early as February 1971 the Pythons were each getting about £80 per episode for their own repeat fees on the first season (WAC T12/1,082).

• N •

"new pence" — ("Mrs. Premise and Mrs. Conclusion Visit Jean-Paul Sartre") There were "New Pence" coins stamped in 1971, when decimalization was introduced, which even had "New Pence" stamped on the flip side. On 15 February 1971, the very familiar pound (£), shilling (s), and pence (d) coins began to be phased out in favor of pound units of ten, including half, one, two, five, ten, and fifty pence denominations.

"Sixty new pence for a bottle of Maltese Claret"—The man at the off-licence would of course know this (see entry below for "off-licence"). This somewhat strange rejoinder may be a complaint on Premise's part regarding the reliability of the man at the off-licence, especially if he overcharges for claret. She may also be complaining about the valuation of the new pence in relation to the old coins, since the old penny and new penny were valued differently, and many during this period complained that the currency exchange rate favored the government, and not the individual.

Also, the better clarets (originally yellowish or light red wines) would not have come from Malta but from France, specifically the Bordeaux region, and would have been "mixed with Benicarlo or some full-bodied French wine" (*OED*). This may be a comment on Premise's lack of sophistication, though she seems to understand modern philosophy fairly well. It's later revealed that Sartre also drinks "vin ordinaire" (and

not some expensive premium wine), and lives in a ratty apartment kept neat by a goat, putting all of these characters on a similar social standing.

Njorl's Saga — ("Icelandic Saga") Cf. *Njal's Saga*, in the "Erik Njorl" entry above for more.

"North Malden" — ("Icelandic Saga") There is and has been both an Old Malden and a New Malden, and even a Malden, but not a North Malden. The various Maldens are located on the edge of Greater London and Surrey, about 6.5 miles north of the M25, and just 1.8 miles from Thames-side docking. Twickenham, the St. Margaret's Road high street area stood in for North Malden for this episode. At the Battle of Maldon in the tenth century in Essex the locals were defeated by Vikings, incidentally.

"not at all well" — ("Mrs. Premise and Mrs. Conclusion Visit Jean-Paul Sartre") This phraseology is used a few times in *FC*, including Ep. 29, when the jugged rabbit fish has been "coughin' up blood" just the night before, and later in *HG*, when the old plague victim complains that he's "not dead," and may even be "getting better." The man carrying him (Cleese) rejoins: "You'll be stone dead in a moment."

"not the way the BBC works" — ("Icelandic Saga") As early as 1957 shows *were* being broadcast on British television just to sell products, though perhaps not by the BBC. *Jim's Inn* (A-R, 1957–1963) was just such a show, where characters actually discussed products and prices in a homey, fictional setting. By 1963, this so-called Admag format—a television program created around commercials—was made illegal by order of Parliament. Other titles included *About Homes and Gardens* (ATV, 1956), *What's in Store* (ABC-TV, 1956), and *Slater's Bazaar* (ATV, 1957–1959). See Gable's *The Tuppenny Punch and Judy Show—25 Years of TV Commercials*, as well as entries in Vahimagi's *British Television* for more on the admag phenomenon.

This same indirect-sell approach will be used later in *FC* with the "Trim-Jeans" weight-loss pants sketch. During the period when the *FC* shows were being written (1969–1974), these same concerns were being voiced about children's programming and advertising, but in the United States, and specifically in relation to Saturday morning cartoons being made to sell breakfast cereal and toys.

• O •

"off-licence" — ("Mrs. Premise and Mrs. Conclusion Visit Jean-Paul Sartre") A shop where alcohol is sold that can be legally consumed off the premises; a liquor store. In Ep. 19, it is the man from the off-licence

(Palin) who gamely but lamely stars in Mr. Dibley's version of *Finian's Rainbow*.

"Oui" — ("Mrs. Premise and Mrs. Conclusion Visit Jean-Paul Sartre") Yet another Monty Python monumental narrative build-up that leads almost nowhere, in diminution, as in the *"Black Eagle"* sketch (Ep. 25), the *"Is There?"*–type panel discussion sketches about life after death (Ep. 36), and the proposed new BBC television channel (Ep. 37). This deflation takes the place of the usual payoff punchline, sending the narrative slouching into the following scene. The denouement for the feature film *The Meaning of Life* also ends very anti-climactically, with the Lady Presenter (Palin) reading from a card: "Try and be nice to people, avoid eating fat, read a good book every now and then, get some walking in, and try and live together in peace and harmony with people of all creeds and nations."

• P •

"Pan Am" — ("Court Scene [Viking]") An American airline company, Pan American was founded in 1927, and was originally meant to serve the entire Americas—North, South, and Central—at affordable prices. In 1970, Pan Am was one of the largest airlines in the world.

Chapman's version of PC Pan Am appeared in Ep. 17, in the "Chemist Sketch."

Part III — ("Court Scene [Viking]") Actually, this is attempt number three to start *Njorl's Saga*, though it fails to materialize at all, instead moving into a modern-day courtroom setting. The narrative tyrannies continue.

There is also no sign of a crest above the judge in this courtroom setting—this may or may not be a Crown Court, and could be a Magistrates Court.

"personal possessions" — ("Mrs. Premise and Mrs. Conclusion Visit Jean-Paul Sartre") Perhaps a better fit is found in Sartre's *Being and Nothingness* (1943, trans. 1965), section 2, "Doing and Having": "Generosity is nothing else than a craze to possess. All which I abandon, all which I give, I enjoy in a higher manner through the fact that I give it away. . . . To give is to enjoy possessively the object which one gives."

"popularity is what television is about" — ("Court Scene [Viking]") There has been a long-standing debate in and around the BBC as to what role a state-owned broadcaster should adopt—purveyor of education or entertainment, straight-ahead news or "managed" news, etc. The fact that the BBC is and has been funded by license fees attached to each television and radio sold gives the people of the UK—shareholders, essentially—a significant voice in the discussion. So Mr. Birchenhall (Chapman) is merely arguing the shareholders' case for a more responsive, representative BBC.

"press is here" — ("Court Scene [Viking]") Meaning, they are being watched, and if they fail to follow exact courtroom procedure, the snafu will end up in the tattle pages of the newspapers. This hints at a deeper collusion, of course, between the law enforcement and judicial entities of England, a suspicion that many in the UK entertained during this period.

"proposed M25" — ("Icelandic Saga") This is an "orbital" roadway that encircles London, and is approximately 117 miles in circumference. This orbital road around London was first proposed in 1937, then again in the "Abercrombie Plan" of 1945 (a five-road proposal), which eventually became the Greater London Development Plan, which included the M25 ring. Construction would begin three years after this episode aired, in 1975, and it was essentially a city bypass road. See more on the Greater London Development Plan in notes to Ep. 35.

• R •

"Rainiers" — ("Mrs. Premise and Mrs. Conclusion Visit Jean-Paul Sartre") Essentially the King of Monaco and his wife, Grace Kelly. Officially, he was Rainier III, Rainier Louis Henri Maxence Bertrand Grimaldi (1923–2005), and was the hereditary Prince and Head of State of the Principality of Monaco. He married the American actress Grace Kelly (1929–1982) in 1956.

"Randall, Michael Norman . . . Felix James Bennett" — ("Court Scene—Multiple Murderer") Following are as many identifications of these listmembers as possible, with the usual acknowledgment that some of the names on such Python lists are invariably made up, while others denote actual (often obscure) persons, some even close acquaintances of the particluar writer. The long list of closing credits for "Timmy Williams" in Ep. 19 is an earlier example of this structure:

"Charles Patrick Trumpington"—The Trumpington name figures prominently into the history of Cambridge University and its environs. There is a Trumpington Hall and a Trumpington Road at Cambridge, thanks to Crusader namesake Sir Roger de Trumpington (d. 1289).

"Marcel Agnes Berstein"— "Marcelle Bernstein" was an author and writer for, among others, the *Observer*, the color supplement to the *Times*.

"Lewis Anona Rudd"—Lewis Rudd was an executive producer for the children's program *Magpie* in 1968, a Thames TV production that ran through 1980.

"John Malcolm Kerr"—A "Malcolm Kerr" is introduced by Cleese's character in the "Theatre Critic" sketch from *The Frost Report* (1967).

"Nigel Sinclair Robinson"—There is a "Nigel Robinson" listed by BT as living in southeast London in 1971.

"Norman Arthur Potter"—Norman Potter wrote *What Is a Designer: Education and Practice, A Guide for Students and Teachers* (1969). There is also a "Norman A. Potter" living in southwest London in 1971, according to period telephone directories.

"Felicity Jayne Stone"—There is an "F.J.F. Stone" listed as living in Kingston Upon Thames in 1971.

"Stephen Jay Greenblatt"—A very real person. Cambridge-educated Greenblatt (b. 1943) would have been a contemporary of the Pythons, graduating from Pembroke College (where Idle matriculated) with his A.B. in 1966 and M.A. in 1968. Greenblatt was a Renaissance scholar at UC Berkeley (1969–1997), thence at Harvard (1997–), publishing prolifically, and is responsible for the flowering of New Historicism in the United States. He was already well published and his work much talked about as early as 1969, and certainly by 1972. Greenblatt also took advanced degrees from Yale, and was a Fulbright scholar and Guggenheim fellow.

"Karl-Heinz Muller"—Luftwaffe Unteroffizier shot down in a new type of plane, the Jul88, near Hemley, in Suffolk on 15 October 1943. Muller was actually mortally wounded by the hostile British fire, and was pushed out of the crippled plane, with open parachute, in hopes that he might live. Two others were taken into custody by a local police constable.

"Belinda Anne Ventham"—There are two "B.A. Ventham" listings in southwest London for 1971. Actress Wanda Ventham appeared in contemporary shows *Dixon of Dock Green*, *Z Cars*, *Doctor Who*, and *Doctor at Large*, the same shows where the Pythons cast many of their own extras. Wanda also appeared, coincidentally, in Idle's *Rutland Weekend Television* in 1975.

"Lord Kimberrley [*sic*] of Pretoria"—Sir John Wodehouse, Fourth Earl of Kimberley (1924–2002), and his then wife Margaret Simon (he was six times married, five times divorced) would have been Lord and Lady Kimberley in 1972, though neither of them died at the hands of a mass murderer. The Earl (known as Johnny Kimberley) was much in the news during this period, sleeping around, spending millions of pounds, and getting sacked from the House of Lords, as both his memoirs and obituaries tell. The fourth Earl's grandfather—John Wodehouse, first Earl of Kimberley

(1826–1902)—was significantly involved in colonial affairs, becoming Secretary of State for the Colonies, and after the great diamond discovery in South Africa, the town of Kimberley was named after him.

"The Right Honourable Nigel Warmsley Kimberley of Pretoria"—To be termed "Right Honourable" is an entitlement for Privy Council members, Barons and Earls, some Lords Mayors, etc. A number of the Kimberleys qualified.

"Robert Henry Noonan"—Robert Noonan was the pen name of Robert Tressell (1870–1911), a fin-de-siècle painter and socialist novelist, producing the well-respected *Ragged-Trousered Philanthropists* (1914), which, after it became quite popular in the 1930s, may have helped Labour win the General Election in 1945. The novel's "angry working class" themes and effusive, laborite socialism likely attracted the Pythons in their university days. Noonan also spent a number of years in South Africa, working in/on union affairs. A BBC production of Noonan's novel aired in May 1967 on BBC 2. Some days after the broadcast there appeared a small but interesting piece in the *Times* describing how Noonan's daughter sold her father's 1600-page manuscript for £25 in 1913, not long after his death. The book would become a hit, reprinted many times, and Miss Noonan received an additional £25, and nothing more. The manuscript was kept in a biscuit tin under a bed, she remembered ("Sold Rights to Classic for £25," 5 June 1967: 3).

"Felix James Bennett"—There are several "F.J. Bennett" listings in the period phone books for the Greater London area. Felix Bennett was also a popular reggae band sax player in this period, and may have been known by Idle.

"ratings conscious" — ("Court Scene [Viking]") This would not have been even a factor when BBC was the only TV network available (1936–1955), but after the appearance of ITV (Independent Television) in 1955, and its offshoots (including Granada in 1956, serving the north and west of England), viewing choices were possible. In 1968, ITV was reviewed and broken into regional broadcasters, including Thames TV, London Weekend TV, Yorkshire, Granada, and ATV.

BBC Light Entertainment would itself gather and peruse a weekly audience survey report, looking at estimated audience size, audience opinions of the target episode (everything from "fresh" and "brilliant" to "rubbishy" and "offensive"), and audience responses to the performers themselves (WAC T12/1,428).

"Revisionist" — ("Mrs. Premise and Mrs. Conclusion Visit Jean-Paul Sartre") Generally, a revisionist is a historian who reinterprets accepted, institutionalized history in the wake of, for example, new eras/theories like post-colonialism, feminism, queer theory, etc. History can be experienced as one thing, then retold as another, with the goals being the challenging of events as they "actually" occurred and/or challenging the "authoritative" interpretations of that history (in history books, for example).

Mrs. Conclusion's (Chapman) somewhat vehement response is actually a bit curious here, given that Sartre himself was attempting to revise Marxism as it was then practiced in most so-called Marxist countries, and he may have been comfortable with either being called a Marxist, or entertaining visitors who were similarly revision-minded.

Apropos of the Sino fixation of a number of Python sketches, it's relevant that Mao and the Communist Party of the People's Republic of China appropriated the term "revisionist" during the Cultural Revolution to define themselves in opposition to the Soviet Union. PRC official Lin Biao (already mentioned in Eps. 19 and 23) had the following to say in 1967, addressing a Peking Rally commemorating the October Revolution:

> The modern revisionists, represented by Khrushchev and his successors, Brezhnev and Kosygin and company, are wildly opposing the revolution of the people of the world and have openly abandoned the dictatorship of the proletariat and brought about an all-round capitalist restoration in the Soviet Union. This is a monstrous betrayal of the October Revolution. This is a monstrous betrayal of Marxism-Leninism. It is a monstrous betrayal of the great Soviet people and the people of the whole world. . . . It is our good fortune that Comrade Mao Tse-tung has comprehensively inherited and developed the teachings of Marx, Engels, Lenin and Stalin on proletarian revolution and the dictatorship of the proletariat. (6 Nov. 1967)

This is the type of rhetoric that defined Sino-Soviet relations for this period (and filled the pages of contemporary newspapers), so it's no surprise that Mao, Lin Biao, the PRC, and the Russians Khrushchev, Kosygin, and others make their presence felt in *Flying Circus* episodes.

"rickety rackety roo" — ("Stock Exchange Report") The respectful, staid delivery of this business information (which would have occurred on BBC radio and TV every day) devolves/evolves into Seuss-ian nonsense by the end, becoming more infantile. This also may be a comment on the silliness not only of the straight-ahead delivery of most BBC presenters, but also on the types of commodities that are traded in stock markets, including tin, canola, and frozen concentrate orange juice futures. See Idle's appearance as the reader in the *Book at Bedtime* in Ep. 38 for more bedtime story nonsense.

Roads to Freedom — ("Mrs. Premise and Mrs. Conclusion Visit Jean-Paul Sartre") A series of novels published 1945–1949, in *Roads* Sartre argued that freedom did have a purpose, and that since the subject of literature had always been "man in the world," the writer "must show the reader his power to make, or to unmake, in short to act—for man is to be reinvented every day." And what was the task of the writer? Certainly "to struggle in favor of the freedom of the person and of socialist revolution." So action is essential, meaning the Pepperpots must make their trip to Paris, and confront the author himself.

"Rotter" — ("Mrs. Premise and Mrs. Conclusion") Julian Rotter (b. 1916) is a psychologist who coined the phrase "locus of control" in the 1960s, which here coincides neatly with Conclusion's and Premise's disagreement about Sartre's intentions regarding man's freedom and action.

Rotter looked at people and their ways of defining *control* in their world. He asked questions about agency and power, and whether we (a) take credit for the "good" things that happen to us, or (b) blame some outside force for the "bad" things, etc. Rotter's "Locus of Control" test was designed to help determine whether the examinee was an "internaliser" or an "externaliser." His "Locus of Control Scale" was published in *Psychological Monographs*, Volume 80, 1966. He also published *Social Learning and Clinical Psychology* (1954), where he showed that an individual *and/in* his environment were essential in shaping the individual.

The fact that it was Rotter who placed the whoopee cushion under Sartre might reflect the degree of control and free will that he felt, and would fit well into Sartre's world of man answering to himself and within his own sphere of action/influence, and not some higher power.

"*Rues à Liberté*" — ("Mrs. Premise and Mrs. Conclusion Visit Jean-Paul Sartre") *Roads to Freedom*, Sartre's trilogy written between 1945 and 1949.

• S •

"Sartre, Jean-Paul" — ("Mrs. Premise and Mrs. Conclusion Visit Jean-Paul Sartre") Sartre (1905–1980) was a French philosopher, essayist, playwright, and novelist. He lived with but never married Simone de Beauvoir (1908–1986). He was awarded the 1964 Nobel Prize, but declined, saying he did not want to become an institution.

Sartre embraced and redefined the existentialist movement in the postwar years, building on Husserl's

(1859–1938) phenomenology and Kierkegaard's version of man's existential being. Sartre believed in a world without God, where man's ultimate responsibility and condemnation is his freedom, his ability (and sentence) to choose. In the Python group, Cleese seems to be the one most sympathetic to Sartre's ethos. (See Cleese's comments in both Morgan's *Monty Python Speaks!* and the more recent *The Pythons* by McCabe.)

shot of a modern road sign: "North Malden—please drive carefully" — (PSC; "Icelandic Saga") This is an example of what would have been called an "unnatural break" in early commercial TV in the UK. From very early in the life of commercial TV in Britain, viewers, regulatory personnel, and Members of Parliament lodged complaints regarding just what constituted a "natural break," or the proper place for a commercial during a broadcast show on ITV, for example.

"so many people" — ("Court Scene—Multiple Murderer") This character, Michael Norman Randall (played by Idle), is certainly a reference to the recent UK mass murderer John Reginald Haliday Christie who was blamed for at least eight murders between 1943 and 1953. Christie would be executed in 1953 for at least one of those murders. Local papers covered the investigation, arrest, conviction, and execution with eagerness, including as many lurid details as decency would allow.

Christie's crimes were made even more memorable when the film *10 Rillington Place* was released in 1971 (and starring Richard Attenborough, not coincidentally), just months prior to this episode being written. See the entry for "does a Dickie Attenborough" for more on this conflation of real and re-enacted life.

"Sorrento" — ("Mrs. Premise and Mrs. Conclusion Visit Jean-Paul Sartre") A popular southern Italian resort city situated on the Sorrento Peninsula, overlooking the Bay of Naples. This is the type of nearby yet still exotically foreign resort town that beckoned to flocks of postwar British travelers who couldn't travel far due to spending money restrictions (see Morgan's *Britain since 1945*).

"spirit . . . original text" — ("Icelandic Saga") Most of the Icelandic sagas were written in plain, unforced language, without much description or flowery verbiage, but with clipped descriptions of *actions* (and not necessarily *intents*). In this way, the North Malden version is somewhat more like the original texts—heroic men and deeds, and careful descriptions of legal and social matters, commerce, and industry.

Stock shot of Eiffel Tower — (PSC; "Mrs. Premise and Mrs. Conclusion Visit Jean-Paul Sartre") This film footage is from Elstree Studios, "World Backgrounds," and is titled "Eiffel Tower" and "French Street" (WAC T12/1,426).

"string remained confident" — ("Stock Market Report") To this day traded commodities on the stock markets are often anthropomorphized, as if they have a life and sentience of their own as they rise and/or fall. Commodities and the market itself can be "strong" or "weak," "safe" or "volatile," etc., as the market allows.

• T •

"Thameside docking facilities" — ("Icelandic Saga") The facilities nearest the Maldens are yachting-type facilities (to the west), for the most part, and not industrial. As larger roadways like the M25 came into use in and around Greater London, however, and lorry transport replaced river/canal transport, the desirability of such docking facilities—except for leisure use—diminished considerably.

• U •

". . . um" — ("Icelandic Saga") If this is actually Eric Njorl reading his own account, then the narrative hijacking begins very early in this episode, and remains the strongest motif of the show. The next time Eric Njorl appears, he is played by Jones, and his name is spelled "Erik."

There is a saga from this same period called *The Tale of Eirek the Traveller*, wherein Eirek is also called "Eirek the Norwegian." See earlier entries in this episode for much more on the sagas. The "Online Medieval & Classical Library" hosted by the University of California, Berkeley graciously offers translations for these and other sagas. See sunsite.berkeley.edu.

"usher" — ("Court Scene [Viking]") An officer of the court. The usher works under the direction of the Court Clerk, normally. The "card" the usher carries would have the oath written down on it, so that a witness being sworn in could read along, hand on the Bible, and affirm to tell the truth.

• V •

"Vadalesc" — ("Icelandic Saga") This is probably a misspelling, but if not, then the fact that here it is spelled without the medial "l" (in the original recitation it was "Valdalesc") may account for the textual revision. Jones's voiceover contains no other change or emendation from the original recitation by Idle's character other than the new *spelling*.

"vin ordinaire" — ("Mrs. Premise and Mrs. Conclusion Visit Jean-Paul Sartre") "Ordinary wine," French wine for everyday use.

Voice — (PSC; animated link out of "Court Scene—Multiple Murderer") The "Voice" (singing "which nobody can deny") sounds like and probably is Gilliam, who continues on with the animation.

• W •

"waterfall" — ("Icelandic Saga") This backdrop appears to be a waterfall at Glencoe, West Highlands, Scotland, where there are a series of falls leading into Loch Achtriochtan and the River Coe.

"We'll ask him" — ("Mrs. Premise and Mrs. Conclusion Visit Jean-Paul Sartre") Just that simple, like the "Man from the Hay Wain" walking up to a Titian painting and being able to talk to the Father/Solomon figure. Woody Allen will borrow this set-up in his 1977 movie *Annie Hall*, where he is able to pull television critical studies professor Marshall McLuhan (1911–1980) from out of nowhere to back up a point of discussion on broadcast theory.

Whicker's World — ("Whicker Island") Alan Whicker (b. 1925) hosted his travel/interview shows around the world, working for the *Tonight* program in the 1950s, then producing such shows as *Whicker Down Under*, *Whicker on Top of the World*, *Whicker Down Mexico Way*, and at least six more similarly titled shows by 1972 (see note for end credits just below). *Whicker's World* appeared in 1959, and ran consistently through 1988. Whicker also appeared in the Peter Sellers's film *The Magic Christian* (1969), for which Chapman and Cleese provided material.

"Windsor, Duke and Duchess" — ("Mrs. Premise and Mrs. Conclusion Visit Jean-Paul Sartre") The tenants in this Paris apartment are as incongruous as the rest of this scene:

Former King Edward VIII (1894–1972) and his American wife Wallis Simpson (1896–1986) did have a Paris villa, near the Bois de Boulogne, where she lived until her death in 1986. Edward had abdicated his throne in 1936 to marry Simpson, and had gone to Paris to escape the press and to allow his younger brother (George VI) the full spotlight as the new king. During the war, the couple lived abroad in the Bahamas, where they were known as the Duke and Duchess of Windsor. After WWII, they returned to France.

"Yves Montand"—Montand (1921–1991) was a French actor. The Pythons here are probably pulling out names of French personalities, as this is an eclectic bunch only connected by their celebrity. Montand's films of this period were *Tout va bien* (Jean-Luc Godard; 1972), *La folie de grandeurs* (1971), and *Le cercle rouge* (1971).

"Jacques Cousteau"—Cousteau (1910–1997) was an underwater adventurer, inventor of the SCUBA system, and well-known television personality by this time. His *The Undersea World of Jacques Cousteau* ran on American TV from 1966 through 1973. Cousteau will be mentioned again in Ep. 30, wrestling for documentary film broadcast rights and repeat fees.

"Jean Genet and Friend"—See note on Genet above. Incidentally, Genet's longtime "friend," Abdallah Bentaga, had committed suicide in 1964. Three years later, Genet would attempt to take his own life. He spent the rest of his life championing radical political and social causes (the Black Panthers, for example) around the world, sneaking across the Canadian border into the United States after being repeatedly denied a visa as a "sexual deviant." It wouldn't be until 1974 (well after this episode is written and broadcast) that Genet would start a new, long-lasting relationship.

"Maurice Laroux"—Maurice *Leroux* (1923–1992) was a composer for such films as *Le ballon rouge* (1956), *Le salaire du péché* (1956), *Les mistons* (1957), and the Godard film *Le petit soldat* (1966). That Godard's name continues to show up isn't coincidental, as he was a prolific and highly controversial political filmmaker, and whose sometime pretentiousness the Pythons had already deflated (see the "French Subtitled Film" in Ep. 23).

"Marcel Marceau . . . Ltd."—Marceau (1923–2007) was a French mime, whose most recent film appearance had been, interestingly enough, *Barbarella* (1968). Marceau performs whiteface mime, and his character's name is "Bip." His trademark is his very subtle and believable "walking against the wind" routine, and which the Pythons (namely Chapman) spoofed in Ep. 13.

"Indira Gandhi"—Gandhi (1917–1984) was Prime Minister of India from 1966 to 1977 and again 1980–1984. Educated at Oxford, there seems to be little reason for her to be living in this Paris flat, except that it's silly, and she would have been quite topical.

• Y •

"you were wilfully and persistently a foreigner" — ("Court Scene [Viking]") The level of xenophobia in the UK seems to have been elevated during this period, with immigration acts passing into law in 1962, 1968, and 1971. Conservative Opposition Cabinet member Enoch Powell would lose his post after speaking his mind about the perceived threat in 1968 (Eps. 5 and 12), when thousands of Kenyan Asians were *legally* entering Britain, many finding their way onto the welfare rolls.

In general, immigration acts passed by Conservative governments tended to tighten immigration policies (i.e., including a demand for employment vouchers), which limited immigrant numbers, while Labour government immigration acts (as in 1968) tried to ease those restrictions, amending the more draconian elements of the Commonwealth Immigrant Act of 1962, for example. The Wilson government did, however, try and stem the legal (but importunate) flow of Commonwealth immigrants, which caused a stir when this hypocritical tack was outed in the press. See the Commonwealth Immigrants Act of 1968 for specific amendments, emendations, and limitations. In Ep. 25, the foreign nationals wandering the streets of London are Hungarian, and thus not strictly affected by the various Commonwealth immigration acts.

Episode 28: "Trim-Jeans Theatre"

Kon Tiki, Ra 1 and Ra 2: Mr. and Mrs. Brian Norris' Ford Popular; **Emigration from Surbiton to Hounslow**; *Animation: Surbiton to Hounslow map*; The Norris' reach Hounslow Central; Nude organist, "And now . . ." Man, and "It's" Man and *titles* (silly Palin v/o); Schoolboys' Life Assurance Company; *How to Do It*: How to rid the world of all known diseases; Mrs. Niggerbaiter explodes; Vicar who is also a salesman; Dynamite can cure athlete's foot; *Animation: Anatomical model walks off the edge of the cartoon*; *Farming Club*: "The Life of Tschaikowsky"; A music critic and famous hairdresser; Tschaikowsky XXI coverage; **Sviatoslav Richter performs Tschaikowsky** as he escapes from a sack and chains; **"Trim-Jeans Theatre"** presents *Murder in the Cathedral*; The Trim-Jeans version of *The Great Escape*; *Animation: Compère's mouth escapes*; **Fish-slapping dance**; World War One: *Animation: Nazi fish swallows British fish, and Chinese fish sinks ocean liner*; Sinking ocean liner: Women, children, red Indians, spacemen and Renaissance men first; "The BBC is short of money"; The Adaptation of "Puss in Boots"; Breaking the set; *Horse of the Year Show* in the Kelly's flat; "BBC 1 are in the kitchen"; Closing credits; "It's" Man show *It's*—with Lulu and Ringo Starr—interrupted

• A •

"AA book" — ("Emigration from Surbiton to Hounslow") Motor guide book from the British Automobile Association. The location of a handy AA office—in the case of nuclear attack—is of great concern to Mrs. S.C.U.M. in Ep. 44, "Mr. Neutron." A yellow AA sign is seen in Ep. 15, when Reg (Chapman) and the BBC Man (Cleese) are driving to a new sketch.

"abattoir" — (*Life of Tschaikowsky*") A slaughterhouse. Mentioned prominently earlier in Ep. 17, in the "Architect Sketch."

"Abide-a-Wee" — ("Emigration from Surbiton to Hounslow") A play on a Northern phrase meaning to stay awhile ("bide-a-wee"), to "wait a bit." The Norrises' home even sports a sign that reads "Abide-a-Wee," though it's not highlighted; it's not finally clear whether the propmaster put up the sign, or the homeowner has actually named his dwelling. Walter Scott employs the phrase in several of his novels, including

Rob Roy (1829) and *Old Mortality* (1816). Scott and his works will be featured in Ep. 38. In *The Bullwinkle Show*, the "Bide-a-Wee Funeral Parlor" is a sponsor for one of Boris Badenov's dastardly schemes (season 2).

The Abide-a-Wee location house is found at 14 Arlington Road, Twickenham. While in Twickenham they had also recorded portions of the "Erik Njorl" saga for Ep. 27—only two blocks away.

"Absolve all those you have excommunicated" — ("Trim-Jeans Theatre") Other than the attackers, only Edward Grim witnessed this murder firsthand, and he recorded the following in *Vita S. Thomae, Cantuariensis Archepiscopi et Martyris* (c. 1170–1177):

The knights came back with swords and axes and other weapons fit for the crime which their minds were set on. . . . The knights cried out, "Where is Thomas Becket, traitor to the King?" Becket . . . in a clear voice answered, "*I am here, no traitor to the King*, but a priest. . . . I am ready to suffer in His name . . . be it far from me to flee from your swords." Having said this, he turned to the right under a pillar . . . and walked to the altar of St. Benedict the Confessor. . . . The murderers followed him; *"Absolve," they cried, "and restore to communion those whom you have excommunicated and restore their powers to those whom you have suspended."* He answered, "I will not absolve them." "Then you shall die," they cried. (italics added)

The Pythons borrow from the Eliot play *Murder in the Cathedral* for their source (see Eliot note below). The play premiered in November 1935. The text as Eliot wrote it for the stage is as follows (original playscript structure not retained), and it's easy to see how Python adapted the scene for their "Trim-Jeans" admag infomercial:

> Thomas: I am here. No traitor to the king. I am a priest.
> A Christian, saved by the blood of Christ,
> Ready to suffer with my blood.
> This is the sign of the Church always,
> The sign of blood. Blood for blood.
>
> First Knight: Absolve all those you have excommunicated.
> Second Knight: Resign the powers you have arrogated.
> Third Knight: Restore to the King the money you appropriated.
> Fourth Knight: Renew the obedience you have violated.
> (2.2)

all in trim-jeans — (PSC; "Trim-Jeans Theatre") Contemporary, local productions of *Murder in the Cathedral* are myriad. A December 1970 production by the Brize Norton Theatre Club in Brize Norton, Oxfordshire; in 1971, the Studio Theatre Club (Salisbury) also performed the play; there is also record of performances in 1955 and 1972 of the play at Brockenhurst County High/Grammar School (meaning other secondary educational institutions, especially Catholic ones, would also have performed the play), the production value of which may have given the Pythons ideas about their own version. The Pythons themselves, as students, *may* have performed in such a play, as well, though the secular nature of the subject matter makes it unlikely.

Becket (Chapman) is the only one on stage not wearing the product, signaling his otherness.

"And now . . ." — (link out of "Emigration from Surbiton to Hounslow") The setting for this season's "And now . . ." moments (with Cleese at the announcer's desk) was located on the southwest portion of the grounds of Norwich Castle, a structure which will double for Edinburgh Castle later in Ep. 38. The Bell Hotel (at 5 Orford Hill) in Norwich can be glimpsed over Cleese's shoulder.

"Anton Chekhov can certainly write" — ("Trim-Jeans Theatre") Clever marketing ploy here, giving weight loss credit not to the product, but to the writer and

production. This might be seen as a way to avoid litigation if the product proves defective or unable to fulfill its promises (though Sauna Belt's many days in court would seem to belie that possible protection).

Apollo-type monograph — (PSC; "*Life of Tschaikowsky*") The backdrop flat is made to look like an Apollo news coverage set from the BBC's extensive coverage of the U.S. space program.

"arrogated" — ("Trim-Jeans Theatre") The fact that there is rhymed verse perhaps unintentionally echoes the affected, alliterative poetic speech used by the critic/hairdresser (Palin) earlier. Unless they are singing or staging portions of a rhymed play, the Pythons tend to avoid rhymed speech. There are multiple versions of this death scene (from Grim through Tennyson and Eliot), with the Pythons choosing the rhyming Eliot version.

"Ascot water heaters" — ("Vicar/Salesman") There exist Ascot hats, dresses, ties, etc., all suitable for wearing to the Royal Enclosure at Ascot. The Ascot Gas Water Heater was a smaller, often single-tapped water heater prevalent in starter homes, council and student housing, etc. They would, perhaps, have been small enough to sell door-to-door. Size aside, the Ascot water heaters were clearly seen as attractive home sales or rental enticements, as they are mentioned by name in scores of real estate classifieds.

"biros"—Generically meaning a ballpoint pen.

"noddy dog"—Dog figurine with a bouncy head.

• B •

bare light bulb — (PSC; "The BBC Is Short of Money") The darkened set is a reference to the nationwide power shortages experienced by the UK in December 1970, brought on by work-to-rule strikes across the country. Power would be reduced as much as 40 percent in many areas, with hospitals being forced to use candles and flashlights (see *Guardian Century Year 1970*).

There is a remarkably similar political cartoon by Stanley Franklin in the *Daily Mirror* (4 Nov. 1966) depicting BBC Director-General Hugh Greene (1910–1987) in a bare office, reading the news under a single light bulb. The cartoon is titled "BBC Plan Economy Cuts." Between 1964 and 1969, at least, the Wilson government saw the BBC, under Greene, as something of an enemy (identifying the BBC as "anti-Labour," specifically):

> Labour had an uneasy relationship with a BBC in the throes of the "Greene revolution," the Director

General's successful attempt to modernise the corporation and to compete more effectively with ITV. In opposition Labour had benefited from the BBC's new-found dynamism as the latter sought to shrug off its stuffy image. A programme like the notorious *TW3* was "anti-pomposity, anti-sanctimony, anti-snob and—blatantly—anti-Conservative." The problem was that it was only a fine line between being anti-Conservative and being anti-government, *any* government. (Freedman, 25)

(Ironically, Tory Winston Churchill had always seen the BBC as a *Leftist* bastion, and in private conversation, opined for a chance to shut the medium down.) As a result, license fee changes, structural reorganizations, and even threats of license revocation were whacked about like political shuttlecocks. One of the more challenging ordeals was PM Wilson's reluctance or refusal to raise the license fee, since he saw the BBC as biased in favor of the political right, leading to cutbacks in BBC production and program availability in 1966–1967. (Alternately, Wilson seemed "comfortable" with the bosses at ITV, which made many feel his bias had to be personal against Greene and the BBC [28].)

"BBC are short of money" — ("The BBC Is Short of Money") The Goons had already questioned the financial stability of the BBC more than a decade earlier. In one of the show's introductory sections, the BBC announcer is taking tips (or handouts) whenever he speaks, and in another, Harry Secombe announces that the BBC have been sold for ten shillings. In another episode, the performers admit that the BBC have agreed to save money by combining sound effects (a car and a bagpipe will make the same sound to cut costs, for example). The fact that the BBC relied on the license fee (affixed to every radio and TV set sold in the UK) meant that as consumer discretionary spending went, so went the fortunes of the BBC, and the postwar era is known as a very challenging time for the British economy.

By 1969, Lord Hill and Harold Wilson's Labour government were preparing to trim the ranks at BBC, including hiving off significant Radio 3 orchestra personnel. The newspapers of the period (including articles, op-ed pieces, and political cartoons) covered the story and public and union outcry from about May through at least September 1969. A cartoon from "Jon" for 25 September 1969 depicts a BBC radio newsreader about to offer a repeat of the previous day's news to save money (*Daily Mail*, 25 Sept. 1969). See the British Cartoon Archive for more.

"BBC has to pay an actor twenty guineas if he speaks" — ("The BBC Is Short of Money") There were precise amounts affixed to walk-on and extra roles,

with speaking parts generating more in payment than others. In the Goons' "Tay Bridge Disaster" episode, one of the band members speaks (with an alarmingly bad Scots accent), and Seagoon (Secombe) comments: "There he goes folks, he and a speaking part fee of two guineas" (9 Feb. 1959).

"BBC Publications" — ("Trim-Jeans Theatre") Companion (printed) publications accompanying many BBC productions, the BBC Publications office was located at 35 Marylebone High Street, London, during this period. In the late 1960s and early 1970s, BBC Publications released titles that included Roger Fiske's *Chamber Music* (1969), Whitting and Bryer's *Byzantium* (1968), and Richard Hooper's *Colour in Britain* (1965). *Byzantium*, for example, was the companion text for a twelve-part BBC Radio broadcast in 1968.

"Becket, Thomas" — ("Trim-Jeans Theatre") Becket (1118–1170) was a clerk, Chancellor, and eventually became Archbishop of Canterbury during Henry II's reign. He had been rather hedonistic and even thug-like prior to his appointment to the deaconship, riding with Henry into battle and enjoying the pomp and fruits of power. He was a great friend to Henry (who was twelve years his junior), and his change surprised, confused, and eventually angered the monarch (not unlike Shakespeare's Prince Hal becoming Henry, and leaving old pal Falstaff dumbfounded and dejected). When Becket began to show more allegiance to God than his king (Henry saw it as betrayal to popery), the end was set for Thomas.

big liner sinking — (PSC; "World War One") This is a miniature special effect shot featuring a model labeled "Titanic." The WAC records indicate that Movietone Library footage from *Titanic* was utilized here, including images A17702-126, A17654-1076, A17709-126, and A17636-1073 (WAC T12/1,427). See the appendices for all stock film (and stock music) used during the run of the show.

The *Titanic*, of course, wasn't sunk by hostile fire. There were a number of passenger ships lost to German attacks during WWI, including the *Lusitania*, *Arabic*, *Sussex*, and *Laconia*.

"Big School" — ("How to Rid the World of All Known Diseases") Generically, the next level of schooling (i.e., secondary school for an elementary pupil).

Blue Peter — (PSC; "How to Rid the World of All Known Diseases") Long-running children's television program (BBC1, 1958–), *Blue Peter* was a children's television magazine show originally presented by Christopher Trace and Leila Williams, followed by Valerie Singleton and Peter Purves (and John Noakes). The show did have a dog, Petra, after 1962 (Vahimagi, 70).

"box girder bridge" — ("How to Rid the World of All Known Diseases") A bridge composed of linked iron boxes, with the four corners of each box connected by angle-irons.

• C •

"capitalist dog" — (animated link into "World War One") Mentioned in Mao Tse-tung's writings and speeches often, with Mao characterizing any anti-revolutionary or revisionist element as "Imperialist running dogs" and the like. For example: "The imperialists and their running dogs, the Chinese reactionaries, will not resign themselves to defeat in this land of China" (from Mao's "Address to the Preparatory Committee of the New Political Consultative Conference" [15 June 1949], *Selected Works* 4:407).

"People's Republic"—The People's Republic of China was established in 1949 by Mao Tse-tung and his Red Army, with Mao installed as the chairman of the central government council.

The fact that China had little or nothing to do with the WWI events and combatants depicted in this animation exhibits the significant contemporary threat (or at least fascination) that Mao's China must have represented, at least for/to Gilliam—here the contemporary Chinese can impose themselves on historical events in which they had no historical part.

"car-swapping belt" — ("Emigration from Surbiton to Hounslow") A kind of regional appellation, like the "Bible Belt" across America's deep south. Some car enthusiasts in the UK practice car-swapping during road rallies, changing cars as clues are discovered. This is probably meant to be a joke, since few would find swapping into a Ford Popular much of a thrill.

cathedral interior — (PSC; "Trim-Jeans Theatre") Historically, Canterbury Cathedral was where Thomas was murdered. This scene was staged in Ealing TFS, where larger set needs could be fulfilled (see "School Prize-Giving," *The Bishop*, and "Accidents Sketch," for example).

Others in this scene include Priests John Hughman, Ian Elliott (*Paul Temple*; *Doctor Who*), and Paul Lindley (*Dixon of Dock Green*), and Waiting Ladies Elizabeth Broom (*Dixon of Dock Green*) and Naomi Sandford (WAC T12/1,428).

"chartered accountancy" — ("Emigration from Surbiton to Hounslow") This dull, uninspired, and wholly inoffensive man is the prototypical Python "type" for a chartered accountant, played often by Palin, and seen earlier in Ep. 2 ("Marriage Guidance Counsellor") and Ep. 10 ("Vocational Guidance Counsellor").

In the featurette "The Crimson Permanent Assurance" prior to *Meaning of Life*, it is the old and beaten-down accountants who swashbuckle their way to financial glory.

"chemists" — ("Emigration from Surbiton to Hounslow") A film developer, often in a pharmacy setting. Boots the Chemist has been popular in the UK for many years, as was the ABC Pharmacy chain, and Harts before that.

Chinese Fish — (animated link into "World War One") This is a bit of an anachronism. The Chinese during WWI were not part of the Kaiser's war effort (internal political turmoil occupying China's factions), and it wouldn't be until WWII and after when Mao and the Communists would figure significantly into world politics. The Chinese Fish is characterized by slanted eyes, buck teeth, and yellow skin/scales—stereotypes not unlike the traditional WWII-era cartoons featuring Axis characters.

"choice" — ("Trim-Jeans Theatre") The freedom to choose and define oneself is perhaps the most significant theme of existential thought. In the Python world, choices have consequences, and they are often fatal. If you ask to see a neighbor die, he will (Ep. 1, "Famous Deaths"); if you agree to attack the self-defense instructor with a banana, you will be shot (Ep. 4, "Self-Defence"); if you choose to see "a Scotsman on a horse," he'll appear (Ep. 2); if you choose to believe in the fantasy block of flats in which you're living, they will remain standing (Ep. 35, "Mystico and Janet"); if you choose to answer honestly that you are, indeed, a "fairy," you will also be shot (Ep. 33, "Biggles Dictates a Letter"); and if you choose blue as your favorite color, then change your mind to yellow, you'll be catapulted to your death (*Holy Grail*).

clips a face — (PSC; animated link into "Farming Club") This looks very much like a cut-out photo of then-FBI director J. Edgar Hoover (b. 1895), who ran the FBI for forty-eight years. This episode was recorded in January 1972, and Hoover would die in May of the same year.

"Cobbley, John" — ("Farming Club") Cobbley was a tenor horn player who, with his G.U.S. Footwear Band Quartet, won the British Open Quartet Championships in Oxford 1966–1968. He may have been known to the Oxfordians (Cleese and/or Palin) in the troupe. The other members of the quartet were John Berryman, David Read, and Trevor Groom.

"Musical . . . Director"—George Solti (1912–1997) was the musical director for the Royal Opera House, Covent Garden from 1961 to 1971. Colin Davis (b. 1927) became musical director there in 1971.

"Covent Garden"—Area in London (near Trafalgar and Leicester squares) where fruit and garden markets had historically been located, as well as the Royal Opera House. The site had been the abbot of Westminster's convent garden when Charles II established the area in 1671.

"complete photographic record" — ("Emigration from Surbiton to Hounslow") No spouses made the Kon Tiki or Ra expeditions—no women at all, actually—so the photographic record was fairly shared by whomever was holding the camera at any particular time. It is possible that Heyerdahl's wife shot some photos of her own as Ra II left its Moroccan port, but she clearly remained behind. Crew member Carlo Mauri shot 16mm film of the Ra II journey, while Heyerdahl notes that even the ship's cook took photographs en route.

"Coover, Gary" — ("Trim-Jeans Theatre") Gary Coover is an actor featured in actual Trim-Jeans TV and print advertisements of this period. Mark Edwards and Jean Wennerstrom also appeared in both print and TV ads. The Pythons were careful to mimic but not copy the ad lingo in their version.

"Cup final tickets" — ("Vicar/Salesman") There is an English Cup final played at Wembley every year, and a World Cup series of matches played internationally every four years.

• D •

"duckety-poos" — (*Life of Tschaikowsky*) Probably a term of endearment, based on "ducky." The following affected alliterations can be read as elevated, effeminized verse, and correspond well with the hairdresser, his "drag queen" voice and bright costume. All of these indicators coalesce to form the "type" the Pythons (and many on TV during this period, including *Laugh-In*'s Alan Sues) project as "gay":

"semi-Mondrian"—Piet Mondrian (1872–1944), an abstract painter—a neoplasticist—eschewed naturalism in favor of angular shapes and primary colors. He was very influential for the later Bauhaus and International Style groups. Since Mondrian was only twenty-one when Tchaikovsky died, and it wasn't until 1910 that Cubism could influence him away from naturalism, the possibility of Tchaikovsky living in a house reminiscent of Mondrian's later work or influence is, well, impossible.

"Lily life"—Also, note that much like the Second Presenter (Cleese) just above who speaks aloud his parentheticals, Maurice (Palin) seems to be doing virtually the same thing—he's saying aloud what could be left in parentheses, and essentially adding merely alliterative words that don't necessarily modify the words that follow them. The sentence reads quite straightforwardly with the words removed: "Here Tschaikowsky wrote some of the most super symphonies you've ever heard in the whole of your life."

The "not-parentheticals" are also all just fairly common first names: Robin, Harry, Tammy, Sammy, Henry, Lily, Sally, Patsy, Adrian, Conny, Vera, Peter, and Fanny. These are followed in his last speech below by "Dickie," "Colin," "Patsy," "Gertie," and "Percy." This is not unlike Ep. 12 wherein the policemen characters must speak/shout in different registers, tempos, even pitches to be properly understood among each other. This type of miscommunication is a Python trademark, with characters having learned or having to learn the particular speech idiosyncrasy before communication is possible.

Lastly, speech-language pathologist Caroline Bowen, Ph.D., gives a quick rundown of what it might mean to "sound gay," and it's as if the Pythons read the primer, then wrote these flamboyant characters. Bowen identifies the subtle prolonging of /l/, /s/, and /z/, the emphasizing and increased aspiration of final stop consonants, lisping, upward inflections, prolonging vowels ("extraooordinary") and consonants ("Ssssammy sssuper sssymphonies"), pursing lips at word initiation, rising voice pitch, and "breathing through sounds." Finally, she identifies the use of vocabulary and expressions that have been culturally flagged as "gay" (the critic/hairdresser refers to Tchaikowsky as "she"), as well as "the adopting of a high camp demeanor." Language, expression, and appearance, then, continue to be oft-used tools as the Pythons construct ready-made types for quick audience identification. See Bowen for more.

• E •

"EBW 343" — ("Emigration from Surbiton to Hounslow") License plate number of the Ford Popular, and probably a play on the designations "Ra I" and "Ra II," etc.

"Eliot, T.S." — ("Trim-Jeans Theatre") Thomas Stearns Eliot (1888–1965) was a poet, essayist, and playwright, whose interests moved from the desolation of *The Waste Land* (1922) to religiosity and even some hope for the salvation of humanity, as exhibited in his 1935 play *Murder in the Cathedral*.

Eliot was influential to the Pythons as he focused on two major themes in much of his work: primitive and metropolitan life—which the Pythons also explore and satirize throughout *FC* and beyond, into the feature films. (See Crawford's *The Savage and the City*.) Eliot's portrait of London in *The Waste Land* is also compelling, as is his use of nontraditional language and imagery. The Pythons clearly mined the tavern scene in the poem earlier, in Ep. 3. See the entry for "hire purchase" there for much more.

"encyclopaedias" — ("Vicar/Salesman") This gag is also found in the magazine *Private Eye* (July 1962), and was first broached in *FC* in Ep. 5, when an encyclopedia salesman poses as a burglar just to get into a home and make a sale.

Concern (or frustration) regarding these door-to-door salesmen reached the highest levels of government, obviously, as in February 1966 the House of Commons took up the matter. Mr. Morris of Manchester, Wythenshawe (Labour) pointed out that some such companies schooled their salesmen to "conceal their purpose"; Mr. Darling of Sheffield, Hillsborough (also Labour) noted that any law passed would be nearly possible to enforce on a door-by-door basis; Mr. Emery of Reading (Conservative) suggested that his honorable colleagues were nearly door-to-door salesmen themselves, and hoped "the prospectus presented by us will be one accepted by the Consumer Council as honest and straightforward"; and finally, Mr. Goodhart of Beckenham (also Conservative), calling many such tradesmen "unscrupulous," described a doorstep confrontation he'd experienced:

> Not long ago a gentleman engaged me in conversation. He said he wished to seek my advice as a recognized leader in education. This was an irresistible opening gambit. Within 60 seconds I discovered he wished to sell me an encyclopaedia. The conversation closed within another 60 seconds.

This was all part of the first reading. The bill was approved for a second reading, meaning it could move forward and be formally discussed. ("Checking the Doorstep Rogues," *Times*, 26 Feb. 1966: 12).

Episode 28 — Recorded 28 January 1972, and broadcast 26 October 1972. These people were scheduled to appear at Television Centre 6 (TC6) on 28 January 1972 for extras work: Julia Breck (*Q5*), Graham Skidmore (*Dixon of Dock Green*), Jeremy Higgins (*Doctor in Charge*), Frank Menzies (*Doctor Who*), Eric Kent (*Doctor in the House*), Terence Sartain (*Doctor Who*), Chris Hodge (*Softly Softly*), Geoffrey Brighty (*Emma*), Keith Ashley (*Doctor in the House*), Harry Tierney (*Doctor Who*), Douglas Hutchinson, Freda Jeffries (*Z Cars*), and *FC* semi-regular John Hughman (WAC T12/1,428).

"escape from a sack" — ("*Life of Tschaikowsky*") It is possible that since pianist Richter (1915–1997) was a Soviet citizen and not free to travel without permission (or collateral), he may have been seen as an

escape artist of sorts as he performed in the West. In fact it took significant time and convincing of Soviet authorities to allow Richter his first trip to America. As with other artists (dancers, musicians, filmmakers) from the Soviet Union, the international goodwill potential for the Communist state often outweighed the possibility (and actuality, sometimes) of a defection. (Celebrated dancer Rudolf Nureyev [1938–1993], for example, defected in 1961.)

The visual symbols of chains and a suffocating bag would have been eminently recognizable to those in the West who were living with the fears of the Red menace and the Cold War.

"handcuffs"—This leans more toward a Harry Houdini (1874–1926) feat than Richter, but the incongruous combination of the two seems about right for Python. Refer back to a government minister performing a burlesque dance while citing foreign agricultural trade policy in Ep. 20.

"exeat form" — ("Schoolboys' Life Assurance Company") A permission slip, essentially, to leave the school's premises.

"extremely naughty for his time" — ("*Life of Tschaikowsky*") Referring to Tchaikovsky's homosexuality, of course, which troubled him throughout his life—some scholarship even claiming it was the reason behind his death by suicide. For more, see entry for "Glenda Jackson" below.

• F •

"*Farming Club* special, the life of Tchaikowsky" — ("*Life of Tchaikowsky*") The very popular radio show *The Archers* (1950–) had begun as a sort of Ministry of Agriculture mouthpiece, where listeners could be reminded of postwar rationing limits, the "English way" of doing things in the face of the thriving European market, and agricultural tips for gardens and farms. It was an organ of the government, designed to make postwar scarcity and thrift more palatable.

first piano concerto — (PSC; "Farming Club") This is not, in fact, Tchaikovsky's first concerto, which will be heard later in the episode as the pianist Sviatoslav Richter (Jones) escapes from chains.

The track being used here is a portion of the first movement of Tchaikovsky's "Symphonie Pathetique," his sixth symphony ("Adagio—Allegro non troppo" section), his final and most poignant work. The symphony was written after he turned fifty, and as he struggled with failing health and what he feared was an evaporating musical gift; he wrote to his nephew that he was suffering "torments" (Orlova). This was the "tortured old ponce" the Pythons were treating here, and someone in the troupe picked the appropriate musical work for the moment. Tchaikovsky would die just a few days after the symphony's premiere.

This specific performance is by the USSR Symphony Orchestra ("Symphony No. 6 in B Minor Allegro non Troppo") (WAC T12/1,427).

"foot and mouth" — ("Farming Club") Also called FMD (foot and mouth disease, or "hoof and mouth"), the disease is less rampant than it was, but is still usually fatal (meaning animals must be quarantined and put down).

"Ford Popular" — ("Emigration from Surbiton to Hounslow") Ford automobile built in the UK between 1953 and 1959, the Popular was a very basic car, with few amenities, and designed for the "austerity" period after WWII. There were more than 150,000 produced during this period for the eager postwar buyer, and was hailed as the cheapest new car available (priced at £390 in 1953).

"Forty minutes . . . Brentford" — ("Emigration from Surbiton to Hounslow") The Richmond-to-Hounslow leg is actually about a sixteen-minute train ride, and traveling via "Clapham, Fulham and Chiswick" (well east of Hounslow) would take the Norrises well out of their way, unless they were headed for Ealing. As indicated in the "Railway Timetables" sketch in Ep. 24, of course, finite accuracy isn't the benchmark the Pythons often aim for.

The Brentford Football Ground was where various works of fine art gather to take a strike vote (Ep. 25).

"four knights" — ("Trim-Jeans Theatre") These are the four knights who acted on Henry II's rash cry for Becket's life. Becket was allegedly stabbed and hacked to death in the cathedral itself on 29 December 1170. The knights by name: Hugh de Morville, William de Tracy, Reginald Fitz Urse, and Richard Le Bret.

Fox, Paul Jnr — (PSC; "Emigration from Surbiton to Hounslow") Paul Fox (b. 1925) was at this time Monty Python's boss, essentially, and a generation older, at least. Fox was, with Bill Cotton, head of BBC Light Entertainment, which oversaw *FC* and other comedy programs. Fox will actually be lampooned later in the episode ("The BBC Is Short of Money"), played by a made-up Jones.

The Pythons had clashed with Fox at the beginning of the broadcast run of the second season, when their time slot was slated for an "opt out" slot in most regions, and most regions were opting out and not carrying the show (WAC T12/1,418). Opt-outs allow for regional or even local programming in place of national shows.

The bad feelings didn't just go away, obviously, as a September 1972 memo from Duncan Wood to Ian MacNaughton (then in Bayern, Germany, for the *FZ* shooting) asks if the continued use of a cut-out image of Paul Fox in the animations is really a good thing, or just "an in-house joke gone too long" (WAC T12/1,428).

"Francis, Kevin" — ("Trim-Jeans Theatre") Francis was a production manager for the Python film *And Now for Something Completely Different* (1971), which the Pythons shot while on hiatus between season two and three of *FC*. Jones and John Hughman play the part in the "Trim-Jeans Theatre" sketch.

"Fritz" — (animated link into "World War One") Shortened version of Friedrich, and used as a nickname for German soldiers in World War I. The epithet "Jerry" was used more in World War II. It's not entirely clear why this sketch is set in/called "World War One," except that the ship being sunk may be a *Lusitania*-type passenger liner, several of which fell prey to German U-boats in WWI.

• G •

"GDBDMDB" — ("Emigration from Surbiton to Hounslow") Probably a play on early computer lingo ("GDB," "MDB"), part of the jabberwock language often spoken by Python characters.

"excess . . . tamping"—Again, silly speak, since a "wopple" is actually a bridle lane and "tamping" means to pack a blast hole above the charge. This is symptomatic of Idle's consistent playfulness with words and language, as heard in the "Stock Exchange Report" in the previous episode.

General panic and dramatic music — (PSC; "World War One") The dramatic music as the ship sinks is from Theme Suites, Vol. 11, "Under Full Sail" by Johnny Pearson (WAC T12/1,427).

"generated independently" — ("Emigration from Surbiton to Hounslow") Heyerdahl had originally gone to the Marquesas Islands in 1937–1938 to study the transoceanic flora and fauna, finding that it was far more reasonable to assume that ancient travelers had made their way to the South Pacific with the help of the strong currents, and began to debunk the reigning theory that Southeast Asian ancients had found a way to struggle against the currents to reach the islands. So it was a similarity and commonality in plant and animal life that first piqued Heyerdahl's interest, *then* the search for human-made similarities would begin.

Heyerdahl's work was published in 1941 and 1952. In the Galapagos (1952) and Easter Island (1955–1956) expeditions, Heyerdahl's discoveries include Incan and pre-Incan tools and instruments (including navigational instruments), and stone carvings similar to those found in Peru, further supporting his theories.

"Gielgud, Sir John" — ("Trim-Jeans Theatre") Gielgud (1904–2000) was a well-respected British actor and, coincidentally, portrayed Louis VII in the 1964 film about Thomas, *Becket*. The role of Becket was played by Richard Burton, while Peter O'Toole played Henry.

This mention of Gielgud (and *Home*) was likely prompted by the airing of the David Storey play *Home* on BBC 1 in January 1972, starring Gielgud and Ralph Richardson. Gielgud was also appearing at the Royal Court in *Veterans* with John Mills (Ep. 23) in 1972, garnering very favorable reviews.

Golden Egg or Wimpy — (PSC; "Emigration from Surbiton to Hounslow") Golden Egg was a chain of low-priced restaurants (owned by Philip Kaye and family) where drinks, coffee, or a meal could be had. Begun in the 1950s, they were described as "colourful, cheap and homogenous: the same layout whether you were in Dover or Dundee" (from "Designing Britain"). Golden Egg franchise outlets were originally located in Aberdeen, Bath, Birmingham, Bournemouth, Brighton, Colchester, Coventry, Great Yarmouth, Norwich, and Liverpool.

The "Wimpy" name came from J. Wellington Wimpy of *Popeye* fame, and was a high street restaurant franchise begun in the UK in 1954 (imported by J. Lyons).

In the film it's clear that they are dining in a restaurant called "Egg Nest," with some slightly garish red lighting inside. This is the Egg Nest then located at 24 New Broadway in Ealing. The restaurant was just a block from Ealing TFS, and a few steps from both The Broadway and Uxbridge Road, areas where the Pythons shot many of their high street–type exteriors for the first and second seasons.

Great Escape, The — (PSC; "Trim-Jeans Theatre") Hollywood feature film based on a true story of the escape of seventy-six prisoners from Stalag Luft III in 1944, directed by John Sturges, and starring Steve McQueen. The signature music was composed by Elmer Bernstein for the film. The book was written by Paul Brickhill, who was himself an escapee of Stalag III. This film/book was referenced earlier in Ep. 18, "Escape (From Film)." This escape footage was shot in the Oban area while the Pythons were shooting in Scotland.

The signature music is performed by Geoff Love and Orchestra, from the album *Big War Movie Themes*, and was composed by Elmer Bernstein (WAC T12/1,427).

• H •

"Hello Pianist" — (*Life of Tschaikowsky*) The title of "Hello Sailor" (same homosexual connotation) was used in Ep. 2, and later spoken in a very effeminate manner in Ep. 14, the "New Cooker Sketch" (by a flamboyantly gay cross-dresser). As seen in earlier episodes, this is the clarion call of the poofy presenter, the academic, the politician, even the historical icon—in short, the sexual orientation of any establishment type is immediately in question in the Python world. It also doesn't hurt that "pianist" can sound a lot like "penis" or "pee"—good for a chuckle in the boys' room.

Horse of the Year Show — ("Puss in Boots") Britain's yearly indoor equine event, the show includes showing, jumping, and stunt and trick riding.

"Hounslow" — ("Emigration from Surbiton to Hounslow") South and west of the City, in Greater London, near Heathrow Airport. The Egg Nest restaurant where Mr. and Mrs. Norris (Palin and Chapman) dine was found in Hounslow.

"Hounslow 25 Miles" — ("Emigration from Surbiton to Hounslow") Surbiton and Hounslow are only about eight miles apart, so Mr. Norris (Palin) was obviously already well off course. Later, Mr. Pither (also Palin) will find Soviet Russia on his tour of Cornwall (Ep. 34).

How to Do It — ("How to Rid the World of All Known Diseases") A spoof of the 1966–1981 Southern TV (est. 1958) children's show *How*, offering "facts and fun" for the younger viewer. The hosts were Bunty James, Fred Dinenage, Jack Hargreaves, and Jon Miller (see Vahimagi, *British Television*, 148).

The happy music played beneath these titles is from the Theatre Orchestra Light Intimations, "Days Work," by Mike McNaught (WAC T12/1,427).

In a likely nod to the production and transmission of the show *How* itself (and *Blue Peter* et al.), this sketch begins with an "iris-out" wipe. This is the kind of precious, obvious transition (it's an electronic edit, with the switcher pulling a handle on the control board to accomplish the move from camera to camera) that draws attention to itself, and has been used in sitcoms since the days of *I Love Lucy*.

Hughman, John — ("Trim-Jeans Theatre") It almost never happens that an extra is mentioned by name in the scripts, but Hughman's tall, very gaunt frame was just what the Pythons were thinking when they wrote the "after" character for this Trim-Jeans promo image. A bit actor, Hughman appears in several *FC* episodes, including Eps. 14 and 41, and later in *Whoops Baghdad!* and *Time Bandits*. Hughman also poses for the "Naughtiest Girl in the School" photo (in string vest and skirt) in Ep. 26, has appeared in a bit speaking part as a Gasman (Ep. 14) and an embarrassed Chemist customer (Ep. 17), and will finally play the Poet Laureate Tennyson in Ep. 41.

• I •

"Italian Grand Prix at Monza" — ("Schoolboys' Life Assurance Company") A car race event initiated in 1922, this Formula One series event in 1971 featured the fastest average speed in the history of the race, a record that still stands. Peter Gethin won this 1971 race, and Emerson Fittipaldi would win the 1972 event.

In 1972 Fittipaldi became the youngest driver (age twenty-five) to win a Formula One championship, a possible reason for the inclusion of the race in the Python sketch about youngsters doing adult things.

It's — ("The BBC Is Short of Money") There were a number of shows beginning with "It's" on British TV, including *It's a Knockout* (1966), *It's a Square World* (1960–1964), and *It's Only Us* (1968). See notes for Ep. 2 for more uses in *FC*.

• J •

"Jackson, Glenda" — ("Trim-Jeans Theatre") Born in 1936, Jackson is an actress who performed an uncredited bit part in the early Angry Young Man film *This Sporting Life* (1963), she played both Elizabeth I and Mary Queen of Scots in 1971, and appeared in Ken Russell's *The Music Lovers* (1971). This was Russell's version of the tumultuous life of Tchaikovsky, and the inclusion/mention of Jackson connects this Becket sketch back to the Tchaikovsky sketch seemingly finished earlier.

jolly music of Edward German — ("Fish-Slapping Dance") One of the few times in the printed scripts that the Pythons are so specific in their incidental music cues. Edward German (1862–1936) was perhaps the first professional British film music composer, and his orchestral works obviously inspired this inclusion. The WAC records for the episode do not mention German, meaning the music used was found elsewhere (perhaps more affordably), and the Pythons were likely referring to German's "Seasons" or "Merrie England" compositions for the needed "jolly" jauntiness.

Jolly showbiz music — (PSC; "Trim-Jeans Theatre") The music used under the opening titles of this infomercial is Anthony Mawer's "Theatre Overture" (WAC T12/1,427). The Pythons would go back to

Mawer for some of the incidental music for the feature film *Holy Grail*, using a portion of his composition "Countrywide." The serene theme can be heard in *HG* when the opening credits change to the more sedate mode, prior to the producers being "sacked" again.

• K •

"Kierkegaardian moment" — ("Trim-Jeans Theatre") Thomas must choose between his longtime friend Henry and the friendship they once knew, and the responsibilities of leading the Church and serving God. Philosopher Søren Kierkegaard (1813–1855) writes in the "Equilibrium between the Aesthetic and the Ethical" chapter of *Either/Or*:

> But the reason why it can seem to an individual that he could constantly change yet remain the same, as if his inmost being were an algebraic entity that could stand for whatever it might be, is to be found in the fact that he has the wrong attitude; he has not chosen himself, he has no conception of doing so, and yet even in his lack of understanding there is an acknowledgment of the eternal validity of personal existence. For someone with the right attitude, on the other hand, things go differently. He chooses himself, not in a finite sense, for then this "self" would be something finite along with other finite things, but in an absolute sense. And still he chooses himself and not another. This self he thus chooses is infinitely concrete, for it is himself, and yet it is absolutely different from his former self, for he has chosen it absolutely. The self did not exist previously, for it came into existence through the choice, and yet it has been in existence, for it was indeed "he himself." (517)

This "choice" made by Thomas—to abandon the reprobate person he was and follow God—means he has become, by choice, a new and distinct self, a new Thomas. Henry is upset because the Thomas he knew and loved is gone forever, essentially betrayed and even destroyed by the new Thomas. Shakespeare demands that young Prince Hal make this same choice when he "grows up," abandons Falstaff and his old tavern acquaintances, and becomes "Henry," his father's kingly son. Falstaff feels betrayed, like Henry II, but cannot act to diminish the betrayal.

For the Pythons, choice can and does bring into existence all sorts of things, as mentioned above in the "choice" entry. In Ep. 9, a "straight man" (Idle) wants to become more funny, and his choice leads to him becoming the butt of all the following jokes. Perhaps even more interesting is the appearance of Bob's twin (both characters played by Idle) after Sir George Head (Cleese) wills him into existence for the viewer—the new Bob is "absolutely distinct from his former self," so much so that he is very much ready to embark on the trip his twin has just refused.

"Kingston by-pass" — ("Emigration from Surbiton to Hounslow") Built in the 1930s to reduce the traffic congestion on old Portsmouth Road.

"Kon-Tiki" — ("Emigration from Surbiton to Hounslow") A modern "primitive" log raft built and sailed in 1947 by explorer/archaeologist Thor Heyerdahl. His goal: to prove his own thesis that ancient South Americans first settled Polynesia, and could have sailed from Peru to the Tuamotu Archipelago, part of French Polynesia. Heyerdahl wrote a very popular book about the voyage, called *Kon Tiki*, which was released in 1950.

As a precedent, in the *Goon Show* episode "Drums along the Mersey," Neddie (Secombe) attempts to prove that the people of Wales originally came from across the sea:

> Grytpype (Sellers): Neddie, we have just discovered, through the courtesy of Mr. Bentine, that you are a Peruvian!
>
> Seagoon: What? But mother said I was born in South Wales!
>
> Grytpype: Of course! Didn't you know that Cardiff originally came from Peru on a raft?
>
> Seagoon: This is wonderful, man. But how can I prove that all Welsh people come from Peru?
>
> Grytpype: Really, it's quite simple. You sail from South America to Cardiff on this cardboard raft . . .
>
> Seagoon: Aye.
>
> Grytpype: . . . and the million pounds is yours to spend right away. Moriarty?
>
> Moriarty (Milligan): Oh, yes sir, yes. Yes indeed, little Welsh blubber. You try this Kon-Tiki type craft at once. (11 Oct. 1956)

• **L** •

"left at Barnes" — ("Emigration from Surbiton to Hounslow") Barnes is in Greater London, Richmond Upon Thames, and these are confused directions, at best. The A308 does run west, but from Hampton Court west, while Norbiton is actually north and east of Surbiton, so Mr. Norris (Palin) would be well off course going that route. Directions have been confused in *FC* since the first episode, when Picasso tried to paint while competing in a bike race, and continuing through Sir George Head's attempts to get from London to Africa in Ep. 9, and Neville Shunt's railway timetable plays in Ep. 24.

"Life and Loves of Toulouse-Lautrec, The" — ("Trim-Jeans Theatre") There was a Brazilian TV film from 1963 called *Moulin Rouge, A Vida de Toulouse Lautrec*, written and directed by Geraldo Vietri, as well as a 1939 German film called (in its U.S. release) *The Life and Loves of Tchaikovsky*. Toulouse-Lautrec was previously mentioned/shown in Ep. 1.

"London Electricity Board" — ("The BBC Is Short of Money") A formerly government-owned (nationalized in 1947) utility that has since been privatized. Many of the nation's most critical industries were brought into central control during or after the war, in the hopes of controlling production, security, and prices.

In February 1972, the Board was publishing "power cut" notices in newspapers and on leaflets, as well as posting helpful blackout diagrams, street by street, in Board showroom windows. The coal miner strike had decimated coal supplies which fueled most of the country's power stations. Customers were given levels of "disconnexion" likelihood per week—two days of "high risk," two days of "medium risk," and two days of "low risk" (*Times*, 9 Feb. 1972: 2). So-called critical industries—health care, sewage treatment, water and gas pumping, etc.—were not affected by these potential disconnections. Train service, however, was affected, and late trains became more common. Power stations had officially run out of their coal stocks on February 7, and heavy industry began to shut down the following day.

Long Day's Journey into Night — ("Trim-Jeans Theatre") Eugene O'Neill (1888–1953) play written and presented to his wife in 1941, but not produced until 1956, three years after his death. Sir Ralph Richardson (mentioned elsewhere in this scene) appeared in the acclaimed 1962 film version directed by Sidney Lumet.

"Lose inches . . . abdomen" — ("Trim-Jeans Theatre") In 1970–1971, the Trim-Jeans product and company (Sauna Belt Inc.) were the focus of a lawsuit alleging false advertising, misrepresentation of the product's effectiveness, safety, etc. The British Consumers' Association magazine *Which?* had even group-tested both the Trim-Jeans and Sauna Belt in summer 1971 and found that contrary to the devices' claims of weight and inches loss, many testers actually *added* an inch or so during the test period (*Times*, 12 Aug. 1971: 2). A California court would find on 20 January 1971 that the complainants failed to prove sufficiently the charges against Sauna Belt, and that Sauna Belt had already altered its advertising claims to ameliorate the situation.

In October 1972, however, a further proceeding reversed the earlier decision, and found for the complainants, ordering "remedial" steps be taken against Sauna Belt Inc. for false advertising, obtaining money through the mail fraudulently, etc. The full text of the proceedings can be found on the usps.com/judicial website.

Perhaps the fact that the Sauna Belt company was under such intense scrutiny gave the Pythons license, they felt, to openly satirize the company and its products and pitch techniques. English libel and slander laws were/are known for favoring the plaintiff, meaning the Pythons certainly could have gotten into trouble for this possible defamation (as the editors of *Private Eye* did, regularly), but the extant legal troubles for Sauna Belt probably kept their attention off the Pythons.

Lulu — (PSC; "*It's*") Pop singer and actress born in 1948 in Glasgow, she appeared in the movie *To Sir, with Love* (1967), and sang the title song, as well as co-winning the Eurovision Song Contest in 1968 with the song "Boom Bang-a-Bang."

"lying like a silver turd" — ("Emigration from Surbiton to Hounslow") The Thames has been poetically treated in literature for centuries, and even in the squalor of the modern, industrial city, T.S. Eliot can ask "Sweet Thames, run softly, till I end my song" (which is itself a borrow from Spenser), and much of *The Waste Land* is dedicated to this artery of the city.

The Thames had, of course, been the dumping ground for the city's human garbage, industrial waste, medical waste, offal, abattoir leavings, and on and on—and provided drinking water all the while—until well into the nineteenth century, meaning, by composition, the Thames was very much "like a silver turd." Ackroyd points out that Spenser, Herrick, Pope, and Drayton all described the Thames with the "silver" epithet, meaning the Pythons would have found the simile in their assigned classical readings (*London*, 532–33).

• M •

"married to Vern Plachenka (Julie Christie) but secretly deeply in love . . ." — ("*Life of Tschaikowsky*") This thumbnail sketch of the plot sounds very much like a spoof of the recent hit film *Dr. Zhivago* (1965), starring Omar Sharif and Julie Christie.

"Metropolitan Railway" — ("Emigration from Surbiton to Hounslow") Britain's national rail service for the Greater London area, and including the underground sections. The Metro Railway opened in January 1863.

This station is in Twickenham, and permission for what looks like early morning shooting had to be obtained from British Railways. These shots were made on 4 November 1971 (WAC T12/1,482).

"Minister for Overseas Development" — ("Mrs. Nigger-Baiter Explodes") The Ministry for Overseas Development was set up in 1964 as a separate minis-

try to develop and oversee colonial economic matters. This ministry was a combination of the Department of Technical Cooperation, as well as "the overseas aid policy functions of the Foreign, Commonwealth Relations and Colonial Offices" ("DFID Historical").

By 1970, though, the ministry was again dissolved and its functions transferred to the Secretary of State for Foreign and Commonwealth Affairs, with the overseas work then under the aegis of the Overseas Development Administration (ODA).

During the period this sketch was written/performed (1971–1972), the man filling this ministerial position was the Right Honorable Richard Wood (1970–1974). There is no indication that Wood lived with his aged mother in this way, but he was in the news as he traveled to Pakistan after a particularly devastating cyclone in December 1970, ostensibly to bring millions of pounds in relief and aid packages, but instead disingenuously proffering already-promised funds with significant interest and restrictive quid pro quo trade agreements attached (*Private Eye* 187, December 1970: 22).

"Ministry" — ("Farming Club") In this case MAFF, the Ministry of Agriculture, Fisheries and Food. James Prior was the minister in place 1970–1972.

Mother Goose — ("Puss in Boots") One of the well-known pantomimes performed during Christmas in Britain; others include *Peter Pan, Sleeping Beauty, Dick Whittington, Aladdin*, and *Snow White*. All feature audience participation, cross-dressing (ugly sisters played by men), pratfalls, song, and broad humor. Python employs the pantomime goose a number of times in *FC*, as well as pantomime horses, and even a pantomime Princess Margaret (see Eps. 29, 30).

"Mrs. David . . . Number 3" — ("The BBC Is Short of Money") Atalanta 3 was a chestnut born in 1948, and had a career including seventy-six starts, twenty wins, seven places, and ten shows. David Barker rode North Flight at the Tokyo Olympics in 1964.

• N •

naked sailor — (PSC; "*Life of Tschaikowsky*") This photo (shot by Robert Broeder) was used earlier, in Ep. 2 (WAC T12/1,427). One of the more pernicious rumors of the period was that Tchaikovsky's intimate relationship with a nobleman's son may have led to the composer's suicide (or even murder) by poisoning.

Nazi Fish — (PSC; animated link into "World War One") These three voices are not identified in the written scripts but are as follows: Nazi Fish—Terry Jones; Britisher Fish—Michael Palin; Chinese Fish—Graham Chapman.

"Nelson's Column" — ("*Life of Tschaikowsky*") Found in Trafalgar Square, the column is 185 feet tall, with a seventeen-foot statue of Nelson atop.

News at Nine — ("The BBC Is Short of Money") Fashioned by the Pythons after ITV's *News at Ten* (ITN, 1967–), which had originally aired in a twelve-minute format at 8:55 p.m. *News at Ten* was one of the top twenty-ranked shows on British TV in 1970–1972. *News at Nine* and anchor Richard Baker will be prominently featured again in Ep. 30, as well as Ep. 33.

"Nigger-Baiter" — ("Mrs. Nigger-Baiter Explodes") Literally, the term used here means one who "baits" or taunts, jabs, or calls out a black. (But, if this is being used as the terms bear-baiting and bull-baiting were utilized in Elizabethan times, then the term actually means "the action of baiting a black with dogs." Neither is a particularly attractive option.) It should also be noted that even in the press of the Pythons' youth these terms were ubiquitous. In a *Time* magazine article from 1941 detailing FDR's actions against wildcat strikers, the columnist identifies "the noisy nigger in the strike woodpile" (16 June 1941). In this article the term is used as an inoffensive colloquialism, and not intended as a bit of inflammatory speech (the magazine's white, upper-middle-class readership acknowledged). By the 1960s the level of sensitivity had increased somewhat, at least in the popular press, and the "nigger-baiter" term is often printed as "race-baiter," instead. (A number of these characters appeared in films looking at American soldiers in WWII, becoming almost a type, or stock character.)

The level of racial insensitivity during this period on British television programs has to be looked at in the context of the times, as the Pythons (and others) felt free to use terms like "Nip," "Jap," "Wop," and "Darkie" without apology and, importantly, without censure. Just a generation earlier the Goons had used black bandleader Ray Ellington as the butt of myriad jokes focusing on his skin color, many of which Ellington himself initiated (at least textually). The cartoons the Pythons (and their viewers and employers) grew up with were also quite racially insensitive, with the major American studios (including Warner Bros., MGM, and Disney) producing countless images of shiftless, lazy, shuffling black characters throughout the 1930s and 1940s. See WB's *Inki and the Minah Bird* (1943), directed by Chuck Jones, for instance. (See Bogle's *Toms, Coons, Mulattoes, Mammies, & Bucks* for more on the subject, and it becomes disturbingly clear just what cinematic and television depictions of blacks the Pythons could draw from.) They grew up reading (or being read to from) *Little Black Sambo*, and eating Robertson's jam with Golly the Golliwog character on the container. Hispanic characters suffered the same

stereotyping in the "Speedy Gonzalez" cartoons, as well. There isn't any indication in the WAC records for the show that the BBC higher-ups—who complained liberally about depictions of Christ and cannibalism and the royals, etc.—ever lodged an official complaint in regard to the depiction of any foreigner, race, or use of racially charged term.

It is worth pointing out, however, that the character with such an offensive name ("Nigger-Baiter by name, Nigger-Baiter by nature"?) is immediately destroyed in the text, as if suffering instant karmic retribution. In the feature film *Meaning of Life* (1983), the charwoman (Jones) cleaning up after Mr. Creosote (also Jones) is textually punished immediately after she admits she's glad she doesn't "work for Jews." The "grinning type monster" Michael Miles character (Cleese) in Ep. 20 is not punished, however, for disliking "darkies," so the Pythons clearly pick and choose their moments.

"not Church people" — ("Vicar/Salesman") This is usually a response to door-to-door evangelizing, but in this case potential converts are actually potential customers, and they're not going to *buy* a product because they don't happen to be members of the Church of England. This equating of organized religion and boundless greed is seen earlier in *FC*. In Ep. 24, the Pythons offer Arthur Crackpot (Idle) as the unapologetic moneygrubber in the guise of an organized religious leader, while in Ep. 6, the vicar is clearly stealing from the donation box.

"not religious"—Again, its not what's for sale, per se, but the fact that something is being sold by a man of the cloth. Here the selling of traditional door-to-door items is equated with the selling of salvation by representatives of the church (ostensibly the Church of England), and of religion in general. In *Canterbury Tales*, Chaucer castigates his seemingly religious characters, including those who offer indulgences like the Pardoner, ostensibly raising funds to support the church. There's no indication here that the Vicar (Idle) is doing anything other than supplementing his own income.

• O •

"old poof" — ("*Life of Tschaikowsky*") Tchaikovsky was in fact a closet homosexual, and spent much of his life fighting against his inclinations, at least publicly. He did even marry, disastrously, and eventually (some scholars have asserted) took his own life rather than be publicly revealed as a practicing homosexual (see Orlova).

"Omalley" — ("The BBC Is Short of Money") Misspelled here in the printed scripts. Harvey Smith placed third on "O'Malley" in the 1963 European Show Jumping Championships.

• P •

***"Panorama* report"** — ("Schoolboys' Life Assurance Company") *Panorama* is a long-running interview/presentation program on BBC-TV (1953–) featuring interviewers Robin Day and Richard Dimbleby, and others. The Pythons often use the *Panorama* "style" for their documentary and interviewing spoofs.

"Parsons Green" — ("Emigration from Surbiton to Hounslow") In Hammersmith, south and west of the City of London. This is not far south of BBC Television Centre in Shepherd's Bush.

"Pasteur" — (link out of "Vicar/Salesman") Dr. Louis Pasteur (1822–1995) was a renowned French chemist who pioneered work in bacteria, Pasteurization, and vaccines. For many, the idea of inoculation (introducing a virus into the host to stimulate antibody production, thus protecting the host) did promote skepticism, even as late as Pasteur's era. So, the Doctor (Chapman) is merely mimicking this treatment regimen, though with dynamite, and more lethal results.

"people explode everyday" — ("Mrs. Nigger-Baiter Explodes") Spontaneous human combustion was much in the news in the UK in the mid-1960s, especially after the publication of a paper entitled "A Case of Spontaneous Combustion" by Dr. David Gee of the University of Leeds. Previously thought to be quite supernatural, the phenomena of people exploding in flames was in 1965 gifted with a critical, academic explanation, and was much-discussed in the contemporary media.

photo of two ballet dancers — (PSC; "Trim-Jeans Theatre") These still photos were taken by Joan Williams, who also contributed photos to Eps. 22 and 26 (WAC T12/1,415).

picture of Tschaikowsky — (PSC; *"Life of Tschaikowsky"*) This photo of the composer is borrowed from the Mansell Collection (WAC T12/1,427).

The Pythons variously spell the composer's name "Tchaikowsky" and "Tschaikowsky" in the printed scripts. Unless the name appears in these pages in regard to a quote or reference by the Pythons, the spelling employed is the more generally accepted "Tchaikovsky."

pigs appear on the screen — (PSC; "Farming Club") These stock pig photos (AG3131 and AG6256) were taken by Thomas A. Wilkie (WAC T12/1,427).

poofy presenter — (*"Life of Tschaikowsky"*) This could be a lampoon of film critic Barry Norman (b. 1933), host of *Film* (BBC1) from 1972 to 2002, or even another

jab at Philip Jenkinson, who was spoofed in Ep. 23, and who will be dealt with rather violently (and gleefully) in Ep. 33.

"Port of Spain" — ("Puss in Boots") In Trinidad and Tobago, on the Gulf of Paria, in the Caribbean. Venezuela ships iron ore through this port regularly.

"Potato Marketing Board" — ("Farming Club") One of many agricultural products marketing boards meant to raise awareness of a domestic product via advertising and information, keeping prices high and providing subsidies for domestic production in the face of international competition. Planting proper acreages—to avoid years of glut, when prices can dive—was also in the PMB's bailiwick. In November 1971 the Board generated unwanted headlines for deploying a light aircraft to spy out "unlicensed potato growers" ("Potato Flight," *Times*, 17 Nov. 1971: 6). By April 1972 it was announced that potatoes had exceeded crop estimates by more than one million pounds.

The Egg Marketing Board had made the news very recently, being scrapped in 1971 due to inefficiency. Overall, these boards as presented by the Pythons seem like a combined "traditional English breakfast" marketing board.

principal boy — (PSC; "Puss in Boots") The principal boy is the leading actor in a pantomime, and traditionally is played by a girl/woman. This role here was originally intended for Beulah Hughes (*The Hands of Orlac*), Carol Cleveland, or Diana Quick (*Complete and Utter History of Britain*), all mentioned by name in notes for the episode, but is instead played by Julia Breck (see WAC T12/1,427 and T12/1,428). Breck appeared with Spike Milligan in his *Q* series, as well as in the controversial Andy Warhol play *Pork* (1971) in its London debut at the Roundhouse.

"Purley and Esher" — ("Emigration from Surbiton to Hounslow") Esher is a residential suburb of London in Surrey, and is often mentioned (interchangeably with Purley) in *FC* as the backwater of the Commonwealth. Purley is south of London along the A23.

"Putney Public Library" — ("Emigration from Surbiton to Hounslow") This library is currently located at 5/7 Disraeli Road SW15 2DR.

• Q •

quayside — ("Fish-Slapping Dance") This scene was shot at Teddington Lock, Richmond upon Thames, just a few miles from Broadcast Centre.

This sketch was one of a handful that appeared (along with linking material) in the *Euroshow 71—May Day Special* ("Pan European May Day") to which the

BBC and the Pythons contributed in 1971, representing British light entertainment television. In that special, this "traditional" dance was said to represent the "ancient town of Lowestoft." (And since Ep. 28 wouldn't be recorded until 28 January 1972, the "Fish Slapping" film likely made its debut in this May Day special.)

• **R** •

"Ra 1 . . . Ra 2" — ("Emigration from Surbiton to Hounslow") The May 1969 Heyerdahl expedition on a reed boat from North Africa to the New World was called "Ra I." This boat began to take on water very near the end of the voyage, and had to be abandoned, though the crew felt it could have continued successfully.

"Ra II"—One year after the Ra I failure (May 1970), the redesigned Ra II set sail, making the voyage successfully, proving that such trips, even anciently, were possible, and that there could have been cross-cultural influences between ancient civilizations long thought to be mutually isolated. A documentary film and book followed the celebrated journey.

Red Indians — (PSC; "World War One") The stereotypical outfit from myriad Hollywood films and television shows (of the *Debbie Reynolds* variety), including feather headdress, face paint, and buckskin leggings.

"Remaindered" — ("Emigration from Surbiton to Hounslow") This means the store is selling the book at a reduced price to be rid of it.

"Renaissance courtier . . . Borgias" — ("World War One") The Borgias were Italians (via Spain), descendants of Pope Alexander IV, and very powerful figures in Italy, attracting poets and artists alike. Lucrezia Borgia (1480–1519) and her brother Cesare (1476–1507) were noted members of the family, and led the Italian (Roman) Renaissance-era court and culture.

The Medicis were Florentine socialites and behind-the-scenes political leaders from the fifteenth century to 1737. The family produced three popes and two queens of France.

A "Renaissance courtier artist" look may have been borrowed from or at least inspired by several paintings in the National Gallery, including *Portrait of a Gentleman* (1550s) and *Knight with His Jousting Helmet* (1530s), both by Giovanni Battista Moroni. (The headdress/hat doesn't match at all, however, especially the tassels.) Raphael's (1483–1520) *Self-Portrait* (1506) and *Self-Portrait with His Fencing Master* (1518) don't fit this look at all, and Leonardo da Vinci's *Musician* (1470s) shows a young Italian artist wearing a simple felt cap and undershirt, tunic, and vest. (There probably wasn't a uniform for courtiers or artists, though, so the Pythons' "impression" approach actually makes some

historical sense.) Stibbert's 1914 book offers significant period illustrations, including "Young Venetian Gentlemen of the 15th Century," none of which precisely match the Python version (*Abiti E Fogge Civile E Militari Dal I Al XVII Secolo*).

There are examples in the mid-fifteenth century of hats much like the one the sailor sports in the episode, but most of the wearers are French aristocrats. (See Jules Quicherat, *Histoire du costume en France*, Paris, 1875.) Stibbert offers at least one example of a young Flemish man (occupation/status unknown) wearing a costume much like the one in the episode, in a print labeled "15 Century Flemish Dress."

Finally, the costume shop request for this week's episode called for Idle to be dressed in, simply, a "medieval outfit," so it's rather interesting to see what they came up with, and how "medieval" became "Renaissance" (WAC T12/1,427).

"Richardson, Sir Ralph" — ("Trim-Jeans Theatre") Richardson (1902–1983) was a noted stage and screen actor and, also coincidentally, appeared in the film version of *Long Day's Journey into Night* (1962), but more recently starring with John Gielgud in David Storey's *Home* at the Apollo Theatre.

"Richmond and Isleworth" — ("Emigration from Surbiton to Hounslow") These cities lie just across the Thames from each other. The bridge(s) in this shot are the Twickenham Rail Bridge and Twickenham Bridge. The Rail Bridge is in the foreground. These scenes were shot in October 1971, according to a memo from crewmember George Clarke. They also shot some of the Norrises' driving scenes on Arlington Road, Chertsey Road, and St. Margaret's Road in East Twickenham (WAC T12/1,428).

"Richter, Sviatoslav" — (*"Life of Tschaikowsky"*) Famed concert pianist (1915–1997) born in Ukraine who performed Haydn, Rachmaninoff, Schubert, Prokofiev, Schumann, Mussgorsky, Beethoven, and others, and was considered the finest Russian pianist of his generation. There is no record of Richter performing (in public) any Tchaikovsky piece after 1960. He performed the piece in December 1940 and January 1941 (in Russia), February 1942, March and May 1950, May 1954, November 1957, February 1958, and December 1960 (see "Sviatoslav Richter Chronology," at trovar.com).

Richter first performed in London at the Royal Festival Hall July 1961, then again in January and February 1963, June 1966 and June 1967, October and November 1968 (Royal Festival and Goldsmith's Hall, respectively), October and November 1969, etc.

ripple — (PSC; "Puss in Boots") Traditional TV special effect that has come to signify an approaching dream sequence, or that a flashback is about to be recounted. The Pythons, of course, draw attention to the usually invisible transition by not completing the transition, and forcing the narrative to go on anyway. The ripple effect was used in Ep. 21, as well, as Mrs. Thing (Chapman) and Mrs. Entity (Idle) discussed Beethoven (Cleese) and his mynah bird.

"Round Table" — ("Emigration from Surbiton to Hounslow") An actual discussion group of similarly minded enthusiasts, the Round Table organization was formed in Norwich in 1927 by Louis Marchesi. See Ep. 10 for more on Round Table.

Royal Albert Hall — (PSC; "*Life of Tschaikowsky*") Located across from Hyde Park on Kensington Gore, in London, and opened in 1871. Richter first played the Royal Albert Hall in 1961.

"Russell, Ken" — ("*Life of Tschaikowsky*") Film director Russell (1927–2011) had already created TV films on Prokofiev, Elgar, Bartok, Debussy, and Tchaikovsky, and was in production on a film about Gustav Mahler in 1971. Being "born in a Ken Russell film" would refer to Russell's penchant for squalor—inner and outer—where characters like Dante Alighieri (*Dante's Inferno*, 1967) struggle with psychosexual problems in the detritus of the postlapsarian world. Tchaikovsky would very much have been one of these tortured characters. Also, Russell's 1970 film *The Music Lovers* (about Tchaikovsky) would have been many viewers' introduction to the composer, meaning he was "born" to them in that Ken Russell world. This film was singled out by conservative groups, incidentally, for consideration of a new BBFC rating, "Y" (or "XY"), to denote "films with violent sexual overtones." Russell's film *The Devils* had also caused concern the previous year.

Russell will be mentioned again in Eps. 29 and 33, his repeated appearances indicating he was something of a front-pager at this time.

Other references in this fictional film cast include:

"Leo McKern"—Actor McKern (1920–2002) had most recently appeared in the David Lean epic *Ryan's Daughter* (1970), and had also appeared in *A Man for All Seasons* (1966), *Help!* (1965), and *The Running, Jumping and Standing Still Film* (1959). He had also played "Third Knight" in the 1952 film version of *Murder in the Cathedral*—based on the death of Thomas Becket—directed by George Hoellering. (See the "Trim-Jeans" notes below for more on this connection.) As a "freelance bishop," this character would be a Bishop somehow not affiliated with any organized religion, or perhaps one who is available to move from see to see. The C of E does not have celibacy vows as part of its dogma, so this Bishop could have been married.

"Julie Christie"—Actress Christie (b. 1941) was by this time internationally known for playing Lara in *Dr. Zhivago* (1965) and Bathsheba Everdene in *Far from the Madding Crowd* (1967).

"Shirley Abicair"—Australian-born actress / singer Abicair (b. 1930) came to the UK to break into TV performance, playing her zither and singing folk and contemporary songs. She appeared on children's shows, variety shows, and in a few films. She also appeared later on the Eurovision Song Contest show.

"Madame Ranevsky"—Character in Chekhov's *The Cherry Orchard*, she has fled Paris for the safety of her home, though the tragedy there and the fate of the orchard combine to prevent her from escaping into her nostalgic memories. Chekhov will be mentioned prominently later, also in the "Trim-Jeans" sketch.

"Norris McWhirter"—Cofounder of the Guinness Book of World Records, McWhirter (1925–2004) also appeared for many years on the *Record Breakers* TV show which appeared in 1972. The fact that the Pythons cast a man into a woman's part shouldn't be surprising, nor was it terribly rare. Leo McKern, for example, had played the role of Duchess in the 1966 *Alice in Wonderland* adaptation for BBC1.

"Eldridge Cleaver"—Eldridge Cleaver (1935–1998) was an American black revolutionary, a "minister of information" for the Black Panthers Party in the late 1960s. Cleaver had appeared in the *Black Panther* documentary in 1969 with fellow members Huey Newton and Bobby Seale, as well as *Eldridge Cleaver, Black Panther* in 1970, the latter an Algerian documentary. Cleaver's book, *Soul on Ice*, was published in 1968 after he was released from prison. Cleaver had been in exile (in Algeria) since 1969, and would not return to the United States until 1975. (The Algerian exile may tie Cleaver to the earlier Sartre reference, the French philosopher very much sympathetic—and vocally so—to the Algerian cause.)

"Moira Lister"—Lister (1923–2007) is a South African-born actress who had appeared in 1968 on *The Eamonn Andrews Show* (Ep. 26). Lister is characterized as playing a "posh lady," which would seem to be the Pythonesque counterpart for Eldridge Cleaver and a character named Stan the Bat. Lister is mentioned, then featured, respectively, on the covers of the 17 and 24 May 1969 *Radio Times* for her appearance in *The Very Merry Widow* (BBC1, Friday).

"Stan the Bat"—This could be a reference to Stan Musial, superstar American baseballer elected to the Hall of Fame in 1969. It also could be "Stan the Bat" is just a silly name along the lines of children's-show characters "Muffin the Mule" (Ep. 22) or Brush" (see notes for "Boom boom!" in Ep. 30). There's even the possibility it's an oblique reference to Stan McCabe (1910–1968), the Australian batsman who stood up so well against the infamous English fast-leg bowlers in the Bodyline series in 1932. (See notes to Ep. 20 for more on this memorable series.) Lastly, and most likely, there are rumblings of a somewhat fearsome table tennis player in the UK who called himself "Stan the Bat," a.k.a. Stanley Battrick (1931–1998), an Essex player who excelled in veteran's play. Battrick's passing is noted in the *Essex Gazette* (14 Dec. 1998).

"Omsk"—Major industrial city/region in Western Siberia; Russia, also a home for political prisoners beginning in the nineteenth century, including Fyodor Dostoevsky. Omsk has already been mentioned in passing by the Newsreader (Cleese) in Ep. 3 as he's being stolen from TV Centre.

"Eddie Waring"—British TV and sporting news personality, Waring (1910–1986) is first mentioned in Ep. 1, in the "Famous Deaths" sketch. Waring also appeared in episodes of *The Goodies* (1973, 1975) and *It's a Knockout* (1966). In this sketch Eddie is portraying the entire city/region, it seems.

"Anthony Barber"—There is also a prominent Australian television personality of this name, and very active during this period, but this is more clearly a reference to the Right Honourable Anthony Barber (1920–2005), a front-page Conservative politician and Cabinet member. Barber will be mentioned again and his picture shown (as a potential "loony") in Ep. 38. Barber had been named Chancellor of the Exchequer by Heath in 1970, meaning he was the focus of the British public's anger and frustration during the economic malaise of the early 1970s, especially as National Health Service cutbacks and charges were introduced.

"Russians and the Chinese" — ("How to Rid the World of All Known Diseases") During this period, the nuclear and conventional saber rattling between the Russian and Chinese governments was at its highest following a series of nasty border wars in 1969, and Russia's agreeing to a 20-year "friendship pact" with India, an emerging power in the region. The positive side of this tension had to be the prospects of improving relations between China and the U.S. during this same period, with President Nixon's historic visit to China in February 1972 marking the acme of this new relationship, and the nadir for Sino-Soviet friendliness. See the notes for "Revisionist" in Ep. 27.

• S •

"sceptical about my work" — (link out of "Vicar/Salesman") A reference back to Heyerdahl's difficulty convincing established academicians as to the worth of his theses, viz., that ancient maritime technology was sufficiently advanced for trans-Atlantic journeys, and/or that allegedly less-advanced peoples could make such a perilous trip at all.

school . . . caps — (PSC; "World War One") This is the same schoolboy outfit Chapman will wear in Ep. 29 ("Salvation Fuzz") when he announces he's found another "dead bishop on the landing."

scrubland — (PSC; "Trim-Jeans Theatre") This looks to be on the premises of a BBC transmission tower, and is likely the Booster Station near Gallanach (WAC T12/1,428). These scenes were recorded in October 1971. In the first two seasons, location shooting was completed by summer, for the most part, meaning that by the time the Pythons got around to shooting these scenes it was quite a bit colder, especially farther north in Scotland. Many of the scenes exhibit trees that are leafless or at least autumn-colored leaves on those trees (for example, the documentary fight scenes in Ep. 30).

"scuppers" — ("Puss in Boots") The opening on a ship's deck that allows water to drain from the surface of the deck.

"Seagull . . . Chekhov" — ("Trim-Jeans Theatre") Anton Chekhov (1860–1904) was a Russian dramatist and short story writer. The Moscow Art Theater produced his play *The Seagull* in 1898. He died of tuberculosis at age forty-four in Germany.

semi-detached house — ("Emigration from Surbiton to Hounslow") Two houses joined together (built as one, duplex-style), and originally identical on either side. Using the conveniently placed light pole as divider, the shot mentioned here makes it look as if they've created a split-screen effect, when in fact it's a non-process shot. This scene was actually shot in Hounslow (WAC T12/1,428).

"sent to Moscow" — (*Life of Tschaikowsky*) Tchaikovsky moved to Moscow in 1866 to teach at the Moscow Conservatory, after three years teaching privately in the St. Petersburg Conservatory.

"Shazam" — (PSC; "Mrs. Nigger-Baiter Explodes") "Shazam" is the magic word spoken by Billy to become Captain Marvel, and first appeared in Whiz Comics in 1940.

Showbiz music — (PSC; "It's") The music is "Theatre Overture" by A. Mawer, which has become a popular cell phone ring tone recently.

"Sleeping Beauty . . . Fanny forte" — (*Life of Tschaikowsky*) All Tchaikovsky compositions. *Sleeping Beauty* composed 1875–1876; "Pathetique" (Symphony No. 6) composed 1893; the "1812 Overture" composed 1880. He composed myriad pieces for the pianoforte (the instrument that replaced the harpsichord and clavichord), as well as several for piano and violin.

Slightly eerie music — (PSC; "Puss in Boots") The accompanying music underneath the Captain's (Jones) scary story is from "Theatre Overture Dramatic and Horror," "String Suspenses" by Paul Lewis, while the (unsuccessful) transitional music is from Harp Solos, "Descending Glissando," by Gareth Walters (WAC T12/1,427).

"small rat" — ("Puss in Boots") Presaging the small white rabbit that will wreak so much havoc in the cave scene of *Holy Grail*.

"Smith, Harvey" — ("The BBC Is Short of Money") Famous Yorkshire showjumper of the 1960s and 1970s, Smith (b. 1938) competed in the 1968 Mexico City Olympic games with his horse Madison Time. Fellow Brit David Broome (b. 1940) competed, as well, on Mr. Softee. Smith also competed in the 1972 Olympics on Summertime.

"Smith, Pat Hornsby" — ("The BBC Is Short of Money") Hornsby-Smith (1914–1985) was a Conservative representing Chislehurst, and serving in the House of Commons 1950–1966, and 1970–February 1974, and then in the House of Lords 1974–1985. She was named Dame Commander of the British Empire (DBE), and granted a Life Peerage in 1974. She also held these offices: Parliamentary Secretary, Ministry of Health (1951–1957); Joint Under-Secretary of State, Home Office (1957–1959); and Joint Parliamentary Secretary, Ministry of Pensions & National Insurance (1959–1961).

South . . . state — ("PSC; "World War One") Later this "South American" country is named as Venezuela, but during this period (early 1970s) the so-called police states in South America might have included Chile (under Pinochet), Paraguay (under Stroessner), Uruguay (under Bordaberry), Bolivia (under Suárez), Ecuador (under Lara), and Brazil (under Silva, then, ironically, Gen. Emilio Garrastazú *Médici*).

Venezuela during this period was moderately stable thanks to a president (Raúl Leoni [1906–1972]) who utilized coalition governments to keep many ideologies (left, right, and center) happy and represented.

Starr, Ringo — (PSC; "It's") The former Richard Starkey (b. 1940) makes his only appearance on the show, and would have been an ex-Beatle by this time. The Pythons had working and personal relationships with The Beatles during this period. In Ep. 24, Idle dresses as John Lennon for a vox pop moment, and after *FC*, he would form the mock Fab Four group The Rutles. Another ex-Beatle, George Harrison (with Denis O'Brien) would, in 1978, assist the Pythons in obtaining financing and distribution for their controversial *Life of Brian*, through Handmade Films.

"statement . . . six" — ("Mrs. Nigger-Baiter Explodes") The Rhodesia question had been front and center since

at least 1953, when calls for independence began to be acknowledged by the British government. Rhodesia's white minority would declare unilateral independence in 1965 under Ian Smith (1919–2007), causing concern and consternation to both Conservative and Labour administrations. Cf. Ep. 45 for much more. The Son (Cleese) is preparing to speak in the House of Commons, the lower, elected house of Parliament—such speeches tended to be in favor of finding a way to deal with Smith, to cajole him out of minority rule, and do postcolonial damage control on the international stage (*Eyewitness: 1960–69*, "Rhodesia Unilateral Declaration of Independence 1965"). Contemporary news reports indicate that the subject was broached often in the House of Lords, as well.

Stirring music — (PSC; "Emigration from Surbiton to Hounslow") The music here and later in this film is from New Concert Orchestra, Background Music, "Sinfonia Tellurica" and "Homines" by Trevor Duncan (WAC T12/1,427).

"Storey, David" — ("Trim-Jeans Theatre") David Storey (b. 1933) is a playwright and novelist who first came to attention in 1963 for his working-class, "Angry Young Man" novel *This Sporting Life*, which would then quickly become a movie, as well, directed by Lindsay Anderson. (See notes to Ep. 2 for more on this working-class film/play/novel movement.)

Storey's play *Home* (1970) won the New York Critics Best Play of the Year Award, and became something of a surprising star vehicle for Richardson and Gielgud, who were by this time middle-aged. (*Home* was playing at the Royal Court Theatre from June 1970, and to very strong reviews.)

Lastly, there is a different take possible when this line is listened to/performed, and not read from the script. It sounds as if Gielgud and Richardson are losing inches as they "act" in Storey's home (house), lending a more sexual interpretation to the moment, and perhaps commenting on at least Gielgud's homosexuality (Richardson was married, and father of one child), and/or even Storey's work in *Radcliffe*, featuring a sexual relationship between a gay man and a married man. (Gielgud had been arrested, coincidentally, for "cottaging" in Chelsea Mews in 1953, meaning he was visiting a public lavatory for the purposes of casual homosexual sex. These bathrooms were designed to look like cottages, or small homes.)

stuffed cat — (PSC; "Puss in Boots") Could be Puss from *Puss-in-Boots*, but could also represent the cat from *Dick Whittington*, another very popular pantomime.

"Surbiton" — ("Emigration from Surbiton to Hounslow") Farther south and still west of London than Hounslow, as well, and very near New Malden. As if the set-up for this sketch isn't absurd enough, there is and has been a London United (bus service) route, number 281, that runs from Hounslow to Tolworth via Surbiton.

"Swan Lake" — ("Trim-Jeans Theatre") Another Tchaikovsky mention, *Swan Lake* is his 1875–1876 ballet.

· T ·

tannoy — (PSC; "World War One") Loudspeaker system.

"tassles" — ("World War One") Misspelled version of "tassels." There doesn't seem to have been a precedent for tasseled hats in either Flanders or Italy during the fourteenth to sixteenth centuries, though embroidered chevrons were part of much Renaissance sewing practice during the period.

"fitted doublets"—A tight-fitting garment worn about the shoulders and chest, a kind of early jacket, and could be sleeved or sleeveless. Common between the fourteenth and eighteenth centuries throughout Europe.

"This is BBC 2" — (link out of "Puss in Boots") As early as 1966, PM Wilson was threatening to de-fund and starve to death BBC2, seeing it as an expensive drag on the government, and not a little superfluous: "I don't see why we need to increase licence fees to pay for a programme that no one wants to see—and many can't see even if they wanted to" (Freedman, 30). *Flying Circus*, of course, would be one of these little seen BBC2 shows just four years later.

"Thor . . . Hillary" — ("Emigration from Surbiton to Hounslow") Thor Heyerdahl (1914–2002) was an anthropologist and explorer who studied and then physically attempted to prove the thesis of ancient peoples performing intercontinental travels. Heyerdahl was from Norway.

Sir Edmund Hillary (1919–2008) was probably the first (in recorded history) to reach the summit of the tallest mountain in the world, Mt. Everest, on 29 May 1953, with his guide/companion Tenzing Norgay, a Nepalese Sherpa. Hillary was a New Zealander. More on Hillary and the climb in Ep. 31.

"three-stage model" — ("*Life of Tschaikowsky*") This "Tchaikowsky XII" set-up is fashioned after the often quite enthusiastic Apollo mission coverage on both UK and U.S. television networks. The Apollo XII mission was carried out in November 1969.

In the UK, ITN carried *Man on the Moon* (21 July 1969) and BBC presented *Apollo 11—Man on the Moon* (BBC2), both of which offered live reports and live coverage of the first moon landing. The BBC's coverage stretched from 15 July through 24 July. For the BBC, it was James Burke (b. 1936; Ep. 35) who handled the plastic mock-ups of the Saturn V rocket and lunar module/command ship that could be broken down into constituent parts as the mission proceeded.

"tighter, firmer, neater" — ("Trim-Jeans Theatre") In an extant print ad version of this advertisement, Coover is credited with saying "tighter, firmer, and 10½ inches trimmer." Gary is also shown standing casually, and wearing a dark T-shirt and leather sandals, just like the Pythons in the sketch. The company in the print ad is listed as "Sauna Belt Incorporated," with headquarters in San Francisco, California. There was no London home office for the company during this period. See the "lose inches" entry earlier in this episode for more on the Trim-Jeans phenomenon.

"Tooting" — ("Emigration from Surbiton to Hounslow") Part of Greater London, just east of Wimbledon. Tooting is mentioned by the narrator in Neville Shunt's play *It All Happened . . . in* Ep. 24.

"transmissions for this evening can be continued as planned" — ("The BBC Is Short of Money") It was actually reported that in mid-December 1970 the BBC was actively pursuing what might be termed "innovative" means of prolonging the broadcast day in the face of national power shortages:

Last Monday, the day on which the first power cuts struck the nation, the BBC commissionaires set off round the TV Centre instructing all typists to turn their office lights out. It was explained to the girls that if they all switched off there might be just enough power for *Panorama* to go out that evening. (*Private Eye*, 18 Dec. 1970 6)

This was also the month when Mary Whitehouse officially asked the minister in charge of communications (Christopher Chataway [b. 1931], Minister of Post and Communications) to revoke the BBC's charter. Mrs. Whitehouse demanded that the royal charter be replaced with an Act of Parliament, meaning the corporation could then be accountable "within the confines of the law," so that "nudity, sexual licence and foul language" could be dealt with summarily ("Plea to Revoke BBC Charter," *Times*, 3 Dec. 1970: 2). The proposed revocation never materialized, of course.

"Treasure Island" — ("Trim-Jeans Theatre") See notes to Ep. 25 for more on *Treasure Island* and Long John Silver (and the Pythons' repeated reference to them).

"Trigorin" — ("Trim-Jeans Theatre") He is a writer, and a prolific one, whose lament is that he *must* write, finishing one story and immediately starting another.

He calls it "a dog's life." This may have been how the Pythons began to feel as the show moved on, especially Cleese, who had wanted to explore new ideas and especially venues as early as during the second season. By summer 1971 Cleese was indicating to his agent that he was interested in exploring something other than Monty Python episodes the following year. (The nature of British TV during this period was for more shows and shorter runs, which is why the Pythons could work for so many different shows before and even during *FC*.) The BBC's Duncan Wood had tried to start contract negotiations (via letters to agents) with the troupe for a fourth season (a minimum of six shows) on 20 August 1971 (WAC T12/1,428). Cleese would eventually opt out of this new contract.

Trim Gentlemen of Verona, The — ("Trim-Jeans Theatre") *The Two Gentlemen of Verona* (c. 1592–1598) is seen by many as a minor Shakespeare comedy.

trim-jeans — (PSC; "Trim-Jeans Theatre") An actual line of weight loss products (c. 1967), the identification of which—by actual name—is unusual. Normally, the Pythons will alter the name and just mimic the sales pitch (as in Whizzo Butter, Crelm Toothpaste, FibroVal Soap Powder), perhaps to avoid litigation, copyright problems, etc. See notes for "lose inches" and "tighter, firmer" for more on the Trim-Jeans phenomena.

"Trim-Jeans Theatre **Presents"** — ("Trim-Jeans Theatre") In the early days of U.S. radio and TV, individual shows often were directly sponsored by advertisers like Palmolive, Colgate, Bell Telephone, Texaco, etc. (*The Flintstones* and *I Love Lucy*, for example, were both sponsored by tobacco companies, and the characters smoked the product in title sequences or commercial breaks.) The products may have been mentioned in these slots, but weren't often featured as part of the fictional world of the production. Here the line is certainly crossed as actors wear the Trim-Jeans, not unlike the previous episode (Ep. 27) where North Malden inserted itself into an Icelandic saga.

There were also so-called Admag shows on early British TV, where products and services were presented by characters in a fictional world, like a sales documentary. See notes to Ep. 27 for more on this phenomenon.

"Tschaikowsky" — ("Farming Club") Peter Ilyich Tchaikovsky (1840–1893) was a Russian composer known for numerous operas, concertos, symphonies, and songs. He used European rather than overtly nationalistic Russian "forms and idioms," setting himself apart from his Russian colleagues.

"Tschaikowsky's . . . Minor" — (*Life of Tschaikowsky*") Tchaikovsky's first piano concerto in B Flat Minor (officially the "Concerto for Piano and Orchestra in B flat minor, op. 23") was composed in the winter of 1874–1875 for pianist Nikolai Rubinstein, who hated it after playing it through once. The composition, however, became famous in Europe and the United States very quickly, and even Rubinstein would later work the piece into his performance repertoire for many years.

• U •

"unit-trust . . . facilities" — ("Schoolboys' Life Assurance Company") This scheme represents an investment trust where units can be bought by participants, with the value of these units based on the value of investments. Units can be sold back to the trust, as well. The boys, then, acting as portfolio managers of the trust, were selling more units (ostensibly to other classmates at big school) than they could reasonably buy back at any time.

• V •

vicar with a suitcase — (PSC; "Vicar/Salesman") The thought of a vicar hawking goods and services seems downright silly, of course, but in November 1970 it happened on British TV for the very first time. The Reverend Ronald Stephens, Vicar of Stanstead Abbotts, had agreed to give an on-camera testimonial for Blue Band margarine "provided he could write his own script and preach a sermon," according to Chris Dunkley of the *Times*. The Independent Television Authority (ITA) wrung their hands over the possible conflict of church and public commerce (and potential violation of the Television Act of 1964), but eventually concluded that since the vicar was "simply [making] a perfectly natural passing reference" to both God and margarine, there would be no harm. The ITA representative, Mr. Archie Graham, went on to note that this ad might help underscore the "authenticity of personal testimonials" in the minds of viewers, and finished with a Stork margarine (Ep. 1) reference:

> It may astonish you to hear that those ladies are real who can't tell Stork from butter; and I doubt if you will get your wives to believe it even now. But you can assure them that 380 Cardiff housewives tried to do it when the Stork caravan visited this city, and that only 32 of them managed to win one of those fivers for sorting out all the butters from the marge on half a dozen biscuits. (*Times*, 13 Nov. 1970: 2)

Voice from Back — (PSC; "Puss in Boots") Not credited, but this voice is Idle. The Second Guard is also Idle, and uncredited. The Third Guard, also uncredited in the printed scripts, is Palin.

• W •

wall diagram of two skeletons — (PSC; "Dynamite Can Cure Athlete's Foot") The anatomical chart on the wall (a figure from which will walk off in a moment) is an antique—a 1918 American Frohse Anatomical Chart. Likely a prop from the BBC, the chart is not accounted for in the WAC records.

warning signs — (PSC; animated link into "Farming Club") These same kinds of warning/directional signs have been used in many cartoons, including *Inki and the Minah Bird* (Chuck Jones, 1943), and the *Rabbit Fire* (1951), *Rabbit Seasoning* (1952), and *Duck, Rabbit, Duck* (1953) series from Jones. Dante even employed a warning sign over the entrance to Hell: "Abandon hope, all ye who enter here" (*Divine Comedy*).

"sprocket holes . . . view"—This is a very self-conscious moment where the medium is acknowledged, and the artificiality and limitations of the cinematic world are foregrounded. This is not unlike the self-reflexive cartoon *Duck Amuck* (1953), where Daffy is confronted with the artificial and plastic nature of his ink and paint world, or many of Tex Avery's cartoons (at Warner Bros. and MGM). In one Avery cartoon (*Screwball Squirrel*, 1944), Screwy Squirrel lifts the edge of the frame he's in to see what's going to happen to him next, for example, and in *Duck Amuck*, Daffy ends up getting in a fight with an adjoining frame's version of himself. Most precisely, in the Tex Avery cartoon *Dumb-Hounded* (1943) the wolf character runs off the frame right, past the racing sprocket holes, and into off-screen white space for a moment, before scampering back into the world framed by the film. These cartoons, with their hyperviolence, speed, and reflexivity, obviously had a profound influence on the Goons, first, for radio, and later on, the Pythons and the often cartoony world they created for television.

"Weldon, Huw" — ("The BBC Is Short of Money") BBC Managing Director for Television during this period. The Pythons even joked in internal memos that perhaps Weldon (1916–1986) himself might appear on the episode, playing Paul Fox, if he were asked politely. There is no record that Weldon was actually officially queried about such an appearance (WAC T12/1,428).

well-choreographed . . . toward her — (PSC; "Puss in Boots") The group knows how to react to and perform with this principal boy character, as the rules of the pantomime world are clearly known to the Pythons. From the pantomime *Snow White*, the following is a representative scene:

Wicked Queen: I am the fairest of them all.
Audience: Oh no you're not!
Queen: Oh yes I am!
Audience: Oh no you're not!

The Pythons have created another level of diegetic reality here as the actors shift from their initial roles into roles as pantomime audience members, allowing one narrative to overtake a previous narrative thread. This new reality will also be overthrown when the performance is interrupted by Mrs. Kelly (Palin) and the set is shut down—the characters becoming unemployed actors at that moment.

"Williams, Dorian" — ("Puss in Boots") Show jumping broadcaster and commentator (1914–1985).

"women and children first" — ("World War One") Though treated comically here, of course, Peter Clarke points out that during the early part of the twentieth century, it was the working man in the British household who received most of the food and money, and virtually all of the meager meat portions of the family diet. Women and children were, as indicated comically in this sketch, put to the back of the line because they were not wage earners, and were therefore somewhat expendable. Both women and children were also far more susceptible to tuberculosis and premature death, primarily because of their poor diets. (See *Hope and Glory: Britain 1900–1990*.)

"'Wrong Way' Norris" — ("Emigration from Surbiton to Hounslow") Douglas "Wrong Way" Corrigan (1907–1995) had in 1938 piloted his small plane mistakenly from New York to Ireland, rather than the planned New York to California. His mistake made him quite the celebrity during the hard-bitten times of the Great Depression, and when he arrived back in the United States, the *New York Post* even printed a banner headline—"Hail to Wrong Way Corrigan"—backward on its front page. It's thought by many that Corrigan—who had applied many times for permission to fly nonstop from New York to Ireland, and been denied every time—finally made the trip without permission, and blamed a faulty compass and clouds (David Onkst, U.S. Centennial of Flight Commission).

• Y •

"Yes (successfully)" — ("Emigration from Surbiton to Hounslow") Perhaps a comment on achieving the bottom of the hour (8:30 a.m.), but more likely a sexual double entendre.

Episode 29: *"The Money Programme"*

The Money Programme; "There is nothing quite so wonderful as money" (song); Nude organist, "And now" Man, and "It's" Man; *Titles* (silly Palin v/o); *Erizabeth L*; Inspector Leopard, **Fraud Film Squad**; Luchino Visconti career review; *Animation: Police violence, Many-handed victim*; Salvation Fuzz (The Church Police); "And Did Those Feet . . ."; *Animation: Woman in the sun, Bouncy ball woman*; Jungle restaurant; BBC 1 Colour title: Apology for violence and nudity; **Ken Russell's *Gardening Club*** (1958); The Lost World of Roiurama; What page in the script?; The British Explorer's Club (in the Mall); Crystal Palace 1851 photo; Six more minutes of *Monty Python's Flying Circus*; **Argument clinic**; Abuse; Complaints; Being hit on the head lessons; Inspector Flying Fox of the Yard; One more minute of *Monty Python's Flying Circus*

• A •

"afters" — ("Salvation Fuzz") The course that follows the main course in a meal (*OED*). In the time period perhaps being depicted (WWII-era), "afters" were a thing of the past, as shortages and rationing reduced most Britons' diets to subsistence levels.

"Akwekwe" — ("Jungle Restaurant") Kwekwe is a town founded on the African gold rush in 1902 in Zimbabwe, Africa.

These "jungle" scenes were shot on film at Ealing TFS on 27 and 28 October 1971 (WAC T12/1,428).

"Alliveldelchi Loma" — ("Fraud Film Squad") "Arrivederci Roma," a song written for the 1958 Hollywood musical *Seven Hills of Rome*; the music is by Renato Ranucci, and Italian lyrics by Pierre Garinei and Sandro Giovannini. Perry Como made the song famous in 1966 on his album *Perry Como in Italy*.

"And did these feet in ancient times . . ." — ("Salvation Fuzz") From the hymn "Jerusalem" (lyrics by William Blake), used several times in *FC* episodes, including Eps. 4 and 8.

Animation: Bouncing Queen Victoria — ("*Animation: Woman in the sun, Bouncy ball woman*") This is labeled as

an image of Queen Victoria turned into a bouncy ball (and her natural figure does seem to lend itself to that comparison), but it's not at all clear that Gilliam used a picture of the queen when making the animation. (The script would have been completed, with this direction, long before Gilliam began the animation process, and he often deviated from the original suggestion.)

The face for the bouncing man is taken from one of Gilliam's myriad (and unattributed) photographic sources—likely a batch of old family photos from an antique shop—but the body appended to this face is borrowed from the *Divided We Fought* book, page 67. (Gilliam will use this face again in Ep. 23, in the "undelivered letter" animation.) This same figure (seen earlier in Ep. 19 performing a silly walk across a scene of "Arabian splendour") is depicted here clutching the female bouncing ball, his upper body swapped for the unidentified man's head and shoulders.

The bouncy ball itself (at least one large enough for someone to ride on) was also a very new product at this time. The toy was invented in 1968 and being distributed in Europe and the United States by 1971, at least.

"annex . . . Russia" — ("Salvation Fuzz") "Gerald" (Sir Gerald Nabarro, again) calls for precisely what Hitler did, in fact, prior to WWII. Tory MP Nabarro has been mentioned in Eps. 11, 15, 21, and 23 (and depicted in Ep. 2), and it's no surprise that since he's a Conservative, the Pythons would align him with Hitler and the far-right National Socialists. The "Norman" mention that follows probably continues the right-bashing reference. See "Norman" below.

There were many on both sides of the political aisle (Labour and Conservative) who either allied themselves with the views of the successful National Socialists prior to the war, or who bent over backward to appease the Nazis up to and including the infamous Munich Agreement. Fear of another world war trumped the rights of certain Europeans in the Sudetenland, for example.

Another Voice — (PSC; "Salvation Fuzz") Not credited, but this is Michael Palin, and, as "Gerald," he may be another appearance of/reference to Sir Gerald Nabarro; "Norman's Voice" is also uncredited, but this sounds like Cleese, using a "swishy" voice; finally, the "Man's Voice" is Terry Jones.

"Antonioni, Michelangelo" — ("Six More Minutes of *Monty Python's Flying Circus*") Born in 1912, filmmaker Antonioni's major works were released in the 1960s, including *Blow-Up* (1966), starring the "wooden" David Hemmings (Ep. 8). The films of the various European New Wave directors were very available in the London area, and especially in the West End, meaning the Pythons would have had ample opportunity to see these films. Antonioni died in 2007.

It's interesting that Antonioni's current film work was not gracing myriad screens in and around London between 1970 and 1972; instead, the Pythons were drawing on a number of critical reviews of other filmmakers citing Antonioni's work and influence appearing in contemporary newspapers, as well as film revivals. *Zabriskie Point* (1970) had debuted with a thud in March 1970 at the Empire, most critics asking what happened to the Italian director they'd come to admire in the 1960s (of *Red Desert* [1964] and *Blow-Up* [1966] fame). In summer 1971 both *Zabriskie Point* and *Blow-Up* were playing but in retrospective, double feature settings at specialty theaters (The Other Cinema; Academy Three); in the fall *La notte* (1961) was showing at the Venus; and *L'eclisse* (1962) had shown on BBC 2 in February 1971.

Perhaps most significantly for this episode, in December 1971 (the same month Episode 29 was recorded), film journal *Sight and Sound* released its decennial list of ten-best films of all time, ranked by critics from around the world. Antonioni's *L'avventura* (1960) came fifth. At the end of this episode the Pythons will discuss Antonioni's work in some detail.

"argument please" — ("Argument Clinic") The implication here is, of course, that anything can be pur-

chased, and that there are such places in the modern UK for any kind of person/malady. At this clinic one can also purchase abuse, complaints, and lessons about being hit on the head.

This is one of the Python sketches that owe a debt to both the music hall stage and, latterly, radio (and more specifically the Goons), as it demands little or no visual accompaniment, and could (and does) play well with just the audio alone. This same kind of dialogue-rich and language-driven sketch will be revisited in Ep. 33, in "Cheese Shop," as well as *Holy Grail*, where two castle guards (Chapman and Idle) are being told to guard the prince (Jones). The camera is essentially locked down for the bulk of this "Who's on first?" kind of scene.

"argument . . . proposition" — ("Argument Clinic") Quoted almost verbatim from the *OED*, which defines an "argument" as: "A connected series of statements or reasons intended to establish a position." In Ep. 37, the Pythons will very nearly quote from historian G.M. Trevelyan, specifically from the 1952 edition of *The History of England*. See notes to Ep. 37 for more.

"ask the team" — ("Salvation Fuzz") As Man (Idle) and Woman (Jones) listen to the radio in the tatty kitchen, the show is a play on the *University Challenge* game show (1962–), which was earlier lampooned by Cleese and Chapman on *At Last the 1948 Show* (1967), and even earlier on *ISIRTA*. The Radio Voice actually sounds like Tim Brooke-Taylor, a member of the *1948 Show* team, though WAC archives offer no confirmation of the actual speaker.

• B •

"Bailey, Betty" — ("Jungle Restaurant") Betty Bailey was a professional diver in the 1930s, as well as the name of a popular dress-up doll in the early 1900s.

"Barclaycard" — ("Jungle Restaurant") This line is very hard to hear, meaning the studio audience misses the joke. Barclay's Bank created Barclaycard in 1966, and was the UK's first credit card. By 1972, there may still have been a number of places that did not take this newer card, especially overseas.

"Bath and Wellsish" — ("Salvation Fuzz") This is asked and answered as if Bishops can be identified by the diocese they administer. Located in Somerset, the first Bishop of Bath and Wells was appointed by the Pope in 1244. It was during Henry VIII's reign that the diocese became Anglican.

The Bath and Wells bishop may have been mentioned here by virtue of the long-standing tradition (from Richard I) whereby Bath and Wells assisted on the left hand of the new monarch during coronation, with the Bishop of Durham on the right. Richard Dimbleby's hushed, dulcet tones and stream of "great" qualifiers (see notes to Ep. 23) transmitted over the BBC rendered the images vivid and permanent (*Eyewitness 1950–59*, "The Coronation").

blacked up — (PSC; "Six More Minutes of *Monty Python's Flying Circus*") Made up in black-face, as was done in music hall and vaudeville shows (and early films). Hiring performers who were actually black was quite rare in the early days of film and vaudeville. In Ep. 20, "*The Attila the Hun Show*," Rochester (Idle) is blacked up, as well, even though his namesake was a black man. See notes to Ep. 20. The incredibly popular musical variety show *The Black and White Minstrel Show*—where performers regularly "blacked up"—appeared on the BBC between 1958 and 1978. (There was also a long-running stage version of the show.) The show went on hiatus in about 1969 after the increasing accusations that it was both racist and loaded with racial stereotypes finally niggled the BBC into action. Due to its popularity, however, *BWMS* came back on the air and stayed for another decade.

"British Explorer's Club in the Mall" — (The Lost World of Roiurama") The Explorer's Club was incorporated in 1905, and its London chapter is located at Victoria Court, Knightsbridge. The Traveller's Club (est. 1819) is actually located at 106 Pall Mall.

"Bulldog Drummond" — ("The Lost World of Roiurama") Series of films (and a play, and novels) begun in earnest in 1929 and twice starring Ronald Colman (1891–1958) as a British WWI officer-turned-detective. The character as he appeared in novels was quite brutal, racist, and even fascistic, lending credibility to Python's mention of him here as an example of Britain's failed colonial policies. The Goons had already lampooned the character—as "Bulldog Seagoon"—in "The Emperor of the Universe" episode (3 Jan. 1957).

• C •

Cronaca Di Un Amore — ("Six More Minutes of *Monty Python's Flying Circus*") Antonioni's (see bio above) first film was actually the documentary film *Gente del Po* (1943), which was followed by eight other documentary films before his 1950 feature film, *Cronaca du un amore*. The Pythons would have perhaps been much less aware of Antonioni's earlier nonfiction films, as these were more influenced by the tenets of neo-realism, so less reactionary and more stylistically conservative. Antonioni wouldn't appear in the London media until 1955, for his film *Le Amici*, which

premiered at the Venice Film Festival. In January 1961 the National Film Theatre offered the first Antonioni retrospective. The descriptions provided by the Pythons are fairly accurate for each film, meaning they've spent significant time watching foreign film.

"colour"—Antonioni's first color film was *Red Desert* (1964), and starred Monica Vitti and Richard Harris.

Crystal Palace — (PSC; "The Lost World of Roiurama") The Crystal Palace was built for the Great Exhibition of 1851, inspired awe in thousands of spectators, and eventually burned down. It's clear from the studio audience's non-reaction to the joke (the "Great Expedition" comment prompting an image of the "Great Exhibition" site) that either they did not hear the prompting phrase, or, more likely, the Crystal Palace wasn't nearly as recognizable as the Pythons thought.

Also, the image of the Crystal Palace would have to be viewed in the studio setting on a small television monitor (or even BP screen), meaning the studio audience may have had to look away from the filmed segment to see the insert, and just missed it.

"curlicued" — ("*The Money Programme*") Fantastically curled or twisted, while "filigree copperplating" simply means intricately worked plating on a particular coin.

• D •

"dead bishop on the landing" — ("Salvation Fuzz") This is primarily funny because it's incongruous—church police, dead bishops, rat tarts—and this also continues the theme visited in Ep. 28, where Thomas Becket's murder was lampooned.

"Du-Bakey" — ("Argument Clinic") A misspelled reference to Michael Ellis DeBakey (1908–2008), who was prominent in world news at this time (he was featured on the cover of *Time* magazine on 28 May 1965). DeBakey in 1966 had implanted the first completely artificial heart into a human. Taken in context with the mention of Barnard below, another heart specialist of the period, the reference seems certain. The later episode entitled "Michael Ellis" (Ep. 41) may also have been named in relation to this man.

"Barnard"—A reference to Dr. Christiaan Barnard (1922–2001), the South African heart surgeon who completed the first human heart transplant in 1967. (Barnard was featured on the cover of *Time* on 15 December 1967.) Barnard has already been mentioned in Ep. 22, where the Batley Townswomen's Guild re-enact the first heart transplant. In 1967 and 1968 Barnard found his smiling face in the pages of *Private Eye*, but only as a target for vilification, especially as his much-celebrated patients sickened and died, and Barnard carried on famously.

• E •

ecclesiastical accoutrements — (PSC; "Salvation Fuzz") These appear to include a navy blue or black Latin cassock, white clerical collar, purple gloves (with gold crosses), a green and gold chasuble and stole (without white alb), a cross pendant, and bishop's crook. He looks to be a cross between a Metropolitan policeman and a vicar, naturally.

Elizabethan music — ("PSC; "*Erizabeth L*") This bit of music is from The Early Music Consort of London and the Morley Consort—Two Renaissance Dance Bands playing "Passe & medio & reprise le pingue," "Basse danse," and "Bergeret sans roche" (WAC T12/1,445).

Elizabethan palace — (PSC; "*Erizabeth L*") This somewhat dilapidated "Elizabethan palace" is actually more a Jacobean house, as construction on what is known as Felbrigg Hall, Norwich, Norfolk, began in 1624. The house is shown at such an odd angle because it is attached, on the (viewer's) right side, to another wing built in the classical style some fifty years later. (The inscription above reads, "Gloria Deo In Excelsis.") The Jacobean portion of the house was designed by owner John Wyndham (1558–1645)—twenty-one years after the death of Elizabeth, and one year after James I's death.

As for the actual Tudor palaces and homes, this could be set at any one of about sixty that Henry VIII built, remodeled, or inhabited—including Hampton Court, Windsor Castle, and Nonsuch Palace—during his reign, and that his daughter paid to keep up.

This outdoor shot was recorded on 12 November 1971 (WAC T12/1,428). The interiors are all recorded at Ealing TFS.

"empire building" — ("Six More Minutes of *Monty Python's Flying Circus*") A comment on the depictions of Britain's benignly magnanimous empire in British films of the period, and in this case the focus on the travails of white British explorers in black Africa, where all black characters are either toadying or threatening. It makes sense that the African director Akawumba (Jones, pretending to be Italian director Antonioni) would be aware of the falseness of these colonial or post-colonial depictions, and decry the empire building "shit." The significant thoughts and then texts for post-colonialism appeared in earnest in the early 1950s and on into the 1960s.

This fits here in this particular episode, as well, since the conquest of the Spanish Armada in 1588 led to England's rise to international dominance, when empire building could begin in earnest. Also, the fact that contemporary times witnessed the dismantling of that same empire—much of it in the Pythons' own lifetimes—renders this sketch acutely topical.

Episode 29 — Recorded 4 December 1971, but not broadcast until 2 November 1972. This was actually the first episode recorded for the third season, and it was broadcast fourth.

Light Entertainment head Duncan Wood screened episodes 1–9 in September 1972 as they were preparing for broadcast of the third season, and suggested this order for the strongest schedule: Eps. 7 (Ep. 28), 5 (Ep. 27), 1 (Ep. 29), 9 (Ep. 31), 6 (Ep. 32), 4 (Ep. 33), 10 (Ep. 34), 11 (Ep. 35), and 8 (Ep. 37) (WAC T12/1,428).

Also appearing in this episode, according to BBC records: Fred Tomlinson and Singers, Sheila Bromberg (harpist); (as trumpeters and courtiers) Cy Town (*Colditz*), Ron Tingley (*Doctor Who*), Roy Pearce (*Doctor Who*); (as the gorilla) Reuben Martin (*Carry On Up the Jungle*); (as Africans) Omo Ade, Ajibade Arimoro, and Kyesi Kay; and Peter Kodak, Tony Christopher, Jonas Carr, Jay Neil, Roy Brent, Graham Skidmore, and Robyn Williams (see "*Episode*" entries in eps. 36, 37, and 38 for more on these seven); Chet Townsend (*Man about the House*), Frances Pidgeon (*Softly Softly*; *Doctor Who*), Nicholas Ward, Tony Adams, Raymond George (*Secrets of Sex*), Julie Desmond (*Casanova*), Sally Anne, Jean Clarke (*The Borderers*), Jill Lamas, and Daniel Jones (*Asylum*) (WAC T12/1,445).

"*Erizabeth L*" — ("*Erizabeth L*") The BBC had just produced (and then sent to American television screens) the very popular *Elizabeth R* in February–March 1971, starring Glenda Jackson (mentioned in Ep. 28) as the Virgin Queen. The Pythons clearly modeled their costuming demands on this recent and much-watched series. The title (the elaborate *Elizabeth R*) is also copied by the Pythons here, rendered as en equally florid *Erizabeth L*.

"Evening all" — ("Argument Clinic") Standard greeting of the title character from the long-running folksy BBC police show *Dixon of Dock Green* (1955–1976), starring Jack Warner (1896–1981) as PC/Sgt. George Dixon. The character first appeared in the 1950 film *The Blue Lamp*. See notes to Ep. 7 for more on the helpful, genial policeman figure.

The Pythons may be including PC Dixon for sentimental reasons, of course, but the fact that TV clean-up campaigner Mary Whitehouse had given *Dixon of Dock Green* her tacit approval as wholesome television might figure into these depictions. See notes to Ep. 32 for more on Whitehouse and her campaign to clean up British TV.

• F •

"festering gob . . . tit" — ("Argument Clinic") "Gob" is northern dialect slang for mouth, and a "tit" in this context would mean a fool.

"toffee-nosed"—One who is snobby. The slang is of British military origin (and according to the *OED*, specifically the Women's Auxiliary Air Force).

"filming us" — ("The Lost World of Roiurama") An acknowledgment of the artifice that has become more and more prevalent as the shows have progressed. Part of the troupe's dissatisfaction with the third series was this growing dependence on displaying theseaonman behind the curtain, as it were, the postmodern upending of any narrative track, instead of where they began in 1969—strong gag and character writing, and a healthy dose of irreverence for the television medium. The obvious knowledge of international cinema of the period (Visconti, Antonioni, Godard) betrays the troupe's interest in and perhaps influence from the various New Waves sweeping the film world, and those filmmakers' movement away from traditional narrative structures.

"fins" — ("Salvation Fuzz") A "rabbit fish" (a rabbit with fins) is an animal more like Gilliam's animated creations. In Ep. 10, the shopkeeper (Palin) will offer to do pet conversions (dog to cat, dog to parrot, etc.).

"Fraud Film Director Squad" — ("Fraud Film Squad") There has been a Special Operations Fraud Squad at Scotland Yard for many years, listed as "SO6." The Pythons also couple their inspectors with Flying Squad–type capabilities—officers who respond to crime situations quickly—allowing for trench-coated inspectors to burst through doors and catch folk red-handed, leading to "Flying Fox of the Yard." These "Flying Squad" units are seen in Hitchcock's *Blackmail* (1929), for example.

• G •

"*Gardening Club* for 1958" — ("Apology for Violence and Nudity") *Gardening Club* made its debut on the BBC in 1955, and ran under that title until 1967, when it became *Gardening World* (Vahimagi, 49). Ken Russell's version of *Gardening Club* would, of course, involve more nudity and psychosexual themes and situations. It was Russell's film *The Devils* (1970) that had provoked a call for a new rating ("XY") to account for films both sexual *and* violent. See the entries for Russell in Ep. 28.

Gardening Club music — ("*Ken Russell's Gardening Club*") The theme for *Gardening Club* was adapted, here by the Folk Dance Orchestra, and was originally "The Shrewsbury Lasses" by Thompson (WAC T12/1,445).

gorilla tear a man from his table — (PSC; "The Lost World of Roiurama") The gorilla is played by Reuben Martin (1921–1993), who also played a gorilla in several of the *Carry On* films.

"Götterdämmerung epic" — ("Fraud Film Squad") A reference to Wagner's "Ring" cycle, and means a sort of apocalyptic or disastrous series of events leading to utter destruction. Visconti's film *The Damned* certainly qualifies in this regard.

• H •

"He has oldeled the whore freet into the Blitish Channer" — ("*Erizabeth L*") England's fortunes were indeed all ventured in this gambit, and the victory became a jumping-off point for the spread of English rule around the globe.

A more contemporary reason for the Pythons' inclusion of a sketch ostensibly about the Spanish Armada is the Christmas-time 1969 broadcast of a *Chronicle* (notes, Eps. 19, 20, and 21) episode called, "The Fate of the Armada," which was introduced by Magnus Magnusson (note, Ep. 21).

"horsefeathers" — ("*Erizabeth L*") This is much later (post-Elizabethan), originally U.S. slang meaning "rubbish" or "nonsense."

huge hand descends — (PSC; "Salvation Fuzz") This hand appears to be a blown-up version of the hand of God from the ceiling of the Sistine Chapel, by Michelangelo. It was most likely xerographed at Gilliam's request. The same type of hand appears and strikes dead a high-strung general (Chapman) in *Meaning of Life*. Gilliam's own hand has been pictured a number of times throughout *FC*, continuing the tradition of early animation where the creator was figuratively represented in relation to his character (McCay, Blackton, Fleischer, et al.).

• I •

"I don't think you're Luchino Visconti at all" — ("*Erizabeth L*") This impostor sequence—especially in its crude audacity (note Visconti's Japanese accent)—is perhaps inspired by the celebrated case of Lobsang Rampa, author of *The Third Eye*. (See notes to Ep. 4, "Secret Service Dentists" sketch, for an earlier reference to this impostor.) Rampa, a self-proclaimed Tibetan monk, published his autobiography *The Third Eye* in 1956; it became a strong seller, but in 1958 he was discovered to be one Cyril Hoskin (1910–1981), originally from Plympton, Devon. The revelation caused something of a furore, but Hoskin continued to write and publish strange books (one dictated to him telepathically from his cat) into the 1980s (*ODNB*).

A poster for Rampa's eleventh book, *Beyond the Tenth* (1969), is seen in the bookshop in Ep. 4.

• J •

"jugged" — ("Salvation Fuzz") Food that has been stewed or boiled in a jug (*OED*).

jungle drums — (PSC; "Jungle Restaurant") The drum track is from Guy Warren of Ghana, "African Drums" (WAC T12/1,445).

"just now" — ("Argument Clinic") Here, the Man (Palin) tries to restart the original argument and, in true contradictory form, Mr. Vibrating (Cleese) takes him along another path, frustrating him as he searches for an argument while, ironically, having an argument.

• L •

"Leicester" — ("Salvation Fuzz") The Bishop of Leicester during this period was the Right Reverend Ronald R. Williams. Chapman was born and raised in Leicester.

"Liberal rubbish!" — ("Salvation Fuzz") The husband, Klaus (Idle), is reading the pink *Financial Times*, normally reserved for bowler-hatted denizens of the City, or those seen as owning the country. The fact that his wife calls the Hitlerian answers on the radio "liberal" must mean that she and her husband are ultra-conservative types, far-right nationalists of some kind, but biding their time, as they live in squalor and eat rat tart and rabbit fish. It may not be an accident that Klaus looks a bit more Germanic than English, either.

"ligging around" — ("*Erizabeth L*") Slang term meaning to sit around, to "sponge" (*OED*).

"Light Entertainment" — ("Argument Clinic") Arm of the BBC charged with developing and broadcasting comedy shows, especially, that would please without offending.

"lolly" — ("There Is Nothing Quite So Wonderful as Money [Song]") Slang term for money, and probably short for "lollipop" (*OED*).

"London Brick Company" — (PSC; "The Lost World of Roiurama") Located in Bedfordshire, the London Brick Company by the mid-1930s had become the largest manufacturer of bricks in the world, and 135 chimneys punctuated the Marston Vale skyline.

The filmed image is culled from BBC SKP 1879-1880 or BBC SKP 1816-9 (WAC T12/1,428).

long corridor — ("*Erizabeth L*") This dark wood, square-paneled construction is typical of the Tudor and then Elizabethan-era palaces, and then even homes, and can still be seen in places like Hampton Court (especially in the older, Wolsey-built sections of the palace, begun as early as 1515) and the dining room at Hardwick Hall, Derbyshire (built 1591–1597), Haddon Hall, etc. The long gallery was a significant room in both the castle and manor of the Elizabethan period, with many stretching more than 100 feet.

This scene was shot at Ealing TFS, using some of the same sets as were seen in Ep. 18, "Accidents Sketch."

• M •

"Marxist ways . . . phase" — ("There Is Nothing Quite So Wonderful as Money [Song]") Rather prescient, as in 1972 the demise of Communism as a practical political/economic/social way of life wasn't at all certain. The Brezhnev era had officially begun earlier in 1971, and the Soviet economy (including wages, crops, and factory output) was on the up, at least according to the speeches given at the twenty-fourth Congress of the Communist Party of the USSR in March 1971.

Money Programme, The — ("*The Money Programme*") Made its debut on BBC 2 in 1966, when David Attenborough was in charge, and would become the BBC's longest-running business and market program. *The Money Programme* was created (from an idea by Harman Grisewood; see notes to Ep. 3) to explain the British market to everyday folk, and especially to make sense of au courant terms like "balance of payment" and "devaluation," both thrown around in the media during this economically difficult time. See the *ODNB* entry for Grisewood for more.

The theme music for the actual *Money Programme* is the familiar "Jimmy Smith Theme" (also known as "The Cat") from "The Carpet Baggers" by Bernstein (WAC T12/1,445).

"Monty Python's Flying Circuses" — (PSC; credit link out of "There Is Nothing Quite So Wonderful as Money [Song]") This is the first time in the series that Palin is voicing the title (Cleese had been doing it before), though he's not credited in the printed script.

• N •

native guide — (PSC; "Jungle Restaurant") A black character is in this case actually played by a black actor, which is unusual for Python. The black actors in this scene are Omo Ade (who plays the guide), Ajibade Arimoro, and Kyesi Kay (playing a "pygmy") (WAC T12/1,428 and T12/1,445). A black man appears in another non-speaking role in Ep. 7, as a jazz musician who becomes a Scotsman. When it comes time in the scene for a black character to speak, however, Jones and Palin, both in black-face, take the roles.

The gorilla in the scene is played by Reuben Martin (*Carry On Up the Jungle*) (WAC T12/1,428), who played a gorilla in several other films, as well.

"nicked" — ("Argument Clinic") Interesting colloquial use here, since the word, according to the *OED*, had come to mean "stolen," and not "arrested."

"Nip" — ("*Erizabeth L*") WWII-era slang for a Japanese person. Short for "Nippon" (or "Nipponese") the Japanese name for Japan. According to the *OED*, the Royal Air Force was an early employer of the term.

"wop"—U.S. slang for a person of Italian descent, used especially in East Coast cities.

Norfolk jacket and plus fours — (PSC; "The Lost World of Roiurama") "Our Hero" is described as wearing a "Norfolk jacket," a sporting jacket made popular by the Prince of Wales in the nineteenth century, and "plus fours," pants cut four inches below the knee that were also popularized by the future King Edward VII.

This sequence looks and feels very much like a classic nineteenth-century melodrama, complete with over-the-top acting, amateur cast, and very obvious stage makeup. The characters in this and the earlier "Lumberjack Song" sketch were clearly drawn from the "Hearts and Flowers" world of the "mellerdrammer" plays like *East Lynne* ("Gone, and never called me mother!").

"Norman" — ("Salvation Fuzz") This somewhat swishy and affected delivery may be a reference to Tory MP Norman St. John Stevas (1929–2012) who never married, loved cats, possessed affectations, and appeared on the Ned Sherrin–produced *BBC3* in 1965. Found on BBC1, *BBC3* was essentially a follow-up to Frost's *Not So Much a Programme. . . .* The mention of Sir Gerald Nabarro in the previous question probably confirms the anti-Conservative bias in this sketch.

It's equally possible that this is a reference to Norman Brook (1902–1967), ultimately 1st Baron Normanbrook, a staunch Conservative who was very visible as he served as Cabinet secretary for fifteen years (1947–1962). Brook was also Chairman of the Board of Governors of the BBC when all of the young Pythons initially worked there, 1964–1967. He had been schooled at the Wolverhampton Grammar School (in

Idle's old stomping grounds) and Wadham College, Oxford. Brook appears over and over again in the "Court and Social" section of the *Times*, attending "gala luncheons" hosted by Lady Churchill, the Lady Mayoress (of London), Harold Macmillan, Anthony Eden, et al. There is a remarkable photo in the *Times* of Churchill's Cabinet from the day he resigned—7 April 1955—and Norman Brook is part of that group (21 Apr. 1955: 8).

"Notte, La" — ("Six More Minutes of *Monty Python's Flying Circus*") The 1961 Antonioni film starring Marcello Mastroianni, Jeanne Moreau, and Monica Vitti (1931), who also appeared in Antonioni's *L'eclisse* (1962) and *L'avventura* (1960).

• O •

"One hundled and thilty-six men of wal" — ("*Erizabeth L*") There were actually about 130 warships and merchant ships converted for the fight, so it's possible to call all of them "man of war" ships, since all were armed.

Organ music — (PSC; "Salvation Fuzz") As Klaus (Idle) is accused by the hand of God, a very short section from Bach's "Fantasia & Fugue in G minor" (BWV 542) is used, and was performed by Helmut Walchive (WAC T12/1,445).

"Ossessione . . . 1951" — ("Fraud Film Squad") *Ossessione* (1943) is Visconti's neo-realist film, and for many, it is the movement's first installment. *La terra trema: Episodio del mare* (1948) is another neo-realist text that looks at the lives of poor fishermen.

The balance of Leopard's (Cleese) arrest explanation also mentions the following:

"*I Bianche Notte*"—The 1957 Visconti adaptation of Dostoyevsky, starring Marcello Mastroianni and Maria Schell.

"Dostoevsky"—Actually, Russian author Fyodor Dostoevsky had died in 1881; his 1848 novel *White Nights* was adapted by Suso Cecchi d'Amico and Visconti for this 1957 film.

"*Boccaccio 70*"—1962 film directed by Vittorio de Sica, Federico Fellini, and Visconti.

"*The Leopard*"—Big-budget 1963 Visconti film examining the collapse of the aristocracy in nineteenth-century Sicily and the rise of Italian unification, and starring Burt Lancaster and Claudia Cardinale.

"Risorgimento"—Meaning renewal or renaissance, the Risorgimento in Italy led to the unification of the country in 1870, with Rome becoming its capital.

"Somerset House"—Home to the General Register Office from 1836 to 1970, where all public records were housed and created. Construction on Somerset House began in 1547. This sprawling building is located on the Strand at the Waterloo Bridge.

"The Damned"—*The Damned* is a film very much as described here by Inspector Leopard, though Berger's (b. 1944, Austria) character isn't so much a transvestite as a pedophilic sociopath, and Charlotte Rampling (b. 1945, UK) is anything but curvaceous (she is decidedly thin).

"Dirk Bogarde"—Born in Hampstead, Bogarde (1921–1999) was christened Derek Jules Gaspard Ulric Niven van den Bogaerde, and began his career on the stage before moving to motion pictures. Bogarde gained prominence appearing in a series of smaller but respectable British genre films directed by Basil Dearden, including *Victim* (1961) and *The Mind Benders* (1963), as well as the Losey-Pinter project *The Servant* (1963).

"elderly poof what expires in Venice"—The plot for *Death in Venice* does involve the death of a homosexual older man in Venice. It is considered by many (including Bogarde himself) as the actor's finest performance.

• P •

polar expedition . . . pass him — (PSC; "The Lost World of Roiurama") The stuffed expedition described in the script is more of an exotic menagerie when it's presented to viewers, and includes what looks to be a stuffed bear, a llama, a dog or two, and perhaps a flamingo. The group of winter-dressed explorers "Our Hero" (Jones) has been sitting with also includes one dead man, seemingly frozen.

"primeval creatures" — ("The Lost World of Roiurama") This was the supposition of various stories about this tepui and others (in Brazil, for example), that prehistoric creatures would be found in this remote, unexplored environment. (The small, hopless frog *Oreophrynella* is one such creature not discovered until 1898, but in existence for millions of years.)

The subject was in the news recently in the UK. In 1971, a British expedition to the North Ridge of Mount Roraima was undertaken, and a filmed version of the event was shown on the BBC's *World about Us*, and called "To Catch an Orchid." New species of frogs were discovered, but no prehistoric beasts.

• R •

"rabbit fish" — ("Salvation Fuzz") Given the WWII-era radio topic (National Socialist policy) and the available food—"rabbit fish" and "strawberry tart"—

this scene references the difficult war and postwar years in Great Britain. Rationing (from January 1940) was a part of life in the UK for many years, with coffee, meats, sugar, butter, bacon, etc., all diminished as the war pushed on—remaining scarce in the frugal postwar years, until at least 1954. (A Milligan character in "The Fireball of Milton Street"—Sir Jim Nasium—asks several times if anyone knows what happened to "that crisp bacon" they had "before the war," and is shot for his troubles.) Beginning in 1940 each family registered with the local government and were given coupons for precisely what they deserved, by age and number of family members, and no more.

In the larger cities especially, where there was less chance of growing a useful garden, Brits had to scrounge and resort to illicit sources for all sorts of items, from cigarettes to tea and, eventually, even bread. Londoners reported many days when bread and milk were the only meals, when housewives had to travel outside the city to buy black market vegetables and dairy products from small farms, and when virtually any kind of animal—including horse—could be justified as a meal (*Eyewitness: 1940–49*, "Wartime Austerity"). Fresh strawberries would have been virtually unknown, of course, and strictly controlled if there were any about.

One of the austerity-inspired dishes created under the auspices of the Ministry of Food was known as "Woolton Pie," a vegetable dish meant to be available from non-rationed home garden ingredients, including potatoes, cauliflower, turnips, carrots, rolled oats, and spring onions. Meat would not have been one of the recommended ingredients, rat or otherwise. (Horseflesh became available in some areas, though many refused to buy it.) The Goons also mention another wartime food, Brown Windsor Soup, served in "British Restaurants" kept open during the war.

"Reichstag" — ("Salvation Fuzz") Located in Berlin, it is the nominal seat of German representative government.

"Roiurama" — ("The Lost World of Roiurama") Misspelled, but Mt. Roraima is in Venezuela, on the border with Guyana and Brazil, and is a flat-topped mountain (tepui) left unexplored into the nineteenth century. It is said to be the inspiration for Sir Arthur Conan Doyle's *The Lost World*, which became a film in 1925.

"thrown up . . . movements"—Actually, the tepuis are sandstone massifs, and have most likely emerged as a process of erosion over millions of years, not upward thrust.

The image used here of the Roraima Plateau is called "South American Expedition," and is from

David Bromhall, Dept. of Zoology, South Park Rd., Oxford (WAC T12/1,428).

"Russell, Ken" — (*"Ken Russell's Gardening Club"*) Born in 1927, Ken Russell had just finished *The Devils* in 1971, starring Vanessa Redgrave and Oliver Reed. (Most contemporary critics skewered the orgiastic film.) See the entry for Russell in Ep. 28.

The audience would certainly have recognized Russell's name. *The Devils* was only allowed for release with an "X" rating after very significant editing, in accordance with the British Board of Film Classification demands, and was even proposed as the first film with an ever harsher "XY" rating from the BBFC. It also received an "X" rating in the United States. Ken Russell passed away in 2011.

• S •

sings to piano accompaniment — (PSC; "There Is Nothing Quite So Wonderful as Money [Song]") The song "Money, Money, Money" is sung live by Idle, and accompanied by the Fred Tomlinson Singers and harpist Sheila Bromberg. The music was written by Fred Tomlinson, with lyrics by John Gould (WAC T12/1,445).

"Slit Eyes Yakamoto" — ("Fraud Film Squad") Fairly run-of-the-mill Python use of racial slur to refer to a person of Asian descent, in this case structured like a gangster's name.

"smell of the rain-washed florin" — (*"The Money Programme"*) This build-up sequence is written very much like the introduction to the "I'm a Lumberjack" song from Ep. 9, though the earlier song was written by Jones, Palin, and McGuffie.

"society is to blame" — ("Salvation Fuzz") The idea of a "permissive society" was quite prevalent at this time, with more conservative elements in the UK (e.g., Mary Whitehouse) certain that the tolerant liberality of these so-called permissives was to blame for the younger generation's immorality, drug use, disrespect of values and tradition, etc. Whitehouse and friends targeted the media, particularly. Contemporary psychiatrists and sociologists were often using "society" (obviating personal choice and accountability) as the hook upon which to hang the blame for troubled teens, seeing, essentially, a lost generation. (See Aldgate's *Censorship and the Permissive Society*.)

There is a quote in the 1952 film *Europa '51* directed by Roberto Rossellini that echoes this sentiment: "If you must blame something, blame our postwar society."

"Spare-Buttons" — ("Jungle Restaurant") Mr. Spare-Buttons is perhaps a quip at the long-standing use of personal attributes, occupation, or area of origin to name Englishmen—for example, Chapman (meaning "merchant"), Norton (meaning "north town"), etc. Also, this may be in reference to colonial native populations naming their new white friends by virtue of their skin color, hair color, or even apparel or accoutrements they carry.

steamy tropical jungle — ("Jungle Restaurant") The mood music is from Dave Lindup, "Elephant Herd," as well as the New Concert Orchestra playing "Background Music 'Stings'" by Alan Langford (WAC T12/1,445). These "Stings" are used when the explorers are seeing shocking images of the volcano, Roiurama, the brick factory, and Crystal Palace.

Stock film of Houses of Parliament — ("The Lost World of Roiurama") This is from the BBC's own archives, BBC 3SKP20 (WAC T12/1,428). The music is Elgar's "Pomp and Circumstance March," which is used at least a dozen times in *FC* (and at least once leading to a threatened lawsuit by Elgar's executors).

"Suffragan or diocesan?" — ("Salvation Fuzz") A suffragan is a bishop "considered in regard to his relation to the archbishop or metropolitan, by whom he may be summoned to attend synods and give his suffrage" (*OED*), while a diocesan is a bishop of a diocese, and more often considered in relation to that diocese.

"sullearist" — (*"Erizebeth L"*) This may be Yakamoto's betrayal of his impersonator status, as Visconti was *not* known for employing surrealist elements (as Bunuel, Fellini, and even Godard were, in this period). The bulk of the surrealist films appeared in the 1920s and 1930s, from Antonin Artaud, Salvador Dali, Luis Bunuel, Rene Clair, Man Ray, and Jean Cocteau, for instance. Elements of surreality in films thereafter are often confined to dream sequences, drug-induced hazes, or other "altered" points of view. Disney's "Pink Elephants on Parade" sequence in *Dumbo* (1941) is a fine example of the surrealists' impact on feature filmmaking—where the narrative justifies the surrealist escapade via the characters' accidental inebriation.

The Pythons will revisit this surrealist world in their final feature film, *Meaning of Life*, specifically in the "Find the Fish" sequence.

• T •

"Tattooed on the back of his neck" — ("Salvation Fuzz") As if the Church would exercise its ownership of bishops by indelibly marking each, much the way the First Pepperpot (Chapman) argues that zoo animals are stamped on the bottom of their feet at birth (Ep. 22).

Though tattooing has a long tradition in the British Isles, as early as 787 AD the Holy Church banned body marking of any kind as a pagan practice. Later adventurers in the Orient and the South Pacific brought tattooing back into Britain's public consciousness, and it became almost de rigueur for the highest and lowest classes, interestingly, including the two royal princes Albert Victor and George Frederick Earnest Albert, both tattooed while serving in the royal navy on HMS *Bacchante* in 1879 (*ODNB*).

Perhaps this is also an idea borrowed from the low-budget sci-fi movie *Invaders from Mars* (1953), where the aliens surgically marked each of their human zombies on the back of their necks. (This isn't really a stretch, considering the Pythons portrayal of church types throughout *FC*.)

"there's violence to be done" — (*"Animation: Police violence"*) The thief who is bested by the many-armed City Gent in the Gilliam animation emerges from the doors of Morpeth Arms, a pub/brewery at 58 Millbank Street (and Ponsonby Place) in London. The image looks like one of a series of inner city images, all taken near the center of London.

Another identifiable building in this series of photographs is the Limebank House (168 Fenchurch), then headquarters to Barclay's, which was finished in 1969 and demolished in 1998. An existing building at the corner of Cornhill and Lombard streets, in the City, can also be seen, as well as Trafalgar Square and the National Gallery.

"tosh" — (link into "One More Minute of *Monty Python's Flying Circus*") A vague epithet that can have little intended derogatory meaning, according to the OED, almost a filler word.

three trumpeters play a fanfare — (PSC; *"Erizabeth L"*) This is Spencer Nakin's "Trumpet Calls" from the album *Towers & Spires*. These three actors pretending to play horns are Cy Town (*Colditz*; *Star Wars*), Ron Tingley (*Doctor Who*; *Z Cars*), and Roy Pearce (*Z Cars*;

Doctor Who), who also play courtiers in the following scene (WAC T12/1,445).

two nuns run in — (PSC; *"Ken Russell's Gardening Club"*) The subject matter for Russell's *The Devils* is religious and sexual hysteria, with most of a nunnery participating in graphic, carnivalistic sexual activity with each other, bones, crucifixes, etc. The basis of the story is Cardinal Richelieu (Eps. 3 and 13) attempting to quash a political rival in Father Grandier.

· V ·

"Visconti, Luchino" — (*"Erizabeth L"*) Italian film director influential in the neo-realist movement of the postwar era. He then moved into a more realist and even romantic period.

"volcano of Andu" — (*"The Lost World of Roiurama"*) Perhaps referring to portions of the Flinders Range in South Australia, which would continue this batch of shows' references to Australia. The photo is from the BBC collection, BBC SKP 2812A-6 (WAC T12/1,428).

"Vo-oorale" — (*"Erizabeth L"*) "Volare," a song made famous by Dean Martin.

· W ·

Welsh . . . costume — (PSC; "There Is Nothing Quite So Wonderful as Money [Song]") The female Welsh national costume (tall black hat, long skirt, white apron, and a shawl) was popularized as such in the nineteenth century by figures such as Lady Llanofer.

Welsh harpist—A Welsh Harp is a triple-strung harp (here a Challen Upright 74947), and is played for this sketch by Sheila Bromberg. This sketch was recorded on 4 and 5 December 1971 at TC6 (WAC T12/1,428).

"we must to Tirbuly" — (*"Erizabeth L"*) Tilbury was the site where Elizabeth spoke to her troops prior to the land battle that most feared would follow the naval engagement.

Episode 30: *"Blood, Devastation, Death, War, and Horror"*

Blood, Devastation, Death, War and Horror; The man who speaks in anagrams; Anagram versions of Shakespeare; Nude organist, "And now" Man, "It's" Man; *Titles* (anagram version of title, Cleese v/o); *Beat the Clock*: Anagram Quiz; Merchant Banker at Slater-Nazi; The donation; Viking cutaway; Pantomime Horses fight to the death; Life and death struggles nature documentary (sea lions, limpets, wolf and ant, and documentary filmmakers fighting); Pantomime horses fight; Pantomime Goose kills Terrence Rattigan; Pantomime Princess Margaret kills her breakfast tray; *Animation: Pantomime flea eats man, carnivorous dining and bed rooms, killer houses, The House-Hunters and NCP Car Parks*; "The makers of this film would like to thank . . ."; Mary Recruitment Office; Durham Light Infantry and interior décor; Bus conductor sketch; The man who makes people laugh uncontrollably; Army captain as clown; "Is the Queen Sane?": Gestures to indicate pauses in televised talk; BBC 1 Colour: Neurotic announcer; "The News with Richard Baker" (with gestures); **The Pantomime Horse Is a Secret Agent** Film; Narrated closing credits (anagrams)

• A •

"anagrams" — ("The Man Who Speaks in Anagrams") An anagram is the purposeful transposition of letters in a word or name to make a new word or name. The character here is actually not making real words (except by accident, occasionally, as will be shown); he's most often merely jumbling the letters.

See the entry for "Peter Scott" below for another anagram mention.

"anagram version" — ("The Man Who Speaks in Anagrams") There have been and continue to be multiple versions of Shakespeare plays—in modern dress, in non-Anglo cultures, supporting or attacking one political persuasion or another—The Bard's are perhaps the most adapted theatrical pieces in the history of staged spectacle (see Dollimore and Sinfield's *Political Shakespeare*). In *FC* there is an underwater production of Shakespeare (Ep. 22) as well as Hamlet brought onto a contemporary psychiatrist's couch (Ep. 43). In the first of two *Fliegender Zirkus* episodes made for Bavarian TV, a dairy herd from Bad Ischl and a troupe of chickens from Kaiserlautern attempt adaptations of

The Merchant of Venice, with varying degrees of success, according to a critic (Idle).

This kind of soft subject was the caliber of topic seen on the earlier episodes of *Man Alive*, before "they got all serious" according to Herbert Mental (Jones) in Ep. 26, that or a regional report on the equally fluffy *Nationwide*.

Animation: Killer Houses — ("*Animation: Pantomime flea eats man, Carnivorous Dining and Bed Rooms, Killer Houses, The House-Hunters and NCP Car Parks*") The building on the hill behind the unsuspecting woman (who is eaten by the house) is Carlton House Terrace, which has been used earlier in an Ep. 6 animation. The following image features several buildings, the one on the right being a reappearance of Her Majesty's Theatre, seen earlier in Ep. 22.

"art . . . revival" — ("Mary Recruitment Office") William Morris (1834–1896) was a Victorian-era art and architecture luminary whose work led to the Arts and Crafts movement. The twentieth-century Art Nouveau movement was inspired by Morris's exploration of the medieval and Arts and Crafts movements.

• B •

backdrop of a circus ring — (PSC; "Army Captain as Clown") The music in the background is "Acrobats" by Keith Papworth from the album *The Big Top* (WAC T12/1,442).

Baker, Richard — (The News with Richard Baker [Vision Only]") Baker (b. 1925) was the presenter for the first BBC television news broadcast in 1954, and he continued in that position until 1982.

Nine O'Clock News—BBC TV's *Nine O'Clock News* went on the air on 14 September 1970.

The Pythons were able to convince two prominent contemporary newsreaders—Baker and Reginald Bosanquet—to bring their sober and respected on-air credentials into the service of *FC* via these bits of self-deprecating, reflexive humor. *Rowan & Martin's Laugh-In* (1967–1973) had plied these waters earlier with the appearances of President Richard Nixon, newscaster Hugh Downs, sports broadcaster Vin Scully, and uber-presenter David Frost, for example, and even earlier the Goons several times welcomed BBC newsreader John Snagge (before whom Walt Greenslade would truckle). Baker plays the gesticulating character straight, as does Bosanquet in his earlier appearance, effectively underscoring the incongruous silliness.

beat the clock — (PSC; "Anagram Quiz") There was an American TV game show called *Beat the Clock* (1969–1974) where couples attempted to perform feats within certain time constraints.

Bols Story, The — (PSC; link into "Gestures to Indicate Pauses in a Televised Talk") This title has absolutely nothing to do with the piece that follows it, precedes it, or appears anywhere in the episode—which is becoming more the case in *FC*. Bols is an Amsterdam-based spirits company, established in 1575. It may be that Mr. Orbiter-5 (Palin) fully intends to talk about Bols, but he speaks around the topic before being cut off completely.

The music beneath this intro is De Sik's "The Windmill Song" from the *Greensleeves* album (WAC T12/1,442).

"Boom boom!" — ("Bus Conductor Sketch") This was the signature line for the glove puppet character Basil on *The Basil Brush Show* (BBC1, 1968–1980), a children's show. The catchphrase also turns up a number of times in *ISIRTA*.

• C •

carnivorous house — (PSC; animation link out of "Life and Death Struggles") Gilliam uses sections from the songs "Prairie Vista" by Dudley Simpson and "Bright Lights" by Roger Webb in this animated link (WAC T12/1,442).

cartoon-type hammer — (PSC; "Anagram Quiz") Again acknowledging the influence that cartoons had on the Pythons, an influence which has been evident to this point, but not stated outright in the printed scripts.

"Champion" — ("Merchant Banker") Horse ridden by Gene Autry (1907–1998), star of dozens of TV and film Westerns. Autry also wrote and performed dozens of songs, including "Here Comes Santa Claus." Champion died in 1990.

"Trigger"—A horse ridden by another American "singing cowboy," Roy Rogers (1911–1998). Trigger died at the age of 33 in 1965. Rogers and Autry appeared in films and TV shows together, as well.

CHAMRAN KNEBT — (PSC; link into "Merchant Banker") The jaunty music beneath this unscrambling is "Droopy Draws" from the album *Selling Sounds* by Barry Stoller (WAC T12/1,442).

"chum" — ("The Man Who Speaks in Anagrams") One of the few words that Man (Idle) actually renders anagrammatically. The others are "sit" from a mispronunciation of "that's it," "mating" from "taming," and "thing" from "night."

City Gent — ("Merchant Banker") This is one of the first times that a type known as "City Gent" has been allowed to participate in a sketch to a significant degree. City Gents have generally appeared in Vox Pops segments, blathering ultra-Conservative comments or just plain blathering. In this case, the City Gent (Cleese) is allowed to continue his traditional rightist, upper-middle-class, profit-at-any-cost litany in a sketch setting. The result is the same, however: the City Gent is by the Pythons indicted (or self-indicted, really, by his own admissions of his obscene wealth, his detachment from the common man, etc.).

In this indictment that the Pythons have pressed throughout the series, they continue to build on the Modernist artists who so often shared and promoted this anti-establishment cause, but just as often with venality, not humor. Artists like George Grosz (1893–1959)—who survived WWI and was forever changed—were certain that the evils of the capitalist machinery that led to the war hadn't becalmed after the bloody saturation, leaving this disillusioned painter to see, especially in his native Germany, that Berlin (and the capitalist world) was still "owned by four breeds of pig: the capitalist, the officer, the priest and the hooker, whose other form is the socialite wife" (Hughes, 75–78). While not giving in to despair or outright loathing, the

Pythons clearly target these same "pigs" in their typological humor, satirizing the City Gent, the "What's All This Then?" Policeman and martinet Colonel, any Church representative, and women in general throughout *Flying Circus*.

In the Pythons' *May Day Special*, one of the new sketches is a dance sequence, poking fun at these monied elites:

> Narrator (Cleese): The City of London also reflects the spirit of joy through rebirth at its world famous stock exchange, where May Day is honored by the spring dance of the futures brokers. This charming variation on the merchant banker's hornpipe expresses the deepest yearning of all financiers for more and more money. This strangely touching dance offers up—in a surprising climax—a fervent prayer that one day each financier shall find some meaning in his life outside this round of eternal acquisition, and that this meaning shall bring him liberation from the whole grisly process. (*Euroshow 71—May Day Special*)

The dance is performed by all the Pythons, excepting Gilliam, dressed as City Gents, on the steps of a columned financial building.

collage of photos appear — (PSC; "The News with Richard Baker [Vision Only]") The photos appearing in the green screen circle behind Baker (as appearing in the printed script) include:

"Richard Nixon"—Seen earlier in Ep. 5, and mentioned again in the feature film *Holy Grail*, this American vice president and president was a consistent target of left-leaning artists and activists, and it must have been immeasurably galling that he was able to be elected not once but twice during this tumultuous period. Nixon (1913–1994) had traveled widely in his capacity as a two-term vice president as well, meaning he had been in the worldwide public eye for a generation by this time.

"Tony Armstrong-Jones"—Antony Armstrong-Jones, first Earl of Snowdon (b. 1930) was a professional portrait photographer and, most notably here, Princess Margaret's husband—he's already been mentioned by Timmy Williams (Idle) in Ep. 19 as "the lovely Snowdon." Armstrong-Jones was an Eton and Cambridge grad.

"the White House"—Just a standard shot across the front lawn. The opening shot of this newscast, where the title is featured, is a 16mm film clip of New York City, and specifically the United Nations building. These shots are probably included to mimic a typical evening newscast of the period, though the Princess and Lord Snowdon did make an unofficial visit to the LBJ White House in November 1965.

"Princess Margaret"—The younger sister to the Queen, Margaret (1930–2002) married Armstrong-

Jones in 1960, and they were divorced in 1978. The Pantomime Princess Margaret will appear later in this episode, as well as in a cameo role in Ep. 33. Baker may be miming the mixing of a drink when Margaret's picture is shown, but it's not clear, and the rumors of her profligate lifestyle seem to have not been confirmed. See Margaret's various obituaries, including comments from Margaret's "friend," who tries to separate her reputation from reality (*Observer*, 17 Feb. 2002). According to WAC records, this very popular costume/ prop was first requested for construction on 23 September 1971 (WAC T12/1,445). The unhappy couple appear on the 14 August 1970 cover of *Private Eye*, and are given equally unflattering dialogue balloons:

> She: What's all this about us rowing in public?
> He: Shut up you fat bitch and keep smiling!

"parliament"—Standard upriver shot of the famous building, and there's no obvious connection between the photos displayed yet. This juxtaposition may be an allusion, though, to Margaret's attempts to marry Air Force pilot Peter Townsend in 1955. Townsend was much older than Margaret, and had been divorced, and it seems that the Queen was advised to discourage the match, including threatening Margaret's place in the succession, etc. Even at the time there were knitted brows over just who controlled the rights to succession, with Britain's left-leaning *New Statesman and Nation* arguing that it was not Canterbury or the Queen, but Parliament alone, and everyone else should clear off:

> It raises sharp constitutional issues. The Princess declared that she has been "aware that, subject to my renouncing my rights of succession, it might have been possible for me to contract a civil marriage." This seems to imply that a civil marriage could have been possible only if the succession were renounced. But who has made her "aware" of any such thing? Is it even true? The right of succession is *peculiarly a matter for Parliament*. (qtd. in *Time*, 14 Nov. 1955)

With this very public and increasingly acrimonious debate still warm, the juxtaposition of Margaret and Parliament makes more sense.

"naked breasts"—This partial nude may be Karen Burch, who signed a "partial nude" (or "use of skin") appearance contract and posed on 18 November 1971 (WAC T12/1,445).

"a scrubbing brush" followed by *"a man with a stoat through his head"*—The serious news has given way to the oddball, or perhaps human interest, the famous stoat appearing or being mentioned in Eps. 5, 6, and 26. Gilliam sported the stoat in Ep. 26.

"Margaret Thatcher"—Back to the hard news, with the Iron Lady perhaps considered an archenemy of the

more liberal Pythons. The fact that her image follows the man with a stoat through his head and precedes a toilet indicates just where the Pythons would rank the high-ranking Tory. Thatcher (b. 1925) would have been front-page news at this time. In the summer of 1971 she endorsed an end to the free milk program for schoolchildren over the age of seven, part of an enormous cuts package (including health and public services) pushed by the Conservative government and approved in September 1971.

"a lavatory"—A standard toilet, the photo was probably taken right there in Television Centre.

"a Scotsman lying on his back with his knees drawn up"—Chapman will assume this position as the "Unexploded Scotsman" in Ep. 38. This photo was probably taken in Norwich, where the Pythons shot location footage for part of the third season, including the exterior work for "Kamikaze Scotsmen" at Norwich Castle.

"a corkscrew"—Taking the previous photo into consideration (a supine, spread-eagled Scotsman), it's probably safe to assume the corkscrew may be included for its sexual connotations.

"Edward Heath"—Conservative Heath (1916–2005) had been PM since the surprising June 1970 General Election, but the economy had been in the doldrums before and since, meaning he was something of an unpopular figure by this time. The recent drastic cuts in government spending (including the milk reductions mentioned above) were also weighing heavily on consumer/voter confidence in 1971–1972. The recent 1971 Industrial Relations Bill, meant to hamstring big labor, had also created a very hostile environment between 10 Downing, Parliament, and the TUC.

"a pair of false teeth in a glass"—The juxtaposition here may be that Heath is too old and out of touch to do the country any good. (He would have been fifty-five at this time—younger than many former PMs, but old enough to be untrustworthy to the younger generation of the late 1960s.) Heath had surrounded himself with a sort of "usual suspects" gang of Cabinet members and influential Ministers, probably reeking of cronyism to young liberals like the Pythons and the editors of *Private Eye*.

Without dialogic comment, these juxtaposed images are not unlike the famous pictorial experiments performed by Lev Kuleshov's workshop in the 1920s. Kuleshov and his students juxtaposed the unchanging image of a man's face with separate, unrelated images to determine how an audience "reads" these juxtapositions. In this case, the Python audience is asked to read images of well-known politicians and public figures intermixed with images of everyday items and silliness, with a third element being Baker's mimes that also "comment" on the images.

"consequently bad television" — ("Life and Death Struggles") An acknowledgment that even in documentary filmmaking—where a realistic representation of life is the supposed hallmark—there must exist an entertainment factor if the viewer is going to stay tuned in. Mr. Birchenhall (Chapman) in Ep. 27 went to jail arguing this very point—that viewers won't stand for evenings of straight ahead televised documentaries; they want entertainment. With this in mind, documentary filmmakers like Cousteau, Scott, and Seilmann have to pick subjects with viewability in mind—among other considerations—then capture images that they hope will be editable into compelling television. One of the often misunderstood elements of documentary film is this very selective, very objective-driven editing process where the "story" of the characters is revealed (or coaxed, coerced, and often created). The specter of aggressive male versus aggressive male, of competition within an ecosystem, of, yes, life and death struggles in the animal world, is the focus of many of Seilmann's and Cousteau's documentaries of this period.

In the end, of course, they aren't arguing about point of view or subject matter or potential manipulation or observational technique—they're brawling over profits, which clearly makes for good television.

"Cousteau, Jacques" — ("Life and Death Struggles") Already mentioned in Ep. 27, where he is found living in Paris in the same building as Jean-Paul Sartre, Cousteau was the preeminent name in televised nature documentaries. See notes to Ep. 27 for more on Cousteau.

credits roll — (PSC; end credits) They managed a few anagrams from the names and titles in the closing credits, but the bulk are just jumbles. The successful anagrams include: "Rice" for "Eric," "Lied" for "Idle," "Lapin" for "Palin," and the brilliant "Torn Jersey" for "Terry Jones," They also are able to create another very believable name from Gilliam's first and last names—"Marty Rigelli."

". . . crreoct" — ("The Man Who Speaks in Anagrams") "That is correct." (Translations are provided herein—the taped version offers no subtitles.) This is a very different sketch from "The Argument Clinic," because the text as delivered almost demands that there is a reader, and not just a listener. Most of the jumbles are difficult if not impossible to decipher without a printed script, so the payoff has to be the fact that the guest (Idle) leaves in a huff, and not in comprehension of the dazzling mis-speak that Idle employs.

"Cumberland" — ("The Man Who Speaks in Anagrams") One of the northernmost counties of England, situated along the Scottish border. Cumberland is in county Cumbria.

• D •

dinky little set — ("Blood, Devastation, Death, War and Horror") The uncredited music behind the Interviewer's introduction is from the Lansdowne Light Orchestra, "Newsroom" by Simon Campbell (WAC T12/1,442).

Dobbin — (PSC; *"The Pantomime Horse Is a Secret Agent* Film") There are several possibilities here. Besides the well-known pantomime horse figure, Dobbin was a coach horse fondly eulogized in *The Post Boy* in April 1699; "Dobbin" is also the name of a traditional rocking chair (with horse head and reins) still available in the UK; finally, a Dobbin is traditionally a steady old horse, a work horse, a horse gentle enough for a child, etc. This last meaning is found in a poem by Walter De La Mare (1873–1956), and others, especially those poems set in the bucolic English countryside of the recent past. In short, "Dobbin" as the name for a recognizable horse figure seems an easy choice.

"does gardening" — ("Blood, Devastation, Death, War and Horror") The emphasis for this sentence as spoken by Palin is on the word "does," for some reasoning, which elicits quite a laugh from the studio audience. Perhaps the juxtaposition of a gardener—quite a common sight on British TV—with such a bloody-themed show is the reason.

dog fight . . . blazing — (PSC; "Blood, Devastation, Death, War and Horror") The order and variety of these shots as shown is slightly different from the printed script: (1) Head-on train wreck (silent film footage); (2) 1930s car crash and burn (probably from a gangster film); (3) train falling from a trestle bridge (special effects footage from a silent film); (4) exploding volcano; (5) burning, sinking ship (this is the *Torrey Canyon*); and (6) forest fire footage. There is no "RAF" or "Spanish hotel" footage used in the film.

The sources for these photos/film stock is as follows (some footage was used, some was not): trains crashing (Philip Jenkinson, *Casey Jones*), hotel blowing up (Movietone E9536 [1040]), volcano erupting (BBC CL 45072), car crashing and exploding (BBC SP1891 or EMI E1740 [red sports car]), train on collapsing bridge (P. Jenkinson), and forest fires (BBC NPA 6688) (WAC T12/1,428).

"Douglas-Home, Sir Alec" — ("The Pantomime Horse Is a Secret Agent Film") Formally, Sir Alexander Frederick Douglas-Home, fourteenth Earl of Home, Baron Home of the Hirsel of Coldstream (1903–1995). Douglas-Home sat in the House of Commons, was a parliamentary undersecretary to Neville Chamberlain, an undersecretary of state for foreign affairs for Churchill, and became Prime Minister in 1963. Home

(pejoratively called "Baillie Vass" in *Private Eye*) is certainly one whom the Pythons would have seen as a "teeth-in-the-glass" Tory. A Conservative (and thus a Python target), his tenure was dogged by a very poor economy and the shrinking of the Empire, and he was succeeded in 1965 as party leader by Edward Heath, who would later become Prime Minister.

"Duke of Kent to the rescue" — (*"The Pantomime Horse Is a Secret Agent* Film") The Walton "Orb and Sceptre" piece, originally written for Elizabeth's coronation in 1953, is heard as Rattigan and the Duke of Kent arrive in the open car.

The fact that it is the Duke of Kent (b. 1935) who saves the day may be due to his position as President of the Royal National Lifeboat Institution (RNLI), an organization featured in Ep. 33, but the fact that he was also serving in active duty in Cyprus in 1970 and then Northern Ireland in 1971 would also keep him much in the news. There was some real concern that the Duke would be either killed, or—worse—kidnapped and used as leverage by IRA forces in Northern Ireland.

"Durham Light Infantry" — ("Mary Recruitment Office") Created in 1881, the DLI served in Gibraltar, the Boer War, WWI, and beyond.

"orange"—The Durham Light Infantry color is green, primarily, with some white and tan.

• E •

"edge of the sailor's uniform, until the word 'Maudling' . . ."** — ("Gestures to Indicate Pauses in Televised Talk") Once again, with "Hello Sailor" being the clarion call for the gay male on the hunt in the Python world, Reginald Maudling—a noted Conservative and Cabinet member to Heath—is painted with the "sexual deviancy" brush so often used in *Flying Circus*.

"Edward VII" — (*"The Pantomime Horse Is a Secret Agent* Film") In Ep. 1, King Edward VII is an unseen contestant in "Famous Deaths," where he achieves the lowest score. Edward VII (1841–1910) was Queen Victoria's eldest son, and was a man of great appetites in women, entertainment, food, and all pleasures of the flesh. His hunt clothing favorites (Norfolk jacket and plus fours) have been featured in the previous episode.

"effeminate" — ("Mary Recruitment Office") Most depictions of the military in *FC* begin in earnest, then move to humor and eventually brutality or effeminization (or both), including soldiers who "camp it up" in close-order drills (Ep. 22), and the lecturing

Brigadier (Cleese) in Ep. 35 who can talk informatively about modern dance troupes, etc. Some depictions are more swishy from the get-go—like Air Chief Marshal Sir Vincent "Kill the Japs" Forster (Cleese) in Ep. 14, who's flaming (cross-dressed, campy, effeminate) right out of the gate.

"dead butch"—An expression meaning *not* homosexual, in this context.

Episode 30 — Recorded 11 December 1971, and broadcast 9 November 1972. This episode was recorded second and broadcast fourth.

Also included on the later "repeat cost" lists: Richard Smith (*Van Der Valk*), Brian Codd, Frank Lester (Ep. 40; *Dixon of Dock Green*), Desmond Verini (*Doctor Who*), Mike Reynell (*Doctor Who*), and Jane Cussons (*Nine Tailors*).

Lastly, Steve Peters (*Daleks' Invasion Earth*), Anthony Hamilton, Gerry Alexander (*Z Cars*), Reg Turner (*The Goodies*; *Z Cars*), Barry Kennington (*Doctor Who*), Clive Rogers (*Z Cars*), and Fred Davis (*It's the Bachelors*) were brought in on 25 October 1971 to play the Coolies, Panto horses, a Panto goose, etc., at Black Park (Fulmer, near Slough, Buckinghamshire). This location was also used on 3 November 1971 (WAC T12/1,428).

"Every one a Maserati" — ("Bus Conductor Sketch") This hackneyed catchphrase is also voiced in *ISIRTA* ("Jack the Ripper"), and from an equally inept jokester.

exciting chase — (PSC; "*The Pantomime Horse Is a Secret Agent* Film") The music beneath the love scene in the boat is "Love in Slow Motion" by Reg Tilsley and the International Studio Orchestra; beneath the car chase scene is "Devil's Gallop" by the Queen's Hall Orchestra; and beneath the rickshaw chase sections is "Viet Theme" by Roger (WAC T12/1,442).

• F •

fish down the trousers — ("Bus Conductor Sketch") Yet another of the tried-and-true vaudeville and music hall gags, with the following bucket of whitewash and finally the custard pie as the coup de grâce. (The original ending of Terry Southern–penned *Dr. Strangelove* was to have featured an all-in custard pie fight in the War Room, but the scene did not make the final cut.) The Pythons' *Live at the Hollywood Bowl* stage show also featured a pie-in-the-mush tutorial sketch. It would generally have been the authority figure getting this kind of ridiculous treatment, though here a befuddled straight man works just as well.

On American television in this period, *Rowan & Martin's Laugh-In* (1967–1973) had been recycling these music hall gags with gusto (and go-go dancers)

to great audience and advertiser delight almost two years before *Flying Circus* aired for the first time.

• H •

"harsh and bitchy world of television features" — ("Life and Death Struggles") The music selections underneath the complete documentary sequences include: "The Rite of Spring" by Stravinsky, performed by L'Orchestra de la Suisse Romande; "Coach and Pair" and "Camel Team" by Merrick Farran; "Orb and Sceptre" by Walton, performed by the Royal Liverpool Philharmonic Orchestra; "Theme and Variation" by R. Tilsley; Today's World "Walk Tall" by Keith Papworth; "Gong Sinister" by J. Gunn; "Waterbuck Koala" by Sam Sklair from "Cartoon Capers"; and "Hearts and Flowers" by Czibulka, W. Warren, performed by the London Symphony Orchestra (WAC T12/1,442).

"has not been able to announce since our youngest, Clifford, was born . . ." — ("Neurotic Announcers") Not to put too fine a point on it, but Jack may be suffering a loss of confidence due to his wife's sexual unavailability since childbirth, not an uncommon situation, and one that renders Jack "impotent" and unable to perform before the BBC microphone.

• I •

"I don't understand" — ("Merchant Banker") The Merchant Banker as depicted here (and perhaps especially by the somewhat leftist and mercurial Cleese) is incapable of understanding pity, empathy, even charity—he is the prototypical heartless, money-grubbing City (of London) Gent Conservative. The Merchant Banker is certain that orphans are a viable developing market, that Mr. Ford (Jones) wants a loan and not a gift, and that said gift must be just a clever way of avoiding taxes. They are on completely different wavelengths, communication-wise, a situation not uncommon in the Python oeuvre, and might as well be speaking/hearing at different pitches ("Silly Voices," Ep. 12).

"I know I'm pausing occasionally" — ("Gestures to Indicate Pauses in Televised Talk") Palin does a masterful job of precisely stepping back from actually beginning his presentation with every refinement he attempts to communicate. First "we" are going to talk, then he qualifies that to "I," then from the future tense ("I *am* going to . . .") to the present ("I *am* talking about it . . ."), then to clarify he hasn't begun actually talking about the subject, but he is still talking, and on and on.

The structure here is very much like the convoluted, qualifying, clarifying, and even extirpating narrative structure in Sterne's *Tristram Shandy*, which spends page after page attempting to relate the facts surrounding Tristram's birth, but digressions abound and overwhelm the narrative thread—and the novel and characters know it. It is Volume III before we reach the (somewhat) blessed event. Mr. Orbiter-5 (Palin) never does get to talk of Bols, however.

"I'm not unusual" — ("Mary Recruitment Office") Adapted from the Tom Jones 1965 hit song "It's Not Unusual." Jones has already been referenced in Ep. 24 by the fast-talking Art Critic (Cleese).

"Inniskillin . . . Regiment" — ("Mary Recruitment Office") An Irish regiment that came to contemporary prominence in 1965 when they were trapped in a blockaded Rhodesia after Ian Smith declared independence (*Eyewitness: 1960–69*, "Rhodesia Unilateral Declaration of Independence 1965"). The Anglian Regiment was formed in 1964 from several existing regiments.

"Is the Queen Sane?" — ("Gestures to Indicate Pauses in Televised Talk") This banner hangs behind the presenter. There is a similar headline in the 7 May 1971 *Private Eye* asking "Is the Queen Dead?"

"I stom certainly od. Revy chum so" — ("The Man Who Speaks in Anagrams") Translation: "I most certainly do. Very much so."

". . . Wersh"—"Yes, yes—that is correct. At the moment I'm working on *The Taming of the Shrew*." *Shrew* is Shakespeare's 1593–1594 comedy.

"Nay"—It's not clear why he uses "nay" here, since it's not anagrammatic (except for "any") or even jumbled, though perhaps it is a nod to the Elizabethan English found in the plays being discussed, and not therefore jumbled at all.

". . . Venice"—"*Two Gentlemen of Verona, Twelfth Night, The Merchant of Venice*." All Shakespeare plays, *Verona* was written/produced in 1592–1593, *Twelfth Night* in 1601–1602, and *Merchant* in 1596–1597 (see Evans's *Riverside Shakespeare*).

". . . nestquie"—"*Hamlet*. 'To be or not to be, that is the question.'" *Hamlet* was produced in 1600–1601.

"thrid"—Another perhaps accidental anagram here, as "thrid" is an obsolete version of both "third" and "thread." *Richard III* was written/produced by Shakespeare in 1607.

"shroe"—An obsolete word for "shrew" (*OED*), so this would qualify as an anagram, though perhaps unintentionally. This quote is from Shakespeare's *Richard III* (5.4.7), which has already been quoted in Ep. 25, the "Hospital for Over-Actors" sketch.

• J •

James Bond style opening titles — (PSC; "*The Pantomime Horse Is a Secret Agent* Film") Gilliam would have provided the titles, which look very much like those he created for Ep. 17, "The Bishop." The distinctive Bond titles referenced here were produced by Maurice Binder (1925–1991).

• K •

kicking . . . shins — (PSC; "Pantomime Horses") Perhaps at least partially inspired by the painters Rubens (*A Lion Hunt*, 1616), Gericault (*Race of Riderless Horses*), and perhaps especially Delacroix (*Arabian Horses Fighting in a Stable*, 1860), whose paintings featured horses in violent scenes, and many of which were available in the National Gallery. *The Lion Hunt* had been on display there since it was purchased in 1871. Here, of course, the Pythons have deflated the nobility of the act in favor of silliness.

"King Haakon of Norway" — ("*The Pantomime Horse Is a Secret Agent* Film") King Haakon VII (1872–1957)—formerly Christian Frederik Carl Georg Valdemar Axel—married the youngest daughter of Edward VII, and Haakon became newly independent Norway's first king in 1905.

"Corpse-Haakon Production"—Implying that Douglas-Home is the "Corpse" or lifeless partner in this partnership (though Haakon had been dead and buried for more than a decade by this time), which fits the Pythons' generally anti-Conservative bent.

• L •

"limpet" — ("Life and Death Struggles") *OED*: "A gasteropod mollusc of the genus Patella, having an open tent-shaped shell and found adhering tightly to the rock which it makes its resting-place."

The film footage in this sequence is from the following sources: Sea lions fighting (BBC Bristol 8917); limpets ("Seashells," Educational Foundation for Visual Aids or "Animals of the Rocky Shore" [Rank 5689222]); "wolf" (static shot, thirty-four seconds long), a slide from Windrose Dumont Time; and "honey bears" from Phillip Ware (WAC T12/1,428).

"sprightly opponent"—Neither limpet is actually doing much of anything in these shots, which adds to the incongruity.

loony get up — (PSC; "*The Pantomime Horse Is a Secret Agent* Film") This insert was shot in the Glencoe area, when the Njorl "Iceland" scenes were being recorded for Ep. 27. The Pythons would record enough outdoor material for an entire season (or more) at a single location, including links, inserts, and exterior continuation shots, saving money and travel time.

• M •

"Maudling" — ("The News with Richard Baker [Vision Only]") Referring once again to Sir Reginald Maudling. See entries in Eps. 12, 16, 20–22, 26, and 36 for more on Maudling and his recurring presence in *FC*, as well as the pages of newspapers and satirical organs like *Private Eye*.

"merchant banker" — ("Merchant Banker") One who engages in credit and financing for businesses, as opposed to individuals.

music hall comedian — (PSC; "Bus Conductor Sketch") Probably meant to reference comedians like Arthur Askey (1900–1982) and George Robey (1869–1954), both active during the Pythons' formative years. Stage and screen comedian (and songwriter and ukelele player) George Formby should also be included here. Formby (1904–1961) was a top drawer film star during the war, and will appear in a short clip in Ep. 42.

• N •

nuns — (PSC; "Mary Recruitment Office") A nun reference again, this after the previous episode where Ken Russell's salacious treatment of the world of Cardinal Richelieu and nonconforming priests and nuns in *The Devils* is highlighted (in the "*Ken Russell's Gardening Club*" sketch). In early 1971 producers of the film were advertising heavily in *Private Eye*, taking out half- and full-page ads.

• O •

"off we go again" — ("Pantomime Horse") Another nod to the constructed nature of the performance, this link is much more artificial and visible than if it had been announced as a link. Again, with Cleese involved, the façade is almost cynically broached, and the theatrical corner-cutting becomes more and more blatant.

Orbiter-5 — (PSC; "Gestures to Indicate Pauses in a Televised Talk") The Lunar Orbiter 5 was a NASA-created orbital moon vehicle launched on 1 August 1967. The Orbiter was sent to photograph the moon's surface, assess meteoroid impact data, and measure radiation in preparation for manned lunar missions. Orbiter-5 was the last of the unmanned Lunar Orbiter missions to the moon.

• P •

"pantomime horse" — ("Pantomime Horse") Significant figure in English pantomime tradition, along with various barnyard animals (e.g., geese). Pantomimes are performed regularly at Christmas in the UK, both live and on TV.

pantomime music — (PSC; "Pantomime Horses") The bit of music used here is Reg Wale's music hall riff from the *Looney Tunes* album, a so-called walk on, walk off selection (WAC T12/1,442).

"pantomime Princess Margaret" — ("Life and Death Struggles") This larger-than-life figure will appear again in Ep. 33, and is often played by Cleese.

Margaret (more fully, HRH The Princess Margaret, Countess of Snowdon, 1930–2002) was the younger sister of Elizabeth, and was frequently in the news thanks to her lifestyle and love life. She was even called "that wayward woman" by noted antimonarchists of the day, and her dalliances with younger men, divorced men, other women, drug use, and high society in general kept her a tabloid favorite for many years. One prominent author/critic, Richard Hoggart (b. 1918), described the cultural paucity of the period using Margaret as the plinth of mediocrity:

> Society in the fifties was a sort of feeble continuation of society before the fifties, with little, tentative innovations . . . it was a lukewarm or less than lukewarm bath, artistically, of such things as the plays of N.C. Hunter [*A Day by the Sea*, 1955], and the late, watered works of Noël Coward. It was a period when the great, infashionable, smart drink was mateus rosé, and *Princess Margaret was a leader of society and fashion, and almost passed for an intellectual*. . . . (Audio transcription, *Eyewitness: 1950–59*, "Fifties Society")

Margaret was also prominently featured (as a young woman) on the first BBC news broadcast in 1954 as she visited Lancashire for charitable purposes.

She was most likely included in this sketch, however, thanks to her well-documented appearances in Windsor Castle pantomimes as a child, where she played "Aladdin," for example, during the war. These broadcasts were made available to the besieged British public.

"punch-up" — ("Life and Death Struggles") A fight, a brawl.

• Q •

"Queen Juliana of the Netherlands" — (*"The Pantomime Horse Is a Secret Agent* Film"*) Juliana (1909–2004) became the monarch in 1948, and showed herself as a pacifist, so this rather bloodthirsty action-adventure film might not have been her first choice, were she a film director. By the 1960s, she looked very much like a prototypical Pepperpot with her print dresses, neat hats, and clutch handbag. Juliana retired from the throne in 1980.

• R •

RAF — (PSC; "Blood, Devastation, Death, War and Horror") The Royal Air Force took the upper hand from the German Luftwaffe during WWII in sustained aerial attacks on German bombers, buzz bombs, and fighter planes.

rather tatty revue — (PSC; "Bus Conductor Sketch") The music hall tradition thrived 1850–1960 in the UK, with public houses across the country creating space for the variety performances. London featured the most and largest such houses, but towns like Leeds, Bradford, and the Isle of Man boasted their own purpose-built music hall spaces. A smaller venue like Collins Music Hall in Islington Green, London, may be the "rather tatty" type the script describes.

"Rattigan, Terence" — ("Life and Death Struggles") Mentioned earlier in the notes to Ep. 1, Terence Rattigan (1911–1977) was a playwright and screenwriter, contributing the screenplay for *Goodbye Mr. Chips* in 1938. He was schooled at Harrow (on scholarship), then Trinity College, Oxford. Rattigan was homosexual, and may have given the Pythons their inspiration for the Pepperpot character from his "Aunt Edna" creation.

Rattigan is even earlier mentioned by the Goons in their episode "The Flea," when Bluebottle (played by Peter Sellers), quips: "Well, we've given them enough Terence Rattigan–type dialogue." The dialogue had been particularly bland and silly, of course, up to that point—featuring Bluebottle's somewhat successful attempts to humiliate Eccles.

For more on Rattigan, see notes to Eps. 1 and 32.

"redundancy scheme" — ("Pantomime Horse") The Redundancy Payments Act of 1965 requires certain employers to pay a lump sum to dismissed employees. Called "severance pay" in the United States.

"repeat fees" — ("Life and Death Struggles") Schedule of payments if a TV show is picked up for foreign distribution, or just rerun on domestic TV. The BBC keeps very accurate records of just who appeared in what show for the purposes of calculating and paying repeat fees. Much of this material is kept in the WAC records.

"Rothwell, Talbot, and Mirielle Mathieu" — (*"The Pantomime Horse Is a Secret Agent* Film"*) Rothwell (1916–1981) was a principal writer for the popular TV series *Up Pompeii* (BBC, 1969) and many installments in the *Carry On* motion picture series (1963–1983). Both of these shows were more like the standard situation comedies the Pythons had created *Flying Circus* to react against, so this is probably not an homage to or flattering mention of this writer.

Mathieu (b. 1946) is a French singer who rose to prominence in the early 1960s, and by 1965 her first album was well on its way to the one million sales mark. She appeared on *Toast of the Town* in 1966. She would have been featured prominently on British radio during this period. In June 1972 Mathieu was appearing in the "Gala Evening Franco-Britannique" performances held at the Albert Hall. Cliff Richard (Ep. 18) and Katie Boyle (Ep. 38) also appeared.

"RSM" — ("Mary Recruitment Office") Regimental Sergeant Major. The character in the "self-defence" sketch in Ep. 4 was an RSM (played by Cleese), and the hospital in Ep. 26 is run by RSM types.

• S •

"school fees" — ("The Man Who Makes People Laugh Uncontrollably") Many schools in the UK charge significant tuition for attendance and/or boarding, ranging into the tens of thousands of pounds annually. These fee-paying schools are distinct from the state and county schools, which are supported by public means (taxation). This jeremiad from the City Gent (Jones) is a familiar one in the UK of this period, when many lower- and middle-class families scrimped and saved so that their children could at least try and have the same experience as the children of the elite.

"Scots Guards" — ("Mary Recruitment Office") A regiment in the British army originally formed in 1642 by Charles I.

"Scott, Peter" — ("Life and Death Struggles") Sir Peter Markham Scott (1909–1989) was a naturalist, artist, author, adventurer, and filmmaker. His interests tended toward ornithology, primarily, and he made a number of TV docs on the subject around the world. One of the films the Pythons may have been referring to is titled *To the South Pole with Peter Scott* (BBC and Time-Life Films, 1967), a self-narrated journey from Cape Crozier to McMurdo Base at the South Pole. Scott was the son of Capt. Robert Falcon Scott, who successfully made the Pole trip in 1912.

In keeping with the anagram theme begun earlier, it is interesting to note that Scott is also remembered for later naming the Loch Ness monster so that it could be registered as an endangered species. The scientific name he chose—*Nessiteras rhombopteryx*—means "the wonder of Ness with the diamond shaped fin," but also happens to be a clever anagram of "Monster hoax by Sir Peter S." (See *Word IQ Dictionary* entry for Peter Scott.)

"Sielmann, Heinz" — ("Life and Death Struggles") Writer, director, and noted host of animal documentaries, including *Masters of the Congo Jungle* (1960), *Galapagos: Trauminsel im Pazifik* (1962), *Wonderen van het Afrikaanse woud* (1968), and *Mystery of Animal Behavior* (1969). Sielmann (1917–2006) was born in Germany.

"Slater Nazi" — ("Merchant Banker") Equating bloated capitalists with bloodthirsty fascists is commonplace in more leftist fare, and is employed throughout *FC* whenever Conservatives (City Gents, specifically) are depicted. This man can't even remember his own name—his profession has overtaken his personality and identity.

The "Slater" mentioned here is likely based on the now legendary UK investor Jim Slater (b. 1929), whose Slater Walker Securities (a secondary bank) turned £2000 to £200 million in just eight years (1965–1973), only to see it all crumble by 1974. The "Walker" was Peter Walker (b. 1932–2010), the oft-satirized (in *Private Eye*) Conservative MP and Cabinet member at this time. Walker is credited with creating the PEG, or "price earnings to growth ratio," a formula which looks at projected prices and expected earnings, and is based significantly in speculation. This financial rigamarole fits well with the Merchant Banker's spiel as the skit began.

"some kind of a sign, like this" (*makes a gesture*) — ("Gestures to Indicate Pauses in Televised Talk") The problem here and in Ep. 33 when Captain Biggles (Chapman) attempts to dictate a letter is literality—characters in the Python world (perhaps not unlike Sterne's Uncle Toby) can be so literal that they cannot appreciate double meanings, inflections, etc., leading to the camera cutting away here, and Biggles's secretary to type what he's *not* dictating. The Marriage Registrar (Idle) in Ep. 19 also suffers from the literalness. Again, miscommunication fuels many of the Python scenarios, indicating how significant communication or the lack of communication—between generations, from seats of power to the masses, between the sexes, etc.—loomed in this period.

"split hairs" — ("The Man Who Speaks in Anagrams") Putting a fine point on it, the presenter (Palin) hasn't worried about the guest's "jumble" as opposed to anagram usage thus far. This is clearly a way to get out of the sketch without a proper punchline, as the arrests at the end of the previous episode claimed. More and more sketches will just end—abruptly and trailing off—as the series continues.

"spoonerism" — ("The Man Who Speaks in Anagrams") *OED*: "An accidental transposition of the initial sounds, or other parts, of two or more words." The *OED* credits Oxfordians in the late nineteenth century for promoting its usage. "Ring Kichard" is a spoonerism. Not a surprise that it's one of the troupe's Oxfordians, here Michael Palin, who identifies the spoonerism masking as an anagram.

Stock colour film — (PSC; "Blood, Devastation, Death, War and Horror") All the clips are actually in black and white.

· T ·

"timber ant" — ("Life and Death Struggles") Probably referring to the carpenter ant, which tunnels through wood but doesn't eat the wood.

Torrey Canyon — (PSC; "Blood, Devastation, Death, War and Horror") The *Torrey Canyon* was a bulk oil carrier that ran aground on the Seven Stones Reef between Lands End and the Islands in March 1967 with 120,000 tons of Kuwaiti oil aboard. The Wilson government decided to set the oil ablaze rather than just let it drift into coastal areas. In all, forty-two bombs were dropped on the wreck, and the oil was eventually burned away. The fact that roughly 25 percent of the bombs missed the target was fodder for the newspapers and the opposition party in the following weeks.

This stock is from a Navy newsreel film (WAC T12/1,428).

turning his back on city gent — (PSC; "The Man Who Makes People Laugh Uncontrollably") Since before (but notably including) Pope and Jonson, derision and scorn of the powerful and mighty via laughter has been the stock-in-trade of the poet, playwright, and librettist, and here the Pythons have to do nothing more than objectify their oft-seen City Gent to disarm him as a symbol of power. He cuts a ridiculous figure, of course, in costume and erect, but if it's considered that his presence renders others powerless to act in/on their own control, then the City Gent could conversely be re-read as an incredibly powerful symbolic figure, one well beyond the slings and arrows of satire. The fact that his boss "collapses in helpless mirth" underscores the latter reading, which may actually be a(n unconscious) Python comment on the inevitability (and power) of such figures and sociopolitical constructions in the modern world.

"turn the paper over" — ("Gestures to Indicate Pauses in Televised Talk") These types of "fold-ins" appeared at the back of every issue of *Mad Magazine* since 1964.

"typical . . . documentaries" — ("Life and Death Struggles") An acknowledgment of the artifice, this type of self-conscious moment is not unusual in *FC*, where the nuts and bolts of television are often revealed. Also, "these documentaries" would include the similar docs and nature films being released during this same period from others like Jacques Cousteau (*World without Sun* [1964]) and Walt Disney Studios (*Yellowstone Cubs* [1963]).

• V •

Voice Over (John) **(German accent)** — (PSC; "Life and Death Struggles") Not credited in the printed scripts, but this is voiced by Cleese in a very Dr. Strangelove–type nasal voice, à la Peter Sellers. The German accent is most likely meant to mimic the voice of documentary narrator Heinz Sielmann, discussed above. The narrators with these types of accents used by Sielmann included Dutchman Herman Niels (*Lords of the Forest*, 1959) and German Ernst Zeitter (*Lockende Wildnis*, 1962).

• W •

waiting to answer his phone — (PSC; "Merchant Banker") By this time in the course of *FC*, the acknowledgment of the artifice becomes common, becomes the norm, and it even appears, occasionally, that the actors are a bit bored with the convention of "pretending" to answer the phone, talk to someone offscreen, create the illusion of offscreen space, etc. This is particularly true for Cleese, who embarked on the third season with some reluctance. See McCabe and Morgan (1999). By Ep. 37, a character pays for a purchase with "in-visible money," obviously counting out nothing and handing nothing to the salesman.

"weak ending" — (*The Pantomime Horse Is a Secret Agent* Film") For much of *FC*, the necessity of having an ending at all was eschewed in favor of upsetting the traditional "sketch format comedy show" structure. Most of the episodes just end without much fanfare at all. The lack of ending, then, becomes the structure, and yet another rigid parameter is constructed. Constantly reacting to such restrictions fueled the show, at least through the first two seasons. The ending of Ep. 41 is actually chosen by the characters, after they run through a list of possible endings. See Morgan (1999) for more comments from the Pythons as to the structure of *FC*.

"What's the Welshman doing under the bed?" — ("Bus Conductor Sketch") A well-worn music hall joke revisited by the Goons, as well. The leek is a national emblem of Wales.

"Women's Royal Army Corps" — ("Mary Recruitment Office") Formed in February 1949, the green-uniformed WRAC members occupied primarily administrative and support positions for most of the organization's life.

"work for one of our announcers" — ("Neurotic Announcers") Announcers and interludes (stock shots with music between shows) were common on the BBC, especially during the 1950s when much of the broadcast material was live. These announcers tended to stick to what had just been watched, what was immediately following, and what was to be expected later in the broadcast day (and sometimes what was on over on the other BBC channel). Announcers continued to be used for transitions well into the 1980s, and can still be heard today, though the practice of showing the BBC World symbol and just hearing the announcer didn't take hold until the 1960s. (See Crisell [2002] and Vahimagi for more.)

As technology improved, fewer announcers were of course needed, since an announcer could both announce and run his/her own sound board, work which may be what Jack (Cleese) is lamenting as "a bit thin." (See Crisell [2002].)

Episode 31: "The All-England *Summarize Proust Competition*"

Nude Organist, "And Now" Man and "It's" Man; Titles; (silly Palin v/o); **"1972 All-England Summarize Proust Competition"**; Closing credits; Everest climbed by hairdressers; Ricky Pule's Salon cinema advert (some *animation*); *Film trailer: A Magnificent Festering*; Fire brigade; **Our Eamonn**, back from Dublin; Fire Brigade visits on Friday night; *Party Hints with Veronica Smalls: What to do when an armed Communist uprising occurs*; *Animation: Communists under the bed, Putrid Peter Doll*; Language laboratory: Sandy Wilson's version of *The Devils*; **Travel agent** office; Can't say the letter "C"; The Tourist's rant (Watney's Red Barrel); Theory on brontosauruses by Anne Elk (Miss)

• A •

"A La Recherche du Temps Perdu" — (*"Summarize Proust Competition"*) Literally, *In Search of Lost Time* (c. 1913–1927), the work is a seven-novel epic by Marcel Proust (1871–1922), three of which were published posthumously. Many believe the novel(s) to be the finest example of narrative fiction ever produced. And as has been and will continue to be seen throughout *Flying Circus*, the Pythons themselves expend a great deal of energy and time searching out, dusting off, and examining closely the remembrances of their own collective pasts, from their Pepperpot mothers to Gumby working fathers to cricket and football heroes and the Great Men of English history.

As fanciful as the subject of summarizing Proust might seem, future *Beyond the Fringe* co-creator Alan Bennett, while at Exeter College, Oxford, had written a satirical cabaret that included references to Proust; he had even jotted a poem (lifted from a cabaret lyric) into the Exeter College Junior Common Room "suggestions book," which was saved and eventually bound for the Bodleian Library:

Marcel Proust had a very poor figure,
He hadn't the chest for sexual rigour.
He lay with Albertine tout nu;

Ce n'est seulement le temps qu'il a perdu. (qtd. in Carpenter 2000, 26)

The necessary translations demonstrate the following public schoolboy witticism: "He lay with Albertine *entirely naked; It was not only time that he lost."* (Thanks again to Prof. Daryl Lee.) It is certainly possible that either or both Jones and Palin, while at Oxford just after Bennett, had read the inscriptions or seen/heard about the revue, and filed the idea away for future use.

This is also the book that Praline (Cleese) is ready to fight for with Man (Palin) for a perceived slight in the "Fish Licence" sketch in Ep. 23. In that sketch, the sickly Proust is well enough to have his own hobby—he keeps a haddock.

"All-England" — (*"Summarize Proust Competition"*) There are myriad "All-England" sporting and music competitions, from badminton and billiards to dancing and (horse) show jumping.

animated sketch — (PSC; animated film out of "Everest Climbed by Hairdressers") This amorous photo couple appear to be Greer Garson and Errol Flynn from *That Forsyte Woman* (1949), directed by Compton Bennett and based on the John Galsworthy book (already mentioned in Ep. 21). Flynn and Garson play Soames and Irene Forsyte in the film version.

61

As the Hollywood lovers coo, an image of John Wayne from *Sands of Iwo Jima* (1949) passes behind them—along with a handful of stock battle images—in Gilliam's animated sequence.

"armed communist uprising near your home when you're having a party" — ("*Party Hints* with Veronica Smalls") This sounds very much like an actual account given by the "respectable" Mrs. Dorothy Raynes Simpson, who, along with supper guest Mrs. Kitty Hesselberger, fought off a band of armed Mau Mau terrorists in the front rooms of her home in Kenya, January 1953. As Joanna Bourke writes (and Tim Pigott-Smith narrates), "Englishness" during this period became identified by order and structure, with "the British media represent[ing] the colonial war in Kenya in terms of guarding English domesticity against an alien other." "Domestic order," Bourke continues, "was an increasingly important marker of Englishness." The sedate, sober account of the attack and defense of home as recounted orally by Mrs. Simpson is both chilling and oddly funny; the smaller, seemingly insignificant details (e.g., "sweets," "a nut") color the telling, as if Veronica Smalls (Idle) were narrating:

> Mrs. Hesselberger and I were in the sitting room, and I was having a light supper in the sitting room, and Mrs. Hesselberger had just turned on the wireless at nine o'clock to hear the BBC news. And after she had turned it on and got the signature tune she came over to the table where I was having sweets. She took a nut off the table and cracked it when the houseboy came through rather hurriedly—made us a little bit suspicious—we looked up, and I said, "They're here." There was a number of figures in the room, all strangers. I leapt out of my chair, and luckily, I had my revolver next to me, and I shot at the first boy that was coming towards me, and then I heard Mrs. Hesselberger saying "Be careful." I turned to her, and I saw one of the boys on top of her [here it seems Mrs. Simpson shoots the boy and her own dog, who is intervening] . . . it was all over in a matter of seconds. When Mrs. Hesselberger was free, we dashed out, and there was, so it seemed, another attack was coming towards us, and in the darkness Mrs. Hesselberger fired, and shot another boy. (audio transcription, *Eyewitness 1950–59*, "Kenya")

According to *State of Emergency* accounts regarding the incident, the ladies killed at least three of the machete-wielding invaders, and wounded at least one other, successfully putting down the uprising, at least for the evening. The Mau Mau uprising continued to terrorize settlers and the British reading public alike for many months, and this disquieting news occupied newspapers daily.

"Arthur" — ("*Summarize Proust Competition*") Yet another Python character given the name Arthur, a fallback name used so often in the first and second seasons. In the very popular *Beyond the Fringe* (1961) satirical revue, several of the mentioned (but unseen) characters are named "Arthur," including Arthur Tinty and Arthur Grodes.

• **B** •

"Bagot, Harry" — ("*Summarize Proust Competiton*") Perhaps accidental, but there was an extant Harry Eric Bagot, Seventh Earl Bagot (1894–1973). There is also the possibility that the fact he was living helped the BBC decide that "masturbation" was not an acceptable hobby for Bagot (Chapman), badly inserting the dubbed "strangling animals and golf" after the fact.

There is a precedent for such possible action, of course. When the Cobham family complained that Shakespeare's beloved but ignoble character John Oldcastle (from whom the Cobhams descended) was demeaning to their family name and heritage, Shakespeare made the change to "Falstaff." Interesting, then, that Falstaff the fictional character would be able to enjoy such narrative and even historical control as a created character, where Oldcastle would have certainly been more tied to history and appropriate behavior. See Bergeron and Larsen for more.

"Balleys of Bond Street" — ("*Theory of Brontosauruses by Anne Elk [Miss]*") There is a "Bally" of Bond Street, offering fine shoes since it opened in 1881. The original building there on Bond Street was completely refurbished in 1965, which may account for Bally being prominently mentioned here.

"brogue"—A more country- or sports-type shoe, as opposed to a formal dress shoe.

"Bedser, Alec and Eric" — ("*Summarize Proust Competition*") Alec Bedser (1918–2010) was the Wisden Cricketer of the Year in 1947, and was eventually knighted for his contributions to cricket. Eric Bedser (1918–2006) was Alec's twin brother, and also played for Surrey. Both were right hand batters.

The other panelists include the following:

"Stewart Surridge"—Stuart Surridge (1917–1992) was a Surrey right hand bat, and Wisden Cricketer of the Year in 1953.

"Omar Sharif"—Sharif (b. 1932) is an Egyptian actor who had most notably appeared in the David Lean epic *Dr. Zhivago* (1965) and the later *Funny Girl* (1968). The detailed plot outline offered by the Art Critic (Cleese) in Ep. 28 was at least partially borrowed from *Dr. Zhivago*.

"Laurie Fishlock"—Fishlock (1907–1986) was a Surrey left hand bat, and Wisden Cricketer of the Year in 1947.

"Peter May"—May (1929–1994) was a Surrey right hand bat, and Wisden Cricketer of the Year in 1952. It seems clear that these men would have been the sports heroes for at least some of the Pythons in their youth, perhaps especially Jones, who lived in Claygate, Surrey, for almost fifteen years (McCabe, 45).

"Yehudi Menuhin"—Menuhin (1916–1999) was an American-born violinist who became a British citizen, peer, and knight. His Yehudi Menuhin School was established, perhaps not coincidentally, in Surrey in 1962. Menuhin also has at least a distant connection to the Pythons' generation in that he was one of the first paying members of the Peter Cook satirical club "The Establishment," set up on Greek Street in Soho, London, in 1961 (Carpenter 2000, 131). There's no indication as to whether or not he actually went to the club, or that any of the Pythons actually met/saw him there.

Clearly, Surrey-ite Jones contributed a great deal to this sketch, with a number of semi-autobiographical references. For Idle's version of this favoritism, centered instead on the West Midlands, see the "Travel Agent" sketch, as well as notes below.

"Bingley" — (*"Summarize Proust Competition"*) Bingley is in West Yorkshire County.

"Birmingham" — ("Travel Agent") Industrial city of the English West Midlands, Birmingham is the second-largest city in England. Idle would have known this area and its people very well, having gone to boarding school just west of Birmingham, at the Royal Wolverhampton School, West Midlands. This entire venting is replete with references to West Midlands locations and personalities, betraying Idle's participation in the sketch's creation, as well as the perhaps nostalgic significance of the Pythons' various backgrounds to their comedy and to *Flying Circus* specifically.

"bitching in the tents" — ("Everest Climbed by Hairdressers") Not just a joke, the reports of personal/personnel conflicts in the Himalayas have significant historical support. The 1971 expedition led by Norman Dyhrenfurth and including climbers from more than a dozen countries ran into "oneupsmanship, personality conflicts, and organizational problems" (everestnews.com). The climb was split into at least two groups, and a rescue party was to be dispatched when a storm paralyzed the climbers. One man died as a result of exposure.

"bodega" — ("Travel Agent") Typically, a wine cellar/shop in Spain, where the Tourist (Idle) would have seen and loathed the ubiquitous symbol of Great Britain's fading (now corporate) empire—the Red Barrel. See the entry for "Watney's" below for more. Cultural maven Richard Hoggart makes this same sort of elitist argument as he describes the social wasteland of 1950s England, where a vulgar common man's drink—the Portugese bulk wine mateus rosé —served as mock evidence of high culture (*Eyewitness: 1950–59*, "Fifties Society").

"bog" — ("Travel Agent") A vulgarization of "boghouse," meaning a privy or toilet.

"bolour supplement" — ("Travel Agent") The "colour supplements" were mentioned earlier by Harry "Snapper" Organs (Jones) in Ep. 14. These supplements are colored pages in newspapers, often indicating advertising sections. A typical color supplement from the *Radio Times* advertised holiday trips to places from Paignton to Ulster to Colwyn Bay (Carpenter 2003, 4). Similar color supplements (tipped-in to the magazine) can be found in period *Private Eye* issues, also advertising trips to exotic but affordable continental locales.

"Bolton Choral Society" — (*"Summarize Proust Competition"*) There was a Bolton Catholic Amateur Operatic & Dramatic Society (so named in 1962) that had been functioning in various capacities since 1925. There are also literally hundreds of choral societies up and down the UK, from Bath to Wimbledon, and from Bristol to Wokingham.

"Bounder of Adventure" — ("Travel Agent") In the very popular "Billy Bunter" magazine, comic, and film series there was a character named Herbert Vernon Smith, who was known as the Bounder. The "Billy Bunter" character appeared in hundreds of stories (1908–1940), then comics (1940–), and finally television episodes (1952–1961). These same characters even appeared in a few Christmas stage performances. (See Vahimagi.) Sir Gerald Nabarro also confessed to being a bit of a "bounder" (or a loveable cad) in his military life, politics, and business ("Nabarro," *ODNB*).

"Bournemouth" — (*"Summarize Proust Competition"*) Located on the south coast in Dorset. The Pythons shot most of their location footage in this area for the first season, including dune-area scenes for "Famous Deaths" and "The Funniest Joke in the World" (Ep. 1), and "Undressing in Public" (Ep. 4).

"Boys' Brigade" — ("Our Eamonn") A UK organization founded in October 1883 by William Smith, designed to give boys discipline and self-respect in a structured environment, and was influential to Baden-Powell's later Boy Scout organization. Their motto was "Sure and Steadfast," and their credo: "The advancement of Christ's Kingdom among Boys and the promotion of habits of Reverence, Discipline, Self-Respect, and all that tends towards a true Christian Manliness" (*ODNB*). Mervyn, of course, sees them as useless, since they aren't firefighters.

"Briddock, I.T." — (*"Summarize Proust Competition"*) Dave Briddock was a character played by Simon Cuff (*Z Cars*) on the popular *Doctor in the House* (1969–1970), for which Bill Oddie, Chapman, Cleese, and David Sherlock (Chapman's life partner) contributed material.

"British Shoe Corporation" — (*"Travel Agent"*) Established by Charles Clore (1904–1979), and in the early 1960s expanded into multiple countries with additional manufacturing plants ("Clore," *ODNB*).

"Brixton" — (*"Everest Climbed by Hairdressers"*) There are a number of Brixtons, including one in Greater London, and one in Devon near Plymouth. The Pythons spent a good deal of time shooting in the Plymouth area for previous shows.

"Brylcreem" — (*"Travel Agent"*) Trademarked name of a hair gel patented in 1929 (in Birmingham, UK, incidentally).

"bungalow" — (*"Our Eamonn"*) Perhaps also a nod to the artificial nature of these sets, since there would not have been a second floor in the studio. In Ep. 17, the "Chemist Sketch," the characters discuss the actions involved when a character runs off camera, pretending to either "nip down to the basement" or out of the chemist's shop after a "fishy requisite," revealing the nuts and bolts of the creative geography employed by the television medium.

One-story bungalows were built by the thousands during and after the war, including more than 150,000 pre-fabs between 1944 and 1948, and were much-desired as single-family homes. The housing crunch forced local councils to opt for semi-detached, row-house, and tower block projects, however, all providing more living space and occupying less open space.

• C •

"calamares . . . two veg" — (*"Travel Agent"*) If "meat and two veg" is an idiom for a traditional (in this case, probably unimaginative, too) English meal, then "calamari and two veg" (fried squid and two vegetable side dishes) must be the Majorcan equivalent whipped up for the British tourist crowds.

"Charlie George Football Book" — (*"Our Eamonn"*) Charlie George (b. 1950) played for the Arsenal Football Club from 1969 to 1975, becoming so popular that there were songs written about him, and even a café named after him. Arsenal had won the FA Cup in the 1970–1971 season.

"chiropodists" — (*"Everest Climbed by Hairdressers"*) One who treats corns and bunions. There were

and are all sorts of climbers who make the Everest attempt, including trained mountaineers (Ep. 9), wealthy businessmen, extreme sports types, and just groups of interested outdoor enthusiasts.

Cinema-style advert with still photos — (PSC; "Ricky Pule's Salon") Some of the photos used here are actually from Hillary expeditions, including a rather famous photo of Hillary and Norgay sitting next to each other and enjoying a hot drink, having conquered Everest. Gilliam has removed the base camp clutter from around and behind them, including a tent and containers, likely to make it look as though they're sitting at the summit. The other even more famous photo follows this one, of Norgay standing on the top of Everest, photographed by Mallory.

The photos are listed as coming from the Alfred Gregory Camera Press, and are labeled "Nepal 161A" (T12/1,441). Gregory (1913–2010) accompanied the Hillary expedition to almost 28,000 feet, snapping many notable still photos.

"cornplaster"—Popular treatment for corns. Worrying about corns was less a concern than equipment like shoes, tents, and oxygen gear wearing out or malfunctioning on the subzero slopes.

"Dr. Scholl"—A UK foot doctor, it was Scholl's nephew William Howard Scholl who pioneered fashionable orthopedic shoes, especially the very trendy "Dr. Scholl's clog" (a sandal, of sorts) in the mid-1960s.

"cloth caps . . . cardigans" — (*"Travel Agent"*) The "cloth cap" is known as a "flat cap," and was very popular in both the UK and United States, but was particularly associated with the British Northern working-class man in the twentieth century. There are innumerable photos to document the cap's popularity, with one in particular depicting a smithy in Slaidburn (photo number BU04734A, Bertram Unné, Unnetie Digitisation Project). The smithy and his co-worker and customer all sport the same cap.

A "cardigan" is a sweater that zips or buttons down the front.

"cotton sun frocks"—Similar to the simple, flowered outfits the Pythons dress themselves in as Pepperpots, probably colorful and thin enough for the hot Mediterranean days.

Competition — (*"Summarize Proust Competition"*) There had indeed been celebrated attempts to summarize Proust's masterwork, including a three-word summary by Gérard Genette in *Figures III* (Paris: Seuil, 1972): "Marcel devient écrivain" ("Marcel becomes a writer"). See tempsperdu.com.

"constitutional settlement" — (*"Our Eamonn"*) This is one of only a handful of instances in all of *FC* that the "troubles" (violence perpetrated by Protestant and Catholic combatants) in Northern Ireland are really broached. (The others include: Ep. 32, where a minister is busily engaged in "dealing with the Irish situation," and the other is in Ep. 41, when Reverend Ian Paisley types are lecturing about Irish sovereignty at a department store counter.)

There is a conspicuous absence in *FC* of pointed jabs at Ireland or Northern Ireland, especially as both Scotland and Wales take it on the chin regularly. It may be that since so many deaths were associated with the struggle in Northern Ireland (for the better part of the century), the issue had become politically taboo, especially in the Light Entertainment division. More routinely, the Poet-Reader-cum-Weatherman (Palin, Ep. 17) mentions that a front is arriving from Ireland, the Ian Paisley types talk to themselves in Ep. 41 (the audience seems to miss the allusion), and the *Radio Times* had early described the nascent *Flying Circus* program as a "history of Irish agriculture"—that's the extent of Ireland and the Irish in *FC*.

Even the BBC found significant opposition to a planned "in-depth" program on Northern Ireland in December–January 1971, with various ministers warning (and even threatening) BBC Director-General Lord Hill that such a program could only damage prospects for peace in the region (reported in the *Times*).

The *Northern Ireland Constitutional Proposals* would be published in March 1973 (after this episode was written and broadcast), and were an attempt to define the problem in Northern Ireland relative to the monarchy and the quest for a free Northern Ireland (rejoined with the Republic of Ireland). A poll was held in early March 1973, with electors voting 591,820 to 6,463 in favor of Northern Ireland remaining a part of the United Kingdom.

These constitutional reforms were undertaken in an effort to stop the intimidations, bombings, assassinations, and executions that had become part of everyday life in Northern Ireland since the "troubles" began. In January 1972, for example, an IRA bomb blast in Belfast killed fifty-five people.

Perhaps also built into the structure of the sketch is the fruitlessness of the ongoing talks in Northern Ireland, as Eamonn (Chapman) here tries unsuccessfully and for the third time to explain conditions in Dublin, and as various phone conversations go nowhere (and the futility spreads to other sketches, as well). Eamonn never does get to anything beyond the possibility of a "constitutional settlement" in his interrupted answers, and the sticky subject is both commented on and ultimately avoided.

contrapuntally, in madrigal . . . until they rallentando — (PSC; "*Summarize Proust Competition*") Tomlinson's singers are essentially combining their melodies and

rhythms in counterpoint, though they don't really rallentando (begin to slow down) as much as they are cut off by the fifteen-second gong.

"Cuba Libres" — ("Travel Agent") A lime juice and rum drink, sometimes topped with iced Coca-Cola, probably something the Tourist (Idle) would dislike, as well.

Cut to stock film of people actually climbing Everest — ("Everest Climbed by Hairdressers") This BBC film stock is only accounted for by number: K26544, K26545, and K26546, which may mean that it's all actually K2 footage, and not Everest (WAC T12/1,441).

• **D** •

"dago" — ("Travel Agent") Slang for someone of Spanish, Portuguese, or Italian origin, one of the many such slang terms employed by the Pythons.

"bandy-legged"—Legs that curve inwardly, perhaps indicating dietary deficiencies.

"dead" — ("Our Eamonn") Mervyn (Cleese) doesn't comprehend metaphoric or allusive language, a trait seen later in Mr. Wensleydale (Palin) in the "Cheese Shop" sketch in Ep. 33. This also could be a reference to Cleese's stated preference for wordplay sketches, where characters would generally be expected to use such euphuistic language with ease.

Devils, The — ("Language Laboratory") Film directed by Ken Russell, who had also directed a film version of Sandy Wilson's *The Boy Friend*, a version Wilson reportedly detested. *The Devils* (1971) depicts the rise to power of Cardinal Richelieu, and the priest who stands in his way, the latter portrayed by Oliver Reed. Parts of the film—especially its attempts at historically accurate production design—were obvious inspirations for the later *Monty Python and the Holy Grail* (1975).

Russell has already been mentioned in Ep. 29 ("Ken Russell's *Gardening Club*") and will be mentioned again in Ep. 33, "Sam Peckinpah's *Salad Days*." See entries to those episodes for more on Russell, *The Devils*, and his attraction for the Pythons.

"doctor encouraged me" — ("Summarizing Proust Competition") Summarizing Proust, then, acts like a trip to the mineral water spa or a drier climate, and must also be equated with "strangling animals, golf, and masturbating," as those are also Bagot's (Chapman) hobbies.

"Do you want to go upstairs?" — ("Travel Agent") As discussed back in Eps. 13 and 14, this Mae Westian "Come on up and see me sometime" line was known in London as a Soho come-on used by working girls who lived/worked above the shops. In Ep. 13 the cinema adverts promise "models" on the second floor, and in Ep. 14 the customer (Idle) misreads posted cards hoping for a sexual liaison.

ducks-on-wall house — (PSC; "Our Eamonn") A metaphor meaning "cheaply decorated," the phrase will be found in a Kinks' song, "Ducks on the Wall," just three years later. The phrase is meant to be a shorthand from the Pythons for the set designers and property masters, who will then scour the BBC prop collections for the proper decor.

In the 17 July 1970 issue of *Private Eye*, the phrase is invoked. After PM Wilson (called "Wislon" by *PE*) lost to Heath, it was rumored that Mrs. Wilson was slow to move out of 10 Downing Street:

> For over a fortnight after the Grocer's [Heath] election triumph she kept coming back for bits and pieces left behind. . . . The situation so exasperated Anthony Royle, one of Baillie Vass's [Alec Douglas-Home] stooges at the Foreign Office that he was heard to remark: "If that woman isn't out of here by tomorrow, I personally will come and shoot the f***ing ducks off the wall." (14 Aug. 1970: 5)

• E •

"Enterovioform" — ("Travel Agent") An anti-diarrheal medication now banned in the United States due to its connection to nerve damage in many patients.

Episode 31 — Recorded 24 April 1972, and broadcast 16 November 1972. This episode was recorded ninth and broadcast fifth.

The music gathered for this episode included the following, according to WAC records: (in-studio) "Stage Struck" by Jack Parnell; "World Trip for Big Orchestra No. 1, Pizzicata Milanese" by H. Kressling; New Concert Orchestra playing "Pistons" section from *Crankcraft* suite by Trevor Duncan; music dubbed to film: London Philharmonic Orchestra playing "Sinfonia Antartica" by Vaughn Williams; "Theme from Glorious West"; London Studio Group's "Inner Reflections Gentle Touch" by Reg Wale; International Studio Orchestra playing "Military Preparation" by Hugo de Groot; "Culver City Title" by Jack Shaindlin; and "Dramenasuspence No. 5" by R. Sharples (WAC T12/1,441).

This does not mean that each one of these pieces was eventually used in the particular episode. Occasionally, two episodes' worth of music cues and even actors (extras) are combined in a single episode file; also, at times the music cue is asked for (by the Pythons in the script) but is either not found or is found to be prohibitively expensive, and a similar, generic piece of music replaces it. This last reason is why there is a surfeit of British light music in these shows (from composers Reg Tilsley, Trevor Duncan, Keith Papworth, Reg Wale, et al.)—the music was available and affordable for quick acquisition, mostly from LPs already in the BBC collection.

• F •

"fat German businessmen pretending they're acrobats" — ("Travel Agent") English travel writer Waugh mentions the Germans encountered on his trip, seeing a sister tourist ship of German registry docked at Naples:

> Her passengers were all middle-aged Germans, unbelievable ugly but dressed with courage and enterprise. One man wore a morning coat, white trousers, and a beret. Everyone in the *Stella* felt great contempt for this vulgar ship. (*Waugh Abroad: Collected Travel Writing*, 45)

fire engine — (PSC; "Fire Brigade") Rather than bring in equipment for the set or shoot in a firehouse somewhere on location, they employ an inexpensive rear screen projection of a firehouse interior, and add appropriate costumes.

fire engines skidding out of the fire station — (PSC; "Our Eamonn") These fire engine location scenes were shot in Jersey with the Jersey Fire Brigade in March 1972 (WAC T12/1,428). Much of the "Dennis Moore" footage (Ep. 37) was shot on the island, as well.

"five principles" — ("Language Laboratory") There were "five principles" (plus one later) outlined by the British government in 1965, designed to lead Rhodesia to majority rule, and are as follows:

1. Unimpeded progress to majority rule must be maintained and guaranteed.
2. There must be guarantees against retrogressive amendment to the constitution.
3. There must an immediate improvement in the political status of the black population.
4. There must progress towards ending racial discrimination.
5. The constitutional proposals must be acceptable to the people of Rhodesia as a whole.
6. There must be no oppression of the majority by the minority or of the minority by the majority.

The fifth principle seemed to be a major sticking point, since Smith and his ilk could reasonably claim that they were unhappy with the prospect of majority rule, and they were part of "the people of Rhodesia as a whole." The sixth principle was added in 1966. Ian Smith (Ep. 45) and the minority white government in Rhodesia declared unilateral independence in 1965, leading to international sanctions. See more at "Smith," who will also be mentioned by Mr. Smoke-Too-Much (Idle) later, as well as in Ep. 45. There, Mrs. S's son (Cleese) is on his way to the Commons to deliver an address on Rhodesia when Mrs. Nigger-Baiter (Palin) explodes.

Fourth Booth — (PSC; "Language Laboratory") Not credited in the scripts, this actor is Gilliam. The Fifth Booth actor is also left uncredited—he is probably a Fred Tomlinson Singer. Others in the booths include Fred Tomlinson and his various singers.

"Franco" — ("Travel Agent") Generalissimo Francisco Franco (1892–1975) and his fascist government ruled Spain from 1939 to his death in 1975. Franco assumed power after the Spanish Civil War, after having served in military positions on the Balearic Islands between 1931 and 1933.

"from this cinema" — (animated link out of "Everest Climbed by Hairdressers") There was significant local advertising in both UK and U.S. movie theaters during this period, with adverts shot on film and run prior to the feature film. The ads were directed at both local villagers and urbanites, and were primarily from local merchants. One such title card, from an American drive-in theater c. 1960, asked viewers to "patronize the following leading merchants for quality merchandise and expert service," then offered a series of ads for local stores and services. In the UK, local coffee shops and restaurants often advertised in these theaters. After a significant hiatus, this kind of local advertising in movie theaters is returning.

• G •

"Glasgow . . . Choir" — ("Everest Climbed by Hairdressers") The Glasgow Orpheus Choir was active for a half century under the direction of Sir Hugh Robertson. The name chosen by the Pythons may have been an amalgamation of the Glasgow choir combined with the Grimsby and Cleethorpes Orpheus Male Voice Choir, begun in 1949.

Separate groups of Danes, French, Englishmen, Americans, Norwegians, Chinese, Russians, etc., made various unsuccessful assaults on the world's tallest mountain from the 1920s through the early 1960s. Some of these groups had permission, some did not; some had state-of-the-art equipment for the period,

others came down nearly dead, if they came down at all. Legitimate sponsoring groups for these expeditions included the Alpine Club, the Royal Geographic Society, the Swiss Foundation for Alpine Research, the National Geographic Society, etc.

"greengrocer" — ("Travel Agent") Simply, one who deals in fruit and vegetables. In other words—a common, working man. The satirical magazine *Private Eye* had been calling Conservative leader Edward Heath "Grocer Heath" or just "The Grocer" since 1962. (Heath represented Bexley, southeast of London, not Luton.)

• H •

"Hillary, Sir Edmond" — ("Everest Climbed by Hairdressers") Hillary (1919–2008) is mentioned in passing in Ep. 28, the "Emigration from Surbiton to Hounslow" sketch.

"Sherpa Tensing"—Tenzing Norgay (1914–1986) was a Nepalese Sherpa who led Hillary on the first successful climb of Everest in 1953, and who had made a number of reconnoitering climbs in the decades prior to reaching the summit.

"Hoddesdon" — (*Summarize Proust Competition*") Located in Hertfordshire, just north of Greater London near Hertford.

• I •

"I can't get the fire brigade Mervyn" — ("Fire Brigade") Not just an incongruity, relations between No. 10 Downing Street and labor had become so strained that even fire brigade unions had gone on strike during Heath's Tory administration, along with other critical care–type professions, many striking for the first time in history.

"Industrial Relations Bill" — ("Our Eamonn") There are two references that inform this mention. The first is the Industrial Relations Act of 1946 that set labor and wage policy for, specifically, Northern Ireland's industry. The act was revisited and revised over the years. Secondly, various industrial relations bills considered during this period had primarily pitted the sitting governments (Wilson, then Heath) against the TUC (Vic Feather, Clive Jenkins, et al.), the political significance of which is represented by well over 200 surviving political cartoons (see the British Cartoon Archive). Most recently, the Conservative government's Industrial Relations Bill of December 1970 had created a firestorm of protest from trade union activists, leading to strike actions and labor unrest across the nation. Heath addressed the significance of the industrial relations changes in a 6 December 1970 speech:

> Within six months of coming into office, we have introduced the most important and the most far-reaching part of our legislative program, the Industrial Relations Bill. And already, as we expected, it has raised a storm of ill-judged protest. But I want to promise you this: that your government is not going to bow before this storm. (*pause for applause and "Here, here!" calls from the assembled audience*) We will persevere and we will come through it. We shall win the arguments, and we shall win the votes, and the bill will become law. This is the storm before the calm. (Audio transcription, *Eyewitness: 1970–79*, "Industrial Relations Bill 1971")

This was immediately followed by the passing into law of the Industrial Relations Act (1971), which greatly curtailed the powers of the trade unions.

"Instamatic . . . *Daily Express*" — ("Travel Agent") Kodak's first Instamatic brand-name camera was sold in 1963, and the ensuing versions sold millions through the late 1980s. It would have been a typical, affordable tourist's camera of this period.

Dr. Scholl's "exercise sandals" sold in the millions as well in 1968, the success of which may be the reason the Tourist mentions them here; this also accords with the mention of the sandals being fit for chiropodists climbing Everest earlier in the episode.

The *Daily Express* was a Conservative paper started by the future Lord Beaverbrook, and by the 1930s had become the nation's highest-circulating newspaper. No surprise here that the Tourist's targets would be clutching this paper, an icon of Englishness in the remnants of the shrinking postcolonial Empire.

interior of hairdresser's salon — ("Everest Climbed by Hairdressers") This beauty shop is located on Moore Street in Jersey, and was used with permission from K. Moser (of Charles of Switzerland). The salon location was used 28 March 1972.

• J •

"Jenkins, Clive" — ("Language Laboratory") Welshman Jenkins (1926–1999) was a white-collar union activist who spoke for and led the Association of Scientific, Technical and Managerial Staffs to huge membership numbers and industry prominence. He was a darling of the Labour Party, and represented the new left of big labor for many years. Jenkins is depicted dozens of times (usually antagonizing the Tory government somehow) during this period in political cartoons. See the British Cartoon Archive.

"Jensen" — ("Language Laboratory") Cars manufactured in West Bromwich, West Midlands, near Birmingham.

Jersey — (PSC; "Everest Climbed by Hairdressers") One of the Channel Islands off the coast of France, and perhaps 100 miles south of Weymouth, the States of Jersey is much closer to France (only fourteen miles offshore) than to the UK. The entire cast and crew set up shop here for location shooting 19–29 March 1972. Most of the exterior footage for the latterly episodes of the third season is recorded on the island.

• K •

"Keble Bollege Oxford" — ("Travel Agent") Keble *College* Oxford was founded in 1870. The two Oxfordians in the troupe attended Brasenose (Palin), and St. Edmund's (Jones) colleges. Python mate and author Humphrey Carpenter (1946–2005) graduated from Keble.

"K2 . . . Vidals" — ("Everest Climbed by Hairdressers") K2 (the second peak surveyed in the Karakorum range) is the second-highest peak in the world at 28,250 feet, and is found on the China-Pakistan border. It was first climbed successfully in 1954. Annapurna is actually a massif of the Himalayas, with two major peaks, Annapurna I and Annapurna II. Annapurna I was first climbed in 1950 by a Frenchman named Maurice, coincidentally.

"Vidal" would be Vidal Sassoon, the very influential hair stylist of the 1960s and beyond. See the entry for "Teasy-Weasy" for more. Vidal's head office during this period was in New Bond Street in London.

"Kettering and Boventry" — ("Travel Agent") Kettering and *Coventry* are within a few miles of each other, and both east of the larger city of Birmingham, and both within Idle's sphere of influence as he grew up—the West Midlands being the locus for much of this rant.

• L •

lady with enormous knockers — (PSC; "*Summarize Proust Competition*") This is Julie Desmond (*Casanova*), who was one of several actors to sign the "use of skin" clause demanded by the BBC for permission to exhibit "more" of themselves on camera (WAC T12/1,445). The others signing such contracts during the third season included Sally Anne, Reuben Martin, and Karen Burch.

"la maladie . . . chose" — (*"Summarize Proust Competition"*) The translation for this phrase reveals the typical jabberwock the Pythons often offer as spoken French: "The imaginary invalid of recondition and of all surveillance is soon one and the same." Providing this translation, Professor Daryl Lee (Brigham Young University French & Italian Dept.) also points out that the phrase "malade imaginaire" is most likely drawn from Molière's play of the same name, and perhaps reminds us of the frail physical condition of Proust.

"Leicester" — (*"Summarize Proust Competition"*) Chapman's hometown, Leicester is in Leicestershire, and is north and east of Birmingham, and well north of London. It was the Bishop of Leicester who was discovered, in Ep. 29, on the landing in the "Salvation Fuzz" sketch. Leicester (the city, the bishop, and the diocese) is mentioned in eleven separate episodes.

"local Roman ruins" — (*"Travel Agent"*) There are a number of surviving Roman sites on these islands, including burial sites, an amphitheater, a bridge, and the sites around ancient Pollentia. Tour companies made regular pilgrimages to these sites, ushering tourists from ruin to ruin as quickly as possible.

loony leans into the camera — (PSC; "Everest Climbed by Hairdressers") The printed scripts give no indication as to who this might be (though Gilliam often takes these kinds of roles), but WAC records indicate that Frank Lester took the part this time (WAC T12/1,441). The audience response (mostly silence) indicates that there's an uncertainty as to how to respond to the odd interjection, perhaps partly because he is interacting with a projected image, and the studio audience misses the "effect" witnessed by the viewing audience at home.

"Luton" — (*"Summarize Proust Competition"*) Approximately thirty-two miles from London, Luton is home to an international airport, and the site where Dinsdale Piranha set off a nuclear weapon in Ep. 14. Luton is mentioned again below, by the Tourist (Idle), as he rambles on about boorish West Midlands tourists on the continent, where it is cited as the example of a typical, middle-class north-of-London city producing benign, self-absorbed Englishness in its citizenry.

"Luton airport" — (*"Travel Agent"*) Opened in 1938, by 1969 Luton was handling a full one-fifth of all "package tour" flights to the continent, was the "most profitable" airport in the UK by 1972, and would have been the place the Tourist or even Idle himself (and family) might have embarked on such a vacation. (See London-luton.co.uk.) The shorter runways at the Birmingham International Airport (closer to home for the "adenoidal typist" and others) did not allow for larger planes—its smaller planes servicing Scotland, Ireland, etc., instead—meaning Luton became the international (and certainly Mediterranean) hub in the 1950s and 1960s for the entire West Midlands.

• **M** •

"Majorcan" — (*"Travel Agent"*) Of or from Majorca. The larger of the Balearic Islands chain (Majorca is also spelled "Mallorca"), Menorca, Ibiza, and Formentara are also major islands in the chain. In Ep. 33, Biggles (Chapman) will be reminded that he recently took a Spanish holiday (like so many of his fellow countrymen) in Ibiza, though he'll counter that such a visit doesn't count as a trip to Spain. It seems that the more familiar the destination becomes, and the more English-tourist-friendly, the less it becomes an exotic destination—it is essentially colonized and co-opted, and can be dismissed. This, of course, is much the reason the Tourist (Idle) seems so worked up—he travels to a foreign land and only to encounter his unliked neighbors in every queue, his own culture pasted into Mediterranean streets.

"Malaga" — (*"Travel Agent"*) Coastal city of Andalucia, Spain, and obviously the destination point of the flights carrying package-tour tourists originating at Luton.

"Maybe It's Because I'm a Londoner" — (*"Travel Agent"*) Written by Hubert Gregg late in the war (1944–1945), during the last months of the V-rocket blitz:

> Maybe it's because I'm a Londoner, that I love London so.
> Maybe it's because I'm a Londoner, that I think of her wherever I go.
> I get a funny feeling inside of me, just walking up and down.
> Maybe it's because I'm a Londoner, that I love London Town.

The jolly British POWs in Ep. 18 begin to sing this refrain as the "Escape (From Film)" begins. See the entry in Ep. 18 for more on the traditional song that wouldn't become a hit until after the war.

"Memorial Baths, Swansea" — (PSC; *"Summarize Proust Competition"*) Swansea is in Wales on Swansea Bay. This is probably modeled after the celebrated War Memorial Swimming Baths in Windsor, opened by the Queen in 1963. (*Private Eye* had earlier reported a Miss Neasden contest originating from the "Stafford Cripps Memorial Baths, Neasden" [4 Dec. 1970, 13].)

This is a curious moment. Generally, the printed scripts' *mise-en-scène* sections do not try and participate in the obfuscation—there can be quips and asides to the other Pythons, but when a setting is announced, it's usually fairly accurate. Example: just a bit later in the episode the description tells us that the setting is a garden in Jersey, which is exactly where the Pythons shot the scene. In the case of the "Summarize Proust" sketch, however, the description tells the reader the setting is Memorial Baths, Swansea, while the spangly Mee (Jones) announces they're in the Arthur Ludlow Memorial Baths in Newport. There is also no indication in the WAC records that the Pythons did any shooting—location, studio, or otherwise—anywhere but the following areas: Devon, Norfolk, Greater London, Scotland, and Jersey. (In actuality, they likely shot this in Television Centre, as it's recorded on tape. With the exception of the occasional bumps to Golders Green and Ealing TFS, the Pythons didn't shoot on tape outside of TC.)

"Mervyn" — ("Our Eamonn") Perhaps drawn from Terence *Mervyn* Rattigan, and just continuing their slighting references to the well-known playwright begun in Ep. 30—Mervyn here is depicted as fairly dim.

"Milo" — ("Everest Climbed by Hairdressers") A chocolate drink from Nestlé (introduced in 1933), and often served warm for breakfast.

"Mt. Everest. Forbidding. Aloof. Terrifying." — ("Everest Climbed by Hairdressers") This is yet another Python skewering of an English sacred cow, in this case the sixty-year quest by the British government to reach the world's highest mountain before any other nation. Gordon Stewart discusses the significance to "Empire" that Everest represented between 1890 and 1953, and the serendipitous fact that Hillary's ascension coincided neatly with Elizabeth's accession propped up—at least in newspapers and the public imagination—Britain's continuing presence as a superpower and a real player in world politics. Stewart notes that Everest was a watershed moment:

> In Britain the Everest triumph was viewed as a symbolic event which revealed significant things about contemporary British culture, about the values which had been conventionally associated with Britain's rise to world power in the nineteenth and early twentieth centuries, and about the British identity in the modern world. (170)

As with earlier ridiculing references to Elizabeth I, Drake, Shakespeare, Nelson, and others, the Pythons undercut the Everest expedition by belittling and deriding it, toppling Empire-building (or Empire-shoring-up) at a single stroke.

The Goons had also rendered silly the Everest adventure, with Seagoon (Secombe) certain that if he manages to eat the highest peak in the world Hollywood will come calling, and he'll be rich and famous ("The Mountain Eaters," 1 Dec. 1958). The Goons had also performed an episode entitled "The Ascent of Mount Everest" on 28 April 1953, and this was reworked as *Telegoons* episode in 1963, as well.

Music starts, continuity-type music — (PSC; "*Summarize Proust Competition*") This brief snippet of music is from World Trip for Big Orchestra No. 1, "Pizzicata Milanese" by H. Kressling (WAC T12/1,441).

· N ·

"never thought about that" — ("Travel Agent") There is a significant audience laugh at this point, indicating that something's been edited out. In the audio version of this sketch, and in the original script, the Tourist (Idle) finishes by saying, "What a silly bunt." "Bunt," of course, stands in for "cunt" here (continuing the initial "b" and "c" switching trope), and when Duncan Wood (then Head of Comedy at BBC) screened the first nine episodes in September 1972, he specifically demanded that the line be removed. (The line has also been elided from the printed scripts.) See cover of *Private Eye* (19 Apr. 1963) for an earlier satirical reference to the term.

Interesting that the clumsy removal of the word "masturbating" (also demanded by Wood in his September 1972 memo) at the beginning of this episode has been cited many times since as an example of the BBC's censorship practices, but the excision of this second, veiled crudity often goes unmentioned.

"new theory about the brontosaurus" — ("Theory on Brontosauruses by Anne Elk [Miss]") Beginning in about 1964, the scientific community and then the public imagination were caught up in this excitement as new discoveries changed the way dinosaurs were perceived. The discovery and identification of deinonychus in 1964 (by John Ostrom) meant that the pantheon of enormous, lumbering, cold-blooded dinosaurs had to make room for the more bird-like, warmer-blooded hunters like the raptors. (See one of Ostrom's many articles on the subject—"*Archaeopteryx*: Notice of a 'New' Specimen"—in *Science* 170.3957 [30 Oct. 1970]: 537–38.)

"North Col" — ("Everest Climbed by Hairdressers") Discovered and climbed by George Mallory (1896–1924) and his team in September 1921, and became the key to making the northern ascent. Mallory would die on the slopes of Everest, his body not discovered until 1999.

• O •

"one dozen communist revolutions" — (PSC; *"Animation: Communists under the Bed, Putrid Peter Doll"*) Nikita Khrushchev (1894–1971) appears first, then the "Communists under the bed" include: Joseph Stalin (1878–1953), then Leonid Brezhnev (1906–1982), who was the Soviet leader in 1972. The partially hidden man next to Brezhnev is likely supposed to be Leon Trotsky (1879–1940), but this isn't certain. Trotsky will figure significantly into Ep. 34. Khrushchev is next, followed by a hidden, mustachioed man who might be Prince Georgy Lvov (1861–1925), the first post-Imperial Russian Prime Minister. Next is Alexei Kosygin (1904–1980), the First Deputy Premier of the Soviet Union in 1972, and V.I. Lenin (1870–1924). Lenin will also be mentioned—by Gulliver (Jones) when he thinks he's Trotsky—in Ep. 34. Khrushchev had died just about seven months prior to the recording of this episode, and had been removed from power well earlier, in October 1964. It's no surprise that leaders of the Soviet Union, the other great superpower during this period, appear often in these episodes, given their high profile in British newspapers and on the international stage.

Given the long break between seasons and even episodes—almost fourteen months between the recording of Ep. 26 and the recording of Ep. 29, the first episode recorded for the third season—it's not unlikely that Gilliam completed this animation before Khrushchev died, or not long after. In 1971 the Pythons used their break to, among personal projects, complete the two German *Fliegender Zirkus* episodes for Bavarian television.

As the animation continues, the following scene involves the selling of Communist revolutions, with the background being a conglomerate (assembled by Gilliam) of 19th-century London high street buildings (note the horse-drawn carriages), and what appears to be the Salisbury Cathedral in the background. The following image (where the chortling Lyndon B. Johnson is seen) is set in front of portions of the Kremlin. Former American president Johnson (1908–1973) had decided to not run for re-election in 1968, and in 1972 was in ill-health but still in the news, having recently endorsed the presidential aspirations of George McGovern. (Johnson would die in early 1973.)

The wind-up "Barry Bigot" doll seen here features the head of Union General W.F. Barry (the image borrowed from *DWF*, 382), who appeared earlier as a laughing figure in "The Spot" animation sequence, Ep. 19.

"our Eamonn" — ("Our Eamonn") Probably borrowed from the popular *The Eamonn Andrews Show* (1964–1969) on BBC-TV, starring Eamonn Andrews. Andrews (1922–1987) became known for not only presenting shows such as *What's My Line?* (1951–1963), *This Is Your Life* (1955–1987), and *Crackerjack* (children's show; 1955–1964), but also for his off-the-cuff non sequitur linkings that made no sense, and which Python would satirize over and over again in *FC*. Andrews has already been referenced in Ep. 26.

"Dublin"—Eamonn Andrews was born in Synge Street in Dublin, Ireland, and became the first head of the state-run RTE Authority in 1961, which governed television in Ireland.

• P •

"package tours" — ("Travel Agent") English travel writer and novelist Evelyn Waugh (Eps. 2 and 10) produced the book *Labels* in 1930, an account of his honeymoon travels but presented as the experiences of a lone Englishman exploring the Mediterranean. He explains the "tourist," or the Englishman trapped in the "package tour" nightmare:

> Every Englishman abroad, until it is proved to the contrary, likes to consider himself a traveler and not a tourist. As I watched my luggage being lifted on to the *Stella* I knew that it was no use keeping up the pretence any longer. My fellow passengers and I were tourists, without any compromise or extenuation; but we were tourists—and this brings us back to our original argument—of a new kind.
>
> The word "tourist" seems naturally to suggest haste and compulsion. One thinks of those pitiable droves of Middle West school teachers whom one encounters suddenly at street corners and in public buildings, baffled, breathless, their heads singing with unfamiliar names, their bodies strained and bruised from scrambling in and out of motor charabancs, up and down staircases, and from trailing disconsolately through miles of gallery and museum at the heels of a facetious and contemptuous guide. How their eyes haunt us long after they have passed on to the next phase of their itinerary—haggard and uncomprehending eyes, mildly resentful, like those of animals in pain, eloquent of that world-weariness we all feel at the dead weight of European culture. Must they go on to the very end? Are there still more cathedrals, more beauty spots, more sites of historical events, more works of art? Is there no remission in this pitiless rite? Must reverence still be done to the past? (*Waugh Abroad: Collected Travel Writing*, 37–38)

panning shot across mountains in CinemaScope format — (PSC; *"Party Hints* with Veronica Smalls") CinemaScope is a widescreen process utilizing an anamorphic lens to project 35mm film at a 2.66:1 aspect ratio. This effect was used primarily as a means to combat the rise in television's influence on American viewers, ideally bringing audiences back into movie theaters for spectacular visual effects not available on TV. Other widescreen processes used in Westerns from other studios included Todd-AO (*The Alamo*), Super Panavision 70 (*Cheyenne Autumn*), and VistaVision (*The Searchers*).

This particular title sequence is actually inspired, however, by the *Cinerama* uber-Western-film *How the West Was Won* (1963), directed by the troika of Henry Hathaway, John Ford, and George Marshall, and starring everyone from Henry Fonda and Karl Malden to Jimmy Stewart, John Wayne, Debbie Reynolds, and Spencer Tracy—twenty-four name stars in all. The Cinerama widescreen technology is fundamentally different from those mentioned above. The process involves three separate filmed images connected, side to side, for an unprecedented and not a little disconcerting widescreen effect—the "forced" perspective draws attention to itself—especially in a panning move, or if a character moves into the foreground or background of the shot.

The music underneath is the "Theme from Glorious West," and the film stock is borrowed from EMI, and called *Cowboy Western* (WAC T12/1,441).

"permanent strike" — ("Travel Agent") As part of the student- and worker-led strikes sweeping across France, air traffic controllers at Orly joined other trade unions and originally went out on strike in May 1968. Afterward and to this day, strikes have been used whenever working conditions demanded it, often shutting down transportation systems and entire cities across France, and having a ripple effect across Europe. (As perhaps a nudge to the Pythons in writing this sketch, TUC took its coal miners out on strike in January 1972, their first such walkout in half a century. By mid-February, lights were being turned off across the country to save power.)

photo of Everest — (PSC; "Everest Climbed by Hairdressers") The stock photo is from the Alfred Gregory Camera Press, "Nepal 161A" (WAC T12/1,441). The superimposed dots graphic motif is borrowed directly from the BBC's celebrated coverage of an Old Man of Hoy climb in 1967, and would have been quite familiar to this studio audience.

"Powell, Enoch" — ("Travel Agent") Powell entered Parliament in 1950 as a Conservative from Wolverhampton (Idle's school home), and would champion ultra-conservative and rigidly nationalistic policies throughout his stormy career. Powell (1912–1998) was born and raised in Birmingham, taught university in Sydney, and studied Urdu in his early quest to become the Viceroy of India (*ODNB*).

Both Powell and Ian Smith are mentioned in this sketch as exemplars of what the Pythons must have seen as Britain's last attempts at colonial control in a rapidly changing world. Both are depicted as ideologues or "racialists" (see Ep. 5, "Vox Pops") who want to transplant or resuscitate the British way of life and authority into/onto Third World countries.

"pretty bad there" — ("Our Eamonn") This episode was recorded in April 1972, and followed close on the heels of the infamous "Bloody Sunday" (30 January 1972), where twenty-seven civil rights demonstrators were shot by British soldiers in Derry.

The fact that Eamonn (Chapman) is completely decked out as an African warrior is perhaps a reference to the wildness, the other-ness with which Northern Ireland was perceived by many Englishmen during this period. Admittedly, if he *were* dressed as an identifiable Irishman, the BBC and Television Centre may have become a target for IRA reprisals, and/or the sketch would never make it to air.

"Proust" — ("*Summarize Proust Competition*") Marcel Proust (1871–1922) was a sickly youth who spent a great deal of time recuperating and writing. See the note for "*A La Recherche . . .*" above for more.

"Proust's novel . . . intemporality" — ("*Summarize Proust Competition*") The quick summary by Harry Bagot (Chapman) is quite accurate, the Pythons betraying their appreciation of this significant Modernist work.

"Pules" — ("Everest Climbed by Hairdressers") "Pule" actually means to whimper or whine, which works well with the poncing nature of the characters here. The highest permanent structure in this area (below Everest base camps) is most likely the Rongbuk Monastery, at about 20,900 feet above sea level.

· R ·

"rabbitting" — ("Travel Agent") Shortened colloquialism meaning to talk on and on incessantly, and deriving from the rhyming slang "rabbit-and-pork," meaning "having a conversation."

"Rhyl" — ("Travel Agent") Located on the north coast of Wales, Rhyl is a beach town just a few miles up the coast from Colwyn Bay, where Jones was born.

· S ·

"Saxones" — ("Our Eamonn") There were at least nineteen Saxone Shoes outlets in the Greater London area in the late 1960s and early 1970s. One of these stores—located at 399 Strand in Romano House—can be seen in the 1969 James Mason-narrated "documentary" *The London Nobody Knows*.

"shooting anyone under nineteen" — ("Travel Agent") Spanish dictator Franco's policies were quite oppressive, as he outlawed even political parties and raised the Catholic Church to the status of a state religion, complicit with and even perpetuating his fascistic policies. There were approved Francoist youth movement organizations, including the Phalange. All other groups were outlawed, though there seemed to have been a number of such groups, including active but hidden cadres of more politicized Boy Scouts.

Showbiz music, applause . . . — (PSC; "*Summarize Proust Competition*") This music is Jack Parnell's "Stage Struck" (WAC T12/1,441).

"sodding" — ("Our Eamonn") A vague epithet, here almost equivalent to "damn." The term will be used again with more of its sexual connotation in place in Ep. 45. Earlier, in Ep. 17, Cleese's "sod" was replaced prior to taping with a voiced raspberry; standards have changed, clearly, with the increased popularity of the show.

"soldering a crystal set" — ("Fire Brigade") A radio (often homemade) that employs a crystal detector. Crystal radios were very popular hobby store items during the Pythons' younger years.

"South Col" — ("Everest Climbed by Hairdressers") "South Col" was the route used by Hillary and Norgay in 1953. It is the site of the highest camp before making the summit—Camp IV, at about 26,000 feet.

"Lhotse Face"—A wall of glacial blue ice that must be traversed when using the southeast approach.

"North Ridge"—They'd be way off course here. After Lhotse Face, the stops and/or landmarks traditionally are Yellow Band, Geneva Spur, South Col, Southeast Ridge, South Summit, Cornice Traverse, Hillary Step, and finally the Summit.

"Smith" — ("Language Laboratory") Referring to Ian Smith, nominal and controversial leader of Rhodesia during this period, who led the unilateral independence movement of Rhodesia from Great Britain. See below for more.

"Smith, Mr." — ("Travel Agent") Two real possibilities here. Sir Dudley Smith was a Tory MP who represented Warwick and Leamington, a West Midlands parliamentary constituency, during this period. Idle would have grown up hearing and reading about Dudley Smith, and his conservatism may have appealed to the Tourist's take on the ignorant British tourist.

But given the following mention of Enoch Powell (see entry above), the "Smith" reference probably actually refers to Ian Smith (1919–2007), who had taken Rhodesia under white minority control in 1965 (and held it until 1979)—perhaps the Tourist is hoping Smith can do the same for Spain and her islands, and then even Britain. These policies reflect the hopes and promises of the British Union of Fascists, though BUF hadn't been an effective political concern since the 1930s, and was actually banned in 1940. (See the recorded entries on British fascism as part of *Eyewitness 1930–39*, beginning with "Fascism in Britain.")

"Spanish tummy" — ("Travel Agent") A colloquial, catch-all (and less alarming) way to refer to stomach and intestinal problems associated with visits to Spain and the Continent. In 1664–1665, it was the bubonic and pneumonic plague that resurged in London, killing as many as 70–100,000 (of a total population of less than 500,000) before giving way to the cleansing destructiveness of the Great Fire in 1666. London's great cholera epidemics actually occurred in the nineteenth century, killing thousands, then hundreds, and then dozens in successive outbreaks. The last great London cholera epidemic ravaged the city in 1854, and was blamed on a contaminated well in Broad Street.

"Guardia"—A quasi-military police force in Spain, originally formed in 1844, and used by General Franco to enforce the government policies in Fascist Spain. See entry for Franco.

stock film of Everest — (PSC; "Everest Climbed by Hairdressers") The film stock here is BBC film stock, and titled "K26544, -45 and -46," and may actually be of K2, and have been taken of a 1965 expedition (WAC T12/1,441).

"strangling . . . masturbating" — ("*Summarize Proust Competition*") This latter word was actually edited out of the broadcast, leaving the studio audience to seemingly respond (with belly laughter) to the audibly mangled "golf and strangling animals." Duncan Wood of BBC Light Entertainment had a meeting with several of the Pythons, telling them that the term "masturbating" was not going to pass muster. This is one of the few times that a finished episode was actually edited/censored for content on BBC brass demand. See Morgan (1999) and McCabe for more.

Along a similar vein, noted British philosopher Bertrand Russell mentions that as a lonely adolescent his keen interests in "sex, mathematics and religion" kept him from suicidal thoughts (see *The Autobiography of Bertrand Russell*, 38–39). Russell admits that masturbation allowed him to survive between ages fifteen and twenty, when he finally fell in love. See Ep. 32 for more on Russell—as a curmudgeonly, free-thinking, sexually obsessed scientist/philosopher/activist/gadfly, he probably very much appealed to the Pythons.

Sunday Mirror — ("Travel Agent") Popular Sunday edition of the *Daily Mirror* (Eps. 10, 24) founded in 1915, and became the *Sunday Mirror* in 1963. Seen as a "paper of the people," appealing to a broad middle-class English readership, which is why Idle's Tourist would denigrate it. See notes to Eps. 10 and 24 for more on the *Daily Mirror*, its readership and features.

• T •

"Teasy-Weasy" — ("Everest Climbed by Hairdressers") "Mr. Teasy-Weasy" was Raymond Bessone, a.k.a. "Raymond of Mayfair," the owner/operator of a hair salon in posh Mayfair that claimed a long list of celebrity clients. Bessone was the most popular hair stylist of 1950s London, and gave the young Vidal Sassoon his start in the business.

The reference to celebrity hairdresser "Roger" in Ep. 14 ("*Face the Press*") is likely a nod to Raymond, who was by this time popular enough to go by just his given name. His salon was located at 18 Grafton Street, W1.

The combination of hairdressing and mountain climbing seems just absurd, but is certainly based on Bessone's own announcement in 1957 that his "Shangri-La Style" was inspired by his view of the Alps and thoughts of Everest after a skiing accident in Switzerland. A memorable newsreel available at British Pathé depicts the campy, poncing Raymond in his full glory. See the British Pathé website.

thirties routine — ("Language Laboratory") Meant to indicate a 1930s-era Hollywood musical number, like those found in the films *Golddiggers of 1933* or *42nd Street*, both produced by the American studio Warner Bros., and both choreographed by Busby Berkeley.

Thrust — ("Theory on Brontosauruses by Anne Elk (Miss)") Meant to mimic probing and/or current affairs news shows like *Panorama*, then airing on BBC1 since 1953. *The World about Us* (BBC2; 1967–1986) was also running, but this show focused on natural history. The combination of current affairs and natural history actually seems quite apropos as Anne Elk (Cleese) discusses her unusual brontosaurus theory.

"Timothy White's suncream" — ("Travel Agent") Skin protection cream popular during the Pythons' youth, the company (Timothy Whites and Taylors Ltd.) had been acquired by chemist giant Boots in 1968, so this is probably a bit of a nostalgic reference.

There were still many Timothy White stores (more than thirty) in the Greater London area in 1969.

Tomlinson, Fred — ("*Summarize Proust Competition*") Tomlinson and his singers appear in Eps. 22, 25, 26, 29, 36, and 37. They will also appear later in this episode in the "Language Laboratory" sketch.

"transistor radios" — ("Travel Agent") To listen to their favorite BBC shows, news, and perhaps especially sport, rather than the local media. Much of this diatribe reads like a postcolonial antagonism, wherein the speaker blasts the vestiges of British imperialism carted along with tourists like so much essential baggage.

"Transworld International" — ("CinemaScope" link into "*Party Hints* with Veronica Smalls") The broadcasting arm of the U.S. sports marketing group IMG, run by Mark McCormack (1930–2003), TWI was set up in the 1960s to tape and broadcast golf, initially.

Keeping in mind the Python penchant for mixing real Mortimers with fake ones (the debt to Shakespeare acknowledged), the other entries in this list of fanciful credits include:

"*Nimrod Productions*"—A biblical figure purported to be a great hunter, "Nimrod" has also become a pejorative term, perhaps thanks to Bugs Bunny's usage in reference to Elmer Fudd in several Warner Bros. cartoons.

"*Arthur E. Ricebacher*"—A European-sounding (and most likely Jewish) name for a typical Hollywood movie mogul, like Larry and Irving R. Saltzberg in Ep. 6.

"*David A. Seltzer Production*"—A play on the name of film producer/studio owner David O. Selznick (1902–1965), producer of such films as *Gone with the Wind* (1939) and *Spellbound* (1945).

"*Hasbach Enterprises*"—A municipality in Germany, though there has also been a Hasbach GmbH (performing industrial sanitary services) in operation in Datteln, Germany, since 1928. This could have been a name the Pythons picked up during their time in Bavaria shooting the first of two German episodes of *Fliegender Zirkus* in 1971. There is a noticeable gap in the *FC* recording dates for the 1972 season, with no activity noted in February or March—they were in Germany during most of this period. Upon their return to BBC in late March or early April, the Pythons went back to recording, with episodes 37 and 31 recorded in April 1972.

"*Pulitzer Prizewinning Idea*"—The Pulitzer Prize is awarded every year (since 1917) for achievement in journalism, drama, poetry, photography, etc.

"*Daniel E. Stollmeyer*"—No certainty here, but there were Stollmeyers who played cricket for the West Indies in the 1950s and 1960s, Jeffrey and Vic. Jeff Stollmeyer (1921–1989) was captain of the team, and the West Indies won the first two Tests (of five). This series may have been a memorable one for the youngish Pythons as it featured incidents of fan violence, official team complaints about rulings, substitutions, etc., and generally caused lots of friction between the countries. See Wisden. (Incidentally, there are no "Stollmeyer" entries in any extant London-area phonebook between 1965 and 1975.)

"from Robert Hughes's Novel"—Hughes (b. 1938) is a Sydney-born art critic and historian who has been publishing *nonfiction* since 1966, and has been art critic for *Time* magazine for many years. He is perhaps now best known for his influential book and TV series *The Shock of the New*, which looks at modern art in the age of commercialism.

"Louis H. Tannhauser"—This (and the "Vernon D. Larue" that follows) sounds much more like the made-up names from earlier lists ("Juan-Carlos Fernandez," "Thor Olaf Stensgaard") picked for how they sound, and not as a direct reference to any historical person. The name Tannhauser has a significant Cambridge connection, however, as occultist Alisteir Crowley (1875–1947) matriculated there (Trinity College), and would go on to write his own version of the Tannhauser story as a sort of "progress of the soul." This was also the name of a Wagner opera of 1845.

"Selzenbach-Tansrod Production"—A sort of half-hearted jumble of Seltzer-Hasbach and Tannhauser-Nimrod, though not unlike some of the co-named production companies of the day, including "Prodimex," a company used by Roger Corman (*Little Shop of Horrors*) for Spanish- and Italian-language exploitation pictures in the 1970s. Another portmanteau-ish example: the home that Mary Pickford and Douglas Fairbanks shared was called "Pickfair."

"Victor A. Lounge"—Though this is likely to be a reference to Victor Mature (mentioned earlier in Ep. 28), husband-and-wife Charles and Ray Eames had made a film in 1956 called *Eames Lounge Chair*, an experimental film looking at their newly designed and very popular piece of Modern Art furniture.

"Rolo Nice Sweeties"—A Nestle chocolate-and-caramel candy. This is a certain return to actual references to actual people/products—the balance of the list is documentable.

"Fison's Fertilizers"—A proprietary name for a weed killer and fertilizer available in the UK in the 1950s and beyond.

"Time Life Innit-for-the-Money Limited"—The *Time-Life* company has been in business since 1961, and had been packaging books with records (LPs) since 1966. This crawl, then, is directly inspired by the 1963 film *How the West Was Won*, which proudly pro-

claimed on its lobby posters: "Suggested by the LIFE series!" The serialized story *How the West Was Won* appeared in *LIFE* magazine in 1959. See "panning" note above for more on this film.

"Trustees of St. Paul's Cathedral"—The Cathedral was designed by Christopher Wren, and built between 1675 and 1708. The trustees would have been in charge of any and all decisions regarding use or upkeep of the property, and continue to do so today.

"Ralph Reader"—Broadway choreographer (1903–1982) who also produced *The Gang Show Gala* (1970), which starred Peter Sellers. His early *Gang Show* productions were amateur variety shows.

"Ralph Nader"—American consumer activist and author, Nader (b. 1934) was during this period campaigning for better safety equipment in American automobiles, including seatbelts. His influential report was called "Unsafe at Any Speed," and appeared in 1965.

"The Chinese Government"—Included because China was emerging on the world stage in a very big way during this period. See entries for some of the many other Mao and China/Chinese references in Eps. 18, 19, 21, 23–25, 28, and 34.

"Michael's Auntie Betty in Australia"—Palin did have an Auntie Katherine (Palin Greenwood), but this is more likely a variation on a *Goon Show* bit, where Eccles (Milligan) tells Bluebottle (Sellers):

Eccles: I been to the doctor and he said I've got (incoherent mumbling)—I got an uncle in Australia! You be careful what you say to me, I got an uncle in Australia! ("The Sleeping Prince," 14 Feb. 1957)

• U •

usual late-night line-up set — ("Theory on Brontosauruses by Anne Elk [Miss]") *Late Night Line-Up* (BBC2, 1964–1972) starred Joan Bakewell (Ep. 5), Denis Tuohy, Michael Dean, and Nicholas Tresilian. The "usual set" was a simple two-chair interview set, with backdrop. The show ran as many as six and seven nights per week, and looked at current trends in television, film, literature, music, etc. *Late Night* also featured a section called *Plunder*, where the vast BBC archives were raided for amusing pre-1955 TV clips, very much as Python would do when they had access to those same archives (Vahimagi, 129).

The music underneath this exchange is Trevor Duncan's New Concert Orchestra playing "Pistons" from *Crankcraft*, a suite written about trains (cf. the "Neville Shunt" section of Ep. 24). British composer Duncan's (1924–2005) light orchestra music can also be heard in Eps. 28 and 45.

• V •

Voice Over (John)— (intro link into "The All-England *Summarize Proust Competition*") This is a mistake in the script, as Palin has by this time essentially taken over the "*Monty Python's Flying Circuses*" recitation chore.

• W •

"wallop" — ("Language Laboratory") A colloquialism for "mild beer," perhaps Australian, and used by Orwell in *1984* (1949), and earlier by J.B. Priestley in *Three Men in New Suits* (1945).

"wasp farm" — ("Theory on Brontosauruses by Anne Elk [Miss]") *Wasp Farm* was the title of a fairly popular book published in 1963 by Howard Ensign Evans of Cornell University. The book looked at the lives and activities of, especially, the solitary digger wasps.

"Watney's Red Barrel" — ("Travel Agent") Catering to British tourists, this Spanish shop sells English food and the English drink, Watney's Red Barrel. A pale lager brewed by the sprawling Watney's Brewing empire during the 1960s and 1970s, the quality of this mass-produced beer was always in question, and the CAMRA organization (Campaign for Real Ale), founded in 1971 to combat the disappearance of individual breweries in the UK, was certainly helped along by Red Barrel's pedestrian infamy.

"Well I'll go . . . Ee ecky thump. Put wood in 'ole muther" — ("Language Laboratory") Traditional or stereotypical Yorkshire sayings and accent, as delivered by northerner Palin. "I'll go to the foot of our stairs" is a Northern exclamation of surprise, not unlike "Well I'll be," while "Put wood in 'ole, muther" means "shut the door, mother," both delivered in the heaviest of Yorkshire Dales dialect.

"Thump" is a Yorkshire festival, but can also be a feast or wake, and "Eckythump" (Lancastrian martial arts) would become a classic *Goodies* episode (1970–1982). This phrase may have been borrowed from Python colleague Bill Oddie (b. 1941 in Lancashire), star of *The Goodies* (1970–1981). Oddie worked with several of the Pythons (Chapman, Cleese, Idle) on *At Last the 1948 Show* (1967), and attended Cambridge, knowing Chapman, Cleese, and Idle there. The phrase is also heard in *ISIRTA*, where both Oddie and Cleese wrote and performed, and Idle occasionally contributed.

Whistling wind, stirring music — (PSC; "Everest Climbed by Hairdressers") This music seems to be borrowed from Vaughn Williams's "Sinfonia Antarctica," probably the Epilogue section (WAC T12/1,441). This is the musical score from the 1948 film *Scott of the Antarctic*, which the Pythons spoofed in Ep. 23. The performance here is by the London Philharmonic Orchestra.

Wilson, Sandy — ("Language Laboratory") Wilson (b. 1924; educated Harrow, Oriel College, Oxford) was a composer and lyricist of what has been called "lighter" theatrical fare. Wilson may have come to the Pythons' attention when he wrote music for Peter Cook's various revues, including *Pieces of Eight*.

Episode 32:
"Expedition to Lake Pahoe"

Tory Housewives Clean-Up Campaign; Pepperpots at war: Nude Organist, "And Now . . ." Man, and "It's" Man; *Titles* (silly Palin v/o); Harley Street: **Gumby brain specialist**—"My brain hurts"; Gumby brain surgeons; *Animation: The meaning of life, badly framed*; All-Essex Badminton Championship promo; *Molluscs*—Live TV documentary; The mollusc's sex life; *Animation: The carnivorous baby; Today in Parliament*: The Minister for not listening to people; Classic serial becomes the Tuesday documentary becomes children's story becomes a party political broadcast; *Match of the Day* (hugging); Apology for politicians; Expedition to Lake Pahoe; *Animation: Groovy Royal Navy advert*; "There's no cannibalism in the Royal Navy"; The Magna Carta: The silliest interview we've ever had, stopped; The silliest sketch we've ever done, stopped; Closing credits

• A •

"Aberdeen versus Raith Rovers" — ("The Silliest Interview We've Ever Done") Aberdeen FC competes in the Scottish Premier League, and was formed from multiple Aberdeen-area clubs in 1903. Raith Rovers FC was formed in 1883, and play in Stark Park in Fife, Scotland. The Rovers are part of Bell's Scottish Football League Division 1.

Raith Rovers did play Aberdeen during this period, though never to a 0–0 tie.

Ambulance racing — ("Gumby Brain Specialist") This film footage is listed as reference numbers NP/NT73292 and NP/NT65980 (WAC T12/1,446).

armoured vehicle — ("Tory Housewives Clean-Up Campaign") This is the same tank and location used in Ep. 21, "Mosquito Hunters," and is located at the main gate, Army School of Transport, Longmore, Liss, Hampshire (WAC T12/1,430).

art gallery exterior — (PSC; "Tory Housewives Clean-Up Campaign") The location for this shot appears to be the columnar façade of the Tate Britain, on Millbank in London.

art gallery interior — (PSC; "Tory Housewives Clean-Up Campaign") In January 1970, police entered the London Arts Gallery and removed lithographs by/of John Lennon and Yoko Ono, citing the Obscene Publications Act of 1959, and following filed complaints.

London's museums had also been much in the news in 1971–1972, with the sweeping implementation of admission fees to formerly free national museums and galleries, as well as the imminent arrival of the "King Tut" exhibit to the UK. See the British Cartoon Archive.

"arthropods" — ("Molluscs—'Live' TV Documentary") Arthropods are, indeed, the largest phylum of animals.

• B •

"Badger" — ("The Silliest Sketch We've Ever Done") Badger (Idle) will appear again, in Ep. 35, as a would-be hijacker ("Bomb on Plane"), there offering to *not* interrupt the show for various small sums of money.

"Batley" — ("The Minister for Not Listening to People") Home of the earlier-mentioned Batley Townswomen's

Guild and their famed and muddy historical re-enactments (see Eps. 11 and 22). Batley is in West Yorkshire.

"battle like bingo boys" — ("Tory Housewives Clean-Up Campaign") "Bingo boys" is actually slang for a heavy drinker, especially of brandy, which is a purposely ironic appellation for the Victorian-throwback Tory housewives (*OED*).

This could also be a slight and even purposeful misspeaking, and Idle could have been referring to the "Biff Boys." These were "stewards," or hired muscle, used by noted British fascist Sir Oswald Mosley in the early 1930s to protect the meetings of his New Party, an ultra-conservative nationalist party separate from any established party or platform. Mosley, who actually stood successfully for the Conservative party in Harrow (1918), would become disenchanted with the government's handling of the Irish situation and switch first to independency and then Labour in the early 1920s. Still dissatisfied with the sitting government, Mosley studied fascism and switched again. His New Party candidates would have no success in the 1931 elections, and he would go on to form the British Union of Fascists in 1932. (See *ODNB* and *Eyewitness 1930–39* for more.)

"Bell's whisky" — ("The Silliest Interview We've Ever Done") In 1970, Bell's was the leading whisky brand in Scotland, and had been in business in Scotland since the 1840s.

"big bad rabbit" — ("Tuesday Documentary/Children's Story/Party Political Broadcast") This same "bad-tempered rodent" will appear in the feature film *Holy Grail*, and will be destroyed by the Holy Hand Grenade of Antioch. The "killer rabbit" character—as silly and absurd as it seems in the hearing—may be traced to a marvelous sequence in Modernist novelist D.H. Lawrence's *Women in Love* (1921), where a pet rabbit reacts to being handled by Winnie and Gudrun:

> They unlocked the door of the hutch. Gudrun thrust in her arm and seized the great, lusty rabbit as it crouched still, she grasped its long ears. It set its four feet flat, and thrust back. There was a long scraping sound as it was hauled forward, and in another instant it was in midair, lunging wildly, its body flying like a spring coiled and released, as it lashed out, suspended from the ears. Gudrun held the black-and-white tempest at arms' length, averting her face. But the rabbit was magically strong, it was all she could do to keep her grasp. She almost lost her presence of mind. [. . .]
>
> Gudrun stood for a moment astounded by the thunder-storm that had sprung into being in her grip. Then her colour came up, a heavy rage came over her like a cloud. She stood shaken as a house in a storm, and utterly overcome. Her heart was arrested with fury at the mindlessness and the bestial stupidity of this struggle,

her wrists were badly scored by the claws of the beast, a heavy cruelty welled up in her. (chapter 18)

As early as Ep. 2, in the "Working-Class Playwright" sketch the Pythons display their knowledge of the England of D.H. Lawrence.

"black spot" — ("Expedition to Lake Pahoe") In *Treasure Island*, those that are meant to suffer or die are given or "marked with" a black spot. The captain fears his mutinous crew is preparing a spot for him, as they want his chest. When Jim asks the captain what a black spot might be, the captain merely answers: "That's a summons, mate. I'll tell you if they get that" (13). When Blind Pew does slip the black spot into the captain's hand, the captain dies immediately.

A black spot has figured prominently in a censored Gilliam animation in Ep. 19. See notes for "The Spot" in that episode.

"Blenheim Crescent" — ("Expedition to Lake Pahoe") There are at least fourteen Blenheim Crescent roads in the UK. In London, it can be found between Elgin Crescent and Cornwall Crescent near the Notting Hill area (W11). There is also a Runcorn Place just a block or so south and west of this same Blenheim Crescent.

British director David Lean (1908–1991) was born in Blenheim Crescent, Croydon. A Lean-like director (Ross, played by Chapman) appears in Ep. 1.

"Blind Pew" — ("Expedition to Lake Pahoe") An evil, wounded pirate character in Stevenson's *Treasure Island*, Pew seeks the map and treasure. Jim describes Pew in their first painful encounter: "I never heard a voice so cruel, and cold, and ugly as that blind man's. It cowed me more than the pain, and I began to obey him at once" (15).

"Squire Trelawney"—The character in Stevenson's *Treasure Island* (1883) who finances the treasure hunt, and who also inadvertently gives away the plan to the bad guys.

These are just the latest of the many references to this obviously seminal text in *FC*, probably as a result of the novel having become a very popular Christmas pantomime years earlier.

"boy's bedroom" — ("Tuesday Documentary/Children's Story/Party Political Broadcast") A do-it-yourself moment (DIY), which a number of British cultural observers have identified as particularly English, including Jeremy Paxman in a 1998 *Sunday Times* article (see the author's *MPSERD*, 22).

"British" — ("Tory Housewives Clean-Up Campaign") Interesting reference to the entire colonial empire, or at least the islands of the United Kingdom, as being "British" (of greater Britain) and not "English."

Perhaps, though, Whitehouse and her Conservative allies were trying to refashion the "British" empire into an "English" one, excluding or transforming the darker, foreign-born, other-tongued interlopers and their white enablers and apologists.

"British Common Market" — ("Tory Housewives Clean-Up Campaign") The tongue-in-cheek term for the proposed European Common Market (or European Economic Community, as it was called), which Britain would join in January 1973, and then reaffirm at the polls two years later (June 1975) via national referendum. Heath and the Labour Party had led the way for Britain's place in the Market, with France's de Gaulle being against Anglo membership in overriding votes in 1963 and 1967. One of the concerns closely held by many Gaulish EEC members was that English would immediately become the de facto language of business in the EEC, and that Britain would never be "European enough."

burning books — (PSC; "Tory Housewives Clean-Up Campaign") There seems to be no evidence that Mary Whitehouse actually destroyed books or films, being more focused on television depictions of sexuality during this period, and setting her sights on the BBC and its "permissive" director, Hugh Greene (and his underlings, including the pictured Robert Robinson). Whitehouse had, in late 1970, unsuccessfully asked the government to revoke the BBC's charter.

"Bertrand Russell"—Russell (1872–1970) was a British mathematician and philosopher, and an outspoken liberal and critic of nuclear arms and the Vietnam War. Russell would also have angered the conservative Christian world with his comments in *Why I Am Not a Christian: And Other Essays on Religion and Related Subjects* (1927). Russell has been mentioned in the notes to Ep. 30, in relation to one of his early hobbies—masturbation. See entry for "Jean . . . Genet" below for more on Russell.

"Das Kapital"—Karl Marx's seminal work would have made the list for its godless, stateless Marxism (he's appeared as a gameshow contestant and in a homosexual encounter with Che Guevara already).

"The Guardian"—This has long been a left-of-center British newspaper, supporting the State of Israel in 1948, for example.

"Sartre"—See the notes to Ep. 27 for reasons the Tory Housewives would disapprove of the French existentialist.

"Freud"—Father of modern psychoanalysis Sigmund Freud's translated writings on sexuality and the unconscious had become part of the popular culture mélange between the wars, and, coincidentally, his books were also burned by Nazi stormtroopers in 1933 Germany.

On the side of the pile is a paperback copy of the infamous Kim Philby's *My Silent War* (1968). Philby was the high-ranking MI6 man who reported secrets to the Soviets for many years before defecting in 1963.

(Incidentally, this book burning image/theme may be what prompts the inclusion of Irish author Edna O'Brien later in the show. See below.)

The final two books pulled from the pile before being consigned to the flames are titled *Plato* and *Two Gentlemen Sharing*. Perhaps the Pythons are painting Plato and Socrates with the same broad brush, since Socrates was found guilty of corrupting the youth of Athens and was executed. The last (and almost unreadable) title is *Two Gentlemen Sharing*, a 1963 book by David Stuart Leslie (which would become a 1969 film) that posits a white, uptight advertising type having to share a flat with a Jamaican cricketer. The title implies a homosexual relationship, but the novel is more about race relations in restrictive middle-class London.

"Business is booming" — ("Tory Housewives Clean-Up Campaign") For a very enlightening look at the *economic* impact of Modernist art(s) and literature(s) see Laurence Rainey's article "The Cultural Economy of Modernism" in *The Cambridge Companion to Modernism*, edited by Michael Levenson. Briefly, this was the period when *ars gratia artis* reigned, and modern artists enjoyed gala showings and equally impressive sales to private collectors. See Hughes's *The Shock of the New* for more on the cultural temblors in commercial/fine art during this period.

"But it's an ordinary house" — ("Expedition to Lake Pahoe") Organizations including the Greater London Industrial Archaeology Society, HADAS (The Hendon & District Archaeological Society), the London Underground Railway Society, the City of London Archaeological Society, the London Museum, and myriad university-affiliated archaeological societies in Greater London have for many years conducted digs in and under the houses, buildings, and streets of Greater London, so the prospect of an expedition coming to a basement apartment in the Notting Hill area isn't unusual at all. In 1972 in Morville Street, E3, for example, an archaeological dig produced Roman pottery in burial pits and ditches dating to the first and second centuries.

This underwater shot was made in a pool at Butlin's Holiday Camp, Bognor, on 18 October 1971. The Pythons and the show's crew are chided in extant communications from local safety officials about not preparing adequately for scuba gear use, improper safety personnel, etc. (WAC T12/1,428).

"by-elections" — ("Tuesday Documentary/Children's Story/Party Political Broadcast") Regional interim elections that can often foretell the voting public's approval or disapproval of the sitting government's policies and accomplishments, but most often are based on more local issues and personalities. Part of the reason Labour was surprised by their 1970 loss to the Conservatives was based on a lack of identifiable dissatisfaction in the electorate in recent by-elections. Wilson confidently then scheduled the June 1970 election to cement the Labour mandate, but a seemingly insignificant downward-trending economic forecast in May and early June swayed voters back to the Tories (*Eyewitness 1970–79*, "General Election, 18 June 1970").

• C •

Camera pans across a bleak landscape — ("Apology [Politicians]") These scenes, as well as the background for the following sketch, were shot while the cast and crew were in the Glencoe, Scotland, area.

"cannibalism . . . British Navy" — ("Expedition to Lake Pahoe") An 1845–1850 expedition led by Sir John Franklin ended, it seems, in cannibalism and starvation for the 134 men on HMS *Terror* and HMS *Erebus*. The men had been looking for the Northwest Passage, and had probably lost their ships to crushing ice. A letter from one explorer who followed Franklin's trail a decade later wrote back to the Admiralty: "From the mutilated state of many of the corpses and the contents of the kettles, it is evident that our wretched countrymen had been driven to the last resource—cannibalism—as a means of prolonging existence" (John Rae, cited in the *Times* [23 Oct. 1854]; see "Franklin, Sir John" in *ODNB*). See entries in Ep. 26 for more on this same subject.

carrying a plywood flat with portion cut out to represent TV — ("Molluscs—'Live' TV Documentary") There were initially a number of competing (and often impoverished) regional independent television entities to bring commercial TV to the British viewer, including Associated-Rediffusion and Associated Television (for London), Associated Television and ABC Television (for the Midlands), and Granada and ABC Television (for the North) (Crisell 2002, 85). These groups tended to lose money between 1955 and 1957, when viewership began to increase dramatically, eventually exceeding the BBC in audience by as much as 3 to 1.

In the case of Zorba (Cleese) having to come into the Jalins' home and entertain, the Pythons were likely pointing up the BBC's struggles to keep viewers where those viewers had a choice between ITV and the Beeb.

Children's Story — ("Tuesday Documentary/Children's Story/Party Political Broadcast") There was a popular and long-running children's show *Jackanory* (1965–1996), where limited budgets meant that storytellers of all kinds took center stage—like Idle's direct-address used here—and not re-enactments. Both Spike Milligan (*The Goon Show*; *Q5*) and Alan Bennett (*Beyond the Fringe*) were readers for *Jackanory* during its early years.

"chlorpromazine" — ("Expedition to Lake Pahoe") Also known as Thorazine, chlorpromazine is a low-potency anti-psychotic drug, often used to treat delusions and hallucinations.

"Classic Serial" — ("Tuesday Documentary/Children's Story/Party Political Broadcast") *Classic Serial* and the more general radio serialization of classic works have run on BBC Radio since at least 1938, according to Robert Giddings, author/presenter of the lecture "Dickens and the Classic Serial" at a Staff Research Seminar, School of Media Arts and Communication, Bournemouth University (15 Nov. 1999). Giddings speaks of growing up listening to these serials, and the effect they had as they were interwoven into the fabric of British life. For more see Giddings and Selby's *The Classic Serial on Television and Radio*.

This nostalgic, state of an ever-present, stream-of-consciousness effect is seen in the Python text, as well, as the various radio and TV stories weave in and out of the textual foreground.

"Clermont-Ferrand" — ("Tuesday Documentary/Children's Story/Party Political Broadcast") Home of Blaise Pascal, French mathematician and philosopher mentioned in Ep. 1 during the "Whizzo Butter" sketch.

"council" — ("Expedition to Lake Pahoe") This referring to the local housing council, where such complaints (water damage, infestations) would have been reported. In the 14 August 1970 edition of *Private Eye*, editors contribute a biting exposé on the shoddy building standards in Britain's council housing tracts. Specifically, the article "Condensation St." looks at the new building standards that reduced or eliminated venting in the homes (block flats and bungalows) and especially near the furnaces, leading almost immediately to elevated humidity levels, then dripping and running condensation, then mold and rot, etc. It was estimated that 97 percent of new homes being built during this period featured inadequate ventilation and suffered from "the damp" (16–17).

"Cunningham, Sir John" — ("Expedition to Lake Pahoe") Sir John H.D. Cunningham was Admiral of the Fleet 1946–1948.

• D •

"D'Arcy . . . man" — ("Tuesday Documentary/Children's Story/Party Political Broadcast") A borrowing from *Pride and Prejudice*, when Darcy reveals to Elizabeth in the famous letter that Wickham isn't as pure as might have been imagined or hoped for. A version of this oft-staged classic appeared on the BBC in 1967.

David — ("Tory Housewives Clean-Up Campaign") There has been a *David* cast replica of the original statue housed at the Victoria & Albert museum since 1857 (when it was called the South Kensington Museum). The V&A website reports that upon receiving the unannounced gift, Victoria was so shocked by the nudity she commissioned a fig leaf to be made, and ordered that it be installed before any royal visit. It seems the Pepperpots and Mary Whitehouse may have had something of a patron saint in their Queen Victoria.

Desdemona . . . Othello — ("Tory Housewives Clean-Up Campaign") Othello is, of course, a Moorish character, and cavorting with a white woman.

This depiction of the Conservatives as the party willing to "whiten" Britain is interesting, especially as it's remembered that Harold Wilson's Labour government worked just as hard in the later 1960s to stem the tide of Asian immigrants from Kenya, for example, responding to calls from constituencies being flooded with refugees, essentially. See notes to Ep. 27 for more on this convenient double standard.

"Dorset" — ("The Silliest Interview We've Ever Done") Dorset is in Dorchester on the southwestern coast of England, known as "Thomas Hardy country," near where the Pythons did significant location shooting for the first season.

Dr. Kildare — ("Gumby Brain Specialist") "The *Dr. Kildare* Theme" here is played by John Spence and Orchestra, as composed by Jerry Goldsmith (WAC T12/1,446). *Dr. Kildare* was a long-running and very popular NBC drama, starring the young Richard Chamberlain. It debuted on BBC 1 in November 1961. The show was featured on the cover of *Radio Times* in October 1961 and October 1963, and the Pythons borrow the music at least once in each of the four seasons.

• E •

"endless overtime" — ("Tory Housewives Clean-Up Campaign") Continuing unrest in British labor and a moribund economy kept the Heath government from governing as successfully as Heath had envisioned,
though his foreign endeavors seemed to bear fruit while domestic policy and support withered on the vine. In the weeks leading up to the devastating January 1972 coal strike, miners had actually refused overtime in their dispute over the government's refusal to raise wages more than 7.9 percent, a sort of work-to-rule tactic.

Episode 32 — Recorded 21 January 1972, and broadcast 23 November 1972. Additional cast members and extras for this episode: Lyn Ashley (also known as Mrs. Idle), John Scott-Martin (*Wednesday Play*; *Crimson Permanent Assurance*), George Ballantine (*Emma*); (appearing on film) Frank Lester (the "looney" in Ep. 31), Desmond Verini (Ep. 30; *Doctor Who*), Mike Reynell (Ep. 30; *Doctor Who*), Harry Tierney (*Doctor Who*), Terry Leigh (*Doctor Who*), Johnny Champs, Danny Sinclair, Cy Town (Ep. 29; *Z Cars*), Laurence Rose, Bill Leonard (first season), Bill Hewitt (*Play for Today*), David Freed (*Doctor Who*), Stephen Cass, Dennis Balcombe (*Timeslip*), Michael White, Pippa Hardman (*Hair*), Marion Park (*Law and Order*), Geoffrey Brighty (*Emma*), Chris Holmes (*Softly Softly*), Wolfgang von Jurgen, Ian Elliott (*Paul Temple*; *Emma*), John Hughman (Eps. 14, 28, 41; *Whoops Baghdad*), Rosemary Lord (*Softly Softly*), Jay Neil (*Softly Softly*), Roy Brent (*Some Mothers Do 'Ave 'Em*), Robyn Williams (*Jackanory*), Terence Denville (*Play for Today*; *Doctor Who*), Jack Dow, Jack Campbell, David Peece, Milton Cadnam, Peter Desmond, Nicholas Coppin (*Omega Factor*), Isobel Gardner (*Sutherland's Law*), Desi Angus (*Omega Factor*) (WAC T12/1,446).

"Euthymol toothpaste" — ("The Minister for Not Listening to People") Toothpaste that would have been around when all the Pythons were growing up after the war. Now manufactured by Pfizer.

• F •

"feet clean" — ("Tory Housewives Clean-Up Campaign") This long-running joke has British tourists certain that the bidets they encounter on visits to the continent are actually for foot-washing.

• G •

"Gastropods! Lamellibranchs! Cephalopods!" — ("Molluscs—'Live' TV Documentary") There are actually nine classes of mollusca, with the largest group being gastropoda.

"Glencoe vox pop" — (link out of "Molluscs—'Live' TV Documentary") One of the inserts shot while on location (for shooting the "Njorl's Saga" scenes) in and around Glencoe, Scotland, in October 1971 (WAC T12/1,428). This is one of the very few times that the location of the shot is mentioned—perhaps here to make sure the production team looks in the right place for the film.

"Grable, Betty" — ("Expedition to Lake Pahoe") Pin-up girl Grable (1916–1973) had made her name in Hollywood musicals, but was perhaps better known in the 1960s for her television commercials for Playtex girdles.

All three of these Hollywood starlets mentioned in the "Expedition to Lake Pahoe" sketch—Grable, Jane Russell, and Dorothy Lamour—were pin-up girls during the war years, their posters decorating barracks in many countries.

"Grenville" — ("Tuesday Documentary/Children's Story/Party Political Broadcast") There is a Lord Grenville character in Powell and Pressburger's *The Elusive Pimpernel* (1950). *The Elusive Pimpernel* was also a 250-minute miniseries that aired on BBC in 1969.

· **H** ·

Harley Street — (PSC; "Gumby Brain Specialist") Harley Street has been a locus of dentists, physicians, and surgeons, as well as a number of hospitals for many years.

Heath, Edward — (PSC; "Tory Housewives Clean-Up Campaign") Leader (Prime Minister) of the Conservative Party 1970–1974, after the Tories defeated Wilson's Labour government in the 1970 elections. Heath had championed Common Market membership since at least 1963. He was replaced as PM by Harold Wilson when, after the 1974 elections (and myriad labor strikes and economic setbacks at home as well as strife in Northern Ireland), he failed to create a coalition government.

The film stock found for Heath was acquired from the documentary TV series *Omnibus* (WAC T12/1,446).

"Hegelianism" — ("Tory Housewives Clean-Up Campaign") The product of Hegel's life work (not usually meant to include Hegel [1770–1831] himself, but responses to him), he may be rejected by the Tory Housewives for his obscurantism—he's just too complicated for comprehension. Also, the fact that he's a foreigner would render him suspect for the PP brigade.

"Liebnitz [*sic*] to Wittgenstein"—Ludwig Wittgenstein (1889–1951) had trained under Bertrand Russell, whose books the ladies were burning earlier, and his

homosexuality and left leanings might explain his mention here. It seems that Gottfried *Leibniz* (1646–1716) would have been preferred by these Housewives, as he included deity in his "Principles": "God assuredly always chooses the best," though he was still a "nasty continental" (Loemker, 311).

"Home Office" — ("The Minister for Not Listening to People") The building housing the department of the Secretary of State for Home Affairs, which is located at 2 Marsham Street, London. The much-maligned Reginald Maudling was the current Home Secretary, his office embroiled in a restriction of immigration from Commonwealth countries imbroglio during these months. Maudling would resign and be replaced by Robert Carr in July 1972, just four months after this episode was recorded.

"Houses of Parliament" — ("The Minister for Not Listening to People") Iconic building on the Thames River in the City of Westminster, London, where the House of Commons and House of Lords conduct parliamentary business. The buildings are in the shadow of the tower containing the bell, Big Ben. Part of the structure dates from the eleventh century, while most of the buildings were rebuilt in the mid-nineteenth century in the Gothic Revival style.

The photo is BBC 3SKP20 (WAC T12/1,428), and is one of the standard shots of the structure seen in myriad evening newscasts of the period.

"hunger marches . . . 1931" — ("Tuesday Documentary/Children's Story/Party Political Broadcast") The Labour government under Ramsay MacDonald resigned in 1931 under intense economic pressure, thanks to the effects of the Great Depression, including massive unemployment and civil unrest ("Ramsay MacDonald" in *ODNB*). Hunger marches began as early as 1932, most often in response to attempted governmental change in social programs meant to combat the effects of the Great Depression. Many of the labor marches began in coal mining towns in Wales and the north of England, including Jarrow (see entry below), which were particularly hard hit by the Depression.

Rather than resign, MacDonald would abandon his party and create a coalition government consisting of Labour, Conservatives, and Liberals, and would win the next election by a wide margin. This may be the reason behind the inclusion of MacDonald as a closet transvestite in Ep. 24—on the outside he appeared to be a staunch defender of the working man, but he would refuse to support militant strikers or even his own party. See the BBC's coverage of these events in "A History of Labour," at bbc.co.uk, and Miller's "British Unemployment Crisis of 1935," and the "MacDonald" entry below.

• I •

"increased productivity" — ("Tory Housewives Clean-Up Campaign") There were significant grumblings during this period about the surge in economic prosperity of countries on the continent (including the economic miracle in the defeated and rebuilding Germany), even as Great Britain continued to see decreases in productivity, and huge increases in inflation, taxation, and government spending to support the welfare state.

A 9 January 1972 coal miner strike—four months before this episode was recorded, and the first massive coal walkout in half a century—was a devastating blow to Heath's promises of increased productivity and lower prices. The strike led to power shortages, plant and industry idlings and even closures, and a fed-up electorate.

Into the oblivion of animation — (*"Animation: The meaning of life, badly framed"*) As the man tries to speak about the meaning of life he appears in several settings, the third being yet another appearance of Plate 28 from *Perspective* by de Vries. In this case, his head has been placed on the body of a wrestler, and a woman is throttling him.

"Irish situation" — ("The Minister for Not Listening to People") The second and final mention of the "troubles" in Northern Ireland. See notes for Ep. 31 for more. The other oblique reference (lost on today's viewers) to the Irish problems is the depiction of versions of the vociferous Reverend Ian Paisley in Ep. 41. See those notes for more.

• J •

"Jarrow" — ("Tuesday Documentary/Children's Story/Party Political Broadcast") Unemployed workers marched from Jarrow to London in 1936 to meet with Prime Minister Stanley Baldwin, who essentially turned them away. Jarrow was experiencing unemployment rates as high as 65 percent during this period, with many already out of work for eight years and longer (*Eyewitness 1930–39*, "The Jarrow March"). This same year would see riots in the East End of London, including the Battle of Cable Street, sparked by fascist group(s) marches and their mostly Jewish opponents mentioned in the "bingo boys" note above. There had been an unsuccessful general strike in 1926, as well, pitting the Trades Union Congress (TUC) against the sitting government, with the hopes that coal miners' wages and standard of living could be increased. (See Morgan's *Oxford History of Britain*.)

The stock film footage used here is called "Jarrow Marchers" (K22514/5) (WAC T12/1,446).

"Jean . . . Genet" — ("Tory Housewives Clean-Up Campaign") Bertrand Russell and Jean-Paul Sartre co-organized a tribunal in 1966–1967—the Russell Tribunal—to bring to light what they saw as the United States' war crimes in Vietnam.

That their works of art might make good kindling is no surprise. Sartre was, of course, both an atheist and French, more than enough to condemn him for Whitehouse and others; Russell's *Marriage and Morals* (1929) advocated sex outside of marriage and "compatibility" marriages—he was a lifelong anti-Victorian, essentially; Genet was a homosexual, and his writings trumpeted both homosexuality and criminality.

• L •

"Lake Pahoe" — ("Expedition to Lake Pahoe") The mountain lake found in the Sierra Nevadas in the United States is called Lake Tahoe, and there is also a Lago Pahoe, a glacial lake in the Chilean Highlands. The expedition is also referencing the 1969 one-man sub dive into Loch Ness by Dan Taylor, and more contemporarily the Academy of Applied Science Expeditions begun in 1972, which included the use of sonar machines in the fabled loch. Both expeditions went into the water looking for "hitherto unclassified marine life," as Sir Jane (Chapman) indicates. There have been calls for many years for the Royal Navy to conduct an extensive Loch Ness survey, as well.

"Lamour, Dorothy" — ("Expedition to Lake Pahoe") Lamour (1914–1996) starred with Bob Hope (Ep. 28) and Bing Crosby in the celebrated "Road" pictures (*Road to Bali*, 1952), and during this period was making guest appearances on American TV shows like *Love, American Style* and *Marcus Welby, M.D.*

"Lancet" — ("Gumby Brain Specialist") An international, independent medical journal published in New York and London.

Long John Silver jacket — (PSC; "Expedition to Lake Pahoe") Again, one of the Pythons' favorite characters reappears, having already shown up in Eps. 5, 10 (in animation), 23, 25, and 28.

• M •

MacDonald, Ramsay — (PSC; "Tuesday Documentary/Children's Story/Party Political Broadcast") Prime Minister for the Labour government, Ramsay

(1866–1937) was PM in 1924, and again 1929–1935. His years at the head of the government during the Great Depression were the most trying, and he was faced with constant civil unrest, both at home and in Ireland. A working-class man by birth, MacDonald was first elected from Leicester in 1906.

The "stock film" used here is "Ramsay MacDonald," film reference "BBC News WPA16133/A" (WAC T12/1,446).

"Magna Carta" — ("The Silliest Interview We've Ever Done") The 1215 legal document that outlined the rights and responsibilities of the king, landed barons, and even the church in England.

man-trap — (PSC; "Expedition to Lake Pahoe") These types of traps have been illegal in England since the nineteenth century, and is more the type seen in cartoons than used for hunting or poaching deterrence.

Match of the Day — ("Tuesday Documentary/Children's Story/Party Political Broadcast") By this time a fixture on BBC 2, *Match of the Day* was first broadcast 22 August 1964, a football match introduced by Kenneth Wolstenholme. Liverpool beat Arsenal 3–2 on that day, and there were approximately 20,000 viewers, according to bbc.co.uk.

The hugging and kissing portions of this sketch appeared earlier in a special the Pythons created as the BBC's entry into *Euroshow 71—May Day Special*. The "Fish Slapping Dance," "All-In Cricket," and a "Batley Townswomen's Guild" performance also appeared as part of this one-off special.

"Molluscs . . . Cephalopods" — ("Molluscs—'Live' TV Documentary") The nature documentary begun in earnest in Ep. 30—where bull limpets face off on a rock—but which falls into disarray as characters and producers get into a fist fight, indicates that the world of television documentaries might indeed be unwatchable without something extra. (This was also broached in Ep. 27, when BBC man Mr. Birchenhall [Chapman] complains that primetime viewers don't want documentaries, just entertainment and sport, like they were getting from the commercial networks.) In this case, the sex lives of the documentary subject is the only thing that keeps the Jalins watching (and offended, but still watching).

This may be a response to the much-ballyhooed introduction of a graphic sex education documentary film (showing a married couple engaging in intercourse) for UK schools in 1970. The film was written and directed by Dr. Martin Coles, Aston University. Also, in May 1971 a radio broadcast of a portion of a schools' sex education film, *Growing Up*, that described the masturbation process for boys and girls was decried as unnecessarily graphic and titillating

by Mary Whitehouse and NVLA. There were calls for increased ministry control of the radio broadcast for school programs thereafter.

• N •

"nasty continental shows" — ("Tory Housewives Clean-Up Campaign") After the introduction of BBC2 in 1964, the possibility of increased foreign programming reaching British households became much more likely. The government worked to keep the BBC ahead of the independently owned (commercial) stations by placing quotas on foreign programming, and even specifying generic appropriateness in purchased foreign shows (Museum of Broadcast Communications). In 1965, the suddenly very conservative (and perhaps xenophobic) Labour government allowed that just 2 percent of programming could come from the Continent (14 percent from the United States; 1.5 percent from the Commonwealth) (MBC).

naval-lib badge — ("Expedition to Lake Pahoe") A play on the au courant terms of social and sexual protest, including "Gay Lib" (see the Judge's complaint in Ep. 27), and "Women's Lib," among others. It seems that ratings like Dorothy Lamour (Idle) want to liberate the navy from hair cuts, rank discipline, and the taboo against cannibalism.

"navy's out of sight man" — ("Expedition to Lake Pahoe") By this time, the absence of conscription powers and the cessation a generation earlier of National Service meant that the British armed forces were relying on enlistment, and standards necessarily suffered. One visible accoutrement of the hippie generation—long sideburns (or sideboards)—were a constant source of consternation to career military men and those who'd "fought the war."

Also, news footage from the United States would have presented the loud, slangy, hip reaction to the unpopular Vietnam War, with soldiers being interviewed who just wanted to go home. There was also a case of two U.S. soldiers on a gunboat (described as "hippies" by their comrades) who mutinied and deserted, seeking asylum in Cambodia.

Newsreel footage — (PSC; "Tory Housewives Clean-Up Campaign") The music beneath this footage is "Queen of the Fleet" by George S. Chase (WAC T12/1,446).

newsreel voice — (PSC; "Tory Housewives Clean-Up Campaign") The cadence and jocular word choice is characteristic of the wartime newsreels presented to Britain's beleaguered population, the commentators ever-positive and spinning the news in favor of a rosy outcome. In one such newsreel, combat motorcyclists are pictured going through camouflage-draped maneuvers:

> The one-time footsloggers have turned kickstart pushers. . . . The left right, left right folks have got both feet off the ground at the same time. They are part of Britain's mighty mobile mountain. All keen welcomers of Adolf when he drops in for a cup of tea and a cream bun. (qtd. in Wilson 2005, 403)

"Nine O'Clock News" — (link into "Molluscs—'Live' TV Documentary") The men of *Nine O'Clock News* (including *FC*-participant Richard Baker) were featured on the cover of the BBC's *Radio Times* in late 1970.

"No! Don't touch it!" — (*"Animation: Omnivorous baby"*) In the "omnivorous baby" animation, there is a portrait of actor and director Erich von Stroheim from *Foolish Wives* on the back wall.

This warning—"No, don't touch it!"—will also be ignored in Gilliam's later film *Time Bandits*, just before Kevin's parents touch the smoldering chunk of evil and are exploded.

Nurse — ("Gumby Brain Specialist") Played by Lyn Ashley, or Mrs. Idle, as the credits sometimes refer to her (WAC T12/1,446).

• O •

"O'Brien, Edna" — (link into "Molluscs—'Live' TV Documentary") There is a photo of the transplanted Irish writer Edna O'Brien (b. 1930) included with her mention, but the audience doesn't verbally respond to the image. She was known somewhat dubiously at this time for having all her books banned in her native country, the first even burnt by her local church authorities, according to the *Telegraph*. It may be that she wasn't as well known as some of the other celebrities mentioned in *FC*, though she may have been known to at least Idle for her participation in the Peter Whitehead documentary on "Swinging" London's night scene, *Let's All Make Love in London Tonight* (1967). Also appearing in that documentary were David Hockney (mentioned in Ep. 14) and Julie Christie (Ep. 28).

In many of her works, O'Brien's frank protrayals of sexuality in (and outside) marriage, and from a woman's point of view, led to her books being sometimes banned and even burned, and perhaps merits her mention by Monty Python in relation to a mollusc documentary that only gets interesting when deviant sexuality is introduced.

ordinary suburban living room — (PSC; "Molluscs—'Live' TV Documentary") This "ordinary" living room

features very popular V.G. Tretchikoff (1913–2006) paintings on the wall. Tretchikoff's work found its way into print form and onto thousands of middle-class walls, thanks to popular art tours in the US and Canada, then the UK, where his work appeared at Harrods. The famous blue-green "Chinese Girl" painting is also mentioned in the "Art Gallery" sketch of Pete and Dud, and can be seen in a setting for an early *Benny Hill* sketch, is in a *Doctor Who* episode, an album cover, and the film *Alfie*. The Tretchikoff will reappear in Ep. 35.

• P •

Party Political Broadcast — ("Tuesday Documentary/Children's Story/Party Political Broadcast") Party Election Broadcasts began in 1951, with Lord Samuel delivering the first speech. Both major parties were given equal time on BBC air and radio waves. Printed texts for many of these broadcasts are available online through Keele University's UK Elections website. A choreographed Party Political Broadcast from the Conservatives is the first sketch in Ep. 38, though only in the printed scripts.

"Penrose, Roland" — ("The Minister for Not Listening to People") Penrose (1900–1984) was a British surrealist painter credited with bringing surrealism to Britain. His coterie of associates included fellow artists Picasso, Miró, Man Ray, Ernst, and Tapies. A number of Penrose's works are currently in the Tate Modern in London.

pepperpots — ("Tory Housewives Clean-Up Campaign") All are reading copies of the *Daily Telegraph*, which has been derisively called the "Daily Torygraph" for its fairly consistent Conservative editorial positions.

"permissive society" — ("Tory Housewives Clean-Up Campaign") The postwar society of television, where many (like Mary Whitehouse) saw the erosion of traditional morals and values being caused by permissiveness in entertainments like TV and film, novels and plays, and even art shows. Increases in drug use, the appearance of the birth control pill, the public visibility of homosexuality and promiscuity, all were part of this permissive society, and all could be blamed on television's negative influence. See Aldgate's *Censorship and the Permissive Society*.

Photo of a French construction site — (PSC; "Classic Serial Becomes the Tuesday Documentary . . .") This French construction site (featuring a sign "De L'Hotel Des Dhuys") is now the Hotel Des Dhuits on Route Nationale 19, 52330 Colombey-les-Deux-Églises. This photo was not requested in the WAC records for the episode or season, and there is no indication where it may have come from.

picketing with slogans — ("Tory Housewives Clean-Up Campaign") *"Fair Pay"*—In the mid-1960s the Seamen's Union struck for pay increases, less hours, and a "fair deal"; teachers at Durham School went out over wage stagnation and a demand for smaller class sizes; in 1970–1971 it was nurses, postal workers, British European Airways employees, and even farmers demanding higher subsidized agriculture prices. During this period strike actions (whether official strikes or just work-to-rule actions, wildcatting, demonstrations, etc.) kept either party from claiming big gains in employment and monetary policies—there were just too many labor fires to put out.

"Less Profits"—There have been demands for curtailed (or just better shared) profits from industry since the earliest days of the Industrial Revolution. Many strike placards in the 1955–1975 period ask for a more fair division of the corporate spoils.

"Parity"—This variably meant prices set at reasonable levels, and job pay also fine-tuned for comparability between regions, trades, etc. One political cartoon of the period (depicting Dagenham Ford strikers in 1971) offers workers opining for parity—as a result of their next big strike—with entertainer Tom Jones (Eps. 24, 30). This cartoon is from Bernard Cookson, and originally appeared in the *Evening News* (2 Feb. 1971). See the British Cartoon Archive.

"No Victimization"—Referring to the worker as the scrap of food between hungry dogs. As early as 1955 British newspaper cartoonists like Michael Cummings were depicting big labor *and* big government as well-dressed bullies with equally menacing clubs (*Daily Express*, 25 Nov. 1955). See the British Cartoon Archive.

Certainly the biggest concerns during this period leading up to Britain's entry in the Common Market were the great unknowns about the pending too-close-for-comfort relationship with the historically untrustworthy Continental. In a 5 July 1971 article in *Time*, the London correspondent summarized the common fears:

> The average Briton is still afraid of the EEC's high food prices and fearful of losing British sovereignty to the Brussels-based Eurocracy. Britain's most powerful trade union leaders are dead set against the EEC. The pressures already are so great that the Labor Party may soon be forced to take an anti-Market position.

pictures and statues — (PSC; Tory Housewives Clean-Up Campaign") Referring to the presence of exploitative sex and sexuality on TV, Whitehouse is quoted

as saying, "I object to having strange male nudes in my living room." The Pythons here have merely extended this objection to male nudes in art galleries and museums. Chapman plays just such a strange male nude in Ep. 17, where he is being interviewed by Derek Hart (Cleese) and blasting the slumping morals of television.

"plastic arts" — ("Tory Housewives Clean-Up Campaign") Art that involves a medium that can be physically molded, shaped, formed, etc., like sculpture and painting.

"POLITICIANS . . . PROGRAMME" — ("Apology [Politicians]") The continuing unfavorable opinion of Ministers of Parliament and the Government (and Shadow Government) in general is also a carryover from other comedy/satire shows like *The Goon Show* (1951–1960) and *Beyond the Fringe* (1961). In the first instance, a Minister without Fixed Address (played by Harry Secombe) often wanders about getting into mischief, and in the latter, there are scathing impersonations of Harold Macmillan, the then sitting Prime Minister, as well as Cabinet members bumbling through a nuclear deterrent lecture, and instead of convincing a Russian to praise Macmillan, the man raspberries instead. The questionable antics and ethics of government men like Reginald Maudling, Alec Douglas-Home, and Peter Walker (all mentioned or referenced earlier in Ep. 30), among others, probably increase the ferocity of this roller caption.

The music heard underneath the apology roller is Elgar's "Pomp and Circumstance" played by the London Symphony Orchestra, the use of which led to a bit of a punch-up. The trust that controls Elgar's music complained that "P&C" had been used illegally, in a slanderous way, and asked for damages. The BBC legal department countered that since the music had been used straight and without editing or manipulation, that it was in no way defaming Elgar or the music, and told the trust to shove off, essentially (WAC T12/1,446).

"Porky" — ("Tuesday Documentary/Children's Story/Party Political Broadcast") A reference to the Warner Bros. cartoon character Porky Pig, but the story being told sounds more like Disney's 1933 cartoon *The Three Little Pigs*, which would also be satirized a decade later by Tex Avery in the MGM cartoon *Blitz Wolf* (1942). The cartoony violence employed by the Pythons indicates a significant cartoon influence on the troupe.

Idle, Jones, and Palin had all written for and acted in the children's show *Do Not Adjust Your Set* (ITV, 1967), just prior to coming together to form Monty Python.

P.P. — (PSC; "Tory Housewives Clean-Up Campaign") "Pepper Pot." The image here is, of course, meant to be reminiscent of other fascist groups (Hitler's SS troops, Mussolini's Black Shirts, even Britain's own British Union of Fascists) wearing identifying armbands.

• R •

rating — (PSC; "Expedition to Lake Pahoe") The script identifies the man about to eat the leg as a "rating," which is a naval term for an enlisted man. It is normally confined to plural usage (*OED*).

"Rattigan, Terence" — ("The Minister for Not Listening to People") The previous-generation playwright already mentioned in Eps. 1 and 30, Rattigan (1911–1977) wrote serious, dramatic plays like *The Winslow Boy* (1946) and *The Browning Version* (1948), though his plays would fall out of favor when the Angry Young Men types stormed the scene in the late 1950s. Rattigan became a target of more progressive elements and was labeled an outdated Conservative trapped in an imagined past, which may account for his several appearances in *Flying Circus* (see especially Ep. 30, "*The Pantomime Horse Is a Secret Agent* Film" sketch).

Red Devils — (PSC; "Tory Housewives Clean-Up Campaign") A memorial mistake (but see below for more on that). The Red Devils were an Army aerial acrobatic team, by this time performing organized *parachute* jumps at air shows around the UK. (John Bilsborough wrote a poem titled "Albert and the Red Devils" in 1971 about the team, featuring his recurring character Albert Ramsbottom.)

The planes shown in this clip are actually Korean War–era jets (perhaps American F-86A-5 Sabres, FJ-4 Furies, or even British Lightnings) flying in formation. This footage may be an example of the proper or needed photo/film clip not being located in time for the show, and the show going on anyway.

What the Pythons intended to include here was not "Red Devils" but "Red Arrows," the Royal Air Force's aerobatic team—they didn't jump out of their planes, opting for close formational flying. The footage reference number is "BBC News Southampton 458" (WAC T12/1,446).

"Regent Street" — (PSC; "Tuesday Documentary/ Children's Story/Party Political Broadcast") Major shopping street and thoroughfare in London's West End, connecting into Piccadilly Circus. The area is a magnet for visitors during the Christmas season. The stock film footage is from the BBC vaults, and is called "Christmas Lights" (74630) (WAC T12/1,446).

Religion Today — ("Tuesday Documentary/Children's Story/Party Political Broadcast") Significant religious programming has been and continues to be available on the BBC radio and TV outlets, including the BBC's *Songs of Praise* (1961–), and myriad discussion-type shows.

Robinson, Robert — (PSC; "Tory Housewives Clean-Up Campaign") This is one of those moments in *FC* where the viewer (especially today's viewer) would be hard-pressed to identify the humor or topicality behind the photo reference. A writer and presenter, Robinson (1927–2011) is perhaps best remembered for the satirical show *BBC-3* (BBC, 1965–1966), and for enduring the use of the "f-word" on this same show by author/critic Kenneth Tynan (broadcast November 1965), the first time that word had been uttered on British television. Robinson and the show immediately became targets of Mary Whitehouse and her organization. See bbc.co.uk/comedy for more on the show and controversy.

"Robson, particularly, in goal" — ("The Silliest Sketch We've Ever Done") Probably a nod to Bryan "Pop" Robson (b. 1945), who in 1971 had signed what was then an enormous contract to play for West Ham. Robson had earlier played for Newcastle United.

"Russell, Jane" — ("Expedition to Lake Pahoe") Hollywood film actress famed for her voluptuousness, Russell (1921–2011) appeared in Howard Hughes's racy Western *The Outlaw* (1943) and *Gentlemen Prefer Blondes* (1953). The latter film is mentioned in Ep. 15, in a smoke signal version.

Later in her life (primarily after her movie career) Russell appeared in Playtex bra commercials, while fellow pin-up Grable (see above) appeared in girdle ads for the same company. By the early 1970s these former starlets were perhaps all better known for their small-screen work (TV ads and guest appearances), and only vaguely remembered for their luminous movie careers.

• S •

"selling them again" — ("The Minister for Not Listening to People") There was a very active black market both during the war and afterward, through the years of rationing, when shortages of essentials were rampant, and ration books necessary until 1954.

"Shadow Minister" — ("The Minister for Not Listening to People") A minister representing the political party not currently in power. During this period (1970–1974), Labour would have provided the shadow government. Typical (and actual) Shadow Ministerial titles include Shadow Minister for Northern Ireland, Shadow Minister for Social Security, and Shadow Minister for Defence, Foreign and Commonwealth Affairs.

"Shiver me timbers" — ("Expedition to Lake Pahoe") This phrase is borrowed from Robert Louis Stevenson's famous pirate in the book *Treasure Island*. See the entry for "black spot" above for more.

short sequence of footballers in slow-motion kissing — (link into "Apology [Politicians]") This sequence has earlier appeared in the *Euroshow 71—May Day Special* produced by the Pythons for continental television. Also included in that short episode were "All-In Cricket," "Fish Slapping Dance," and one of the "Batley Townswomen's Guild" performances, along with some new material filmed in the smaller villages of Bray, Holyport, and Littlewick Green, and also back in Ealing. The romantic music here is from the well-known Mantovani Orchestra playing "Charmaine," by Rapee and Pollack (WAC T12/1,466).

"sneaky second channel" — ("Tory Housewives Clean-Up Campaign") BBC2, brought on-line in 1964, went to full color in 1967. BBC2 broadcast more serious and challenging fare from the beginning, and has been a proving ground for new shows before they migrate to BBC1. The more frank depictions of sexuality and violence upset Whitehouse's group from the channel's inception, and, ironically, the first show to be broadcast by BBC2 was the children's program *Playschool* (1964–1988).

The men in control of BBC2 during this period—and who would have been on the receiving end of the NVLA and Clean Up TV campaign attentions—were: Michael Peacock (1964–1965); David Attenborough (1965–1969); and Robin Scott (1969–1974).

"spotty continental boys" — ("Tory Housewives Clean-Up Campaign") Referring to the fact that a number of very young and even pimply "agitators" plaguing various sitting governments in the UK had actually been foreign nationals, including Daniel Cohn-Bendit (b. 1945), a French-born German-Jew and student in France at the University of Nanterre. Cohn-Bendit, 23, had almost single-handedly organized the student revolts that would eventually ripple across France, creating a general strike that nearly toppled the de Gaulle government. After being expelled from France in late May 1968, Cohn-Bendit came to Great Britain on 11 June 1968 on a twenty-four-hour visa, and ended up staying a fortnight. He arranged and led a sit-in at the BBC's Television Centre in Wood Lane, and visited Karl Marx's grave. He would later become a German citizen. See news.bbc.co.uk.

"stirring music" — ("Gumby Brain Specialist") The music being played underneath is "Main Titles and Openers: Wide Screen Title" by Jack Shaindlin (WAC T12/1,446).

"sub-aqua head" — ("Expedition to Lake Pahoe") Following the mass production of scuba gear (co-created by Jacques Cousteau [Ep. 30]), "sub-aqua clubs"—essentially, diving clubs—began to appear throughout the UK in the early 1960s.

• **T** •

"tatty, scrofulous old rapist" — ("Molluscs—'Live' TV Documentary") The lamellibranch (scallop) is characterized as scruffy ("tatty") and morally corrupt ("scrofulous")—scallop are hermaphroditic, which may account for the species' "depravity" as described by Zorba (Cleese). The term and characterization "rapist" is used twice by the Pythons—once in this episode, and once in *FZ* where the joke is stretched into a sketch—indicating that the sensitivity and public reaction surrounding the term was either diminished or just ignored during this period. There are no mentions of public or in-house reaction to the term's usage, for example, in WAC records. This kind of "insensitive" humor (racial epithets, sexist language and depictions), then, can be helpful as this period is studied, hinting at cultural biases, perceptions, allowances, etc.

"firm-breasted Rabelaisian"—Like author O'Brien mentioned earlier, François Rabelais (1494–1553) also had most of his books banned, though in France, but also because of the books' licentious, satiric treatment of monasticism.

"Fanny Hill"—Title character in John Cleland's scandalous 1749 novel, Fanny becomes a prostitute, a mistress, and just plain sexually active to survive in a man's world. The book was eventually banned in the UK and United States alike.

"like a dead Pope"—This comparison may also be two-edged, as there were a number of popes who behaved in questionable ways, including offering sinecures, soliciting murder, currying political favor, and engaging in bacchanalian sexual depravity—their dissolute lives might have shamed someone like Fanny Hill, actually. Also, in the "Cadaver Synod" (897 AD), nine-months-dead Pope Formosus was exhumed, put on trial, found guilty, his corpse desecrated and dumped into the Tiber. His dead body was then rumored to have performed miracles. Thus, a dead Pope could have been surprisingly active and vital, not unlike Fanny herself.

"whelk"—Another gastropod whose only fault might be its carnivorousness, the characters here crush it because of its alleged homosexuality. In Ep. 33 Algy (Palin) will be killed when he boldly admits his same-sex attraction. Again, the insensitive humor (killing women or homosexuals simply because they are female or homosexual) wasn't insensitive for the period, the genre, the medium, or there might have been more of a recorded reaction.

The words are quite large and easily readable . . . — (PSC; "Apology [Politicians]") One of the few very obvious directorial/technical elements included in the scripts, this command is obviously intended for whomever will be physically turning the roller caption machine (still cranked by hand during this period).

"Timothy Whites" — ("The Minister for Not Listening to People") A chain chemist's shop found in Midland-area towns like Preston (Lancashire), Seaham (Durham), and Bromsgrove (Worcestershire). Timothy Whites is also mentioned by the ranting Tourist (Idle) in Ep. 31 (see notes). This particular chain store seems to have found its way into the hearts and memories of many in the Midlands; this is obviously the name of the chemist that most of the Pythons grew up with, as "Timothy Whites" is mentioned at least twice in *FC*, and Boots the Chemist isn't mentioned at all.

Today in Parliament — ("Tuesday Documentary/ Children's Story/Party Political Broadcast") Radio 4 has produced this show since 1945, offering insights on the comings and goings in Britain's legislative bodies.

"Tory Tours" — (PSC; "Tory Housewives Clean-Up Campaign") The Conservative Party has carried the nickname "Tory" since c. 1830, when "Conservative" became the name of choice. "Tory" had been in use since about 1689 to refer to royalists. The term can be used both affectionately and in a more derogatory manner, depending on the user.

"Trade Practices Bill" — ("The Minister for Not Listening to People") Standard bit of legislation before Parliament in the area of international trade. There would be a significant Restrictive Trade Practices Act drafted in 1976, following others in 1974, and a Trade Descriptions Act 1968 which made it "an offence for a trader to apply, by any means, false or misleading statements, or to knowingly or recklessly make such statements about services." Similar bills and acts can be found making their way through former Commonwealth members India and Australia during this same period.

"Tuesday Documentary" — ("Tuesday Documentary/ Children's Story/Party Political Broadcast") A BBC weekly TV show, featuring titles like "Christians at War," "The Price of Violence," and "Last Night An-other Soldier," all about the continuing slaughter in Northern Ireland. These episodes were broadcast 5 October 1971, 14 November 1972, and 4 December 1973. *Tuesday's Documentary* is featured on a late 1969 cover of the BBC's *Radio Times*.

"two-up, two-down house" — ("Tuesday Documentary/Children's Story/Party Political Broadcast") More likely this is describing what the ordinary English worker lives in, a terrace house set in rows of other terrace houses. Enormous, soulless housing blocks were actually being built around Paris (Sarcelles) after the war to deal with the population boom, and the burgeoning migration to the capital.

· U ·

undercrank — (PSC; "Tory Housewives Clean-Up Campaign") The film camera would be "cranked" (actually run by an electric motor) slower than twenty-four frames per second, meaning the projected image would appear to move faster than usual.

· V ·

V-sign — (PSC; "Expedition to Lake Pahoe") The "palm-back V-sign" offered by the woman (Jones) is an insult meaning "up yours," and has been used in the UK for generations.

· W ·

"war against pornography" — ("Tory Housewives Clean-Up Campaign") Drawing parallels between the militant campaign of NVLA and the armed, fascistic military campaigns being waged around the world at that time, probably including at least the Israel-Egypt Six Days War (1967), Vietnam, and the still-stinging Suez Crisis (1956), where British gunboat diplomacy was effectively humbled, and her second-tier world power status was confirmed (*Eyewitness: 1950–59*, "Aftermath of Suez").

"weetabix" — ("Expedition to Lake Pahoe") UK cereal company founded in 1932.

Whitehouse, Mary — (PSC; "Tory Housewives Clean-Up Campaign") A strident defender of public morality, Whitehouse (1910–2001) was the founder and president of the National Viewers and Listeners Association (NVLA), a public television and radio morals watchdog group. The first public meeting she addressed took place in Birmingham, coincidentally, and her target was the "permissive" BBC and its director Sir Hugh Greene. It's been reported that thirty-seven coachloads of supporters accompanied her. Whitehouse (a native of Wolverhampton, like Idle) would later lock horns with the Pythons over the "blasphemous" film *Life of Brian* (1979).

"windmills" — ("Tory Housewives Clean-Up Campaign") A reference to the character Don Quixote de La Mancha from Cervantes's novel *Don Quixote* (1605, 1615), and fairly typical of the kind of pop-allusive language used in these newsreels. It also indicates that these ultra-conservative crusaders aren't in their right minds, at least to the Pythons.

• Y •

"young people" — ("Tory Housewives Clean-Up Campaign") In Ep. 31, the Tourist alluded to General Franco's mistrust and mistreatment of young people in postwar Spain, and that theme is carried over here, to Whitehouse and her Clean Up TV campaign. One of the well-known posters created during the May 1968 student demonstrations in France depicted a young person with his mouth being covered by a sinister adult (a silhouette of de Gaulle) from behind, and the caption: "Sois Jeune et Tais Toi" ("Be Young and Shut Up").

• Z •

Zorba — (PSC; "Molluscs—'Live' TV Documentary") Probably drawn from Anthony Quinn's memorable depiction of Zorba in *Zorba the Greek* (1964). The presenter's name is never spoken, so this is yet another moment lost on the viewer, but available to the reader.

Episode 33: *"Salad Days"*

The Adventures of Biggles: "Part 1, Biggles dictates a letter"; *Animation: The domino effect*; **Climbing the north face of the Uxbridge Road**; New Haven Lifeboat: "It's not a lifeboat, it's this lady's house"; Old lady snoopers; "Morning teas" on the lifeboat; *Storage Jars*; *Animation: TV is bad for your eyes, and Program Control fairy*; "The show so far"; **Cheese Shop**; *Rogue Cheddar* (1967); Philip Jenkinson on Cheese Westerns; Sam Peckinpah's *Salad Days*; Closing credits over Philip Jenkinson's murder; BBC apology; BBC denies the apology; "The News with Richard Baker"; Seashore interlude film

• A •

. . . a very noisy and violent animation sketch — (link out of *Biggles*: "*Animation: The Domino Effect*") The first identifiable background in this sequence can be seen when the Sopwith Camel hits the top of an obelisk, knocking off an orb decoration. This background is another image from Giuseppe Galli Bibiena's *Architectural and Perspective Designs*, this one Part V, Plate 7. Gilliam has used Bibiena's work before, in animations for Eps. 2, 14, and 19.

Gilliam has adapted the original work for his animation purposes. First, he has cropped the image from the left, right, and bottom, removing all tiles and stairs, and leaving just the colonnade that had jutted past the center of the original work. Second, he reduced the length of that colonnade and pulled in the background buildings and the left obelisk into the center of the new rendering. The purpose was to leave room above for the plane and its action. There is no orb at the top of the obelisk in the original rendering.

The following image is a seesaw setting, mostly original, followed by a Union mortar battery. This 1864 image (also from *DWF*, page 371) was originally part of a stereographic pair (like many of these Civil War photos). Gilliam cut out everything in this original photo except two men and the cannon, including eight other men, a stack of ammunition, the mortar

platform, and the Petersburg countryside. The mortar ball knocks Harold the Flying Sheep (Ep. 2) out of the skies, and the audience gives a hoot of recognition.

Another following sequence features a row of houses that gets knocked over, domino-style, by a car. The photo looks like it was taken in the neighborhoods around the Fulham FC stadium and Stevenage Road, where portions of Ep. 10 were shot. This is followed by the last shot, the toppling of rather famous buildings, including St. Martin-in-the-Fields, Her Majesty's Theatre, St. Paul's, the recognizable onion-domed Brighton (Royal) Pavilion, et al.

"accoutrements" — ("Climbing the North Face of the Uxbridge Road") All necessary components for rock climbing during this period, and many would have been carried by the intrepid hairdressers climbing Everest in the previous episode. "Carabino" is actually "carabiner" (or even "karabiner"), and is a device for connecting looped ends of ropes or for hooking onto a piton, which is a spike driven into a rock fissure.

"Algy" — ("Biggles Dictates a Letter") Algernon Montgomery Lacey, Biggles's close friend in the W.E. Johns's adventures. See entries below for "Biggles" and "Johns" for more.

Animation: television is bad for your eyes — (animated link into "The Show So Far") The music used under this link is from the International Studio Orchestra, "Sea Music," "Ripcord" by Julius Steffaro (WAC T12/1,444).

"Ark Royal" — ("Lifeboat") The only really modern aircraft carrier in the Royal Navy at the outbreak of WWII, *Ark Royal* was in service 1938–1941, when she took a U-boat torpedo hit and sank off Gibraltar (see Colledge). The film stock used in this sequence is "*Ark Royal NP78078*" (WAC T12/1,444).

• B •

"bad for your eyes" — ("Bad for Your Eyes" animation) During this animation sequence, a fairy godfather figure appears, claiming to be from "Program Control." The face Gilliam used here is of Paul Fox, BBC Controller, a man the Pythons crossed swords with more than once in regard to regional time slots and repeat airings for the episodes. Duncan Wood (Head of BBC Comedy through the third season) had asked in a September 1972 memo (somewhat rhetorically) whether it wasn't time to put away the Paul Fox bashing in the animations, seeing it by the third season as a kind of reflexive "joke gone too long" (WAC T12/1,428). (The editors of *Private Eye* also lament Fox's continuing presence at the BBC [18 Dec. 1970, 5].)

In Ep. 28, the naughty book Mr. Norris (Palin) is reading, *The Lady with the Naked Skin*, is authored by "Paul Fox Jr."

"BBC cameras" — ("Climbing the North Face of the Uxbridge Road") In 1966, the BBC did cover an assault on the Old Man of Hoy, giving over much of the broadcast day to the climb, and popularizing both the sport of climbing and the climbing of the various "stacks" in Scotland. Another similar BBC broadcast followed in 1967.

"Biggles" — ("Biggles Dictates a Letter") Actually James Bigglesworth, he was a character created by author W.E. Johns (see below) in 1934 for the long-running series of flying adventures books. Palin admits to reading the books as a youngster, fascinated by the books' exotic foreign settings (McCabe).

"Biggles Flies Undone" — ("Biggles Dictates a Letter") A play on actual Biggles titles such as *Biggles Flies Again*, *Biggles Flies East*, etc.

"Biggles, Mary" — ("Biggles Dictates a Letter") Biggles did fall in love with Marie Janis in the story "Affair De Coeur" in *The Camels Are Coming* (1932), a romance retold in the later book *Biggles Looks Back* (1965).

"bouzouki" — ("Cheese Shop") A Greek mandolin instrument, the bouzouki is being played by Alan

Parker, who has continued to play bouzouki (and Oud) gigs to this writing. The song is "Grecian Nights" (WAC T12/1,444).

Buckets of blood burst . . . — (PSC; "Sam Peckinpah's *Salad Days*") The blood flows generously in this sequence, of course, as has been specifically requested by director Ian MacNaughton. In a note to the production design team, MacNaughton emphasizes that the vast quantities of blood "cannot be overdone" (WAC T12/1,445).

• C •

Capote, Truman — ("Philip Jenkinson on Cheese Westerns") Mercurial, eccentric novelist (*In Cold Blood*), Capote (1924–1984) was also flamboyantly, even stereotypically gay. His birth name was Truman Streckfus Persons. During this period (1971–1972), Capote was serializing portions of a forthcoming novel, *Answered Prayers*, in *Esquire* magazine, angering and alienating his socialite friends by outing their lavish and debauched lifestyles.

"Cheese Westerns" — ("Philip Jenkinson on Cheese Westerns") There were straight-ahead Hollywood Westerns like *Shane* (George Stevens, 1950), and *My Darling Clementine* (John Ford, 1946), noodle Westerns including Akira Kurosawa's *Yojimbo* (1961) and *Sanjuro* (1962), and even spaghetti Westerns—Sergio Leone's memorable *A Fistful of Dollars* (1964), *For a Few Dollars More* (1965), and *The Good, the Bad, and the Ugly* (1966).

"courtesan" — ("Biggles Dictates a Letter") Not in the original sense of the word, she's not. "Courtesan" actually means a lady of the court. Here it is clearly used to mean a prostitute.

"Crippen" — ("Climbing the North Face of the Uxbridge Road") "Doctor" Peter Hawley Harvey Crippen (1862–1910)—of 39 Hilldrop Crescent, Camden Town, London—killed his wife, Belle Elmore, in 1910, dismembering and burying her beneath the house, and then took his secretary and tried to escape to America. Crippen would be caught by use of Marconi wireless telegraph as he and his secretary (disguised as a boy) sailed across the Atlantic. He was found guilty and hanged in 1910. Crippen was the subject of a 1962 film called *Dr. Crippen*, starring Donald Pleasance in the title role. Finally, Crippen is also mentioned by the Goons in the "Lurgi" episode.

The mention of this name and the following lines are stumbled over badly in the film (significant traffic noise and ambient sound), and the audience probably misses the historical allusion, as there is little or no reaction.

Cut to the deck of a lifeboat — (PSC; "Lifeboat") The structure here has acquired a sort of stream-of-consciousness, with the dream state (the illusion earlier of a lifeboat deck) becoming reality as Mrs. Neves (Jones) exits her home to the deck of that same lifeboat. The illusion was originally denied by Neves, as she claimed there was no lifeboat "out there," but then confirmed as she entered that world, seemingly without noticing any disruption. This reality will continue until a new one replaces it.

The "Elizabethan Pornography Smugglers" sketch (Ep. 36) will follow a similar progression, crossing between real and imagined worlds and across time, in that case, until a sort of revolving-door-ever-present is possible. Several of the sketches in the latter season attempt these more sophisticated structures, playing with time and space, and move away (at least temporarily) from the gag-laden bits.

• D •

"do you have any cheese at all?" — ("Cheese Shop") Coincidentally, cheese was something of a headline item at this time. After Britain had managed to finagle the necessary votes to gain entry into the European Common Market (yes, after de Gaulle was out of the way), an unforeseen hurdle presented itself. According to a *Time* magazine report from 5 April 1971, the whole deal was about to go sour because Commonwealth member New Zealand demanded guarantees that its dairy farmers could continue to sell the bulk of their cheese (and butter) to the UK, by far their biggest market. Other European countries with dairy interests complained that protectionism was just what the Common Market was trying to overcome (with the French saying "sink or swim" to the New Zealand proposal), and it took an eleventh-hour deal to keep both the negotiations and the cheese flowing ("Common Market: Breaking Out the Bubbly," *Time*, 5 July 1971; and "French Attitude Becomes More Relaxed," *Times*, 12 May 1971: 6).

• E •

"Ee I were all hungry like" — ("Cheese Shop") Communication difficulties, again, but this time based on class, upbringing, and regionalization. An elementary school teacher in an urban Lancashire classroom (c. 1905) noted that since children had no access to a cultural clearinghouse like BBC radio, meaning no real aural or verbal contact with the rest of England, they had no idea anyone spoke any differently than they did. The teacher describes having to consciously switch from her London-based English to a broad Lancashire accent in order to be understood on even the simplest terms, a process that steepened the learning curve significantly, and set these children well behind others (*Eyewitness 1900–09*, "Education in a Slum School").

"eels" — ("Biggles Dictates a Letter") Eels have been a part of many Englanders' cuisine for generations; jellied eels can still be bought from street vendors in East London.

Episode 33 — Recorded 7 January 1972, and broadcast 30 November 1972. This episode was recorded fourth and broadcast seventh.

In-studio taping was performed on 7 January 1972 at TC6, and the following guests and extras were called in: Richard Baker (*News at Ten*), Nicki Howorth (*Not Tonight Darling*), and Alan Parker (musician); extras included: Clinton Morris (*Z Cars*), Steve Ismay (*Softly Softly*), Roy Pearce (Ep. 29; *Doctor Who*), Ron Tingley (Ep. 29; *Doctor Who*; *Z Cars*), Ken Halliwell (*Z Cars*), Terry Sartain (Ep. 28; *Doctor Who*), and David Waterman (*Doctor Who*).

On film for this episode: Pippa Hardman, Marion Park, Beulah Hughes, David Wilde, Richard de Meath, Jean Clarke, Elaine Carr (*Fashion Time*), Francis Pidgeon, Alan Hutchinson, and Richard Baker (WAC T12/1,444).

"explosion . . . Lords" — ("The News with Richard Baker") By this time, there had been more than 100 explosions of various devices planted by various factions in the fight for control of Northern Ireland. A bomb planted in the Post Office tower in London was detonated in 1971, with no injuries. The early 1970s saw elements of the IRA taking its fight for independence out of Northern Ireland and into the streets of London, especially with bombs and mortar attacks.

Much earlier, the Gunpowder Plot of 1605 was an attempt to blow up the Houses of Parliament, kill James I, and bring Catholicism back to England, all in one fell swoop. The plot was discovered, the gunpowder removed, and the conspirators tortured and executed (*ODNB*).

• F •

First World War fighter planes in a dog-fight — (PSC; "Biggles Dictates a Letter") The film footage here is "Dog Fight" VisNews 2266 (WAC T12/1,444). The "[h]eroic war music" is from the Royal Liverpool Philharmonic Orchestra, and is William Walton's "Spitfire Prelude & Fugue" (WAC T12/1,444).

• G •

"Ginger" — ("Biggles Dictates a Letter") The third member of the comrades-in-arms group in the Biggles books, Algy and Biggles meet Ginger after the war and eventually form an air transport company. There is no indication that any of the three were homosexual, at least in Johns's characterizations. Here the Pythons have taken homosociality and elevated it to homosexuality, simply because it's funnier.

"Greek rebel leader" — ("Storage Jars") Greece had, in fact, undergone significant political turmoil and change in recent months and years. A military junta had seized power from the monarchy in April 1967, and King Constantine II was forced into exile. The military leader who took control was Colonel George Papadopoulos, who would eventually try to legitimize and even soften his rule by surrendering his military post to become Prime Minister, then president. Unsuccessfully trying to quash cultural embellishments like long haircuts and miniskirts, Papadopoulos would be ousted in a coup just a year after this episode was broadcast (November 1973). See Papadopoulos's obituary in the *London Times* (July 1999), and the article "The Poly-Papadopoulos" in *Time* (3 Apr. 1972).

guerrilla leader . . . gun — (PSC; "Storage Jars") This is a still frame (or, more likely, a publicity still) of Warren Beatty as Clyde Barrow from the Warner Bros' 1967 film *Bonnie and Clyde*. This is the kind of "new Hollywood" film of the late 1960s and early 1970s—darker, edgier, bloodier, more sexualized—that the Pythons spoof in the *"Salad Days"* sketch, as well as when Jenkinson (Idle) is gleefully shot later in this same episode. The bullet-riddled and slow motion "death" sequence in *Bonnie and Clyde* had already caused an uproar, and been copied and recopied by lesser filmmakers.

"Gunfight at Gruyère Corral" — ("Philip Jenkinson on Cheese Westerns") A play on the Western film title *Gunfight at the O.K. Corral* (1957), directed by Preston Sturges and starring Burt Lancaster and Kirk Douglas. Gruyère is a salty cheese from Switzerland.

"Ilchester '73"—A play on the western film title *Winchester '73* (1950), directed by Tony Mann and starring Jimmy Stewart. The Ilchester Cheese Company creates cheeses blended with beer and spices.

"The Cheese Who Shot Liberty Valance"—A play on the film title *The Man Who Shot Liberty Valance* (1962), directed by John Ford and starring Jimmy Stewart and John Wayne.

It's not surprising that so many Hollywood genre films of the 1940s and 1950s (Hollywood's "Golden Age") are mentioned in *FC*. During the war years, film imports fell off dramatically in the UK and across Europe. It wasn't until 1946 that the flood of backlogged Hollywood films could burst into European theaters, providing comedies, Westerns, historical epics, gangster pictures, musicals, and love stories for a war-weary audience. The young men who would become the leaders of the French New Wave, for example, watched all these films one on top of another—cinephiles in the UK would have done much the same.

"guttering" — ("Climbing the North Face of the Uxbridge Road") A play on some of the standard but perhaps unfamiliar rock climbing jargon that would have been part of the 1966–1967 BBC broadcasts of the Hoy assault. This refers to terms like "barn-dooring" (swinging out from the rock like a barn door), "edging" (moving along a narrow edge) and "scumming" (a crack-climbing technique).

• H •

"Haakon" — ("Biggles Dictates a Letter") King Haakon is earlier mentioned in Ep. 30 as producer (with Sir Alec Douglas-Home) of the film *The Pantomime Horse Is a Secret Agent*. It's curious again to have mentioned Haakon here, as he had died in 1957. See notes to Ep. 30 for more. Haakon's last state visit to the UK took place in 1951, followed by a state visit from Queen Elizabeth to Norway in 1955.

"hardship . . . glove" — ("Climbing the North Face of the Uxbridge Road") This may be based on the posttrek accounts of these types of adventurers, who would give interviews and write books and articles about the reasons behind the climb, the journey, the sacrifice, etc. Sir Edmund Hillary's book was *High Adventure* in 1955, and Thor Heyerdahl's were *Kon-Tiki* (1950), and *The Ra Expeditions* (1971). (See notes to Ep. 28 for more on both Hillary and Heyerdahl.) The publication of all three followed close on the heels of the actual events depicted.

This sketch may also have been influenced by the appearance in 1971 of a popular and very serious climbing book, *The Black Cliff: Clogwyn du'r Arddu* by Crew, Soper, and Wilson.

"HMS Defiant" — ("Lifeboat") Not an active or even recently active royal naval vessel. *HMS Defiant* is the title of the 1962 film starring Alec Guinness and Dirk Bogarde, and is set during the Napoleonic wars. Bogarde was mentioned earlier for his virtuoso performances for director Luchino Visconti, including his swan song in *Death in Venice* (Ep. 29). *Defiant* is also the name of a wooden sailing ship converted to a Royal Navy torpedo training vessel in about 1899.

"HMS Eagle" — ("Lifeboat") *Eagle* was commissioned in October 1951, and was part of the Audacious-class of carriers. *Eagle* was decommissioned as part of the Royal Navy downsizing in 1972—just when this episode was being written, recorded, and broadcast—and ultimately scrapped in 1978.

Howorth, Nicki — ("Biggles Dictates a Letter") A model and actress, Howorth appeared in *Not Tonight Darling* (1971) and *Are You Being Served* (1977), as well as appearing in the erotic Pirelli calendar in 1973. She is one of the few actual females to appear on *FC* in a significant speaking role, along with Carol Cleveland, Connie Booth, Marjorie Wilde, Rita Davies, and Julia Breck.

• J •

Jenkinson, Philip — ("Philip Jenkinson on Cheese Westerns") Jenkinson was a writer for the TV series *Horne A'Plenty* and *Marty*, both in 1968, and would later appear on *Rutland Weekend Television* (1975). Jenkinson also interviewed Alfred Hitchcock for the BBC in 1966. In 1971–1972 Jenkinson was hosting *Film Night*, as well as working behind the scenes on Ken Russell's (Ep. 28) film *The Boy Friend*. See the BFI website for a more complete list of Jenkinson's credits.

The Pythons would access various stock film footage titles from what appears to be Jenkinson's collection throughout the run of *Flying Circus*. See the entry for "pederast vole" below for more.

"Johns, Captain W.E." — ("Biggles Dictates a Letter") Johns (1893–1968) wrote almost 100 Biggles books between 1932 and 1970 (the character being created for an earlier *Popular Flying* magazine), himself a veteran of the Gallipoli, Suez, and Salonika campaigns, and he later joined the Royal Air Force. (See *ODNB* for more on Johns.)

"Julian Slade's *Salad Days*" — ("Philip Jenkinson on Cheese Westerns") Born Julian Penkivil Slade (1930–2006; Eton and Trinity College), Julian Slade was a musical writer of some accomplishment, and began composing musicals and incidental music for productions at Cambridge.

Salad Days is a Slade musical that premiered at the Bristol Old Vic (Ep. 2) in 1954, then moved to the Vaudeville Theatre in London on 5 August of that year. It ran for more than 2,280 performances. *Salad Days* is mentioned here because of what it was not—a messy, contemptible, violent bloodbath of a production. It was instead a breezy, "whimsical" musical, seen by many as just the type of British musical that might nudge

the popular American musicals off of British West End stages ("Julian Slade Obituary").

• K •

"Kup Kakes" — ("Lifeboat") This was a trademark brand name from the J. Lyons company (est. 1887), a baking interest in Hammersmith, London. Lyons catered events at Buckingham Palace, Windsor Castle, London's Guildhall, Wimbledon, etc. By 1972, Lyons was stretching across the globe with packing plants, frozen food plants, even hotel chains. The difficult 1970s (oil shortages, recession) would hit Lyons hard, according to Peter Bird, as Lyons was heavily overextended just when interest rates skyrocketed worldwide. Easy to see how the Pythons could put a Lyons-type shop on a lifeboat, then, given Lyons's ubiquitousness during this period.

There was a Lyons Teashop at 54 Uxbridge Road during this period, just down the street and around the corner from Television Centre.

• L •

lifeboatmen — ("Lifeboat") The men who eventually fill Mrs. Neves's (Jones) kitchen include Clinton Morris (*Z Cars*), Steve Ismay (*Softly Softly*), Roy Pearce (*Doctor Who*), Terry Sartain (*Emma*), Ron Tingley (*Play for Today*; *Z Cars*), David Waterman (*Doctor Who*), Ken Halliwell (*Play for Today*; *Z Cars*) (WAC T12/1,444).

"loopy brothel inmate" — ("Biggles Dictates a Letter") What follows is a now-typical Python trope of listing, and in this case the use of metaphoric or poetic terminology for a sexual object. Miss Bladder (Nicki Howorth) is a "loopy brothel inmate," "not a courtesan"; she is a harlot, "paramour, concubine, *fille de joie*," and a "bit of tail." But rather than be one-sided about this stereotypical name-calling, the Pythons turn the tables on the "men" in the conversation. Miss Bladder is allowed to interject and then go on the offensive, calling Biggles a "demented fictional character," then Algy a "fairy," a "poof," and finally a "mincing old RAF queen." All of these later appellations, in the world of the sketch, turn out to be accurate, by the way, giving the narrative power to Miss Bladder—a true female, purposely and actually attractive—which is unusual for the Pythons. Even more unusually, she is not punished, textually, for her cheek.

The allusive language continues, with terms like "old fruit," "ginger beer" (rhymes with "queer," see note below), a "terrible poof," and finally Biggles's celebration of England's regained masculinity in his sort of "John of Gaunt" speech (see "salt of the earth" below for more).

• M •

"Major Dundee" — ("Philip Jenkinson on Cheese Westerns") 1965 Sam Peckinpah film starring Charlton Heston.

"*Wild Bunch* and *Straw Dogs*"—The hyperviolent anti-Western *Wild Bunch* (1969) brought Peckinpah to international acclaim, and the equally disturbing rape-and-revenge film *Straw Dogs* (1971) cemented that reputation. Peckinpah often said that he wanted to make Westerns the way Akira Kurosawa made Westerns, obviously being very influenced by Kurosawa's over-the-top violence in *Yojimbo* (1961) and especially *Sanjuro* (1962), which Peckinpah's films tend to resemble, as well as Sergio Leone's influential "spaghetti Westerns" *A Fistful of Dollars* (1964), *For a Few Dollars More* (1965), and *The Good, the Bad, and the Ugly* (1966).

montage of photographs — (PSC; "Cheese Shop") This set of photos was shot in a narrow alley between 19 and 20 King Street in Richmond, Surrey. Behind Mousebender (Cleese) can be seen two King Street businesses—the British School of Motoring (BSM) and the *Richmond & Twickenham Times*. BSM was located at 12 King Street; the *R&T Times* at 14 King Street.

Mousebender — ("Cheese Shop") Perhaps a reference back to the "bent" character Cleese portrayed in Ep. 2's "The Mouse Problem" sketch, who felt more comfortable dressed as a mouse. Mr. Mousebender's name is never mentioned by the characters in the sketch, which is often the case in *FC*, remaining a sort of lifelong in-joke for the script writers and readers. A "mouse bender" could also occur, of course, if a mouse happens to get loose in a cheese shop.

Finally, "Mousebender" might also be an oblique reference to the then-prominent psychic and kineticist Uri Geller (b. 1946), a so-called mindbender who demonstrated a mental utensil-bending ability on various TV shows and public appearances between 1969 and 1972.

Mrs. Pinnet type — ("Lifeboat") References the character, also played by Jones, who appeared back in Ep. 14, in the "New Cooker Sketch." She is essentially a Pepperpot, but not nearly as fussy, more like a sweet mother type. The Pythons here have gone a step further in their reflexivity, their self-referentiality—they've moved from a clear, long-held British TV (and literary) type (the fussy, middle-aged woman), to referencing one of their own refinements of that type, "Mrs. Pinnet." Production designers could then eas-ily access the generic construct "Mrs. Pinnet," greatly facilitating wardrobe, makeup, and even prop and set dressing decisions.

• N •

naked quartet — (PSC; titles) The single chord played by this fright-wigged quartet is borrowed from "String Quartet in G minor" by Debussy (WAC T12/1,444).

"never even been to Spain" — ("Biggles Dictates a Letter") Perhaps because by this period, travel to the Spanish coast wasn't really considered international travel by the English tourist, it had become so traditional.

"Ibiza"—A Spanish Mediterranean island mentioned previously in Ep. 27 as the vacation spot where Mrs. Premise (Cleese) and Mrs. Conclusion (Chapman) met Jean-Paul Sartre and his wife (Palin), Betty-Muriel. See notes to Ep. 27.

"Newhaven" — ("Lifeboat") The Newhaven Lifeboat Station was founded in 1803 to serve England's south coast. It is located sixty miles west of Dover, the area where the Pythons were shooting exteriors for this season. The Pythons and crew shot with the crew of Newhaven Lifeboat on 20 October 1971, all for a £20 donation to the Newhaven branch of the RNLI (WAC T12/1,444).

"no better than you should be" — ("Biggles Dictates a Letter") A phrase taken from various sources, including Beaumont and Fletcher's *The Coxcomb* (act 4, scene 3; perf. 1612), and Henry Fielding's *The Temple Beau* (also 4.3; perf. 1730). In the first, the young lady in question is being accused of being a thief and perhaps more, and in the latter she is an unsavory match for a monied young man based on her "flaw"—alleged sexual libertinism. In both, the meaning is clear: Once a sullied woman, always a sullied woman—and the sullied woman will ever act the part.

Also, this phrase appears in Joyce's *Ulysses*, coming from Deasy as he is regaling Stephen about foot and mouth and the curse of the Jews:

I have put the matter into a nutshell, Mr Deasy said. It's about the foot and mouth disease. Just look through it. There can be no two opinions on the matter. . . . May I trespass on your valuable space. That doctrine of laissez faire which so often in our history. Our cattle trade. The way of all our old industries. Liverpool ring which jockeyed the Galway harbour scheme. European conflagration. Grain supplies through the narrow waters of the channel. The pluterperfect imperturbability of the department of agriculture. Pardoned a classical allusion. Cassandra. *By a woman who was no better than she should be.* To come to the point at issue. (*Ulysses,* Episode 2—"Nestor"; italics added)

(And yes, the above does sound very much like the topics and even cadence of the "Farming Club" and *"Life of Tschaikowsky"* sections of Ep. 28. The influence of Modernist writers like Joyce and Stein and Eliot on the Pythons has been pointed out and discussed. See notes to Eps. 1, 12, 13, 17, 23, 25, and on.)

In the Biggles sketch the Secretary sits "provocatively" and wears a short, form-fitting dress, emblematic of her "should be-ness." She is very much a biological, sexualized woman in this raving cast of transvestites (Biggles when he's dressed as his wife), homosexuals (Algy), and flamboyant glam-rock crossdressers (Ginger). This "type" casting is typical of Python, and has been seen with other types, including City Gents, Rustics, Pepperpots, etc.

"No longer used in the West" — ("Storage Jars") This is often the case in developing countries. In Cuba, for instance, big American cars of the 1950s were used for many years as "new" cars—none were being imported from the United States, so those abandoned when Bautista's government fell in 1959 had to be made to last.

• O •

"one of my favourite film directors, Sam Peckinpah" — ("Cheese Westerns") Jenkinson had interviewed another American Western filmmaker, John Ford, in 1970 for *Listener* (12 Feb. 1970).

Ordinary simple Philip Jenkinson at a desk set — (PSC; "Cheese Westerns") The large photo behind Jenkinson (Idle) is a Keystone Cops image, c. 1913. Some of the recognizable comic actors include Roscoe "Fatty" Arbuckle (far right), Al St. John (fourth from right), and Nick Cogley (on the phone).

• P •

Pantomime Princess Margaret — ("Biggles Dictates a Letter") Pantomime Princess Margaret has appeared in Ep. 30, as well, where she harpooned her breakfast tray, then stomped the tea service to death. Cleese is playing the part in this scene (WAC T12/1,444).

Peter Ackroyd notes that a German visitor to England for the coronation of George IV recorded that the king "was obliged to present himself, as chief actor in a pantomime" (*London,* 146). It is also mentioned earlier that the young girl Margaret performed in pantomime for Christmas broadcast during the war, though

admittedly not as a "dummy." See notes to Ep. 30. The Pythons' massaging, then, of Princess Margaret from royal to player to "pantomimetic royal person" is not as ridiculous as it may have seemed.

"Peckinpah, Sam" — ("Philip Jenkinson on Cheese Westerns") Peckinpah (1925–1984) was indeed born in Fresno, California, and would die returning to California from Mexico, after living and working abroad in England, as well.

pederast vole — (PSC; "Cheese Shop") These comments comparing Philip Jenkinson to a hybrid Truman Capote/pederast vole would have been for the other Pythons only, really, and those who had to prep the script for the taping of the show. It's interesting that these textual comments were never excised from the printed scripts, as they may have represented actionable slander under UK law. Perhaps it is because the scripts weren't originally intended for publication. It also could be that since the comments in question occur in the scenic directions and aren't voiced by any character, printed on the screen, or visually/aurally depicted in any way, the benchmark for slander wasn't reached? Or, the characterization could have been a good-natured joke among friends. Whatever the reason, the Pythons comparing their contemporary Jenkinson to a gay, pedophilic rodent has remained in the *FC* printed scripts since 1972.

"phone up" — ("Apology") In *That Was Satire, That Was* Humphrey Carpenter (1946–2005) reports that BBC viewers have a long tradition of making their feelings known via phone and mail, with significant complaints lodged over especially satirical shows like *That Was the Week That Was, Benny Hill,* and *FC* later. The British Board of Film Censors (BBFC) and the Lord Chamberlain's office also fielded hundreds of calls and mail items in regard to controversial filmed productions from this period, including *Look Back in Anger, The Entertainer, Room at the Top, Billy Liar, A Taste of Honey,* and so on. Both the BBFC and the Lord Chamberlain's Office (for theater) were quite considerate about responding—and civilly, respectfully—to all such complaints. See Aldgate.

As a sort of sideways testament to this careful viewer attention the BBC enjoyed, there are a number of letters (and telegrams) from *Flying Circus* viewers in the WAC records for the show, asking for tickets, offering jokes and new characters and "funny" storylines, showering congratulations and clucking tongues alike. By sheer number, most letters are offering written material, which the producers kindly and thankfully decline, saying the troupe writes all its own material. Many BBC comedy shows accepted and then employed outside material, meaning the practice was fairly usual, if the material was worthwhile (see Carpenter).

"puzzle her" — ("Biggles Dictates a Letter") Perhaps he is referring to the use of "Saxe-Coburg" rather than "Windsor," if he is talking about Margaret's immediate family. Both are adopted surnames, anyway.

• R •

"Red Leicester" — ("Cheese Shop") A cheese originally made in Leicestershire. This section of the sketch seems to be a ready-made in-joke, poking fun at Cleese's propensity for writing wordier, even encyclopedic sketches. It is also the "most failed transaction" of all of the Pythons' myriad failed transactions in *Flying Circus*. This "list" scenario will be revisited in Ep. 37, and has become legendary (even by 1972) thanks to the success of the "Dead Parrot" sketch in Ep. 8.

Of all the cheeses mentioned, thirteen are from the UK; twelve from France; four from Italy; three from Switzerland; two each from Holland, Denmark, and Czechoslovakia; and one each from Norway, Austria, and Germany. Remarkably, "Venezuelan Beaver Cheese" seems to be the only "made-up" cheese in the entire spiel. In most lists ("Timmy Williams," *The Black Eagle*," "Court Scene—Multiple Murderer") there are a few names that are clearly real, and then many just as clearly cobbled together from multiple sources. The cheese list itself isn't meant to be funny—real cheeses, proper pronunciations—it's the sheer length of the list and the willful persistence of the participants where the humor emerges. In Tex Avery's *Blitz Wolf* (1942), the new secret weapon meant to destroy Nazi Germany and Fascist Japan simply looks like a big cannon—it's not funny until the camera "pans" along the barrel for a full thirty-one seconds, and it seems as if it's never going to end. (The Pythons will revisit this "waiting" structure of humor in *Holy Grail*, when Lancelot [Cleese] runs toward Swamp Castle's front gate over and over again.)

At last this sketch may be about optimism—the customer (Cleese) is content to push on through the cheese list on the real possibility that the shop actually sells cheese, and the proprietor (Palin) good-naturedly allows the customer his full range of ordering potentiality, knowing from the outset that there is no cheese to be had. In the end, both seem to agree that the gunshot is an acceptable ending to the failed transaction.

"Rhyming slang—ginger beer" — ("Biggles Dictates a Letter") "Ginger beer" is a Cockney rhyming slang phrase for "queer." It's said that so-called Cockneys created this secret rhyming language so they could converse about their nefarious affairs in front of any-

one, including a constable. This would have lasted only as long, of course, as it took the authorities to learn the slang.

In Ep. 7 the Compère (Palin) uses another Cockney rhyming slang, "lager and lime," slang for "spine," in that case.

Ginger beer was and is both a brewed beer and a soft drink. Dickens mentions it several times.

"rock buns" — ("Lifeboat") Simple drop cakes made of flour, butter, sugar, dried fruit, eggs, and milk.

"*Rogue Cheddar*" — ("Cheese Shop") This short film sequence is borrowed from EMI's *Cowboy* C2 859 (WAC T12/1,444).

"*Rogue . . . Walpole*" — ("Cheese Shop") Actually, *Rogue Herries* (1930) was written by *Hugh* Walpole (1884–1941), part of his Cumberland family saga. *Horace* Walpole (1717–1797) lived much earlier, and nearly single-handedly created the Gothic novel genre with *The Castle of Otranto* (1764), and was the son of Robert Walpole, the former first Prime Minister.

And speaking of lists, Horace Walpole had set up a printing concern at his Strawberry Hill estate, publishing, among other things, catalogs and list-like materials, including *Catalogue of Royal and Noble Authors of England* (1758), *Anecdotes of Painting in England*, and *A Catalogue of Engravers* (1762–1771).

• S •

"salt of the earth" — ("Biggles Dictates a Letter") Borrowed from the New Testament, Matthew 5:13. The balance of the declamation is perhaps Biggles's version of John of Gaunt's stirring "this realm, this England" assessment of the English character in *Richard II*; that, or Henry's "Once more unto the breach" speech on the eve of St. Crispin's Day and the Battle of Agincourt depicted in *Henry V*. Algy soon joins his worthy English predecessors in noble death, of course.

"stout fellow"—Guest star Valentine Dyall uses this phrase several times in *The Goon Show* episode "The Giant Bombardon" (17 Nov. 1957), there describing the essence of British military manhood, Colonel Splun, who also lost his life in "battle."

"Saxe-Coburgs" — ("Biggles Dictates a Letter") Name taken from a German duchy, and was the royal house for a number of European monarchies, including the Wettins (now called Windsors). For the English portion of this large royal family, the German surnames and titles were dropped during the First World War, for obvious reasons, and "Windsor" was adopted. This family name will be mentioned again in Ep. 36, in the "Tudor Jobs Agency" sketch.

"canasta"—A card game (of Uruguayan origin) combining portions of both rummy and pinochle (*OED*).

"self-righting models" — ("Lifeboat") Lifeboats that were designed to right themselves even after being overturned in heavy seas came into regular service in the UK as early as 1881, and would have been standard by the 1970s.

show-off angles — ("Cheese Shop") This form—still photos shot "artily"—was used by French "film essayist" Chris Marker (b. 1921) in his landmark 1962 film *La jetée*, as well as hundreds of school films and slide show presentations of the period.

This is also clearly a reference to the early Cleese and Gilliam collaboration in a 1968 *Help!* magazine panel story (*fumetti*), wherein a man (Cleese) falls in love (and eventually has relations) with his daughter's Barbie-type doll. *Fumetti*, or photo novels, are laid out like a comic book set-up, complete with thought balloons, speech bubbles, and written sound effects. For "Cheese Shop," just the arty photos are employed.

silver stars — (PSC; "Biggles Dictates a Letter") Gilliam's flashy attire here is a throwback to the transgendered "Mod" crowd of the 1960s, but more precisely to the more current fashions in the Glam Rock movement popular in the UK. Note the title of a Tyrannosaurus Rex album from this period: "My people were fair and had sky in their hair but now they're content to wear stars on their brows." Gilliam here looks very much like Marc Bolan of T-Rex fame, circa 1972.

sou'wester — (PSC; "Lifeboat") A large, waterproof hat (formerly made of oilskin).

Spanish soldier's outfit — (PSC; "Seashore Interlude Film") This is a shot recorded during the shooting of the seaside portions of the soon-to-be-aired Ep. 36, where Sir Philip Sidney (Palin) fights Spanish porn merchants. These exterior, on-location "inserts" were generally done in one or two goes, at the beginning and middle of the various seasons, then parsed out as needed for each episode. The "lemon curry" inserts were shot in the Glencoe locations in October 1971, for instance, then held for Ep. 33.

"strife-torn Bolivia" — ("Storage Jars") According to the *Columbia Encyclopedia*, Bolivia has endured at least 190 coup attempts since 1825, with the 1960s and 1970s being particularly uneasy. There was an overthrow in 1964, another in 1969, and widespread nationalizations of essential industries in between. A rightist junta overthrew the 1969-inaugurated government in 1970, but was only able to keep power for a single day, when a leftist coup assumed control. This leftist government was itself unseated in 1971 by a U.S.-friendly government, and on and on.

The still photo is from the Colour Library International, "G.V. La Paz" 60914 (WAC T12/1,444).

• **T** •

"Tee Hee" — ("Sam Peckinpah's *Salad Days*") This is the Pythons enjoying the sight of one of their targets "getting his," while at the same time perhaps covering themselves in case Jenkinson actually is offended by the depiction. (See the entry for "pederast vole" above for more on this curious and potentially actionable slander.) If the latter case, the subtitle acts as the "SATIRE" subtitle in Ep. 17 ("Architect Sketch") and the "A Joke" flashcard in Ep. 24 ("Conquistador Coffee Campaign") where the seriousness of the on-screen depiction of a Ronan Point–type disaster (Ep. 17) is undercut by satiric humor that is also carefully underscored.

"terpsichorean muse" — ("Cheese Shop") Terpsichore is the muse of dancing.

"thank you, love" — ("Old Lady Snoopers") This could be a comment on the media watchdogs seen earlier in Ep. 32, Mary Whitehouse and her friends at the National Viewers and Listeners Association (NVLA). More simply, it could just be a send-up of the typical nosy neighbor scenario.

"Thurmond Street" — ("Cheese Shop") There is a cheese shop, Bloomsbury's, very near Broadcast House, on the corner of Leigh Street and Judd Street, WC 1.

• **U** •

urgent documentary music — (PSC; "Storage Jars") This "urgent" music is P. Gerard's "Riot Squad" from the Standard Music Library (WAC T12/1,444).

"Uxbridge Road" — ("Climbing the North Face of Uxbridge Road") This busy main road is found in Shepherd's Bush, W12, just near BBC Production Centre; however, according to Palin, the scene was actually shot on South Ealing Road, W5. This is not far from Lammas Park (both the park and the adjacent road), where portions of the "Bicycle Repair Man" sketch were shot for Ep. 3. Due to budgetary constraints, most of the neighborhood exteriors for *FC* were shot within a ten-mile radius of BBC Television Centre, Shepherd's Bush.

The Pythons are not, of course, shooting on that busy Uxbridge Road thoroughfare; instead they set up their cameras along the South Ealing Road, in front of number 177 (at the corner of North Road). Young's Bakeries and A.E. Rodd can be seen across the street (both can be found in period phone books on this street). This is one of the handful of shooting locations that guide Michael Palin visits in the short subject "Pythonland," part of the *Life of Python* DVD set.

• W •

"what about that" — ("Biggles Dictates a Letter") The dangers of (mis)communication are illustrated here again, as in Ep. 30, where pauses in televised speech have to be precisely described and delineated from actual or finished speech.

• Z •

Zabriskie Point — ("Sam Peckinpah's *Salad Days*") Michelangelo Antonioni's 1970 film looking at late 1960s America and the emerging youth culture. (London newspaper critics weren't kind to this film, by the way, seeing it as pretentious and—worse—dull.)

Antonioni and his films are discussed at length in Ep. 29. It's worth noting that even though the Pythons are sending up Peckinpah and American excess in film, they are asking that the scene be shot in the manner of a noted Italian director, which may just mean that stylistically Peckinpah had yet to leave a memorable visual signature to be copied. These same London critics who have grown tired of Antonioni's excessive longueurs and beauty shots, laud Peckinpah as the only man who should be allowed to direct (or write) westerns; even Peckinpah's faults and failings, they say, make for better cinema than most.

slow motion—This is the same kind of violence being asked for by the American producer (Idle) in Ep. 23, in the "*Scott of the Antarctic*" sketch. This level of violence, and the "geysers of blood," had really begun with the influence of the final sequence in Kurosawa's anti-heroic samurai Western *Sanjuro* (1962), and was taken to new heights in *Bonnie and Clyde* (1967), *Wild Bunch* (1969), and *Straw Dogs* (1971)—the latter two Peckinpah films.

Episode 34: "The Cycling Tour"

Mr. Pither falls; Banana and cheese sandwiches; "The pump caught in my trouser leg"; Tizer; Mr. Gulliver and safer foods; Clodagh Rogers and "Jack in a Box"; The dangerous hospital; Trotsky; Lenin's "If I Ruled the World"; Smolensk; The YMACA; Bingo-crazed Chinese; Moscow and the 42nd International Clambake; Trotsky sings "I'm Just an Old-Fashioned Girl"; Firing squad; "So it was all a dream!"; Eartha Kitt; "Scene Missing"; *Animation: Monsters dance* to "Jack in a Box," and closing credits

• A •

"agent in the town" — ("Trotsky") After he was expelled from Russia, Trotsky was a fairly consistent target for assassination. He was exiled in 1927 to the far-flung remoteness of eastern Russia, then had to flee to Istanbul, several locations in France, Norway, and finally Mexico, according to his own work and that of biographers. (Trotsky wrote seemingly non-stop throughout his lifetime.) There was either political pressure everywhere he went, viz., Stalin and supporters pressing local governments, or agents to watch and report on Trotsky's movements and associations. It was 1940 when agents with orders to kill were finally sent, and sent successfully.

• B •

"Bakewell's tart" — ("Bingo-Crazed Chinese") Long-popular English confection.

"bloodstained shadow of Stalinist repression" — ("Jack in a Box") Trotsky had said—when favorable comparisons were being made between Lenin and Stalin after Lenin's death—that a "river of blood" (1927) separated the two men, as it separated Stalinism from Bolshevism.

Trotsky and his Left Opposition group were all expelled from the Communist Party in November 1927, and he was deported in 1929 to Istanbul and then France. He would eventually be assassinated in Mexico.

"Bovey Tracey" — ("Mr. Pither") Small town in Devon north of Newton Abbot on the B3387 and the A382.

Brun, M. — (PSC; "Trotsky") "Brun" simply means "brown," and is probably meant to indicate a kind of standard surname. This could be a reference to the noted electronic music composer and performer Herbert Brun (1918–2000), who was internationally active in 1972.

"Bude" — ("Clodagh Rogers") One of the few locations mentioned by Pither that is actually in Cornwall, Bude is a coastal town.

"Budleigh Salterton" — ("Mr. Pither") City on the coast a little north and west of Bovey Tracey in Devon, Pither would have had to cross the Exe (or navigate the Dawlish Marshes) to reach this site, a distance of about twenty-six miles.

"bugged or unbugged" — ("Smolensk") The Soviet Union of the Cold War era (c. 1949–1989) employed clandestine intelligence-gathering both at home and abroad, as outlined in, for example, the KGB's "Annual Report" for 1967, where the installation of "electronic monitoring devices" in at least thirty-six foreign buildings is discussed. The goal of such monitoring was identified as "improvement of counterintelligence work inside the country . . . so as to ensure more efficient struggle with military, economic and political espionage." Hotels in the Soviet Union frequented by foreign visitors (especially Western foreign visitors) were regularly bugged and guests photographed. Reports of Soviet spies in the West being identified and either put on trial (if they were British citizens) or deported (if they were foreign nationals) regularly appear in contemporary London newspapers.

The crossed-out pictures behind the Clerk include Robert Baden-Powell (1857–1941), founder of the Boy Scouts. Powell may be here because he represents what many in the Sino-Soviet bloc during this period saw as a "sleeper" paramilitary organization—the Boy Scouts—or because he was a member of the British secret service during his military career.

Secondly, the middle picture seems to be of St. Tikhon of Moscow (1865–1925), the Russian Orthodox Church Patriarch from about 1917 to his death. Tikhon would spend time in prison/house arrest for speaking and writing against the excesses of the Soviet government.

"Bulganin" — ("Jack in a Box") Nikolai Bulganin (1895–1975) was a Soviet soldier, secret police member, WWII general, and eventually Prime Minister of Russia when he and Khrushchev toured the UK in the late 1950s. He was a Marshal during and just after WWII. During the 1950s, as Defense Minister Bulganin was one of the most heard, most militant voices of the bristly Soviet government. He warned over and over again about the dangers of "United States' imperialism," of the "aggressive Anglo-American bloc" working to re-militarize both Japan and Germany against Russia, and the need for the Fatherland's strength and continued vigilance supporting the Soviet industrial and war machines. Bulganin and First Secretary Khrushchev visited Great Britain in April 1956, a visit marked by angry protests from Russian and Eastern European exiles, as well as myriad letters to the editor haranguing the invitation. PM Eden's reputation took significant hits, since the invitation was his, and many saw the visit as serving the public relations needs of the USSR, and not for the betterment of those living in the shadow of Soviet Communism across Eastern Europe.

"Charlie" was the name of Edgar Bergen's ventriloquist doll. This image—a powerful military or political figure with a ventriloquist's dummy—was a common sight in political cartoons of the period, including a 1962 cartoon from Fritz Behrendt featuring Khrushchev with Janos Kadar (Hungary) and Mao with Enver Hoxha (Albania). Both dummies are screaming epithets at the other, while their manipulators look

away (*Observer*, 2 Dec. 1962). See the British Cartoon Archive.

Burgess and Maclean — ("Jack in a Box") These names appear on a poster in Pither's Moscow cell. Guy Burgess (1911–1963) and Donald Maclean (1913–1983) were British diplomats when they disappeared in 1951, only to reappear in Moscow in 1956, and their careers of spying for the Soviet Union became banner headlines.

The U.S. government's extensive files on Burgess, Maclean, and the rest of the so-called Cambridge Five spy ring (who had been suspect in the Americans' view for many years) are now available from the FBI.

• C •

Camera pans very slightly — ("Mr. Pither") Pither is the type of character who sees the world in his own way. He never takes offense, even when offense is intended; he misses facial and body cues that signal the end of conversations or the subtle discomforts of another; he is also invincible, seemingly protected by the hands of God (not unlike Harry Langdon's character in his early Frank Capra–directed films for Columbia). In the Python world, this type of character will survive and even flourish in spite of himself.

What Smollett wrote of his character Roderick Random (from *The Adventures of Roderick Random*) fits Pither quite well:

> [In creating and presenting the character Roderick] I have attempted to represent modest merit struggling with every difficulty to which a friendless orphan is exposed, from his own want of experience, as well as from the selfishness, envy, malice, and base indifference of mankind. (*Letters*, 8)

See the entry for "Tobias Smollett" in the *ODNB* for more on the author and his picaresque characters.

chemist's shop — ("Mr. Pither") The sign on this pharmacy clearly reads "West Park Pharmacy" and "Cheapside Post Office," meaning these scenes were shot on location in the St. Helier area, Jersey, along with most of the exterior work for these later third season episodes. This shot appears to be taken at 3 Pierson Road, where West Park Pharmacy still operates today.

"Compton, Denis" — ("Clodagh Rogers") Compton (1918–1997) was both a cricketer (for England) and footballer (Arsenal), setting records in the immediate postwar years. He has earlier been mentioned in Ep. 21.

"continue in English" — ("Jack in a Box") An acknowledgment of the standard practice in British and

American films and TV of having all central characters—no matter their native tongue—speak English with pronounced accent to approximate a foreigner.

Cook, Peter, and Dudley Moore — ("Jack in a Box") Listed on a jail cell poster as appearing in the Moscow Praesidium, Peter Cook (1937–1995) and Dudley Moore (1935–2002) had been performing together since the early 1960s, when they joined Alan Bennett and Jonathan Miller in *Beyond the Fringe*. The show's satirical edge and wordsmithing were clear influences on the Pythons. In 1972 when this episode was being produced, Cook and Moore were on tour together in Australia, incidentally.

"crunchie" — ("Jack in a Box") According to Cadbury, the Crunchie bar was first sold in the UK in 1929. The "Mars bar" (from Mars, Inc.) mentioned earlier appeared in 1936 in the United States.

"Cycling Tour" — ("Mr. Pither") After thirty-three hodge-podge episodes, where central characters come and go seemingly at random, this nearly unilinear narrative follows Mr. Pither from start to finish, perhaps signaling a change in mood for the Pythons. They have never attempted to maintain interest via a single character's storyline, and this episode may have been a chance to test the writing chops—and certainly served to shake things up generally—as they create this sort of picaresque journey for the unflappable Mr. Pither (Palin).

Pither is very much crafted in the vein of earlier celebrated peripatetic literary characters, including Cervantes's Don Quixote, Fielding's Joseph Andrews and Tom Jones, Smollett's Humphry Clinker, and even Sterne's Uncle Toby (who doesn't go very far but does talk a good deal of his experiences). Astride his Rocinante, a rickety ten-speed, Pither moves from experience to experience, living out the empiricist theory (à la Locke) as he observes the natural world, "senses it," and then reflects upon those observances and sensations for himself, the viewer, and anyone who'll listen during his journeys.

Pither is a sensory being, certainly, as will be seen, especially as he repeatedly falls from his mount, then describes in very real and tactile language the results of those experiences—after a crash his lunch has "grit all over it" and "small particles of bitumen in the chocolate kup kakes" from the "tarmacadam surface" of the roadway, etc.

This episode ends up being one of the oddest but also most philosophically centered in all of *FC*, as the Pythons—perhaps unconsciously—create a classically inspired picaresque, neatly adorned with the twentieth-century philosophies that so influenced them.

• D •

Dawlish Road — ("Mr. Pither") The Dawlish Road runs south from Exeter in Devon, where the Pythons shot location footage for the first season. Urban and suburban Exeter is the setting for a number of exterior scenes in Ep. 42, as will be seen.

Devon countryside — ("Mr. Pither") These outdoor scenes were actually recorded on the island of Jersey.

District Hospital — ("Clodagh Rogers") The depictions here also keep the text close to Tobias Smollett's world, especially with the treatment of the hospital as the last place one would go when sick or injured. In volume one of *Humphry Clinker*, Bramble writes to Dr. Lewis that the waters of Bath can't possibly be a cure-all, and that the man who subscribes to the myth of Bath "sacrifices his precious time, which might be employed in taking more effectual remedies, and exposes himself to the dirt, the stench, the chilling blasts, and perpetual rains" (23). See also Bramble's lengthy complaint to his doctor when he arrives in Bath, calling it a "national hospital," and then enumerating its unhygienic and even dangerous faults (33–35).

This entire episode is a cleverly updated version of the picaresque-type novels of eighteenth-century England, including *Tom Jones*, *Joseph Andrews*, *Humphry Clinker*, and *Roderick Random*.

"Dr. Wu" — ("Clodagh Rogers") There has been concern and discussion for many years in the UK regarding the quality of doctors and critical-care nurses in regional and especially rural National Health Service facilities. Based on the views expressed in hundreds of letters to various newspapers and now websites and blogs, it's still assumed by a large portion of the British public that the NHS struggles to entice the highest-qualified medical personnel into less lucrative and seemingly provincial state service—and it gets worse the farther one happens to be from London. Example: In Webster's *The National Health Service: A Political History*, figures indicate that the Southwestern region (Devon and Cornwall) had consistently run well beneath fiscal allocation goals between 1963 and 1975. Over this same period, however, the Metropolitan regions (Greater London) consistently ran above the allocation goals. A series of government Green Papers on the subject (briefly mentioned earlier in Ep. 26) had been in the public forum since 1970.

Though backhanded, this reference to an Asian doctor in a slap-dash rural hospital might be a hint at this still-smoldering issue in UK healthcare. When the doctor (played by Cleese) appears, of course, it's clear he isn't Asian, nor even "acting" like one, which Chapman will do later in the episode.

• E •

Episode 34 — This nearly single-narrative episode was recorded 4 May 1972 and broadcast 7 December 1972. It was the tenth episode recorded, and the eighth broadcast, with most of the exterior work accomplished between March and May 1972.

Walk-ons for this episode include: Ron Gregory (*Dixon of Dock Green*; *Z Cars*), John Beardmore (*Softly Softly*; *Colditz*), Charles Saynor (*Blue Lamp*; *Man in the White Suit*), Desmond Verini (*Day of the Daleks*), Aldwyn Francis Davies (*Under Milkwood*), Peter Brett (Eps. 38, 45; *Dixon of Dock Green*), Pat Cleveland, Beulah Hughes (*Hands of the Ripper*), Charlotte Green; (as Maoists) Arnold Lee (*Doctor Who*), George Laughing-Sam, Kelwin Sue-a-Quan and C.H. Yang (both findable in period Greater London–area telephone directories), Jack Tong, Ken Nazarin (*A Casual Affair*), Carey Wilson, Richard Gregory (*Paul Temple*) (WAC T12/1,440).

• G •

"Gulliver" — ("Mr. Pither") Well-known character from Swift's *Gulliver's Travels*, it's no surprise that this character name appears in this episode so clearly indebted to eighteenth-century literature and philosophy. Lemuel Gulliver was a traveler, to be sure, but his encounters being termed by Swift as the "great foundation of Misanthropy" were not the ends sought by the Pythons. Gently satirizing the cheerful, dopey English traveler as well as Communist fervor is perhaps shooting fish in a barrel, but it's the incongruity of a jangling Pither meeting Clodagh Rodgers, Trotsky, Chinese insurgents, Soviet Communist party members and executioners, and others, and blissfully living through it all that drives the narrative.

Once Mr. Gulliver (Jones) joins Pither on his adventures, the tale takes on a sort of *Humphry Clinker* feel to it, with the letter-writing Matthew Bramble and Humphry on the road through rural Britain. Bramble is gouty and complaining, of course, and shackled with a lovesick niece and a maiden sister, so he's no Pither, who is the picture of blind optimism.

Smollett's focus on illness, medicine, and healing in *Humphry Clinker* is also borrowed by the Pythons here. Pither will be nearly injured as he consistently falls from his bike, he'll visit a doctor in a rural town who can only give him directions, his travel partner Gulliver will be injured and go to a very dangerous hospital, as well as undergo several personality changes, Pither will nearly be executed, etc. Part of the Pythons' satire here must be the inadvisability of traveling into Britain's provinces, where both hospitality and hospitals fall well short of reasonable (southern, as in London?) expectations. Smollett would have agreed with this, certainly.

Gulliver dashing through the trees — ("Clodagh Rogers") Very much a Swiftian character trait, in chapter 1 of "A Voyage to Brobdingnag," Lemuel Gulliver confesses to being "condemned by Nature and Fortune to an active and restless life" and leaves his wife and children for yet another maritime adventure (63).

• H •

"Hackney Star" — ("Bingo-Crazed Chinese") The Hackney Empire Theatre had been an early television studio before becoming a bingo hall in 1963.

The "Top Rank Suite" theater in Doncaster, for example, hosted first-tier concerts including Pink Floyd (1971), Ziggy Stardust (David Bowie, 1972), and The Velvet Underground (1972).

Heath, Ted — ("Eartha Kitt") In November 1972, following power shortages, mine and general labor strikes, big business struggles, an unpopular Industrial Relations Bill, and the consistent fumbling of the economic ball, Heath and government had instituted a wage and salary freeze, cellaring their already-low opinion ratings among working families. The Conservatives would be not-so-politely ushered out of office in 1974, in favor of Wilson's Labour coalition. See Morgan's *Britain since 1945* for more.

This particular speech was most likely delivered in about June 1972, when the government had given concessions to coal miners.

hospital — ("Clodagh Rogers") This exterior location is the General Hospital found on Gloucester Street, in St. Helier, Jersey.

"Housey! Housey!" — ("Bingo-Crazed Chinese") This was a kind of alert call from street vendors in Hong Kong (and India) announcing a game of "tambola," a lotto-type game. The postwar craze for bingo in an otherwise impoverished, rationed, and grey Britain is discussed in the "Popular Culture" section of *Eyewitness: 1950–59*.

"How do you know so much about cycling?" — ("Mr. Pither") Pither has intricately connected his food experience and appreciation with his cycling avocation, meaning it becomes difficult to see where one leaves off and another begins. In the same vein the "Trim-Jeans" users losing pounds and inches in performance owe their weight loss to the *writing* abilities of Chekhov, according to the announcer (Palin), and not necessarily exercise or even the Trim-Jeans product.

• I •

"I'd be happier with a bugged one" — ("Smolensk") Curious, unless it's considered that the likelihood of home invasion from authorities in a totalitarian state is probably greatly reduced if that authority knows exactly what's going on in the home. In the science fiction film *THX-1138* (dir. George Lucas) released in 1971, most men of this future (and stiflingly oppressive) society choose the certain, comfortable safeties of oppression over the unknown waiting "out there." For the Soviet citizen under Stalin, Malenkov, Khrushchev and finally Brezhnev, a bug likely meant nothing controversial is ever discussed, therefore no need for special attentions from the state.

"Iddesleigh" — ("Mr. Pither") In West Devon.

"I decided to check . . ." — ("Smolensk") This is a very interesting moment, narratively, what Gérard Genette would call a "narrative metalepsis," and what sets this episode apart from most of the previous thirty-three. Pither for the first time in the narrative speaks to "us" (or his own narrating voice) when he thanks the Military Man (Idle) for providing directions just when he needs them; the voiceover (also Pither) then continues to the "all the way from Monte Carlo" line, and the Military Man interrupts, helpfully again, to which Pither (on his bike) says "thank you" again. With that thank you, the "live" Pither continues on with "I decided to check . . . ," only to be interrupted by the voiceover Pither saying the same thing. Here we have multiple levels of possible narration and story progression tripping over one another for a brief, fascinating moment. These progressions of course are always flowing, at the diegetic and metadiegetic levels, at least, but we generally only hear from one at a time to avoid such confusions. Genette notes such "second-degree narratives" in *Tristram Shandy* and *Manon Lescaut*, and "in [Brontë's] *Wuthering Heights* (Isabella's narrative to Nelly, reported by Nelly to Lockwood, noted by Lockwood in his journal), and especially in *Lord Jim* [Joseph Conrad], *where the entanglement reaches the bounds of general intelligibility*" (*Narrative Discourse*, 232–33; italics for emphasis added). The Pythons merely slip their toe into these less-fathomed waters, then allow the ever-gracious Pither to bow out and let his voiceover self continue the exciting narration.

"Ilfracombe" — ("Clodagh Rogers") A fairly small Devon town in the North Devon Coastal area.

Imperial music — (PSC; "Bingo-Crazy Chinese") The music used here is "Pomp and Circumstance" by Elgar (from Marches No. 1 in D major) (WAC T12/1,440).

• J •

"Jack in the Box" — ("Clodagh Rogers") This particular recording of the song is from "Unaccompanied Artists" and was written by David Myers and John Worsley (WAC T12/1,440).

• K •

"Kerensky" — ("Clodagh Rogers") Alexander Fyodorovich Kerensky (1881–1970) was an anti-Tsarist revolutionary instrumental in toppling the Russian monarchy. He was a major figure in the coalition government(s), before being himself unseated when the Bolsheviks (under Lenin) seized power. He would later live out much of his life in exile in the United States, and is buried in England. One of the handful of active early Soviet figures still alive in the 1960s, Kerensky had recently published *Russia and History's Turning Point* in 1966.

"Kitt, Eartha" — ("Jack in a Box") Kitt (1927–2008) was an American singer who came to prominence in the 1950s. She is perhaps included here because in 1968 she had offended the White House with anti-war remarks, and her American bookings dried up. She went to Europe and successfully continued her career. It's also likely that she's included here based on her recent appearance in the Frankie Howerd vehicle *Up the Chastity Belt* (1971). Ned Sherrin (Ep. 5) produced the film.

• L •

large Chinese crowds — (PSC; "Bingo-Crazed Chinese") This film stock is "Red Guards 1376/67" and "961/67" from VisNews (WAC T12/1,440). These newsreels would have been recorded during the mass demonstrations in places like Wuhan, China, in July 1967.

"Lenin" — ("Clodagh Rogers") V.I. Lenin (1870–1924) led the Soviet state 1917–1924. The footage used when Lenin "sings" is Pathe film stock (WAC T12/1,440). Lenin earlier appeared as a befuddled contestant on *Communist Quiz*, and wasn't able to utter a word (Ep. 25).

The depiction of Trotsky's relationship with Lenin is significant here. Stalin and comrades moved against Trotsky as Lenin tried to recuperate from several strokes, and Lenin over and over again wrote from his bed that Trotsky was essential to the future of the Soviet Union he'd (Lenin) envisioned, characterizing such dismissive moves as the "height of stupidity" (Document 106, *The Unknown Lenin*). So Gulliver as Trotsky having some kind of an emotional connection to Lenin is in character for both men and historically justifiable.

"line of gentlemen with rifles" — ("Jack in a Box") During Stalin's purges in the 1930s, thousands of "disloyal" and "counterrevolutionary" types were executed by firing squad, most innocent of the charges brought against them, but caught up in Stalin's consolidation of power machinations. Estimates of those killed during Stalin's purges and recriminations mount into the tens of millions (*EBO*).

"Little White Bull" — ("Clodagh Rogers") A song from the film *Tommy the Toreador* (1959), and written by Lionel Bart, Michael Pratt, and Jimmy Bennett. The film starred Tommy Steele.

"Lyons, Joe" — ("Bingo-Crazed Chinese") Joe Lyons Corner Houses were ubiquitous food establishments, catering royal gatherings and becoming Europe's largest food company before falling prey to the recession of the 1970s. Lyons' Kup Kakes are mentioned prominently in Ep. 33, when Mrs. Neves (Jones) has gone to sea for cakes and macaroons.

• M •

Mao-suited Chinese people — ("Bingo-Crazed Chinese") These actors include Arnold Lee (*Doctor Who*), George Laughing-Sam, Kelwin Sue-a-Quan, C.H. Yang, Jack Tong, and Ken Nazarin (*A Casual Affair*). These actors were cast simply because they were Asian, and were even from a different talent agency than most of the other extras the show acquired (WAC T12/1,440).

"me Blitish consul" — ("Bingo-Crazed Chinese") Continuing the Python (and music hall) tradition of outrageous racial stereotyping, substituting "r" for "l" and squinting for an Asian character (last seen and heard in Ep. 29), though the presence of Chinese infiltrators becomes the more interesting specter here. Again, relations between the Russians and the Chinese were deteriorating at this point, with differing socialist interpretations (Soviet Marxism vs. Chinese Maoism) leading to border concerns as the Chinese military flexed its muscles, and the USSR flexed right back. In this case the Chinese have killed the British ambassador, replaced him, and Chinese minions are actually hiding in the woodwork, emerging at the call of "Housey!"

Mix through to British Consulate — (PSC; "Bingo-Crazed Chinese") The "British Consulate" (where Pither [Palin] enters) is actually Jersey government buildings in Royal Square, St. Helier, Jersey.

"Monte Carlo" — ("Smolensk") The helpful Military Man (Idle) has trouble distinguishing direction, especially the difference between west and east. Monte Carlo, Monaco, is about 100 miles south of Turin, Italy, about 177 miles (along the coast) *west* of Pisa, Italy (not east), and about 520 miles *east* of Bilbao, Portugal (not west).

Shakespeare, of course, provides similarly bad (and probably memorial) directions in *Richard III*:

> [He confuses] travel directions from Northampton to London: "Last night, I [hear], they lay at Stony-Stratford/ And at Northampton they do rest to-night. / Tomorrow, or next day, they will be here" (2.4.1–3). Following these directions it certainly would not be tomorrow or the next day; one would find the Irish Sea quicker than the city of London. Phyllis Rackin offers that Shakespeare's dubious geography was certainly "careless only because he had better things to do with his settings than plot their locations on a map. . . ." (Larsen, *MPSERD*)

As has been seen, Python has relied less on hyper-accurate research and more on the group memory of names, places, and events. In Ep. 33, for instance, Mousebender says he's been reading *Horace* Walpoling, when he clearly meant he'd been reading *Hugh* Walpole. See notes to the "Cheese Shop" sketch.

• N •

"North Cornwall" — ("Mr. Pither") Though he says he's enjoying North Cornwall, most of the locations Mr. Pither mentions are in Devon, where the Pythons spent a great deal of time shooting locations in May 1970. In additon, every bit of the country he's currently riding through is found on the island of Jersey, where the Pythons spent much of the March–May 1972 period.

• O •

"Okehampton by-pass" — ("Jack in a Box") Okehampton is in Devon just north of Dartmoor.

"old fashioned girl" — ("Jack in a Box") Lyrics from the 1957 song "Just an Old-Fashioned Girl" by Marve Fisher.

"Ottery St. Mary" — ("Mr. Pither") Also in Devon, Ottery St. Mary lies about ten miles east of Exeter.

• P •

"Permanent Revolution" — ("Jack in a Box") A concept adapted by Trotsky from Marx's writings, Trotsky defines "permanent revolution" this way:

> The complete victory of the democratic revolution in Russia is conceivable only in the form of the dictatorship of the proletariat, leaning on the peasantry. The dictatorship of the proletariat, which would inevitably place on the order of the day not only democratic but socialistic tasks as well, would at the same time give a powerful impetus to the international socialist revolution. (*Permanent Revolution*)

Part of the purpose of Trotsky's definition—placing all power in the hands of the working proletariat and shared with the peasantry, and pressing for social revolution worldwide—was to illumine the dangers of Stalin and Bukharin's centralized grab for power in the late 1920s. Stalin would, of course, eventually win that battle, too, and then have Bukharin (b. 1888) executed in 1938, and Trotsky in 1940.

Trotsky probably didn't intend the concept to be as sensual as delivered by the Eartha Kitt character here, however. Kitt—American television's "Catwoman"—was known to "purr" a sultry introductory "I'm here" when she took the stage in concert. Kitt had performed in stage plays, appeared on variety shows, and headlined at the Queen Elizabeth Hall, all in Great Britain and all in 1972—she was very high profile all year.

Petrograd . . . Moscva — ("Jack in a Box") St. Petersburg was only known as Petrograd between 1914 and 1924, when its name was changed officially to Leningrad.

"Lewgrad" is a reference to Sir Lew Grade (1906–1998), producer of myriad entertainments—movies, television, theater productions, etc.—in the UK, and founder of ATV. The Goons mention Lord Grade ("Lew Grade in rags?"), as well.

"Lesliegrad" is a reference to Lew Grade's brother, Leslie (1916–1979), a partner in Grade's production company.

Pither is writing up his diary — (PSC; link into "Trotsky") Portions of this Pither character may be a parody of Palin himself, as he was and is a devoted diarist. The first volume (1969–1979) was published in 2006.

"Pogrom" — ("Smolensk") A pogrom is an official or at least officially *tolerated* riot action against the Jewish population in Russia.

• R •

Red Book — ("Bingo-Crazed Chinese") The collection of Mao's writings made official and required reading, and called *The Quotations of Mao Tse-Tung*, first printed in 1964.

"reputedly self-sealing" — ("Mr. Pither") A terrific example of Pither's empiricist philosophy (see "Cycling Tour" entry above). His a priori knowledge turns out to be secondhand, of course, and therefore unreliable when the real-world experience—where the Tupperware hits the road—presents itself to him after a cycling crash. The lesson learned is that firsthand experience counts in the world, and he even attempts to prepare himself for the next (and inevitable) crash by asking the Woman (Cleese) where she keeps her eggs. English philosopher John Locke (1632–1704) notes that it is only through "sensation" and "reflection" that we acquire ideas; and Pither is certainly the wide-eyed "white paper" Locke describes where experience is written.

Locke has already been mentioned by the Pythons in Ep. 22, where he is one of the subjects to be taught by the new Bruce, Michael (Jones) at the University of Woollamaloo. Locke is also mentioned as a member of the defeated English football team in the second *Fliegender Zirkus* episode.

"Rich, Buddy" — ("Clodagh Rogers") American jazz and Big Band drummer. Rich (1917–1987) had appeared on BBC 2 just prior to the Eurovision Song Contest broadcast (on BBC 1) in March 1972, and in November he and his band headlined at Ronnie Scott's, both times to solid reviews by London music critics.

Rodgers, Clodagh — ("Clodagh Rogers") Irish-born singer whose "Jack in the Box," Britain's entry in the 1971 Eurovision Song Contest (3 April 1971) held in Dublin, came fourth. This is the song Pither is talking about when he tries to comfort her as she becomes Trotsky: "Did enjoy your song for Europe, Clodagh."

Russian 42nd International Clambake — ("Jack in a Box") The First International (International Working-men's Association) was convened in Geneva in 1866, and at later Internationals Trotsky would argue his anti-Stalinist policies, essentially sealing his own demise.

• S •

"SCENE MISSING" — ("Jack in a Box") In the early days of film censorship, offending reels of film or just shots were often removed (by local or national review boards, or even projectionists) with little thought to continuity. This removal creates a deus ex machina for Pither and Gulliver, allowing them a fantastical escape. In this case, the narrative metalepsis or disruption means that the characters necessarily miss the execution scene, which is cut from the film, and end up safe and happy in the Devon (well, Jersey) countryside, no worse for the wear.

"Smolensk" — ("Smolensk") A Russian city approximately 190 miles *east* of Minsk (not west), about 289 miles north of Kursk, and 1,644 miles west of Omsk. Smolensk is also about 1,544 miles from Tavistock, give or take a few miles.

"Solzhenitzhin" — ("Jack in a Box") Most of this Russian is gibberish, but there are a few recognizable words, including a variation of the name of the noted author and former prison camp inmate Aleksandr Solzhenitsyn (1918–2008), author of *One Day in the Life of Ivan Denisovich* (1962). Solzhenitsyn was awarded the Nobel Prize in 1970.

"oblomov"—The central and titular character in *Oblomov* by Ivan Goncharov (1858).

"Stalin has always hated me" — ("Trotsky") Cricket journalist and adept world historian C.L.R. James, writing in *World Revolution 1917–1936* (1937), defined this particularly venal enmity:

Yet, as Lenin, quite obviously saw, the immediate origin of the danger was personal. Lenin did not say so in so many words. *The Testament* is very carefully phrased, but all through the civil war there had been clashes between Trotsky and Stalin. Stalin, with Zinoviev and Kamenev, who supported him at first, hated Trotsky, but Stalin hated him with a hatred which saw in him the chief obstacle to his power; Zinoviev and Kamenev Stalin knew he could manage. (chapter 6)

Stock film of Kremlin — ("Jack in a Box") The stock film is a Pathé reel called "Kremlin." The music in this transition is "Variety Playoff" by M. Hunter (WAC T12/1,440).

• T •

"Taisez-vous" — ("Clodagh Rogers") "Who's there?" Translations of the balance of the sometimes fractured Python French:

M. Brun (Cleese): "Taisez-vous. Qu'est-ce que le bruit? C'est impossible! ("Who is it? What's that noise? It's impossible!")

Mme. Brun (Idle): "Mais oui—c'est Clodagh Rogers!" ("Yes, it's Clodagh Rogers!") . . . "C'est Clodagh Rogers la fameuse chanteuse Anglaise." ("It's Clodagh Rogers the famous English singer!")

Genevieve (Chapman): "Excusez-moi Madame Clodagh. Ecrivez-vous votre nom dans mon livre des hommes célèbres, s'il vous plait. Là, au-dessous de Denis Compton. Maman! Ce n'est pas la belle

Clodagh. ("Excuse me, Madame Clodagh. Could you write your name in my book of male celebrities. There, below Denis Compton. Mama! This isn't the beautiful Clodagh!")

Mme. Brun: "Quoi?" ("What?")

Genevieve: "C'est Trotsky le révolutionaire." ("It's Trotsky, the revolutionary!")

Mme. Brun: "Mais Trotsky ne chante pas." ("But Trotsky doesn't sing.")

M. Brun: "Il chante un peu." ("He sings a little.")

Mme. Brun: "Mais pas professionalement. Qu'il pense de Lenin." ("But not professionally. Then you'd think of Lenin.")

M. Brun: "Ah! Lenin!! Quel chanteur." ("Ah, Lenin! What a singer.")

M. Brun: "Et aussi Monsieur Kerensky avec le 'Little White Bull', eh?" ("And Mr. Kerensky with 'The Little White Bull,' eh?")

And moments later when the lovers are in the car:

Frenchman: "Je t'aime." ("I love you.")

French Girl: "Maurice! Regardez! C'est la chanteuse anglaise Clodagh Rogers." ("Maurice! Look! It's that English singer Clodagh Rogers.")

Frenchman: "Ah mais oui! Jacques dans la boîte. . . ." ("It is! 'Jack in the Box'. . . .")

"tarmacadam surface" — ("Mr. Pither") "Tar penetration macadam" is a highway surface type, which essentially means "asphalt."

"Taunton" — ("Clodagh Rogers") Taunton is in Somerset, while the A237 runs through Greater London and runs south from Wandsworth, and past Croydon.

"Tavistock" — ("Mr. Pither") Pither falls off in front of The Peirson on Royal Square in St. Helier, Jersey, and not in Tavistock, Devon.

"ten woods" — ("Mr. Pither") Colloquialism for half a pack of cigarettes.

Theme music — ("Mr. Pither") Pither's cycling theme music is a snippet of the Vienna Philharmonic playing "Waltz from Faust" by Gounod (WAC T12/1,440).

through the streets — ("Jack in a Box") The music behind this chase scene is the London Symphony Orchestra playing "Gayaneh Ballet Suite: Dance of the Young Kurds" and "Fire" by Khachaturian (WAC T12/1,440).

The frantic ending to this film plays very much like a Peter Sellers or even Terry-Thomas film of the 1950s and 1960s (or a Fleischer Brothers Betty Boop cartoon from the 1930s).

tiny village high street — ("Mr. Pither") These scenes were actually shot on Jersey, in and around St. Helier and St. Ouen.

"Tiverton" — ("Mr. Pither") Tiverton is also in Devon, on the Exe and Lowman rivers.

"Tizer" — ("Mr. Pither") A soft drink; in December 1972 A.G. Barr had purchased the Tizer brand. Interestingly, the reviled Slater Walker Trust (called Slater Nazi in Ep. 30) had held Tizer through Armour Trust up until about 1971.

The Tizer brand had also made the huge leap into the US market as of June 1972, with the confidence that it could compete favorably with giants Coke and Pepsi in its first test market, California. (The author/editor was an 8-year-old in central California at this time, and, for the record, has no recollection of Tizer on supermarket or convenience store shelves. The author/editor also admits that as an 8-year-old he may not have been the best source for period information.) See "Full of Fizz," *Times*, 20 June,1972: 19.

"Tonblidge Wells" — ("Bingo-Crazed Chinese") Tunbridge Wells is in Kent, south of London. Baden-Powell (mentioned above) went to school in Tunbridge Wells.

train wheels in the night — ("Jack in a Box") The incidental music under this unnamed film stock is played by the International Studio Orchestra, from the album *Modern Transport*, and is called "Long Haul" by Keith Papworth (WAC T12/1,440).

transport café — ("Mr. Pither") Essentially, a truck stop (or lorry stop).

"Trotsky" — ("Clodagh Rogers") Leon Davidovich Trotsky (1879–1940) had, with Lenin, spent time in London planning their revolutionary activities, and then became the military mind of the Revolution. It was in the period 1922–1923, when Lenin's health was failing, that Stalin and friends consolidated their power against Trotsky. Stalin would later have most of those same "friends" eliminated, as well. It's somewhat ironic that one of the charges leveled against Trotsky in 1924 (by Stalin's associates) was that he had "distorted" his role in the October Revolution—raising his level of action and reducing the influence of others (a charge that could have been laid at Stalin's door, as well). In other words, he changed as the current situation demanded, not unlike Gulliver-Clodagh-Trotsky-Eartha Kitt in this episode.

• W •

Watney's pub — ("Mr. Pither") Pubs that sold the line of Watney beers, including the Red Barrel so loathed by the Tourist (Idle) in Ep. 31. A noteworthy conflation has to be a 1971 advertising campaign employed by Watney's. Billboards featuring Khrushchev, Mao, and Fidel Castro, each drinking a heady glass of Red Barrel, along with an invitation to "Join the RED Army," graced some London hoardings.

• Y •

"Young Generation" — ("Clodagh Rogers") The Young Generation were actually performing with Engelbert Humperdinck in 1972 for a West German television variety show, not with Buddy Rich. The Young Generation had also appeared fairly recently on the BBC in *Christmas with the Stars* (December 1971), appearing with Engelbert Humperdinck (Eps. 18 and 19) and Lulu (Eps. 21 and 28).

"Young Men's Anti-Christian Association" — ("Jack in a Box") The YMCA had been in Russia since 1900, but as an admitted evangelical Christian society, was officially shut down by Soviet authorities in 1919.

The Desk Clerk's (Gilliam) later "Lack of God!" oath is another reminder of the so-called godless society of Soviet Communism.

Episode 35: "The Olympic Hide-and-Seek Final"

Bomb on plane; "I won't ruin your sketch for a pound"; "A Naked Man"; "And now" Man being interviewed, and "It's" Man; *Titles* (Gumby Palin v/o); Ten seconds of sex; "We'll be continuing with *Monty Python's Flying Circus . . .*"; Housing project built by characters from nineteenth-century English literature; M1 interchange built by characters from *Paradise Lost*; Mystico and Janet—Flats built by hypnosis; Accidental executions; *Mortuary Hour*; *Animation: How to animate cut-outs, St. Anthony on a break, WWI helmets*; The Olympic hide-and-seek final; Butlin's Redcoat compère; The Cheap-Laughs; *Probe*: Bull-fighting; The British Well-Basically Club; *Animation: A simple little push of a button, two trees, and Hitler*; Prices on the planet Algon; Interrupting the show with closing credits

• A •

"accidentally hanged" — (*"Mortuary Hour"*) There may have been an "accidental" hanging in the UK, and fairly recently. In April 1962, James Hanratty was hanged for murder and attempted murder, in the so-called A6 Murders, a crime for which another man, Peter Alphon, later allegedly confessed. Hanratty's family and many others campaigned actively for years to exonerate him. This followed the conviction and execution of Timothy Evans, well known for his alleged role in the 10 Rillington Place murders referenced in Ep. 27. Evans was characterized by many as mentally deficient, offering several different accounts of the deaths, eventually accusing a neighbor, John Reginald Christie. Evans was hanged in March 1950. Christie would be found to have killed a number of women and hidden them around his house just a few years later. Writer Ludovic Kennedy (see notes to Ep. 37) championed Evans's innocence for many years.

Adam and Eve — ("M1 Interchange Built by Characters from *Paradise Lost*") These two actors—Paul Barton and Laurel Brown—signed "nudity" contracts with the BBC to appear partly clothed here. This scene seems to have been filmed on 16 March 1972 (WAC T12/1,460). In a clever, easily missed throwaway gag

in the middle background, Eve gives Adam a bite of something as they work in the trenches together.

"Aldebaran" — ("Prices on the Planet Algon") This bright star is actually in the constellation Taurus and, connecting it back to the Brigadier's (Cleese) rant, is called "The Bull's Eye."

Algon 1 — ("Prices on the Planet Algon") Launched in March 1972, on 15 July 1972 the *Pioneer 10* spacecraft passed through the asteroid belt on its journey toward Jupiter, and was the subject of much media coverage and intense scientific speculation. *Pioneer 10* is currently on the way toward Aldebaran (see above), which is more than sixty-five light years distant—scientists estimate the trip can be made in about two million years (*EBO*). There were many print and aired stories covering the trip past Jupiter, with many speculations as to just what might characterize the planet's atmosphere, surface, and even bacterial life. The concurrent concern about the costs of these explorations may have contributed to the Pythons' "prices on a distant planet" narrative.

The Apollo program (1969–1972) had completed six manned missions to the Moon by this time. This frenetic, over-the-top coverage is yet another jab at the BBC's exhaustive coverage of the recent Apollo lunar landings, which James Burke (see "M'Burke" below) also covered.

"an 1100" — ("Prices on the Planet Algon") This could be either a Morris or Simca 1100, both small cars available in the UK at this time. The Morris was a British car, which makes it the more likely reference, and the Simca was built by Chrysler for the Continental market.

Animation: with Gilliam's hands in shot — (PSC; "*Animation: How to animate cut-outs*") There are several recognizable figures in this animation. First, the character waiting in the wilderness is St. Anthony from Dürer's *St. Anthony Reading* (1519). The artist Albrecht Dürer has figured significantly in the initial *Fliegender Zirkus* episode (earlier in 1971), as well. Gilliam will again draw this character (and many others) from various Dürer and Hieronymus Bosch sources as he prepares for the animated sequences in *Monty Python and the Holy Grail* (1974). Additionally, the French general whose neck elongates is General Joseph Gallieni (1849–1916). Gallieni would die from natural causes during the war. The floating tin helmets are attached to British WWI infantry (specifically, the Royal Irish Rifles) waiting in a trench. This is a much-reprinted photo of the devastating Somme campaign, and has appeared in many period history books. Lastly, the "surprised" general whose helmet flies off (with deadly results) is Count Franz Conrad von Hötzendorf (1852–1925), an Austro-Hungarian army Chief of the General Staff during WWI.

"Antony has his Cleopatra" — ("Mystico and Janet— Flats Built by Hypnosis") This photographic still is from the Mansell Collection, "Anthony & Cleopatra" B127 (WAC T12/1,443).

"Archangel Gabriel" — ("M1 Being Built by Characters from *Paradise Lost*") An angel of mercy, Gabriel actually captures Satan attempting to seduce Adam and Eve to evil, and forces him to leave their presence (*Paradise Lost*, chapter 8).

"asbestos-lined ceilings" — ("Housing Project Built by Characters from Nineteenth-Century English Literature") It was just recently, in 1971, that the installation of asbestos materials in construction was banned in the United States. These nineteenth-century characters, however, would have carried on the asbestos installation without pause—it was ubiquitous as an insulation material after the advent of the Industrial Revolution.

Asbestos was much in the news during this period, especially as ships like the celebrated *QE2*, being built in the financially struggling Clyde shipyards, experienced lengthy delays as installed asbestos linings

(approved in 1968, declared hazardous not long after) had to be completely removed by special covered saws (*Private Eye*, 2 July 1971: 20). Stopgap funding from the sitting Labour government helped pay for these snafus. The Asbestos Regulation Act of 1969 had been implemented in 1970.

Austin 30 — (PSC; "Mystic and Janet—Flats Built by Hypnosis") A small car introduced in 1951 from the Austin Motor Company.

• **B** •

Badger, Mr. — (PSC; "Bomb on Plane") With this appearance and his previous appearance in Ep. 32, Mr. Badger (Idle) has begun living up to the metaphoric meaning of his name, as he tends to good-naturedly badger anyone he contacts.

"Bassey, Shirley" — ("*Mortuary Hour*") Welsh-born singer Bassey (b. 1937) had recently performed the hit song "Diamonds Are Forever" from the James Bond film of the same name (1971). The song was composed by John Barry. Bassey had also appeared on television at least twice in 1972, once with Rolf Harris and once with Segment.

"Battersby" — ("*Mortuary Hour*") Roy Battersby (b. 1936) had produced and directed a landmark film, *The Body* (1970), which took viewers on an unprecedented, endoscopic guided tour of the human body. Battersby had worked for the BBC in the Science and Features area since at least 1963, and is also credited with co-founding *Tomorrow's World*, a show mentioned in Ep. 20.

"Bergsonian" — ("Naked Man") Theorist Henri Bergson (1859–1941) has been mentioned a number of times in *FC*, especially by and in relation to Cleese. Specifically, Bergson wrote:

> Laughter is, above all, a corrective. Being intended to humiliate, it must make a painful impression on the person against whom it is directed. By laughter, society avenges itself for the liberties taken with it. It would fail in its object if it bore the stamp of sympathy or kindness. . . . In this sense, laughter cannot be absolutely just. Nor should it be kind-hearted either. Its function is to intimidate by humiliating. Now, it would not succeed in doing this, had not nature implanted for that very purpose, even in the best of men, a spark of spitefulness or, at all events, of mischief. Perhaps we had better not investigate this point too closely, for we should not find anything very flattering to ourselves. (chapter V)

So if in Bergson's terms rigidity is the comical, and laughter is its corrective, then the Pythons clearly share that definition. With a certain glee of "spitefulness" they puncture straight-laced types in every level of society—from middle-class Tory Housewives to the Upper Class to the Monied Elite (City Gents and Merchant Bankers), and any inflexible organization—the Church, the Military, the Monarchy, the Constabulary—in British society or history.

"Bob Cratchett on his father's back" — ("Housing Project Built by Characters from Nineteenth-Century English Literature") A mistake here, probably intended to be "Tim Cratchett on his father's [Bob's] back." Tim is played by the child actor Balfour Sharp, who was attending the Corona Stage School (26 Wellesley Road, W4), and his mother may have picked up his check, according to BBC payroll records (WAC T12/1,460). The Pythons also switched the Walpoles, Horace and Hugh, earlier in Ep. 33. Shakespeare did this fairly regularly, as well, especially in his history plays. In *1 Henry IV*, for example, he mixes his Mortimers, moves battles around to suit his chronological and dramatic needs, and changes ages of his characters when necessary.

See notes to *1 Henry IV* in Evans's *The Riverside Shakespeare*, as well as Larsen's *MPSERD* for more.

brief funny noises — ("*Mortuary Hour*") Shows from BBC1 deejays like Bob Callan, whose theme song—"Can You Dig Bob Callan?"—is of the ilk the Pythons seem to be lampooning here, complete with inane radio babble and sound effects. Early BBC1 deejays Tony Blackburn and David Gregory could also qualify for this dubious honor. The *Guardian* stood with the Pythons, reporting in October 1971: "Radio 1 and 2 were the deeper part in the warm sea of mediocrity" (quoted at radiorewind.co.uk, where clips of these shows can be heard). Blackburn and Gregory are featured on a 1970 "Top of the Pops" cover of the *Radio Times*.

"Brontë, Anne" — ("Housing Project Built by Characters from Nineteenth-Century English Literature") A Northern-born author (Yorkshire), Anne (1820–1849) was the younger sister of authors Emily (*Wuthering Heights*) and Charlotte (*Jane Eyre*). Anne's *The Tenant of Wildfell Hall* appeared in 1848, not long before she died at Scarborough. See the *"Tenant . . ."* entry below for more on the novel.

"building site" — ("Housing Project Built by Characters From Nineteenth-Century English Literature") This construction site was found at Sussex Gardens and Southwick Street, where Wates Ltd. were building both the towers and the shorter (five stories) apartment blocks that framed the site. These first few images are taken inside the common green area of one

of these developments. The shots were recorded on 16 March 1972.

• C •

castle — (PSC; "The Olympic Hide-and-Seek Final") Don (Chapman) is hiding in Mont Orgueil Castle in Jersey, and specifically in the Long Cellar, also called the Crypt Chapel of St. George.

"Clochmerle" — (link into "The Cheap-Laughs") *Clochemerle* was a short-lived (nine episodes, all in 1972) BBC2 comedy about a French town that builds a urinal as a war memorial. The show was co-produced by Bavarian television (Bavaria Atelier GmbH, which produced the *Fliegender Zirkus* episodes in 1971), and was shot on location in France, which would have greatly increased production costs in relation to other contemporary BBC shows.

"Coward, Noël" — (PSC; "Naked Man") Noël Coward (1899–1973) was the quintessentially English playwright, novelist, screenwriter, singer, and songwriter, who breathed life back into British live theater in the 1920s and then carried the stage through the Depression and war years. By the 1950s, though, the bloom was off his rose, leading social critics like Richard Hoggart to dismiss him as hopelessly passé. (See the entry for "pantomime Princess Margaret" in Ep. 30 for more on Hoggart's dim view of the decade.) By 1972 he was the venerable old man of London stage and screen letters, and is seen by the Pythons, at least, holding court like Dr. Johnson or John Dryden might have. The Goons mention Coward's work often—kiddingly, "Noël Coward–type dialogue"—whenever their subject matter is less than urbane.

current-affairs-type programme — (PSC; "Bull-Fighting") The music used here is from "Music for Technology," "Industrial Sounds" by Walter Scott (WAC T12/1,443).

Cut to a brigadier — (PSC; "The British Well-Basically Club") The portrait next to the mincing brigadier (Cleese) appears to be of General Douglas Haig (1861–1928), was a British senior officer during World War I. Haig is likely included here due to his reputation as a field commander who lost thousands of troops during the Somme battle, and became known as "Butcher Haig."

Cut to an animated sketch — (PSC; "*Animation: A simple little push of a button, two trees, and Hitler*) The original song in this sketch was the source of some controversy. In the WAC records there is a copy of a letter from the renowned animation team Halas and

Batchelor (dated 20 Dec. 1972; WAC T12/1,413). The letter asserts that in the show transmitted 14 December 1972 (Ep. 35) a sound track was used in violation of copyright. The song initially appeared, it seems, in the "two growing trees" animated sequence that leads into the "Remember 1937/Hitler" section, and then the Planet Algon sketch. The letter complains that the song was from a German TV spot created by HB, and they want to know how and why Gilliam lifted it without permission. There is no record of a return letter, or of specific/recuperative action taken by the BBC, except that the song was likely replaced for rebroadcast. Music rights forced the change of a number of episodes for rebroadcast, and was (and still is) common at the BBC and other TV producers of the time.

cut to Trafalgar Square — (PSC; "The Olympic Hide-and-Seek Final") The stirring music used here is Jack Trombey's "March Trident" as played by the International Studio Orchestra (WAC T12/1,443). This track can be heard at the DeWolfe website. (The DeWolfe catalogue of program music would provide much of the incidental music for *Holy Grail*, incidentally.)

• D •

donkey jacket — (PSC; "Housing Project Built by Characters from Nineteenth-Century Literature") The character is wearing a "donkey jacket," a workman's jacket designed for warmth and rain protection.

Don Roberts hails a cab — ("The Olympic Hide-and-Seek Final") The music here is from the Pul Piotet et son Grand Orchestre, "Dance Mood Music, Les fous de soleil" by St. George (WAC T12/1,443).

• E •

"East Scottish Airways" — ("Bomb on Plane") A fictional airline. BEA had taken over regional airlines like Scottish Airways in 1947. Scottish-based Caledonian Airways had been founded in 1961.

"eighteen-level motorway interchange" — ("M1 Interchange Built by Characters from *Paradise Lost*") A reference to the then new and novel (and celebrated) "four-level stack" interchanges that began appearing in the UK in 1966, when the Almondsbury, Bristol, stack opened at the M4-M5 exchange. As with many other hobbies in the UK, there is at least one website dedicated to spotting and cataloging these interchanges (see, for example, cbrd.co.uk/reference/interchanges).

There were also negative reactions to this progress, of course, with many complaining that such roadways and especially the sprawling, unappealing interchanges devalued the countryside and villages around them, creating inner-city American ugliness. In the election for the Greater London Council and Inner London Education Authority of 9 April 1970, candidates aligning themselves with the "Homes before Roads" group and policies appeared on ballots in all inner and outer London boroughs. HBR candidates' collective goal was to save Greater London from the scheduled "London Development Plan" with its vast array of "ringways." In late March 1970 the GLC confessed that the new motorways and widening projects would destroy about 20,000 homes in the Greater London area. In the ensuing election, no HBR candidates were successful in unseating either the Conservative or Labour incumbents or candidates. (In the end, the GLC remained Conservative while the ILEA swung to Labour.)

Episode 35 — This episode was recorded ninth in the third season, on 11 May 1972, and was broadcast on 14 December 1972.

Also appearing in this episode as extras or in photos: Paul Lindley (Eps. 3, 14, 29; *Dixon of Dock Green*), Henry Raynor (*Dixon of Dock Green*), Emmett Hennessy (*Doctor Who*; *Softly Softly*), Laurel Brown (Ep. 39), Frank Lester (Eps. 31, 36, 37, 40; *Jackanory*), Alf Coster (*Law & Order*); on film: Marie Anderson (photo work, too), Laurel Brown, Balfour Sharp (child; *Till Death Do Us Part*), Cyma Feldwick (*Doctor in the House*), Paul Barton (*Z Cars*; *Doctor Who*), David Pike (*Survivors: Lights of London*), Katie Evans (*Softly Softly*) (WAC T12/1,443).

• F •

Frank Bough man — (PSC; "The Olympic Hide-and-Seek Final") Bough (b. 1933) presented *Grandstand*, *Sportsnight*, and *Nationwide*, and was already a ubiquitous television personality, and very much connected to sport.

• H •

"hanged at Leeds" — ("Mystico and Janet—Flats Built by Hypnosis") The death penalty had been abolished in the UK in 1965, so this execution would truly have been a miscarriage of justice. Leeds had been a site for state executions since the nineteenth century.

This fascination with accidental or summary executions might be connected to the speed with which the English court system often heard cases, passed judgments, and executed its criminals. In June 1957 a young man murdered another young man during a robbery in June, and was executed in December 1957. In 1959, a young man found guilty of murdering a retired military man on about 14 January 1959 was hanged even more quickly—on 14 May of that same year. (See the entry "Burlington Wall-banger" in Ep. 43 for more on this latter case.) The death penalty would be done away with in 1965.

Heathcliff and Catherine — (PSC; "Housing Project Built by Characters from Nineteenth-Century Literature") The love-tossed characters from the novel *Wuthering Heights*, who were earlier satirized in the "Semaphore Version of *Wuthering Heights*" sketch, in Ep. 15.

"Here's your pound" — ("Bomb on Plane") This is borrowing from Bugs Bunny's classic turnabouts performed, most memorably, with Daffy Duck (*Rabbit Fire* [1951]; *Rabbit Seasoning* [1952]; *Duck! Rabbit, Duck!* [1953]), where the argument is completely reversed by Bugs' taking the opponent's position in the middle of the debate. Bugs also uses this topos with the umpire in *Baseball Bugs* (1946), and the stranded men on the desert island in *Wackiki Rabbit* (1943). Cartoons admittedly played a profound influence on both the Pythons and their comedy mentors, the Goons. See the "squawk" entry in the notes for Ep. 1 for more on the cartoon connection to both the Goons and *Flying Circus*.

High-rise development area — ("Mystico and Janet—Flats Built by Hypnosis") This building site is in Sussex Gardens, and was being constructed by Wates Ltd. when shooting took place on 16 March 1972 (WAC T12/1,428). Mystico is specifically pictured in front of The Quadrangle, Sussex Gardens, between Southwick Street and Norfolk Crescent. This set of buildings was completed in about 1968.

"Hinckley in Leicestershire" — ("The Olympic Hide-and-Seek Final") Hinckley lies between Birmingham and Leicester, near where Chapman grew up.

"his brain is so tiny" — (*Mortuary Hour*) Another in a long line of jabs at the upper class, this one very much in line with the scathing depictions in "The Upperclass Twit of the Year" discussed earlier in Ep. 12. A similar brain difficulty is troubling British "Great White Hope" boxer Ken Clean-Air Systems (Cleese) in Ep. 18, with removal of the brain being the only sure remedy.

huge hammer strikes him on the head — ("The British Well-Basically Club") This sort of violent, cartoony, retributive action—to beat the campiness out of a character—goes right along with the often violent, retributive actions taken against homosexuals (the Mason in

Ep. 17, the "Rabelaisian" clam squashed flat in Ep. 32, the admittedly "gay" Algy shot in Ep. 33) and women ("She" in the "Science Fiction Sketch") in *FC*. The character Alex (Malcolm McDowell) was subjected to violent therapies in *A Clockwork Orange* (1971), ostensibly to rid him of his violent, sexualized, antisocial behaviors.

"Huntingdon, Arthur" — ("Housing Project Built by Characters from Nineteenth-Century Literature") Arthur Huntingdon is a character from Anne Brontë's *The Tenant of Wildfell Hall* (1848); the visitor Huntingdon does pore over a series of Miss Hargrave's drawings in chapter 17, all the while making "clever" and "droll" remarks. Anne's older sister Emily's 1847 novel, *Wuthering Heights*, is featured in Ep. 15 in semaphore version.

• I •

"Is this character giving you trouble?" — ("Bomb on Plane") Identifying the artificial nature of the narrative, the poorly received performance of a Scottish character is blamed for the demise of the sketch, not the writing or production value. In Ep. 1 a guest being interviewed is similarly labeled and summarily tossed off the interview set ("Arthur 'Two-Sheds' Jackson"). So rather than work out a difficult character situation within the narrative, the Pythons increasingly bring in deus ex machina–type characters and situations (the intruding Scotland Yard detectives in Ep. 29, the "Missing Scene" in Ep. 34, for example) to bring scenes and episodes to a close.

• J •

"Janet" — ("Mystico and Janet—Flats Built by Hypnosis") Marie Anderson plays the character of Janet, appearing on film and in still photos (WAC T12/1,460).

• K •

"Khan, Professor Herman" — ("Prices on the Planet Algon") Khan (1922–1983) was a RAND Corporation military thinker, and can be credited with popularizing the MAD theory—the "Mutual Assured Destruction" scenario should the Soviets attempt an all-out preemptive nuclear strike against the United States. Khan may have been especially frightening to many because he talked openly about "winnable" nuclear wars, and has been seen by many as the influence for the military mindset exhibited in *Dr. Strangelove* (1964). See Bruce-

Briggs's *Supergenius: The Mega-Worlds of Herman Khan* for more.

This frightening man is rendered silly and perhaps less threatening here as he discusses sexy women's underwear—a typical Python method of Bergsonian diminution for the inflexible authority figure.

"Kilmarnock" — ("The Olympic Hide-and-Seek Final") Town in East Ayrshire, Scotland.

• L •

"Little Nell from Dickens' *Old Curiosity Shop"* — ("Housing Project Built by Characters from Nineteenth-Century Literature") Peter Ackroyd points out that girls of Nell's age would most definitely have been working in 1841 London, but that child prostitution would have been their trade, primarily. She would have been the "young woman . . . betrayed by the great metropolis," and mourned by the Victorian reader (*London*, 621). In Dickens's work she is found wandering at night by the narrator, and taken to her "grandfather." The actress here may have been adolescent Cyma Feldwick, who, along with Balfour Sharp (playing Tiny Tim), attended the Corona Stage School in London when they were cast for this brief appearance (WAC T12/1,460).

"*Tess of the D'Urbervilles*"—Thomas Hardy's 1891 novel. In Ep. 17, Hardy (1840–1928) was a novelist installed in the Housewife's (Jones) bedroom ("Poets"), and he is also featured on a Monty Python LP, where he is attempting to begin a new novel in front of a large football-type crowd ("Novel-Writing" from *The Monty Python Instant Record Collection* album). The "farm-hands" depicted would be the Dorset-area people he grew up with and spent his life writing about as inhabitants of his fictional "Wessex." The novel calls into question Victorian morality and judgment, which is perhaps why it is included here.

"Mrs. Jupp, from Samuel Butler's *Way of All Flesh*"—Another Northerner (like the Brontës), Butler (1825–1902) was born in Nottinghamshire and finished this almost anti-Victorian novel in 1885, though it would not be published until after his death in 1902.

"Milton's *Paradise Lost*"—John Milton's magnum opus, *Paradise Lost* is a seventeenth-century English poem of epic proportions, and also upset traditionalists as he looked creatively at the pre- and postlapsarian existences.

• M •

making rather a noise — (PSC; "Mystico and Janet—Flats Built by Hypnosis") The radio is playing a version of "Jack in a Box," as sung by the Pythons. The Clodagh Rodgers song was featured prominently in Ep. 34.

M'Burke, James — (PSC; "Prices on the Planet Algon") BBC Science correspondent James Burke (b. 1936) covered the Apollo missions for the network in 1969 and beyond, and has already been spoofed in Ep. 28. It's not clear why the printed script terms him "M'Burke," except as a simple joke. Burke was also the cohost for *Tomorrow's World*, mentioned in Ep. 20. It's possible that the Pythons are Africanizing Burke's name—an Edgar Rice Burroughs character in the Tarzan series is named "M'buku," for example—just as they created Scots names in Ep. 2 ("McWoolworths"), and Jewish-sounding names in Ep. 6 ("Chapmanberg").

"Mrs. Equator sort of lady" — ("The Cheap Laughs") One of the standardized "type" requests possible as the show goes on—the production design team merely has to seek out wardrobe and hair and makeup requests for Ep. 9, "The Visitors" sketch. Many of these requests and the weekly costuming needs forms are part of the archival WAC collection.

Mystico at wheel of his little Austin **30** — (PSC; "Mystico and Janet—Flats Built By Hypnosis") Mystico and Janet are parked in Cambridge Square, The Quadrangle, Sussex Gardens buildings in sight behind them.

• N •

Nelson, Mr. Beadle — (PSC; "Housing Project Built by Characters From Nineteenth-Century Literature") Admiral Nelson has already made an appearance in *FC*, while Mr. Bumble the Beadle—from Dickens' *Oliver Twist*—makes a first appearance. These characters aren't seen long enough or clearly enough amid the scaffolding and smoke to really be identifiable. Most of the actors are just dressed in period clothing.

"new town site" — ("M1 Being Built by Characters from *Paradise Lost*") A New Town is a purpose-built, planned town, generally away from existing cities, and which became vogue especially in Europe and the UK after the destruction and social upheaval of WWII. These types of "new towns" were just the answer, for Modernists, to the Victorian dilapidation of England's larger cities, providing the opportunity to tear down miles of maze-like structures and design clean, orderly, and efficient spaces for the working poor. The Gustave Doré etching *Over London by Rail* (1870) illustrates the cramped, sooty, oppressive neighborhoods London's working classes called home. New towns like Milton Keynes, Stevenage, and Peterborough were just such planned cities, the last emerging just before *FC* went on the air, in 1968.

"new world record time" — ("The Olympic Hide-and-Seek Final") This may be a comment on the interminable cricket test matches, the record for which was set in 1939 at more than forty-three total playing hours over eleven days. Test cricket is played to a limit of five days, generally. It wouldn't be until 1963 that one-day cricket was introduced, mostly to try and bolster sagging attendance figures across the UK.

"no need to panic" — ("Bomb on Plane") Yet another swipe at one of the Pythons' favorite targets, the Scots, treating the plane's Glaswegian destination as if it is Havana or the Middle East in a hijacking situation.

"note from the Council" — ("M1 Being Built by Characters from *Paradise Lost*") After the Ronan Point disaster in 1968, the local Council made sure gas supply was cut off to the entire development (nine buildings), and the residents had to wait for electric appliances to be installed. See the British Cartoon Archive for editorial page mentions of the problem.

Local or borough councils were (and often still are) charged with providing adequate housing for their citizens, whether the structures are high-rises or apartment blocks (both Ep. 17), semi-detached houses (duplexes; see Ep. 28), bungalows (Ep. 31), or rowhouses (Mrs. Pinnet's house, Ep. 14).

nude organist — (PSC; "A Naked Man") This and the following introduction scenes (including the "It's Man") were shot in Jersey, in the same area as the Reg Pither's "Cycling Tour" scenes. The Organist (Jones) is in a recently harvested cauliflower field; the "And Now" Man (Cleese) is in a commercial tulip field; and the "It's" Man (Palin) looks to be in an area between harvesting fields (there are harvest boxes around him). These scenes were shot in late May 1972, when many of the island's row and field crops would have been in harvest.

• O •

"Olympic Hide-and-Seek" — ("The Olympic Hide-and-Seek Final") The silliness of this event may be in response to the upcoming appearance in the 1972 Summer Olympics of events like handball, slalom canoeing, and water skiing. The episode was recorded in May 1972, months before the 26 August 1972 opening ceremonies in Munich. In these summer Olympics Britain managed four gold medals—sailing, equestrian (two), and women's pentathlon.

"Onan, Clement" — ("Mystico and Janet—Flats Built by Hypnosis") Hardly a surprise that this "well-dressed authoritative person" is tagged by the Py-

thons as a sexual deviant. Onan is a character in the Old Testament who was destroyed by God when he "spilled his seed" rather than impregnate his brother's widow. See Genesis 38. A Chapman character admitted his onanism back in Ep. 31, when Harry Bagot listed his hobbies at the "All-England *Summarize Proust Competition*."

"Oppenheimer spy ring" — ("Mystico and Janet—Flats Built by Hypnosis") Klaus Fuchs (1911–1988) and others who worked with Robert Oppenheimer (1904–1967) at the Los Alamos site in the war years were eventually arrested and tried for spying for the Soviet Union, but not until 1950.

• P •

palm court set — (PSC; link out of "Ten Seconds of Sex") This "palm court set" description in the printed script is a shorthand for the show's production designers to build a very simple chair, table, and curtained backdrop set, designed for a presenter (or linkman) only. The Pythons will use it often, and it will comprise the final set for their final feature film, *The Meaning of Life* (1983).

"Paraguay" — ("The Olympic Hide-and-Seek Final") Paraguay wouldn't send an athlete to the Olympics, summer or winter, until 1988. The Pythons may also be referencing Great Britain's medal paucity in the 1968 and 1972 Olympics, the proud nation accounting for only 31 medals in both games. By comparison, the United States took home 107 medals in 1968 and 94 medals in 1972, and Australia even accounted for 34 medals over the same two games. This same kind of British athletic performance lamentation is also seen in Ep. 7, when the UK must rely on a Scotsman (Palin) to defeat extraterrestrial blancmanges and win Wimbledon.

peer of the realm — (PSC; "*Mortuary Hour*") One who is a member of the peerage, who can sit in the House of Lords. This Peer (Palin) is probably a duke, since he is called "Your Grace." This treatment is similar to what the Upperclass Twits receive in Ep. 12—as a class, the aristocracy (to the Pythons) seems just too collectively dim to even survive.

"perspicacious Paraguayan" — ("The Olympic Hide-and-Seek Final") Probably just a bad word choice, when the character probably meant to use "peripatetic," which both continues the alliteration and the hide-and-seek theme.

"Peterborough" — ("Housing Project Built by Characters from Nineteenth-Century Literature") North of

London, Peterborough was designated a New Town in 1968, with the new townships to be Bretton, Orton, and Paston/Werrington. See the entry for "new town site" above for more.

"plane" — ("Bomb on Plane") Skyjackings began in earnest in about 1961, with a number of domestic American flights being rerouted to Cuba. Skyjacking was seen as a significant political tool for smaller, leftist terrorist cells such as the Popular Front for the Liberation of Palestine (PFLP), which began skyjacking planes in 1968, the first an international El Al flight from Rome to Tel Aviv. The phenomena had become so prevalent during the late 1960s that *Time* magazine devoted its 21 September 1970 cover to these "Pirates in the Sky."

This particular sketch may well have been spurred by the infamous skyjacking in the northwestern United States of 24 November 1971, where a man initially identified as "D.B. Cooper" indicated to a flight attendant that a bomb on the plane would explode unless he was given money and parachutes at the next stop. Mr. Badger (Idle), naturally, isn't given the foresight to consider bringing a parachute or foment any kind of escape strategy. Cooper had demanded (and received) $200,000, and is assumed to have jumped from the plane. In Ep. 16, a Gunman (Palin) hijacks a plane to Luton, but then decides it's less bothersome to be thrown out over Basingstoke.

"prefabricated concrete slabs" — ("Housing Project Built by Characters from Nineteenth-Century Literature") This was the very type of construction—prefab concrete—that would be at least partly to blame for the collapse at Ronan Point. The joining and bolting procedures weren't properly followed in that high-rise project, and the vulnerable seams came right apart in the moderate gas explosion in May 1968 that killed four. See notes to Ep. 17.

Pre-fabricated concrete slabs were also key to the Bauhaus-inspired (thus continental in origin, thus suspect) design and construction dreams of the Modernist architects of the 1930s and beyond in England. These architects embraced the prefab simplicity of concrete slabs, piecing together new buildings onsite, and fairly quickly. (And for the homeowner, Alborough of Surbiton was advertising prefab concrete garages in the early 1960s.) Government embraced the new technology as well, since Labour had promised to build myriad new homes after the 1964 General Election:

> In the next five years we shall go further. We have announced—and we intend to achieve—a target of 500,000 houses by 1969/70. After that we shall go on to higher levels still. It can be done—as other nations have shown. It must be done—for bad and inadequate hous-

ing is the greatest social evil in Britain today. (Dale, *Labour Manifesto*, 1964)

The shadow government Conservatives were also making big promises for thousands of new homes, and the Pythons had already lampooned this hyperbole in Ep. 14, when an interviewer asks pointedly about the government's promise to build "88 million, billion" homes in a single year. The cross-dressed minister answers in a high-pitched squeal.

For more, see the series of articles on Modernism and Modernist architecture—"From Here to Modernity"—at the Open University website.

"Premier Chou En Lai" — (*"Mortuary Hour"*) Probably referring to the "major breakthrough" that was the February 1972 "Shanghai Communiqué," signed by the United States and China, pledging mutual work toward normalized relations. This was Nixon's backdoor way to improved security not only in Southeast Asia, but farther north and west, as a U.S. friend in China meant the Soviet's sabers had to rattle more quietly.

"provided of course people *believe* in them" — (*"Mystico and Janet—Flats Built by Hypnosis"*) Certainly another comment on the still-fresh events at Ronan Point, when a high-rise block partially collapsed after a faulty cooker blew up. See notes to Ep. 17, the "Architect Sketch" for more on that disaster. Local councils continued to "believe in" these high-rises (tower blocks) because they housed so many people so efficiently, and they also believed a greatly reduced cost-per-tenant ratio (whether in the end that was true or not) for towers as opposed to rowhouses was a main consideration. The 1956 Housing Act had even put subsidies on the table for local councils willing to build higher than five stories, so there was great incentive to go skyward during this period.

Also, in 1967, the Wilson government had devalued the pound after many months of denying that any such move was imminent, with Wilson asking, essentially, that the British people still believe in the value of the pound in their "pocket or purse," and that better financial times were just ahead. The pound would be floated again in June 1972, during the Heath administration, just days after Chancellor Anthony Barber had reaffirmed the government's position against such a move on the BBC's *Panorama*.

• R •

"Radio Four" — (*"Mortuary Hour"*) BBC Radio 1, 2, 3, and 4 went on the air on 30 September 1967. Tony

Blackburn was the morning DJ on Radio One, having worked for a pirate radio station previously.

Redcoat — (PSC; link into "Cheap-Laughs") Described in the printed script as a "Redcoat," which is the nickname for hosts at Butlin's Holiday Camps. Palin has already appeared as a Redcoat in Ep. 7, introducing the "Science Fiction Sketch," and the crew shot the Lake Pahoe scene at the Butlin's Holiday Camp pool in Bognor Regis on 18 October 1971 (WAC T12/1,428). These camps would have entertained millions of families on school and bank holidays, and were generally within driving (or train) distance for most in at least the south.

"Robinson, Roger" — ("The Cheap-Laughs") This could be a reference to the Roger Robinson who attended Cambridge at the same time as the Pythons. Coincidentally, Robinson would edit the Pan Classics 1976 edition of Samuel Butler's *The Way of All Flesh*. (See entry for "Mrs. Jupp . . ." above.)

"rota" — ("Housing Project Built by Characters from Nineteenth-Century Literature") A rotation of persons, simply.

• S •

Sardinia — ("The Olympic Hide-and-Seek Final") Castelsardo is a prominent castle in Sardinia, and was probably the inspiration for the location in Jersey where Don Roberts (Chapman) actually hides.

"Scottish money" — ("Bomb on Plane") The Scottish pound is, indeed, numbered, meaning it can be traced.

"self-generating" — ("Housing Project Built by Characters from Nineteenth-Century Literature") The obsession for self-perpetuating machines in the nineteenth century was quite unequaled in history, and wouldn't cool until the law of conservation of energy was discovered/published in the early 1840s, and then slowly disseminated to the world. *Wildfell Hall* appeared in 1848, though the setting is 1827, so Mr. Huntingdon could very well have still been quite enamored of this supernal energy potential.

"shtoom" — (*"Mortuary Hour"*) Already heard in Ep. 14, when Vercotti (Palin) is on the phone, the word is used here in its Cockney vein, generally meaning "shut it." Mr. Wang (Cleese) just wants Battersby (Jones) to shut up and prepare for the peer's visitation.

"sorry about Mon-trerx" — (link into "The Cheap-Laughs") In 1971 the Pythons were invited by the BBC to submit a compilation episode to the Golden Rose of Montreux competition. They then compiled a sort of "best of" the available episodes and set about reshooting (to put everything on film stock). They did not win, finishing behind an Austrian-produced show, and brought home a silver rose. *The Marty Feldman Comedy Machine* show would win the prize the following year.

The compilation episode included the following sketches, most reshot specifically for the competition, in this order: *"Scott of the Sahara,"* a drag minister, "The New Cooker Sketch," "Conrad Poohs and His Dancing Teeth," *"It's the Arts,"* "Wuthering Heights/ Julius Caesar," the fig leaf animation, the "Exploding Version of the Blue Danube," "Newsagent Shop," "Silly Walks," "Birdman," "Butterfly Man" animation, "Blackmail," "Newsreader," "Erotic Film," the Women's Institute footage, "Upperclass Twits," and the end credits run over "Battle for Pearl Harbor" footage, and ending with "Ramsay MacDonald" (WAC T12/1,413). Most of the scenes were shot in late March 1971, and the show was aired 16 April 1971.

Others appearing in this reshoot included: Derek Chafer (*Doctor Who*), John Hughman, David Ballantyne, and Stanley Mason (all Gasmen), Helena Clayton (*The Sex Killer*) as the "Blackmail" dominatrix, and twenty extras (to play Gasmen on 24 March 1971). The Gasmen were: Richard Lawrence (*Doctor Who*), Ivor Owen, Donald Campbell (Eps. 27, 28), William Curran (Ep. 3), David Pike (Ep. 35; *Survivor: Lights of London*), John Baker (*Doctor Who*), Richard Kirk (Ep. 39), Bob Raymond (Eps. 40, 42–45; *Secrets of Sex*), Mike Urry (*Public Eye*), Roger Minnis, Michael Earl (*Doctor in the House*), Terry Leigh (Ep. 32; *Doctor Who*), Leslie Bryant (Eps. 25, 40; *The Wednesday Play*), Alan Wells (*Doctor Who*), Bill Richards (*Dixon of Dock Green*), David Melbourne (*Z Cars*), Harry Tierney (*Doctor Who*), Emmett Hennessey (*Doctor Who*), Eric Kent (*Doctor Who*), and Reg Lloyd (*Softly Softly*). Daphne Davey (*Troubleshooters*) also appears in an insert (WAC T12/1,413).

SUPERIMPOSED CAPTION: 'MR K. V. B. LIAR' — (PSC; "Mystico and Janet—Flats Built by Hypnosis") Mr. K.V.B. Liar (Palin) is being interviewed in front of one of the three Edward Woods Estate buildings (in Hammersmith and Fulham), tower blocks completed in 1967, and probably Stebbing House, specifically. The Pythons will use Flat 79 in Stebbing House for the Tenant and Wife (Idle and Chapman) scene, on 13 March 1972.

"Swalk, Harry 'Boot-in'" — ("Mystico and Janet—Flats Built by Hypnosis") Another indictment of the police as simple thugs ("Boot-in"), "Swalk" isn't even a name, but an ironic acronym for "Sealed with a Loving Kiss."

"Housing Project
nth-Century Lit-
Brontë's second
ator reviewed the
orbid love for the
e estranged wife
ntingdon asserts,
ies and convince
for more on the
rks.

the Pythons—the
he novel starring
he Day the Earth
rly 1969.

Hide-and-Seek
across the street
location permis-
Trafalgar Build-
tted. Permission
ncil, 30 Millbank,
nd noon (WAC

xxxxx   mpic Hide-and-
Seek Final") A central London road that runs north-
south. This area was known for electronics (hobby)
shops for many years. This sketch was shot in both
London and Jersey.

Tretchikoff picture of the Chinese girl — ("The Cheap-
Laughs") This odd, green-and-blue-faced portrait has
been used in previous episodes, most recently behind
the documentary presenter (Cleese) in the "Molluscs"
sketch for Ep. 32. It is also on the cover of an LP of
light music from this period, and was a very popular
framed print after its original painting in 1950. See the
entry "*ordinary suburban living room*" in Ep. 32 for more
on this painting, artist, and phenomena.

In this scene she's been given a penciled-in mus-
tache, probably low art's (and Monty Python's) version of the famous Duchamps treatment of the *Mona
Lisa* in the portrait *L.H.O.O.Q.* (1919).

"train" — ("Bomb on Plane") This is a mnemonic device designed to allow Mr. Badger to correctly remember just where he's put the bomb.

"two separate strands of existence" — ("Naked
Man") Probably a reference to the fairly recent and
(for some) revolutionary book, William Carlo's *The
Ultimate Reducibility of Essence to Existence in Existential
Metaphysics* (1966), where Carlo (1921–1971) examines
the metaphysics of St. Thomas Aquinas. Carlo's writing and reputation may have been more prominent

during this period due to his untimely death at age
fifty in 1971. Carlo was a visiting professor at Oxford
1959–1961. (Jones was at Oxford 1961–1964.)

• U •

"Unless you give me the bomb" — ("Bomb on
Plane") This befuddled-would-be-criminal-meets-
helpful-victims scenario is seen a few years earlier in
the Woody Allen film *Take the Money and Run* (1967),
where earnest but nervous bank robber Allen has to
help the bank staff decipher his scrawled stick-up
note.

• W •

"Whitby" — (*Mortuary Hour*) Whitby is in Yorkshire, but has no record of a significant assize history,
unlike York, for example. There is a traditional song
called "The Whitby Lad" about a ne'er-do-well who,
after punching up a woman, is condemned at the assizes to Botany Bay, the Australian penal colony.

• Y •

"Yeovil, Somerset" — (link out of "Mystico and
Janet—Flats Built by Hypnosis") North and east
of Paignton and Torquay, where the Pythons shot
significant second season footage. Not far off the
A303, the Pythons could have traveled through the
town on their way to and from these locations and
London.

"Younger Generation" — ("British Well-Basically
Club") The Brigadier (Cleese) offers a list of active and
semi-active dance troupes in the London area, circa
1972:

"Lionel Blair Troupe"—Some of the Pythons would
have met dancer/choreographer Blair (b. 1931) when
he choreographed *The Magic Christian* (1969), for
which Chapman and Cleese contributed material.
Blair and his dancers appeared in The Beatles' 1964
film *Hard Day's Night*, as well.

"Irving Davies Dancers"—Welsh-born Davies
(1926–2002) was also a dancer and choreographer
who appeared on Ed Sullivan's *Toast of the Town* (1955)
and choreographed for Cicely Courtneidge (Ep. 6) and
even Twiggy.

"Pan's People"—Dance troupe attached to the very
popular *Tops of the Pops* (1964–2006), the BBC's long-
running pop music show. Their choreographer was

Flick Colby. Both Colby and Pan's People have already been mentioned in the printed scripts, in Ep. 21.

"SAM missiles"—These are Surface-to-Air Missiles, and they can be launched from silos. These missiles became newsworthy during the early years of the Vietnam War (beginning in 1965), when Soviet-made missiles manned by North Vietnamese forces began shooting at (and shooting down) American jets. Also during this period, the Soviets deployed myriad SAMs in underground silos around Moscow, Leningrad, Kiev, for example.

"send in Scottish boys with air cover"—One such regiment has already been mentioned prominently, the Argyll and Southern Highlanders, deployed to Aden in 1967 during mass uprisings. See notes to Ep. 26 for more.

"George Balanchine and Martha Graham"—Balanchine (1904–1983) was a Russian émigré who led American ballet from the 1930s through the 1960s, while Graham (1894–1991) was an American-born ballet dancer and choreographer during that same period.

"Sadler's Wells"—A dance and performance theater in Clerkenwell—there has been a theater space on the property since the late seventeenth century.

"auxiliary role in international chess"—The chess world began to "hot up" in the 1970–1972 period, when a Python-aged grand master would emerge and tweak the nose of international chess. American sensation Bobby Fischer (1943–2008) would beat Soviet champion Boris Spassky (b. 1937) in Reykjavik, Iceland, in September 1972, a few months after this episode was recorded. Leading up to this world championship match, however, the international interest in this mercurial and erratic but entirely watchable young challenger boomed as Fischer beat virtually all comers by staggering margins. He would string together twenty consecutive wins during this period (*EBO*).

Fischer is also significant in his connection to the Worldwide Church of God and the Armstrongs (Ep. 24), all in the news in May 1972. He would donate a large portion of his winnings in September 1972 to the church, but later renounce both the church and its infighting leadership.

Episode 36:
"The Life of Sir Phillip Sidney"

Tudor Jobs Agency; Pornographic bookshop; *The Life of Sir Phillip Sidney*; Elizabethan pornography smugglers; *Animation: Aldwych Theatre's* Gay Boys in Bondage, *and Nude Organist*; Silly disturbances by the Rev. Arthur Belling; Nude Organist, "And now" Man, and "It's" Man and *titles* (Palin Gumby voice); *Animation: Arcade target shooting, mixing a drink, a kiss at the pub*; The free repetition of doubtful words sketch, by an underrated author; *Animation: Folding and posting a letter to the BBC; Is There? . . . life after death?*; The man who says words in the wrong order; **Thripshaw's disease**; Film clips; Silly noises; Sherry-drinking vicar; Closing credits; BBC 1 Colour announces E. Henry Thripshaw t-shirts

• A •

"Acton" — ("Pornographic Bookshop") Acton is a part of Greater London, and is just west of Shepherd's Bush, where BBC Television Centre is located. The Uxbridge Road (Ep. 33) runs through Acton. The Goons had memorialized the city in "The Missing Boa Constrictor" episode, by waxing poetic, as Seagoon decides where to hide: "In the corner of some foreign field . . . that is forever Acton" (apologies to Rupert Brooke).

Aldwych Theatre — (PSC; "Elizabethan Pornography Smugglers") The Aldwych Theatre was the home of the Royal Shakespeare Company of Stratford-upon-Avon between 1960 and 1982, and the "Theatre of Cruelty" in the mid-1960s (see below).

The 1950s and 1960s saw a significant increase in the sexual frankness of London stage plays, including Joe Orton's *Entertaining Mr. Sloane* (1964), which raised the hackles of many in the London theater industry, while encouraging as many others. The so-called Theatre of Cruelty season at the Aldwych Theatre in 1964 also upset and disturbed many, with *Marat/Sade* (Peter Weiss) drawing condemnation from the establishment types, though audience members leaving the theater voiced support for the production, as well as optimism for the future of the English stage

(*Eyewitness: 1960–69*, "'New Writing' and the 'Theatre of Cruelty' Season").

An animated excerpt from this little known Shakespearian masterpiece — PSC; "*Animation: Aldwych Theatre's Gay Boys in Bondage, and Nude Organist*") For this animated sequence Gilliam borrows some of Eadweard Muybridge's still photographs of nude men (c. 1885), as well as portions of two de Vries perspectives.

Gilliam takes most of Plate 42 (seen earlier in the season one credit sequence) and combines it with a bit from Plate 15, which is here being used for the first time. He has colored portions of Plate 42, including the blue water in the medium distance. From Plate 15 Gilliam borrows the arch element at the left of the original, flips it, and places it over the fountain on Plate 42. This creates a proscenium space, of sorts, where the "Shakespearian" nudes can act and recite. The arch element is then slid away as if it were simply a piece of theatrical scenery, a flat, revealing the second actor.

In the following, brief scene, a nude on roller skates (the nude doesn't appear to be a Muybridge image) stands at the edge of a hole, and the shrubbery is clearly borrowed from a Dürer engraving. Specifically, Gilliam used a portion of the bottom left corner of Dürer's *John before God and the Elders* (1498), then colored it, as well. The work of Dürer, Bosch, and loads of images from Gothic manuscripts will populate Gilliam's notes and eventual animations for *Monty Python and the Holy Grail*.

Animation link . . . — ("*Animation: Folding and posting a letter to the BBC*") Again the bulk of the Python troupe have no idea and give no clues to the content of this animated sequence, except that it should act as a link. The horse used in the animation is actually a borrow from the Muybridge collection, as well. Gilliam used the discrete images of a horse walking, captured by Eadweard Muybridge in the 1880s, rephotographing them a frame at a time to create the illusion of motion. In this same episode Gilliam uses Muybridge photographs of a man walking and a man climbing stairs, as well, in the *Shakespeare's Gay Boys in Bondage* animation.

· B ·

"Bridget—Queen of the Whip" — ("Pornographic Bookshop") Some actual erotic titles from the period include *Love Lottery* (1961), *Sleep-In Maid* (1968), and the almost-too-good-to-be-true *Hillbilly Nympho* (1961). The Frankfurt, Germany, office of Olympia Press (see below) published titles that included *Königin der Lust* (*Great Balls of Fire*) in 1970 and *Die Sexfarm* (*Meanwhile, Back at the Sex Farm*, 1971).

· C ·

"Call My Bluff" — ("Thripshaw's Disease") A BBC2 quiz show debuting in 1965, the show ran to 1988, and featured celebrity guests presenting real and fake definitions for *Oxford English Dictionary* words.

"cleaned up a packet" — ("Elizabethan Pornography Smugglers") A colloquialism meaning to obtain (illicitly) a large amount of money.

· D ·

"de Vega, Lope" — ("Elizabethan Pornography Smugglers") Spain's most accomplished and prolific playwright, de Vega (1562–1635) was also a well-known womanizer throughout his life, even after taking vows. He wrote what many call "cloak and sword" plays and poems steeped in intrigue and Spanish history.

"Devon and Cornwall" — ("Pornographic Bookshop") The area in the southwestern portion of England where Pither had supposedly been riding in "The Cycling Tour" (Ep. 34), and where the Pythons had spent weeks shooting location footage for the first season.

"Devonshire Country Churches" — ("Pornographic Bookshop") John Stabb published the trilogy *Some Old Devon Churches* in 1908–1916 (London: Simpkin), a fairly exhaustive examination of area churches as they existed in the Edwardian era.

"Dirty books, please" — ("Pornographic Bookshop") The Obscene Publications Acts of 1959 and 1964 were created to control "the publication of obscene matter; to provide for the protection of literature; and to strengthen the law concerning pornography." The acts test the obscenity of an "article" (picture, magazine, book, film, etc.) as well as provide punishment guidelines for those convicted of publishing and/or distributing such matter. These rather strict laws forced many publishers of pornography in the UK to either close shop or move to more favorable climes, including the Netherlands and Germany.

"doing five years bird" — ("Elizabethan Pornography Smugglers") "Bird-lime" is rhyming slang for "doing time," and often shortened to just "bird."

"Drake" — ("Tudor Jobs Agency") Sir Francis Drake (1540–1596) led Elizabeth's navy against the Spanish Armada in 1588, and was also a bit of a privateer and explorer. Drake was last mentioned in Ep. 29 by Elizabeth (Chapman) in the sketch "*Erizabeth L.*" Lawrence James notes that as late as 1628, however, and the publication of a life of Drake, readers were being encouraged to abandon "this Dull or Effeminate Age to follow his noble steps for Gold and Silver"—a promise of rich employment indeed.

· E ·

Elizabethan music — (PSC; "Elizabethan Pornography Smugglers") These two musical pieces (here and under the credit) seem to be "Lady Margaret's Pavan" and "Sir William Galiard" by composer Gareth Walters (WAC T12/1,447).

"Elizabeth, we supplied the archbishops for her coronation" — ("Tudor Jobs Agency") Elizabeth I (1533–1603) was crowned in January 1559 after the death of her half-sister Mary. According to histories of the period, the church officials needed for the coronation were very nearly "temped" out, since the requisite bishops were severally unavailable. The Archbishop of Canterbury had died just months before, and the remaining high-ranking clergy were, according to Collinson, "either dead, too old and infirm, unacceptable to the queen, or unwilling to serve" (*ODNB*). The bishop of Carlisle eventually carried out the ceremony, clearly temping for Canterbury.

Episode 36 — Recorded 25 May 1972, and broadcast 21 December 1972. This episode was recorded thirteenth, and transmitted tenth.

Others appearing in this episode (or billed to this episode by BBC accountants) but not officially credited include: The Fred Tomlinson Singers, The Cittie Waites (a Tudor Minstrel group), Frank Lester (Eps. 31, 35–37, 40; *Jackanory*), Caron Gardner (Ep. 39; *The Saint*), Peter Kodak (Eps. 27, 29; *Doctor Who*), Graham Skidmore (Eps. 27–29; *Dixon of Dock Green*), John Beardmore (Ep. 34; *Softly Softly*), Bob Midgley (drums), Ralph Dollimore (piano), and Rosalind Bailey (WAC T12/1447). Some of these have been "charged to another episode," but Bailey appears here as the crying Elizabethan Girl, according to IMDb .com. Midgley had played drums on the Frank Sinatra track "Roses of Picardy" in 1962, from *Sinatra Sings Great Songs from Great Britain*. Dollimore had played piano on many albums for the Studio to Stereo label, and in Eric Winstone's band.

• F •

"Frances" — ("Elizabethan Pornography Smugglers") Frances Walsingham (1569–1631) married Sir Philip Sidney in 1583. Her father, Sir Francis Walsingham, was Elizabeth's head of secret police activities. See "Walsingham" entry below.

"Free Repetition of Doubtful Words" — ("The Free Repetition of Doubtful Words Sketch") "For free repetition of doubtful words" is a standard phrase from the bottom of Post Office Telegram pages. The entire line reads:

> For free repetition of doubtful words telephone "TELEGRAMS ENQUIRY" or call, with this form at office of delivery. Other enquiries should be accompanied by this form and, if possible, the envelope.

There are two telegrams included in the early pages of *Monty Python's Big Red Book* (1971), as well.

• G •

"Gargoyle Club" — ("Pornographic Bookshop") Located on Meard Street in Soho, the club was by this period a low-rent bar. The Club had been the hangout for artists and writers in the 1950s, including Dylan Thomas, Francis Bacon, and journalist/presenter Dan-

iel Farson, and was frequented by men seeking the company of other men (or boys).

"Gilbert, Sir Humphrey" — ("Tudor Job Agency") Explorer and politician Gilbert (1537–1583) served under Philip Sidney and was Walter Raleigh's half brother, both mentioned elsewhere in this scene. Gilbert shares the Northwest Passage exploration honors with a number of other explorers.

"Cabot"—Sebastian Cabot (1484–1557) and his father John Cabot (c. 1450–1499) had also looked for the fabled Northwest Passage. Both made significant discoveries in the New World.

"Cathay"—The period name for China.

"Gloucester" — ("Pornographic Bookshop") Probably a reference to Shakespeare's Gloucester in *1 Henry VI*, who appears together with Warwick in the play's opening scene.

group of Spanish singers — ("Sherry-Drinking Vicar") These are the Fred Tomlinson Singers, and the song, "Amontillado," was penned by Tomlinson. The taping was scheduled for 25 May 1972 (WAC T12/1,428).

• H •

"Hamlet" — ("Elizabethan Pornography Smugglers") Written and performed about 1601.

"Harley Street" — ("Thripshaw's Disease") The area in London where myriad medical offices are found.

"Fleet Street"—The center of Britain's publishing industry until the late twentieth century, it was named for the River Fleet.

• I •

"Imperial War Museum" — (*"Is There? . . . Life after Death?"*) A London museum featuring exhibits from various British military campaigns, and located in Lambeth in the former Bedlam Hospital.

The museum was at this time assisting in the production of the epic *World at War* documentary series that would debut on Thames TV in 1973.

"Introduced by Roger Last" — (*"Is There? . . . Life after Death?"*) Roger Last is one of the Floor Managers for the show during this period, often responsible for props, and he appeared in the lingerie shop sketch in Ep. 10.

"J. Losey"—Joseph Losey (1909–1984) was an American-born expatriate who led Britain's New Wave filmmakers into the 1960s and beyond, directing class-conscious social satire films like *The Servant* (1963) and

Accident (1967), both written by Harold Pinter (Eps. 2 and 10).

"L. Anderson"—British filmmaker Lindsay Anderson (1923–1994) has already been mentioned in Ep. 19, where his controversial 1968 film *If. . . .* is satirized.

"S. Kubrick"—Another American expatriate director working in the UK, Kubrick (1928–1999) had recently directed the infamous *A Clockwork Orange* (1971). A *Flying Circus* speaking part extra from the first season, Katya Wyeth, also appeared in a small part in this film.

"P.P. Pasolini"—Pier Paolo Pasolini (1922–1975) was an Italian New Wave director who had directed some of the most important (and Marxist) films of the recent past, including *Accatone* (1964) and *The Decameron* (1971). The authentic, coarse "look" of Pasolini's medieval films influenced the Pythons significantly as they planned and then produced their later feature film, *Monty Python and the Holy Grail*.

"O. Welles"—Iconic American film director and actor Orson Welles (1915–1985).

"B. Forbes"—Bryan Forbes (b. 1926) is a British actor/writer/director already mentioned in Eps. 20 and 23.

"Is There?" — ("*Is There? . . . Life after Death?*") The music under the closing credits for *Is There?* is from Prokofiev's "Symphony No. 3," as performed by the London Symphony Orchestra (WAC T12/1,447).

This panel of experts set-up is probably modeled after the popular radio and then TV program *The Brains Trust* (1955). Topics included questions like "What Is Civilisation?" for example, and various eminent church men, philosophers, scholars, novelists, and even Dr. Bronowski (Ep. 22) appeared on the show (Vahimagi, 47).

"I think I will" — ("Elizabethan Pornography Smugglers") Here, Gaskell (Palin) crosses over not only into the appearance of the Elizabethan world, but allows himself to become part of that world by admitting its possible existence, and eventually partaking of its niceties. And whether Gaskell is actually Sidney isn't important—for most of the remainder of the episode he *is* Sir Philip Sidney. He is either acting the part, which is quite possible, or we have crossed the fringes of time (as is apt to happen in the world of Python) and are back in Tudor times.

• J •

"job on the buses, digging the underground" — ("Pornographic Bookshop") As recently as the 1950s, the UK government had resorted to inviting/imploring Caribbean workers to staff the buses, trains, and underground service positions in London, due to a severe shortage of interested native workers (Judt, 335–36). This welcome mat would be yanked in the early 1960s, when the flood of former-colonial-now-Commonwealth-workers inundated the UK work force, making even menial labor very hard to come by for native Englishmen. The immigration problem became so vexing that even the sitting Labour government took up the cause, sponsoring laws to curb Commonwealth immigration—a damaging public relations move for the party of the underrepresented.

• K •

knights sack a village, looting, pillaging, burning and murdering — (PSC; "Thripshaw's Disease") The clips are borrowed from a 1960 Polish film depicting a 15th-century battle. The film is *Knights of the Teutonic Order*, or *Black Cross*, and is directed by Aleksander Ford (1908–1980). (Thanks to Tomasz Dobrogoszcz.) The WAC material does not account for these clips.

The music appended to the clip is accounted for in the archives—it's from Sergei Eisenstein's film *Alexander Nevsky* (1938). Specifically, portions are from the "Battle on the Ice" sequence, and was composed by Prokofiev.

• L •

"London 1583" — ("Elizabethan Pornography Smugglers") It was during this period that Sidney was doing more writing than courtly duties, and he wouldn't be married until September 1583 ("Philip Sidney" at *ODNB*).

loud silly noises — ("Silly Disturbances [The Rev. Arthur Belling]") The hooting Belling (Palin) voices are borrowed from the "Language Laboratory" (Ep. 31). The episodes were recorded approximately one month apart.

• M •

Maddox pauses only to pick a book from the bookcase near the door — (PSC; "Pornographic Bookshop") The scope of the corruption discovered in the Flying Squad and Metropolitan Police rank and file during the "Soho porn merchants" investigations in the early 1970s led to approximately 400 actions against officers—ranging from reprimands to reassignments to criminal prosecution. Maddox (Chapman) is offering an accurate example of the contradictory nature of the times—the policemen in charge of ferreting out pornography and pornographers were often themselves enjoying and profiting from that same industry. Many in the police force seemed to believe that as long as the pornography wasn't targeting or exploiting children, for instance, then it should be monitored but essentially left alone (*Eyewitness 1970–79*, "The Oz Trial"). See the entry for "sad I am" below for specifics on the Soho investigations.

Former Labour MP Raymond Blackburn (1915–1991) in October 1972 claimed the following as he was attempting to have police "forced" to crack down on Soho pornography:

> [P]olice officers of the pornographic materials department at Scotland Yard were on the most friendly terms with the men who owned or controlled virtually all the bookshops selling the extreme hard pornography in Soho . . . this was common knowledge in Soho, because no attempt was made to conceal it. ("No Early Hearing of Pornography Claim," *Times*, 14 Oct. 1972: 5)

magazines in racks — ("Pornographic Bookshop") Most of these are images from actual "dirty books," but the magazine prominently displayed behind the Second Assistant (Idle) is *Woman & Home*, a popular (and non-pornographic) UK ladies' magazine still published today. Straight ahead men's magazines in plain view include *Tip Top* and *Spontan*.

man emerges from a barrel — (link out of "Thripshaw's Disease") This transitional gag had already been seen on *The Benny Hill Show* (BBC, 1955–1989), Cook and Moore's *Not Only . . . But Also* (1965), as well as the American comedy show *Laugh-In* (1967). In recycling the recognizable gag, the Pythons could be reminiscing with the audience, relying on the gag's commonality.

"master joiners and craftsmen" — ("Tudor Job Agency") A joiner is a woodworker, not unlike a finish carpenter. The Globe Theatre was built in 1599, then destroyed by fire and rebuilt in 1614. Joiners and craftsmen would have been much needed as the Globe was originally built from the timbers and material of The Theatre (owned by the Burbages), having been completely dismantled and moved from Shoreditch to Southwark.

messenger on a horse — ("Elizabethan Pornography Smugglers") The horse for this sequence was acquired from Henry Woodley at Elm Farm, Boveney (still a riding/stable business today), and was shot on 6 April 1972 (WAC T12/1,428).

minstrels in attendance — (PSC; "Elizabethan Pornography Smugglers") These minstrels are The Cittie Waites (WAC T12/1,447).

"morass of filth" — ("Elizabethan Pornography Smugglers") Historically, of course, Sir Philip Sidney did fight the Spanish, and he was also a Tudor gentleman, scholar, poet, and courtier. The Pythons are shaping a new history for and with the admittedly Petrarchan Sidney, drawing here, instead, on coarser, *Ovidian* elements in Sidney's work. It is known that Sidney was more than a little taken with the physical attributes of his fancy, Penelope Rich, so much so that some recent analysis of his "Astrophil and Stella" sonnet sequence purports to reveal a man corporeally obsessed. In 1991 Paul Allen Miller may have unconsciously supported Python's reading of Sidney when he argued that rather than the announced Petrarchan tradition of chaste love from afar, Sidney just as often embraced the Ovidian fascination with body parts and sexuality (see Miller's "Sidney, Petrarch and Ovid, or Imitation as Subversion"). This attraction to the body is a noteworthy element when the specter of Python's Sidney as a fighter *against* pornography ("where the female body is objectified for its sexual parts") is presented in the Python sketch. Miller sees Sidney's approach as descriptive of Bakhtin's later phenomenon of "grotesque degradation," or the "bringing down" of both the object of affection/obsession and the objectifier.

So is Python appropriating Sidney the respected public figure, the gentleman who lives up to his station and waxes Petrarchan in writing? This Sidney would naturally, rightfully, be against the practice of pornography and "porn-merchanting." Or is this the more licentious, Ovidian Sidney who lusts where he cannot love and describes in what must have been considered at least mildly pornographic detail ("her belly," her "Cupid's hill," "spotless mine," and "her thighs") the object of his unfulfilled carnal desire for a married woman? For the Oxbridge-educated Pythons, the more "earthy" Sidney must have been at least unconsciously appreciated, and the irony of Sidney the porn fighter then becomes possible.

"My particular prob or buglem bear" — ("Thripshaw's Disease") Once again, the source of the conflict here is miscommunication, as was seen just moments before in the stilted "vignette" scene. This Python trope often involves at least two people and their inability to effectively communicate, leading to confusion and, sometimes, dire consequences. Python characters create offensive sales campaigns (Ep. 24), use mistranslated Hungarian phrasebooks (Ep. 25), ask pop culture questions of Marxist leaders (Ep. 25), speak only certain parts of words (Ep. 26) or in hopelessly fractured English (Ep. 29), or even in anagrams and jumbles (Ep. 30). The comedy of "misunderstanding" (as discussed in the author's *MPSERD*) is ubiquitous.

• P •

"Panther, Maudling" — ("Pornographic Bookshop") Police dog names here ticked off by the flustered Gaskell, but earlier "Panther" was Inspector Leopard's (Cleese) original name (Ep. 29), and "Maudling" is yet another reference to the unpopular Conservative Home Secretary. Maudling would be forced to resign less than three months after this episode was recorded, when the Metropolitan police opened an investigation into one of his former business partners, John Poulson (*ODNB*).

"Parkhurst" — ("Elizabethan Pornography Smugglers") A prison on the Isle of Wight. The Kray brothers (Ep. 14) spent time in Parkhurst.

"Penshurst" — ("Elizabethan Pornography Smugglers") Penshurst Place was the Sidney ancestral home in Kent.

"Philip of Spain" — ("Tudor Job Agency") Born in 1527, Philip ruled Spain from 1556 to his death in 1598, and was in power during Spain's most expansive colonial, military, and mercantile endeavors.

"porn merchant" — ("Elizabethan Pornography Smugglers") The definition of pornography would have been quite different in Elizabethan times. According to Lynda Boose, pornography in the time of Shakespeare and Elizabeth was "a language not of lascivious delight but of sexual scatology—of slime, poison, garbage, vomit, clyster pipes, dung, and animality—that emerges connected to images of sexuality in the vocabulary" (193). The Pythons, then, have transposed the pornography of the twentieth century into Elizabethan times, an anachronistic incongruity common for the troupe. The fear of sexual license for Elizabeth's subjects was very real, of course, but only as it threatened to contaminate and confuse lineage lines with bastard children making inheritance claims. The homosexual (or "sodomitical," in the period terminology) exploits of men, especially, were less threatening—no procreation, simply recreation—so dallying with a catamite or ingle was frowned upon, but not often punished. See the author's chapter six in *MPSERD* for more.

"Professor Thynne" — (*Is There? . . . Life after Death?*) Maybe a reference to the well-loved *Goon Show* character Hercules Grytpype-Thynne, played by Peter Sellers. In the episode "The First Albert Memorial to the Moon," he is known as "Professor Thynne" for at least a few moments.

• R •

"Raleigh, Sir Walter" — ("Tudor Job Agency") Adventurer and courtier to Elizabeth I, Raleigh (1552–1618) commissioned the first *Ark Royal*, and established settlements in the New World in the years before the Armada. Raleigh was last mentioned in Ep. 29, in the "*Erizabeth L*" sketch.

"Royal College of Surgeons" — ("Thripshaw's Disease") The RCS received its Royal Charter in 1800.

running into a church — ("Silly Disturbances [The Rev. Arthur Belling]") This setting is The Old Place, Boveney, Windsor, and was used before as a location for Ep. 2.

• S •

"sad I am to see you caught up in this morass of filth" — ("Pornographic Bookshop") The image of a "fighter against filth" being caught up in the trafficking of that same material is likely a very contemporary reference to Detective Chief Inspector George Fenwick and his relation with the Soho pornographic industry. Fenwick had led the investigation and arrest of the *Oz* publishers in 1971 for obscenity, but was himself soon thereafter revealed as the controller of a "Soho porn merchant" ring that the Metropolitan Police had been ignoring altogether or assisting outright. Another police official, Flying Squad Chief Kenneth Drury, had been on holiday to the Continent with a Soho porn merchant in 1972, it was discovered. Both Drury and Fenwick would eventually be arrested, tried, and imprisoned by the mid-1970s, along with a dozen other policemen (*Eyewitness: 1970–79*, "The Oz Trial").

second Spaniard leaps out — ("Elizabethan Pornography Smugglers") This second costumed actor is Cleese, who has already appeared in this very costume and in this very location in Ep. 33, when he admits that the show's run long and the audience needs to trundle on home. They would have shot as much seashore footage as they might have needed for the entire third season in this location.

"Seltzer, David O." — ("Thripshaw's Disease") The stock Hollywood producer name used before by the Pythons, and modeled after David O. Selznick, producer of *Gone With the Wind* (1939), and earlier adventure films like *Prisoner of Zenda* (1936) and *Viva Villa!* (1934).

"Shakespeare's latest works" — ("Elizabethan Pornography Smugglers") In 1583, Shakespeare was just meeting/forming up with the Queen's Company, and was several years away from professional playing and writing in London (commencing about 1587). Sidney was getting married this year, and would be dead in three years from a wound received in the battle he'd so hoped for in the Netherlands.

sherry — ("Sherry-Drinking Vicar") A Spanish fortified wine. The Pythons may have been thinking of the popular (low-priced and available) QC brand of sherry.

"Amontillado"—A wine produced originally in Montilla, it is a more mature sherry than the "dry" sherry mentioned by the Vicar (*OED*).

"Sidney, Sir Philip" — ("Pornographic Bookshop") Sidney (1554–1586) was a poet, a man of the court, and an accomplished soldier. The title misspells his name as "Phillip."

sign reads "Tudor Job Agency" — (PSC; "Tudor Job Agency") The dirty bookshop the Customer (Chapman) enters is located at 280 Uxbridge Road, and is now the Café Tuga, just next to 278 Uxbridge Road (then West London Radio), W12. The radio shop (which can be seen in the episode) has become a dental office.

"since 1625" — ("Tudor Job Agency") It's not clear why the Tudor job market would last this long, since the Tudor era officially ended with Elizabeth's death in 1603, and the Stuart era (under James) began that same year. James would die in 1625, which may be the reason this date is mentioned, but then Charles ascended the throne, and the (Carolean-) Stuart period continued until 1714.

This may also be alluding to the Tudor Job Agency actually putting Charles I on the throne in 1625. A temp job, certainly—Charles would lose both the job and his head in 1649, signaling the beginning of the Interregnum.

"Sir Philip! Not alone!" — ("Elizabethan Pornography Smugglers") Historically, Sidney had been frustrated many times in his attempts to gain Elizabeth's favor and secure both a knighthood and important foreign service, so this moment of bravado isn't out of character.

Soho dirty bookshop — (PSC; "Pornographic Bookshop") Located in the West End of London, Soho has been the home to illicit (meaning sexual) activities since the area was left out of upscale development in the sixteenth and seventeenth centuries, and a mixed immigrant and English working-class population flourished. Popular entertainment venues dotted the streets, including music halls and pubs and houses of ill repute, and soon these included "dirty bookshop"–type stores, as well. The sex trade (prostitutes, clip joints, sex shops) called Soho home for much of the latter half of the twentieth century. See Ackroyd.

"Spaniards have landed in the Netherlands" — ("Elizabethan Pornography Smugglers") Probably a reference to the then-notorious Maurice Girodias (1919–1990), owner/publisher of Olympia Press in Paris. Girodias was watched carefully by British authorities, and was hounded from Paris to Denmark to the United States. His "dirty books" were intercepted and destroyed on a regular basis as pornography. Among the naughty titles were also included other innovative, more avant-garde works, as well. Python mate Terry Southern (*The Magic Christian*; *Dr. Strangelove*) was published through Girodias's Traveller's Companion press (within Olympia), as were luminaries including Genet and Beckett.

stock film of Elizabethan London — (PSC; "Elizabethan Pornography Smugglers") The WAC records for this episode offer no source for this film stock, nor for the later shot of a seventeenth-century sailing ship. It appears that sometimes, when the film stock or photograph is from the BBC Library, the official request/copyright notation does not appear on the paperwork that normally includes all cast members, extras, musicians, film and photographic stock, and music clips charged to that particular episode. This may be the case when there is no need to request copyright permission for an item already owned by the BBC.

"St Loony up the Cream Bun and Jam" — ("Silly Disturbances") The Silly Disturbances couple (Cleese and Cleveland) make their way into St. Brelade's Rectory on La Route des Camps, Jersey. Much of the later parts of the third season were filmed in the St. Helier and St. Ouen, Jersey, areas, between 20–29 March 1972. This scene was filmed on 20 March 1972 (T12/1,428).

stock film of marauding knights — (PSC; "Thripshaw's Disease") This is the same film stock used in Ep. 20 for the *Attila the Hun Show* sequence, and is simply titled "*Attila the Hun*" in the BBC records. It may have been borrowed from film critic Philip Jenkinson's film stock collection, who is lampooned in Ep. 33.

Straight into animated sketch — (PSC; "*Animation: Arcade target shooting*") This is the second of three animated sequences in this episode, the first being "Aldwych Theatre's *Gay Boys in Bondage*."

In this animated arcade setting multiple images are targeted including a mandrill, two sheep (Basil and The Kid, from the earlier "Arthur X" sketch, Ep. 20), a parrot (also from Ep. 20), the marauding Mutated Cat from Ep. 22, a lion, a panto horse (Ep. 30), an elephant, another, less terrifying cat, the same parrot, a Mickey Mouse figurine, the polka dot piggy bank (Ep. 32), a Bear Country Jamboree bear (from Disneyland, see below), and the hatted Muybridge "walking man." This is the same man seen earlier in the "*Gay Boys in Bondage*" animation.

The "Big Al" character sang "Blood on the Saddle" in the show, ironically, and the Country Bear Jamboree would have been quite new at this point, having opened at Disneyland in March 1972 (and at Disneyworld in October 1971).

The leafy background is comprised, partly, of trees and shrubs (and one surprise) from Albrecht Dürer prints. More precisely, most of Dürer's *The Flight into Egypt* (c. 1502–1505) is used for the foliage (including the date palm at the left), with the holy family removed completely. The surprise is that one of the broad-leafed plants (at the bottom front, tinted light green) is actually a bit of inverted heavenly flame or glory from Dürer's *John before God and the Elders*. Lastly, Gilliam's replaced some of the holy family with a fruiting tree borrowed from another work, *The Knight and the Lansquenet* (1497). Dürer's work is employed in Eps. 22, 25, 35, and 37, as well as in the first *Fliegender Zirkus* episode.

string quartet — ("The Free Repetition of Doubtful Words Sketch, by an Underrated Author") These men are most likely some of Fred Tomlinson's singers, pretending to play Mozart's "String Quartet in G" (K.516), originally played by the Weller Quartet (WAC T12/1,447).

"Stuart period nothing. Hanoverians nothing . . ." — ("Tudor Jobs Agency") The Stuart line began with James I and continued to 1714, followed by the German-bred Hanoverians from 1714–1901 (including Victoria), and the Saxe-Coburgs (also German, through Prince Albert), before Windsor was chosen as the English royal family name in 1917, during the height of WWI.

• T •

"That's all you say?" — ("Tudor Job Agency") It's unclear whether this is a reference to the printed script for the sketch itself, which has been referred to in past shows (Eps. 17 and 29, for example), or if this is the first cracking of the "Tudor" façade with the customer. The back-and-forth trading of code phrases was last seen in Ep. 4, and was already a staple of the pulp spy film/novel genre.

"the most sherry they can ship" — ("Sherry-Drinking Vicar") The Duff Gordon sherry brand was running a promotion in 1968–1969, challenging *Times* readers to come up with better, more creative anagrams using "Duff Gordon's El Cid Amontillado," and other similar slogans. The prize—for every winner published in the *Times*—was *six bottles of sherry*. The winner displayed in early December 1968—from P.A.G. Keith of Pinner, Middlesex—was "Flog Aunt's Old Diamond for El Cid" (12 Dec. 1968: 20); and for January 1969, from a Miss J. Chamberlain of Eastbourne: "Medici-

nal? Lord no—Good stuff lad!" (2 Jan. 1969: 18). In all it seems the good folk at Duff Gordon shipped about 200 free bottles of sherry to thirty or so different consumers.

Thripshaw at a desk evidently in a castle — ("Thripshaw's Disease") The Hollywood-ization of historical subjects has been going on since the movies began, and "biopics" had been a staple of various studios' output since *The Life of Moses* (1909; J. Stuart Blackton), *I Am a Fugitive from a Chain Gang* (1932), and *The Life of Emile Zola* (1937).

"thy sharp-tongued wit" — ("Elizabethan Pornography Smugglers") His sharp-tongued (and sharp-penned) reputation did get Sidney into trouble on a few occasions, as, for example, he quarreled with the earl of Oxford over a tennis court at Greenwich Palace, essentially since the higher-born Oxford hadn't said "please." The Queen would later "remind" Sidney of his place, and the row subsided (Woudhuysen, *ODNB*).

"'tis a story of man's great love for his . . . fellow man" — ("Elizabethan Pornography Smugglers") The homoerotic was not nearly as stigmatized during the Elizabethan period as it has become, mostly due to the fact that same-gender sexual activity (man-to-man, even man-to-boy) couldn't upset bloodlines and introduce bastards or multiple claimants to the gentry's fortunes. See the entry for "porn merchant" above for more.

"Tudor" — ("Tudor Job Agency") The Tudors were the ruling family named for Owen Tudor (1400–1461), who married Henry V's widow.

• U •

"underground" — ("Tudor Job Agency") The colloquial name for London's subway system, which opened in 1863.

• V •

"vittler" — ("Tudor Job Agency") One who provides food and drink.

• W •

"Walsingham" — ("Elizabethan Pornography Smugglers") Francis Walsingham (c. 1530–1590) was Elizabeth's spymaster, rooting out Popish types and any family (especially the old Catholic-leaning nobility in the north) who might be inviting Catholic priests and/or spies into England. Sidney—Walsingham's son-in-law—is said to have found safe haven in Walsingham's Paris home as a Protestant refugee in the early 1570s.

"Warwick" — ("Pornographic Bookshop") Ambrose Dudley, third Earl of Warwick (c. 1528–1589) was Master-General of the Ordnance with Philip Sidney in 1585–1586, and another favorite of Elizabeth I.

"We live in Esher" — ("Thripshaw's Disease") As in previous episodes, Esher seems to be the center of the swinging London borough lifestyle.

• Y •

"You'll do time for this" — ("Elizabethan Pornography Smugglers") The Obscene Publications Acts of 1959 and 1964 did outline sentencing guidelines, including prison sentences lasting up to three years, as well as fines, probations, etc. Technically, however, since the Acts also determine that "[a] prosecution . . . for an offence against this section shall not be commenced more than two years after the commission of the offence," Maddox may have a hard time making the charges stick almost 400 years after Sidney/Gaskell allegedly committed them.

Episode 37: "Dennis Moore"

Boxing Tonight—Jack Bodell v. Sir Kenneth Clark; "And now" Man, Nude Organist, and "It's" Man in the ring; *Titles* (Gumby Palin v/o); **Dennis Moore**; Lupins; "Dennis Moore" song; What the stars foretell; Doctor stick-ups; *Animation: Ambulance running over City Gent, frog/man explodes*; *The Great Debate*: "TV4 or Not TV4?" discussion; BBC 1 and 2 promos; Dennis Moore, Episode 3, "The Gathering Storm"; Ideal Loon Exhibition; Judging; *Animation: Stealing cut-outs, moveable black hole*; Off-licence; Dennis Moore's swag; *Prejudice*; "Shoot the poof!"; Dennis Moore redistributes wealth, and closing credits; Weepy judges

• A •

a couple of minutes of animation — ("*Animation: Stealing cut-outs, moveable black hole*") By this time—nearly the end of the third season—the Pythons have given up attempting to predict or match the animated sequences that Gilliam would concoct, likely a combination of certainty in Gilliam's eventual accomplishment and boredom (Cleese would quit after Ep. 39).

The recognizable buildings behind the wheeled burglar include St. Martin-in-the-Fields and Her Majesty's Theatre, both images used several times prior to create animated cityscapes. The authority figure watching the burglar is hiding behind Dürer shrubbery, again, and again the shrubbery is an agglomerate of several items, all from the oft-used print *John before God and the Elders*. Coloring green inverted portions of not flora but cloud and flame (God's glory, right and left of frame) and combining it with grass from the bottom of the frame creates a practicable shrubbery arrangement.

In the following frames, the buildings on the hill include glimpses of St. Paul's and its environs, as well as another Dürer landscape. The line of shrubbery running toward the buildings and the shrub-crested hillside at the left are taken from *John before God*, as well. The original work is to the left of the castle structure seen at bottom center.

"all so meaningless" — ("Dennis Moore") Here Moore slips the twentieth-century philosophy of Jean-Paul Sartre into the eighteenth century, spouting the Paris coffee-house nihilism of Sartre's *Being and Nothingness*, the hopeless anxiety of the academic and the intellectual in a godless and technological world that festered into student riots in the late 1960s.

"Amalgamated Money TV" — ("*TV4 or Not TV4* Discussion") Since at least the early 1950s there had been ongoing discussions in the UK regarding commercial television. The BBC and various sitting governments (Wilson, Heath) had been very concerned about the effect commercial TV would have on the electorate, and whether the subsidized BBC could survive in the new commercial world. Labour spent a good deal of time pointing at the big money owners of various independent television networks, seeing a Conservative mouthpiece at each commercial-driven channel. See Buscombe, Crisell (2002), and Freedman for more.

Part of the Pythons' reasons for blasting commercial television might be similar to their dislike of David Frost—perhaps a modicum of professional jealousy? In the 27 June 1972 edition of the *Times*, Associated Television Corporation (ATV) took out a full-page ad proclaiming its sterling new season as well as its recent awards. One of the trumpeted shows was Sir Kenneth Clark's new series, *Romantic Versus Classic Art*, while the awards included two Montreux awards (one from the festival, the "Golden Rose," and one from the city itself) for *Marty Feldman's Comedy Machine*. The Pythons had won the "Silver Rose" (second place) in 1971. See the entry for Sir Clark below, as well.

"Amontillado" — ("Off-Licence") See the entry in Ep. 36 for more on sherry, the "Sherry-Drinking Vicar" sketch.

• **B** •

"Basil" — ("What the Stars Foretell") Basil was the name of the clever sheep in Ep. 2, "Flying Sheep." The star sign for 21–22 June is actually Cancer.

"Bodell, Jack" — (*Boxing Tonight*) Played by Nosher Powell (b. 1928), who went on to perform stunts and act as stunt coordinator for James Bond films and *Star Wars* (1977). Powell also did stuntwork for Leone's spaghetti Westerns and *The Magic Christian* (1969), where he probably met at least Chapman and Cleese.

"British and Empire Heavyweight Champion" — Indicating that the fighter holds the titles for both Britain and the Commonwealth. In 1959, for example, the British and Empire Heavyweight Champion was Henry Cooper, who had defeated Brian London (already mentioned in Ep. 13) in January.

Braddon, Russell — (PSC; "Prejudice") The printed script notes that this character is Russell Braddon (1921–1995, Australia), who wrote the novel upon which the camp film classic *Night of the Lepus* (1972) was based. Braddon also wrote the celebrated *The Naked Island* (1952), detailing the horrors of his four years in a Japanese concentration camp. Braddon's play of the same name (and based on portions of the book) played in Liverpool in 1960, while in 1971 publisher Michael Joseph advertised Braddon's recent novel, *Prelude and Fugue for Lovers*. By November 1972, Braddon's most recent work, *End Play*, was garnering fascinating, cryptic reviews, like the following from the *Times*:

> The author has developed some perfectly maddening Faulknerian mannerisms. And is probably fuming at all the misprints that puncture his suspense. But there is suspense, as the Motorway Maniac stabs his fourth blonde hitch-hiker and the police close in. How did her corpse find its way to a seat in the stalls of the local cinema during the big picture? Like many stories of its kind, it is neatly turned and almost completely unreal. Two brothers, a ship's officer and a paraplegic javelin champion, plumb the depths of sibling tension as the investigation opens up some very old wounds. ("End Play," 9 Nov. 1972: 11)

The *Daily Telegraph* would call it "damnably readable." Braddon was living and working in the UK during this period.

"Bremen and Verdun" — ("Lupins") Sweden had ceded both Bremen and Verdun to George in his capacity as Elector of Hanover, and these were significant northern ports for the landlocked Hanover.

Incidentally, Jones had read English and Palin modern history at Oxford, and they had worked together writing the London Weekend Television show *The Complete and Utter History of Britain* (1969).

"Buckingham" — ("Lupins") There were multiple Buckinghams, though only two from the eighteenth-century period depicted in "Dennis Moore"—George Nugent-Temple-Grenville (1753–1813) and his son, Richard Temple-Nugent-Brydges-Chandos-Grenville (1776–1839).

• **C** •

"cell'd" — ("Off-Licence") A poetic contraction meaning enclosed within a cell or cellar, the wine would have been aged in caves in the region.

"vinous soil"—Meaning the soil has the "nature" of wine.

"Pluto's hills"—There is an area in Fuentes de Andalucia Sevilla known as "Pluto."

"Charles XII" — ("Lupins") Charles (1682–1718) was indeed the central figure in the Great Northern War, campaigning as king of Sweden against Denmark, Poland, Russia, and collections of northern forces banding together to answer Charles's overreaching foreign policy.

"Clark, Petula" — ("What the Stars Foretell") Born in 1932, Clark is a British singer and actress already mentioned in Ep. 3.

"Clark, Sir Kenneth" — (*Boxing Tonight*) Lord Clark (1903–1983) was an author, presenter, museum director, and academic, and for many years was Britain's most visible and respected critical art figure. His 1969 television series *Civilization* (BBC2) was a hit in both the UK and United States, and Clark's reputation and stature would have been enormous in 1972, when this episode was broadcast.

Clark does indeed wander around as he lectures in *Civilization*, hands in pockets under a casual tweed jacket—Chapman mimics this quite well.

". . . cock may chance an arm" — ("Off-Licence") This trumped-up Elizabethan stage dialogue is a cobbling of Shakespeare and Marlowe mixed in with Lewis

Carroll–type frippery. Idle did this once before, in Ep. 3, as the Olivier-like prisoner trying to beat a parking ticket. The *Beyond the Fringe* group also created a full mock-Shakespeare sketch called "So That's the Way You Like It." See the entry for "Olivier impression" in Ep. 3 for more.

"Colwyn Bay" — ("Ideal Loon Exhibition") Jones was born in Colwyn Bay, Wales.

"Concorde" — ("Dennis Moore") This name elicits a generous laugh from the studio audience, perhaps because the horse's namesake—the still new Concorde SST aircraft—was very much in the public's view and imagination. There are, for example, more than 300 political cartoons treating the subject (Concorde's noise levels, cost overruns, the challenges of cooperating with the French, the expense of operating even one plane, etc.) that appeared in English newspapers during the 1964–1972 period. Also, the significant experienced and projected costs (and cost overruns) for the cooperative program had many asking how such a boondoggle could be justified in times of inflation, and preservationists worried about the sonic booms' deleterious effect on fragile stone cathedrals and churches throughout the country (*Private Eye*, 9 Oct. 1970: 21–22).

The horse ridden by Cleese appears to have been obtained from Chris Le Boutillier of Le Chassine, St. Ouen, Jersey, and was used 21, 26, and 29 May 1972 (WAC T12/1,460).

"crofter's daughter" — (link out of "*TV4 or Not TV4*") Victoria (1819–1901) was, of course, the daughter of a duke and a princess, and thus not a commoner. The show *Victoria Regina* had been produced in 1961 for American television on George Schaefer's Showcase Theatre, with Julie Harris in the title role.

Probably a well-worn comedy phrase (it's heard in *The Goon Show*, for example), the *Private Eye* staff earlier describe PM Macmillan as a "humble crofter's grandson" (Ingrams, 82). Macmillan (1894–1986) was actually born well and married even better, leading a patrician life that provided ample ammunition to his opponents.

The photo used is an un-retouched image of Victoria at Balmoral, posing with a spinning wheel, which she likely learned how to use as a child. The photo is dated c. 1875, and is accounted for in the WAC records as coming from Keystone Press, number CF 14728-3 (WAC T12/1,460).

"Curtis, Tony" — ("What the Stars Foretell") In 1972 the American Hollywood star Curtis (1925–2010) was appearing with Englishman Roger Moore (b. 1927) in the British television show *The Persuaders* (Tribune Productions/ITC, 1971–1972), and would have been featured in the very newspapers being read by Mrs. Trepidatious and Mrs. O. This show was part of the full-page 27 June 1972 Associated Television (ATV) ad appearing in the *Times*, as well (along with *Marty Feldman's Comedy Machine*), having been awarded a "Sun Newspaper Award." Stars Tony Curtis and Roger Moore received some kind of individual awards, as well. See the "Amalgamated Money TV" entry above for more on that rubbing-it-in moment for commercial television.

• D •

Daily Express — ("Ideal Loon Exhibition") Long-standing Conservative-leaning newspaper, the *Express* would have been both run by and favorable to the Heath-led "loons" the Pythons lampoon in this sketch.

"Derry and Toms" — ("What the Stars Foretell") A popular Kensington High Street department store that had just closed in January 1972, and was earlier mentioned in Ep. 35.

"digger duffer" — ("Ideal Loon Exhibition") Probably a colloquialism meaning a luckless, fortune-less miner. The editors of *Private Eye* had nicknamed Australian media mogul Rupert Murdoch "Digger" and "Dirty Digger" (*PE*, 1 Jan. 1971: 3).

DJ — ("*Boxing Tonight*") Dinner Jacket. This is also the uniform of BBC announcers as portrayed by the Pythons.

doctor is lowered on a wire — ("What the Stars Foretell") In Groucho Marx's (1890–1977) popular television show *You Bet Your Life* (1950–1961), the "Secret Word Duck" would drop from above if the secret word was uttered, though brother Harpo (1888–1964) also made an entrance this way at least once. Mr. and Mrs. Bun (Idle and Chapman) arrived into and then departed the "Spam" sketch in this same manner in Ep. 25. A Hertz rental car commercial from 1960s American television introduced its driver and passenger in the same way.

Down Your Way — ("*Prejudice*") The printed script describes this set-up as the visual equivalent ("a TV version") of *Down Your Way*, a popular and long-running BBC radio show (1946–1992). The show had been hosted by Richard Dimbleby (Ep. 23) and later Brian Johnston (Ep. 21), and focused on life and people in smaller English villages and towns, not the big cities or New Cities being built after the war. (Hence, the sketch begins "from the *tiny village* of Rabid in Buckinghamshire.") The Pythons' joke, then, could be either (a) the backward provinciality of these simpler folk allowed for time-honored ignorant bigotry or (b) the squeaky-clean "hominess" of the characters and settings (the show was broadcast Sundays at teatime) were a perfectly incongruous backdrop for such bald-faced prejudices.

• E •

"Eddy, Duane" — ("What the Stars Foretell") Eddy is an American born in 1938, and had become known for myriad instrumental hits, and for his rock-and-roll "twangy" guitar-playing.

By 1975 Eddy is being described in "has-been" terms, with partly-sold concert venues standing in the way of his attempted comeback. His major hits appeared in the late 1950s and early 1960s, of course, when he was voted more popular in the UK than Elvis Presley. The critic does give Eddy credit for making the rock-and-roll movement possible, saving it from the "skiffle" wave ("Duane Eddy at the New Victoria," *Times*, 29 July 1975: 7).

Edward Heath opening something — ("Ideal Loon Exhibition") This film footage is BBC stock, titled "Heath & Queen at Ideal Home" (WAC T12/1,460). Heath was Prime Minister from 1970 to 1974, and, as a Conservative, a constant target of the Pythons.

"Empire Pool, Wembley" — (*Boxing Tonight*) Empire Pool is the nickname of Wembley Arena, and is across the street from Wembley Stadium in Greater London.

empties his wallet — ("Doctor") In Britain the National Health Service (NHS) had been providing socialized medicine since 1948, with every citizen able to receive "free" medical treatment from cradle to grave. This universal coverage led to long waiting times for treatment (and especially surgery) as well as dips in levels of service quality and the quality of people willing to embark on medical careers. (See Klein for more.) However, forcing the patients to pay for expensive procedures has not been one of the NHS's real problems, though "co-pay"–type charges (minimal fees for dental visits and prescriptions, for example) have been utilized for many years to offset the enormous expense of truly "universal" NHS coverage.

Also, so-called amenity beds have become available for those with sufficient funds to pay for more services and comfort, especially in hospitals. The state of London-area and provincial hospitals is broached in Eps. 26 and 34, as well.

Episode 37 — Recorded 17 April 1972, and broadcast 4 January 1973. The episode was recorded eighth and broadcast eleventh in the season.

Others included on the BBC's repeat list (for royalty payment purposes) include: Frank Lester (Eps. 31, 35–37, 40; *Jackanory*), Henry Rayner (Ep. 35; *Dixon of Dock Green*), Paul Lindley (Eps. 3, 14, 28, 35), Francis Mortimer (*The Brontes of Haworth*), Michael Fitzpatrick, Derek Allen, Richard Burke, Adrien Wells, Reid Anderson (*Secrets of Sex*), Adam Day, Micki Shorn, Nosher Powell, Peter Roy (*Engelbert with The Young Generation*), Fred Tomlinson, Helena Clayton (*FC* Montreux episode; *The Agony of Love*), Jean Clarke (Eps. 29, 33, 39; *The Borderers*), Frances Pidgeon (Eps. 29, 33; *Value for Money*), and Peter Kodak (Eps. 27, 29, 36; *Doctor Who*) (WAC T12/1,460).

"Erratum" — (link out of *"Prejudice"*) This bit of errata is correct—Bodell was born in Swadlincote, Derbyshire in 1940, and not Lincolnshire. Derbyshire is west of Lincolnshire, in the East Midlands.

• F •

"Flan-and-pickle" — ("What the Stars Foretell") An unusual dessert combination, at the least, and here pronounced more like "flannem pickle."

fop — (PSC; "Lupins") An eighteenth-century foolish-dandy character of the stage and page, the fop is based originally on Sir Fopling Flutter from Etherege's *Man of Mode* (1676).

"Frederick William busily engaged" — ("Lupins") Again, the Pythons have plundered eminent historian Trevelyan and given a fair accounting of Frederick William's travails regarding Silesia, an Austrian province, which would include the Seven Years' War. Note the linguistic similarity of Buckingham (Jones) and Grantley's (Palin) description of the period to Trevelyan's, from *The History of England*:

> During the Seven Years' War, Frederic was engaged in defending against the three great military powers of Europe the Silesian province, which he had seized in the War of Austrian Succession in spite of his pledged word. The heroism of the defence covered the baseness of the original robbery. Yet even Frederic must have succumbed but for Pitt's subsidies. (544)

The Pythons are quoting Trevelyan (the 1952 edition), essentially, as they've done before—though previously with acknowledgment (see Ep. 26).

"Pitt's subsidies"—Britain was one of Frederick's few allies during this period, with William Pitt arranging ample subsidies to support Frederick's efforts and underscore Britain's burgeoning Continental and even global influence.

"Free French" — ("Ideal Loon Exhibition") The Free French forces fought against the Axis forces during WWII, generally outside of established war zones. Exiled General de Gaulle claimed at least nominal leadership of these forces.

"Frost, David" — ("What the Stars Foretell") The one-time Python associate and boss, Frost (b. 1939) by this time was appearing in another of his own shows, *The Frost Programme*, and was well-known enough to already be featured on *This Is Your Life* in 1972, and regularly travel on the Concorde between London and New York. See the earlier entries (Eps. 10 and 19) for the ubiquitous and successful Frost—the Pythons' simpering, glad-handing, and irritatingly successful bête noire.

• G •

Gathering Storm, The — (*George I* link out of "Doctor") This is the title of the first volume of Sir Winston Churchill's six-volume work covering WWII and the immediate pre- and postwar years, the entire series published between 1948 and 1953. The title will be soberly used again in the "Penguins" section of Ep. 38.

"George" — ("Lupins") A reference to George III (1738–1820) and his involvement in the post–French Revolution struggles in Europe against the seemingly unstoppable Napoleon Bonaparte (Eps. 2, 5, 12, 13, 23, 35, and 44).

Gilliam animation — (PSC; "*Animation: Ambulance running over City Gent*") In this animation Gilliam includes a Securicor "ambulance," a background of Trafalgar Square (photographed from Cockspur Street, looking northeast), as well as some landscape scenery borrowed from an Albrecht Dürer print.

Securicor was a security company, of course (head office, Chelsea Embankment), and ran armored cars, security, and surveillance schemes. Matching the firm with an ambulance makes perfect sense for the preceding "cash for cure" sketch. The trees and landscape in the following frame (as the ambulance approaches the home) is borrowed from Dürer's *John before God and the Elders*, a source already used in Ep. 36. The following scene—where the stationary City Gent eventually gets run over by the ambulance—also employs Dürer work, and is also from the margins of *John before God*, this time the left and bottom left of the frame. The man/frog scene that follows uses grasses and the background landscape from the foreground of this same Dürer work.

Dürer's work can be seen throughout *MPFC*, and he is featured in the first *Fliegender Zirkus* episode, as well as in publications like *Monty Python's Big Red Book* (1971), *The Brand New Monty Python Bok* (1973), and *Animations of Mortality* (1978). Gilliam was obviously a big fan.

"Grantley" — ("Lupins") The Baron Grantley during this period was William Norton (1742–1822).

"green, scaly skin . . . arid subtropical zones" — ("What the Stars Foretell") This fanciful description is somewhat close to the Komodo Dragon of Indonesia, though thirty feet is a bit long even for these top-of-the-food-chain predators.

• H •

"Hanover" — ("Lupins") English kings George I, II, and III were all Electors of Hanover, a German city in Lower Saxony. The Hanoverian line has been mentioned in Ep. 36, in the "Tudor Jobs Agency" sketch. The German "Saxe-Coburg" heritage of the English royal house was officially made unofficial during WWI, when the more politically correct "Windsor" became the family name.

"height of the English Renaissance" — (*Boxing Tonight*) Inigo Jones (Ep. 7) is given credit for instigating this renaissance movement in English architecture, with the designs for Covent Garden and the Banqueting House at Whitehall (Ep. 40).

"He seeks them here" — ("Lupins") Adapted from Baroness Orczy's very popular *The Scarlet Pimpernel* (1905):

> They seek him here, they seek him there
> Those Frenchies seek him everywhere
> Is he in heaven or is he in hell?
> That demned elusive Pimpernel.

The hero of that work, Sir Percy Blakeney (a.k.a. "The Scarlet Pimpernel"), played a dandified fop character to hide his true identity from evil Revolutionaries.

highwayman — ("Dennis Moore") Moore may be patterned after the Robin Hood–like English highwayman Humphrey Kynaston (1474–1534), who is said to have robbed the rich to help the poor. Kynaston's mount was allegedly called "Beelzebub."

"hip injuries" — ("Ideal Loon Exhibition") Though not made clear in the sketch, this comment must refer to the dangers of counter-marching near another player wearing a very large bathtub.

• I •

"Ideal Loon Exhibition" — ("Ideal Loon Exhibition") The *Daily Mail* (not *Daily Express*) has sponsored the Ideal Home Exhibition (now Ideal Home Show) since 1908. New furniture, appliance, and decorating ideas galore greeted Ideal Home attendees. The *Daily Mail*, along with the *Daily Express*, have been termed "conservative" (and even "nationalist") British newspapers. In 1972, the Ideal Home Exhibition started its twenty-three day run on 2 March, at Olympia, London. More than one million were expected to visit the displays.

"I know one of them isn't" — ("Dennis Moore") At this point Moore digresses from the narrative trajectory, and even after all the verisimilitude of eighteenth-century costumes, props, and overall production design, we're quickly thrust sideways into the world of Laurence Sterne's Uncle Toby and Tristram (from *Tristram Shandy*) where diversions, backtracks, and self-conscious narrative hiccoughs keep the story from ever actually progressing. (Palin did this earlier, in Ep. 30, "Gestures to Indicate Pauses in a Televised Talk," where he qualifies and hedges and qualifies some more, creating brackets of reference and speech within other brackets.)

In this the Pythons are anticipating their feature film *Holy Grail*, where the grimy reality of the sets and Middle Ages design are consistently undercut by the temporal and spatial narrative transgressions—the appearance of coconuts, argumentative peasants, a film production member's death (the Animator), and the "out of bracket" Historian who attempts to narrate the story, only to be killed by someone "inside the bracket."

The digressions in "Dennis Moore" also suffer digressions (as seen earlier in "Njorl's Saga"), with the discussion moving from the remaining loaded pistol to Moore's accuracy to his practice schedule to the target to size of the target hillock to the particular tree that can be hit to how often he can hit that target tree. They then disagree which tree Moore might be aiming at, and then discuss trees in general. The narrative doesn't get retracked until Moore takes control of the situation again, narratively, sidetracks the sidetracking digressions, and reminds the coach travelers that they are his victims. Still later, the out-of-bracket chorus will sidetrack Dennis yet again as they make him aware of his taking-from-the-poor-and-giving-to-the-rich status (calling him a "stupid bitch"), forcing him to retool, narratively, and try and reestablish his idiom. (Lancelot [also Cleese] suffers from this idiomatic slippage as well in *Holy Grail*.) In the Modern-cum-Postmodern world of the Pythons there is rarely stable narrative footing.

"Ikon" — ("What the Stars Foretell") This spelling of "icon" is generally not used, but this also could be a reference to the Ikon Gallery, a modern art gallery in Birmingham, opened in the city's Bull Ring section in the 1960s. It also may be that the well-publicized end of production for Zeiss Ikon cameras in April 1972 stirred this reference. Also, the figure of a "Mrs. Trepidatious" may actually have become iconic by this time, in the Python world at least, meaning a fussy, ratbag of a mannish-woman.

"it's all so meaningless" — ("Lupins") This existentialist moment is certainly an intrusion of the twentieth-century on the eighteenth, with Moore (Cleese) voicing the Sartrean discipline already covered in Ep. 27 by the Pepperpots, where possessions and the "wants" of life can only preclude or put off the search for a meaningful existence. With further prodding, however, Moore switches to a more practical mode of existence, outlining "the usual things" he and everyone wants—home and marriage—the sort of cheerful "hearth, children and home" trope seen so often in the eighteenth-century English pastoral tradition (see Thomson's "The Seasons," and Grey's "Elegy Written in a Country Church-Yard").

• L •

"Ludovic Ludovic" — (*TV4 or Not TV4* Discussion") This is more than likely a reference to the working journalist/author Ludovic Kennedy (1919–2009), an Oxford grad who would become a newsreader for ITV and a presenter/interviewer for the public affairs program *This Week*.

"Ludo" Kennedy was also the screenwriter for *10 Rillington Place* (1971), starring "Dickie" Attenborough, the film detailing the John Christie murders alluded to in Ep. 27, the "Court Scene—Multiple Murderer" sketch. In summer 1972 Kennedy was involved in a tit-for-tat newspaper editorial bout with Aldershot MP Julian Critchley (1930–2000) after Kennedy took party political broadcasts to task—to Critchley's mind, quite disingenuously (Kennedy had run and lost for a seat in the 1950s). Kennedy was presenting at this time on the BBC's *24 Hours*, which was about to be canceled. See "Putting Broadcasters Back in Their Box," *Times*, 2 June 1972: 14.

• M •

"Massed Pipes and Toilet Requisites" — ("Ideal Loon Exhibition") There are many Massed Pipes and

Drum groups in the UK, often appearing at Military Tatoos and Highland games.

McGough — (PSC; "Off-Licence") The poet named in the scripts as "McGough" (Idle) is certainly based on Roger McGough (b. 1937), the Liverpudlian poet/playwright who was also a member of the 1960s music/poetry group The Scaffold. McGough would later appear in *All You Need Is Cash* (1978), written by Idle. McGough and friends may have been at least partly the inspiration for the Scottish poet McTeagle seen earlier in Ep. 16.

The short rhyme beginning with "Just one bottle . . ." is much like McGough's playful poetry, for example, his 1967 poem "Cake":

i wanted one life
you wanted another
we couldn't have our cake
so we ate each other. (*The Mersey Sound*)

"Mike Sammes Singers" — ("What the Stars Foretell") Originally a working solo backup singer, Sammes founded his backup group and performed almost non-stop on commercials, jingles, pop records, and on until the mid-1970s.

Sammes and his singers were performing with Petula Clark in 1970 on *Petula*, a 1970 American television special.

"Millichope" — ("Doctor") Ray Millichope was the editor for much of the run of *Flying Circus*.

Miss World — (PSC; "Ideal Loon Exhibition") The printed script mentions that this judging scene is to mimic the "Miss World" pageant look, which debuted in the UK in 1951. In April 1972 the pageant's owners had won a highly visible court case against several newspapers, including the *Guardian* and the *Manchester Evening News*, both of which had alleged the 1970 event was "rigged."

"Moore, Roger" — ("What the Stars Foretell") Soon-to-be popular British TV and film actor who in the following year would take on the James Bond role in *Live and Let Die* (1973). In 1972, however, Moore was merely a mid-level television actor appearing with former Hollywood star Tony Curtis in *The Persuaders*.

"Mrs Ikon" — ("What the Stars Foretell") It's not clear why Mrs. Trepidatious (Chapman) has become Mrs. Ikon, nor why she doesn't correct the doctor, except perhaps that this is a comment on the strained doctor-patient relationship in the inefficient and overburdened National Health Service. Since the creation of the NHS in 1948 there have been lingering complaints about waiting lists for certain treatments and extended waiting times for appointments and in doctors' offices.

The robbery going on in the following scene may just be this particular doctor or hospital trying to make ends meet, since budgets for state-owned and funded medical services were/are always at least meager, and certainly cost-conscious.

"Mrs. Trepidatious" — ("Doctor") Mrs. Trepidatious (identified in both the script and by Mrs. O) will later be called "Mrs. Ikon" by the Doctor (Jones). And though "trepidatious" is an overstated way of saying "timid," the character as played by Chapman seems anything but timid or timorous, complaining loudly about her health and arguing with her friend regularly. She doesn't even seem overly frightened when the doctor robs them at gunpoint.

Music starts — (link out of "Doctor") The musical piece used under the *George I* promo is an overture from the Paul Bonneau Orchestra Terpsichoreau Festival by F. de Boisvalle. The music that follows as the nobles chat in "Dennis Moore" is "Musiques pour les fetes d'eau face" (WAC T12/1,460).

• N •

"Nae Trews" — ("Ideal Loon Exhibition") Literally, "without trousers."

"Nesbitt" — ("What the Stars Foretell") The name Nesbitt has been used at least twice to indicate a Pepperpot type, in Eps. 24 and 26, and Mrs. Trepidatious (Chapman) appears to fit that profile well.

• O •

"On ITV now the" (*sound of a punch*) — ("*George I*" link into "Dennis Moore") The possibility of a BBC announcer giving programming information for the rival networks is remote, and punished here rather finally.

"Oxford Professor of Fine Art" — ("*Boxing Tonight*") In the immediate postwar years, Sir Kenneth Clark was the Slade Professor of Fine Art at Oxford. In Ep. 25, Clark is mentioned as a volunteer negotiator between museums and the striking artworks.

• P •

"Palladio's villas" — ("*Boxing Tonight*") Ornate, groundbreaking, and, yes, "ordered" villas designed by the Italian architect professionally known as Palladio (1508–1580), whose influence would be carried into England by Inigo Jones and Christopher Wren

(1632–1723). In Ep. 17 the City Gent-cum-Mason Pythons hopped past a Wren church on Ludgate Hill.

pan across idyllic countryside — ("Dennis Moore") The music underneath this opening is "Early Dusk" from the album *Pastoral Music* by Ivor Slaney (WAC T12/1,460).

"party feeling" — ("Lupins") A specialized phrase meaning action in favor or support of partisanship. According to the *OED*, the phrase dates just to the early nineteenth century, though Trevelyan—whom the Pythons are very nearly quoting in this scene—does employ the phrase. This indicates that the eighteenth-century characters portrayed by the Pythons are actually speaking in the later vernacular of their chroniclers, like Trevelyan.

phony mouthing way — (PSC; "Dennis Moore") This refers to the time-honored stage and television tradition of secondary actors speaking sotto voce when the microphones are hot and only the principals are meant to be heard. Rather than mic up everyone in the scene (time-consuming and costly), the overhead boom mic is placed as near the action as possible, so all "crowd" actors have to pretend to talk normally—which often does look quite phony, since these actors tend to overplay their dumb-show to compensate.

postilion — (PSC; "Dennis Moore") This man essentially "rides shotgun" on the coach, though this doesn't seem to fit the historical demands for the job—which was to ride along with multiple-horse carriages as an assistant.

"Pretty Girl Is Like a Melody, A" — ("Ideal Loon Exhibition") This performance is by Stanley Black, and the song is composed by Irving Berlin (WAC T12/1,460).

pulls out a stethoscope — ("Doctor") This is a very clever sight gag—a doctor being frightened of a snake-like stethoscope—the likes of which are disappearing as the series progresses, in favor of either non-sequitur moments/transitions or just more homogenous narrative structures.

• R •

"redistribution of wealth" — ("Lupins") This may be a comment on the UK's non-proportional income tax, where incomes above certain levels take on more and more of the tax burden, with that money being "redistributed" via social programs, creating a kind of "Robin Hood" (or here, "Dennis Moore") effect. Trade unionists (and syndicalists, even) made similar demands of owners of industrial concerns in this period,

that profits should be more evenly distributed among workers and owners. Economist and former Harvard professor Simon Kuznets (1901–1985) had won the Nobel Prize in October 1971 for his work along these lines (income inequality and economic growth correlations), the notoriety of which may account for the Pythons' treatment of the subject.

Rhodesian police — ("Prejudice") The Rhodesian situation has been treated before (Eps. 28 and 31), and will be again (in Ep. 45). The Rhodesian police force had gained quite a reputation for firm crowd control tactics and enforcing the white minority government's segregation laws. The Judge (Chapman) in Ep. 15 wishes aloud that he could emigrate to Africa and "get some real sentencing done."

• S •

"skivers" — ("Prejudice") Those who shun their duties; the lazy and shiftless.

song is heard — ("Dennis Moore") There are numerous songs about highwaymen (most dating from the nineteenth century), including "Whiskey in the Jar," and "Brennan on the Moor." The song used by the Pythons was originally titled "Robin Hood" and penned by Fred Tomlinson, and is sung by the Fred Tomlinson Singers (WAC T12/1,460).

Sports programme music — (PSC; "Boxing Tonight") This recording on film is the Scots Guard playing "Drum Majorette" by Steck (WAC T12/1,460).

"Stand and Deliver!" — ("Dennis Moore") According to Alexander Smith in his 1714 book on English highwaymen, this was the well-known and much-feared cry of the rogue beginning his work.

"stars in the paper" — ("What the Stars Foretell") The newspaper Mrs. O (Idle) and Mrs. Trepidatious (Chapman) appear to be reading is the *Daily Express*. One visible article concerns the continuing search for "Ginger" Marks, a low-level gangster from London's East End who'd disappeared in 1965. Marks's alleged killer, Frederick Foreman, was an enforcer for the Kray brothers (Ep. 14). The police followed many leads, dug up many vacant lots and even a filled-in pond, but never did find the body.

Another story on this same page bears the headline: "Rebel No. 8 Tells Wilson He Quits." This was likely a reference to the unexpected resignation of Roy Jenkins (1920–2003), the then-Shadow Chancellor of the Exchequer. Jenkins had quit this and the deputy Labour leader post over the party's support of a European Economic Community referendum.

"Stars Spangled Banner" — (PSC; "Ideal Loon Exhibition") This music used here is listed in the printed scripts as "Souza's Star Spangled Banner," but is actually Sousa's (proper spelling) "Stars and Stripes Forever." (Francis Scott Key, of course, wrote the poem that would become "The Star-Spangled Banner," while the music was contributed by John Stafford Smith from an existing tune.) This particular performance is by the Band of Royal Military Academy, Sandhurst (WAC T12/1,460).

Stern music — ("*TV4 or Not TV4* Discussion") This and the closing titles music are short clips from Shostakovich's "Symphony No. 12, First Movement" performed by the Leningrad Philharmonic Orchestra (WAC T12/1,460).

swag — (PSC; "Lupins") Slang for ill-gotten booty.

"sward" — ("Dennis Moore") A green, grassy slope (*OED*), and probably only used because it nearly rhymes with "Concorde."

• T •

"through that stage" — ("Lupins") Though this obviously sounds like a very modern, psychoanalytic phrase, the *OED* makes it clear that as early as the fourteenth century this more abstract usage of the term was extant, though not common.

traditional eighteenth-century coach and horses — (PSC; "Dennis Moore") The coach appears to be a Red Rover Coach and two, and the faded painting on the back indicates a Southampton to London route. They likely brought this large item with them (on the ferry), and it was also likely BBC property for use on period shoots.

It appears that at least their gear and vehicles (including the prop coach) made the crossing to Jersey aboard the Duchess of Normandy, which was "standing by" in St. Ouen Bay on 19 March 1972, at a cost of £60 for the wait (WAC T12/1,460).

"Treaty of Westphalia" — ("Lupins") Already argued about in Ep. 13, the Treaty ended the Thirty Years' War, and did cede significant northern lands to Sweden.

"trencherman" — ("Off-Licence") A preparer or purveyor of food. Sir Philip Sidney (Ep. 36) uses the term in *Arcadia* (1586).

TV4 — ("*TV4 or Not TV4* Discussion") There never has been, technically, a TV4 in Britain. The third and fourth BBC television channels (by number) wouldn't appear until 2002–2003. The proliferation of commercial channels via the Independent Television Authority was active during this period, which did lead to debate concerning the need for myriad broadcast channels and those channels' sometimes spurious, commercially driven content.

"Two say will" — ("*TV4 or Not TV4* Discussion") Again, as in the previous episode where life after death is briefly discussed, the terseness of the scene might indicate the Pythons' waning interest in writing more complex sketches, though the cleverness of the announced *Great Debate* episode being "cancelled mysteriously" is admitted, and saves the scene from the cynicism it seems to embrace.

• V •

"Velasquez" — ("Lupins") Spanish painter Diego Velasquez (1599–1660) was a baroque artist; he highly influenced the later Impressionists. According to biographers, Velasquez was a fairly well-kept secret outside of his home country until the nineteenth century, meaning well after Dennis Moore's peasants could have demanded his work for the loo (*Gardner's*).

For the Pythons' reference, however, Velasquez work has been displayed in the National Gallery since at least 1846. The Female Peasant (Jones) may be referring to Velasquez's earlier work, as well, where depictions of "tavern scenes" and the common life abounded—just right for her "outside loo," perhaps.

"very good about the spectacles" — ("What the Stars Foretell") A comment on the generalized nature of many newspaper-based horoscopes, which could with finessing fit any reader, as well as the willingness of horoscope readers to overlook these vagaries and embrace any accidental specificity.

• W •

What's My Line? — ("Prejudice") BBC television game show appearing in 1951 in the UK (after its debut in the US in 1950), and which would run through 1962.

"Wiltshire" — ("Off-Licence") County just east of Somerset, where Cleese was born and raised. There were a number of noted Wiltshire highwaymen, including a man known as "Biss," one William Davies, and another Thomas Boulter, who allegedly cut quite a nice figure (expensive clothes, impeccable manners, etc., not unlike Dennis). See Spraggs's *Outlaws and Highwaymen* for more.

"Wops, Krauts, Nigs..." — ("Prejudice") A laundry list of insulting appellations: "Wops": Italians; "Krauts":

Germans; "Nigs": blacks; "Eyeties": Italians; "Gippos": Egyptians (and/or gypsies); "Bubbles": Greeks; "Froggies": French; "Chinks": Chinese; "Yidds": Jews; "Jocks": Scots; "Polacks": Poles; "Paddies": Irish; and "Dagoes": Spanish/Portuguese. Use of such terms was still fairly common on British radio and television (especially comedies)—listen to or watch *The Goon Show*, *Benny Hill*, *Beyond the Fringe*, and *Not Only . . . But Also*, as well as just run-of-the-mill situation comedies, etc., for more.

"Wyngarde, Peter" — ("What the Stars Foretell") Wyngarde (b. 1933; France) was appearing in the spin-off series *Jason King* in 1972, after having created the role in *Department S* (1969). His role is that of a pleasure-seeking womanizer, which may account for the Pepperpots' negative reaction to the mention of his amorous attentions.

• Y •

"Your money, your jewellery . . ." — ("Lupins") Spraggs and others note that with the advent of bank checks in the later eighteenth century, the instances of wealthy travelers carrying chests of cash and goods dropped significantly, one of the reasons that highway robberies began to trail off in the same period.

Moore here is covering his bases, then, asking for all manner of valuables that still might be carried on their persons.

"snuff"—Generally, powdered tobacco.

• Z •

"zodiacal signs" — ("What the Stars Foretell") The mention of the "horoscopic fates" here (Aries, Taurus, Gemini, etc.) initiates one of the show's few "on the nose" thesaurus moments, even to the point of a placard descending from above to continue the list and allow audience participation. In previous sketches, including "Cheese Shop" (Ep. 33), the thesaurus structure is at least woven into the fabric of the diegetic world, but here that list element is forwarded in all its artificiality. Other listings include:

"genethliac prognostications"—The castings of nativities (fortune-telling, to some).

"mantalogical [*sic*] harbingers"—Misspelled here, a "mantologist" is one who practices divination.

"vaticinal utterances"—Utterances that are prophetic, "vatic."

"fratidical [*sic*] premonitory uttering of the mantalogical omens"—Another misspelling here, "fatidical" utterings are those that are prophetic.

Episode 38:
"BBC Programme Planners"

(Party Political Broadcast—Choreographed); *Titles* (Gumby Palin v/o); *A Book at Bedtime—Redgauntlet*; **Kamikaze Scotsmen**; Kamikaze Advice Centre; No Time to Lose Advice Centre; *Animation: No-Time Toulouse*; "Towards the Russian bolder"; *Animation: 2001: A Space Odyssey spoof*; *Frontiers of (Penguin) Medicine*: "The Gathering Storm"; Tennis scientists; **BBC programme planners**; *Animation: Penguin invasion*; Unexploded Scotsman; *Spot the Loony*; Rival documentaries; Closing credits and more loonies; (BBC 1 Colour promos: *Dad's Doctors*; *Dad's Pooves*)

• A •

"abandoned in 1956" — ("Penguins") Australians Lew Hoad and Ken Rosewall were dominating men's international tennis in 1956. See their biographical entries below.

"All Answers Verified by Encyclopaedia Britannica" — ("Spot the Loony") This may be a slight, actually, since this was the era when *EB* was owned and operated by American business interests, and when the scholarly thicket of entries was consistently winnowed for the more modern reader's understanding and accessibility. In other words, these "silly" facts and identifications of loonies may be just what the American editors thought the publication needed to command a larger *paying* audience.

animated line showing the route — (PSC; *2001* animation) The music Gilliam uses in this *2001: A Space Odyssey* send-up is the Scholar Canforiuno of Stuttgart singing "Lux Aeterna, New Music for Chorus" by Ligeti, followed by "The Blue Danube" by Strauss (WAC T12/1,462).

This incongruous juxtaposition isn't as unusual as it might appear, even three years after the movie's debut. After the release of Kubrick's 1968 film, fashionable handbag maker John Romain released a movie tie-in poster that featured a star-dotted backdrop;

a beautiful, leather-clad, floating model clutching a modish handbag; and a small insert of a *2001* lobby title card. This particular card, however, depicts the pod (piloted by Dave Bowman) retrieving the dead body of Bowman's shipmate Frank Poole. The leaping model and the floating, spacesuited body do look similar, even ethereally beautiful, but it probably indicates the ad agency had not screened the film before choosing the image.

"Ann Sewell's *Black Beauty*" — ("*Book at Bedtime*" link into "*Dad's Doctors*") Anna Sewell (1820–1878) published *Black Beauty* in 1877–1878, just before her death.

• B •

"Ben Medhui" — ("*Spot the Loony*") Actually spelled Ben *Machdui*, it is the highest peak in the Cairngorms (and the second-highest in Scotland), connecting this reference right back to the *Redgauntlet* reading earlier in the episode. This is also a reference to the Himalayan theme in Ep. 31 ("Everest Climbed by Hairdressers"), though here it's a bit of a mock heroic, since Machdui is just under 4,300 feet high.

This scene was shot on the troupe's location visit to the Oban area in Scotland, where much of the exterior work for the "Walter Scott" bits, "Rival Documentaries," and "Expedition to Lake Pahoe," etc., was recorded for the third season.

Book at Bedtime, A — ("*A Book at Bedtime*") Title of a long-running BBC4 radio show, selected books have generally been read by well-known actors.

"Britain's timber resources" — ("Rival Documentaries") According to the Royal Scottish Forest Society, forests covered only about 4 percent of Scotland during Sir Walter Scott's lifetime, which seems to be the time period being struggled over here. By 1972, when the faux documentaries are being produced, that number had risen to somewhere around 14 percent.

• C •

Close ups of soldiers — (PSC; "Kamikaze Scotsmen") Idle's Kamikaze Scotsman "waterskiing vox pop" is actually shot in Norwich, not Edinburgh. The Norwich Tower can be seen behind him.

"common parlance" — ("Kamikaze Scotsmen") Again, communication between seemingly compatible people (military men) is always a struggle in the Python world. There is the possibility that the rank and class of these individuals—one a captain, the other a sergeant major—figures in, preventing them from speaking the same language, while the lowly, suicidal Scotsman recruit can't be reached at all.

"coniferous cornicopia" — ("Rival Documentaries") This verbiage harks back to Ep. 27 and "Whicker Island," where jetsetting interviewer Alan Whicker is satirized for his recognizable euphuistic language.

"Conservative and Unionist" — (PSC; "Party Political Broadcast [Choreographed]") The official name of the Conservative Party, and which stresses the significance of Ireland, Wales, and Scotland as part of the kingdom. This entire opening sketch is missing from the more recent (1999 and beyond) editions of *Flying Circus* on VHS and DVD, likely due to a bad film/video transfer (as opposed to any censorship).

Crescendo of music — ("*Spot the Loony*") The intro music for *Spot the Loony* is "Opening Number" by Len Stevens (WAC T12/1,462).

"Curb inflation, save the nation" — (PSC; "Party Political Broadcast [Choreographed]") The years 1971–1972 were fairly unforgiving to British workers, with some wages being risen artificially to stay ahead of "rising prices," and unemployment reaching record post-Depression numbers in January 1972. Heath's government attempted intervention by spending—that is, increasing capital expenditures in national industries to stimulate the economy via new cash and employment—but inflation figures forced businesses to hive off workers and downsize to stay competitive. This cycle kept prices high and jobs scarce.

The "wages spiral" had been lamented since at least the late 1950s, when Macmillan's Conservative government struggled with the specter of rising wages and wage demands in a time of poor economic performance, with Lord Cohen's (1900–1977) Council on Prices, Productivity and Incomes reports offering sometimes painful solutions. (See the entry for Lord Cohen in *ODNB* for more.) Chancellor of the Exchequer Anthony Barber gave a speech in April on this very subject, with unions, union leadership, and their "industrial actions" (strike actions) shouldering most of the blame from the Conservative mandarin ("Mr. Barber Says Pay Offer Is 'Fair,'" *Times*, 14 Apr. 1972: 2). And according to financial statistics provided by HM's government, the inflation rate in 1972 (a little over 7 percent) was a bargain compared to the rates of 16 percent and more than 24 percent by 1974 and 1975, respectively. Again, the sagging economy played into the Opposition's hand (as it had in 1970 for the Conservatives), this time bringing Labour back into power in 1974.

Cut to film (no sound) of Edward Heath — ("*Spot the Loony*") This footage is not accounted for in the WAC records, but is likely that mentioned in requests for Ep. 32.

• D •

"Dad's Pooves" — (PSC; "*Dad's Pooves*") Like the opening "Party Political Broadcast" sketch, this trailer sketch is missing completely from the latest (1999) DVD and earlier VHS versions of this episode. As it doesn't seem particularly more naughty or libelous than anything else in the third season, it's likely that the scenes are missing due to a film transfer oversight. (This scene *is* included on the laser disc versions of the episodes, which represent an earlier transfer.) One particular show—*Dad's Army*—may be the target here due to *Flying Circus* losing out to *Dad's Army* for the Light Entertainment Production award at BAFTA in 1971. The Pythons had won two special awards from BAFTA in 1970, but not in any of the usual (read: prestigious) categories.

"Dame Elsie Occluded" — (PSC; "*Spot the Loony*") The printed script lists this character as being played by Palin, but it isn't, and instead looks very much like John Hughman.

diving rugger tackle — (PSC; "Rival Documentaries") This competition between documentarists has appeared before, in Ep. 30, when documentarists Heinz Sielmann, Peter Scott, and Jacques Cousteau get into a punch-up with the Duke of York, Terence Rattigan, and the Dummy Princess Margaret over repeat fees.

The competition the Pythons could have been referring to was the struggle for primetime viewing slots not only between documentary shows, but between Light Entertainment fare and drama or documentary productions—all equally interested in the largest British viewing audience. The Pythons complained over and over again with the BBC programmers (whom they take to task in this episode) for the erratic scheduling and repeat broadcast difficulties. There are memos and letters throughout the WAC archives from the Pythons and their representation as well as responses from BBC departments in regard to programming.

• E •

"Edinburgh Castle" — ("Kamikaze Scotsmen") This castle is actually Norwich Castle, in Norfolk, and the scene was shot on 9 November 1971, just before principal photography was set to begin. WAC records indicate that the keepers of Edinburgh Castle (likely the Ministry of Defence) had politely declined to allow the Pythons access for filming purposes in October 1971 (WAC T12/1,428). The exterior scenes (where the RSM [Jones] drives MacDonald [Chapman] in the lorry) were also shot around the Norfolk-area castle.

Episode 38 — Recorded 18 December 1971, and broadcast 11 January 1973. The episode was recorded third in the season and broadcast twelfth, meaning there passed a very long period (about thirteen months) between its initial recording date in mid-December 1971 to its transmission in mid-January 1973.

The entire first sketch for this episode—"Party Political Broadcast for the Conservative and Union Party"—is missing from most surviving video copies of Ep. 38, as is the Wilson and Heath dancing animation that follows. Variously, compilers of the recent A&E versions of the shows (on VHS/DVD) have stated that the original prints they were provided for copying purposes were missing bits and pieces, but also that due to "rights issues" some changes had to be made.

Also appearing in this episode: (in-studio) John Hughman, Karen Burch, and Peter Kodak (Eps. 27, 29, 36, 37; *Doctor Who*) (all scheduled to appear at TC 6 for taping on 18 December 1971); Robyn Williams (Ep. 29, 32; *Jackanory*), Jeff Witherick (*Doctor Who*; *Z Cars*), Roy Pearce (Ep. 29, 33; *Doctor Who*; *Z Cars*), Kevan Morgan, David Waterman (Ep. 33; *Doctor Who*),

Ron Tingley (Eps. 29, 33; *Z Cars*); (on film) Bernard Mistovski (*Colditz*), Colin Richmond (Ep. 29), Sabu Kimura (*Tenko*), Omo Aide (Ep. 29), Kock Chuan, Peter Moore, Graham Skidmore (Eps. 27–30, 36; *Dixon of Dock Green*), Peter Kodak; (in Norwich) Anne Hall; (and dancers) Arthur Sweet (*Slipper and the Rose*), Peter Walker (*Doctor Who*), David Ellen, and Christopher Robinson (WAC T12/1,462).

The complete list of music requests for this episode (many of which are identified elsewhere in these notes by their final place in the recorded show) includes the following:

Music dubbed onto film: M. Burgess "Lament for Viscount Dundee"; Orchestra de Suisse Romande, French Overtures: Orpheus, "Scenic and Romance: Desert Morning" by Cliff Johns, and "Industrial and War: Action Line" by David De Lara, and "Scenic and Romance: After Midnight" by James Harpham; Moscow PO "The Execution of Stepan Razin" by Shostakovich, and "Dramatic Background: Approaching Menace" by Neil Richardson; "I Belong to Glasgow"; ISO Pastoral Music "The Big Country" by Keith Papworth; "Locations and Comedy: Comic Giggles" by John Pearson, and "Viennese Party" by Harry Wild; Ensemble de Guivres de Paris "Fanfares de tour les temps face" by Paul Dukas; "Towers and Spires: Brandle de Bourgogne" by Spencer Nakin; Scholar Canforiuno of Stuttgart "Lux Aeterna New Music for Chorus" by Ligeti, and "Blue Danube" by Strauss; (music on disc) English Chamber Orchestra "Welsh Music for Strings Fifth Movement" by Gareth Walters; Ronnie Aldrich "Silent Movie Piano Suite No. 6: Hearts and Flowers" by Czibulka/Warren, and "Opening Number" by Len Stevens; Queens Hall Light Orchestra "Devil's Gallop"; and London Big Sound "Big City Story: Beyond the Night" by Peter Reno.

Music on records (additional): European Stage Orchestra "Pleasure Spectacle: Picnic in the Park" by Syd Dale; Das Orchester Heinz Kiessling "A la bonheur"; London Studio Group "Looney Tunes: Pit Overture" by R. Wale, and "Luva Duck" by Peter Reno; LSO "P&C" by Elgar; "Selling Sounds: Skip Along" Barry Stoller (WAC T12/1,462).

Complete music requests for all episodes are listed in the appendix.

• F •

fanfare as for historical pageant — (PSC; "*Spot the Loony*") The fanfare used is Spencer Nakin's "Brandle de Bourgogne" from "Towers and Spires" (WAC T12/1,462). Nakin's fanfares have been used before, in Ep. 29.

few bars of bagpipe music — ("Kamikaze Scotsmen") The music here is M. Burgess's (most likely Pipe Major John Burgess) performance of "Lament for Viscount Dundee" (WAC T12/1,462).

"fifth state" — ("Kamikaze Scotsmen") There was an approximately thirty-day training course for kamikaze pilots, and it's reported that their practiced positive attitude (including smiling) and stoicness in the face of sure death kept most pilots focused on their goal suicide, but the destruction of enemy materiel and personnel, and furthering of the war effort.

"Fleming, Sir Alexander" — ("Penguins") Fleming's discovery of penicillin was, indeed, something of an accident, when his culture dishes became contaminated after being left out. Fleming (1881–1955) and others had been working to find antibacterial agents since at least the end of WWI.

"James Watt"—Scottish inventor Watt (1736–1819) didn't invent the steam engine, but did modify and improve steam power to make it more industry-friendly.

"Albert Einstein"—Einstein's (1879–1955) cleverness improved upon existing theories of Galileo and Lorentz, among others, in producing the special and general theories of relativity in the first years of the twentieth century.

"Rutherford"—Ernest Rutherford (1871–1937) first split the atom in 1919.

"Marconi"—Marconi (1874–1937) developed a practical radiotelegraph system, and would win the Nobel Prize in 1909.

A commonality exists for most of these mentioned: Einstein, Rutherford, Fleming, and Marconi were awarded Nobel Prizes for their work. (James Watt lived and worked before the institution of the Nobel Prize, but he was a Scotsman.) See Watson's *The Modern Mind* for more on most of these inventors and innovators and the ideas that shaped the world of the twentieth century. The Pythons continue to betray a fascination with and deep knowledge of the great ideas of their century, flavoring their "silly" narratives with astute cultural references and recognizable philosophic undertones.

There is also a structural unity here, the "rule of three," or a staple of the comedic monologue (and, incidentally, speech and oratory in general). The Presenter (Cleese) mentions Fleming and his accomplishments, Watt and his accomplishments, and Einstein and his accomplishments—all fairly straight ahead and even accurate—immediately followed by a comedic twist ("if he hadn't been clever"). The comic cadence is "set-up, set-up, set-up, pay-off." There is then an interstitial bridge, a pause ("All these tremendous

leaps forward have been taken in the dark"), followed by the next threesome: Rutherford, Marconi, and the generalized "amazing breakthroughs"—followed by the comedic "Of course not." The same cadence is heard in Ep. 7, when the Camel Spotter (Idle) admits that he's (1) seen one yeti, (2) seen a little yeti, (3) seen a picture of a yeti, and, finally, he's (4) only heard of a yeti, and after only three, four, five, and actually seven years of spotting. This is the classic set-up and pay-off structure of the stand-up comedian, monologist, mythology, and fairy/folk tales (see Propp), memorable addresses ("Life, liberty, and the pursuit of happiness"), and, very often, Python's humor in *Flying Circus*. Even as the Pythons admittedly attempt to fly in the face of conventional comedic structures, they very often obey those time-honored tenets.

"Frontiers of Medicine" — ("Penguins") This mock documentary is inspired by earlier and memorable BBC programming, including Laurens van der Post's *The Lost World of the Kalahari* (1957), which includes the author's Afrikaans-tinged voiceover narration, as well as the series *Frontiers of Science*, which appeared on the BBC in the late 1950s, and then BBC2 in the late 1960s. *Frontiers of Science* themes were primarily space- and environmentally oriented.

• **G** •

Gathering Storm, The — ("Penguins") Once again, this is the title of the first volume of Churchill's massive WWII book project. The music under this title is "Industrial and War: Action Line" by David De Lara (WAC T12/1,462).

Gentle classical music — (PSC; "Rival Documentaries") The printed script mentions accompanying music to this section, but there is none provided in the final broadcast version of the episode.

"going from 'unemployment' through 'pensions'" — (PSC; "Party Political Broadcast [Choreographed]") This entire scene has been elided from recent broadcast and recorded versions of the episode. It wasn't until 1972 that the British Pensioners and Trade Union Action Association was formed, to organize and mobilize millions of retired trade union members into continuing political action. These voters tended to lean toward Labour and promises of full employment, higher wages, and increased pensions.

"group of mad medicos" — (PSC; *Dad's Doctors* [Trail]") *Dad's Doctors* is a variation on the very popular BBC sitcom *Dad's Army* (1968–1977), which featured the exploits of the old and creaky Home Guard in London during WWII. The *Dad's Army* humor was often warm and broad, just the type of show for the Pythons' incongruous sexually deviant remakes.

"RAMC"—The Royal Army Medical Corps. These references may also point to the currently popular *Doctor at Large* series, contributed to by Chapman and Cleese in 1971, or even the award-winning Robert Altman film *M*A*S*H* (1970).

"Guy Mannering" — ("Rival Documentaries") One of Scott's "Waverley" novels, and published anonymously in 1815.

• H •

"Heart of Midlothian" — ("Rival Documentaries") *Heart of Midlothian* was not one of Scott's "Waverley" novels, but was gathered in a series called "Tales of My Landlord," and originally appeared in 1818. *Old Mortality* (1816) was part of the first series of "Tales" novels, and was set in West Scotland in the late seventeenth century. What both are "preserving," probably, is the Scottish language and way of life of the recent past.

• I •

"I can't go on with this drivel" — ("Kamikaze Scotsmen") Another moment of self-consciousness, with the usually controlled and unflappable BBC announcer (Palin) actually critiquing the words he's hired to read. Earlier, in Ep. 30, BBC Announcers are reminded that they aren't to think about what they're reading ("Neurotic Announcers"). The silliness of MacDonald's suicide attempts just following supports the announcer's assessment of the drama.

"it's so much harder with the words" — ("Party Political Broadcast") In the "Colour Section" of *Private Eye*, where actual news tidbits are offered for their innate silliness, the goings-on in preparation for the Conservative Party political broadcast (probably for a 1965 by-election) were described:

> Something that seemed to sum up the election campaign was seen in a BBC studio last week.
> Mr. Heath was rehearsing for his party political broadcast. On the tele-prompter could be seen the words:
>
> I CARE DEEPLY ABOUT . . .
>
> The word "deeply" was underlined no less than three times. (Ingrams, 132)

Again, this sketch has been left out of most recent versions of Ep. 38 on DVD or VHS, and can only be found in the printed scripts.

Ivanoe — (PSC; *"Spot the Loony"*) Spelled correctly on the screen, in the printed scripts, the subtitle reads "Ivanoe," which is a misspelling of Scott's very popular historical adventure novel *Ivanhoe* (1819).

• J •

"Jacklin, Tony" — (*"Spot the Loony"*) Well-known British golfer (b. 1944) who's already been mentioned by two ranters—the abattoir architect (Cleese) in Ep. 17, and the Tourist (Idle) in Ep. 31, both of whom see owning "Tony Jacklin golf clubs" as a significant and execrable British status symbol.

"Anthony Barber"—Barber (1920–2005) was the Chancellor of the Exchequer during the Heath administration, thus a Conservative and certainly a potential "loony" to the Pythons. Throughout 1972 inflation was rising dramatically in the UK, and Barber was persona non grata to many who felt the pinch of their weakening purchase power. Barber has already been mentioned (in Ep. 28) as appearing in a Ken Russell film where he, "sadly, was unable to cope," a comment on his perceived ineffectiveness at the helm of Britain's listing economic ship. Barber was much in the news in 1972, having recently reaffirmed the government's position against floating the pound. (It would be floated just four days later, 23 June 1972.)

"Edgar Allan Poe"—A noted American poet, Poe (1809–1849) is probably the only celebrity in this list of possible "loonies" who might have actually fit the appellation, given his alleged penchant for alcohol and drug abuse, his morose published work (and life), and untimely death.

"Katie Boyle"—Boyle (b. 1926) was indeed a television presenter, hosting *It's a Knockout* in 1966. Boyle would also host the Eurovision Song Contest in 1968, and was likely the inspiration for Idle's "Girl" character in Ep. 22 who hosts a similar international singing contest. It may well be that the Pythons pulled back on this "loony" reference to Boyle to avoid complaints from the BBC and/or attorneys representing Boyle or the various popular shows she hosted.

"Reginald Maudling"—Yet another Conservative figure. Due to a financial scandal that indirectly implicated him, Maudling (1917–1979) had resigned as Home Secretary in July 1972, before this episode was broadcast (but long after studio recording had been accomplished, in December 1971). Barber (mentioned above) had served as Financial Secretary to the Treasury under Maudling in the early 1960s.

One name missing from this list as broadcast was Morris [*sic*] Wiggin (actually Maurice Wiggin), "country book" author and contributor to the *Sunday Times*, specifically as an often acerbic TV critic. The latter may be where he ran afoul of the Pythons and became a "looney." Wiggin had also been tapped by the BBC to chat up the BBC 2 conversion to color in 1968. His photo was requested for the "Loony" line-up, but was either not filled or they changed their minds and didn't include him. The *Sunday Times* said this about their man in a promotional ad in January 1961:

PRO-WIGGIN?
or
ANTI-WIGGIN?
Maurice Wiggin, Television Critic of the *Sunday Times*, and acknowledged leader of television criticism, writes with such personality that the sampling of one article will place you in the pro-Wiggin or anti-Wiggin camp. Probably the former if your approach to the box is at all similar to his strict, unbemused attitude. Try him this Sunday—if you go anti-Wiggin you'll probably want to continue to read him just to have something solid to champ at. And it'll be good for you to work off those tensions! ("This Week in the *Sunday Times*," *Times*, 6 Jan. 1961: 6.)

It's likely the Pythons were leaning anti-Wiggin.

There were also "US presidential hopefuls" requested, but not included (T12/1,444). Leading up to the 1972 election, the "hopefuls" would have included incumbent Nixon, of course, but also Democrats George McGovern (b. 1922), Hubert H. Humphrey (1911–1978), George Wallace (1919–1998), and Edmund Muskie (1914–1996). (Muskie will be mentioned in Ep. 39, while Nixon is a favorite flogging post for the Pythons.) Republican hopefuls included John Ashbrook (1928–1982) and Pete McCloskey (b. 1927). Nixon would win by a landslide, capturing almost 87 percent of the popular vote.

• L •

"late Pleistocene era" — (PSC; closing link out of *"Dad's Pooves* [Trail]") Probably pulling a geological era out of the blue, the Pythons have identified this fairly recent epoch as the time when Britain's rock strata was forming. However, the earliest formations in the islands date back at least 2.7 million years (especially in Scotland). The Pleistocene epoch in Great Britain, more precisely, was a time of ice ages and glaciation.

"Limestone, Dear Limestone"—The sappy title is a play on the popular *Father, Dear Father* (1968), a Thames TV farcical comedy about a single father and his rambunctious household. The show was a star vehicle for Patrick Cargill (1918–1996), who also appeared in *The Magic Christian* and *The Frankie Howerd Show*.

Most of the UK's limestone was formed during the Jurassic period, much earlier than the Pleistocene. There are small limestone deposits in the northern area (Oban, Scotland) where the Pythons were shooting this location footage, but much larger ones to the south, especially in southern Scotland and northern England.

"Leicester . . . Gatwick" — (*"Spot the Loony"*) Leicester is Chapman's birthplace and is found in Leicestershire, Buxton is located in Derbyshire, and Gatwick is in Crawley, West Sussex, and is really just the name of the airport located there (and the medieval manor house in the area).

lorry emerges — (PSC; "Kamikaze Scotsmen") This lorry travels down the main road from Norwich Castle.

The swelling music underneath is "Scenic and Romance: Desert Morning" by Cliff Johns (WAC T12/1,462).

• M •

Map with an animated line — (PSC; "Kamikaze Scotsmen") Wartime documentaries and animated training films featured this type of animated map work. See the "Why We Fight" series (1943–1944), *Memphis Belle*, and Disney's *Victory Through Air Power* (both 1943) for myriad examples.

Morris Minor speeds up — (PSC; "Rival Documentaries") The music used in this chase sequence is "Devil's Gallop" played by the Queens Hall Light Orchestra (WAC T12/1,462). This chase music was also used in the wrap-up for "The Spanish Inquisition" sketch in Ep. 15, as well as a similar chase scene in Ep. 30, *"The Pantomime Horse Is a Secret Agent* Film" sketch. Also, Janet (Marie Anderson) and Mystico (Jones) drive a Morris in Ep. 35.

Mr. Gilliam's animation shows penguins infiltrating important positions everywhere — (*"Animation: Penguin invasion"*) The first image appears to be taken at Windsor Castle where the Queen's Guards stand watch. This image of the Queen and Prince Philip (where the Duke of Edinburgh is replaced by a penguin) appears to have been taken during the royal tour of Australia in 1963. The following image depicts sitting Prime Minister Ted Heath being replaced with a penguin, to audience laughter, followed by sitting American President Richard M. Nixon being replaced, to audience cheering. It's not clear whether the cheer is prompted by the disappearance of a disliked foreign leader, or the appearance of a penguin holding a copy of *Monty Python's Big Red Book*, which was published in 1971. The next image features the contemporary leaders of the USSR, Brezhnev, Kosygin, and Gromyko, and all are replaced, as is the entire (likely) May Day parade they are reviewing—they all become penguins.

• N •

"no time to lose" — ("Kamikaze Scotsmen") The Pythons often take something very familiar—a bedtime story, a stock market report, a newscast, a colloquialism—and defamiliarize it for comedic purposes. The horror film genre, of course, performs the same type of defamiliarization, but for uncanny results (a harmless stuffed doll becomes a threat, for example). Additionally, just spending time examining a word or phrase serves the same purpose, detaching that phrase from its context and rendering it abstract, thus difficult to comprehend. Later, Man (Palin) will struggle greatly with this seemingly simple phrase, putting the emphasis on the wrong word, etc., and demonstrate no ability to understand how to "turn a phrase."

This entire stilted conversation will be revisited in the feature film *Life of Brian*, when Pontius Pilate (Palin) and Centurion (Cleese) attempt to discuss Brian's fate, with Centurion mishearing, but responding anyway.

The music under the animation following this sketch is from the Orchestra de Suisse Romande's album *French Overtures*, "Orpheus in the Underworld" (WAC T12/1,462).

• O •

"On the Dad's Liver Bachelors at Large" — (PSC; *"Dad's Pooves* [Trail]") Certainly a reference to another Chapman and Cleese show (where they contributed as writers), *Doctor at Large*, starring Barry Evans, and appearing on London Weekend Television (LWT), followed by *Doctor in Charge* (premiering in April 1972). Only Chapman contributed material to this latter season.

• P •

"Party Political Broadcast" — (PSC; "Party Political Broadcast [Choreographed]") Broadcast time given to the major political parties prior to elections. The staginess and stiffness of the (especially) earlier broadcasts from both parties is well documented, with surviving party broadcast scripts available through the "UK Elections" site at Keele University. Some of these broadcasts featured carefully written and rehearsed scripts with trained actors, vox pops, and the party

leaders themselves trying to smile through the clumsy staged events. In the lead-up to the 1970 General Election, the Conservatives created a *News at Ten*–lookalike set on which their presenters were to act, with presenters delivering the anti-Labour message like coverage of a rail disaster:

> Voice Over: Last night Mr. Heath spoke in Birmingham, one of his themes was care and compassion. And that's the theme of tonight's edition of "A Better Tomorrow."
>
> Geoffrey Johnson Smith: We're hearing a lot about care in this election. Mr. Wilson calls it compassion, and you'd think he'd invented the word. But just how much does Mr. Wilson's caring count?
>
> Christopher Chataway: The fact is that today after five years of Labour government the poor are getting poorer, things are actually getting worse. Two million families are living in sub-standard conditions, yet this year fewer homes are being built than when Labour took over.
>
> G.J. Smith: As for people on pension, well Labour meant well. When they came to office, they put pensions up by four shillings in the pound.
>
> C. Chataway: The only trouble was that in the next five years prices rose faster than pensions . . . ("UK Party Election Broadcasts 1970: Conservative Party")

These in-studio portions were matched by man-on-the-street Vox Pops moments with disaffected folk in parks or at the shops, and usually ended with a short address by Heath himself. The Conservatives would surprise Labour and win the 1970 General Election, largely on the basis of the electorate's hope that the ailing economy could be "fixed."

penguin pool — (PSC; "Penguins") This scene was shot at Penguin Pool, Children's Zoo, Hotham Park, on 18 October 1971, with permission received from the Bognor Regis Urban District Council (WAC T12/1,428).

"Penguins, yes penguins" — ("Penguins") The affordable and attractive line of pocket-sized Penguin books (est. 1935) featuring readable titles from myriad authors and genres—titles from *Lady Chatterley's Lover* to *Gidget*—made Penguin books a national phenomenon. These color-coded (orange, green, maroon, blue) and unadornedly printed books were, literally, everywhere as the Pythons grew up. In *FC*, penguins appear in as many settings—in stage shows, on TV sets, in boardrooms, and as killer creatures in bad Hollywood films. See notes to Eps. 4, 5, 22, and 23 for more.

Lastly, the celebrated case in the UK when Penguin Books was taken to court for violating the Obscene Publications Act of 1959 with the belated publication of *Lady Chatterley's Lover* brought penguins into court, literally, and forcing the name into the public consciousness.

"Phillips-Bong" — (*"Dad's Pooves* [Trail]") The character Kevin Phillips-Bong (Palin) appeared in Ep. 19 as a candidate from the Slightly Silly Party, and received no votes.

"post-Impressionists" — ("No Time to Lose") Toulouse-Lautrec is considered to be a member of the post-Impressionists, with notable others including Gauguin, Cezanne, Van Gogh, and Seurat. If they can be described as "lawless," it must be due to the post-Impressionists' purposeful move away from the rules of classical composition, use of color, and perspective.

• Q •

"Queen's Own" — ("Kamikaze Scotsmen") Indicating that the unit or materiel belongs to the government (*OED*).

• R •

"Ratings Game, The" — (PSC; *"Dad's Pooves* [Trail]") *The Dating Game* was a very popular American game show that made its debut in 1965.

Redgauntlet — (*"A Book at Bedtime"*) Sir Walter Scott's 1824 novel looks at a further return to Scotland by Bonnie Prince Charlie.

Red Square — ("Unexploded Scotsman") The transition music under this title and footage is Shostakovich's "The Execution of Stepan Razin" as played by the Moscow Philharmonic Orchestra (WAC T12/1,462).

"remember you're cabinet ministers" — (PSC; "Party Political Broadcast [Choreographed]") Prime Minister Heath's Cabinet included Robert Carr, Quintin Hogg, Anthony Barber (Ep. 28), Alec Douglas-Home (Ep. 30), Reginald Maudling (Eps. 12, 22, 36, etc.), Jim Prior, Lord Carrington (Ep. 42), Margaret Thatcher (Ep. 30), and others.

"Rosewall" — ("Penguins") Australian tennis player Rosewall (b. 1934) competed at the international level from the 1950s through the 1970s. What follows is another laundry list of professional tennis players first visited in the initial season, in Ep. 7, when alien blancmanges winning Wimbledon was the subject.

"Laver"—Rod Laver (b. 1938) was of the tennis generation just following Rosewall; he was also Australian, and held the number one ranking for five consecutive years.

"Charles Pasarell"—American Pasarell (b. 1944) and partner lost to Rosewall and partner in the 1969 U.S. Open.

"Dr. Peaches Bartkowicz"—American Jane Bartkowicz (b. 1949) had retired from tennis very recently, in 1971.

"Dr. Kramer"—Born in 1921 and still very much alive at the time this episode was produced, Jack Kramer was a star player and then promoter for/of international tennis. Kramer wouldn't pass away until 2009.

"Dr. Lewis Hoad"—Yet another Australian tennis player, Hoad (1934–1994) and Rosewall were a very successful doubles team, and Hoad won the singles title at Wimbledon in both 1956 and 1957.

• S •

"Sapper" — ("Kamikaze Scotsmen") A "sapper" is the colloquial or unofficial term for a private in the Royal Engineers (*OED*).

"Scott, Sir Walter" — (*"Spot the Loony"*) Noted Scot novelist (1771–1832) whose Waverley novels popularized historical fiction and especially "folk" romance fiction involving "real" Scottish families and settings. As for being "disllusioned and embittered," Scott seems to have escaped that fate, with the exception of some financial concerns that kept him writing for a living well into his retirement years.

"Charles Dickens"—Victorian novelist Dickens (1812–1870) produced all of his major works much later than Scott (his first, *The Pickwick Papers*, appeared in 1836), and his settings and characters were inseparably connected to the south and especially the city of London.

The Pythons (and/or their set designers) have thoughtfully placed William Hogarth (1697–1764) images behind author Dickens, who was an admirer and collector of Hogarth's work. The images appear to be from Hogarth's *Marriage à-la-mode* set, and include, from left to right, *The Tête à Tête, The Inspection*, and *The Bagnio*, all dated 1743.

six male dancers — (PSC; "Party Political Broadcast [Choreographed]") These dancers (none pictured in the latest episode versions, however) include Arthur Sweet (*The Slipper and the Rose*), David Allen (*40 Pounds of Trouble*), Chris Robinson, and Peter Walker (*Amahl and the Night Visitors*), who also dances in Ep. 39.

sixty-six feet high penguin — ("Penguins") This model as built by the BBC prop crew measured about 10 feet tall and 16 feet wide (WAC T12/1,445). The giant penguin motif was last seen in Ep. 23, *"Scott of the Antarctic."*

"Spot the Looney" — (PSC; *"Spot the Loony"*) In the printed scripts, "loony" is more often spelled "looney."

On the set created for the sketch, for example, it is spelled "Looney" in flashing lights.

stock film of penguins — (PSC; "Penguins") This footage is listed as "GR 2091A Reduction Print from T/R" in the WAC records (WAC T12/1,462). Much of the stock footage used in this episode—for example, the Kremlin and the "investiture of the Prince of Wales"—is not source-identified in the WAC records.

"stop the rising unemployment at a stroke" — (PSC; "Party Political Broadcast [Choreographed]") Part of Heath's proposed political platform for his eventual (and surprising) Conservative government win in the 1970 General Elections was a drastic upswing in the economy: "This would, at a stroke, reduce the rise in prices, increase production and reduce unemployment." This sweeping comment on the effects of reduced taxation was actually deleted from Heath's speech when delivered as part of a political party broadcast, but the line remained in the material given to the press, and was printed in most newspapers. The line became fodder for op-ed pages and cartoonists, especially as the Heath government struggled through the economic crises of 1971 and 1972. The oft-heard joke became "At a stroke, lose your jobs," etc. See the British Cartoon Archive for these UK political cartoons.

As printed in the *Times* on 17 June 1970, the entire section of the platform reads quite optimistically:

> But there is a very real alternative which ought to be pursued immediately. That alternative is to break into the price/wage spiral by acting directly to reduce prices. This can be done by reducing those taxes which bear directly on prices and costs, such as the selective employment tax, and by taking a firm grip on public sector prices and charges such as coal, steel, gas, electricity, transport charges and postal charges. This would at a stroke reduce the rise in prices, increase production and reduce unemployment. It would have an immediate effect of moderating the wage/price spiral which would far outweigh any effects from higher pressure of demand for labour. ("Heath Warning of Squeeze, Freeze and Perhaps Devaluation to Come," 4)

sunlit university quad with classical pillars — (PSC; "Rival Documentaries") This shot was actually recorded way back on 12 November 1971 at Felbrigg Hall, where the exterior shot for *Erizabeth L* (Ep. 29) was also shot (WAC T12/1,428). The specific location is the stables and courtyard area at the extreme east of the structure.

"sunset was dying over the hills . . ." — ("*A Book at Bedtime*") This is an imagined passage from an imagined Scott novel, no doubt, as it appears nowhere in

Redgauntlet or in any of Scott's existing works. There is a similarly themed passage which the Pythons may have remembered as they wrote the sketch, from the opening paragraph of "Letter IV":

> The whole was illuminated by the beams of the low and setting sun, who showed his ruddy front, like a warrior prepared for defence, over a huge battlemented and turreted wall of crimson and black clouds, which appeared like an immense Gothic fortress, into which the lord of day was descending. His setting rays glimmered bright upon the wet surface of the sands, and the numberless pools of water by which it was covered, where the inequality of the ground had occasioned their being left by the tide (35).

As can be seen, the imagery is very similar, but without the specifics of "Edinburgh Castle," for example. Coincidentally, the origination for this letter in the Scott novel is "Shepherd's Bush," where BBC Television Centre would be built some 136 years later.

· **T** ·

tennis courts in the background — (PSC; "BBC Programme Planners") These tennis court scenes were shot in Salt Hill Park, Slough (WAC T12/1,428).

"That's where you'll get the balloons and the ticker tape, Chris" — (PSC; "Party Political Broadcast [Choreographed]") The "Chris" mentioned by the Choreographer (Idle) is likely to refer to Chris Chataway (b. 1931), a presenter on *Panorama* and *ITV News* and who appeared in Conservative Party Political Broadcasts leading up to the 1970 General Election. Chataway has already been mentioned in Ep. 28, in relation to campaigner Mary Whitehouse.

"Toulouse" — ("No Time to Lose") Larger city (population of about 475,000 in 1968) located in southwest France.

"Toulouse-Lautrec"—Noted French painter, the diminutive Toulouse-Lautrec (1864–1901) has already been mentioned (and spoofed, riding a tricycle while painting) in Ep. 1. His favorite subjects were the "real" people in the lower-class Montmartre section of Paris, and especially the theaters and brothels.

tragic, heart-rending music — (PSC; "No Time to Lose") This is Ronnie Aldrich's (1916–1993) "Silent Movie Piano Suite No. 6: Hearts and Flowers" by Czibulka/Warren (WAC T12/1,462).

"trans at eight, so nobody be late" — (PSC; "Party Political Broadcast [Choreographed]") Once again, the sing-song delivery of a gay male is the "type" identifier, along with the dance and "luv" references. "Trans" is the diminution of "transmission," though it may not be accidental that it also bears sexual connotations.

• U •

Unexploded Scotsman — ("Unexploded Scotsman") There were thousands of unexploded bombs—known as "UXB"—left in and under England after WWII, and hundreds remain under London homes and buildings today, untouched and undetonated. Reports of these devices appear regularly in period newspapers, scattered across the country. For example, between 1963 and 1972, bombs were dredged up in fishing trawler nets, found by holidaymakers on beaches, and discovered during new building works in and around London, Coventry, etc. Most were safely removed and detonated.

The music under the defusing of the Scotsman is Neil Richardson's "Dramatic Background: Approaching Menace," which was also used by the popular BBC quiz show *Mastermind* (1972–).

"Up the Palace" — (PSC; "*Dad's Pooves* [Trail]") *Carry On . . . Up the Khyber* (1968) and *Carry On . . . Up the Jungle* (1970) were part of a series of slapstick, Empire-bashing film comedies starring Frankie Howerd, who also later starred in the popular *Up Pompei!!* television series for the BBC. The Pythons, of course, quite easily connect these ribald, pratfall-rich sources with the investiture of Charles as the Prince of Wales (by his mother, the Queen), accomplished in July 1969, just as the first season of *FC* was being cobbled together.

• V •

"Very good sergeant major" — ("No Time to Lose") This structure is a revisitation of the "Being Hit on the Head Lessons" section from Ep. 29, "Argument Clinic." The repetitiveness of the writing and structure of the show is what put Cleese off as early as midway through the second season (see Morgan [1999]).

Very impressive stirring music — ("Spot the Loony") The music used in the first part of the sequence is Keith Papworth's "The Big Country," from DeWolfe Music (WAC T12/1,462). This same music will also be used later in the feature film *Holy Grail*. Budgetary constraints precluded hiring a composer, and the fallback—paying very reasonable one-use licensing fees for program music—had worked very well for *FC* (and myriad BBC shows).

The music changes to "Locations and Comedy: Comic Giggles" by John Pearson (WAC T12/1,462).

Voice Over — (PSC; "Kamikaze Scotsmen") The printed script lists this as being voiced by Palin, but it clearly is not Palin in each speech. The WAC records don't indicate directly who took the role in the "conditions of extreme secrecy" speech, but it may have been (actual Scotsmen) director Ian MacNaughton or even cameraman James Balfour.

• W •

"What makes these young Scotsmen so keen to kill themselves?" — ("Kamikaze Scotsmen") Yet another swipe at the easy targets to the north (and once again avoiding similar attacks on the Irish, for example), the typical young Scot, it seems, will fall prey to the British military's recruiting drives that actually do mention sports and fun as part of service. The good money quote, of course, is silly in that the dead Scotsmen won't be spending his paycheck anyway.

But lack of jobs could have also played a significant part in this willingness to join the military. In January 1972 *International Socialism* announced that unemployment in Great Britain and Ireland had exceeded one million, and in Scotland, unemployment among men stood at more than 9 percent in that same year, second only to Northern Ireland (*International Socialism* 51 [April–June 1972]: 31). Suicide rates in Scotland were also increasing rapidly during this period, and would continue to rise into the 1980s, according to NHS figures.

The *Times* proclaimed in a rather somber headline "A Million Out of Work" in January 1972, the first time that level had been breached "in a generation." Scotland's own figures bear this out, and then some—even though Scotland could claim only 9.6% of the population it was home to 15.8% of the total unemployed (21 Jan. 1972: 13).

• Y •

"Yes excellent" — ("No Time to Lose") The Consultant (Idle) is kneeling away from Man (Palin) and everything else, indicating he's about to have the sixteen-ton weight dropped on him, but there is a cutaway before the weight drops. This was either cut out during the editing for the show or, more likely, did not make the transfer cut when the latest DVDs were being produced. The opening scene and following animated link also suffered the same fate, disappearing before transfer to DVD.

Episode 39: "Grandstand"

Thames TV introduction; Nude Organist, "And now . . ." Man, and "It's" Man; *Titles*; *Light Entertainment Awards*, starring Dickie Attenborough; The remains of Sir Alan Waddle; **The Oscar Wilde sketch**; *Animation: Swell party, bathroom noises, Charwoman*; David Niven's fridge; Pasolini's film *The Third Test Match*; Cricket critics; New brain from Curry's; Blood donor; International Wife-Swapping; *Come Wife-Swopping*; *Grandstand* match highlights; Credits of the Year; "The Dirty Vicar Sketch"

• A •

"Are you the man from Curry's?" — ("New Brain from Curry's") The Cleese character is wearing a hat with a very prominent tag that reads "L.H. Nathan." L.H. Nathan was actually a costumier who had recently costumed for the film *Carry On Henry* (1971) and *The Lion in Winter* (1968).

Around the World in 80 Days' *music* — (PSC; "David Niven's Fridge") Niven's 1956 film based on Jules Verne's novel, and scored by Victor Young (1899–1956). The Pythons do use a snippet of the popular theme from the film, but that use isn't accounted for in the WAC records for some reason.

Composer Victor Young would score this film using all sorts of recognizable musical cues—including *Rule Britannia*, *Yankee Doodle*, and *La cucaracha*—a technique the Pythons obviously picked up on as they approached "scoring" the *Flying Circus* series.

Attenborough, Dickie — ("*Light Entertainment Awards*") Richard Attenborough (b. 1923) is an actor, director, and producer who was busy directing *Young Winston* in 1972 (which was nominated for but lost the Academy Award). His 1969 film *Oh! What a Lovely War* had been nominated for a BAFTA award in 1970. In 1972, Attenborough's co-star in *10 Rillington Place*, John Hurt, had been nominated for a best supporting actor BAFTA, while Attenborough wasn't, even

though he was the "star" of the film. Dustin Hoffman (*Little Big Man*), Dirk Bogarde (*Death in Venice*), Albert Finney (*Gumshoe*), and Peter Finch (eventual winner, for *Sunday, Bloody Sunday*) had been the best actor nominees that year.

Attenborough is earlier lampooned, also by Idle, in his portrayal of the multiple murderer in Ep. 27.

audience standing in a rapturous applause — (PSC; "Dickie Attenborough") The film stock of the applauding audience is EMI's "Theatre Audience" (WAC T12/1,461).

awful continuity music — (PSC; "*Light Entertainment Awards*") This canned music is "Aces to Open" by Syd Dale (WAC T12/1,461).

• B •

"Best Foreign Film Director" — ("David Niven's Fridge") As the BAFTA awards were earmarked for British performers and performances, there were no foreign film categories.

The winner of the "Best Foreign Language" film award in the 1972 Academy Awards was Vittorio de Sica's *The Garden of the Finzi-Continis* (1970). The same award in 1971 was also collected by an Italian film, though not directed by Pier Pasolini, while Costa Gavras's *Z* (1969) took the award the year before.

Bough, Frank — (link out of "International Wife-Swapping") Frank Bough (b. 1933) presented *Grandstand* (1958), *Sportsnight* (1968), and *Nationwide* (1969), among others. Bough was depicted earlier, also by Palin, in Ep. 35, presenting "The Olympic Hide and Seek Final."

"Boycott, Geoff" — ("Pasolini's Film *The Third Test Match*") Boycott (b. 1940) was a Yorkshire and English cricket player who went on to become a cricket broadcaster. According to cricinfoengland.com, Boycott's Test batting average (for his career) stands at 47.72.

"Fred Titmus"—Another cricketer, Titmus (1932–2011) was a cricketer and footballer. Titmus played for England, and in 1964 batted with Boycott against Australia in Nottinghamshire, which is probably the match the Pythons are referencing.

"Ray Illingworth"—Born in 1932, Illingworth played for Yorkshire, Leicestershire, and England, and was the English national cricket team captain during this period. (See cricinfo.com and *Wisden* for much more.)

British Showbiz Awards — ("*Light Entertainment Awards*") On 4 March 1971 the "British Screen Awards: A Gala Night for Television and Film" were held in the Royal Albert Hall, and hosted by Richard Attenborough. This show was broadcast on BBC1. On 23 April 1972 Attenborough hosted the "British Screen Awards," also known as the "Society of Film and Television Arts Awards," also at the Royal Albert Hall. These awards actually were aired on Thames Television, for ITV.

The title picture is a nighttime shot of Piccadilly Circus, though given the type of cars visible and the signage, the time period looks to be the late 1950s. (The Coca-Cola sign, for example, had been in place since about 1954, the BP sign appears in 1959, and the Bovril and Guinness signs would be gone by the late 1960s.)

• C •

"Come Wife-Swapping—North West v the South East" — (link out of "International Wife-Swapping") Spoofing the *Come Dancing* ballroom dance show that made its debut on the BBC in 1949. Regions of England competed against each other. *Come Dancing* was presented by Peter West and Brian Johnston, among others. This long-running and popular interregional competition show has already been mentioned in the "Test Match" sketch in Ep. 20. This dancing sequence appears to have been filmed at the former Galtymore Ballroom, 184 Cricklewood Broadway, NW2 (T12/1,460). The building has since been torn down.

Incidentally, the title "Come Wife-Swapping" is misspelled on screen, being printed as "Wife-Swopping."

Cotton, Bill — ("Light Entertainment Awards") Born in 1928, Cotton was the head of BBC Light Entertainment and is credited with giving Cleese and the Pythons a shot at a new BBC show in 1969.

Cotton appears in the WAC archives for *Flying Circus*, but only for his responses to some of the show's lapses in "good taste," as well as fielding memos from agents asking/demanding more money and better time slots for their clients (the Pythons, severally).

"Curry's" — ("New Brain from Curry's") Currys was an electrical appliance store chain in the UK, with stores conveniently close to the Pythons in Uxbridge, Staines, Harrow, Pinner, Ruislip, and the nearest located in Southall.

• D •

"Dirty Vicar Sketch" — ("The Dirty Vicar Sketch") This set-up may be a poke at BAFTA awarding *The Benny Hill Show*—flatulence, jiggling breasts, and "wink-wink" jokes—with the Light Entertainment Award in 1972 for the best comedy program *and* best comedy script.

Also, *Jude the Obscure* (based on the Hardy novel) appeared on the BBC in 1971, with the requisite setting (Victorian) and characters (including a "Chivers" and a vicar) for the Pythons to have borrowed. The serialized book was greeted with much public denunciation due to its "libertine" and sexualized characters, something not lost on the Pythons as they created their Vicar character.

"Doncaster" — ("Wife-Swapping") Doncaster was one of the sites for ITV's (horse) race coverage of the *ITV Seven*, while Cheltenham was actually a BBC-covered event for the more affluent horse racers (see Aylett).

"dose of clap" — ("The Oscar Wilde Sketch") The term "clap" has been in common (albeit vulgar) parlance since the late sixteenth century, at least. The widespread presence and virulence of venereal diseases in the UK, and especially larger cities, had been reported and fretted over for generations. The numerous Contagious Disease Acts enacted, re-enacted, reinforced, and reinvigorated in the nineteenth century alone attests to an almost epidemic infection rate in the crowded metropolis. Hundreds of professional books and articles were published in the UK and on the Continent on the subject, and the ravages of syphilis became the stock-in-trade of many dramatists and literary types, including Voltaire, Shakespeare, Swift, Hogarth, and Charlotte Brontë, and hundreds of lesser scribes and broadside balladeers. The royal hospital

St. Bartholomew's (where Chapman had worked) was a well-known venereal disease treatment facility through much of the preceding two hundred years.

• E •

Episode 39 — This episode was recorded on 18 May 1972, and first broadcast 18 January 1973. It was the twelfth episode recorded and was broadcast thirteenth, and was Cleese's last official (broadcast) episode as a full member of the troupe. His written contributions would continue into the abbreviated fourth season. He is even scheduled to appear in Ep. 42, but does not, with Douglas Adams appearing in his place.

The assorted extras and walk-ons appearing in this episode include: Giovanna de Domenici, Gillian Phelps (Eps. 12, 17, 32), Annetta Bell (*Microbes and Men*), Jill Shirley, Cathy Holland, Alison McGuire (*Dial M for Murder*), Antonia McCarthy, Jack Fulton, Barry Ashton (*Doctor Who*), Roy De Wynters, Richard Kirk, Colin Thomas (*Doctor Who*), Jenifer Nicholas, Laurel Brown (Ep. 35), Emmett Hennessey (Ep. 35; *Z Cars*; *Softly Softly*), Clive Rogers (Ep. 30; *Z Cars*) (WAC T12/1,461).

• F •

"five-and-a-half" — ("New Brain from Curry's") This reflexive moment connects the audience back to the obviously remembered and popular (they applaud and laugh) moments in Ep. 31, the "Our Eamonn" sketch, when characters answering the phone have to give their shoe sizes in a string of "yes" answers. Other reflexivities—Spiny Norman, Cardinal Ximinez, the Nudge Nudge Man, Richard Baker—continue to erase boundaries between episodes and create a sort of ever-present in the *Flying Circus* world. All this being said, the show continues to separate itself from most of its predecessors in that by late in its third season it still does not rely on long-running characters or obvious familiarities—instead, the framework tropes of miscommunication, absurdity, unsuccessful transactions, and narrative undercutting support the show.

four screens of naughty activity — (PSC; link out of "International Wife-Swapping") The *Grandstand* titles did feature a similar four corners effect, but with different sports depicted in each section.

"friends of the society" — (*"Light Entertainment Awards"*) Meaning the "Society of Film and Television Arts" established in 1958.

• G •

"Graham Chapman and Mr. Sherlock" — ("Credits of the Year") David Sherlock is acknowledged here as Chapman's partner, or spouse. Sherlock was a writer for *Doctor in the House* (1973) and *Doctor in Charge* (1969), and has spoken for Chapman in Python-related interviews since Chapman's death in 1989.

Grandstand — (introductory titles) *Grandstand* was a popular BBC sports show that made its debut in 1958, and was hosted by Frank Bough and David Coleman, among many others.

• H •

Hamilton, David — (PSC; "Thames TV Introduction") Hamilton (b. 1939) was a Thames TV announcer, specifically for ABC Weekend Television (ATV), the broadcast organization awarded a license by the government to conduct weekend programming in London beginning in 1956. This same license was given over to London Weekend Television (fronted by David Frost) in 1968. Hamilton also announced for the popular *Top of the Pops*, and would have been a very familiar face to the Pythons' studio and home audience.

hansom cabs — (PSC; *"Light Entertainment Awards"*) This film stock is from the British Movietone News Library (WAC T12/1,461).

"he has sent his fridge" — ("David Niven's Fridge") Just two months later, in March 1973, Hollywood icon Marlon Brando would send an actress dressed as an American Indian to reject his Academy Award for Best Actor.

HRH The Dummy Princess Margaret — (*"Light Entertainment Awards"*) At the 1971 "British Screen Awards: A Gala Night for Television and Film" show, Princess Anne (b. 1950) actually served as the royal guest, not Margaret. This is the third episode where Margaret has appeared in this "pantomimetic" form.

There is no indication in the WAC records that either the princess or the royal family officially or unofficially complained about these continuing, unflattering references to the Queen's younger sister. Perhaps Margaret's more public (and sometimes profligate) lifestyle made such barbs inevitable, and the royal family and equerry took them as unavoidable.

• I •

"I never said that" — ("The Oscar Wilde Sketch") The friendship and competition between Wilde and

Whistler is attested to in each man's own words from the period, as well as in many incidents recorded by friends and associates. Desmond McCarthy (a member of the Bloomsbury Group) notes that Wilde did indeed host and attend the type of socially and artistically elevated parties as depicted by the Pythons, and that Wilde's goal wasn't ridicule or scorn, necessarily, but to "play others off the stage" in good fun (see Nelson's *English Wits*, 50). Wilde would come to such events prepared with witticisms and bon mots; his stories and amusements were carefully crafted to lead to a witty finish, to the delight of all in attendance. In *The Whistler Journal* by E. R. and J. Pennell (1921), one such party conversation moment is recorded, with the theatricalized and rehearsed Wilde being suddenly upstaged, to Whistler's great satisfaction. From the Pennells:

> A characteristic of a still different mood and manner was a story John Alexander [an American painter, 1856–1915] used to tell. He was dining at the Walter Gays [Gay was also an American painter, 1856–1937] and Whistler was there, though at the other end of the table. Alexander was recalling another dinner some years before where he met Oscar Wilde. As usual Wilde's talk was designed to lead up to carefully prepared witticisms. In the midst of it the lady he had taken in to dinner asked, "And how did you leave the weather in London, Mr. Wilde?" and that was the end of the talk and the witticisms. Alexander had no idea that Whistler was listening or even could hear, but, at this point he heard the familiar "Ha! Ha!" and Whistler leaning over said to him, "Truly a most valuable lady!" (228; bracketed descriptions added)

It is just this type of elevated one-upmanship that the Pythons employ in the sketch, with the target being the good-natured Prince of Wales (Jones), and Shaw (Palin) getting played off the stage.

One such potential gathering is announced in the *Times*, a sort of "welcome back" and even "get well" dinner for Edmund Yates, held at the Criterion Restaurant on 30 May 1885. Yates (1831–1894), a respected novelist and dramatist, had recently served a seven-week jail sentence on a libel charge, and the literary cognoscenti clearly wanted to celebrate his freedom. Invited gentlemen guests (a veritable who's who of London's men of art, law, and letters) include both Whistler and Wilde, of course, but also the Earl of Dunraven (1841–1926), Lord Houghton (1809–1885), Lord Randolph Churchill, MP (1849–1895), Henry de Worms, MP (1840–1903), and the host was newspaper publisher and MP Algernon Borthwick (1830–1908).

Ironically, G.B. "Shaw-y" Shaw was not on the list of invited stewards.

ink all over Mr. Heath — (PSC; *"Light Entertainment Awards"*) On 22 January 1972 a young woman (a native German living in London) approached PM Heath in Brussels and splattered him with ink. Heath was in Belgium to sign the accession pact (along with Ireland, Norway, and Denmark) for entry into the European Union. Political cartoonists of the day had fun with this incident for weeks afterward (see the British Cartoon Archive). The woman was reportedly upset about the proposed redevelopment of Covent Garden Market, and not Britain's entry into the Common Market.

The film stock is BBC Film DO23/72/41 "Heath" ("WAC T12/1,461). The photo of the attack graced the front page of hundreds of newspapers and magazines, as well.

• J •

John Rickman type person — ("International Wife-Swapping") Rickman (who died in 1997) was ITV's host for its popular racing program, *ITV Seven*, which featured seven horse races, and went on the air in 1969. The audience obviously recognizes the caricature, laughing as soon as Palin appears.

• K •

"Keighley" — (Rugby link into "Credits of the Year") Keighley and Hull Kingston Rovers played for the Yorkshire Cup, a county cup, though Keighley never won the cup. Hull K.R. won the cup in 1971–1972, defeating Castleford 11–7, after having won the Yorkshire in 1966–1967 and 1967–1968.

• L •

lady rushes across the street — ("International Wife-Swapping") An accident report was filed with the BBC for this episode, according to WAC archives. Actress Antonia McCarthy fell and skinned her knee (on 13 March 1972) as she ran from one house to another on Aldbourne Road, Hammersmith, Greater London, where this scene was shot. Though it's not identifiably Miss McCarthy, one woman in the far background can be seen falling to her knees in the street toward the end of the filmed sequence. After a visit to the "surgery," she returned to the set to work (WAC T12/1,428).

"latest play" — ("Oscar Wilde Sketch") Wilde's *The Importance of Being Earnest* made its premiere in February 1895, to strong reviews (excepting Shaw's, co-incidentally) and full houses. Unfortunately, Wilde's homosexuality was soon to be revealed, and his career took a fairly precipitous downward spin thereafter (including a trial for sodomy and then prison).

"Light Entertainment Award" — (*"Light Entertainment Awards"*) In 1972, BAFTA gave its "Best Light Entertainment Performance Award" to Ronnie Corbett and Ronnie Barker of *The Two Ronnies*, with the runner-up nod going to *Benny Hill*. The "Best Light Entertainment Production Award" went to *The Benny Hill Show. Monty Python's Flying Circus* did not make the final nominations.

FC had been nominated twice the previous year at the same awards show. Cleese was nominated for the "Performance" award but lost out to Eric Morecambe and Ernie Wise (*The Morecambe and Wise Show*), while *FC* was nominated for the "Production" award, losing to the atavistic *Dad's Army*. This latter loss may be the reason the Pythons gleefully, deviantly skewer *Dad's Army* in the final scene of Ep. 38, *"Dad's Pooves."*

FC would finally win the award for "Best Light Entertainment Programme" in 1973. See the Internet Movie Database for a complete list of BAFTA winners and nominees.

"like a big jam doughnut" — ("Oscar Wilde Sketch") Both Wilde and Shaw were well-known for aphorisms, epigrams, and memorable one-liners. From Wilde: "Those whom the gods love grow young" (from "A Few Maxims for the Instruction of the Over-Educated," *Saturday Review* [London, 17 Nov. 1894]); and from Shaw: "There are no secrets better kept than the secrets everybody guesses" (from *Mrs. Warren's Profession*). Contemporary newspaper reviews of Wilde's work, for instance, mention (positively and negatively) his reliance on characters who speak in epigrams, no matter the setting or plot.

• **M** •

Mambo music starts its intro — (PSC; "International Wife-Swapping") The music here is from the Edmundo Ros Orchestra album *The Wedding Samba*, "Dance Again" by Ellestein (WAC T12/1,461).

"Manchester United" — (link into "Credits of the Year") Manchester United, Southampton, and Coventry are all English football teams.

man in a brown coat — (PSC; *"Light Entertainment Awards"*) This is Frank Lester, who appeared as a loony in Ep. 31 (WAC T12/1,461).

"Marsh, Alec" — ("International Wife-Swapping") Alec Marsh (1908–1996) was first a jockey then a horse racing official (*ODNB*). "Mrs. Alec Marsh" at this time was Marjorie Minnie Cole, Marsh's second wife. They

had married in June 1972, meaning the starter here had very recently swapped his own wife for a newer model.

"Match of the Day" — (Rugby link into "Credits of the Year") A BBC 2 sports show that appeared in 1964 and broadcast football highlights. David Coleman (b. 1926), mentioned later, assumed the role of presenter in 1970.

"Mountbatten" — ("Credits of the Year") Lord Mountbatten (1900–1979), also known as "Dickie," was a great-grandson of Queen Victoria and the last viceroy of India. The naming of the award here after him might be in reference to the unreleased home movie Charlie Chaplin made with the newly married Mountbattens on their honeymoon in America, titled *Nice and Friendly* (1922), or the later marital infidelities and fireworks the Mountbattens would endure. As early as 1953 many would hint at Mountbatten's allegedly homosexual flings with naval cadets (calling him "Mountbottom"), these sexual indiscretions fitting into the "Wife-Swapping" theme rather well (see Wilson's *After the Victorians*).

Music comes in — ("Pasolini's Film *The Third Test Match*") This dramatic music is from Prokofiev's score for *Alexander Nevsky*, the "Battle on the Ice" (specifically the "Ice Breaks" section) as played by the Czech Symphony Orchestra (WAC T12/1,461).

"Muskie, Senator" — ("New Brain from Curry's") Edmund Muskie (1914–1996) was a U.S. senator from Maine, and had run for vice president in 1968 on the Humphrey Democratic ticket, losing to Nixon and Agnew. During the contentious primaries for the 1972 Democratic Party presidential nominations, Muskie was perceived as crying in an address to the media, and this may have prompted the Pythons to ratchet up the Attenborough "waterworks" as seen in this episode.

• **N** •

"Niven, David" — (*"Light Entertainment Awards"*) Actor Niven (1910–1983) had appeared most recently in *The Statue* (1971), in which Cleese also makes a brief appearance.

"np" — ("New Brain from Curry's") "Old pence" and "new pence" ("op" and "np") indicate the pre- and post-decimalization valuation of the penny in the UK.

• **O** •

"Old Sketch Written Before Decimalisation" — ("New Brain from Curry's") In 1971 the UK adopted the system where the pound was divided into one hundred equal parts, as opposed to the pound being earlier divided into twenty shillings, and each shilling then divided into twelve pence. This Labour-spawned but Tory-managed changeover was such a momentous event that a mass advertising campaign was created by the government, including memorable radio and TV spots. One such announcement offers a shouting Cockney hawker type followed by a musical jingle:

Jingling sound of a new penny dropped on a counter.
Hawker (*shouting*): The new penny! It's lighter than the old penny, it's smaller, and it's worth over twice as much!
Then a jaunty piano and male choir chime in:
Singers: One pound is a hundred new pennies,
A hundred new pence to the pound.
One pound is a hundred new pennies,
A hundred new pence to the pound. (*Eyewitness: 1970–79*, "General Election, 18 June 1970")

Significantly, this mention also points up the increasing delay between the team's writing of the show and the eventual production. For the third season, writing would have been under way in the fall of 1971, with studio recording beginning in December 1971. Broadcasting these episodes for the first time wouldn't be complete until January 1973, eighteen months *after* decimalization.

"only thing worse than being talked about" — ("Oscar Wilde Sketch") A quote actually attributed to Wilde.

• P •

"Pasolini, Peir Paolo" — (*"Light Entertainment Awards"*) Italian New Wave film director Pasolini (1922–1975) had recently directed *Teorem* (1968), *Porcile* (1969), and *The Decameron* (1971), all "experimental" in their approaches to classical filmmaking. Pasolini may have faced this kind of interpretive scrutiny as he created his version of an English treasure, Chaucer's *The Canterbury Tales* in 1972, where he would drift away from Chaucer with his own written material and characterizations.

The Third Test Match sketch is probably satirizing Pasolini's raucous *Il Decameron* (1971), but there are also images (tight close-ups, crash zooms, face offs) borrowed from at least two other Pasolini films, *Oedipus Rex* (1967) and his most rcent, *Canterbury Tales* (1972). It's abundantly clear, for example, that at least some of the Pythons had watched Pasolini's Oedipus adaptation before embarking on the *Holy Grail* film project.

paying him with invisible money — ("New Brain from Curry's") This "pretending" is a fairly new development in the show, where a bit of "business" in a sketch is feigned as opposed to enacted. It could be said that the Pythons are less reliant on fastidiousness when it comes to use of props and common exchanges because they're tiring of the show itself, but it's also arguable that the show is becoming less reliant on normal, accepted theatrical conventions, and edging further into television's avant garde. But the dumb show is hodge podge—just moments before when Mrs. Zambesi is asked to sign the severed leg, she takes a pencil and attempts to do so. She (Chapman) accidentally drops the pencil, then bothers to pick it up and complete the signature, so the skirting of theatrical convention hasn't been completely embraced by (all of) the Pythons.

photo of Picadilly Circus — (PSC; *"Light Entertainment Awards"*) The swelling music beneath this photo and the titles of the show is from "Academy Awards: The Music of Stanley Black" by Stanley Black (WAC T12/1,461).

picking up a catalogue — ("New Brain from Curry's") Mrs. First Zambesi (Chapman) is actually reading from an Empire Stores catalog, not a Curry's catalog. Empire Stores was founded in the early 19th century.

"Prince of Wales" — ("Oscar Wilde Sketch") HRH Albert Edward was the Prince of Wales between 1841 and the death of his mother, Victoria, at the turn of the century, when he became George V. The prince was an avid patron of the arts, and he did have a social relationship with Wilde and even Whistler. The Prince and Princess of Wales, for example, took in a private tour of Whistler's etching exhibition at the Fine Art Society in 1883.

The Prince also answered to a nickname not unlike "Shaw-y"—for G.B. Shaw heard here—the Prince was called "Bertie."

• R •

"Redcar" — ("International Wife-Swapping") There remains a racecourse in Redcar (in Redcar & Cleveland), off of Redcar Road.

"Richard Baker for Lemon Curry" — (*"Light Entertainment Awards"*) This insert appeared originally in Ep. 33, and was most likely recorded during the taping of Ep. 30 (on 11 December 1971), when Baker appears as himself and "gestures" the day's news.

"rotten old BBC" — ("Thames TV Introduction") The government-funded "Auntie Beeb" was often characterized as producing dated, tired, and very "safe" programming, especially during the tenures of John Reith (1932–1939) and Ian Jacob (1952–1959), whose programming choices and management styles tended to mirror their own conservative, even didactic beliefs.

Ironically, the Pythons had only come into existence thanks to a general thaw in this corporate conservatism, when Hugh Greene headed the BBC (1960–1969) and expanded the new show directions into the youth and even counterculture markets. What they are likely complaining about here is the current administration, under Charles Curran (1969–1977), which had regressed back into more conservative and family-friendly programming in the wake of threats and bluster from Mary Whitehouse and her followers.

Lastly, this "rotten old" show so spurned by Hamilton and Thames TV, the "British Screen Awards," would the following year appear on Thames TV, and not on the BBC.

"Russell, Bertrand" — ("New Brain from Curry's") Noted British philosopher and mathematician Russell (1872–1970) was a Nobel laureate, anti-war activist, and anti-nuclear demonstrator. He is mentioned in the notes to Ep. 31, and his writings are being burned by crusading Pepperpots ("Tory Housewives") in Ep. 32.

• S •

"Shaw" — ("Oscar Wilde Sketch") George Bernard Shaw (1856–1950) was an Irish playwright and wit, and younger than either Wilde or Whistler. Shaw had been one of the few critics to react negatively to Wilde's very popular 1895 play *The Importance of Being Earnest*, admitting its engaging qualities but bemoaning its lack of "humanity," but was for the most part a supporter of his fellow Irishman, even campaigning for Wilde's early release from prison and against censorship of Wilde's controversial *Salome*. Both Shaw and Wilde had written for the *Pall Mall Gazette*, developing at least a mutual respect for each other's work there (see Gordon). There seems to be no evidence for the convivial triumvirate of Whistler, Wilde, and Shaw, especially as late as 1895, when Whistler was caring for his terminally ill wife and Wilde was in the early stages of his fall from grace.

"south of Sidcup" — ("New Brain from Curry's") Part of Greater London, Sidcup is in Bexley, about twelve miles from the City of London.

"split the urban Republican vote" — ("New Brain from Curry's") Probably a campaign plan of both Senators Ed Muskie (mentioned moments earlier) and George McGovern, front-runners for the Democratic nomination for U.S. president in 1972. Eventually,

Muskie dropped out of the race, and incumbent Richard Nixon was re-elected.

Suitable classy music — ("Oscar Wilde Sketch") The music clip is from "Strauss at the Waltz" by Harry Wild (WAC T12/1,461).

• T •

Talk-back — (PSC; "Pasolini's Film *The Third Test Match*") *Talkback* was a BBC show designed to let viewers give comments on sports and BBC coverage of sport. The show was presented by Michael Barratt (b. 1928).

Thames Television logo — (PSC; "Thames TV Introduction") Thames was the weekday company serving London for ITV (commercial broadcasting) after 1968. The re-recording (for use here in the show) of the "Thames Opening Symbol" theme sparked plenty of controversy, it seems, with memos flying back and forth between various departments and the BBC legal personnel. The BBC eventually agreed to pay the Musician's Union about £157 (WAC T12/1,462).

"the other side" — ("New Brain from Curry's") Indicating that these Pepperpots still see the available television stations as they would an LP—there are only two sides, BBC1 and BBC2.

"Third Parachute Brigade Amateur Dramatic Society" — ("The Oscar Wilde Sketch") The Third Parachute Brigade was a WWII-era unit that participated in the Normandy D-Day invasion on 6 June 1944.

There are literally hundreds of amateur dramatic and operatic societies in the UK, most, however, associated with municipalities. These societies did (and do) perform Wilde's repertoire. For example, the Macclesfield Amateur Dramatic Society staged a version of *The Importance of Being Earnest* in 1951–1952. The incongruous combination of a military unit and dramatic society may be a result of the well-known dramatic efforts of WWII Allied prisoners of war staging sometimes lavish performances (very often featuring cross-dressed characters). Some of these performances are recounted by participants in *Eyewitness 1940–49*, "Getting Through," with those who took women's parts being described as often assuming feminine qualities and allurements that went with them after the camps were liberated.

• V •

vast applause — (PSC; "David Niven's Fridge") At the 1971 Academy Awards (broadcast in April 1972), Charles Chaplin (1889–1977) received a lifetime achievement award and a lengthy standing ovation.

Chaplin did attend the ceremony in Los Angeles. In the previous year's Oscar ceremony, Orson Welles (1915–1985) was also given a lifetime award, but sent actor/director John Huston (1906–1987) to collect the statuette.

very patriotic music — ("Dirty Vicar Sketch") This is Edward Elgar's "Enigma Variations" as played by the London Symphony Orchestra (WAC T12/1,461).

• W •

Waring, Eddie — (PSC; Rugby link into "Credits of the Year") Idle is listed in the printed script as playing Eddie Waring (1910–1986), who was earlier mentioned in the script for Eps. 1 and 13. Waring is also lampooned a number of times in *ISIRTA*. Waring was a Rugby League commentator for many years.

West, Peter — (PSC; "International Wife-Swapping") Peter West (1920–2003) was a journalist who covered cricket, rugby, tennis, and even dancing for the BBC. West has already been mentioned along with fellow broadcaster Brian Johnston in Ep. 21.

"Whistler, James McNeill" — ("The Oscar Wilde Sketch") American-born painter who spent most of his adult life in the artist colonies of London and Paris, Whistler (1834–1903) did have a much-publicized epistolary and in-person relationship with Wilde, whom many considered Whistler's disciple (including Whistler). The two allowed for the publication of their satiric and witty (and sometimes vitriolic) correspondences in *The World* in 1883 (and Wilde published art criticism in the *Pall Mall Gazette*), and it seems that by this point Whistler was already beginning to worry that his protégé was surpassing him at the forefront of modern British society and as leader of the avant garde (Anderson and Koval). The competition for the crowd's affections as shown in the *FC* sketch is a reflection of the two artists' real-life competition to be the most respected artist in Britain.

In 1895 (when this sketch is said to be staged) Whistler was spending much time in London, where his wife was terminally ill, and Wilde was on the verge of a two-year prison sentence. See entries in the *ODNB* for more on both men.

"Wife-Swapping" — ("International Wife-Swapping") There is a healthy car swapping market in the UK, where interested parties swap cars rather than buying and selling them. The swapping theme was earlier broached in Ep. 28, as was the "Ford Popular" reference.

"Wife Swapping with Coleman" — (link into "Credits of the Year") Frank Bough did replace David Coleman

as the host of *Grandstand* in 1968. See the *"Match of the Day"* entry for more.

Wilde, Oscar — (PSC; "The Oscar Wilde Sketch") During this fin-de-siècle period Wilde (1854–1900)—a very prominent and flamboyant British writer, aesthete, and bon viveur—lived in Paris, where he and Whistler would, indeed, hobnob and exchange witty ripostes with astonishing alacrity. By 1895, however, their mutual acrimony and personal life struggles prevented any real social or personal encounters (Whistler's wife reportedly "loathed" Wilde)—this scene could have better been set in 1880–1883, when they were still at least mostly on speaking terms (see Anderson and Koval).

• Y •

"Yorkshire" — ("Pasolini's Film *The Third Test Match*") The Yorkshire County Cricket Club featured Brian Close, Geoff Boycott, and Ray Illington during the 1960s. These are meant to be Yorkshire cricketers, hence the accents, and the references to popular professional Yorkshire cricketers.

"You will, Oscar, you will" — ("The Oscar Wilde Sketch") Yet another famous riposte by Whistler (allegedly spoken c. 1888), acknowledging his friend/foe Wilde's penchant for incorporating bits and pieces from other wits into his own repertoire. In 1886 Whistler would write to *The World*, illustrating the growing rift between him and former disciple Wilde:

> What has Oscar in common with Art? except that he dines at our tables and plucks from our platters the plums for the puddings he peddles in the provinces. Oscar—the amiable, irresponsible, esurient Oscar—with no more sense of a picture than of the fit of a coat, has the courage of the opinions—of others! (qtd. in Anderson and Koval, 314)

"You might even need a new brain" — ("New Brain from Curry's") This was the miraculous era when heart transplants and artificial hearts, for example, had stormed the news internationally, originating in South Africa and Texas and moving into developed countries around the world. These pioneering surgeons (Barnard and DeBakey) are mentioned in Ep. 29, "Argument Clinic."

• Z •

Zambesi — ("New Brain from Curry's") The Zambezi is a river in Africa, and yet another silly name for a Python character.

SEASON FOUR

Episode 40:
"The Golden Age of Ballooning"

The Golden Age of Ballooning, Episode 1; Montgolfier Brothers; *Animation: Washing with soap and water*; *The Golden Age of Ballooning* promos; Episode 2; Louis XIV; Episode 3; *Decision*; George III (and song); O'Toole's curtain calls; Closing credits; BBC 1 Colour announcement; Party Political Broadcast, Norwegian Party; *The Golden Age of Ballooning*, Episode 6: Ferdinand von Zeppelin; The drawing room, not the sitting room; *Animation:* The Golden Age of Colonic Irrigation; *The Mill on the Floss*

• A •

Animation of balloons ascending — (PSC; "Montgolfier Brothers") Though not mentioned in the printed scripts, the music for the titles here sounds to be Salieri's "La Fiera di Venezia" as performed by the Richard Bonynge English Chamber Orchestra (WAC T12/1,469).

The balloon models Gilliam chooses for the "Golden Age of Ballooning" titles include: The Montgolfier's original September 1783 balloon (the elaborately decorated one); Jean-Pierre Blanchard's balloon (with the wings/fins); a version of J.A.C. Charles's hydrogen balloon that first flew in December 1783; a Jean-Baptiste Marie Meusnier de La Place–looking dirigible; all are used more than once and recolored.

"Annencay" — ("Montgolfier Brothers") Actually "Annonay," the first Montgolfier balloon flight in 1783 was conducted just south of St. Étienne at Annonay in southwestern France. This first balloon was made of paper (the brothers were papermakers by trade), and the next flight in September 1783 carried a duck, a chicken, and a rooster as passengers. The first manned flight occurred on 21 November of that same year.

• B •

"ballcock . . . bang" — ("Montgolfier Brothers") The first is an apropos plumbing reference, as it is a toilet requisite reportedly invented by Englishman Thomas Crapper much later than the Montgolfiers' flight. The latter might refer to the sound of an exploding balloon, or have a sexual context based on the later comments made by Jacques (Jones) as his fiancée hangs from the gas bag. Joseph (Idle) also follows the dictionary entry by saying, "What a position!"

"Bartlett" — ("Louis XIV") It's not clear why Mr. Bartlett (played here by Peter Brett) wants to see the brothers, nor whether he is connected at all to the Glaswegian Louis, nor why the Irishman O'Toole (Chapman) has such a difficult time pronouncing what should be a fairly recognizable name. The continuity breaks in this period piece are myriad, however, and include a modern plumber who narrates (Palin), the introduction of stage hands and projection equipment for voiceover assistance, a Scotsman (Palin again) impersonating a dead French king, etc. The last six shows of the series vary greatly in their cohesiveness and even watchability, as Cleese had long since left for greener pastures, prepping elsewhere for *Fawlty Towers* (1975–1979).

"Bartlett" is also the name of Counsel in Ep. 3, there played by Cleese.

"better things to do" — ("Louis XIV") One of the concerns about a monarch such as Louis XIV was that he did attempt to rule every aspect of his kingdom, making decisions and commands without utilizing a strong network of more regional or local controlling bodies. In short, he took on too much, and the slip-pages (angry dukes, unhappy commoners, unsuccessful military endeavors, unfinished roads) became inevitable (*EBO*).

"Bismarck" — ("Zeppelin") First chancellor of the German Empire, Bismarck (1815–1898) was a driving force behind German unification.

"bits and pieces of balloons" — ("Louis XIV") After the Montgolfier brothers' successful flight, there was an explosion in balloon paraphernalia throughout France, with balloon-emblazoned crockery and figurines available in many French stores.

black and white film of Barry — ("Zeppelin") The tearful piano music used behind this footage is Peter Reno's "The Poor Soul" as performed by Rose Treacher. The scene was shot near Motspur Park, with the South East Gas Holders looming in the background, on 3 October 1974 (WAC T12/1,469).

"Bo-sankway, Reginald" — ("Zeppelin") Reginald Bosanquet (1932–1984) was an ITV newsreader and the BBC's *News at Ten* anchor. Bosanquet has already been mentioned in Ep. 20, and he appears in Ep. 26, standing to attention for the Queen.

• C •

"canal" — ("Louis XIV") In the seventeenth and eighteenth centuries the French did speculate about a canal through the isthmus in Egypt, attempting to counter the dominance of East Indian trade by the Portuguese, Dutch, and then English. The French didn't survey the area until around 1800, however. The Suez Canal—financed by France and Egypt—was finally completed in 1869. Britain, however, would come late and pick up a significant interest in the canal by 1875, culminating in an embarrassing military exercise in 1956 that essentially put the lid on Britain's world power dreams.

"Constance" — ("Zeppelin") Or Konstanz, in Baden, Germany.

Cut to a throne room — ("George III") The music here is from Handel's "Concerto Grosso in C Major, Alexander's Feast, First Movement (Allegro)" as performed by Granville Jones's Philomusica of London (WAC T12/1,469).

• D •

"drawing room . . . sitting room" — ("Zeppelin") This type of corrective badinage ("*Drawing* room") will be

revisited in *Holy Grail*, when King Arthur (Chapman) constantly says "five" and is corrected to "three."

"dukes" — ("Louis XIV") The "dukes" Louis is trailing behind him are played by Frank Lester (Eps. 31, 35–37; *Jackanory*) and Bob Raymond (*FC* fourth season; *Secrets of Sex*) (WAC T12/1,469).

• E •

Edwardian photo — (PSC; "Zeppelin") These black-and-white photos were and are available in London shops and stalls. The advent of photography in the nineteenth century caught the general public's imagination quickly and many—not just the upper class—began sitting for photos. Most of the images Gilliam employs appear to be common folk sitting for dignified "picture portraits." Gilliam mentions that comedian Ronnie Barker (1929–2005) gave him a boxful of the mildly erotic photos—Gilliam called the Edwardian-era models "round and squidgy"—and the photos then begin to appear in his animations (*Gilliam on Gilliam*, 41). A number of these photos and postcards were gathered into books edited by Barker in the later 1970s and 1980s. See the bibliography for those titles.

Episode 40 — This is the first of the last six episodes recorded for the entire *Flying Circus* series, and the episodes are broadcast in the precise order of recording. The Pythons had been officially "separated" since the completion of recording for Ep. 36, which was finished 25 May 1972. The fourth season wouldn't start taping until 12 October 1974, and they were finished just five weeks later, when Ep. 45 would be recorded on 16 November 1974.

Episode 40 "The Golden Age of Ballooning" was recorded on 12 October 1974, and broadcast on 31 October 1974. This episode is also featured on the cover of the *Radio Times* for 26 October 1974, complete with a Gilliam animation and a synopsis of the major sketches. The BBC was also making it clear both in internal memos and advertising blurbs for the final season that the shows were "similar but different" to the previous three seasons, especially in that there was a theme for each episode (WAC T12/1,469).

The BBC had convinced the remaining Pythons (Chapman, Gilliam, Idle, Jones, and Palin) to create a half-season schedule for 1974, but the writing was clearly on the wall. By December 1974, according to the BBC's regularly gathered ratings figures, the percentage of available audience watching *FC* on BBC2 had dropped to 8.4 percent (while competing shows on BBC1 and ITV experienced viewership increases during this same period). Many canvassed viewers commented that without Cleese the show wasn't as funny or appealing, that it had grown completely tasteless and offensive, and seemed to be reaching for shocks, not laughs (WAC T12/1,469).

Various actors brought in and dressed in period costumes for "The Golden Age of Ballooning" include the following: Reg Turner (*Z Cars*), Rory O'Connor (*Blakes 7*), Hattie Riemer (*Z Cars*; *The Wednesday Play*), Leslie Bryant (Ep. 25; *The Wednesday Play*), Leslie Glenroy (*Doctor Who*), Bill Lodge (*Upstairs, Downstairs*), Nicholas Kane (*The Ribald Tales of Robin Hood*), Simon Joseph (*Softly Softly*), Harry Davis (*Dixon of Dock Green*), Cecil Lloyd (*Microbes and Men*), George Lowdell (*The Saint*), John Kimberlake, Bill Earle, Jim O'Neill, Charles Rayford (*Doctor Who*), Raymond St. Clair (*Track of the Moon Beast*), Ronald Musgrove (*Z Cars*), Richard Cash, D. Southern, Les Conrad (*Softly Softly*), Annet Peters (*The Fall and Rise of Reginald Perrin*), Judy Roger, Sylvia Lane, Audrey Searle (*The Debussy Film*), Stella Conway, Mike Barrymore, and Noel Pointing (WAC T12/1,469).

• F •

"failure to buy it" — ("Louis XIV") The Goons dedicated an entire show to the Big Brother–type corporation BBC forcing listeners and viewers (and actors and announcers) to participate, watch, or listen. Listen to the "1985" episode from *The Goon Show* (BBC Radio Collection).

Fanfare. Enter Louis XIV — ("Louis XIV") The fanfare is from "The Fanfares" by Charles Williams (WAC T12/1,469).

"fire balloon" — ("Montgolfier Brothers") The Montgolfiers' creation utilized a fire at the mouth of the balloon to inflate and lift the balloon.

"flannel" — ("Montgolfier Brothers") A colloquialism for "wash cloth," the *OED* points out that it won't be until 1819 that "flannel" appears (in English) in print.

• G •

"George-Brown, Lord" — ("Party Political Broadcast") Higher-up in the Labour Party during the 1960s, George-Brown (1914–1985) had won a Labour seat in 1945 and was in the running for the party leadership before Harold Wilson came to the fore. In 1966, George-Brown became Foreign Secretary, only to lose that position in 1968, and then lose his seat completely in the Conservative-friendly 1970 General Election. It was Brown's alleged increasing dependence on alcohol that prompted *Private Eye* to coin the euphemism "tired and emotional," mostly to avoid libel or slander charges while still taking their shots at the Labour leader.

George III — ("George III") This song is written by oft-contributor Neil Innes (b. 1944), who will go on to get squashed by a catapulted rabbit in *Holy Grail* and write all the songs for Idle's *Meet the Rutles* (1978) parody film. Innes was part of the Bonzo Dog Doo-Dah Band who appeared regularly on the Palin/Jones/Idle pre-Python show, *Do Not Adjust Your Set* (1967).

The historical person George III (1738–1820) was the English monarch from a German background (a Hanoverian king) who at this time (1781–1782) was losing the American colonies to independence. France had signed agreements with the upstart colonies to supply material support in the revolutionary effort, which probably accounts for the international intrigue at the heart of this episode (*ODNB*). George (Chapman) will ask the faux-Frenchman Louis (Palin) to stop this assistance as part of the balloon plan deal.

"George IV" — ("George III") George IV (1762–1830) would act as regent for his father in later years, coinciding with the king's here-and-there mental stability. George III is reported to have disliked his son for his epicurean proclivities, so this mistaken identity might have bothered him even more (*ODNB*).

"Glaisher and Coxwell" — ("Louis XIV") Henry Coxwell (1819–1900) and James Glaisher (1809–1903) did, in fact, reach record heights in 1862 in their balloon. See the entry for Coxwell in the *ODNB* for more.

"Glaswegian" — ("Louis XIV") Louis (Palin) speaks with the accent peculiar to Glasgow, Scotland's largest city, which sits on the Clyde River. Even among the Scots, it seems that a Glaswegian accent is more "coarse" and even "shorthand" than other dialects.

"Golden Age" — ("Montgolfier Brothers") Other similar titles available to the Pythons as they wrote included *The Golden Age of Comedy* (1957), and *Greece: The Golden Age* (1963), the latter narrated by Trevor Howard.

"Golden Years of Colonic Irrigation" — (link out of "Zeppelin") The music under this title card is John Reid's "Market Research" (WAC T12/1,469).

"Government has collapsed" — ("Decision") This is a reference to the recent 1974 General Election that saw the Tories lose many seats (in the House of Commons) while retaining a slim lead over Labour, but not enough to form a government without coalition. When the Liberals didn't cooperate, rendering a coalition impossible, Heath and his group had to resign, bringing Wilson and Labour's return to power. Labour, however, did not enjoy anything like a mandate. (Exact figures on the change of power can be found at Keele's "UK Elections" website.) In the 1974 election, both Northern Irish and Welsh seats were won by local parties/candidates, a startling change that certainly illustrated the government's incapability "of providing any sort of unifying force," as Dividends (Chapman) asserts. The Pythons' Tory bashing continues unabated.

• H •

Hamer, Dr. — (PSC; "George III") In the printed scripts, Gilliam's butler character is named "Dr. Hamer," and there's even a textual comment on the fact that he is to look like a "period butler," and not a doctor. There was a Dr. Neil Hamer at Trinity College, Cambridge (from 1964), who may have been the inspiration for Gilliam's affected performance here, probably as coaxed by the remaining Cantab Pythons, Idle and Chapman.

health and efficiency nudist camp — ("Zeppelin") *Health & Efficiency* is an international nudist magazine.

"heavier than air dirigible" — ("Louis XIV") These types of balloons are typically heavier than the air around them, meaning buoyancy must be created by filling the balloon with heated air, allowing for lift. From a man so obsessed with balloons, of course, Antoinette (Cleveland) should have interpreted this remark as the ultimate compliment.

"hen" — ("George III") A very familiar term, and one which wouldn't usually be used with royalty, which is probably why it's here—the impostor Louis, like the Peasant Dennis in *HG* (both played by Palin), doesn't recognize such things.

He reappears, takes a bow — (PSC; "Louis XIV") The adulation for this seemingly minor character is probably a reference to Angus Hodson, a butler character played by Gordon Jackson in *Upstairs, Downstairs* (1971–1975, LWT), one of British television's "classic" serials.

"Hollweg" — ("Zeppelin") Theobald Bethmann-Hollweg (1856–1921) was German imperial chancellor before and during WWI.

• I •

"I could hardly wash" — ("Montgolfier Brothers") If a washing was sought at all during the late eighteenth century, it usually included face and hands—or just those body parts not covered by thick clothing. Most

people washed only when they had to, and the resulting odors would have been quite the standard. It will become clear that this entire episode does have a lavatorial bent—a plumber-narrator, bathing animation, Joseph in his towel and shower cap, etc.

This is also a traditional (by now) structure for the Pythons—introducing a serious or important historical topic or personage (the first manned balloon flight), then undercutting that seriousness by silliness or diminution (inadequate personal hygiene).

"Ik tvika nasai" — ("Party Political Broadcast") This is jabberwock Norwegian, and actually structured more like a Slavic language than anything Nordic. "Good evening," for example, in Norwegian would be "God aften." The next two lines would translate something like: "De tror det merkelig at vi spør De stemme Norsk på den neste valg" and "Men betrakter fordelene." The Pythons have demonstrated abilities in French, German, and even Spanish and semaphore code in *FC*, but when it has come to Russian and now Norwegian, they have clearly attempted just the "sound" of those languages and avoided trying for any linguistic accuracy.

• K •

"kiddy-winkies" — ("Zeppelin") A little-used colloquialism meaning "children," the term earlier appears in *Private Eye* in Christopher Logue's "True Stories" section, the 6 August 1965 edition (Ingrams, 125).

• L •

"least talented" — ("George III") Not unlike the lesser-known Marx brothers, including Zeppo (1901–1979), who played the straight man and/or romantic lead in several of their films, and Gummo (1893–1977), who appeared in no films at all. The actual Ferdinand Zeppelin had one brother and one sister.

Lord North — (PSC; "George III") Not mentioned by name in the episode, Jones is playing Lord North (1732–1792), who was Prime Minister 1770–1782, and who suffered greatly (politically, personally) when the American colonies were lost.

"Louis XIV died in 1717" — ("Louis XIV") The French monarch (1638–1715) actually died 1 September 1715, at Versailles, thirty-five years before Joseph Montgolfier was born.

In Ep. 3, Inspector Dim (Chapman) points out that Cardinal Richelieu (Palin) has been dead since 1642—"I put it to you that you died"—making it impossible for him to be testifying as a character witness for the also-dead Harold Larch in 1969 London.

"Louis XV" — ("Louis XIV") Louis XV was the great-grandson of Louis XIV, and was just five years old when he assumed the crown (under a protectorate). He would die in 1774, and his grandson would become Louis XVI, and would be the last French monarch. Louis XVI was beheaded in 1793 during the French Revolution.

• **M** •

"make a list" — ("Zeppelin") The Pythons are by now clearly poking fun at the perceived German mania for order and rigor—reading alphabetical listings of food items, correcting room designations, sorting out dead government men by job description, and making lists. German critic and essayist Jürgen Syberberg characterizes the perceived fixation this disturbing way:

> The problem is that Germans are too well organized for the messiness of liberal democracy. We attempt to organize democratic opinion, to keep the system running smoothly and efficiently. When something disrupts the system, or doesn't fit where it's supposed to, there are problems. The concentration camps also belong to this chapter of German thoroughness, of starting from basics, thinking radically, totally, absolutely, getting to the very root of things. Expressed in vulgar terms, this means German orderliness. (*NPQ* 10, no. 1 [Winter 1993])

This outsider's view of the Germans isn't new, either, as a newspaper article from 1914 attests. The correspondent is traveling from Paris to Kiev by train, and notes the approach of the German frontier:

> The world that becomes visible as the sun rises is the ordered world of the Germans. Everything is prim, everything is as it should be; the fields are symmetrical, the palings are vertical and in good repair, the manure heaps are compact; where houses are being pulled down or set up there is no disorder whatever; nothing is scattered about, everything is collected and numbered. (Stephen Graham, "Returning to Russia: German Orderliness," *Times*, 5 Feb. 1914: 7)

Men racing through the gardens — (PSC; "Louis XIV") Very faintly the Wick Scottish Dance Band can be heard (as chase/transition music) playing "Mrs. McLeod of Raasay (Reel)" (WAC T12/1,469).

"Mill on the Floss" — (link out of "Zeppelin") The music underneath this "balloonic" version of George Eliot's novel *Mill on the Floss* (1859) is Sir Adrian Boult and the London Philharmonic Orchestra play-

ing "Symphony No. 2 in E Flat Major" by Elgar (WAC T12/1,469).

The realism that Eliot so often employed in the depicting of characters' lives and worlds is sent up, literally, as the lovers float away gently like balloons.

"Minister for Colonies" — ("Zeppelin") The "State Secretary for the Colonies" for Germany in 1908 was Bernhard Dernburg.

"Mirabeau's . . . 'assignats'" — ("George III") The "assignats" (or a form of paper currency) weren't issued in France until 1789, during the period of the Revolution, or fully eight years after this sketch is said to be set. Honoré Gabriel Riqueti, Comte de Mirabeau (1749–1791) very much believed in the program, which would spiral the country into hopeless inflation by 1795 (*Mirabeau and the French Revolution*, 368–70).

"Montesquieu" — ("Montgolfier Brothers") A leading figure of the French Enlightenment, Montesquieu (1689–1755) forwarded the "separation of powers" theory of government, and his work was very popular in Great Britain (and America). His *Persian Letters* (1722) poked fun at Louis XIV's court, which may be why the Pythons reference both in this episode. (See the entry for Montesquieu in the *Catholic Encyclopedia* for more.) Mozart has already been mentioned in the initial *Flying Circus* episode, hosting a "famous deaths" television show, and in Ep. 21, as the father of Colin Mozart, Ratcatcher.

"Montgolfier" — ("Montgolfier Brothers") Actual historical personages, the Montgolfier brothers—Joseph-Michel (1740–1810) and Jacques-Étienne (1745–1799)—are credited with developing the hot air balloon and conducting the first untethered flights.

Muybridge — (PSC; "Zeppelin") This particular photo does not appear to be a Muybridge photo. Eadweard Muybridge (1830–1904) was an early experimental photographer. Gilliam has used Muybridge's series photography before, however, earlier in this episode (as the Montgolfier brothers wash, supposedly), and even earlier in Ep. 36.

• **N** •

"Necker" — ("George III") Necker (1732–1804) was a Swiss banker and a director general of finance (1771–1781, 1788–1789, 1789–1790) under Louis XVI. The "wee bit of trouble" Louis mentions probably refers to Necker's 1781 financial state-of-the-kingdom report that painted a very positive picture of France's fiscal health, and which would eventually cost him his job (*Catholic Encyclopedia*). He would resign finally in 1790, leaving the country to the devices of Mirabeau and the "assignats" (see above).

"Norwegian Party" — (PSC; "Party Political Broadcast") The printed script notes that Idle is essentially ad-libbing here, and that his "Norwegian" should be "earnestly" delivered as the subtitles pass. This jabberwock approach is used by Idle earlier, in "The Cycling Tour" episode (Ep. 34), when he plays a Soviet compère telling a joke in faux-Russian. In the 1971 *May Day Special* created by the Pythons and submitted by the BBC, Chapman delivers a similar farrago of mock-Swedish, none of it subtitled.

"not a balloon" — ("Zeppelin") Zeppelin observed American balloon reconnaissance activities during the Civil War and determined to create balloons that could be guided, or "airships."

"not supposed to go mad until 1800" — ("George III") Actually, George III was completely overtaken by mental disease in 1810, after severe breakdowns in 1788 (when he tried to kill his son, the Prince of Wales), 1801, and 1804 (*ODNB*).

• O •

"orangery" — ("Louis XIV") A room in many of the more impressive manors in both France and England where orange (or citrus) trees were grown—the glassed-in rooms are kept warmer and very well-lit. Orangeries can be found at both Kew and Kensington.

• P •

palm court orchestra playing — (PSC; "Zeppelin") This small group is pretending to play the Palm Court Trio's version of "On Wings of Song" by Mendelssohn (WAC T12/1,469).

"Party Political Broadcast" — ("Party Political Broadcast") Air time given over to the leading political parties prior to elections. Python lampoons these regular broadcasts in Eps. 12, 32, 38, and 45 (latterly, the Labour candidate performing martial arts in a hallway). See entries in those episodes for more.

Pleasant elegant eighteenth-century music — (PSC; "Montgolfier Brothers") This is a snippet of organ music, specifically Corette's "Concerto in D Minor" performed by the Helmuth Rilling Wurttemberg Chamber Orchestra (WAC T12/1,469).

plumber — ("Montgolfier Brothers") A Plumber (Palin) relates the story of the Montgolfiers, and a plumber is included in every scene at the Montgolfiers' residence, working away in the near background. This privileged view is much like the evidence of memorialized versions of some of Shakespeare's works, wherein all the lines of a minor character like Marcellus (*Hamlet*) are included and even added upon, while other areas/ characters are given significantly less attention. Scholars can conclude, then, that a particular version could have been provided by an actor who had played Marcellus at one point (or been recreated from a particular prompt book), thus the favoritism toward his own lines and his elevated significance in the memorialized version. (See *The Oxford Shakespeare: Histories with the Poems and Sonnets*, xxvi.) The Plumber's version of the Montgolfier story, then, might understandably include otherwise insignificant details about washing and hygiene.

The plumber working in the background in most of the scenes (excepting the initial scene where Palin narrates) is played by Stenson Falke (*Doctor Who*) (WAC T12/1,469).

"Portland, Duke of" — ("George III") The Duke of Portland (1738–1809) was the British Prime Minister from 2 April to 19 December 1783, and again 1807–1809.

"published by the BBC" — ("Louis XIV") The BBC did produce (or provide) accompanying texts to many of its documentary-type programs, with representative titles including *Colour in Britain* (1965), from a radio feature of the same name, and *Europe and the Indies: The Era of the Companies, 1600–1824* (1970), from a multi-part television serial.

• R •

racing through the gardens — ("Montgolfier Brothers") These chase scenes are shot at Bicton Gardens, East Budleigh, Devon on 11 September 1974 (WAC T12/1,469). Much of the location work for the abbreviated fourth season was accomplished in Devon.

"railway between the towns" — ("Louis XIV") Serious talk about railway-building in India didn't begin until the 1840s, and the Lahore sections of railway were constructed in the 1860s, well after this sketch is allegedly set.

• S •

"salle à manger" — ("Louis XIV") A dining hall. Perhaps because the Montgolfiers' butler is Irish

("O'Toole"), they feel they must translate from French to English for him.

"seventeen square feet of body area" — ("Montgolfier Brothers") Since most adults can claim about twenty square feet of skin area, Joseph and Jacques are *still* missing some vital areas in their washing.

"shit" — ("Louis XIV") The Pythons generally used veiled vulgarism, rather than straightforward swearing, but the swearing and violence does increase during the third and especially fourth seasons of *FC*. They have used "merde" in previous episodes, which might have been expected from the Frenchman Joseph, though their butler is obviously an Irishman ("O'Toole") who for some reason struggles with the pronunciation of British-type names like "Bartlett." They have also used "excrement" in Eps. 17 and 19.

"six months later" — ("George III") It's 1781 now, so "six months later" is actually two years earlier than the historical Montgolfier setting. George (1738–1820) was a Hanoverian king who did suffer periods of dementia or "madness" that forced him from the throne for months at a time. In 1781, George's forces in America were losing, and suing for peace would begin the following year.

"sixteen years of work" — ("Louis XIV") The Montgolfiers had been working on balloons since 1782, or about one year.

The question of France being "in the grip of a Glaswegian monarch" is relevant when Louis XIV's Catholicism (or anti-Protestantism, more precisely) allied him with the Scottish Stuarts and their claim to the English throne against William of Orange, who would become William III. So Louis could have been known as a "Glaswegian (French) monarch" more readily than a "Londoner (French) monarch," certainly.

"smartarse" — ("Louis XIV") A would-be clever person, a know-it-all, and one who talks back (*OED*).

some men — ("Montgolfier Brothers") These men who enter carrying film projection equipment are meant to look like black-draped stagehands from the modern theater, but they certainly clash with the otherwise period settings and dress. These two actors are Mike Britton (variously spelled "Bridon," "Briton," or "Brydon" in WAC records; *Secrets of Sex*) and David Wilde (WAC T12/1,469).

"spotty sassenach pillock" — ("George III") Literally, the insult means a pimpled/blemished Saxon fool (or even "dick"), according to the *OED*. Not unlike Shakespeare's often-used three-part insults: "damned tripe-visaged rascal" (*Henry IV*, part 2, 5.4); "scurvy jack-dog priest" (*Merry Wives of Windsor* 2.3); or "foul indigested lump" (*Henry VI*, part 2, 5.1).

"St. James Palace" — ("George III") The official residence of the English monarch was built by Henry VIII, but hasn't been lived in as such since the nineteenth century.

"suppositories" — (link out of "Zeppelin") This simply continues the lavatorial (and now excretory) emphasis of the episode, which will be once again reinforced when the "Golden Years of Colonic Irrigation" title card is presented later.

"Surely he gave you some money for it" — ("Zeppelin") Graf Zeppelin seems to have raised money for his designs and experiments by both private donation and government contracts, mostly for possible military applications of the new airships. (See De Syon.)

• T •

tam o'shanters — ("George III") The Scotsmen posing as the French court are wearing the colorful Scottish caps more often worn by young Scots *women* in the nineteenth century, according to the *OED*. Like the Interviewer (Cleese) slowly becoming a pirate in Ep. 32, the Glaswegian Louis is looking more and more like a Scotsman as the episode moves along.

"thousand francs" — ("Louis XIV") The Montgolfier brothers were essentially self-funded, their family owning a very prosperous paper factory. They did benefit from their close relationship with the French government as an industry of rather advanced technology.

Three black ladies — (PSC; "George III") These performers are Sue Glover, Rosetta Hightower, and Joanna Williams (WAC T12/1,469). Glover would release a handful of solo albums in the mid-1970s in the UK, including *Solo* in 1976; Hightower had been a member of the Ronettes-like The Orlons until 1968, according to the *All Music Guide*; and Joanna (perhaps "Joanne") Williams was a studio background singer who participated in Roger Glover projects, including "Butterfly Ball" in 1974. Dr. Hamer (Gilliam) actually introduces them as "The Ronettes," a 1960s girl group singing rock and roll and the blues, specifically the Motown sound. The real Ronettes were Veronica Bennett, Estelle Bennett, and Nedra Talley.

time-honoured Glaswegian way — ("Louis XIV") This headbutt has become known as a "Glasgow kiss."

"Tirpitz" — ("Zeppelin") Alfred von Tirpitz (1849–1930) was a German admiral and chief builder of the

German Navy prior to WWI. Tirpitz and Hollweg (thrown out next) are given significant historical culpability for World War I and its horrors, which may account for their early (and fatal) exit from the airship.

"Titty" — ("George III") There is a character named Titty in Englishman Arthur Ransome's book series "Swallows and Amazons," about siblings' adventures on school breaks in the wilds of Britain. The book the Reader (Idle) is reading from appears to be a "Little Golden" title (est. 1942).

"Trondheim" — ("Party Political Broadcast" link out of "Zeppelin") Third-largest city in Norway, seat of Sør-Trøndelag fylke (county) and situated in central Norway. Trondheim has already been mentioned in Ep. 25 as the "Spam" Vikings' launch point for coastal invasions.

two naked men boxing — ("Montgolfier Brothers") These images belong to one of Eadweard Muybridge's "Animal Locomotion" series of consecutive still images. A man walking and a man climbing stairs from the Muybridge collection were used in Ep. 36.

• V •

"verified by *Encyclopaedia Britannica*" — ("George III") The Pythons have, in fact, leaned on reference texts in the past, nearly quoting historian Trevelyan in the "Dennis Moore" episode (Ep. 37), after mentioning him by name in Ep. 26. The "facts" found in the game show *Spot the Loony* (Ep. 38) were also allegedly verified by the *American*-owned and controlled *EB*.

Victorian couple in the countryside — (PSC; "Zeppelin") The music beneath this ballooning couple is from Sir Adrian Boult and the London Philharmonic Orchestra playing "Symphony No. 2 in E Flat Major" by Edward Elgar.

"Von Bülow" — ("Zeppelin") Bernhard von Bülow (1849–1929) was the German Imperial Chancellor and Prussian Prime Minister under William II, and was probably elsewhere dealing with the international reputation of his Emperor and country, and not with Zeppelin. His is a recognizable old German name, certainly, hence its inclusion.

"Von Moltke" — ("Zeppelin") Probably referring to the younger von Moltke (1848–1916), who led the German army into WWI. *Karl von Müller* may be the naval officer who was captured by the British and interned in a Nottinghamshire prison camp for the duration of the war. Most of the other names listed (Reichner, Von Graunberg, Zimmerman, Kimpte) don't appear to be

anything other than part of the usual Python laundry listing of historical and made-up names.

• W •

"waggle" — ("Louis XIV") One of the initial problems with the Montgolfier balloons was their instability—test flights indicated that human occupants ("aeronauts") might incur serious injury on even low-altitude ascents, so animals were sent up first. By the time the United States and USSR had achieved extraterrestrial capability in the 1950s and 1960s, it was a dog and then a monkey making the initial space flights, and not humans.

"Will Louis XIV get away with . . ." — ("Louis XIV") This is structured much like a Saturday matinee serial (*Buck Rogers*, *The Perils of Pauline*, both 1934) where a cliffhanger ending keeps the audience waiting for the next exciting episode. This cliffhanger structure and the "burning questions" trope ("Is France really in the grip . . .") were also played up on the long-running *Rocky & Bullwinkle* cartoon series (1959–1973) produced by Bill Scott and Jay Ward for ABC and NBC.

Here also the artifice of using both videotape and film in a continuing narrative is broached. In most cases, the Pythons just have done what other shows also did—cut between tape and film when the characters/story head out of doors, without comment. Most UK audience members would have by this time become quite accustomed to the transition, which may seem quite jarring to modern audiences. Here the film projection equipment is made manifest (the man-behind-the-curtain-is-the-wizard scenario), drawing attention to the filmed images as separate and distinct from the videotaped images. Earlier, characters have discussed filmed images—Ep. 8, stopping a filmed sketch; Ep. 15, as a "link"; Ep. 18 when characters are "trapped" on film; and Ep. 29, when film is capturing the explorer's last words. The introduction of the projector and screen as such an artificial and theatricalized linking device was earlier seen in the "Silly Walks" sketch, though in that instance the character is merely illustrating a referenced point—that other silly walks exist—and the original narrative is rejoined when the film stops.

• Y •

"year 1908 was a year of triumph" — ("Zeppelin") The first successful flight was in 1900, though in 1908 a crash of one of the airships created a rush to donate funds to continue Graf Zeppelin's work, rendering an ironic triumph.

At the end of the episode, the narrator (Palin) mentions that the momentous flight occurred in 1900, not 1908.

"Yours has been the work" — ("Montgolfier Brothers") Spoken in the episode by Jacques (Jones) to Joseph (Idle), the historical accounts seem to support this, as well. Joseph initiated the experiments in 1782 and performed much of the early balloon research (*EBO*).

• Z •

"zabaglione . . . Zakuskie" — ("Zeppelin") Helmut seems to be at the end of a kind of food encyclopedia, yet another "list" moment for these German characters.

Zeppelin — ("Zeppelin") Ferdinand von Zeppelin (1838–1917) was the first major designer and builder of rigid airships for commercial purposes. The initial flight of his airship was on 2 July 1900 near Lake Constance.

Episode 41: "Michael Ellis"

(New) *Animation: Titles*; Closing credits; Department store; Buying an ant; The Paisley Counter; At home with the ant and other pets; University of the Air documentary on ants: "Let's Talk Ant"; Ant communication (restaurant sketch); *Animation: Anatomy of the ant*; Victorian Poetry Reading Hall (Wordsworth, Keats, Shelley and Tennyson); Queen Victoria und her late husband; Toupee hall; Complaints office on fire; End of Show Department: Different endings

• A •

"Abanazar" — ("Buying an Ant") The evil character in the popular pantomime *Aladdin*, as well as Kipling's *Slaves of the Lamp* (from *Stalky and Co.*, 1899). Jones and Palin had written a version of the *Aladdin* panto, and were able to watch a performance of that pantomime in Glasgow in January 1971 (Palin, 51–52).

Albert's coffin — (PSC; "Poetry Reading [Ants]") Victoria's husband HRH Prince Albert died in 1861, leaving the Queen devastated and in seclusion and mourning for years. The first cover photo for *Private Eye* featured the Albert Memorial, characterizing it as a spaceship ready to take Albert into orbit (7 February 1962).

"Allison, Malcolm, Brian Clough . . . Jimmy Hill" — ("Different Endings") Footballer Malcolm Allison (1927–2010) retired from play in 1958. Allison was managing Crystal Palace in 1974. Brian Clough (1935–2004) was a former footballer who was managing Brighton & Hove Albion in 1974.

Former player and coach Jimmy Hill (b. 1928) was presenting the BBC's *Match of the Day* in 1974. Hill had pioneered the panel set program for football discussion when working for London Weekend Television in the late 1960s. He will appear in Ep. 43 dressed as Queen Victoria.

Animated titles — (Opening Credits) For the last five episodes the title as presented on the screen is *Monty Python*, and not *Monty Python's Flying Circus*.

"Ayrshire" — ("Buying an Ant") A breed of cattle from Ayr, Scotland. A "King George bitch" is probably a play on the dog breed "King Charles spaniel." King George III (played by Chapman) is featured in Ep. 40, "The Golden Age of Ballooning." An "Afghan" is a furry greyhound.

• B •

"Blancmange" — ("Buying an Ant") He says "blancmange" because a race of these giant pastries from outer space menaced Earth in Ep. 7, in the "Science Fiction Sketch." This intertextuality pops up occasionally in *FC*, with reappearances of recognized characters from previous episodes, including the "Nudge, Nudge" character (Idle), Cardinal Ximinez (Palin), characters answering the phone and immediately looking at their shoe size, etc.

The Pythons do "quote themselves," as well (just as Shakespeare quoted himself), in revisiting character situations and incidents of miscommunication episode after episode, accessing the show's history as it becomes institutionalized (see *MPSERD*). See notes to Ep. 45, where a character sings a bit of an original song first heard in Ep. 42. This familiarity is part of the reason that the show could build an audience—the flip side is, of course, that troupe members (like Cleese) could quickly tire of the repetitiveness and revisitation.

"book on ants" — ("Buying an Ant") Episode 12 is subtitled "The Naked Ant," which is a play on the Desmond Morris book *The Naked Ape: A Zoologist's Study of the Human Animal*, published in 1967. A poster for *The Naked Ape* is featured prominently in Ep. 4, the "Secret Service Dentists" sketch.

"Bradlaugh" — ("Poetry Reading [Ants]") Charles Bradlaugh (1833–1891) was a well-known atheist and "freethinker" during Victoria's reign.

• **C** •

customer whose back is on fire — ("Department Store") This actor is Tim Condren—listed as "Smoldering Man"—a stuntman who did stunt work for the early Bond films, *Star Wars*, and Gilliam's *Brazil* (WAC T12/1,467). He died in 2006.

The young woman talking to him in this shot is Annet Peters ("Lady in Twin-Set") (WAC T12/1,467).

• **D** •

developing a German accent — (PSC; "Poetry Reading [Ants]") Victoria was of German descent, being from the House of Hanover, and she was taught English, French, and German. The royals would officially put away the Germanic history of the family during WWI, adopting "Windsor" as the family surname. Victoria was never the ruler of Hanover, since German law forbade a female ruler, and that title transferred away from her and to her uncle ("Victoria" in *ODNB*).

The essentially German pedigree of portions of the English royal family is alluded to earlier in Ep. 33, when Biggles dictates a letter to the *"real* Princess Margaret," coyly reminding her of the "Saxe-Coburg canasta evening."

"dinner-wagon" — ("Buying an Ant") A dinner wagon is a wheeled serving table.

• **E** •

"Eighth Floor: Roof Garden" — (PSC; "Department Store") Certainly another reference to the celebrated roof garden at the Derry & Toms department store, which closed in 1972. Derry & Toms has been referenced before in *FC*, in Eps. 23 and 37, and will be mentioned later in Ep. 42. See notes to those episodes for more.

"Ellis, Michael" — ("Buying an Ant") The mysterious Michael Ellis was an assistant editor on Lindsay Anderson's controversial 1968 film *If. . . .,* referenced earlier in Ep. 19. Throughout this *Flying Circus* episode Ellis is a Harry Lime–like apparition—the childhood friend/black marketeer (Orson Welles) to Holly Martins (Joseph Cotten) from *The Third Man* (1949)—who is much talked about and sought-after through the noir-ish streets (and sewers) of postwar Vienna.

ending up in an aerial view of London — (PSC; "Different Endings") This film stock is "Aerial Views of London" from World Background, Elstree Studios (WAC T12/1,467).

Episode 41 — This episode was recorded 19 October 1974, and broadcast 7 November 1974, and was officially titled "Michael Ellis." All six episodes in the fourth season are given titles, long after Light Entertainment higher-ups worried that such subsidiary titles might be confusing to the typical BBC viewer. See notes to Ep. 2 for more on this request, and WAC T12/1,242.

The actors/extras used in the episode include the following: Tim Condren (*Doctor Who; Star Wars*); J. Hughman; Annet Peters and Pam Wardell (*The Avengers*); (extras) Steve Kelly (*Barlow at Large*), Eric French (*Z Cars*), Derrick (or "Derek") Hunt (*Z Cars*), Dennis Hayward (*Play for Today*), James Muir (*Z Cars*), Reg Turner (*Doctor Who*), Keith Norrish (*Doctor Who*), James Haswell (*Wednesday Play*), Alec Pleon (*Up the Chastity Belt*), Lyn Howard, Vi Delmer (*Z Cars*), Peggy Sirr (*Doctor Who*), Vi Kane (an Equity Council rep; *Wednesday Play*), Barbara Faye, Mary Maxted (a.k.a. Mary Millington [1945–1979]; *Doctor Who*), Suzy Mandel (*The Benny Hill Show*), Jackie Street (*A Little of What You Fancy*), Kathleen Heath (*Emma*), Susanne Fleuret (*Z Cars*), Rita Tobin (*Anne of the Thousand Days*), Beatrice Greek (*Frankenstein and the Monster from Hell*), Vi Ward (*Engelbert with the Young Generation*), Eileen Matthews (*Agatha Christie's Miss Marple: Nemesis*), Pat Prior (*Doctor Who*), Bob Raymond (*Softly Softly*), Eve Aubrey (*Mini Weekend*), Elsa Smith (*Arthur of the Britons*), Peter Holmes (*Play for Today*), Simon Joseph (*Softly Softly*), Lionel Sansby (*Doctor Who*), Constance Reason (*Z Cars*), Willie Shearer (*Private Life of Sherlock Holmes*).

• **F** •

Fourth Floor — (PSC; "Department Store") In the "Granite Hall" are non-granitic rocks including "shale" (a sedimentary rock), "alluvial deposits" (which can contain some granite), and "felspar" ("*feldspar*," a mineral-forming rock). Also, there seem to be mountain ranges in this hall, including the "Carpathians" (Central Europe), the "Andes" (South America), and "Urals" (Russia). Though shot in Croydon, this store is modeled on Harrods, the fashionable Knightsbridge department store offering virtually everything—clothing, electronics, food, jewelry, pet supplies, appliances, and legendary service—since the beginning of the twentieth century.

• G •

gaggle of customers — (PSC; "Department Store") These Pepperpots and Customers include Peter Holmes (Man in Bad Suit), Reg Turner, and Alec Pleon (both Pepperpots) (WAC T12/1,467). The extras in the fourth season often appear in multiple episodes, with calls at Television Centre arranged for maximum efficiency. See the WAC records for these episodes for more.

Greek national costume — (PSC; "Ant Communication") The actor is listed as Dennis Hayward, though it looks very much like Terry Jones has taken the role (WAC T12/1,467). WAC records have previously indicated in error a particular actor brought in to play a particular role, so this type of personnel change (sometimes due to an actor missing a call for various reasons) isn't unusual.

• H •

"Half an inch" — ("Poetry Reading (Ants)") A play on the initial lines of Tennyson's *Charge of the Light Brigade*, a very early wax recording of which (voiced by Tennyson himself) was extant at the time the Pythons wrote and performed this episode. The first stanza, as written by Tennyson:

Half a league, half a league,
Half a league onward,
All in the valley of Death
Rode the six hundred.

"Forward, the Light Brigade!
Charge for the guns!" he said:
Into the valley of Death
Rode the six hundred.

Harrods-type store — ("Department Store") The show received permission to shoot much of the episode at Grants Department Store, High Street, Croydon (WAC T12/1,469).

The music used underneath this scene is from Eric Coates, "London Suite (London Everyday): No. 3 Knightsbridge," here played by the Royal Liverpool Philharmonic Orchestra (WAC T12/1,467). This familiar music is also used earlier, in Eps. 7 and 16.

"Hillman" — ("At Home with the Ant and Other Pets") A Hillman was a small car designed to be a competitor to the very popular Mini.

"how about a chase" — ("Different Endings") The music used here is "Devil's Gallop," from the *Dick Barton* series, which was used in Eps. 15 and 30, both in chase sequences.

• I •

"I can assure you they do" — ("Ant Communication") Open University (or University of the Air) broadcasts tended to be prerecorded and then just transmitted at a slotted time, but here the Pythons are positing a more traditional, in-class kind of experience where the teacher can answer questions directly to the students. In this the effectiveness of the Open University model—a single message transmitted simultaneously to thousands of potential recipients—is made far less efficient, becoming a one-on-one teacher-student experience where the teacher also must sit and wait for the student to be available for instruction.

Early on, there was much ridicule of the new educational endeavor, including hundreds of op-ed page cartoons depicting Open University–trained surgeons, non-traditional (as in OAP) student demonstrations, and airtime competition with the likes of Basil Brush, etc. See the many cartoons lampooning the new educational endeavor at the British Cartoon Archive.

"I met a traveller . . ." — ("Poetry Reading [Ants]") Shelley's *Ozymandias*, published in 1818, is a sonnet that reads more precisely:

I met a traveller from an antique land
Who said:—Two vast and trunkless legs of stone
Stand in the desert. Near them on the sand,
Half sunk, a shatter'd visage lies, whose frown
And wrinkled lip and sneer of cold command

Tell that its sculptor well those passions read
Which yet survive, stamp'd on these lifeless things,
The hand that mock'd them and the heart that fed.
And on the pedestal these words appear:

"My name is Ozymandias, king of kings:
Look on my works, ye mighty, and despair!"
Nothing beside remains: round the decay
Of that colossal wreck, boundless and bare,
The lone and level sands stretch far away.

"inflation I'm afraid" — ("Buying an Ant") In 1974, the inflation rate in the UK reached 16 percent by mid-year and was still climbing, peaking at 24 percent in 1975 (UK Composite Price Index). The Heath administration would lose its hold on the government in 1974 due in large part to the very weak economy. The Wilson Labour government wouldn't be able to work wonders with the moribund economy, either, ushering in Margaret Thatcher (Eps. 21–22, 30) and the Tories in 1979.

"intraspecific signalling codes" — ("At Home with the Ant and Other Pets") These would be signals used *within* a certain species, not between species, so from one ant to another ant.

"I wandered . . ." — ("Poetry Reading [Ants]") Wordsworth's Romantic-era poem, written in 1804, and preceding the Victorian age. Instead of "worker ants," Wordsworth (and his sister, autobiographically) saw "daffodils."

This same poem has already been read aloud in Ep. 17, in the "Poets" sketch, from a Wordsworth (Idle) kept under the stairs.

• J •

"Jehovah's witnesses" — ("At Home with the Ant and Other Pets") A well-known proselytizing religious group, the "Watchtower Bible and Tract Society" would have been in the news significantly during this period. In 1969 a mass meeting of Jehovah's Witness faithful at Yankee Stadium was hailed by many as the final gathering of the international church before the end of the world, which was calculated to take place in late 1975, just months after these *FC* episodes were being written and recorded.

The mention of this eschatological sect in the midst of an episode so obviously satirizing a corrupt, debased consumer society is no surprise, nor is the mention that the tiger has consumed the witnessing faithful, further evidence that a cleansing is imminent. In the early 1970s, Witnesses were patiently waiting for "Jehovah God to bring an end to a corrupt world drifting toward ultimate disintegration," according to one of their inedible tracts, *Awake!* (8 Oct. 1968). In fact, this particular issue of *Awake!* (probably meant to spur the faithful to attend the New York gathering) provides a laundry list of the woes of the world—mammon before God, violence, drug use, material worship, pestilences, lawlessness, disobedience to parents—*all* coincidentally encountered by Chris (Idle) as he wanders through the department store and even his home in this episode.

Lastly, *Private Eye* had announced in late 1969 that then-Prime Minister Harold Wilson was converting to the Jehovah's Witness faith (26 September 1969).

• L •

ladies in German national costume — (PSC; "Ant Communication") Suzy Mandel (*Benny Hill*) plays one of these German girls (WAC T12/1,467).

line of ten people — (PSC; "Complaints" link) These actors, according to WAC records, include: "Tyrolean Man"—Keith Norrish (*Doctor Who*); "Icelandic Man"—Steve Kelley; "Greek Man"—Dennis Hayward (*Play for Today*); "Man with Lawn Mower"—Lionel Sansby (*Doctor Who*); "Man with Dog"—James Muir (*Z Cars*); "Bandaged Nose Lady"—Constance Reason (*Z Cars*); "Lady with Pram"—Barbara Fay; "Lady with Tennis Racquet"—Pat Prior (*Doctor Who*); "Man with Cigar"—Simon Joseph (*Sunday Bloody Sunday*); "Man in Bad Suit"—Peter Holmes (*Doctor Who*) (WAC T12/1,467).

• M •

"Mac Fisheries" — ("Toupee") A chain of UK fish shops set up in 1919 by William Lever. The intended insult is likely that the toupee looks woven, like a fishnet.

"mandies" — ("At Home with the Ant and Other Pets") A "mandy" is a dose of the sedative methaqualone, used as a sleep inducer in this period.

mix through to the exterior of the store — (PSC; "End of Show Department: Different Endings") The pulling away shot is actually Grant's of Croydon, where many of the interiors for this episode were shot.

The following image—a dissolve to an aerial view of Big Ben and the Houses of Parliament—is noted in the WAC records as "Aerial View of London," World Background, Elstree Studios (T12/1,467).

"My heart aches . . ." — ("Poetry Reading [Ants]") Inspired by Keats's *Ode to a Nightingale*, the first stanza of which is actually as follows:

My heart aches, and a drowsy numbness pains
My sense, as though of hemlock I had drunk,
Or emptied some dull opiate to the drains
One minute past, and Lethe-wards had sunk:
'Tis not through envy of thy happy lot,
But being too happy in thine happiness,—
That thou, light winged Dryad of the trees,

In some melodious plot
Of beechen green, and shadows numberless,
Singest of summer in full-throated ease.

• N •

"No, I want a *different* assistant" — ("Buying an Ant") This is the beginning of yet another difficult transaction (a communication, of sorts) in the Python world, where it's never as simple as choosing an item, paying for that item, and completing the transaction (that wouldn't be funny, on its own). In many cases, the item isn't available or as advertised ("Cheese Shop," "Tobacconists," "Dead Parrot," "Argument Clinic"), or the exchange is abrogated as the narrative moves off tangentially ("Off-Licence," "Police Station," "Fish Licence"). In this case, Mr. Quinn (Idle) has to go through two assistants (Chapman and Palin) and a manager (Jones) before successfully completing his purchase, one of the few such successful transactions in all of *Flying Circus*. The success is short-lived, of course, as Chris realizes later that the ant is damaged, and he has to return to the store for an attempt (à la the "Dead Parrot" sketch) at a refund.

• O •

"Only useful animal you ever bought, that" — ("At Home with the Ant and Other Pets") Since the "orange-rumped agouti" (a rodent) is about the size of a hare, it's unlikely that this pet would be the one opening the door.

• P •

Paisley — ("Buying an Ant") A department store "Paisley Counter" would have offered items featuring the distinctive Paisley print (ties, scarves, shawls, etc.), created by weavers in the lowland Scotland town of the same name.

Ian Paisley (b. 1926) represented the North Antrim, Ireland, constituency in this period, and was a leading voice in the Irish "situation" for many years. The Reverend Paisley was instrumental in opposing the sharing of power in Ireland with all entities, including England, Ireland, and Northern Ireland. In 1971 Paisley had co-founded the Democratic Unionist Party, as well. Paisley was featured on the cover of *Private Eye* on 31 January 1969.

The lady passing with a bandaged nose in this shot is Constance Reason (WAC T12/1,467).

"pangolin" — ("At Home with the Ant and Other Pets") A pangolin is a scaly (armored) anteater, essentially.

"parky" — ("Buying an Ant") Chilly, cold.

• Q •

Queen Victoria with a fanfare — ("Poetry Reading [Ants]") The fanfare used here is "Investiture Fanfare" by Charles Williams. Victoria's attendants (carrying Albert's coffin) are Bob Raymond and William Shearer (WAC T12/1,467).

• R •

"rag week" — ("Buying an Ant") A university tradition where students help raise money (via sideshow-type performances) for charities. Both Cambridge and Oxford participate in the long-standing "raising and giving" tradition. The student fun and games during rag week could be rather over the top. In 1967 Surrey University rag week participants kidnapped a popular Radio 1 deejay, Tony Blackburn, demanding he play a sort of commercial tape for their rag week activities (see "Radio Rewind," 1967).

"recent discoveries in the field" — ("At Home with the Ant and Other Pets") Both the focus on ants and this specific scientific section are perhaps attributable to the front-page presence of the ant work of Harvard professor E. O. Wilson, who had released *The Insect Societies* in 1971.

Also, poet Sir Osbert Sitwell (1892–1969) had depicted the ant as one of the paragons of humanity's interwar pugnacity.

"Ribena" — ("Buying an Ant") A popular blackcurrant soft drink in the UK.

"rotten ending" — ("Different Endings") The traditional structure of the traditional BBC show is just what the Pythons were intending to upend when *Flying Circus* was being talked about back in early 1969. They have flirted with all sorts of endings in the preceding three seasons, but here is the first time they actually lay bare the various possibilities and weed through them, one by one.

• S •

shopping trolley is smoldering — (PSC; link out of "Ant Communication") This burning lady is Pam Wardell (WAC T12/1,467).

"Snetterton" — ("Buying an Ant") Snetterton is a village in Norfolk, where the Pythons shot location scenes for much of the second season. The "nailed-my-head-to-the-floor" character from "The Piranha Brothers" (Ep. 14) is named Vince Snetterton Lewis.

switches it on and settles down to watch it with Marcus — ("At Home with the Ant and Other Pets") The snippet of introductory music used for the University of the Air is from Benjamin Britten's "Lisbon Bay," and is played by the Members of the English Chamber Orchestra (WAC T12/1,467).

• T •

twenty old televisions — (PSC; "At Home with the Ant and Other Pets") The overarching theme of this episode seems to be rampant consumerism in an existential world, or the materialist, "acquisitive" quagmire bemoaned by many in twentieth-century Western culture. The myriad televisions, the profligate menagerie, and the "anything-you-could-want" department store setting point toward Thorstein Veblen's "conspicuous consumption," or the middle-class accumulation of consumer goods in place of active political or social commitment. See Veblen's *Theory of the Leisure Class*. In Ep. 27 Mrs. Premise (Cleese) and Mrs. Conclusion (Chapman) agree that man can only be free when he's rid himself of his worldly possessions, which Mrs. Premise sees as the central argument of Sartre's *Roads to Freedom*. See notes to Ep. 27 for more on the Pythons' existentialism.

two customers are talking to mirrors in thick Irish accents — ("The Paisley Counter") The customers—both dressed as Ian Paisley—are deep in recitation: "Crush the papist swine with the iron boot of Protestant enlightenment!" This sentiment, of an oppressive mother church in Ireland, echoes through many of Paisley's period utterances. From the 1966 pamphlet "Protestants Remember!":

> Now there are voices raised in our Province today which advocate a course of forgetfulness. They tell us that the sooner we forget the great epochs of history, the sooner we forget about "Derry, Aughrim, Enniskillen and the Boyne" the better for us as a people. . . . Let it be said, and let me say it without fear of contradiction, that there are even leaders in Church and State who are apostles of this doctrine of forgetfulness. . . . This text says, "Remember, thou wast a bondsman in the land of Egypt" . . . if there's one thing Ulster needs to remember it is this, that four hundred years ago they were bondsmen and under the Egyptian slavery of pagan popery. Let me say this: wherever there is bondage,

wherever there is tyranny, wherever there is superstition, wherever the people are subjugated, there you will find the iron heel of the Roman Catholic Church, the jack-boot of the Vatican." (Ian R.K. Paisley)

• U •

"University of the Air" — ("At Home with the Ant and Other Pets") Open University was established in 1969, broadcasting on the BBC, and was designed to offer the university experience to non-traditional students (disabled, non-traditional students, post-grads, distance learners, etc.). Palin is depicted wearing the typically drab "coat-and-kipper-tie" uniform of the early on-air lecturers.

• V •

"Victorian poetry reading hall" — ("Poetry Reading [Ants]") The ladies in the audience in this scene include Lyn Howard, Elsa Smith, Eve Aubrey, Pamela Wardell, Mary Maxted, and Vi Delmar (WAC T12/1,467).

For most of the poets in this line-up, Victoria (1819–1901) would have been an infant when they died, though perhaps she was no more German than when she was very young.

• W •

"Walking into the sunset?" — ("Different Endings") The music used in this romantic moment is "Elm Street" by Johnny Burt (WAC T12/1,467).

"was ist das schreckliche Gepong . . . es schmecke wie ein Scheisshauss . . ." — ("Poetry Reading [Ants]") Essentially, in very fractured German, she's asking: "What is that awful smell? . . . It smells/tastes like a shithouse . . . and so on."

"We are not . . . amusiert?" — ("Poetry Reading [Ants]") The "We are not amused" catchphrase is credited to Queen Victoria by one Caroline Holland in *Notebooks of a Spinster Lady* (London: Cassell, 1919), though its authenticity can certainly be challenged, as the book was originally published anonymously. What cannot be challenged is the phrase's significance to the Pythons in their depictions of the somewhat dour Queen—she is not amused when she's earlier given a hole in her head in a Gilliam animation (Ep. 15), and she's not "amusiert" by the ant references here.

Wordsworth, Shelley, Keats, Tennyson — (PSC; "Poetry Reading [Ants]") All writers included, for example, in Harrison and Bates's 1959 collection *Major British Writers II*, from Harcourt, and yet three of the four are actually from the English Romantic period, which preceded the Victorian Age.

Wordsworth—An English Romantic poet, William Wordsworth (1770–1850) was Poet Laureate the last seven years of his life.

Shelley—Another English Romantic poet, Percy Bysshe Shelley (1792–1822).

Keats—Active in the English Romantic period, John Keats (1785–1821) is also a bit out of place in this Victorian setting.

Tennyson — (1809–1892) He assumed the laureateship after Wordsworth, and was the poet installed in the bathroom in Ep. 17. See entries in the *ODNB* for more on all these writers.

• Y •

"Yes, the book on ants" — ("Buying an Ant") Probably an unintended pun, as the "book on ants" is slammed down *on the ants*. The joke becomes the ants being thoughtlessly crushed, not thoughtlessly crushed by a book on ants. The audience doesn't seem to get the joke, anyway, intended or not.

"You can see the join" — ("Poetry Reading [Ants]") The "join" would be the place where the toupee is supposed to mesh invisibly with the remaining natural hair. In the *Beyond the Fringe* sketch "Bollard," one of the models is fretting about his hair, and another assures him that he can "scarcely see the join." When Chris finally makes it to the Toupee Hall, the assistants' bad hair joins are all quite visible.

"You let them die, then you buy another one" — ("Buying an Ant") This is a moment where the normally unspoken part of the commodity transaction in a consumer culture is voiced—buying for the long-term isn't as good for business as buying, then buying again, and again and again. Watson notes in *The Modern Mind* both the increasing importance of "things" in the twentieth century and the literary/artistic reaction to that acquisitiveness:

> What Joyce, Eliot, Lewis, and the others were criticising, among other things, was the society—and not only the [WWI-era] war society—which capitalism had brought about, a society where value was placed on possessions, where life had become a race to acquire things, as opposed to knowledge, understanding, or virtue. In short, they were attacking the acquisitive society. (186)

The Pythons' firm reliance on the masterpieces and ethoi of the Modernist movement(s) has been mentioned throughout these notes; coupled with the more hopeful existentialism of the postwar Sartre, the Pythons' attacks on consumer society (they grew up in a culture forever changed by capitalism) reach a significant level of maturity in this self-contained episode.

Episode 42:
"Light Entertainment War"

Up Your Pavement; RAF banter; Trivializing the war; Courtmartial; Basingstoke in Westphalia; "Anything Goes In" (Cole Porter song); Film trailer; *"But now . . ."* Monster (animated), Nude Organist, "It's" Man, and titles; Bloody repeats; The public are idiots; Programme titles conference; The last five miles of the M2; *Animation: "What a lovely day"*; Woody and tinny words; More bloody repeats; Show-jumping (musical); Newsflash (Germans); "When Does a Dream Begin?" (song); Closing credits

• A •

"Agnelli, Gino" — (*"Up Your Pavement"*) Italian billionaire Gianni Agnelli (1921–2003) had been the principal owner of Fiat since 1966.

"Alan Jones knocked down poor Judd" — ("Show Jumping [Musical]") Jones (b. 1946) was an Australian Formula 1 driver racing in the UK during this period, and not affiliated with horse jumping. Judd is a character in *Oklahoma!*, and he is mock-lamented in the song "Poor Judd Is Dead."

Animation: **"What a lovely day"** — (animated link into "Woody and Tinny Words") This Gilliam animation, where the "bloody weather" becomes noisily exasperating, will be revisited in *Holy Grail*.

Arsenal — (closing credits) After winning the FA Cup in 1970–1971, Arsenal FC had slipped steadily, and by 1974 were on their way to a sixteenth-place finish.

• B •

"Basing House, burned down . . ." — ("Basingstoke in Westphalia") Basing House (est. 1535) would burn down as a result of the English Civil War in 1645. Cromwell would empty the buildings of valuables, and the local villagers came in and took the bricks to rebuild their homes. Earthworks and some gating still

stand today. See entries for "John Paulet" and "Cromwell" in the *ODNB* for more.

"bored" — ("Woody and Tinny Words") Father (Chapman) here is expressing a Kierkegaardian complaint voiced in *Either/Or*—namely, that for the aesthete—whose life is devoted to the pursuit of pleasure and amusement—boredom is the single greatest evil. When discussing pleasingly "woody" and unpleasant "tinny" words, as well as admiring the fecundity of the "woody" croquet hoops or the sensuality of "woody" words grows tiresome, boredom sets in for Father, and he's off to his tenth bath of the day, or to build another useless Babel, in Kierkegaard's terms:

> The gods were bored, and so they created man. Adam was bored because he was alone, and so Eve was created. Thus boredom entered the world, and increased in proportion to the increase of population. Adam was bored alone; then Adam and Eve were bored together; then Adam and Eve and Cain and Abel were bored *en famille*; then the population of the world increased, and the peoples were bored *en masse*. To divert themselves they conceived the idea of constructing a tower high enough to reach the heavens. This idea is itself as boring as the tower was high, and constitutes a terrible proof of how boredom gained the upper hand. (228)

And when his wife (Cleveland) dissuades him from his next bath, he opts instead to sack a "tinny" (and thus unpleasant) servant, enacting just the type of change (what Kierkegaard called a "crop rotation") that focuses him away from one moment and onto another, an act that can, for a time, stave off boredom.

Bovril — (PSC; "RAF Banter") The character played by Jones is in the printed scripts identified as "Bovril," a proprietary name for a beef extract spread.

"B roads" — ("The Last Five Miles of the M2") A "B" road is a more local road separate from the larger, longer A and AA roads in the UK. The "B roads" series idea might have played better, then, in the regional markets (Midlands, for example), where, ironically, *Flying Circus* tended to struggle, thanks to on-again-off-again programming decisions by individual regions.

• C •

"can't say 'sodding' on the television" — ("The Last Five Miles of the M2") This should be *couldn't* say sodding on television, since the word was elided in Ep. 17, the "Architect Sketch," when Cleese's line reads "Oh (*blows raspberry*) the abattoir," instead of "Oh sod the abattoir," which it had read originally. By the fourth season (several years later) words like "sod" and "bugger" and "shit" were being heard more regularly on *FC*, which led some viewers (general audience and BBC types alike) to lament the too-easy shock value of the formerly creative, edgy show.

"Captain Phillips" — ("Show-Jumping [Musical]") Captain Mark Phillips (b. 1948) was the husband of Princess Anne (Elizabeth's daughter), and won an equestrian team gold medal in the 1972 Munich Olympics. (Princess Anne had officiated at the British Screen Awards in 1971, and was lampooned in Ep. 39, "Grandstand.") According to the United States Event Association, Phillips successfully rode mounts Rock On, Great Ovation, Maid Marion, and Columbus between 1967 and 1974.

"Streuth" is an invective (a contraction of "God's truth") that's been used (mostly by Chapman) several times in the series, including Eps. 1 and 2.

"Caption: '1942 . . .'" — ("Woody and Tinny Words") The British Empire did at one time extend to Africa, the Middle East, and South America, where landed men like Father (Chapman) would have performed foreign civil or military service before retiring to woody pursuits back home.

car park below — ("Programme Titles Conference") This scene was shot from the roof of Clarendon House, Western Way, Exeter, on 13 September 1974 (WAC T12/1,469).

"Carrington, Lord" — ("*Up Your Pavement*") Lord Carrington (b. 1919) was leading the Conservative opposition in the House of Lords after the Labour victory in 1974, and had been Chairman of the Conservative Party between 1972 and 1974, as well as Defence Secretary. His education qualifies him for special vituperation, at least in the Python world: Eton, Sandhurst, and the Guards (see Ep. 20). For the Pythons, Carrington would have been just the stuffy, establishment type—along with a reverend and spouse—to have concocted such a traditional, corny kind of show as the one lampooned.

"Chiropodist" — ("*Up Your Pavement*") This corn and bunion specialization was earlier featured in Ep. 31, when Everest was being climbed by hairdressers and chiropodists.

"Conceived and Written By" — (closing credits) Cleese is given a writing credit here, though not a performing credit. (He is listed as performing in the script, but does not appear in the finished segment.) Neil Innes also receives a writing/conception credit here.

Other tidbits from the "Social Class" credits section include: Another mention of the now-defunct department store ("Derry and Toms"); body measurements for the costumer ("35 28 34"); an f-stop reading for the cameraman ("f8 at 25th sec."); a school mention ("Lower Sixth"); director Ian MacNaughton's drink of choice ("a bottle of Bell's"); and a reference to Eps. 9 and 41 ("Ant").

Crossroads *type theme music* — (PSC; link out of "Woody and Tinny Words") *Crossroads* (ATV, 1964–1988) was a very popular family drama set in a Midlands motel.

• D •

"Dad's Navy" — ("The Last Five Miles of the M2") Playing on well-known extant BBC shows, including *Dad's Army* (1968–1977), already satirized in Ep. 38, and the feature film/BBC play *Up the Junction* (1968), a gritty kitchen sink drama (and *Up Pompeii!*, etc.). Chapman makes fun of himself in mentioning "*Doctor at Bee*," "*Doctor at Three*," and "*Doctor at Cake*," seeing that he contributed significantly (as a writer) to *Doctor in Charge* (1972–1973), *Doctor at Large* (1971), and *Doctor in the House* (1969). *And Mother Makes Three* was a 1971 British comedy written by Peter Robinson, who also wrote for *The Two Ronnies*.

There are bunches of *I Married . . .* titles extant, including *I Married a Communist* (1958), *I Married a Witch* (1942), and *I Married a Heathen* (1974).

"Diamond, Alex" — (*"Up Your Pavement"*) Alexandros Diamantis is a Greek filmmaker whose screen name in the mid-1970s was Alex Diamond.

Diamond enters a doorway next to Richards at 232 High Street in Exeter, Devon.

"Drummond-Hay, Anneli" — ("Show Jumping [Musical]") She's already been mentioned in Ep. 28, when she was jumping with her horse in a family's flat (when the BBC were short of money). See notes to Ep. 28, "Puss in Boots."

• E •

Episode 42 — Recorded 26 October 1974 and transmitted 14 November 1974.

Additional actors for this episode include the following: Neil Innes, Bill Olaf, Marion Mould (rider), Peter Woods (*Morecambe & Wise*), Judy Roger, Angela Taylor, Ann Payot (*Health & Efficiency*), Elsa Smith (*Adventures of Barry Mackenzie*), Annet Peters (Eps. 40–43; *Fall and Rise of Reginald Perrin*), Sylvia Laine (*Thief of Baghdad*), Lyn Howard, Jean Channon (*Z Cars*), Stella Conway, Sylvia Brent, Stuart Myers (*Microbes and Men*), Rory O'Connor (*Blakes 7*), Michael Finbar (*Blakes 7*), Fred Davies (*Blackpool Show*), Ron Musgrove (*Z Cars*), Eden Fox (*Doctor in the House*), Paul Phillips (*Doctor Who*), Les Shannon (*Blakes 7*), Bill Hughes (*Barlow at Large*), Colin Thomas (*Love among the Ruins*), Sue Bishop (*Dad's Army*), Sally Foulger, Belinda Lee (*Are You Being Served?*), Diane Holt, Sally Sinclair (*Doctor Who*), Jackie Street (*A Little of What You Fancy*), Dominic Plant, Tania Simmons, Laura Hannington, Sharon Parmee, Deborah Jones, Matthew Jones, Bob Raymond (*FC* fourth season), John Hughman, Donald Stratford (*Barlow at Large*), Garth Watkins (*The Liver Birds*), Reg Turner (*Doctor Who*), James Haswell (*Z Cars*), Harry Davis (*Dixon of Dock Green*), Kathleen Heath (*Doctor in the House*), Mike Barrymore, Peter Leeway, John Casley, and Cliff Anning.

• F •

"fairy wands with big stars on the end" — ("Trivializing the War") This lighthearted or even disinterested approach to The Great War may be a reference to the fact that in Britain, during 1938–1940, the continental affairs were known as the "Phoney War," since no direct hostilities against or by British troops and installations had been undertaken, nor had the Axis powers directly engaged British interests. Many in the UK felt that as Czechoslovakia, The Netherlands, and even France fell into German hands, it still had nothing to do with Great Britain. Part of the problem was, of course, that British authorities called for wartime measures—austerity, vigilance, gas masks, internment, billeting—a full year before any bomb fell on London.

"4th Armoured Brigade" — ("Trivializing the War") This brigade saw significant action in North Africa, Italy, and Germany during WWII, and was disbanded after the war.

• G •

"gaiters" — ("Courtmartial") Military-issue legwear, specifically to be worn between the heel and knee. Ceremonial attire is usually reserved to swords, adornments, etc.

"Get me the Prime Minister" — ("Trivializing the War") A phrase heard in many of the British WWII films, especially when a discovery's been made (like a decoded communiqué or the identification of incoming "cabbage crates"), and it's always meant "get the PM on the phone." Here, again, Python's penchant for literality is expressed. In Ep. 20, it is the Chief of Police (Ian Davidson) who appears from a morgue drawer just when he's summoned.

"Gorn" — (PSC; "Woody and Tinny Words") Probably a nonce word, but the pronunciation is very much like the Yorkshire version of "go on" or even "gone," and when hearing it (as the audience does), it's probably too homonymic to accurately identify.

In fact, when Mother (Idle) asks, "What's gorn, dear?" and Father (Chapman) answers, "Nothing," she is asking, essentially, "What's gone, dear?" Later in the scene this reading is underscored when Father shoots the caribou, then quips "Caribou gorn."

• H •

high street — (PSC; "Up Your Pavement") The printed script describes the setting as a "high street," which would be the main shopping district in most smaller towns during this period. This high street is in Exeter, Devon, specifically Cowick Street. Easily seen are the Le Roy Funeral, John Holt Carpets, and Kentucky Fried Chicken stores (also findable in period phone books). Incidentally, the KFC is still right where it was in 1972.

"Hills Are Alive, The" — (PSC; "Show Jumping [Musical]") The Rodgers and Hammerstein song performance here is by Ann Rogers with Ainsworth and his Orchestra. The following number from *Oklahoma!* (also

Rodgers and Hammerstein) is performed by Tony Adams and Singers, and then the Black and White Minstrels sing "Let's Face the Music" by Irving Berlin (WAC T12/1,469).

Incidentally, the use of the song from *Oklahoma!* generated an angry letter from copyright holders, though BBC lawyers argued that since the song wasn't parodied there was no recourse either possible or justified (WAC T12/1,469).

Leslie Crowther (1933–1996)—flicked by Drummond-Hay on a jump—hosted *The Black & White Minstrel Show* in 1958.

• I •

"I Married Lucy" — ("The Last Five Miles of the M2") *I Love Lucy* (1951–1957) was the top-rated U.S. television show throughout most of the 1950s, and first appeared in syndication on ITV in early July 1955. During the run of *Flying Circus*, Lucille Ball (1911–1989) was starring in another version of the show, *Here's Lucy* (1968–1974).

impressive college grounds — (PSC; "Up Your Pavement") These are the grounds not of Bicton College, but of the Bicton Park Botanical Gardens, in East Budleigh, Devon, and this footage was shot on 11 September 1974 (WAC T12/1,469).

interior of a bomber — (PSC; "Film Trailer") This sexually confused military film trailer employs a mixture of Imperial War Museum footage and black and white footage from the Pythons. One sequence toward the end—when banjos are being mentioned—features popular music hall and film entertainer George Formby (1904–1961) playing the banjo ukulele and singing to British troops. The shots of the Pythons inside the Lancaster bomber were recorded at the RAF Museum in Hendon on 4 October 1974 (T12/1,469).

The footage here is shot as a straight-ahead dramatic combat scene, with no indication that the sexualized voiceover ("hot bloodedly bi-sexual navigator") has any connection to the characters or images displayed. In this the scene plays much like the 1966 Woody Allen project *What's Up Tiger Lily?*, where Allen and friends remove the soundtrack from a Japanese gangster B-movie and replace it with their own silly, self-conscious, and sexualized dialogue and sound effects.

"It's the World War series . . ." — (link out of "Programme Titles Conference") In addition to the admittedly, unashamedly sentimentalized *Dad's Army*, this may be a reference to the very new *The World at War* series (from Jeremy Isaacs) produced by BBC com-

petitor Thames and sponsored by the Imperial War Museum. The twenty-six-part series made its debut in October 1973 and ran through May 1974—in time for the Pythons to make fun of the series' very sober approach to the war.

• J •

Joseph, Sir K. — (PSC; closing credits) Sir Keith Joseph (1918–1994) was a powerful Conservative politician who helped push Thatcherism into the public eye in the 1970s and beyond. In 1974, Mary Whitehouse lauded Joseph for toting the banner of anti-permissiveness, which is probably why the Pythons mention him here, as well as later in the "Dramatis Personae" for Ep. 43.

Joseph was interviewed rather prominently by Robin Day during the early morning hours of the 1970 General Election. He'd held his seat, but his race didn't reflect the general Conservative "swing," he admitted—he'd won by just about the same number of votes as the previous election.

• K •

Kildare theme — (PSC; "Up Your Pavement") This performance of the well-known "*Dr. Kildare* Theme" (Jerry Goldsmith) is by Johnnie Spence (WAC T12/1,469), and has been used whenever a pseudo-serious medical setting is demanded (Eps. 13, 26, and 32).

The actor playing the doctor here is supposed to have been Cleese, according to the printed script, but since he was no longer attached to the show by this time, the part seems to have been given to Douglas Adams (*Hitchhiker's Guide*). Adams will appear briefly in two more episodes, and get screen credit for Ep. 45. Interestingly, Adams's name does not appear in the BBC records for the series, which is unusual. If nowhere else, the participants' names for repeat fees assignation purposes should be extant—his is not.

"Kissinger, Henry" — ("*Up Your Pavement*") U.S. Secretary of State during this period, Kissinger (b. 1923) was in the headlines often, making agreements with Communist China in 1972 and winning the Nobel Prize in 1973. A German-born American, Kissinger may be implicitly connected to the Hanoverian Victoria's appearance in the previous episode, but he also represents the increasing international presence of the United States, its policies and culture, and the concomitant decline of Great Britain's international significance during this period. Both Kissinger and

Nixon visited Europe and London a number of times between 1968 and 1974.

• L •

large, tasteful, Georgian rich person's house — (PSC; "Woody and Tinny Words") The printed set-up for this shot belies the actual finished shot, with a significant amount of detail included for the reader only:

> *Sound of lawnmowers and cricket in the distance. Laughter from the tennis court. Sound of gardener sharpening spades in the potting shed. Out of vision, a Red Indian struggles to free himself from the rope bonds that bind him.*

There are no lawnmower or cricket or gardener or tennis sounds, and no Indian anywhere. There is the sound of a single-engine propeller-driven plane, however, which may have been "wild" sound (meaning accidentally recorded on location). At some points the Pythons have included such script details for either the production design team (to assist in gathering props and finding locations) or just to amuse themselves—inside jokes for the other Pythons only.

"Len Hanky!" — (*"Up Your Pavement"*) The music beneath this section (as the character emerges from behind the shrubbery) is George Malcolm's "Bach before Breakfast" (WAC T12/1,469).

This lurker is described in the script as "a seedy fellow in a terrible lightweight suit of several years ago which has got all stained and creased around the crutch (Michael)" (2.42.278). Played by Terry Jones, this voyeur and chiropodist is actually wearing a soiled mac and perhaps little else.

This scene is also shot on the grounds of Bicton Gardens.

"lower middle" — ("Woody and Tinny Words") The indication by Mother (Idle) here is that "tinny" words are those spoken by the lower classes, those who would also occupy mock-Tudor homes, and dress in the twin-set-and-pearls outfits seen earlier with Mrs. Elizabeth III (Jones) and Mrs. Mock Tudor (Chapman).

Luke 17, verse 3 — (PSC; "RAF Banter") "Take heed to yourselves: If thy brother trespass against thee, rebuke him; and if he repent, forgive him." Rather than the usual pinup girl nose art and accompanying clever or naughty slogan, the chaplains have chosen scriptural passages. There are actually a few records showing that chaplains did indeed pilot aircraft, including C.S. "Bam" Bamberger, a Jewish Chaplain who was awarded the Distinguished Flying Cross in 1943, and who was Sergeant Pilot, then Squadron Leader. Bamberger took part in the Battle of Britain, significantly. (See battleofbritain.net.)

• M •

"Marquetry" — ("Film Trailer") Intricate carvings, often found in handmade furniture. This type of film trailer was common through the 1960s.

"micturate" — ("The Public Are Idiots") To urinate.

Mock Tudor — (PSC; "The Public Are Idiots") The characters' names here, not voiced, are Mrs. Mock Tudor (Chapman) and Mrs. Elizabeth III (Jones). A "Mock Tudor" is a contemporary version of the well-known Tudor-style home/building—there are countless such homes in the UK and United States. There has been no Elizabeth III, and with the succession clearly leaning toward the male side of the Windsors, at least for the present, there's little chance of a third ruling Elizabeth in the near future.

modern casa-type Italian office — (PSC; *"Up Your Pavement"*) The music beneath this Italian interlude is lifted from the Nino Rota soundtrack for *La Dolce Vita* (1960), and is performed by Gordon Franks and Orchestra (WAC T12/1,469).

momentary flash of a still of each — (PSC; *"Up Your Pavement"*) This stream-of-consciousness structure (photos and narration) was earlier used in Ep. 40 to wrap up the episode.

mounted female rider — (PSC; "Show Jumping [Musical]") The rider/actress is Marion Coakes Mould (b. 1947), the horse is most likely Stroller, and the jumping scenes are being shot at the All English Jumping Course, Hickstead, on 23 September 1974 (WAC T12/1,469). Mould had jumped in the 1968 Mexico City Olympics for Great Britain.

"Mr. Heath" — ("The Last Five Miles of the M2") Ted Heath had resigned the PM position in March 1974 after failing to create a viable coalition government in the wake of a Conservative backslide (in seats, not votes) in the 1974 General Election. Harold Wilson and Labour (with more Commons seats) returned to power in the transition, but without a mandate, and Wilson would resign in 1976, leaving the party leadership (and the country's fiscal mess) to James Callaghan (1912–2005). By 1979, the Tories would be back in 10 Downing Street thanks in great part to a doleful economy. See the University of Keele's "UK Elections" website for more on the pivotal election.

"M2" — ("The Last Five Miles of the M2") The M2 motorway was finished in 1965, reaching into Faversham, Kent, which is what/where these "idiot" viewers would have been watching.

"municipal borough . . . cavalry in 1645" — ("Courtmartial") The information here is accurate, meaning the Pythons probably checked their facts as they wrote, rather than relying on memory. Even the distance between Southampton and Basingstoke is accurate (about twenty-seven miles). In Ep. 37, the historical recitation given by Grantley (Palin) and Buckingham (Jones) is also quite accurate, there drawn from G.M. Trevelyan's work on the period.

music instantly changes to the heroic — (PSC; *"Up Your Pavement"*) This is Elgar's "Pomp & Circumstance March" as played by the London Symphony Orchestra (WAC T12/1,469).

music turns more urgent and transatlantic — (PSC; *"Up Your Pavement"*) The new bit of music is Neil Richardson's "Full Speed Ahead" (WAC T12/1,469).

• N •

Nissen hut — (PSC; "RAF Banter") Quonset-type huts installed at airbases across the UK, used for mess halls, officer's clubs, barracks, etc.

"not only fighting this war on the cheap . . . they're also not taking it seriously" — ("Trivializing the War") American broadcaster Edward R. Murrow (1908–1965) visited London in April 1940 just as the possibilities of Britain's participation in war in Europe were being heatedly discussed, and the baggage-heavy, "peace in our time" Chamberlain government was essentially being shown the door in a Commons no-confidence vote. Murrow reported the following:

> This is London. I spent today in the House of Commons. The debate was opened by Mr. Herbert Morrison, one of the ablest members of the Labour Party. He doubted that the government was *taking the war seriously.* Mr. Morrison said that the Labour Party had decided to divide the House—in other words, call for a vote. Mr. Chamberlain, white with anger, intervened in the debate and accepted the challenge. In fact, he welcomed it. . . . When he had finished, Mr. David Lloyd George rose and placed his notes upon the dispatch box, and members surged into the room through both doors, as though the little, grey, square-shouldered, white-haired Welshman were a magnet to draw them back to their seats. He swept the house with his arm and said: "*If there is a man here who is satisfied with our production of planes, of guns, of tanks, or the training of troops, let him*

stand on his feet." No one stood. (Audio transcription, *Eyewitness 1940–49*, "'No Confidence' Debate")

In this one dispatch from London to America before the war even begins, Murrow voices the concern that the Pythons will comedically lament in this episode—the war is being trivialized *and* fought on the cheap. In the aftermath of the Commons vote, Chamberlain's grip on power was greatly eroded, he resigned, and the king asked Winston Churchill to form a coalition government.

This sketch is also likely an indirect result of significant BBC tongue-clucking over the *"Ypres 1914"* sketch(es) that appeared in Ep. 25. The weekly assessment meetings of the various Light Entertainment shows (attended by higher-ups representing most major departments at the BBC) revealed the dismay with which this episode—and especially the ridicule of the amputee Padre (Cleese)—was met by BBC officials and viewers alike. (Also, the silliness of war-themed comedy shows like *Dad's Army* [1968] may have contributed to the WWII veterans' dismay over their fading public and historic valorization.)

In *Hard Day's Night* (1964), the stuffy gentleman on the train reminds The Beatles that he had "fought the war" for them, a rhetorical flag that had been flown and saluted by WWII vets (and their political reps) for almost two decades by that time, and almost three decades by 1974. In the "Programme Titles" sketch from Ep. 42, the security guard (Gilliam) with the "oriental sword" (read: Japanese) through his head is obviously a WWII-era vet, and wears his battle wounds from the Great War with on-the-sleeve pride—in fact, the wound can't help but be noticed. The "not taking it seriously" malaise may be an indication that the unpopularity and evening news ugliness of the Vietnam War was by this time supplanting the patriotic memories of the WWII generation in the (especially younger) public's eye, and the WWII generation may have begun to miss the limelight.

"not understanding" — ("RAF Banter") The Python-esque miscommunication trope, again. This can be referred back to the sketch in the police station (Ep. 12) where each officer hears in his own way (low pitch, high pitch, faster, slower), meaning they each must learn each other's idiom/delivery in order to communicate, and strangers (like the man trying to report a crime) are left in a sea of babel.

• O •

"oblige them sir" — ("Courtmartial") From the earliest *FC* episodes the specter of "sodomitical" behavior (read: buggery), or man-on/in-man sexuality has been a source of humor for the troupe, even though one of their members (Chapman) was by this time an "outed" gay man active in the gay community. The stigma of gay relationships had lessened recently, with the decriminalization of homosexuality in the UK in 1967, and following the publication of the polarizing Wolfenden Report in 1957, which had recommended the sweeping public policy move. Still, "gay" jokes appear often in *FC* (and *Benny Hill* and many other contemporaneous comedy shows), and seem to go over fairly well with the studio audience, including the later "one man's love for another man in drag" and "night emission" quips.

"198 feet high . . ." — ("Show Jumping [Musical]") The Coliseum is actually about 157 feet high. Why the biblical epic *Ben Hur* (novel 1880; Charlton Heston film 1959) is included as a jump in this event featuring musicals isn't clear. By 1974, the Lew Wallace story had been filmed at least three times.

Opening titles — ("Nude Organist, "It's" Man, and Titles") This new fourth season title sequence features a Renaissance profile (of a man) moving along the ground as if he were a hound. The image is borrowed from *Portrait of an Elderly Man* (c. 1517) by Quentin Matsys (1466–1529). This same image (though colored differently) was already used in Ep. 22, in the "How to Recognize Different Parts of the Body" section, specifically, "the nose."

• P •

"Porter, Cole" — ("Courtmartial") American songwriter Porter (1891–1964) did write "Kiss Me Kate" in 1948, as well as "Anything Goes" in 1934.

"public are idiots" — ("Programme Titles Conference") The premise that British viewers would sit and watch just about anything might not have been far wrong, especially when it's considered what hobbies were/are popular in the UK, including trainspotting and bridge identification. This television audience consideration is also topical—in the fall of 1974 the first cable television experiments were underway in the UK, and concerns ranged from too much programming to too much competition with the BBC to diminished programming variety thanks to the fee schedules.

If anything, however, the BBC as discovered in the WAC records seems overly considerate of the viewing audience, with most of the recorded comments illustrating concern over how portions of the epi-

sodes would be received. The admitted competition with newer, flashier commercial television networks like ITV kept attractive programming very high in the minds of Light Entertainment officials, while at the same time disturbing parliamentary, purse-string powers who wished the BBC to retain her brilliance as a moral beacon.

"PVC" — ("Woody and Tinny Words") An acronym for polyvinyl chloride, a plastic used in construction materials around the world, including mock Tudor homes in the UK. The initials are pronounced "pee-vee-cee," a definite "tinny" sound.

• R •

"repeats" — ("The Public Are Idiots") The Pythons as a group probably liked repeats, actually. As early as 1971 the Pythons were reaping tidy sums from repeats of the first *FC* season (£80 per troupe member), and the WAC files are thick with repeat information in the following months and then years. Paul Fox (Controller BBC1) and David Attenborough (BBC Television's Director of Programmes) were even working overtime, it seems, to make sure that the repeat slots for *FC* were as favorable as possible for a burgeoning audience (WAC T47/216).

• S •

sailor on a ship — ("Film Trailer") These scenes were shot aboard the HMS *Belfast* at Symons Wharf on 27 September 1974.

"sausage squad . . . briny" — ("RAF Banter") These may not have been true RAF banter phrases, but they at least make some sense, and are much more on-the-nose. The first—"Sausage squad up the blue end"—is clearly to be translated as the presence of Germans (eaters of sausage) "up the butt" (meaning many of them). The second is even easier. Since Germans were also known as Krauts (from sauerkraut, which is made from fermented cabbage), the German planes are the "cabbage crates" on their way over the "briny" sea. (The latter may date from WWI, actually.)

So the Pythons are mixing traditional banter with colorful period slurs and just nonsense. The point seems to have been that it didn't used to matter what was said, but it had to be said quickly—it can't be banter if it's slow, or if it's explained. Here, the Pythons have taken the RAF-speak—a privileged vernacular reserved for "members only" as a means of communication and quick identification of other members—and Babel-ized it, meaning even those on the inside, those who allegedly speak the lingo, can no longer understand. Earlier, in the "Architect Sketch" (Ep. 17), the Masonic "language" is used to exclude non-members.

"Second World War has entered a sentimental phase" — ("Newsflash [German]") The sentimentalizing of both the war and its servicemen and women began not long after the war, and continues to a significant degree to this day. The Home Guard portion of the war effort, depicted warmly in *Dad's Army*, which was busy winning entertainment awards (and perhaps inciting a bit of jealousy), may have inspired this reference.

see a momentary flash of a still of each — (PSC; "Up Your Pavement") These still photos are part of the last moments of the *Up Your Pavement*/Alex Diamond sequence. The second candid photo of a Middle-Eastern-looking man was taken on the street, at about 25 Goldhawk Road, Hammersmith and Fulham, not far from TV Centre. The Tuck-Away restaurant seen at the right is still a restaurant. The next photo was taken just a few feet away from the previous one, at the corner of Goldhawk and Bamborough Gardens.

seedy fellow in a terrible lightweight suit — (PSC; "Up Your Pavement") The script describes this character differently from the finished version, and even has Palin playing the part as a sort of Ken Shabby. In the filmed version, Jones takes the part, looking more like one of the "rapists" from *Fliegender Zirkus 1*.

"She's going to marry Yum Yum" — ("Woody and Tinny Words") A song from the comic opera *The Mikado*, which is actually titled "For He's Going to Marry Yum Yum," and penned by Gilbert and Sullivan (Ep. 16).

Shots of big coastal guns — ("Film Trailer") This is Pathé film footage (WAC T12/1,469). All of the stock film in this episode is borrowed from the Pathé film stock archives, though the WAC records do not indicate which particular bits of stock are being used. In past episodes, most film stock is both requested and accounted for, by name and/or file number.

"Show-Jumping from White City" — ("Show-Jumping [Musical])") Show-jumping has already been lampooned in Ep. 28, and the White City Stadium setting was a typical event location. (This location is the All English Jumping Course in Hickstead.) Rider David Broome was actually astride Mr. Softee in the 1968 Summer Olympics in Mexico City, and not Drummond-Hay, who rode Xanthos II to the British Jumping Derby crown in 1969.

White City was a stadium built originally for the 1908 Olympic Games. The stadium is used as a location in *The Blue Lamp* (1950), the film that presented PC Dixon—later of *Dixon of Dock Green*—to the grateful British viewing public.

silver halos . . . stars — ("Film Trailer") This type of fairy has appeared before, in Ep. 13, when policemen became fairies to more successfully fight crime.

Skating Vicar — (PSC; "Courtmartial") The Skating Vicar is played here by Bill Olaf (WAC T12/1,469).

"Somewhere in England" — ("RAF Banter") The exact location of RAF and U.S. military airfields and hangars in the UK were kept as secret as possible during the war, and also far away from London and strategic targets. Many were hidden in plain sight in and near country villages Winkleigh and Okehampton in Devonshire—and the Local Defence Volunteer (Home Guard) units would even remove or rearrange road signs to further confuse any invading German force. A July 1940 newspaper article detailed a tour of Britain's coastline defenses, noting military and civilian readiness, a readiness that included clandestineness:

> It must remain a secret tour through a part of England that was anonymous in fact as well as necessity to anyone who did not know the countryside far better than a German parachutist is likely to know it . . . here, among the winding roads and high hedgerows of rural England, with no signposts, no milestones, and unnamed towns, we might have been anywhere. ("On the Sea Front: Coastal Defences of the Island Base," *Times*, 18 July 1940: 5)

Wartime documentary or newsreel presentations displaying military training and/or Home Guard preparations often echoed this "Somewhere in England" mantra.

Spitfire — (PSC; link into "RAF Banter") This plane was located at the Torbay Airport Museum, and the shot was recorded on 9 September 1974 (WAC T12/1,469). The Spitfire was the star of the Battle for Britain during the early days of WWII.

"Squiffy" — ("RAF Banter") Squiffy has been a nickname for the surname "Asquith."

Steptoe and Son — (PSC; "Up Your Pavement") The printed script mentions that the theme music here is supposed to sound like that of *Steptoe and Son* (1962–1974), a popular BBC comedy starring Wilford Brambell (Paul's grandfather in *Hard Day's Night*), and which later would be adapted into *Sanford and Son* on American television.

The specific title/artist procured is not accounted for, however, in the WAC records for the episode.

stock film of a big car-producing plant — ("*Up Your Pavement*") This stock photo (not film stock) is listed as a photo of a Fiat car factory (WAC T12/1,469).

"studio five" — ("The Last Five Miles of the M2") Actually one of Television Centre's smallest studio spaces, it's unlikely that a WWII drama would have been relegated to the Studio 5 space, which was used for game shows and the like. *Flying Circus* shot most of its in-studio scenes in Studio 6, but also used Studios 1 and 8 and the nearby Ealing Television Film Studio when more space was needed (see WAC records for call locations).

• T •

Tense music — (PSC; "Film Trailer") The mood music here is also from Eric Coates, and called "633 Squadron" (from the 1964 movie of the same name), and is performed by Geoff Love and Orchestra (WAC T12/1,469).

"tinny sort" — ("Woody and Tinny Words") In an episode of *The Goon Show*, a Peter Sellers character mentions the "certain thin" sounds of the studio orchestra, giving a mass or shape to the anticipated music.

"Top-hole . . . Bertie" — ("RAF Banter") Most of this is actually identifiable RAF-speak, though some, as usual, has been manufactured by the Pythons.

"Top-hole" means first rate, "bally" is a euphemism for bloody, while "Jerry" is one of the nicknames given to German troops during the war. To prang something is to smash it, a "kite" is an airplane, and "how's your father" is a euphemism for sex or sexual organs (probably from a music hall derivation). A "hairy blighter" is merely a rude, hirsute fellow, and a "dicky birdie" is a small, inconsequential bird, like a sparrow, which could die and none would notice. See the *OED*.

"trivializing this war" — ("Trivializing the War") Elgar's "Pomp & Circumstance March" is used here again, the same recording as used before in the "*Up Your Pavement*" sketch.

twin-set-and-pearls ladies — (PSC; "The Public Are Idiots") These ladies (Chapman and Jones) are decidedly less frumpy than the normal Python Pepperpot, though certainly no more attractive. Their elevated social position (and membership in the colonial club, as it were) might be indicated by the "Arab Boy remote control" (Gilliam) they've had installed.

• U •

"Up Your Pavement" — ("*Up Your Pavement*") Yoko Ono had produced an experimental film in 1970 called *Up Your Legs Forever*. This type of title has been spoofed before, and is probably based on the popular *Up Pompeii!* and *Carry On*–type films noted in Ep. 38.

• V •

"Vauxhall Vivas" — (link out of "Woody and Tinny Words") Vauxhall is a British car company owned by General Motors since the 1920s. Vivas were small cars built by the thousands during the gas crunch times of the late 1960s and into the 1970s, designed to compete with Datsun, Toyota, and Opel imports.

veers off away — (PSC; "*Up Your Pavement*") This active, restive camera in relation to the supposed narrational object/subject was first glimpsed in Ep. 7, when the first protagonists introduced, Mr. and Mrs. Brain Sample (Chapman and Idle), are found to be too dull, and the camera and narrator veer away to Mr. Harold Potter (Palin), so that the exciting sci-fi story can begin. A similar wandering camera finds a helpful, "moustachioed Italian waiter" in Ep. 26, on its way to Herbert Mental (Jones), who collects birdwatchers' eggs. Nouvelle Vague filmmaker Godard (Ep. 23) employs this type of camera work in *Week End* (1967), as well.

victory-at-sea music — (PSC; "Film Trailer") The printed scripts call for "victory-at-sea"–type music, referring to the 1952–1953 WWII documentary series, *Victory at Sea*. Music for the actual series was created by Richard Rodgers. The stirring music used here is Eric Coates's "Dambusters" played by Geoffrey Love and Orchestra (WAC T12/1,469). Coates's "633 Squadron" will be used later in the episode.

• W •

WAAF — (PSC; "Trivializing the War") A member of the Women's Auxiliary Air Force.

"we never actually see the horses jump" — ("Show Jumping [Musical]") A comment on the budgetary constraints for most BBC shows, constraints that reduced the levels of acceptable verisimilitude for most shows and most genres. (It would also have been quite dangerous to have a shod horse leaping over extras, admittedly.) The "cutaway" shot is the standard obfuscation method for the medium—the Pythons have used it since the first episode, when the

Rustic (Chapman) and the City Gent (Jones) watch and comment upon action taking place well offscreen. This comment also points up the artificiality of the medium, of the episode being taped, filmed, and broadcast.

"Western Front" — ("Trivializing the War") A term not used as readily after WWI, especially in the West. When the Germans during WWII referred to a front, it was the Eastern Front, as they were fighting Russia there. The Pythons may have mixed up their Mortimers here, so to speak (see the discussion on anachronisms in *MPSERD*).

"When Does a Dream Begin?" — ("Trivializing the War") This original song is orchestrated and accompanied by Bill McGuffie and written/sung by Neil Innes (WAC T12/1,469). The orchestra is being led by Bobby Midgley. Later as the "Woody and Tinny Words" sketch begins the printed script mistakenly calls this song "*Where* Does a Dream Begin."

Whitehall war office room — ("Trivializing the War") There were and are subterranean "war rooms" beneath Whitehall and HM Treasury in London, secure locations where the Cabinet, military, and PM could meet and conduct the war.

Williams, Dorian — (PSC; "Show Jumping [Musical]") Author, host, and presenter Williams (1914–1985) was the voice of the BBC's show jumping broadcasts since 1962, as well as the *Horse of the Year* show since 1949.

Wingco — ("RAF Banter") Short for "Wing Commander."

Woods, Peter — (PSC; "Newsflash [German]") Woods (1930–1995) was a BBC reporter and then newsreader.

"woody" — ("Woody and Tinny Words") There is a precedent for this type of seemingly nutty nomenclature. A sound (of a musical instrument, for an example) that is more "dull of tone" can be called "woody," meaning it's not as bright or piercing as a "tinny" sound, which is most often used pejoratively, and refers to a "cheaply contrived" high frequency sound (*OED*).

The "woody" words chosen by the Pythons tend to contain vowels—as found on the International Phonetic Association chart—that are generally voiced toward the "back" and "open" (like "gorn" and "vole"), while the more "tinny" words like "tit" and "leap" are voiced nearer the "front" and more "closed." The "woody" words then sound more rich and full, while the "tinny" words are clipped and even shrill—just the sort of distinction one might make while sitting about with nothing to do (suffering Kierkegaardian boredom, see above) in a stuffy and expensive Georgian drawing room.

• X •

"Xerxes" — ("Programme Titles Conference") A king of Persia (c. 485 BC), and obviously a random thought from the dementia-tinged mind of the planner (Palin). The planner goes from "Joey" to "Xerxes" and finally to "Mr. Heath" as the name of his long-lost pet budgie.

• Y •

"You don't re-heat cakes" — ("The Last Five Miles of the M2") Based on the hand-wringing and general tsk-tsk-ing apparent in the department heads' meetings in regards to broadcast *FC* episodes, the dotty, fuddy-duddy depictions here might be somewhat justified. Comments from these postmorta include words like "disgusting," "over the edge," "awful," "appalling," and "not . . . amusing" (WAC T47/216).

young, inspired and devoted nurse — (PSC; "*Up Your Pavement*") The music changes to a version of Siebert's "Rule Britannia" as performed by the All Star Brass Band (WAC T12/1,469).

Episode 43: "Hamlet"

Hamlet; Bogus psychiatrists; *Nationwide*; Police helmets; Father-in-law in the marriage bed; *Titles*; Hamlet and Ophelia; *Animation: Anatomy monster at the city walls*; Boxing match aftermath; Boxing commentary; Piston engine (a bargain); A room in Polonius's house; Dentists; Live from Epsom; **Queen Victoria Handicap**; *Animation: Grape balloons*; *Hamlet* curtain call; "And then . . ." Man explosion

• A •

Anatomy monster at the city walls — (PSC; "*Animation: ends with a poster . . .*") This monstrous-looking figure looming over the parachutists is a drawing from the landmark anatomy text *De humani corporis fabrica* (*On the Structure of the Human Body*) by Andreas Vesalius (1514–1564).

This entire scene is visually similar to an illustration in Faust Vrancic's *Machinae Novae* (1616), which detailed his multiple technical innovations including the parachute. The illustration depicts a man (likely Vrancic himself) leaping from a castle tower, floating downward under a crude parachute. There doesn't seem to be any firm evidence that Vrancic actually tested the parachute.

"And then . . ." — (link out of "Queen Victoria Handicap") This is Palin, but clearly not the "It's Man" character—perhaps this is an attempt to make this linking role more Shakespearean. The phrase does appear in *Hamlet* on six occasions.

Archers *theme tune* — (PSC; "Piston Engine [A Bargain]") The theme song to the popular radio show *The Archers* is called "Barwick Green" and was composed by Arthur Wood. This BBC Radio drama has been running since January 1951, and was originally created to offer postwar farming and husbandry support to a nation recovering from years of privation, and was even a not-so-subtle reminder of the importance of UK

price supports and subsidies in the face of the flood of incoming European goods (see Smethurst). During WWII, as well, when material and personnel were at a premium in the UK, feature filmmaking could only be truly justified as part of the war effort, and it was with tacit Ministry of Information approval and assistance that such films of Englishness like *Henry V* could be produced, and on such a massive scale.

This crossing of purposes in entertainment shows was not lost on the Pythons, as various sketches have wandered into similarly divergent storylines, including a wrestling match to prove the existence of God (Ep. 2), the Careers Advisory Board hosting of a "Silly Job Interview" (Ep. 5), and all of Ep. 45 as a Party Political Broadcast for the dark horse Liberal Party.

"arrived here by train" — ("Police Helmets") The nearest train station to the Westminster Bridge site is Waterloo, to the south.

Assistant — (PSC; "Boxing Match Aftermath") The Assistant is played by Bob Raymond, who appears in most of the fourth season episodes.

• B •

"bachelor friend" — ("Dramatis Personae") A Victorian-era euphemism for a homosexual man, which fits, considering Chapman's admitted sexuality. Gilliam is credited as being a "butch" bachelor friend to

187

Hamlet—he had been married since the previous year. In the "Dramatis Personae" provided for the actual Shakespeare play, Horatio is listed as "friend to Hamlet" (*Riverside Shakespeare*, 1141).

"bogus psychiatrists" — ("Bogus Psychiatrists") This may be a comment on the significant anti-psychiatry bias that appeared after WWII, especially, and which came to a head in the 1960s and 1970s. The practices of the Nazi, Japanese, and then Soviet mental health communities in regard to political and criminal prisoners as well as mentally ill citizens before, during, and then after the war called into question all invasive and so-called traditional treatments of mental disease.

This section is perhaps a reference to then-infamous American con artist Frank Abagnale, Jr., who had impersonated a teacher, a pilot, an attorney, and even a physician before being apprehended in 1969. Abagnale was in the news in 1974, when he was released from prison to assist the U.S. government in fraud investigations.

boxer on a stretcher — (PSC; "Boxing Match Aftermath") The decapitated boxer is played by Reg Turner (WAC T12/1,468).

The setting, according to the printed script, is New York's Madison Square Gardens [*sic*], and the actors all attempt (with varying success) tough, East Coast American accents.

In a connection with the later mention of Nazis Martin Bormann and Heinrich "Gus" Himmler, author Ladislas Farago (see "Sinatra" note below) is quoted by *Time* magazine as saying: "Even if I bring Martin Bormann back with me personally and exhibit him in the Felt Forum of Madison Square Garden, people will still say it's just another hoax" (11 Dec. 1972).

"Brian" — (link out of "Queen Victoria Handicap") Another reference to Brian Clough, football player, coach, and analyst, who was mentioned and lampooned in Ep. 41, where he slouches through another football analysis.

Burlington Wall-banger — (PSC; link out of "Father-in-Law") This reference is most likely an amalgam. First, Burlington-Ware launched the upscale Burlington Arcade (in Piccadilly) in 1819, a fashionable mall before there were shopping malls. Stores within tended to be very high-end, and would have sold gold-leafed wall-bangers, if such things were available for sale. Secondly, the drink Harvey Wallbanger had been introduced (in the United States) just a few years prior to this episode's creation. The script also mentions that the weapon looks like an "Indian club," which was a piece of athletic equipment (not unlike a thin bowling pin) popular in Victorian times modified from an ancient Indian weapon.

Additionally, a 1959 murder trial covered extensively in British newspapers mentions that the assailant— "an unemployed cinema projectionist"—entered an old man's house in mid-January, took a "Zulu knobkerrie" from its place on the wall, and bludgeoned the retired captain with it. The killer was convicted at the Winchester Assizes. See the *Times*, 28 Apr. 1959: 14. The murderer—Michael George Tatum—was hanged at Winchester on 14 May 1959.

• C •

. . . camera pans across the road, and comes across a couple making love on the pavement. Pedestrians step over them — ("Father-in-Law in the Marriage Bed") This couple snogging on the bridge pavement is reminiscent of an event reported in July 1964. Police blotters indicate that a woman was "posing" at a bus stop on Westminster Bridge (the same bridge the Pythons would use) wearing a "topless dress," and when approached by a constable on duty, she and her husband argued that she was doing nothing indecent, and that they were breaking no laws. An indecency arrest followed, of course, though at the woman's arraignment the judge admitted the case had no precedent, giving the woman a year's "conditional discharge" (probation). She did have to pay court costs—£2 4s. This public display preceded the appearance (and subsequent arrest) on 9 July 1964 of two models in Soho wearing similarly topless dresses, there to promote the underground film *London in the Raw*, mentioned earlier in notes to Ep. 8. See "Topless Dress 'Indecent,'" *Times*, 22 Aug. 1964: 4.

"Chaldeans" — ("Police Helmets") From the Babylonian empire of about the seventh century.

The episode seems to hinge thematically on "authenticity," with credentials proving the qualified psychiatrist, a number and helmet proving the true Metro policeman, Edgeworth's name on the bottom of her chair, and Hamlet's inability to do anything other than what has historically made him "authentic." Previously an authentic BALPA spokesman wore the appropriate cufflinks, etc. (Ep. 16), and a "bona fide" animal lover would not have tried to feed goldfish sausages (Ep. 13). This struggle with authenticity continues the Pythons' fascination (conscious or otherwise) with the Sartrean notion of *choosing* freedom and living life as it can/should be lived.

Charlton, Michael — (PSC; "*Nationwide*") Charlton (b. 1927) was a presenter on *Panorama* (1953–) and reported on both the 1964 General Election and the Apollo 11 landing for the BBC.

"completely bona fide psychiatrist" — ("Bogus Psychiatrists") This fixation on authenticity is also a Sartrean conceit, with the Pythons playing on Sartre's examinations of his own characters as they do or do not live "authentically." Essentially, are they so afraid of the freedoms of this life that they choose (in bad faith) to live by the strictures of class and race and religions and gender, eschewing complete (and frightening) freedom for the comforts of restraint and submission? See Sartre's *Being and Nothingness* for much, much more.

"Cutty Sark" — ("Father-in-Law") A clipper ship commissioned in 1869.

• D •

deafening sound track — ("Bogus Psychiatrists") This chase music is "The Good Word" from Johnny Scott and his Orchestra (WAC T12/1,468).

"Dull, John" — ("Police Helmets") The name here is certainly a comment on the perceived interest level in a show like *Nationwide*, its subject matter, and on-air staff. Besides Frank Bough, others presenting on *Nationwide* in these early years included Michael Barratt, Bob Wellings, and Sue Lawley.

This "John Dull" reference, however, would have meant one of the myriad reporters sent out on assignment across the UK for the show's regional human interest stories. Contributor Philip Tibbenham, for example, reported on the effects of the new three-day work week (thanks to power and goods shortages) on the town of Hartlepool, Durham. Due to a prolonged coal miners' work-to-rule action in 1973, most areas of the country were rationed to three days per week of electricity transmissions by January and February of 1974. This episode of *Nationwide* was broadcast on 18 January 1974 (BFI).

• E •

Episode 43 — Recorded 2 November 1974, and transmitted 21 November 1974, this episode was given the subtitle "Python's Playhouse," indicating the troupe's movement away from the previous three seasons. A quote probably submitted by the show to the *Radio Times*: "Programme Four: Monty Python has decided to change its image. Towards Shakespeare seemed to be the logical departure and the MP Repertory Company present their production of *Hamlet*" (WAC T12/1,468).

Also appearing: Jimmy Hill (*Match of the Day*), Connie Booth; (stuntmen playing Queen Victorias) Marc

Boyle (*You Only Live Twice*), Tim Condren (Ep. 41; *Star Wars*), Billy Horrigan (*Doctor Who*; *Raiders of the Lost Ark*), Tony Smart (*Casino Royale*), and Bob Raymond (Eps. 40–45; *Softly Softly*); (extras) Richard Sheekey (*Some Mothers Do 'Ave 'Em*), Bill Barnsley (*Z Cars*), Victor Charrington (*Dixon of Dock Green*), Martine Holland, Jackie Bristow, Katie Evans (*Softly Softly*), Freda Curtis, Mrs. Kitty, Eileen Rice, Rosemary Parrot, Babs Westcott, Edna Wood (*Wanted for Murder*), Edith Crump, Hilary Abbot, Reg Turner (*Z Cars*), James Haswell (*Doctor Who*), Tony Snell, Michael Dalton, Stuart Myers (*Microbes and Men*); (Asian actors) Vincent Wong (Ep. 22; *Birds on the Wing*), Edgar Hing, Ken Nazarin (Ep. 34; *A Casual Affair*), and Robert Ng; Annet Peters (Eps. 40–42; *The Fall and Rise of Reginald Perrin*), Pamela Wardell (Ep. 41; *Microbes and Men*), Donald Groves (*Jackanory*), Reg Thomason (*Some Mothers Do 'Ave 'Em*), Lionel Sansby (Ep. 41; *Blakes 7*), Michael Finbar (Ep. 42; *Blakes 7*), Michael Brydon (*Doctor Who*), Harry Davis (Ep. 40; *Dixon of Dock Green*) (WAC T12/1,468).

A number of these extras are "locals," meaning they were cast in the areas where the Pythons shot location footage for this final season.

"Epsom" — (link into "Dentists") Epsom Downs is a racecourse that hosts the Epsom Derby, and is the second race of the English Triple Crown.

The racecourse used here is not Epsom, but actually Lingfield Racecourse, Lingfield, Surrey, south of London. The footage was shot on 24 September 1974 (WAC T12/1,469).

"European Cup" — (link into "Dentists") FC Bayern-Munich did win the Cup for the first time in 1973–1974, and would win again the following two championships, beating Leeds United FC 2–0 in the 1974–1975 final match. There were some significant blow-outs during the 1973–1974 European Cup, with established football powers like Club Brugge KV beating Floriana FC 10–0, and the Irish team Crusaders FC losing badly to the Romanian team Dinamo Bucuresti 12–0 (see Motson and Rowlinson).

• F •

Frank Bough type presenter — (PSC; link into "Dentists") Frank Bough (b. 1933) presented for *Nationwide*, *Grandstand*, and myriad sports programs. He has already "appeared" in Ep. 35, covering the Olympic Hide-and-Seek finals, and then in Ep. 39, where he presents rugby league highlights (where Mrs. Colyer is tossed into the scrum).

• H •

Hamlet — ("Bogus Psychiatrists") Shakespearean tragedy written about 1599, the play has become the *locus classicus* for both the Elizabethan revenge tragedy corpus and the "troubled" dramatic character.

Many critics have put Hamlet "on the couch," including J. Dover Wilson in *What Happens in Hamlet* (1935):

> From the *point of view of analytic psychology* such a character may even seem a monster of inconsistency. This does not matter, if as here it also seems to spectators in the theatre to be more convincingly life-like than any other character in literature. (219; italics added)

This very "life-like" character of Hamlet can be assumed, in the Pythons' world, to be so real that he must be obsessed with sex and the body, as indicated by years of Shakespeare scholarship and the Pythons' own penchant for such corporeality. The popularization of Freud's theories of the unconscious—emerging and being engaged by scientists, critics, and laymen alike between the wars—accounts here for the frustrated, sexualized, psychoanalyzed Hamlet.

Harley Street type — (PSC; "Bogus Psychiatrists") Harley Street has been the upscale home of the London medical establishment for many years, and has already been mentioned in the scripts for Eps. 13 and 22. See notes to those episodes for more.

"head came off" — ("Boxing Match Aftermath") This oft-injured fighter could be a very topical reference to the then-heavyweight contender Gerry Quarry (1945–1999), an American fighter who suffered many stopped fights due to facial/head cuts that could not be adequately treated.

"Hill, Jimmy" — ("Queen Victoria Handicap") A football player, coach, and broadcaster, Hill (b. 1928) was hosting *Match of the Day* during this period.

hospital ward — (PSC; "Boxing Commentary") In this scene are bandaged patients (Reg Turner, James Haswell, Donald Grove, and Lionel Sansby), as well as patients Wong, Hing, Nazarin, and Ng (WAC T12/1,468).

• I •

"I am myself indifferent honest . . ." — ("Hamlet and Ophelia") Slightly misquoted from *Hamlet* 3.1: "I am myself indifferent honest, but yet I could accuse me of such things that it were better my mother had not borne me" (3.1.121–23).

The following "O fair Ophelia" lines come from earlier in this same act, so are played here out of order: "The fair Ophelia. Nymph in thy orisons / Be all my sins remb'red" (3.1.87–88).

identically dressed Queen Victorias — (PSC; "Queen Victoria Handicap") This costume is based on the well-known depiction of the mourning Victoria painted by Heinrich von Angeli (1840–1925) in 1899. Albert had died in 1861. There were also several paintings created in the Angeli style (and featuring Victoria in the same black dress) in later years, as well as a few photographs featuring the same attire.

"It's the sex, is it" — ("Bogus Psychiatrists") The long-held bias against Freud's psychoanalytical approach through the subconscious, at least in popular culture, is the seemingly unwavering focus on sex or the libido as the foundation of many/all psychological problems.

• J •

Japanese businessmen . . . Tour de France — (PSC; link out of "Father-in-Law") The "Japanese businessmen" are played by Wong, Hing, Nazarin, and Ng (see Episode 43 notes above for their credits); the "lady American tourists" are Annet Peters and Pam Wardell; the "English gentlemen in pyjamas" are Tony Snell, Donald Grove, and Reg Thomason; the "Tour de France riders" are Michael Dalton and Stuart Meyers; the "Swedish businessmen" are Lionel Sansby, Michael Finbar, and Michael Bridon; and Harry Davies plays the "Winston Churchill" character (WAC T12/1,468).

Joseph, Sir K. — ("Dramatis Personae") Conservative politician already mentioned in the credits to Ep. 42, it's no surprise he's characterized by the Pythons as a "loony." During the lead up to the miners' strike in early 1974, Joseph (then Secretary of State for Social Services) was tasked with refusing supplementary benefits to the families of striking coal miners as a way to force the miners and their union(s) back to the bargaining table. Labour MP Richard Crossman saw the Heath government's hardline positions as the short, sure road to anarchy ("Mr. Heath Leading the Way to Anarchy," *Times*, 30 Jan. 1974: 14.)

• L •

"Let four captains . . ." — (link out of "Queen Victoria Handicap") From Hamlet 5.2, the actual lines, as spoken by Fortinbras, not Victoria:

Fort. Let four captains
Bear Hamlet like a soldier to the stage,
For he was likely, had he been put on,
To have prov'd most royal. . . . (395–98)

lyrical music — (PSC; "Father-in-Law") Even though the printed script calls for transition music here, none is included, and there is no indication in the WAC records that any such music was requested for copyright clearance.

• M •

"Mau Mau, Ronnie" — ("Live from Epsom") A tidbit from recent British colonial history, the Mau Mau Uprising involved Kenyan rebels sniping at the British troops and administrative authority in Kenya between 1952 and 1960, with a number of white settlers gruesomely hacked to death by local insurgents. Earlier references to the Mau Mau incidents occurred in Eps. 9 and 31.

• N •

Natal — (PSC; "Bogus Psychiatrists") Dr. Natal (Idle) isn't named outside of the printed scripts. The Colony of Natal in eastern South Africa was a British Colony throughout the second half of the nineteenth century.

"Nationwide" — (*"Nationwide"*) A very popular current affairs program that adroitly gave attention to most of the regions covered by the BBC, *Nationwide* (BBC1, 1969–1984) was ensured a wide and loyal viewership. Herbert Mental (Jones), the man who collects birdwatchers' eggs in Ep. 26, mentions an appearance as an "eccentric" on the regional section of *Nationwide*.

The *Nationwide* theme music is from Johnny Scott, "The Good Word" (WAC T12/1,468).

Nationwide had made its debut on the BBC less than one month before *Monty Python's Flying Circus* came on the air on 5 October 1969.

New York Times *headline* — (PSC; "Boxing Match Aftermath") The copy of the *Times* is from 29 October 1974.

• O •

"O/C lights" — ("Father-in-Law") Probably from the military, and here means "Officer in Charge" of the lights.

"on aggregate" — (link into "Dentists") In English football an aggregate score is achieved when the scores for two matches are combined, the winner having the higher aggregate score. This can only mean that Wrexham, in the first leg of this match, must have scored more than 4,397 points against Bayern-München.

• P •

"Peter" — ("Queen Victoria Handicap") This is likely a reference to Peter Bromley (1929–2003), the voice of English horse racing, especially on BBC radio, for more than forty years. The "Brian" mentioned may be Brian Moore (1932–2001), another well-known sports broadcaster, but associated with ITV.

"Pinner" — ("Police Helmets") Pinner is a small town in northwest London, near Harrow. Pinner is just west of other *FC* locations, including Golders Green (Ep. 8), Edgware Road, and Willesden (WAC T12/1,416).

policeman runs up to him, grabs his arm, twists it . . . — ("Police Helmets") The insensitive and downright brutal police officer of the *Flying Circus* world appears throughout the series. In Ep. 42 the wheelchair-bound Security Guard (Gilliam) at the BBC is described as looking "neo-fascist." Earlier, in Ep. 29, Inspector Leopard (Cleese) knees his PC (Gilliam) and arrests Queen Elizabeth I because she's handy and "there's violence to be done." Earlier still the testifying policeman (Palin) truncheons everyone within reach (Ep. 27), and in Ep. 17 PC Pan Am (Chapman) arrests a man (Idle) for simply reporting a crime.

The oft-captured images of policemen in the United States, UK, and across Europe (especially in the mid- to late-1960s) dealing with angry "rights" protesters contributed to this easy depiction. More recently and closer to home, a demonstrator (a Warwick University student) had died in June 1974 at an anti-fascist counterdemonstration in Red Lion Square. In this raucous demonstration there were at least three combatant parties—fascists, anti-fascists, and police. The popular claim was that a policeman's club had killed the young man, but no evidence supports any final conclusion. The story was well-covered in period newspapers; see also "On This Day" at bbc.co.uk, 15 June 1974.

Press Photographer — (PSC; "Boxing Match Aftermath") The two press photogs in this scene are played by Michael Bridon and Michael Finbar, while Bob Raymond carries one end of the litter, and extra Ken Cranham may be on the other end (WAC T12/1,468).

• R •

"Real Madrid" — ("Queen Victoria Handicap") Considered to be one of the best football teams in the world in this period (and the twentieth century), Real Madrid had won the UEFA championship 1956–1960 and 1966, and had played for second place in 1962 and 1964.

"Robinsons" — ("Piston Engine [A Bargain]") Based on the Archers family from *The Archers* radio series (1951–), which follows the lives and travails of a farm family in rural (and mythical) Ambridge, England.

The visual cutting from radio set to radio set is probably a comment on the huge radio broadcast presence *The Archers* enjoyed since it first took to the airwaves in 1951—reaching an unprecedented 60 percent market share at one point.

"room in Polonius's house" — ("A Room in Polonius's House") This particular setting occurs in act one, scene three (1.3) and act two, scene one (2.1) in *Hamlet*. Ophelia and Hamlet have no exchanges in these scenes from the original play, and aren't even in the room together.

• S •

"sent off" — (link out of "Queen Victoria Handicap") There is a reason these rather silly send-offs are mentioned here, in the 1974 *FC* season. The "red card" in international football—issued to a player for an ejectionable incident of misconduct—had been instituted in 1970 in FIFA play (along with the "yellow card"). In the 1974 tournament (13 June through 7 July) the first red card was issued to Carlos Caszely of Chile, and he was sent off in the match against West Germany.

"she's all ready for it" — ("Bogus Psychiatrist") The debate rages on today as to the level of sexual intimacy Hamlet and Ophelia may have reached—equally strident voices (on scholarly Shakespeare listserv sites, for example) argue for everything from unblemished chastity to heavy petting to either a hysterical or real pregnancy contributing to the characters' states of mind. It's interesting to note that the surviving quarto and folio versions of the play—Q1, Q2, and F1—also disagree in their characterizations of Ophelia, Hamlet, and their physical relationship, so the Pythons are in good company.

"Sinatra, Frank" — ("Boxing Match Aftermath") The legendary singer Sinatra (1915–1998) was also a lifelong boxing fan, and even co-promoted several fighters over the years. He was ringside in Madison Square Garden in 1971 when Frazier beat Ali (see *Boxing Monthly*, July 1998). Sinatra and actor George Raft (1895–1980), a former boxer himself, attended fights at Hollywood Legion Stadium in the 1940s and 1950s (Springer).

"Martin Bormann"—Bormann (c. 1900–1945) was one of Hitler's most trusted henchmen, and allegedly died in 1945 as Berlin fell. The mention of Nazis Bormann and Himmler (1900–1945) here—as well as the subtitle of this scene—is probably due to the recent and controversial release (in 1974) of the book *Aftermath: Martin Bormann and the Fourth Reich* by Ladislas Farago. The author alleged that Bormann not only survived the war but escaped Berlin and Europe, and as late as 1972 was alive and well in Argentina. A lively denunciation of the book and these "facts" was waged in the newspapers of the time, with an especially interesting exchange found in the *New York Review of Books* between reviewer Hugh Trevor-Roper and Farago attorney Joel Weinberg (14 November 1974 and 20 February 1975). Farago's assertions about Bormann appeared first in a series of articles in the *Daily Express* (as early as 1972), which is where the Pythons may have encountered them.

six pairs of legs — (PSC; "Bogus Psychiatrists") These actors under the prop computer are Tony Snell, Michael Dalton, and Stuart Myers, and there are six legs in toto (WAC T12/1,468).

sports pictures — (PSC; link into "Dentists") The pictures behind the Bough-like character include images of show jumping, cricket, track and field sprinting, Formula 1 racing, and football, as well as an image of Mark Spitz swimming in a butterfly (or the 4 x 100 medley relay) event in the 1972 Olympics.

• T •

Third Jockey — (PSC; "Live from Epsom") The Third Jockey (wearing the green silks) appears to be Neil Innes, who is listed as appearing, per WAC records (WAC T12/1,468).

"To be or not to be" — ("Bogus Psychiatrists") Probably the most famous speech in all dramatic history, this is found in *Hamlet* 3.1. The "too too solid flesh should melt" lines are found earlier, in *Hamlet* 1.2, after Hamlet's been left alone by Claudius and Gertrude:

> *Ham.* O that this too too sallied flesh would melt,
> Thaw, and resolve itself into a dew!
> Or that the Everlasting had not fix'd
> His canon 'gainst [self-]slaughter! O God, God. . . .
> (129–32)

Lastly, the abbreviated mention of the "Alas poor Yorick" is drawn from the fifth act, first scene.

tragic music — (PSC; "Bogus Psychiatrists") The "tragic music" is actually somewhat martial, and is from Walton's "*Henry V* Suite: Globe Playhouse," as played by Walton's Philharmonic Orchestra (WAC T12/1,468).

The chase music that follows is not listed in the records for the episode.

"Tsar's private army" — ("Police Helmets") The Alexander tsars installed "Internal Guard" cadres in the nineteenth century, while earlier and more bloodthirsty black-clad operatives served Ivan in the sixteenth century. The groups were essentially secret police units.

two men in white coats — (PSC; "Bogus Psychiatrists") These actors hustling the Bogus Psychiatrist off are Reg Turner and James Haswell. Their credits are listed above in the "Episode 43" note.

• U •

"University of Oxford" — ("Bogus Psychiatrists") Palin is one of the two Pythons who graduated from Oxford.

"British Psychiatric Association"—The British Psychological Society was founded in 1901, was located at Tavistock House, South Tavistock Square, WC1, and was earlier referenced in Ep. 16 by the BALPA spokesman (Idle).

"Psychiatry Today"—Probably meaning *The British Journal of Psychiatry*, established in 1965 in the UK.

• W •

West End surgery — (PSC; "Bogus Psychiatrists") London's West End has been the home to most of the city's live theaters for many years, and has been a trendy spot for business and living since at least the eighteenth century. The BBC's Portland Place flagship building is not far northwest of the West End.

"Westminster Bridge" — ("Police Helmets") The bridge spans the Thames from Westminster (at the Houses of Parliament) to Lambeth, and is still a very busy bridge.

"wet things" — ("Nationwide") There were some viewers who complained that the regionalized eccentricity of *Nationwide* made for dull, provincial viewing—including roller-skating ducks, and beer-drinking snails—and that serious news was to be had elsewhere. The complex *Nationwide* broadcast structure—where broadcast from Lime Grove Studios (BBC) would be the "home base" and hand-offs to regional broadcast centers would happen periodically—is also touched on in the sketch, as Charlton (Idle) waits nervously for the first such switch.

Nationwide may also have attracted this unwanted attention thanks to the BBC's decision to broadcast "regional" episodes (subtitled *Your Region Tonight*) in black and white as late as 1972.

"What d'you buy that for?" — ("Piston Engine [A Bargain]") The answer: "It was a bargain!" This is a return to a previous episode's fixation of the acquisitive culture (Ep. 41) which had settled in on the UK with the prosperities of the 1950s and beyond. Not only is the engine being casually purchased for no discernible reason, but it's then resold just as casually. In addition, Mrs. Non-Smoker (Jones) isn't consuming her goods; she's using her purchases as weapons, smashing birds left and right.

It's probably no accident that these ladies have been listening to a version of *The Archers*, a radio program originally designed to encourage consumer spending, build consumer confidence, and reaffirm the government's pivotal role in recovering the agricultural economy (and fending off the alliance-happy Europeans and culturally barbaric Americans) during the lean postwar years.

"wondrous strange" — ("Piston Engine [A Bargain]") From Horatio and Hamlet's conversation in act one, scene five, when the Ghost has appeared beneath the stage, demanding they both take an oath (*Hamlet* 1.5.163–90). The Pythons abridge Hamlet's speech quite a bit, eliding most of his lines between 169 (in the *Riverside Shakespeare*) and 187, picking up again at line 188:

Hamlet: The time is out of joint—O cursed sprite,
That ever I was born to set it right!
Nay, come, let's go together. *Exeunt.* (1.5.188–90)

"wouldn't put up much of a fight" — ("Live from Epsom") This specter of forceful redevelopment isn't terribly unrealistic. The influx of Commonwealth foreigners coupled with the postwar baby boom meant housing was at a premium in the UK in the 1960s, while retail (or upscale) expansion tended to trump older apartments and neighborhoods, and there were plenty of unscrupulous types (including the notorious Notting Hill slumlord Peter Rachman) taking advantage of the situation. According to Donald Chesworth (1923–1991), a London Councillor:

There were, however, enormous profits to be made . . . there were people who specialized in getting rid of existing tenants—old people, all kinds of people—and replacing them substantially by newcomers to Britain, who were in desperate need for themselves and their families. . . . They were willing to pay very substantial rents. (Audio transcription, *Eyewitness: 1960–69*, "Rachmanism 1")

Rachman has already been lampooned in Ep. 14, as the low-end gangster Dino Vercotti (Palin) being menaced by the Piranha brothers. See notes to Ep. 14 for more on that real-life intimidation scheme.

Secondly, in the early 1970s there were significant razings of housing in London to take advantage of a new hotel tax break that paid off by the rentable room, and dozens of new hotels began to spring up. Thousands of residents found themselves out of their apartments and, thanks to the rather cozy arrangement between local councils and developers, those displaced had little opportunity to "put up much of a fight," either (*Private Eye*, 20 Feb. 1970: 20–21).

Lastly, the problem of razing undeniably substandard housing and then building replacement homes/blocks consistently ran into the brick-and-mortar wall of reality. The *New Left Review* in 1962 noted sardonically that at even the optimistic razing rates promised by the Ministry and local councils back in 1955, it would take Manchester, Liverpool, and Pembroke forty-six, ninety-four, and a whopping 480 years, respectively, to simply knock down those tracts of unfit houses (qtd. in "Clearing the Slums," *Times*, 17 Apr. 1962: 13).

"Wrexham" — (link into "Dentists") A football club located in Wrexham, Wales, Wrexham FC first appeared in European Cup competition in 1970. Wrexham is about forty-four miles southeast of Colwyn Bay, where Jones was born.

• Y •

"Yes, a private dick!" — ("Bogus Psychiatrists") So, is Hamlet also participating in acts of Sartrean bad faith as he laments his lot in life yet chooses to continue in that lot? The chartered accountant who wants to be a lion tamer (played by Palin) also clings to his dull but safe profession in Ep. 10. (See notes to Eps. 9 and 13 for more of this "bad faith" phenomenon as it appears throughout *FC*.) In the world of the play, of course, Hamlet does act the investigator, the discoverer (meaning he reveals and discloses), as he entertains the Ghost's charges and demands, and seeks out the truth of not only his father's death but his uncle's duplicity and his mother's unwitting betrayal. He also "discovers" the depths of his sadness to Rosencrantz and Guildenstern, as well as Polonius behind the arras (with the point of a sword). But in true "bad faith" form, Hamlet won't free himself of everything and become that private dick, he won't escape his role in this 400-year-old tragedy—instead, he goes to a modern-day anguish manager (a psychiatrist), to deal with the bad faith issues.

"you sure it doesn't put you off?" — (link into "Father-in-Law") The incongruity here, of course, is that this publicly affectionate couple isn't put off by the cold, wet pavement or a busy sidewalk in the heart of workaday London, but will struggle with intimacy when her dad's in bed with them in the following scene.

Episode 44: "Mr. Neutron"

Titles; Tripod and missile float; Post box ceremony; Mr. Neutron (and *animation*); Looking for Teddy Salad (CIA agent); The Prime Minister; The bombing of Enfield; Mr. Neutron in love; *Radio Times* man narration; Closing credits; *Conjuring Today*; World Domination t-shirts

• A •

"a bit flash" — ("Mr. Neutron") Meaning Shirley is a bit showy or ostentatious.

American government building — (PSC; link into "Teddy Salad") The still image used as the headquarters for FEAR is an image of the Federal Reserve Board Building in Washington, D.C. There is no record in the WAC records to indicate a copyright clearance search for this photo.

American military music — (PSC; link into "Teddy Salad") The music here is Sousa's "Stars and Stripes Forever" as performed by the British Grenadier Guards (who also perform every iteration of "Liberty Bell" in the series) (WAC T12/1,469).

"Anouk" — ("Teddy Salad [CIA Agent]") Not an Eskimo but a Dutch name, "Anouk" was probably chosen because (1) it sounds like "Nanook," the star of the Robert Flaherty Eskimo pseudo-ethnography *Nanook of the North* (1922), and (2) Anouk Aimee (b. 1932) is a French actress who would have been known to the Pythons, having appeared in *La Dolce Vita* (1960, musical theme used in Ep. 42) and *8½* (1963).

area of smoking rubble — (PSC; "The Bombing of Enfield") This scene of devastation is likely influenced by a very similar scene in the 1961 British postapocalyptic film *The Day the Earth Caught Fire*. Toward the end of the film the boffins and military have decided to try a radical experiment to shift the Earth back onto its sustainable orbit (and away from the Sun), by detonating "four thermonuclear bombs—the largest ever devised." One of the film's iconic images is of a lone car driving through deserted London, past identifiable landmarks, all tinted red to accentuate the increasing heat.

• B •

"Ballet Rambert" — ("Teddy Salad [CIA Agent]") This company (established in 1935) had by this time switched from ballet to modern dance.

"Petrouchka"—Also "*Petrushka*," this was a controversial (thanks to the avant garde music) Igor Stravinsky ballet first performed in 1911. The Pythons use an audio snippet from another controversial Stravinsky ballet, *The Rite of Spring* (1913)—which, along with its dance, caused a riot—in Ep. 30.

"Fille Mal Gardée"—A late eighteenth-century pastiche French ballet.

"Benidorm" — ("Teddy Salad [CIA Agent]") Another seaside resort town, this one in Alicante, Spain. The other mentioned in this episode is Shanklin, Isle of Wight (see below). The Mediterranean vacation spots have been mentioned several times by the Pythons, most notably by Idle's rambling Tourist (Idle) in the "Travel Agent" sketch in Ep. 31, but also as a past vacation spot for Captain Biggles (Chapman) in Ep. 33.

"bream" — ("Teddy Salad [CIA Agent]") Certain types of bream (bluegill, for example) are found in Canada, so this request wouldn't have been so out of line. Bream was also one of the possible "toilet requisites" proffered by the Chemist (Palin) in Ep. 17.

• C •

C & A twin set — (PSC; "Teddy Salad [CIA Agent]") The uniform of the smart, mid-1970s Pepperpot, this outfit is also employed in the Batley Townswomen's Guild re-enactments, as well as Ep. 41 (in the department store), and the Wife in "The Restaurant Sketch" in the second *FZ*.

"C & A" was a clothing store chain founded in the Netherlands in the nineteenth century, and was considered a high street–type (downtown) store when it reached the UK in 1922. The stores sold moderately priced (and modestly fashioned) clothing ideal for the Pepperpot wanting to step out.

"canelloni" — ("Teddy Salad [CIA Agent]") Misspelled in the printed scripts, "cannelloni" is a meat-stuffed pastry, and has already been mistaken for fish by Mrs. Scum (Jones) in Ep. 20. Mrs. S.C.U.M. will appear later in Ep. 44, also played by Jones, though in her C&A twin set she looks decidedly more modish.

Carpenter is trekking along — ("Teddy Salad [CIA Agent]") The background music here is Sibelius's "Finlandia Op. 26 No. 7," as performed by the London Proms Symphony Orchestra (WAC T12/1,469).

"CIA" — ("Teddy Salad [CIA Agent]") The Central Intelligence Agency was very active internationally during the Cold War. Intelligence gathering and anti-Communist activities dominated the work, with CIA agents and mercenaries active—especially in the Third World—wherever a democratic-styled (or just anti-Communist) government might be losing support, or a Marxist government showing signs of weakness.

The silliness of Teddy Salad and this sketch in general might be a result of incidents like the Bay of Pigs debacle, where the CIA's reputation had been badly tarnished.

There were also concerns, however, that the increasing threat of Arab terrorism, international drug trafficking, and even anarchic trade union movements in the UK could have profound international effects, prompting the CIA to spend more time and energies in 1974 watching Britain.

Prominent British journalist Louis Heren (1919–1995) filed this bleak page one assessment in January 1974, after the *Times* had reported an increasing and active CIA presence in the UK:

From Washington, Britain must now be beginning to look like a Central American banana republic. The most sentimental Anglophile there—and many can be found in the CIA headquarters in Langley, Virginia—must be wondering if Britain is still capable of running its affairs. . . . A civil war has been raging in Northern Ireland for years, with one side receiving assistance from Libya. After years of stop and go, we have yet to prove capable of managing a modern economy. . . . Now it must be seen that the Government is incapable of governing. Militant trade unions are in direct confrontation with authority. . . . Seen from abroad, Britain could be moving into a pre-revolutionary period. ("Increase in CIA Activity in Britain Denied by the United States Embassy," *Times*, 19 Jan. 1974: 1)

contributions of arms from householders — (PSC; link into "Post Box Ceremony") The Firearms Act of 1968 in the UK had banned all sorts of automatic weapons, as well as weapons not deemed ordinary for target shooting or self-defense. This newest Act had consolidated a jumbled handful of earlier ordinances into one, which may account for the array of weapons the housewives are producing. Also, the Firearms Act of 1968 defined a firearm as "a lethal barreled weapon of any description from which *any shot, bullet or other missile can be discharged*" (italics added). This looks like it would include bazookas, grenade launchers, rocket-propelled grenades, etc.

"Corsair" — ("Teddy Salad [CIA Agent]") Originally an African coast pirate, the Ford Corsair was built by American automaker Ford in the UK. This family-style car wasn't made after 1970. (There are, of course, Ford Corsair car clubs in the UK.)

"Cotton, Mr." — ("Teddy Salad [CIA Agent]") Bill Cotton (1928–2008) was the head of BBC Light Entertainment Group, and is the man who had to respond to most of the Pythons' (personally and via their agents) complaints about salaries, repeat fees, broadcast time slots, repeat time slots, and on and on. Cotton would also have been fielding many of the complaints lodged against the show, not only from viewers, but weekly from other heads of BBC departments. It's probably also important to note that Cotton had to perform these services for every other Light Entertainment show, as well. Contemporary letters to the editor columns feature Cotton's responses to, for example, royal variety show participants demanding more money, viewers (and critics) complaining about Python broadcasts being hard to find or too risqué and tasteless, viewers whinging about Peter O'Toole "mocking" Christ (in clips from *The Ruling Class*), or even Cotton simply, nobly defending the notion of the importance of Light Entertainment programming on the public's shilling at all. His was not the easiest of jobs.

· D ·

décor of a rather exclusive restaurant — (PSC; "Teddy Salad [CIA Agent]") Characteristic of this fourth and final season is the escalating budget for each episode. In the first season, for example, blank backdrops or extant sets (at Television Centre, Golders Green, and Ealing TFS) were used for all sorts of set-ups, and even as late as Ep. 29 (third season) the very clever "Argument Clinic" sketch was staged in a bare bones office set. By the latter third of the third season (i.e., Ep. 37 and beyond), costumes and set dressing had become increasingly intricate and baroque, while at the same time audiences were complaining that the show wasn't as funny as it had been, especially without Cleese (WAC T12/1,469).

In this episode there are also at least two (expensive) process shots (masked screen or green screen special effects shots) that had no place in the earlier seasons, when the show's shoestring budget served to ratchet up the creativity level.

disembodied voice — (PSC; "Mr. Neutron") Not unlike a Bond-type villain or henchman, or even a cartoon supervillain of the period, which Mr. Neutron (Chapman) clearly resembles. The recent Bond-spoof films *Our Man Flint* (1966) and *In Like Flint* (1967) may also be precursors to this parody, as was the silly "Captain Fantastic" serial that appeared as a recurring segment in Palin/Jones/Idle's children's show *Do Not Adjust Your Set* (1967).

· E ·

Episode 44 — Titled "Mr. Neutron," this themed episode was recorded on 9 November 1974 and broadcast 28 November 1974.

The additional cast for this episode include: Len and Dot Webb (husband and wife mayor and mayoress), Muriel Evans, Betty Budd, Barry Casley, Mrs. Please, Mrs. Richards, Freda Curtis, Mrs. Bradwell, Rosemary Parrot, Edna Wood (*Wanted for Murder*), Johnathon, Andrew, and David Chandler, Noel Pointing, Araby Rio, Tony Marshall, Jasmine Rio, Helen Fishlock, Reg Turner, Bob Raymond, Eden Fox, Rory O'Connor, Ronald Musgrove (*Colditz*), Bill Hughes (*Z Cars*), Belinda Lee (*Are You Being Served?*), Annet Peters (*The Fall and Rise of Reginald Perrin*), Pam Wardell (*Microbes and Men*), Diana Holt, Alison Kemp, Jane von Arrensdorff, Leslie Conroy, and Bill Earle (WAC T12/1,469). Many of these extras are locals (living outside of Greater London) brought in for location shooting.

"Everyone's really scared of us" — ("Mr. Neutron") This "show of force" or Monroe Doctrine–type men-

tality had been apparent in the U.S. foreign policy since the Spanish-American War, at least, and had reached something of a zenith during the Vietnam and Cold War era, when U.S. military strength (what the Brit press would call "gunboat diplomacy") was constantly on display, even in Britain. (From 1962 the United States had, for example, been supplying the UK with all of its nuclear-tipped ballistic missiles, including the Polaris ICBM, and in return occupied nuclear submarine berths in Scotland.) The diminishing military influence of Britain during this same period simply threw American military and diplomatic muscle into greater relief.

According to the "Department of the Army Historical Summary," however, in 1974 (fiscal year) there were no U.S. combat units "engaged in military action" anywhere in Southeast Asia, for instance, and the armed forces were able to make enlistment quotas without conscription for the first time since 1948 (1). There had been significant military exercises with NATO allies in the recent past which would have made the news, including "Operation Reforger" in fall 1973 in Germany (2.4).

"expensive and lavish scenes" — ("Teddy Salad [CIA Agent]") These episodes were, in fact, much more expensive than previous episodes, and this sketch is most likely a comment on the BBC's continuing prate (via memo) about salaries and costs.

· F ·

"FEAR" — ("Mr. Neutron") There are and were innumerable American military acronyms available for spoofing, including DARPA (Defense Advanced Research Projects Agency), NORAD (North American Aerospace Defense Command), and both LZ (Landing Zone) and FOB (Forward Operating Base), the last two of which would have been mentioned often in newscasts and reports during the recently concluded Vietnam conflict.

"fifty-six stone" — ("Teddy Salad [CIA Agent]") Approximately 784 pounds.

flash, a jump cut — (PSC; "Teddy Salad [CIA Agent]") The special effect sound used here as Mrs. S.C.U.M. is made more beautiful is borrowed from Ilhan Mimaroglu's "Agony," an electronic music piece composed in 1965 (WAC T12/1,469). The prompt for this sound effect is not included in the printed script.

"Fonteyn, Margot" — ("Teddy Salad [CIA Agent]") The prima ballerina of her time, Fonteyn (1919–1991) danced initially at Sadler's Wells Theatre, already mentioned by Cleese in his military/dance rant in Ep. 35. *Les Sylphides* is a non-narrative ballet first performed in 1893, and performed by Fonteyn in 1938 at Sadler's Wells, according to Helpmann's "Prompt Collection."

"Lionel Blair"—Born in 1931, Blair headed his own dance troupe in the 1960s, appearing in *Hard Day's Night* (1964) and myriad variety programs. Blair has also been mentioned in Ep. 35.

"fruit machine" — ("Teddy Salad [CIA Agent]") A fruit machine is a slot machine, in tabloid and underworld lingo. The Piranha brothers strongarm their targets by forcing them to buy overpriced "fruit machines" in Ep. 14; the Kray brothers had practiced a similar shakedown.

• G •

"Gobi Desert" — ("Teddy Salad [CIA Agent]") The Chinese/Mongolian desert is the setting for one of this episode's special effects shots, where a portion of the image is matted out, and a dunescape is inserted.

GPO van — (PSC; "Post Box Ceremony") From the General Post Office, these are still very recognizable red vans. The GPO had actually been dissolved in 1969, with postal service duties being assumed by the Post Office Corporation, formed by an Act of Parliament.

"gunga" — ("Teddy Salad [CIA Agent]") A reference to the water-bearer in Kipling's 1892 poem "Gunga Din," here used as a catch-all for calling the ethnic help.

• H •

"Harrow, Hammersmith, Stepney, Wandsworth and Enfield" — ("Teddy Salad [CIA Agent]") Following this route executes a large "U" around London, and would be an effective bombing path if killing civilians were the goal. The collateral damage of the Cold War was significant—including the support of brutal anti-Communist dictators, death by terrorist and antiterrorist activity, civilians dying in B-52 carpet bombing runs in Southeast Asia, etc.

"hen-teaser" — ("Teddy Salad [CIA Agent]") The Fiat chairman (played by Idle) has already asked this question back in Ep. 42.

his little tadger tiny as a tapir's tits — (PSC; "Teddy Salad ["CIA Agent]") Another example where portions of the printed script are included by the Pythons just for the Pythons, meaning the described action or item never actually appears on the screen (in this case, because it's an alliterative metaphor), and is never spoken by a character. These kinds of "in jokes" are obviously just designed for the mutual amusement of the Pythons, and don't exist for the viewer at all.

"Tadger" is Yorkshire slang for "penis," while a tapir is a tropical climate ungulate.

"Horse of the Year Show" — (*Conjuring Today*") Already mentioned in *FC* in Ep. 28, where the show was being broadcast from the Kellys' flat due to BBC budget cuts. A very popular show in its own right, but with an older demographic, *Horse of the Year* would have been one of those "rubbish" shows to the younger generation.

housewife brings out a rather sophisticated-looking ground-to-air missile — (PSC; link into "Post Box Ceremony") In the immediate months after WWII, only four countries—the United States, Britain, France, and the UK—competed for and with missile technology, much of it brought home from the Nazi works at Peenemünde (Ep. 1). By 1973, however, missiles had proliferated throughout Central and Eastern Europe, across the Middle East and the Asian diaspora, and Khrushchev had even tried to install them in Cuba, instigating the Cuban Missile Crisis in 1962.

The (a) success the North Vietnamese forces enjoyed in deploying and then effectively using ground-to-air missiles against American aircraft in the Vietnam conflict and (b) the significance of Syrian missiles (all Soviet-made) launched against Israel in the Arab-Israeli conflict of 1973 certainly led to this depiction—that anyone, even housewives, could acquire (and successfully use) advanced missile systems.

• I •

"introduce conscription" — (link into "Teddy Salad") The U.S. military had abandoned "the draft" in 1973, after the long and unpopular Vietnam War. In 1974 President Gerald Ford was making headlines by declaring amnesty for many draft evaders.

• K •

"Kellogg's Corn Flake Competition" — ("Mr. Neutron") Kellogg's is a well-known American breakfast cereal company. The Kellogg's Corn Flakes brand cereal has been around since 1906, and Kellogg's began running mail-in and cereal box promotional events during the 1920s.

"King Edwards" — ("Teddy Salad [CIA Agent]") A popular British baking potato.

• L •

"Laine, Frankie" — ("Teddy Salad [CIA Agent]") Laine (1913–2007), an American pop singer, was married to Nan Grey. Laine may have been best known during this period for having sung the theme for the popular television show *Rawhide*.

Lord Mayor is ushered out . . . — (PSC; "Post Box Ceremony") The Lord Mayor and wife are here played by locals Len and Dot Webb, then of 13 Haddington Road, Stoke, Plymouth.

• M •

"Man from the *Radio Times*" — ("Teddy Salad [CIA Agent]") Idle is reading the *Radio Times* edition that featured a *Flying Circus* cover story, dated 24 October 1974 (*RT* 2659). This cover story was an attempt by the BBC to usher in the fourth and final season with as large a viewing audience as possible, and promised a new and improved show.

"Moscow! Peking! and Shanklin" — ("Teddy Salad [CIA Agent]") The seats of power and struggle during the Cold War period, excluding Shanklin, which is a quiet resort town on the Isle of Wight. Moscow (USSR) and Peking (PRC) were alternately at each other's throats and rattling their sabers at their common ideological enemy, the United States.

"Mr. Neutron" — ("Mr. Neutron") This character's name may come from the then-current "neutron bomb" technology and testing, which had been under way since 1962, when the bomb was created by American scientists. The neutron bomb was a *tactical* nuclear weapon, meaning it was designed to be a more focused attack weapon, and not just an umbrella-blast against military installations or even cities, for which larger nuclear devices were designed.

This actually fits the Pythons' positioning of Mr. Neutron (Chapman) in Sutton, a London borough, where "the most dangerous man in the world" can be more concerned about proximity to shops and the West End than global domination, and where his "strike" amounts to attempting to woo away Mrs. S.C.U.M. (Jones) from her husband Ken.

Music: "Rule Britannia" type theme — (PSC; "Teddy Salad [CIA Agent]") This version of "Rule Britannia" is from the All Stars Brass Band, as led by Siebert (WAC T12/1,469).

• N •

"Nous sommes ici . . ." — ("Post Box Ceremony") This translation is fairly accurate, as is the German version that is to follow.

• O •

"Oldham" — ("Teddy Salad [CIA Agent]") In northwest England, and part of Greater Manchester.

"Ottershaw" — ("Mr. Neutron") A village in Surrey, and mentioned in H.G. Wells's *War of the Worlds* as the place where the narrator first hears of the Martian appearances.

• P •

"perfectly ordinary morning" — ("Mr. Neutron") This utopian, bucolic serenity, borrowed from scores of lesser science fiction sources, but also reminiscent of the infamous 1938 radio broadcast of H.G. Wells's *War of the Worlds*, as introduced by a very young Orson Welles:

> With infinite complacence people went to and fro over the earth about their little affairs, serene in the assurance of their dominion over this small, spinning fragment of solar driftwood which, by chance or design, man has inherited out of the dark mystery of Time and Space.

In the case of Wells's original work, the English suburbs were Woking, Ottershaw, Winchester, and Weybridge, etc., and every smaller town "in Berkshire, Surrey, and Middlesex," where the invasion begins (chapter 2).

The "Science Fiction Sketch" in Ep. 7 also begins very much in this form.

photo of Eisenhower — (PSC; "Mr. Neutron") The sitting PM during this period was the newly re-elected Harold Wilson, though Idle is clearly not lampooning him (Wilson was round-faced and sucked on an ever-present pipe), nor the recent Conservative PM Heath. Instead, Idle seems to be reaching back to the height of the Cold War and former Conservative PM Harold Macmillan, who had been such a consistent target of contemporary satirists, including the *Beyond the Fringe* troupe, *Private Eye*, and Frost's *That Was the Week That Was*. Macmillan (distinguished, mustachioed, and eminently deflatable) enjoyed a special relationship with Dwight Eisenhower, both in the war years in Africa and when Eisenhower was U.S. president and

Macmillan was PM. Many (including the Pythons, clearly) saw Macmillan as too much of an American lapdog during this period, especially in military and foreign policy terms. (Macmillan was, coincidentally, half-American by birth.) Many political cartoons of the period echo this concern about Macmillan's "special" U.S. relationship. See the British Cartoon Archive.

The worshipful shrine seen in the sketch isn't so out of left field, either. In his review of Geelhoed and Edmonds' *Eisenhower, Macmillan and Allied Unity, 1957–1961* (2003), Christopher A. Preble of The Cato Institute, notes that "Macmillan deliberately played on British affection for Eisenhower for his own political gain, shamelessly flaunting Eisenhower during a visit to England in August 1959" (see Preble).

"pillar box" — (PSC; "Post Box Ceremony") A postal receptacle shaped like a pillar.

"Post Office . . . complete world domination" — ("Teddy Salad [CIA Agent]") A queer claim seeing that as of 1969 the GPO had ceased to exist as a government department, though maybe the "domination" could only begin when the Post Office became a state-owned company, with the Royal Mail as part of its mandate. This is probably a very tongue-in-cheek reference, also, to the fifteen-year GPO project of assigning postal codes to every corner of the UK, just completed in 1974. The acronym fixation seen earlier can also be credited to this postal code changeover, with acronyms assigned to cities across the country— "CRO" for Croydon, "NPT" for Newport, and "NOR" for Norwich, for example. Between 1959 and 1974 the new system was implemented for the entire country.

"Prime Minister" — ("Teddy Salad [CIA Agent]") Harold Wilson was back in Number 10 Downing Street during this period, Labour having wrested at least a coalition-driven control of the government from the Tories in the 1974 General Election.

• R •

"roses bloom anew" — ("Teddy Salad [CIA Agent]") Perhaps a reference to the popular WWII-era big band song "When the Roses Bloom Again" ("When the roses bloom again / And the fields feel the plough / We will meet again sweetheart / Somehow") by Nat Burton and Walter Kent, and sung (in 1942) by Deanna Durbin, among others.

Ruislip — (PSC; "Post Box Ceremony") According to WAC records, the troupe and crew shot in Harefield, which is about 2.5 miles from Ruislip, Hillingdon, Greater London. The street where the scrap cart is

gathering appears to be in the Exeter area (WAC T12/1,469).

• S •

Sainsbury's — (PSC; "Mr. Neutron") A grocery store chain in the UK.

scrap cart — ("Post Box Ceremony") This cart notion will reappear in the feature film *Holy Grail*, there collecting plague victims.

The music beneath this section sounds like "Serenade for Summer" by King Palmer (WAC T12/1,469).

Secretary of State — (PSC; "Teddy Salad [CIA Agent]") This is most likely either the Secretary of State for Foreign Affairs or Defence, Sir Alec Douglas-Home (1903–1995) or Roy Mason (b. 1924), respectively, in the second half of 1974.

"She's 206!" — ("Teddy Salad [CIA Agent]") Margot Fonteyn's age was a news item during this period—at fifty-three, she was still dancing at peak performance, and wouldn't retire until she was sixty.

Smailes, Frank — ("Teddy Salad [CIA Agent]") An English cricketer, Thomas "Frank" Smailes (1910–1970) played for England in 1946, and for Yorkshire in his early years.

sniffs his left armpit — ("Mr. Neutron") Once again the Pythons are harnessing a powerful leadership presence (in this case military, but just as often political or social) to a diminishing fetish or embarrassing peccadillo. This particular characterization may be related to the preoccupation of General Ripper (Sterling Hayden) with "precious bodily fluids" in Kubrick's 1964 black comedy *Dr. Strangelove*, co-written by Python intimate Terry Southern (1924–1995). In that film, Ripper's paranoia about the sanctity of his (and all Americans') bodily fluids leads him to launch a nuclear strike against those he sees as perpetrating this public health attack, the Soviet Union.

"Staines" — ("Mr. Neutron") In Middlesex, where the initial events of the Martian invasion occurred, the rest of Mrs. S.C.U.M.'s list includes Stanmore, in Greater London; Leytonstone, in Walthamstow; and Deauville, which is quite a bit farther away. The action of this apocalyptic adventure continues to focus on the same areas Wells (and the Martians) targeted in *War of the Worlds*.

The Pythons had shot some location footage at the Staines Recreation Grounds, including at a pool and a ballroom setting, early in the first season (WAC T12/1,086).

stock film — ("Teddy Salad [CIA Agent]") The stock film used in this episode is not accounted for in the surviving WAC records.

sudden explosion — ("Teddy Salad [CIA Agent]") This begins to look and be structured more and more like Kubrick's above-mentioned *Dr. Strangelove* (1964), where hypersexualized, paranoid, and somewhat dim military and political figures (mostly American) end up destroying the world in a nuclear conflagration.

"Supreme Commander" — ("Mr. Neutron") The Chairmanship of the Joint Chiefs of Staff of the United States' military in 1974 was held by two men, Thomas H. Moorer (1912–2004), then George S. Brown (1918–1978). The Supreme Commander of Allied forces during WWII was General Dwight Eisenhower, who will be referenced later in the episode.

"Sutton" — ("Mr. Neutron") A London borough southwest of the City.

• T •

"Time-Life" — ("Teddy Salad [CIA Agent]") The BBC and Time-Life co-produced or shared distribution credits for many expensive/expansive film projects, including the recent and very popular *Ascent of Man* series (from Dr. Jacob Bronowski [Ep. 22]) released in 1973, and *David Copperfield* (1974).

Time-Life has been referenced earlier, in notes to Ep. 30, with *To the South Pole with Peter Scott*, a BBC and Time-Life Film from 1967, as well as Ep. 31, in the "Summarize Proust" sketch.

train stops at the station — (PSC; "Mr. Neutron") The station is in Lingfield, Surrey, where the Lingfield Racecourse is also located. The "Queen Victoria Handicap" (Ep. 43) was shot at this course on 24 September 1974.

"Turner's Parade" — ("Post Box Ceremony") An urban shopping area, similar to a strip mall, usually in a smaller town. There are several in Ealing, for example, where the Pythons shot much of the first season's exteriors (including Lammas Park Road, Elers Road, and Walpole and Lammas Park, all within a stone's throw of Ealing TFS).

• U •

"Ulverston Road and Sandwood Crescent" — ("Post Box Ceremony") A concatenation of locations, since these street names—including Esher Road and Wyatt Road—can be found in multiple towns and counties up and down the UK, from Glasgow south to Devon.

• W •

"Wir kommen hier heute morgen . . ." — ("Post Box Ceremony") It's likely that the multi-language post box announcement here is a nod to not only Britain's entry into the Common Market—which had officially happened 1 January 1973—but the consistently multilingual Eurovision broadcasts so very popular across Europe.

• Y •

"Yellow River" — ("Teddy Salad [CIA Agent]") There is no Yellow River in the Yukon (it's actually in China), but there is a White River. The Yukon Territory is about 2,700 miles from Montreal, meaning this ballet road trip would have been substantial.

"You're not Jewish, are you?" — ("Mr. Neutron") Anti-Semitism hasn't been any more of a fixation in *FC* than any other type of fairly good-natured racial ribbing. And with the more relaxed attention to racial and ethnic slurring on television in general during this period, these barbs would be expected. (See the entries of the cartoony-ness of *FC* in Eps. 1 and 6 for more.) Specifically, a "Jewish Figure" (Palin) is depicted in Ep. 7, though he's no Fagin-ish stereotype—in fact, viewers seem to have not recognized the type at all.

Yukon — ("Teddy Salad [CIA Agent]") These scenes (the ones not in an indoor set) were shot on and around Hookney Tor, Dartmoor, on 18–19 September 1974 (WAC T12/1,469). The Pythons had been here before, shooting, for example, the exterior scenes for "The Semaphore Version of *Wuthering Heights*" for Ep. 15.

Episode 45:
"Party Political Broadcast"

Most Awful Family in Britain; Icelandic Honey Week; *Titles*; Comanche film; The doctor whose patients are stabbed by his nurse; Brigadier and Bishop; *Animation: Slow-motion shell*; Appeal on behalf of extremely rich people; The man who finishes other people's sentences; The walk to Stonehenge; David Attenborough; The walking tree of Dahomey; The batsmen of the Kalahari (and *animation*); Cricket match (assegais); BBC News handovers; Closing credits

• A •

"AA" — ("BBC News [Handovers]") Britain's Automobile Association, earlier mentioned by Mrs. S.C.U.M. (Jones) in the "Mr. Neutron" sketch in Ep. 44.

"Adams, Douglas" — (closing credits) Douglas Adams (1952–2001) was a science fiction writer and avowed technologist, who, in 1974, was a protégé of Chapman's in Cleese's absence, contributing some material to *FC*. Adams would go on to create the popular *The Hitchhiker's Guide to the Galaxy* (1981), originally as a BBC Radio Series program.

Ano-Weet — (PSC; "*Most Awful Family in Britain*") Probably a play on high-fiber cereals from the Weetabix company (est. 1932), a cereal company founded, coincidentally, by South Africans (see "Rhodesia" below). Also, as early as the war years American cereal company Nabisco was marketing its "Nabisco 100% Bran" for its encouragement of bowel regularity: "And that's the reason Nabisco 100% Bran offers such mild, gentle relief from constipation due to insufficient bulk" (Nabisco newspaper print ad, 1944).

The cereal box Dad (Jones) is pouring from is actually a Kellogg's Corn Flakes box (seen and mentioned several times over the course of the show), while an unaltered Kellogg's Bran Flakes box sits on the shelf behind the son (Palin).

"Anything Goes" — (link out of "The Man Who Finishes Other People's Sentences") Another intertextual moment, where the Pythons "quote themselves," Jones's character humming a bit of the "other Cole Porter" song that was first heard in Ep. 42. The audience doesn't seem to respond to the quoting—at least, not nearly as much as when Cardinal Ximinez (Palin) and the Nudge, Nudge Man (Idle) reappeared well after their debut episodes.

"Amazellus Robin Ray" — ("The Walking Tree of Dahomey") Robin Ray (1934–1998) was an actor (*Doctor in Love*; *Hard Day's Night*) and quiz show panelist (*Face the Music*), which connects him to Gascoigne mentioned just below. Nicholas Parsons (see below) was also a cast member of *Doctor in Love*.

"Arborus Bamber Gascoignus" — ("The Walking Tree of Dahomey") Born in 1935, Bamber Gascoigne was quizmaster for the very popular *University Challenge* (Granada, then BBC1, 1962).

Attenborough, David — (PSC; The Walking Tree of Dahomey") Brother to previously lampooned Sir Richard Attenborough (who blubbered through Ep. 39's "*Light Entertainment Awards*"), David had produced the popular nature documentary series *The World about Us* (1967–1986). The music used here is actually the theme from *The World about Us*, and is played by Stuart Crombie and Orchestra (WAC T12/1,469).

• B •

"Batsmen of the Kalahari" — ("Batsmen of the Kalahari") A play on "Bushmen" of the Kalahari. The BBC had commissioned a very popular six-part series in 1956 from Laurens van der Post (1906–1996), called *The Lost World of the Kalahari*, based on his book of the same name. The two batsmen pictured here are Derrick Southern and Ken Tracey (WAC T12/1,469).

"Berkshire" — (*Most Awful Family in Britain*) The "home" to Queen Elizabeth and Windsor Castle, as well as the Second-Most Awful Family, the Fanshaw-Chumleighs, the Royal County of Berkshire is also home to Reading, where the family depicted in the BBC's reality series *The Family* (1974) lived.

Big Country *theme* — (PSC; link out of "Icelandic Honey Week") Performed by Geoff Love and His Orchestra, the movie theme (from *Big Country*, 1958) was composed by Jerome Moross (WAC T12/1,469).

big county grand pavilion — (PSC; "The Batsmen of the Kalahari") This is the Exeter Cricket Club on Prince of Wales Road, Exeter, and the scenes were shot in September 1974 (WAC T12/1,469).

Bishop sitting at a desk typing — ("Brigadier and Bishop") The Bishop (Palin) is wearing the same cope (floor length robe) that enforcer Bruce Beer, the Archbishop of Australia (Cleese) wore in "Crackpot Religions Ltd." in Ep. 24.

"Bogarde, Dirk" — ("Brigadier and Bishop") Actor already mentioned in Ep. 29, Bogarde (1921–1999) appeared in *Death in Venice* (1971) and *The Damned* (1969). The first volume of Bogarde's autobiography, *A Postillion Struck by Lightning*, would not appear until 1977.

"Book of Maccabee" — ("Brigadier and Bishop") Actually Books of Machabees, these are four scriptural/historical texts—two accepted by the Catholic Church as doctrinal, and all treated as apocrypha by most Protestant faiths. This pseudo-scriptural recitation delivered by Palin will be revisited in *HG*, in the "Holy Hand Grenade" scene, and in *ML* in the "Growth and Learning" chapel scene.

• C •

"Cedron" — ("Brigadier and Bishop") Cedron is actually a brook or streambed on the east side of Jerusalem, and is mentioned in the scriptures in relation to King David, King Asa, and in 2 Chronicles and Jeremiah.

Centre Point — (PSC; "Appeal on Behalf of Extremely Rich People") A controversial and empty office build- ing at the writing of this episode, Centre Point had been designed for a single, upscale company tenant, and was sitting empty (as it had been since 1964) when that tenant failed to materialize. Homeless activists (squatters, Ep. 13) had even managed to briefly occupy a portion of the building in January 1974, which may account for its mention in the episode. There are also a handful of political cartoons equating the empty Centre Point with the emptiness of Parliament in 1972. See the British Cartoon Archive. The Centre Point debacle is also addressed a number of times in the pages of *Private Eye*.

"Chandler, Raymond" — ("Brigadier and Bishop") Hard-boiled crime writer Chandler (1888–1959) set many of his stories in the hot, dry streets of Los Angeles, and used similes with great success. Chandler created the Philip Marlowe character, who would, in *Farewell My Lovely*, think: "Her voice came from her mouth sounding like a worn out phonograph record" (101). The Pythons even picked up on the fact that many of Chandler's similes utilized "aspects of the natural world" (Newman).

"China Declares War" — (*Most Awful Family in Britain*) Another mention of the Chinese, a regime that's appeared in some way in at least five other episodes, most of the references hinting at a kind of "sleeping giant" threat.

commentator — ("Batsmen of the Kalahari") This may be a parody of probably the most well-known and beloved cricket commentator of the period, Brian Johnston (1912–1994), who has been mentioned in earlier episodes (Eps. 20 and 21). The hirsuteness of the mask isn't characteristic of "Johnners," but the nose and facial features are nearly identical.

"corn-plasters" — (link into "Icelandic Honey Week") A topical application for the treatment of corns, and earlier mentioned as being worn by French chiropodists trying for the summit of Everest (Ep. 31).

"Council re-housing" — (*Most Awful Family in Britain*) Local city and village councils were faced with re-housing their citizens after myriad slum razings in the post-Victorian era, and which continued into at least the 1970s in the UK. Both the New Towns Act of 1946 and the Town and Country Planning Act of 1947 were instrumental in jumpstarting the postwar re-housing boom, with semi-detached homes and then tower blocks springing up around the country. Entire towns were also laid out, along the newer motorways. See notes for Ep. 14 for more on Britain's postwar housing crunch, as well as notes to Ep. 17 for the tower block phenomenon.

The scarcity of housing even years after the war is demonstrated in Caledon, Ireland, where in 1968 an Irish MP Austin Currie squatted in protest in a council house that had been allocated to a young woman. The nineteen-year-old had been bumped ahead of hundreds of families on the council housing waiting list largely due to her religious affiliation, and protests followed (*Eyewitness: 1960–69*, "Dungannon Housing Protest").

Cut to an animation sketch — (PSC; "*Animation: Slow-motion shell*") The background to this animated sequence (a slow-motion cannon shell shot) is another borrow from Giuseppe Galli Bibiena, the theatrical engineer and architect whose work has already been seen in Eps. 2, 14, 19, 23, and 33 (see index).

The background here is a complicated one. Bibiena has labeled it as an occasional work for royalty:

> The covered Riding School of the Royal Court of Vienna, transformed into a salon by order of Her Majesty the Queen of Hungary and Bohemia on the occasion of the wedding of the most noble Archduchess Marianna with the most noble Prince Charles of Lorraine. This view shows one side of the hall more fully than the other; the chandeliers hanging in the center are omitted. (*Architectural and Perspective Designs*)

Gilliam hasn't retouched too much, simply coloring and tinting the work, and has removed nothing. The cannon (or mortar) is a retouched version of the thirteen-inch "Dictator" Gilliam found in *DWF*, page 371, and used already in Ep. 33, where it shot down Harold the Flying Sheep. (The actual mortar would have fired a round shot, by the way.)

Cowdrey, Colin — (PSC; "The Batsmen of the Kalahari") The printed script compares this performance (the cricketer being impaled) to celebrated cricketer Cowdrey (1932–2000) "caught clean bowled." Cowdrey, still active in 1974, would retire from play in 1976. A "clean bowl" occurs when the batsmen makes no contact with the ball and the wickets are put down.

Cowdrey would have been one of the most recognized cricketers for most of the Pythons' lives, being active in First-Class play 1950–1976; he played for both the Kent and Oxford University teams, as well as England.

• D •

"Dad" — ("Icelandic Honey Week") Dad here is cross-dressed a bit, wearing a sweater vest over a dress, a wig, and obviously a stuffed bra. The characters are Pepperpots underneath, and father, mother, and son on the surface.

"Dahomey" — ("The Walking Tree of Dahomey") The African nation of Dahomey would be renamed Benin in 1975.

"Delaney, Hugh" — ("BBC News [Handovers]") A radio and television presenter.

drawing of Indians attacking a fort — (PSC; "Comanche Film") This is an unattributed print depicting an Indian settlement being attacked by the US Cavalry. It looks to be a Frederic Remington (1861–1909) styled scene (which the Pythons were likely thinking when they made the request), though on closer inspection it's clear that the artist was Charles Schreyvogel (1861–1912). The painting is known as *Early Dawn Attack*, and it's clearly a cavalry raid on an Indian village, and not an Indian attack on a US fort. The Indian about to be shot down in the bottom left corner of the frame has just emerged from a teepee, for example. Again, this photo request was not part of the WAC record for the episode, for some reason.

drinking and celebrating — (PSC; "BBC News [Handovers]") The Liberals did have much to celebrate after the February 1974 General Election, where they picked up an additional eight seats in the Commons, bringing their total to fourteen. The Liberals garnered almost 20 percent of the total vote, indicating how frustrated the average voter had become with the two seemingly inept governments, Tory and Labour, especially in the throes of runaway inflation.

"Droitwich" — ("*Most Awful Family in Britain*") In Worcestershire, Droitwich is a suburb of the greater Birmingham area, and south from Idle's stomping grounds in Wolverhampton.

"Dunaway, Faye" — ("*Most Awful Family in Britain*") Mrs. Garibaldi (Idle) is fielding an offer from a Hollywood studio, obviously, though it's not clear yet that this is a *television* family we're watching. In 1974, American actress Faye Dunaway (b. 1941) had appeared in *Chinatown* and *Towering Inferno*, and had been the most sought-after Hollywood actress since her appearance in *Bonnie and Clyde* in 1967.

"Durham" — ("*Most Awful Family in Britain*") Located in northeast England, Durham has been mentioned in passing in Eps. 24 and 30.

• E •

"East Midlands" — ("*Most Awful Family in Britain*") Essentially Idle's old stomping grounds, growing up in the Wolverhampton area. Idle's "Tourist" rant from Ep. 31 is focused on the Midlands, its people, and places. The "East Midlands Poet Board" also figured into Ep. 17.

"Elsan" — (*"Most Awful Family in Britain"*) A portable chemical toilet, which may mean that this public housing building has no working toilet facilities of its own, which is yet another comment on the situation of both the family and housing in Britain in 1974.

Episode 45 — Recorded 16 November 1974, and broadcast 5 December 1974.

Additional actors and extras appearing in this episode include: Peter Brett (Ep. 40; *Dixon of Dock Green*), Ernest Blythe (*Play for Today*); Bikini Girls: Teresa Wood (*The Office Party*), Diane Holt, Pip (*On the Bright Side*), Alison Kemp; Everett Mitchell, Harold Coward, Bill Shani, Ade Jumal, Fernando Benito, Cecil Calston, Louis St. Just, Tony Regar, Louie McKenzie, Horace McKenzie, Bowle Williams, Derrick Southern and Ken Tracey (both Batsmen), Bola Omoniyi, John Hughman (Eps. 14–15, 17–18, 26, 29–30, 32, 36, 38, 41–42, 45, Montreux compilation), Bob Raymond (Eps. 40–44, Montreux compilation), Douglas Barlow (*Malice Aforethought*).

"Eton" — (*"Most Awful Family in Britain"*) Exclusive school for training Britain's young elite, Eton was established in 1440 by Henry VI, and is mentioned in Eps. 16 and 20.

• F •

"forced to live in conditions of extreme luxury" — (*"Appeal on Behalf of Extremely Rich People"*) In the 13 May 1966 edition of *Private Eye*, the "Personal" section features a similar appeal: "Don't miss the Rt. Hon. Selwyn Lloyd's appeal on behalf of distressed Toryfolk. BBC Home Service. Sunday May 16. 6:30 p.m." (Ingrams, 133). The Tories had been out of power since the 1964 General Election.

"Free Inside—The Pope + Demonstration Record" — (*"Most Awful Family in Britain"*) During the 1960s and beyond a number of breakfast cereal companies included short-play "45s" in cereal boxes as promotional giveaways. The records were also included in the packaging, having to be cut out of the back material by the eager listener. Post, General Mills, and Kellogg's provided such prizes (the records often made of plastic or even cardboard), with songs from groups like The Monkees, The Jackson 5, and teen heartthrob Bobby Sherman.

The fact that the family is at least nominally Italian may account for the inclusion of the Pope in the cereal box, along with a record demonstrating how he works.

• G •

Garibaldi — (PSC; *"Most Awful Family in Britain"*) This spoof is based at least partly on the recent and very popular BBC reality show *The Family*, wherein a real Reading family was the subject of the twelve-part documentary series. The series was initially broadcast between April and June 1974, and was adapted from an American show, *An American Family* (1973). The artificial nature of the setting (when the "show"-ness is made clear) supports this parody of a recent television reality.

"George, Lloyd" — (closing credits) Former Prime Minister David Lloyd George (1863–1945) was often privately (and even publicly) attacked for his "absolutist" demeanor and policies, which is probably why the Pythons surrender producer credit to him. One of the Pythons' favorite historians, A.J.P. Taylor (satirized as "Prof. R.J. Gumby" in Ep. 9, and later in *HG*), describes the former Liberal PM as "the nearest thing England has known to a Napoleon, a supreme ruler maintaining himself by individual achievement" (qtd. in A.N. Wilson, 242). George, then, is just the kind of larger-than-life, politically hungry character the Pythons would have allowed to purloin a producer credit for the episode. Plus, he was a Liberal, the obvious party of choice for this episode.

girls in bikinis — (PSC; "Appeal on Behalf of Extremely Rich People") These actresses/models are Teresa Wood, Diane Holt, Pip, and Alison Kemp. See notes for "Episode 45" for more on these actresses.

"Grimond, Jo" — (closing credits) Grimond (1913–1993) was essentially the public face of the Liberal Party in the 1950s and 1960s, when the party enjoyed a resurgence in popularity and votes. Grimond represented Orkney and Shetland in Parliament.

• H •

He has no iguana on his shoulder — (PSC; "The Man Who Finishes Other People's Sentences") This statement is apropos of nothing that can be seen in the scene, and is merely included for the other Python readers. It follows the absurd textual naming (never uttered) of "Mrs.-What-a-long-name-this-is-hardly-worth-typing-but-never-mind-it-doesn't-come-up-again's-living-room" in the same section of stage direction.

heroic shots of Mrs. Long Name walking — (PSC; "The Walk to Stonehenge") Mrs. Pim is walking to Stonehenge through Exeter, passing, for example, Eastgate House along the way, at the junction of High

Street and Paris Street. The building has more recently been pulled down.

"Hippocratic" — ("A Doctor Whose Patients Have Been Stabbed by His Nurse") A reference to the oath taken by doctors to provide relief and cause no injury, this scene is structured almost exactly like the "Merchant Banker" scene in Ep. 30, except that the phrase being looked up is "inner life" there. This rehearsal of earlier themes and narrative structures is the very reason Cleese (who played the Merchant Banker) left the show after the third season was completed.

"howzat" — ("The Batsmen of the Kalahari") The native fielders respond to Pratt's (Jones) death at the crease with an appeal to the umpire for a ruling on the impaled batsman, called a "howzat."

• I •

"In the spring of 1863 . . ." — ("Comanche Film") Though not led by a "Conchito," the Comanche and allied tribes were active in frontier Texas during spring and summer 1863, but as raiders and cattle rustlers, more often. More active warfare was going on farther north across the Great Plains.

• K •

"Kentucky Fried Chicken" — ("BBC News [Handovers]") KFC opened its first outlet in the UK in 1965, after debuting in the United States (in South Salt Lake, Utah) in 1952. In Ep. 42 the loveable rogues from *Up Your Pavement* (Palin and Jones) saunter past a Kentucky Fried Chicken store on Cowick Street in Exeter before being run down by Alex Diamond (Chapman).

In 1970, KFC had announced an ambitious expansion plan across Europe, and hundreds of new restaurants followed. By 1972 there were ninety KFC restaurants in the London area, and American take-away had come to stay.

• L •

lavender tutu . . . high heels — ("Brigadier and Bishop") A nexus moment for the Pythons and their playful-derision-of-authority-figures hobbyhorse, here they've posited a representative of both the church and the military in ridiculous attire and a compromising sexual situation. Throughout the series the Pythons have diminished such respectable, stentorian figures of "The Establishment" by means of effeminate

dress, effeminate behaviors, and "aberrant" sexualities (including homosexuality, bestiality, self-abuse, etc.). The humor often works so well, as it does in this scene, because the respected figures retain their gravitas even as they ponce about.

"lbw" — ("The Batsmen of the Kalahari") Meaning "leg before wicket," which an umpire can call if the batsmen places any part of his body in front of the wicket to protect it, and the ball hits him. If the wicket is hit, the batsman is bowled out. The fielding team can "howzat" for an appeal (see "howzat" above) if they feel an lbw has occurred.

"Leicester North" — (closing credits) These constituencies listed in the closing credits represent the home towns, essentially, of each of the Pythons.

Leicester North (representing Chapman) was not an official constituency in the October 1974 General Election, but Labour did hold or gain the three Leicester seats—East, West, and South—with the Liberal candidates polling less than 13 percent in each area. For South Shields (Idle), Labour also held easily, though the Liberal candidate polled more than 17 percent. Of the six Sheffield constituencies (Palin), Labour held five and the Conservatives held one in 1974. In Sheffield Park the Liberals came second, an unusually strong showing. Most northern Wales (Jones's Colwyn Bay is situated between Conwy and Denbigh) parliamentary seats were held by the Conservatives during this period.

"Liberal Party" — ("Party Political Broadcast") The Liberal Party has been the atrophied "third leg" party since 1922, when Labour became the official opposition party to the Conservatives—the Labour-Conservative ruling tandem becoming de rigueur, and remaining so. In the 1950s and 1960s the Liberals made a bit of a comeback under Joe Grimond and then Jeremy Thorpe, the latter lampooned by the Pythons later in this episode. In 1970, the Liberals were reduced to six MPs, though under Thorpe's leadership the Liberal Party claimed a total of fourteen seats in the February 1974 election (which then fell to thirteen seats in the October 1974 General Election).

"Liberals a very close third" — ("BBC News [Handovers]") In the October 1974 General Election the Liberal Party managed to garner just over 18 percent of the total votes cast, a *distant* third behind Labour (39.2 percent) and the Conservatives (35.8 percent). The Liberals gained one seat and lost two, for a total of thirteen seats in the Commons. Just five years later the country would witness a significant swing to the Conservative camp (behind the leadership of Margaret Thatcher), when Labour would lose fifty seats, and the Liberals would surrender two seats.

"Lost Deposit" — (closing credits) If the candidate does not receive a minimum number of votes in a particular election, that candidate must forfeit his/ her filing deposit. The "back marker" in many of these elections for many years has been Liberal Party candidates, though fringe candidates (e.g., National Front, Marxist-Leninist) also regularly suffer the same fate.

In the February 1974 General Election, eight Conservatives, twenty-five Labour, and twenty-three Liberal candidates lost their deposits.

• M •

man in a dark suit — ("*Most Awful Family in Britain*") This actor is Peter Brett, who also appeared in Ep. 40.

"Merchant of Venice . . . Virginia Wade" — ("A Doctor Whose Patients Are Stabbed by His Nurse") *Merchant of Venice* (c. 1597) is one of Shakespeare's so-called problem plays, and was performed by the cows of the Bad Ischl Dairy in Python's *FZ 1* (1971); the Treaty of Versailles (signed 1919) put into writing the surrender and then reparations promised by Germany to France and the allies after WWI; Emerson Fittipaldi (b. 1946) was racing Formula One in 1974; and British-born tennis player Virginia Wade (b. 1945) was ranked in the women's top five, winning the U.S. Open and Australian Open, etc.

"Most Awful Family in Britain" — ("*Most Awful Family in Britain*") Depictions of the institution of the family in *FC* have ranged from benign to appalling across the span of the four seasons, but such depictions are primarily conspicuous by their absence. With the exception of myriad dowdy married couples (e.g., Mr. and Mrs. Brain Sample), the nuclear family doesn't figure prominently in *FC*, partly due to the relatively few juvenile roles the Pythons wrote for themselves to perform. There are just a few examples to draw on.

In Ep. 2, the Pythons borrow a scene from Lawrence's *Sons and Lovers* to depict the harsh life of a working-class playwright, with the coal miner son coming home to his father's scorn. This scene is an inversion, of course, of the typical Lawrence drawing room, where the blue-collar father might confront the angry, disaffected son who wants a life outside the mines. In Ep. 9 the extended nuclear family has run into trouble as the grannies take to the streets in "Hell's Grannies"; there's a benign family in Ep. 10, with a "Man" and "Wife" and offscreen "Dad" figure in a walk-on part for the BBC, and Chapman plays a school boy (he wears the typical grammar school uniform) in Ep. 29, "Salvation Fuzz," part of a "Man" (Idle), "Woman" (Jones), and "Son" family grouping. Episode 21 offers Michelangelo (Palin) lost in a sea of

newborns, and his wife is having more, while Mozart wishes his son a better life than that of a composer. In "Salvation Fuzz" the family operates simply as a narrative tool, with each member playing a part in the eventual discovery and arrest of the murderer, the Man (Idle). Most of the familial depictions, then, are narratively useful rather than revealing, and can be traced back to the *Beyond the Fringe*–type scenes typical of the university revues, where the Pythons honed their writing and performing skills.

Finally, it may well be that the other "broadcast families" of the period (including the Archers [BBC Radio], the Richardsons of *Crossroads* fame, and even the denizens of *Hancock's Half Hour*) were so banal and "cosy," as Vahimagi notes, that they just didn't merit parody through most of *FC*, so the depiction in Episode 45 becomes a full-choke shotgun blast at the television family (*British Television*, 123).

Mrs. Long Name leaves — (link out of "Icelandic Honey Week") In Ep. 14, Mrs. G. Pinnet (also Jones) answers the door only to discover she's been watching TV in the wrong house. She clambers outside, across the brick fence, and into the house next door, and the "New Cooker Sketch" can begin. (In the printed script "Mrs. Long Name" is called "Mrs. What-a-long-name-this-is-hardly-worth-typing-but-never-mind-it-doesn't-come-up-again's-living-room," another in-joke for the other Pythons, and not the viewer.)

It seems that here, in addition, Mrs. Long Name (Jones) has been empowered by her ability to finish her own sentences, and she can leave her workaday drudgery and head out into the exciting world (represented by the Exeter-area countryside), perhaps for the first time. She encounters other Pepperpot types doing road construction work as she goes, and eventually ends up staring in rapture at Stonehenge.

• N •

National Health glasses — (PSC; "*Most Awful Family in Britain*") Eyeglasses provided by Britain's National Health Service (NHS), in styles that tended to be quite uniform, sturdy, and unflattering. In episodes of *The Goon Show*, young Neddie (Secombe) can lament his sorry state, and poke fun at the NHS at once:

Neddie: Oh, oh, folks! It was me folks! Neddie Seagoon, folks! All the winter I'd been in Paris, starving folks. No money, no work, no means of support except for my small National Health braces. Oooohoohoh! ("The White Neddie Trade").

Neddie: I had a tough life. Never had a father. Mother got me on the national health. She had an obliging doctor you know (clears his throat) ("The End: Confessions of a Secret Senna-Pod Drinker")

Fair-Isle jersey—Traditional knitted wear from Fair Isle, north of Scotland, near the Orkneys.

• O •

"Odinga" — ("Batsmen of the Kalahari") Jaramogi Oginga Odinga was a popular Kenyan political leader in the 1960s, and was often in the news, including the pages of *Private Eye*.

"P.B.T.R."—An acronym for "Play By the Rules," which the Assegai clearly are flaunting.

"jacksey"—Meaning "arse" or "backside," the term is usually spelled "jacksy."

• P •

"Party Political Broadcast" — (link into "BBC News [Handovers]") A staple on radio and TV for many years in Great Britain, PPBs were designed to give the more prominent political parties free access to the mass listening/viewing voting audience, both just before and in between elections.

Formats were initially rather dull, with a somewhat stentorian delivery by a single, precise voice offering the Conservative, Labour, and Liberal party platforms to anyone who would listen. Martin Rosenbaum notes that after 1955 (certainly due to commercial television's influence) skits, celebrity readers, vox pops, and signature music became part of many of these broadcasts, which is probably where the Pythons found inspiration for the lunacy depicted in their PPB sketches. See Martin Rosenbaum's *From Soapbox to Soundbite*.

played very hesitantly on guitar — (PSC; closing titles) For the first time in the series, the closing "Liberty Bell" theme is not the Band of the Grenadier Guards version.

"Pratt, M.J.K." — ("The Batsmen of the Kalahari") Meant to remind viewers of eminent English cricketer M.J.K. Smith (b. 1933), who had played for Oxford University, Warwickshire (see below) and Leicestershire, as well as England. Cowdrey (see above) followed him as English National Cricket Captain.

"W.G. Pratt"—Styled after the pre-eminent batsman W.G. Grace (1848–1915), who popularized cricket as a mass spectator sport. Noted cricket historian Peter Wynne-Thomas calls Grace "the greatest of cricketers" (1983). Grace's bearded image appears in *Holy Grail* as God calling Arthur to his quest. For more on Grace

and his stature in the cricket world, see "Muscular Christianity and Cricket" (*Eyewitness: 1900–09*).

"Z. Pratt"—Perhaps a reference to noted batsman Z. Harris (1927–1991), who played internationally for New Zealand in the 1950s and 1960s.

• Q •

"Quercus Nicholas Parsonus" — ("The Walking Tree of Dahomey") "Quercus" is the Latin term for "oak," while Nicholas Parsons (b. 1923) is a Brit TV and radio personality who has participated in the BBC radio panel game *Just a Minute* since 1967. Derek Nimmo (mentioned in Ep. 25) was one of the early panelists.

quite appalling accents — (PSC; "*Most Awful Family in Britain*") The upper-crust dinner party participants sound very much like the Upperclass Twits from Ep. 12.

• R •

"recommend you for hospital" — ("A Doctor Whose Patients Are Stabbed by His Nurse") The doctor is running his office here as if it were an English prep school, where test performance can recommend a student to Cambridge or Oxford, or keep a student at one of the newer universities, or out of higher education entirely.

"Rhodesia" — ("*Most Awful Family in Britain*") See entry for "Ian Smith" below. Named in 1965 after Cecil Rhodes, Southern Rhodesia (now Zimbabwe) was hit with United Nations sanctions after Smith's UDI (Unilateral Declaration of Independence), and quickly became an international pariah. See notes for "Rhodesia" in Eps. 3, 10, and 28, as well.

"Rostrum Camera" — (closing credits) A special effects camera platform, allowing precise camera movement across, "into," and "out of" still images, for example, to create animated special effects. This camera was used only in this fourth and more expensive/expansive season. There are two special effects shots in Ep. 44 (composite shots) that may have demanded such a camera.

• S •

saxophone-wearing natives — ("The Walking Tree of Dahomey") A barefaced but still fairly clever comment on the lingering perception of blacks being capable of only performing as either African natives or jazz musicians on British television. Black characters in *FC* are few and far between, however, with Idle putting on a broadly stereotyped "Rochester"-type performance, in black-face, for *The Attila the Hun Show*," and Cleese and extras donning black-face to portray the West Indies' cricket team, both in Ep. 20. Black actors are even scarcer still. This racial mix paucity probably reflects both the "whiteness" of Cambridge and Oxford (and especially their respective dramatic clubs) as well as the BBC in general, which tended to produce shows aimed at its predominantly Caucasian audience. (Just leaf through Vahimagi's *British Television* to view the predictable sea of white faces, spanning broadcast years 1930–1995—and where the few black performers are almost exclusively pictured in relation to jazz music variety shows.)

During this period (1958–1978), the very popular *Black and White Minstrel Show* was also airing on BBC, offering black-face performers singing primarily American music. As early as 1967 there were public outcries for the program's change or elimination, but it stayed on the air for another ten years.

Scun — (PSC; "*Most Awful Family in Britain*") A play on the sensationalistic *Sun* tabloid newspaper, which continues to feature scantily clad women along with some news to this day. The paper had been a fairly Labour-friendly mouthpiece during its early years (1964–1974).

sets off purposefully up the road — (PSC; link out of "Icelandic Honey Week") Mrs. Long Name (Jones) walks "purposefully" to the sounds of the Vienna Philharmonic Orchestra's performance of "Ride of the Valkyrie" by Richard Wagner (WAC T12/1,469).

This same music was used quite effectively a decade earlier in Federico Fellini's *8½* (1963), when Guido is trying to rein in his harem.

This is also reminiscent of the penultimate scene in Pier Pasolini's *Teorema* (1968), when the sanctified Emilia sets out suddenly from the village to go to her "burial" site—she strides purposely, knows just where she's going, and is accompanied by a musical score (from Ennio Morricone), as well.

"Smith, C." — (closing credits) Continuing the Liberal Party slant of the entire episode, Cyril Smith (1928–2010) was the portly Liberal MP for Rochdale 1972–1992.

"L. Byers"—Lord (Charles) Byers (b. 1915) led the handful of Liberal MPs in the House of Lords from 1967 until his death in 1984.

Smith, Ian — (PSC; "*Most Awful Family in Britain*") Leader of the white minority and ruling government in Rhodesia, Smith declared a unilateral independence from Great Britain in November 1965. Smith was vilified by the international community and press for his

party's minority rule policies, and would eventually have to surrender power (in 1979). Smith and the Rhodesia situation have already been mentioned in Ep. 10.

"Spring of 1863" — (link out of "Icelandic Honey Week") A bevy of cobbled-together names and facts. In 1863 the Comanche were fighting battles with other tribes on the Great Plains, with Texas having become inhospitable to the tribe several years earlier.

Stonehenge — (link into "David Attenborough") One of many distinct locations employed by the show during the production of this final season (this one used only as a fleeting link), the Pythons seemed to be less concerned with keeping costs at a minimum by shooting all exteriors in a single geographical area, as had been the case in at least the first and second seasons. For this season they filmed in: Torbay, Exeter, and Hookney Tor, Devon; Bicton, East Devon; Lingfield, Surrey; Turners Hill and Hickstead, West Sussex; Croydon, Greater London; Motspur Park, West London; Hendon, Barnet, Greater London; and Harefield, Hillingdon, Greater London (WAC T12/1,469).

"strewth" — ("Icelandic Honey Week") Again, it's Chapman uttering this mild invective, as he's done in Eps. 1 and 2.

• T •

Thorpe, Jeremy — (PSC; "Icelandic Honey Week") Without the script notation it's probably not clear who this masked figure is supposed to be (and the studio audience's lack of response supports this). Liberal Party leader during this period, Thorpe (b. 1929) was an Eton grad (see above), and had been in the news as he responded to allegations about his alleged homosexuality. Perhaps more importantly, Thorpe rather famously (but politely) said "no" to Heath just after the 1974 elections, when the Conservatives couldn't claim a majority and needed Liberal help to create a government. The letters between the two were reprinted, verbatim, in newspapers of the period. In the *Times* see "Texts of Heath-Thorpe Exchange of Letters," 5 March 1974, page 2. To be more recognizable, the masked Thorpe is also wearing the yellow badge of the Liberal Party candidates. Thorpe represented the North Devon constituency 1955–1975. The rorty celebration here by Liberal Party members might be attributable to the recent gains of six seats from the Conservatives—five in the February 1974 election (Cornwall, Bodmin, Hazel Grove, Isle of Ely, Isle of Wight, and Northumberland, Berwick-upon-Tweed) and one in October (Cornwall, Truro)—as well as three Liberal gains from Labour (Cardiganshire, Rochdale, and Yorkshire [WR], Colne Valley) in February 1974. (The Liberals would then lose two of these seats in October 1974.) This episode was recorded a little over a month after the 10 October General Election.

The satirical magazine *Private Eye* published a cover featuring Thorpe in this very outfit on 15 December 1972.

"Tits and Inflation" — (PSC; *"Most Awful Family in Britain"*) Beginning in 1969, bikini-clad (and then top-less) models began to appear in Rupert Murdoch's tab-loid newspaper the *Sun*, called "Page Three Girls"—they helped the paper's circulation jump significantly in the early 1970s. See note for *"Scun"* above.

· U ·

"Umbonga's hostile opening" — ("Batsmen of the Ka-lahari") A reference to the practice of "fast bowling" in modern cricket. In 1932–1933, the English bowler (and Captain) Douglas Jardine (1900–1958) upset much of the cricket world with his purposefully intimidating bowling style—designed to brush the batsman back and force a bad swing. In the so-called Bodyline series, Eng-lish bowlers attempted to mitigate Australia's highly ef-fective batsman Don Bradman (1908–2001) by throwing the ball directly at him (and other Australian hitters), causing various injuries (including a fractured skull) and leading to a diplomatic row between England and Australia. For Jardine's version of the events (he called it "Fast Leg Theory") see his *In Quest of the Ashes* (1933).

See notes for "Gubby Allen" in Ep. 20 for another reference to the Bodyline Tour.

· W ·

"Walking Tree" — ("The Walking Tree of Dahomey") There are species of trees (including mangroves) that reportedly re-root themselves—very, very slowly—in whatever direction provides the best/better soil. They would have been a suitable subject for a *World about Us*–type show, however.

"Warwickshire" — ("The Batsmen of the Kalahari") The Warwickshire County Cricket Club had won a County Championship in 1972.

woman is dancing on the table — ("BBC News [Handovers]") The rorty celebration here by Carol Cleveland and Liberal Party members might be at-tributable to the recent gains of six seats from the Con-servatives—five in the February election (Cornwall, Bodmin, Hazel Grove, Isle of Ely, Isle of Wight, and Northumberland, Berwick-upon-Tweed) and one in October (Cornwall, Truro)—as well as three Liberal gains from Labour (Cardiganshire, Rochdale, and Yorkshire [WR], Colne Valley) in February 1974. (The Liberals would then lose two of these seats in October 1974.) This episode was recorded a little over a month after the 10 October General Election.

· Y ·

"You mean going to live in Hollywood?" — (*"Most Awful Family in Britain"*) Some of the most inane or inept characters and situations are attached to Hol-lywood throughout *Flying Circus*, including idiots and banking in Ep. 20, the syrupy and racist *The Attila the Hun Show* (also Ep. 20), and anything Twentieth-Century Vole produces. It might be that Hollywood's odd combination of cutting edge 1960s outsider films (*Bonnie and Clyde*, *The Wild Bunch*), edgy television fare from the early 1970s (*All in the Family*, *Maude*), and thousands of hours of pabulum-like game shows, soap operas, sitcoms, and afternoon Million Dollar Movies formed a tidal wave of mass culture that swept aside everything in its path.

Appendix A:
Stock Film Clips and Still Images

Not all of the titles listed below were included in the finished episodes, nor are all of them cited in the pages of this book (though the majority of them are identified and/or discussed). This listing represents every *request* made for film stock and photos during the run of the series. Some requests made for one episode were actually aired as part of another episode, as well. Lastly, not every photograph and bit of film footage used in the series was officially requested, meaning public domain may have applied, or the show's researchers just neglected to ask. (For example, almost none of the myriad photographs, postcards, and film clips used by animator Gilliam are accounted for in the WAC records.)

Listed by BBC WAC file number:

T12/1,082 *Monty Python's Flying Circus* **1969–1971 TX 69.10.05**
Episode 1—Film stock: "WWII Nuremberg Rally" from Associated British Pathé; 49 feet of Library Mt. footage (silent); Neville Chamberlain's piece from VisNews, Ref. No. 1450; Hitler footage from Pathé, Ref. No. 139

T12/1,083 *Monty Python's Flying Circus* **1969–1986 TX 69.10.12**
Episode 2—No film stock or photo requests

T12/1,084 *Monty Python's Flying Circus* **1969–1971 TX 69.10.19**
Episode 3—Film stock: 1969 Scottish Cup Final film, British Movietone News (BMN)

T12/1,085 *Monty Python's Flying Circus* **1969–1971 TX 69.10.26**
Episode 4—No film stock or photo requests

T12/1,086 *Monty Python's Flying Circus* **1969–1971 TX 69.11.16**
Episode 5—Photo: Chichester Cathedral plate from *English Cathedrals in Colour* by A.F. Kersting (London: Batsford, 1960); Film stock: "Girl Bosses Lions"

T12/1,087 *Monty Python's Flying Circus* **1969–1971 TX 69.11.23**
Episode 6—No film stock or photo requests

T12/1,088 *Monty Python's Flying Circus* **1969–1971 TX 69.11.30**
Episode 7—Film stock: "Women's Institute Applauding" (WI) first used/requested, 3 feet of film (about 48 frames, or two seconds at 24 frames per second); 35mm "outer space material" used in "Blancmange" opening ("Science Fiction Sketch") obtained from Technicolour

T12/1,089 *Monty Python's Flying Circus* **1969–1970 TX 69.12.07**
Episode 8—Film stock: VisNews footage of the British Army; British Movietone News, peacetime army drill; "WI Applauding"

T12/1,090 *Monty Python's Flying Circus* **1969–1971 TX 69.12.14**
Episode 9—Film stock: "Women's Institute again"; "*Casino Royale*" from the Shepperton Film Library

T12/1,091 *Monty Python's Flying Circus* **1969–1971 TX 69.12.21**
Episode 10—Film stock: Unnamed stock film footage from the BBC Film Library; BMN clip of the Pope; Photo: Plate from *Gray's Anatomy*, 33rd edition, p. 868, figure 743, "The veins of the right side of the head and neck" (1962, edited by Davies and Davies)

T12/1,092 *Monty Python's Flying Circus* 1969–1971 TX 69.12.28
Episode 11—Film stock: "Mary Bignall," "WI," "Orchestra," and *"Sportsview,"* all monochrome; Audio clip: "Football Crowd Cheering," BMN; Photo: "La Gloria Di Trafalga No. 942, 1805 Trafalga" from the Colour Plate BBC Reference Library

T12/1,093 *Monty Python's Flying Circus* 1969–1970 TX 70.01.04
Episode 12—Photo: "The Emperor" by Meissomer, from *The Life of Napoleon Bonaparte* by S. Baring-Gould (Methuen & Co., 1896 and 1908)

T12/1,094 *Monty Python's Flying Circus* 1970 TX 70.01.11
Episode 13—Film stock: "Cup Final" and "Opera Audience"

T12/1,242 *Monty Python's Flying Circus* 1969–1970 GENERAL: SERIES 1
Photos: Plate from *Gray's Anatomy*, 33rd edition, p. 868, figure 743, "The veins of the right side of the head and neck" (1962, edited by Davies and Davies); colour print "Animals 2548—Roaring Lion," L.404 by N. Myers; and colour transparencies "In the Lael Forest" and "Easter Ross"; Stock film request (from a penciled note): Speeding train in show 8—from A.B. Pathé GER 0444; the Pyramids from the British Movietone, Denham; the battleships (show 9), city gents (show 11), Lords cricket (show 11), swimming races (show 10), and Vatican crowds (show 10) all BBC Library; Hun shots are all from "Attila the Hun"

T12/1,413 *Monty Python's Flying Circus* 1971 TX 71.04.16 MONTREUX
Montreux Special episode: The clips for "blue films" watched by Jones/Cleveland in "Match of the Day": Factory Chimney (427-430); pan up tall soaring poplars, waves crashing (2088-9); fountain (75756); explosion (47624); volcano erupting (45072); rocket taking off (NPA 15438); express train going into a tunnel (SKP 50); torpedo coming out of a tube (26634); dam bursting (99656); battleship broadside (95537); lion leaping through flaming hoop (Pathé); penalty kick into goal net (81800); Richard Nixon smiling (16 6A 48606); milking a cow by hand (K 14392); planes refueling in mid-air (NPA 8508); people charging a door with a battering ram, WI applauding (223/4); tossing the caber (SKP 700-702); plane falling in flames (Pathé); tree crashing to ground (92136); factory chimney (427-430); WI applauding, huge audience applauding (92027); and Wembley crowd applauding (NP 70674 and NP 71102)

T12/1,414 *Monty Python's Flying Circus* 1970 TX 70.12.08 SERIES 2 EP 11
Episode 24—Film stock: VisNews, Ramsay Macdonald (9 secs.), and British Movietone "Goldfinger" E. 9536 (10 secs.)

T12/1,415 *Monty Python's Flying Circus* 1970 TX 70.12.22 SERIES 2 EP 13
Episode 26—Film stock: "Women's Institute" footage

T12/1,416 *Monty Python's Flying Circus* 1970 TX 70.12.15 SERIES 2 EP 12
Episode 25—No film stock or photo requests

T12/1,417 *Monty Python's Flying Circus* 1970 TX 70.9.15 SERIES 2 EP 1
Episode 14—No film stock or photo requests

T12/1,418 *Monty Python's Flying Circus* 1970 SERIES 2: GENERAL
No film stock or photo requests

T12/1,426 *Monty Python's Flying Circus* 1972 TX 72.10.19 SERIES 3 EP 1
Episode 27—Film stock: "Plane taking off" from *Whickers World* (K1418); "Coral Islands" (SKRP65); "Eiffel Tower" and "French Street" from World Backgrounds, Elstree Studios

T12/1,427 *Monty Python's Flying Circus* 1972 TX 72.10.26 SERIES 3 EP 2
Episode 28—Photos: "Pig" photos by Thomas A. Wilkie, AG3131 and AG6256; "Sailor on rug" photo by Robert Broeder; Tschaikowsky picture from the Mansell Collection; Film stock: BBC 48808, SKP 2874A/D, 2868A/B, 2850A/B, 2791A/C, and 2789A/B; Movietone Library of "Titanic" A17702-126, A17654-1076, A17709-126, and A17636-1073

T12/1,428 *Monty Python's Flying Circus* 1972 SERIES 3: GENERAL
Episodes 27–31—Audience laughing (PL 049564 BBC B&W), Heath laughing (BBC K015049), audience applause (WI), Kremlin (Pathé "Moscow" or K 3028 BBC), volcanoes (BBC SKP 2812A-6), chimney stacks in brickyard (BBC SKP 1879-1880 or BBC SKP 1816-9), Houses of Parliament (BBC 3SKP20), Ark Royal (Movietone GR 526A), volcano erupting (BBC CL 45072), Torrey Canyon burning (Navy newsreel film), forest fires (BBC NPA 6688), sea lions fighting (BBC Bristol 8917), limpets ("Seashells" Educational Foundation for Visual Aids or (two just slightly moving on a rock), "Animals of the Rocky Shore" (Rank 5689222), wolf (static shot 34 seconds long) either slide or from

Windrose Dumont Time, honey bears (2 films from Phillip Ware), RAF style dog fight (VisNews 13774), trains crashing (P. Jenkinson "Casey Jones"), hotel blowing up (Movietone E9536 [1040]), car crashing and exploding (BBC SP1891 or EMI E1740 [red sports car]), train on collapsing bridge (P. Jenkinson), plateau of Roiurama ("South American Expedition" by David Bromhall, Dept. of Zoology, South Park Rd., Oxford), "Prehistoric Beasts Attacking" (P. Jenkinson), plane landing (BBC SKP 168), plane taking off (BBC SKP 168, "Air Safety: Unknown Factor"), boat traveling, listing, exploding (Pathé HMS Barham 45/55); Montreux holdover: Map: Phillips Contemporary World Atlas (1956), "The World—Political and Communications"

T12/1,429 *Monty Python's Flying Circus* **1970 SERIES 2 EP 8**
Episode 21—No stock film or photo requests

T12/1,430 *Monty Python's Flying Circus* **1970 SERIES 2 EP 5**
Episode 18—No film stock or photo requests

T12/1,431 *Monty Python's Flying Circus* **1970 SERIES 2 EP 4**
Episode 17—No film stock or photo requests

T12/1,432 *Monty Python's Flying Circus* **1970 SERIES 2 EP 9**
Episode 22—No film stock or photo requests

T12/1,433 *Monty Python's Flying Circus* **1970 TX 70.09.29 SERIES 2 EP 7**
Episode 20—No film stock or photo requests

T12/1,434 *Monty Python's Flying Circus* **1970 TX 70.09.22 SERIES 2 EP 6**
Episode 19—No film stock or photo requests

T12/1,435 *Monty Python's Flying Circus* **1970 SERIES 2 EP 10**
Episode 23—No film stock or photo requests

T12/1,436 *Monty Python's Flying Circus* **1970 SERIES 2 EP 3**
Episode 16—No film stock or photo requests

T12/1,437 *Monty Python's Flying Circus* **1970 TX 70.9.22 SERIES 2 EP 2**
Episode 15—Film stock: Philip Jenkinson's "Chariot Race," from Film Finders Limited

T12/1,440 *Monty Python's Flying Circus* **1972 TX 72.12.07 SERIES 3 EP 8**

Episode 34—Film stock: Pathé: Lenin; VisNews: Red Guards 1376/67, 961/67; Pathé: Kremlin.

T12/1,441 *Monty Python's Flying Circus* **1972 TX 72.11.16 SERIES 3 EP 5**
Episode 31—Photo: Alfred Gregory Camera Press, Nepal 161A; BBC film stock: K26544, -45, and -46; EMI *Cowboy Western*

T12/1,442 *Monty Python's Flying Circus* **1972 TX 72.11.09 SERIES 3 EP 4**
Episode 30 (See T12/1,428 above)—No film stock or photo requests

T12/1,443 *Monty Python's Flying Circus* **1972 TX 72.12.14 SERIES 3 EP 9**
Episode 35—Photo: "Anthony & Cleopatra" B127, from the Mansell Collection

T12/1,444 *Monty Python's Flying Circus* **1972 TX 72.11.30 SERIES 3 EP 7**
Episode 33—Photo: Colour Library International, G.V. La Paz 60914; Stock film: BBC: "Ark Royal" NP78078; EMI's *Cowboy* C2 859; and "Dog Fight" VisNews 2266

T12/1,445 *Monty Python's Flying Circus* **1972 TX 72.11.02 SERIES 3 EP 3**
Episode 29—No film stock or photo requests

T12/1,446 *Monty Python's Flying Circus* **1972 TX 72.11.23 SERIES 3 EP 6**
Episode 32—Film stock: BBC—"Christmas Lights," etc. (74630), "Ambulance" (NP/NT73292 and NP/NT65980), "Ramsay Macdonald" (BBC News WPA16133/A), "Jarrow Marchers" (Ktra514/5), "Red Arrows" (BBC News Southampton 458), and Ted Heath (*Omnibus*)

T12/1,447 *Monty Python's Flying Circus* **1972 TX 72.12.21 SERIES 3 EP 10**
Episode 36—Slides: "Scottish Dancing" from Walton, and "Cactus in the Desert"

T12/1,460 *Monty Python's Flying Circus* **1973 TX 73.01.04 SERIES 3 EP 11**
Episode 37—Still photo: Keystone Press CF 14728-3; Film stock: BBC's "Heath & Queen at Ideal Home Exhibition"; BMN Library No. 259-CY3, "Do It Now"

T12/1,461 *Monty Python's Flying Circus* **1973 TX 73.01.18 SERIES 3 EP 13**
Episode 39—Film stock: BBC Film DO23/72/41 "Heath"; BMN Library "Hansom Cab"; EMI, "Theatre Audience"

T12/1,462 *Monty Python's Flying Circus* **1973 TX 73.11.01 SERIES 3 EP 12**
Episode 38—Film stock: GR 2091A, Reduction Print from Thames Rediffusion

T12/1,467 *Monty Python's Flying Circus* **1974 TX 74.11.07**
Episode 41—Film Stock: "Aerial Views London" from World Background, Elstree Studios

T12/1,468 *Monty Python's Flying Circus* **1974 TX 74.11.21**
Episode 43—No film stock or photo requests

T12/1,469 *Monty Python's Flying Circus* **1974 GENERAL**
Episodes 40–45—Photos: Fiat car factory and "Henry Kissinger"; Film Stock: Imperial War Museum footage; Pathé stock

Appendix B:
Recorded and Live Music Cues

Not all of the items listed below were included in the finished episodes. This listing represents every *request* made for music cues during the run of the series. It is listed by episode.

EPISODE 1

"Liberty Bell" (J.P. Sousa) played by the Band of Grenadier Guard (BGG); "Tratalala Rhythm"; National Light Orchestra, "Saturday Sports" (Wilfred Burns); (89-key marenghi) "All the Fun of the Fairground" and "Baywood Villa"; Handel's *Messiah* Highlights No. 44, "Hallelujah Chorus"; "Rule Britannia"; "In the News" (Peter York); Funeral March (Beethoven, arr. Mayhew Lake); L'Oiseau-lyre: Gigue in G (Mozart) and Mozart Quartets: "Pression No. 3"; Hitler's Inferno "Deutschland Über Alles"; Beethoven Symphonie No. 4.; Miguel Lopez-Cortezo, guitar, "Quando Caliente del Sol"

EPISODE 2

Track from Chaplin's film "In the Park"; Handel's "Concerto No. 3 in G Minor, 4th movement, Allegro"; Rachmaninoff's "Symphony No. 1, Op. 13, Part 4, Allegro con fuoco"

EPISODE 3

Mantovani's Waltz Time—"Charmaine" (by Rapee); "Someone Else I'd Like to Be" sung by GC and JC, live piano by Bill McGuffie, written by Tom Sutton; "Chase martial" from Jack Shaindlin; Holiday Playtime, "King Palmer"; Famous Offenbach Overtures—Orpheus in the Underground, "The Can-Can"; "Music Boxes 1–16" by Eddie Warner; Richard Rodger's Waltzes

EPISODE 4

Fourteen Pictorial Sketches for Orchestra, "Eveil a L'Aube" by Edward Michael; Blackpool Favourites, "I Do Like to Be Beside the Seaside" performed by Reginald Dixon; Dubbed to film: Reg Dixon, "Colonel Bogey March" by Alford; David Rose and Orchestra performing "The Stripper"

EPISODE 5

"Action Station" by Dave Lindup, European Sound Stage Orchestra; "Stars and Stripes Forever," BGG (band 1, side 1)

EPISODES 6 AND 7

"Enigma" variations (no. 9, "Nimrod"), OP 36 by Elgar (conducted by Sir Adrian Boult); "From Russia with Love" by John Barry; "Gay's World" Part Two ('Vitality') by Novello; Dubbed to film: "March of the Insurgents" and "Spectacular" by J. Shaindlin, dramatic and scenic usage, respectively; 12 Etudien Op. 10 (No. 9 in F Minor) by Tamas Vasary; London Suite "Knightsbridge" (March) Side 1, Band 3; "Bonny Sweet Robin" on harpsichord

EPISODE 8

"Jerusalem" by Blake-Parry, performed by Royal Choral Society and Philharmonia Orchestra; Band of the

Scots playing Music of the Two World Wars, World War II, Part I, "Roll Out the Barrel"; Dubbed onto film: "Thunderball" by John Barry; "Gonna Get a Girl" by Harry Bidgood and His Broadcasters Fox Trot; Debussy's "Jeux de Vagues"; "Mantovani's "The Most Beautiful Girl in the World" by Rodgers and Hart; "True to the End" by Van Phillips

EPISODE 9

Dubbed onto film: Melodious Brass "Waltzing Trumpets" by the Fairey Band; "Banjerino" on jugs, washboards, and kazoos; On record: "I Love You Samantha" by the Dudley Moore Trio, from "Genuine Dud"; "Le Marsellaise" by BGG; "Ad Lib" by P. Reno and performed by the Quartet of Modern Jazz, The Studio Group; and Sousa's "Washington Post" march

EPISODE 10

On record: "Dead March" from "Saul" by Handel; "By George," the David Frost Theme and "Frost over London"; "The Dambusters" from the Central Band of the Royal Air Force; "Victory at Sea" by Richard Rodgers; "Fanfare on the RAF Call" by O'Donnell; "Creepy Clowns," Crawford Light Orchestra, by Ronald Hamer; "Mexican Hat Dance" played live

EPISODE 11

Tchaikovsky Piano Concerto No. 1 in B Flat Minor, Op. 23, performed by Julius Katchen with the LSO and Pierino Gamba; Handel's *Messiah*, "Hallelujah" by London Philharmonic Choir with the LPO and Walter Sisskind; Lansdowne Jazz Series, "Oh, Didn't He Ramble" by Terry Lightfoot and His New Orleans Jazzmen; "Music for Vive L'Oompa" Funeral March, Chopin, The London Brass Players; "I'm Gonna Make You Love Me" from "I've Gotta Be Me" by Peter Nero; David Rose and His Orchestra play the Stripper and other fun songs for the Family!, and "Night Train"; The Paris Studio Group, "Batterie pour une foule" by Renaud and Hermel; "Carols From the Kings" by The Choir of King's College Cambridge singing "Ding Dong Merrily," and conducted by David Willcocks; "There's No Business Like Show Business" from "Annie Get Your Gun" by Irving Berlin, performed by Werner Muller and His Orchestra; "Towers & Spires" by Spencer Nakin; "Song of the Universe" from "Seven Symphonic Preludes" from The Music of Edward Michael, The International Symphony Orchestra

EPISODE 12

"Deutschland Über Alles" by BGG, conducted by Harris; "Prelude Richard III" from Walton's "Shakespeare Film Scores for *Henry V, Hamlet, Richard III*," with Sir William Walton conducting the Philharmonia Orchestra; "Hallelujah" from Handel's *Messiah*, London Philharmonia Choir with the LPO conducted by Susskind; "The Rose"—Selection Myddleton, by BGG, conducted by Harris

EPISODE 13

The London Brass Players performing "Music for Vive L'Oompa" Funeral March, by Chopin; Robert Hartow in "Sunday Night at the Palladium" by the London Palladium Orchestra, conducted by Cyril Orandel; "On the Button—Quick Mover" by The Studio Group, directed by Keith Papworth; Petula Clark's "Don't Sleep in the Subway" from "These Are My Songs," arranged and conducted by Ernie Freeman; "Le Marsellaise" by BGG; Rachmaninov Symphony No. 1 in D Minor Op. 13, "Allegro Con Fuoco," by USSR Symphony Orchestra, Yevgeny Svetlanov conducting; Julie Felix's "Going to the Zoo" by The World of Harmony Music; "The *Dr. Kildare* Theme" by Johnnie Spence and His Orchestra; Strings and Things Tilsley Orchestra playing "The Lump," "Return to Summer," and "Venus"; "Great Britain: God Save the Queen" by National Anthems of the World, BGG; "Devil's Gallop" by Queens Hall Light Orchestra, directed by Charles Williams; Theme from "A Summer Place" by Max Steiner, from Percy Faith; "Happy Harp" from Johnny Teupen and His Harp; "Sweet & Singing" by Gene Herrmann and His Orchestra; "Musical Boxes 1–8"; TV & Radio Commercials: "Mother & Baby" and "Bossa Nova Beat"

EPISODE 14

"Warm Hands," Watt Peters Orchestra; "Epic Title" by Jack Shaindlin; "Karelia Suite Op. II, Intermezzo" by Sibelius, Danish State Radio Symphony Orchestra; "Cockney Song" from Silent Film Music

EPISODE 15

"Lullaby" by Gary Hughes, Westway Studio Orchestra; Hungarian Rhapsody No. 2, Liszt, Black Dyke Mills Band; "Aggression," Eric Towren, ISO; "The World Turns," L. Stevens; "Ceremonial March No. 1," John Reids, ISO; "Openings and Endings No. 2," Robert Farnon; "Voice of the Jungle—Tribal Message,"

Freddie Phillips; Offenbach's "Orpheus in the Underworld" ("Can-Can"), Jean Martinau; "God Save the Queen," Synchrofax Music Library; "Devil's Gallop," Charles Williams

EPISODE 16

Music dubbed onto film: ISO "Flute" Promenade by E. Towren; "Long Trail" from Far West Suite by Eddie Warner; Eric Coates and the Philharmonic Promenade Orchestra playing "Knightsbridge March" from London Suite; Pipes and Drums of the Royal Scots Greys: "Scotland's Pride," "Skye Boat Song" and "Road to Isles"; Mantovani's "It's 3 O'clock in the Morning" by Robledo/Terriss; BGG "LB"; On record: Pete Wilsher and Keith Chester's "Eye of Horus" from "Electroshake"; P.M. MacLellan "Clan Campbell's" from Pibroch 1

EPISODE 17

"Star Spangled Banner"; "Grazing Land" and "Vistavision Title" by J. Shaindlin; "Superformance (Impact and Action) by D. Lindup; "Concert" by Concert band of HM's Lifeguards; "Peter Gunn Theme" by Mancini; "Poet Jingle" by B. McGuffie, sung by CC and TJ

EPISODE 18

"Keep the Home Fires Burning" by Ivor Novello; "Bright Lights" by Sam Fonteyn

EPISODE 19

On record: "Roving Report No. 2" by Jack Trombey; "Comic Bugle Call" by Alan Langford; "Late Night" by Roger Webb; "Jeru" by Gerry Mulligan; Dubbed onto tape: BGG "LB"; On film: "Hollywood Title" from "Signature Tunes and Titles" by J. Shaindlin; "News Titles No. 1" by J. Scott

EPISODE 20

On film: Mike Leroy's "With a Little Love" by T. Romeo; "Banjo in the Hollow" and "Back Porch Blue Grass" by D. Allard; "Episodes from the Bible" by Derek Laren and ISO; Westway Studio Ensemble, "Woodland Tryst" by C. Watters; On record: Concert Band of HM's Lifeguards, "The Stripper" by Rose and "Arabian Belly Dance" by John Leach; LSO, "The Land

of Hope and Glory" by Elgar; "The Big Fuzz" from "Impact and Action" by Johnny Pearson; Orchestra of Amsterdam's "Symphonie Fantastique 4th Movement" by Berlioz; London Palladium Orchestra, "Startime"

EPISODE 21

On record: Jimmy Durante, "Schnozzles," "I'm the guy who found the lost chord" by Brent and Durante; LSO, "Casbah" by Keith Papworth and "Overland to Oregon Pt. 1"; LSO "Pomp and Circumstance," "Orb and Sceptre," and "Coronation March"; Franco Chiari Jazz Quartet, "Romantic Theme"; On film: Light scenic Pastorale "Assisi Byways" by J. Shaindlin; Black Bottom, "My Baby Loves to Charleston" by De Sylva, Brown, and Henderson; "The Hunt" (Music for Wind Quintet) by Adrian Bonse; Dubbed from tape to film: "Today" sung by TJ and composed by B. McGuffie with His Orchestra; On film: Symphonia Orchestra's "Elephant Country" and "Heroic Saga," and "Saturday Sport" by Burns; On tape: Mozart's "Eine Kleine Nachtmusik" (G-dur KV525)

EPISODE 22

On record: Peter Dawson's "My Life of Song" for "Waltzing Matilda," arranged by Patterson-Cowan and Thomas Wood; Queens Hall Light Orchestra, "Coronation Scott" by Vivian Ellis; Band of Corps of Royal Engineers "National Anthems (Eire)"; BGG "LB"; On film: "Horrific Sting" by Alan Langford; The Westway Studio Ensemble's "Woodland Tryst" by C. Watters; RCA Victor Symphony Orchestra's "Victory at Sea" by Richard Rodgers, and "The Sugar Plum Fairy" by Tschaikowsky

EPISODE 23

Music dubbed onto film: Sir Adrian Boult and the LPO, "Sinfonia Antartica," First, Third, and Fifth Movements by Vaughn Williams; The Machines "Electronic Screams" by Eric Peters; BGG's "LB"; ISO, "Aggression" by E. Towren, "Pride of the Ride" and "Nathan le prophete" by Edward Michael; Helmut Walcha, Church of Cappel Schnitger Organ, "Prelude & Fugue D. Major BWV 532" by J.S. Bach

EPISODE 24

On record: Autumn Chartbusters "Yummy, Yummy" by Resnick/Levine (MAL 848); Music dubbed onto film: Vienna Philharmonic Orchestra played "Overtures from Fingal's Cave" by Mendelssohn; LPO, "Stars & Stripes" by Sousa (ACL33); ISO, "Man of Power" by J. Trombey (DW LP 2988)

EPISODE 25

On record: "Battle at Sea" by J. Pearson; Syd Dale's "Breaking Point"; Band of the Irish Guards, "There'll Always Be an England" by Parker/Charles; Music played live: Eric Idle on harmonica, "Keep the Home Fires Burning" by I. Novello; Music dubbed onto film: Vienna Symphony Orchestra from "Ace of Diamonds," "Thus Spake Zarathustra" by H. Van Karajan; Pearson's "Battle at Sea"; Johnny Scott's "News Titles"; ISO, "Pastoralia" by E. Towren and "Pastel Pastoral" by Neil Richardson; BGG "LB"

EPISODE 26

On record: Band of Corps of Royal Engineers, "National Anthems" (MALS 1141 Side 1, Band 1); Treorchy Male Choir, from "The Pride of Wales," "All through the Night", arranged by Robinson (HMV CLP 3653); ISO, "On the River" by John Snow (DW/LP 3068A); On film: LSO, "Pomp and Circumstance March" in D Major, Elgar (ACL 137), "Fresh Breezes" and "Open Air" by N. Richardson (KPM 1060), and "Culver City Title" (from "Signature Tunes and Titles") by J. Shaindlin (CMR 301A); London Variety Theatre Orchestra, "Blue Danube" ("Great Waltzes of J. Strauss") by Strauss (STM 6025); Johnnie Spence Orchestra, "The *Dr. Kildare* Theme" by Goldsmith (EMI CLP1565); "Saturday Sport" by Burns (BC 1269)

EPISODE 27

On film: "Quatorze esquisses pittoresques pour orchestra" side 2, track 1: "Au fil de l'eau" by Edouard Michael; BGG "LB"; National, "Monegasque" by Primo di Luca; ISO, "New World—Man of Destiny" by S. Fonteyn; Music on disc: Wally Stott and Orchestra "Rotten Row" from "London Souvenir"; Georgia Brown's "Theme from Roads to Freedom" by James Cellan-Jones and Herbert Kretzmer; BGG "LB"

EPISODE 28

On film: New Concert Orchestra Background Music, "Sinfonia Tellurica and Homines" by Trevor Duncan;

USSR Symphony Orchestra, "Symphony No. 6 in B Minor Allegro non Troppo" by Tchaikowsky; Geoff Love and Orchestra, Big War Movie Themes, "The Great Escape" by Bernstein/Stillman; "Theme Suites Vol. 11, Under Full Sail" by J. Pearson; BGG "LB"; Music on record: Theatre Orchestra Light Intimations, "Days Work" by Mike McNaught; Theatre Overture Dramatic and Horror, "String Suspenses" by Paul Lewis; BGG "LB"; LSO, "Piano Concerto No. 1 in B Flat Minor Op. 23 "Allegro non troppo" and "molto maestos" by Tchaikowsky; Harp Solos, "Descending Glassando," Gareth Walters; "Openings, Closings, Links and Bridges" by P. Moore; Music dubbed onto film: "Theatre Overture" by A. Mawer; "Free Love" and "Man Is Born" by Peter Reno

EPISODE 29

On film: "Jimmy Smith Theme" from "The Carpet Baggers" by Bernstein; BGG "LB"; The Early Music Consort of London and the Morley Consort, "Passe & medio & reprise le pingue," "Basse danse," and "Bergeret sans roche"; Spencer Nakin "Trumpet Calls" from Towers & Spires; D. Lindup "Elephant Herd"; Guy Warren of Ghana, "African Drums"; The Folk Dance Orchestra, "The Shrewsbury Lasses" by Thompson; The New Concert Orchestra, "Background Music 'Stings'" by Alan Langford; LSO "Pomp and Circumstance" by Elgar; R. Sharples's "Shock Treatment" (Side A, Tracks 1 and 3); On record: Helmut Walcha, "Fantasia & Fugue in G minor" by J. S. Bach; Live song: "Money, Money, Money" sung by Idle and the Fred Tomlinson Singers and harpist, music by Tomlinson and lyrics by John Gould; Live performance of "And did those feet . . ."

EPISODE 30

Lansdowne Light Orchestra "Newsroom" by Simon Campbell; "Greensleeves," De Sik, "The Windmill Song," BGG "LB"; Selling Sounds "Droopy Draws" by Barry Stoller; Looney Tunes by Reg Wale, International London Studio Group; The Big Top "Acrobats" by Keith Papworth, ISO; "The Rite of Spring" by Stravinsky, L'Orchestre de la Suisse Romande; "Coach and Pair" by Merrick and Farran; "Camel Team" by Merrick Farran; "Orb and Sceptre" by Walton, Royal Liverpool Philharmonic Orchestra; "Theme and Variation" by R. Tilsley; Today's World "Walk Tall" by Papworth; "Gong Sinister" by J. Gunn; Waterbuck Koala by S. Sklair from Cartoon Capers; "Hearts and Flowers" by Alphons Czibulka, W. Warren, LSO;

"Prairie Vista" by Dudley Simpson; "Bright Lights" by Roger Webb; "Love in Slow Motion" by Tilsley and ISO; "Devil's Gallop" by Queen's Hall Orchestra; "Viet Theme" by Roger

EPISODE 31

Music: "Stage Struck" by Jack Parnell; BGG "LB"; "World Trip for Big Orchestra No. 1, Pizzicata Milanese" by H. Kressling; New Concert Orchestra "Pistons from Crankcraft" by T. Duncan; Tomlinson/Idle's "Proust" sung live, as well as "Boo Boopee Doo"; music dubbed to film: LPO "Sinfonia Antarctica" by V. Williams; BGG "LB" and "Theme from Glorious West"; London Studio Group "Inner Reflections Gentle Touch" by Reg Wale; ISO "Military Preparation" by Hugo de Groot, "Culver City Title" by Shaindlin, and "Dramenasuspence No. 5" by R. Sharples

EPISODE 32

On film: "Queen of the Fleet" by George Chase; BGG "LB"; Mantovani, "Mantovani's Golden Hits," "Charmaine" by Rapee/Pollack; Royal Marines "A Life on the Ocean Wave" by Russell; "Peter Pan" by Hugo de Groot; Main Titles and Openers: Wide Screen Title" by Shaindlin; J. Spence and Orchestra *Dr. Kildare Theme* by Goldsmith; LSO "P&C" by Elgar

EPISODE 33

On film: "String Quartet in G minor" by Debussy; BGG "LB"; Royal Liverpool PO, "Spitfire Prelude & Fugue" by Walton, "Riot Squad" from Standard Music Library by P. Gerard; ISO Sea Music "Ripcord" by J. Steffaro; Julian Slade "Salad Days"; "I Sit in the Sun" and "Oh! Look at Me," both by Slade; "This Division" by Shaindlin; live performance by Alan Parker, "Grecian Nights"

EPISODE 34

Terry Jones singing "Just an Old-Fashioned Girl" by Fisher; LSO "Gayaneh Ballet Suite: "Dance of the Young Kurds" and "Fire" by Khachaturian, "P&C" by Elgar (Marches No. 1 in D major), and Variety Playoff by M. Hunter; Unaccompanied Artists "Jack in a Box" by David Myers and John Worsley; Vienna Philharmonic "Waltz from Faust" by Gounod; ISO, Modern Transport "Long Haul" by K. Papworth

EPISODE 35

Music for Technology "Industrial Sounds" by Walter Scott; BGG "LB"; dubbed to film: ISO "March Trident" by J. Trombey; BGG "LB"; Pul Piotet et Son Grand Orchestre, Dance Mood Music, "Les fous de soleil" by St. George

EPISODE 36

FT Singers "Amontillado" and "Half-a-Bee" both by Tomlinson; Weller Quartet "String Quartet in G" (K.516) by Mozart; LSO Prokofiev's "Symphony No. 3"; ISO "David & Goliath" by Derek Laren; BGG "LB"; Ensemble de Cuivres de Paris, "Fanfares de tous les temps" by Gravure; "Lady Margaret's Pavan" and "Sir William Gaillard" by Gareth Walters; "Fanfare No. 8" by Rene Challan; and "Dark Passage" by R. Wilhelm

EPISODE 37

On record: Leningrad PO "Symphony No. 12 1st Movement" Shostakovich; Paul Bonneau Orchestra, Terpsichoreau Festival (Overture Period), F. de Boisvalle, and "Musique pour les fetes d'eau Face" 461; BGG "LB"; Johnny Pearson "Locations" and "Comedy"; music dubbed onto film: Scots Guards "Drum Majorette" by Steck; BGG "LB"; ISO "Early Dusk" (Pastoral Music) by Ivor Slaney and "Flashing Blade" (Arena March); Stanley Black "A Pretty Girl Is Like a Melody" by Berlin; Band of Royal Military Academy, Sandhurst, "Stars and Stripes Forever" by Sousa; Fred Tomlinson Singers with piano, "Robin Hood"

EPISODE 38

Music dubbed onto film: BGG "LB"; M. Burgess "Lament for Viscount Dundee"; Orchestra de Suisse Romande, French Overtures Orpheus Scenic and Romance "Desert Morning" by Cliff Johns, and "Industrial and War: Action Line" by David De Lara, and "Scenic and Romance: After Midnight" by James Harpham; Moscow PO "The Execution of Stepan Razin" by Shostakovich, and "Dramatic Background: Approaching Menace" by N. Richardson; "I Belong to Glasgow"; ISO Pastoral Music "The Big Country" by Papworth; "Locations and Comedy: Comic Giggles" by J. Pearson, and "Viennese Party" by Harry Wild; Ensemble de Guivres de Paris "Fanfares de Tour les Temps Face" by Paul Dukas; "Towers and Spires" Brandle de Bourgogne" by Spencer Nakin; Scholar

Canforiuno of Stuttgart "Lux Aeterna New Music for Chorus" by Ligeti, and "Blue Danube" by Strauss; (music on disc) English Chamber Orchestra "Welsh Music for Strings 5th Movement" by Gareth Walters; Ronnie Aldrich "Silent Movie Piano Suite No. 6: Hearts and Flowers" by Czibulka/Warren, and "Opening Number" by Len Stevens; Queens Hall Light Orchestra "Devil's Gallop"; BGG "LB"; London Big Sound "Big City Story: Beyond the Night" by Peter Reno

EPISODE 39

Music dubbed onto film: "Strauss at the Waltz" Harry Wild; Czech PO "Fight on the Ice from 'Alexander Nevsky'" Prokofiev; BBC SO Collages "La Nativite du Seigneru" Massaien; Edmundo Ros Orchestra, The Wedding Samba "Dance Again," Ellestein; London Festival SO "Nutcracker Suite" Tchaikowsky and "Time Marches On: Wide Screen Title" by Shaindlin, and "Soft Touch" by R. Tilsley; On records: ISO "Academy Awards: The Music of Stanley Black" by Stanley Black, and "Aces to Open" by Syd Dale; Band of Scots Guards "News Scoop" by Stevens; LSO "Enigma Variations" by Elgar

EPISODE 40

BGG "LB"; Vienna PO "Ride of the Valkyrie" by Wagner; Geoff Love and His Orchestra, "The Big Country" by Neff-Lewis-Moross; The New Concert Orchestra, "A Little Suite March" by T. Duncan; The Westway Novelty Ensemble, "Hawaiian Party"; Pro Arts Orchestra, "Vanity Fair" by Collins; Stuart Crombie and Orchestra, "The World about Us"; "George III" (Neil Innes)

EPISODE 41

On film: BGG "LB"; Royal Liverpool PO, "Knightsbridge" by E. Coates; "Elm Street" by Johnny Burt; music on disc: BGG "LB"; Members of the English Chamber Orchestra, "Lisbon" by Britten; "Devil's Gallop" and "Investiture Fanfare" by Charles Williams

EPISODE 42

B. McGuffie's "When Does a Dream Begin" sung by N. Innes; Johnnie Spence, "*Dr. Kildare* Theme" by Goldsmith; Neil Richardson "Full Speed Ahead"; LSO "P&C March" by Elgar; All Stars Brass Band, "Rule Britannia" by Siebert; George Malcolm "Bach before Breakfast"; Gordon Franks and Orchestra "La Dolce Vita"; Geoff Love and Orchestra, "The Dam Busters" and "633 Squadron"; Tony Adams and Singers, "Oklahoma" by Rodgers-Hammerstein; Black & White Minstrels, "Let's Face the Music" by Berlin; London Festival Orchestra, "Love theme from Ben Hur"; Ann Rogers with Ainsworth and His Orchestra, "The Sound of Music" by Rodgers-Hammerstein; Wurttenburg Chamber Orchestra, "A Musical Joke—Rondo" by Mozart; LSO, "P&C March" by Elgar; Terry Jones sings "Anything Goes" by Cole Porter

EPISODE 43

BGG "LB"; Johnny Scott and his Orchestra, "The Good Word"; Philharmonia Orchestra and Sir William Walton, "*Henry V* Suite—Globe Playhouse"

EPISODE 44

BGG "LB" and "Stars & Stripes Forever"; London Proms SO, "Finlandia Op. 26 No. 7" by Sibelius; All Stars Brass Band, "Rule Britannia" by Siebert; "Agony" by Ilhan Mimaroglu; Continental Theatre Orchestra, "In the Party Mood" by Jack Strachney; "Serenade for Summer" by King Palmer

EPISODE 45

BGG "LB"; Vienna PO "Ride of the Valkyrie" by Wagner; Geoff Love and His Orchestra, "The Big Country" by Neff-Lewis-Moross; The New Concert Orchestra, "A Little Suite March" by T. Duncan; The Westway Novelty Ensemble, "Hawaiian Party"; Pro Arts Orchestra, "Vanity Fair" by Collins; Stuart Crombie and Orchestra, "The World about Us"

Appendix C: Sketch, Animation, and Link Listing

This comprehensive listing of sketches, animations, and links in *Monty Python's Flying Circus* includes entries from both volumes of this book. To find more information about each episode, refer to volume 1 for episodes 1–26 (seasons 1 and 2) and volume 2 for episodes 27–45 (seasons 3 and 4).

"42nd International Clambake" Ep. 34

"Accidental Executions" Ep. 35

"Accidents Sketch" ("Prawn Salad Ltd.") Ep. 18

Ada's Snack Bar ("And now . . ." Man link) Ep. 9

"After-shave" ("Toilet requisite") Ep. 17

"Agatha Christie Sketch" Ep. 11

"Agatha Christie Sketch (Railway Timetables) Ep. 24

"Albatross" Ep. 13

"All-England Summarize Proust Competition" Ep. 31

"All-Essex Badminton Championship" (promo) Ep. 32

"All-In Cricket" Ep. 11

"Amazing Kargol and Janet" Ep. 2

"Anagram Quiz" Ep. 30

"Anagram Versions of Shakespeare" Ep. 30

"An Appeal on Behalf of the National Truss" Ep. 21

"And Did Those Feet" (song); Link into "England's Mountains Green" Ep. 4

"And Did Those Feet . . ." (arrest hymn) Ep. 29

"And now for something completely different" (links) Eps. 2, 9, 21

"And now for something completely different" Man (intros/links): Ep. 9—Ada's Snack Bar; Ep. 14—Zoo cage; Ep. 15—Rocky beach; Ep. 16—Window cleaner's platform; Ep. 17—Propellered desk; Ep. 18—Grill-o-Mat snack bar; Ep. 19—Smithee; Ep. 20—Projected over Hun film; Ep. 22—Bikini-clad; With a pig; Ep. 23—Paignton; Ep. 24—Seaside; Ep. 25—Night-time beach; Ep. 26—At attention (for the Queen); Eps. 27–33—Norwich Castle; Ep. 35—Inter-

viewed in a flowery field; Ep. 36—Norwich Castle; Ep. 37—Boxing ring; Ep. 38—Norwich Castle; Ep. 39—Flowery field

"And then . . ." Man (link) Ep. 43

Animations (*in the order each appears, by episode*): Ep. 1—Escaping pig; Whizzo Butter; "Sit up!" photos; Ep. 2—"I think therefore I am"; Harold the flying sheep; Carnivorous pram; Ep. 3—Link into Donkey Rides; Purchase a past; Ep. 4—Tumor operation to palanquin link; Ep. 5—Pulling old lady apart; Charles Atlas's "Dynamo Tension"; Ep. 6—Escaping scribble; Link out of *It's the Arts*; *Thrills and Adventure* comic book; Criminal pram; 20th-Century Vole; Ep. 8—"Full Frontal Nudity Vol. 2"; "An Intimate Review"; Meat grinder to dancing Botticelli's Venus link; Ep. 9—Encyclopaedia salesman; Kewpie doll carnival game; Brian Islam and Brucie; Ep. 10—A Chippendale writing desk; Humor, the new permissiveness, and animals eating animals; Ep. 11—Flushing head; Violent nudes; Tenement coffins; Ep. 12—Falling people; The Great Fred; Falling apart; Animals from a pipe; Ep. 13—Feeding the birdman; Ambulance on the loose; "What a terrible way to end the series!"; Ep. 14—Vintage model European monarchs; Straight razor shave; Ep. 15—Can-can diversion; Civil War cannons; "I confess!"; Ep. 16—"I am somebody's lunch hour"; Ep. 17—Cocoon to compère butterfly; "How to give up being a Mason"; Bouncing on naked lady; Jack and the Beanstalk; Five Frog Curse; Ep. 18—Monopod woman; Men escaping the film; Color separation link (walking general Civil War robots, Last Supper ruined, Hand of God rescues Sir William, WWI fighter cloud); Teddy and Neddy want to hunt piggybanks; Ep. 19—Enoch Powell head; Lights out; Additional prizes, including a deadly samurai made into a meal; Michelangelo's Adam in a sandwich;

Train and naked girl; "Welcome All Sexual Athletes"; Mona Lisa says "Hello Tiger; Bloody lipstick; The Prince and the Black Spot; *Election Night Special* titles; Ep. 20—"Arthur X, leader of the Pennine Gang"; Parrots announcing TV programs; Attila the Bun; Ep. 21—Building and decay; Luxury Flats; A toe-elephant; Giant football in Wembley; Mugsy Spaniel and Eggs Diamond; *Raising Gangsters for Fun & Profit*; Ep. 22—Dancing generals; Suicidal man; Bus stop eyeball; "The Killer Cars"; Atomic-Mutated Cat; Ep. 23—Stepping on people; Conrad Poohs and His Dancing Teeth; A letter undelivered; Ep. 24—Overrun by Chinese Communists; "Domino Theory"; Crelm toothpaste; Shrill petrol; Cartoon Religions Ltd.; Ep. 25—Picketers and *2001: A Space Odyssey*; "I wonder just how much Molly knew?"; Characters leaving paintings; Venus de Milo: ". . . bloody consultation!"; Over-actors; Bombs creating flowers; Ep. 26—Crelm toothpaste; The surgical garment; Madonna balloon bomb; "Fire Mrs. Nesbit!"; Cannibalism; Ep. 27—Into the criminal body; Davis and the Inspector in the criminal body; Teleporting Mrs. Cut-out; Ep. 28—Surbiton to Hounslow map; Anatomical model walks off the edge of the cartoon; Compère's mouth escapes; Nazi fish swallows British fish; Chinese fish sinks ocean liner; Ep. 29—Police violence; Many-handed victim; Woman in the sun; Bouncy ball woman; Ep. 30—Pantomime flea eats man; Carnivorous dining and bed rooms; Killer houses; *The House-Hunters*; NCP Car Parks; Ep. 31—Communists under the bed; Putrid Peter doll; Ep. 32—The meaning of life, badly framed; Carnivorous baby; Groovy Royal Navy advert; Ep. 33—The domino effect; TV is bad for your eyes; Program Control fairy; Ep. 34—Monsters dance; Ep. 35—How to animate cut-outs; St. Anthony on a break; WWI helmets; A simple little push of a button; Two trees; Hitler; Ep. 36—Aldwych Theatre's *Gay Boys in Bondage*; Arcade target shooting; Mixing a drink; A kiss at the pub; Folding and posting a letter to the BBC; Ep. 37—Ambulance running over City Gent; Stealing cut-outs; moveable black hole; Ep. 38—No-Time Toulouse; 2001: A Space Odyssey; Penguin invasion; Ep. 39—Swell party and bathroom noises; Charwoman; Ep. 40—Washing with soap and water; *The Golden Age of Colonic Irrigation*; Ep. 41—Anatomy of an ant; Ep. 42—"What a lovely day"; Ep. 43—Anatomy monster at the city walls; Grape balloons; Ep. 44—Mr. Neutron; Ep. 45—Slow-motion cannon shell; Batsmen of the Kalahari

"Another Indian massacre at Dorking Theatre" (link) Ep. 6

"Ant Communication" ("Restaurant Sketch") Ep. 41

Anti-communist (link) Ep. 3

"Antonioni Career Review" Ep. 29

"Anything Goes In" (song) Ep. 42

"Apology for Violence and Nudity" Ep. 28

"Apology (Politicians)" Ep. 32

"Appeal on Behalf of Extremely Rich People" Ep. 45

"*Archaeology Today*" Ep. 21

"Architect Sketch" Ep. 17

"Argument Clinic" Ep. 29

"Army Captain as Clown" Ep. 30

"Army Protection Racket" Ep. 8

"Art Critic" Ep. 4

"Art Critic Strangles His Wife" Ep. 8

"Art Critic: 'The Place of the Nude'" Ep. 8

"Art Gallery" Ep. 4

"Art Gallery Strike" Ep. 25

"Arthur Ewing and His Musical Mice" Ep. 2

"Arthur Figgis" Ep. 6

"Arthur Tree" Ep. 10

"Arthur 'Two-Sheds' Jackson Interview" Ep. 1

"At Home with the Ant and Other Pets" Ep. 41

The Attila the Hun Show" Ep. 20

"Attila the Nun" Ep. 20

"Audit" Ep. 7

"BALPA Interruptions" (and "Corrections") Ep. 16

"Banana and Cheese Sandwiches" Ep. 34

"Bank Robber (Lingerie Shop)" Ep. 10

"Basingstoke in Westphalia" Ep. 42

"Batley Townswomen's Guild Presents the Battle of Pearl Harbour" Ep. 11

"Batley Townswomen's Guild Presents the First Heart Transplant" Ep. 22

"Battle of Trafalgar with Prof. R.J. Canning" Ep. 11

"BBC 1 and 2 Promos" Ep. 37

"BBC 1 Colour Promos" (*Dad's Doctors* and *Dad's Pooves*) Ep. 38

"BBC 1 Previews Trailer" Ep. 21

"BBC Apology" (and the BBC's denial of that apology) Ep. 33

"BBC Entry for the Zinc Stoat of Budapest" Ep. 6

"BBC Head of Drama" Ep. 27

"BBC Is Short of Money" Ep. 28

"BBC News Handovers" Ep. 45

"BBC Newsreader(s) Arrested" Ep. 5

"BBC Programme Planners" Ep. 38

"BBC TV News" Ep. 20

BBC walk-on role (link) Ep. 15

"BBC Would Like to Apologize" by the Gumbys (link) Ep. 17

"*Beat the Clock*" Ep. 30

"Being Thrown into a River" Ep. 19

"Beethoven Finds 'The Lost Chord'" Ep. 21

"Beethoven's Mynah Bird" (and Shakespeare, Michelangelo) Ep. 21

"Bicycle Repair Man" (Mr. F.G. Superman) Ep. 3

Bicycling Picasso map (link) Ep. 1

"Biggles Dictates a Letter" Ep. 33

Bikini girls (intro link) Ep. 22

"Bing Tiddle Tiddle Bong" (song) Ep. 22

"Bingo-Crazed Chinese" Ep. 34

"The Bishop" (titles and film, repeated) Ep. 17

"Bishop Rehearsing" ("Oh, Mr. Belpit") Ep. 16

"The Black Eagle" Ep. 25

"Blackmail" Ep. 18

"Blancmanges Playing Tennis" Ep. 7

"Blood, Devastation, Death, War and Horror" Ep. 30

"Blood Donor" Ep. 39

"Bloody Repeats" Ep. 42

"Bogus Psychiatrists" Ep. 43

"Bomb on Plane" Ep. 35

"The Bombing of Enfield" Ep. 44

"Book at Bedtime" (*Redgauntlet*) Ep. 38

"Book-of-the-Month Club" prizes ("Dead Indian," "The M4") Ep. 19

"Bookshop" Ep. 4

"Borrow your head for a bit of animation?" (link) Ep. 15

"Boxing Match Aftermath" (and Radio Broadcast) Ep. 43

"Boxing Tonight" (Jack Bodell v. Sir Kenneth Clark) Ep. 37

"Brigadier and Bishop" Ep. 45

"Britain's Entry Joke for the 'Rubber Mac of Zurich Award'" Ep. 9

"Britain's Great Pre-War Joke" Ep. 1

"British Explorer's Club" Ep. 29

"British Rail Complaints" Ep. 8

"British Well-Basically Club" Ep. 35

"Bruces" (Philosophy Department, University of Woolamaloo) Ep. 22

"Bull-Fighting" (*Probe*) Ep. 35

"Burglar Who Is an Encyclopaedia Salesman" Ep. 5

"But it's my only line!" Eps. 4, 8

"But now . . ." (link) Ep. 42

Butlin's Redcoat (intro/link) Eps. 2, 3, 7, 35

"Buying a Bed" ("Don't say mattress") Ep. 8

"Buying a Piston Engine" ("A Bargain") Ep. 43

"Buying an Ant" Ep. 41

"Buzz Aldrin" (photo link) Ep. 17

"Camel Spotting" (and Yeti and Train Spotting) Ep. 7

"Camp Square-Bashing" (and "Close-Order Swanning About") Ep. 22

"Careers Advisory Board" Ep. 5

"Cheap-Laughs" Ep. 35

"Cheese Shop" Ep. 33

"Chemist Sketch" ("An Apology," and "A Less Naughty Chemist") Ep. 17

"Children's Stories" Ep. 3

"Choice of viewing on BBC television" (link) Eps. 14, 17

"Church Police" (Salvation Fuzz) Ep. 29

"Cinema Adverts" (Luigi Vercotti and La Gondola Restaurant) Ep. 13

"Classic Serial Becomes Tuesday Documentary Becomes Children's Story Becomes Party Political Broadcast . . ." Ep. 32

"Climbing the North Face of the Uxbridge Road" Ep. 33

"Clodagh Rogers" Ep. 34

"Coal Mine in Llanddarog" (Historical Argument) Ep. 25

"Colin Mozart, Ratcatcher" Ep. 20

Colonel cues the "telecine" cartoon, and stops a sketch (links) Ep. 8

"Colonel Stops the Program" Ep. 4

"Comanche film" Ep. 45

"Commercial Possibilities of Avine Aviation" Ep. 2

"Commercials"

"Communist Quiz Show: *World Forum*" Ep. 25

"Complaint Letters Address" Ep. 7

"Complaints" Ep. 29

"Complaints Office on Fire" Ep. 41

"Confuse-a-Cat" (and Pantomime Show) Ep. 5

"Conjuring Today" Ep. 44

"Conquistador Coffee Campaign" Ep. 24

"Constable Runs to the Scene" Ep. 25

"Corner of a Bed Sitter" (link) Ep. 12

"Cosmetic Surgery" Ep. 22

"Court Scene (Charades)" Ep. 15

"Court Scene (Dirty Hungarian Phrasebook)" Ep. 25

"Court Scene" (Erik Njorl) Ep. 27

"Court Scene" ("Laurence Olivier"; Mrs. Fiona Lewis; Witness in Coffin; Cardinal Richelieu) Ep. 3

"Court Scene—Mass Murder" (and BBC on trial) Ep. 27

"Courtmartial" Ep. 42

"Crackpot Religions Ltd." Ep. 24

"Credits of the Year" Ep. 39

"Cricket Critics" Ep. 39

"Cricket Match (Assegais)" Ep. 45

"Crossed-Out Pig" Ep. 1

"Crossing the Atlantic on a Tricycle" Ep. 24

"Crunchy Frog" (and Inspector Parrot link) Ep. 6

"Cuidado llamas!" Ep. 9

"Current Affairs" (Mr. Praline) Ep. 18

"Cut-Price Airline" Ep. 22

"Cycling Tour" (Mr. Pither) Ep. 34

"Dad's Doctors" (and *Dad's Pooves*) BBC Colour Promos Ep. 38

"Dame Irene Stoat" Ep. 19

"David Attenborough" Ep. 45

"David Niven's Fridge" Ep. 39

"David Unction and a 'Special Good Evening'" Ep. 10

"David Unction reads *Physique*" Ep. 10

"Dead Indian" Ep. 19

"Dead Parrot" Ep. 8

Dead pig (link) Ep. 1

"Dear BBC" letters Ep. 5

"Death of Admiral Nelson" Ep. 1

"The Death of Mary Queen of Scots" (radio version) Ep. 22

"Death of Genghis Khan" (and Bruce Foster, Admiral Nelson) Ep. 1

"Decision" ("Lord Interest and Sir Dividends") Ep. 40

"Dennis Moore" (and song) Ep. 37

"Dentists" ("Live from Epsom") Ep. 43

"Department Store" Ep. 41

"Derby Council v. All Blacks Rugby Match" Ep. 23

"Derek Hart Interviewing a Nude Man" Ep. 17

"Detective Sketch Revisited" Ep. 11

"Dickie Attenborough" (*British Showbiz Awards*) Ep. 39

"Different Endings" ("End of Show Department") Ep. 41

"Dirty Hungarian Phrasebook" Ep. 25

"Dirty Vicar Sketch" Ep. 39

"Doctor and Patient 'Relationship'" Ep. 22

"Doctor Stick-Ups" Ep. 37

"Doctor Whose Patients Are Stabbed by His Nurse" Ep. 45

"Documentary on Boxer" ("Ken Clean-Air Systems") Ep. 18

"Documentary Time: Invasion of Normandy" Ep. 26

"Donation" (for orphans) Ep. 30

Donkey rides (link into) Ep. 3

"Dormitory in a Girls' Public School" Ep. 26

"Dramatic Off-Licence" Ep. 37

"A Duck, a Cat and a Lizard Discussion on Customs Policies" Ep. 5

"Dull Life of a City Stockbroker" Ep. 6

"Dung" (at a dinner party) Ep. 19

"Durham Light Infantry" (interior décor) Ep. 30

"Dynamite Cures Athlete's Foot" Ep. 28

"Eartha Kitt" Ep. 34

"Eighteenth-Century Social Legislation" Ep. 11

"Election Night Special" (Silly and Sensible parties) Ep. 19

"Elizabethan Pornography Smugglers" Ep. 36

"Emigration from Surbiton to Hounslow" Ep. 28

"England's Mountains Green (It's a Man's Life)" rustic monologue Ep. 4

"Episode 12B: Full Frontal Nudity" Ep. 8

"Episode 12B: How to Recognize Different Types of Trees from Quite a Long Way Away" Ep. 3

"Episode Arthur, Part 7, Teeth" Ep. 4

"Episodes 17–26: The Naked Ant" Ep. 12

"Epsom Furniture Races" Ep. 20

"Erizabeth L" Ep. 29

"Ernest Scribbler" ("World's Deadliest Joke") Ep. 1

"Erotic Film" ("Match of the Day") Ep. 5

"Escape (From Film)" Ep. 18

"Ethel the Frog: The Piranha Brothers" Ep. 14

"Europolice Song Contest" Ep. 22

"Evening Class: Italian Language" Ep. 1

"Everest Climbed by Hairdressers" Ep. 31

"Expedition to Lake Pahoe" Ep. 32

"Expensive Captions" Ep. 6

"Exploding Animals" Ep. 16

"Exploding Penguin on TV Set" Ep. 22

"Exploding Version of 'The Blue Danube'" Ep. 26

"Face the Press" Ep. 14

"Falling from Building" Ep. 12

"Famous Deaths" Ep. 1

"Farming Club" Ep. 28

"Father-in-Law" Ep. 43

"Film Critic" Ep. 23

"Film Director (Teeth)", a Writer/Dentist Ep. 24

"Film Trailer" Ep. 42

"Films of Sir Edward Ross" Ep. 1

"Finian's Rainbow—Starring the Man from the Off-Licence" Ep. 19

"Fire Brigade" Ep. 31

"First Man to Jump the Channel" Ep. 10

"First Underwater Production of *Measure for Measure*" Ep. 22

"Fish Licence" (Mr. Praline) Ep. 23

"Fish-Slapping Dance" Ep. 28

"Flaming Star" (Archaeology drama and musical) Ep. 21

"Flasher" Ep. 8

"Flying Lessons" Ep. 16

"Flying Sheep" Ep. 2

"Foreign Secretary Tells about Canoeing" Ep. 19

"Fraud Film Squad" (Inspector Leopard née Panther) Ep. 29

"Free Repetition of Doubtful Words Sketch, by an Underrated Author" Ep. 36

"French Lecture on Sheep-Aircraft" Ep. 2

"French Subtitled Film" Ep. 23

"Fruit Self-Defence class" Ep. 4

"Funny Bus Conductor Sketch" Ep. 30

"Furniture Playing Cricket" Ep. 20

"The Gathering Storm": "Dennis Moore, Episode 3," Ep. 37; "Frontiers of (Penguin) Medicine," Ep. 38

"Gavin Millar, Critic" Ep. 24

"George III" (and song) Ep. 4

"German V-Joke" Ep. 1

"Gestures to Indicate Pauses in a Televised Talk" Ep. 30

"The Golden Age of Ballooning" (and "Promos," and "The Golden Age of Colonic Irrigation") Ep. 40

"Good evening" and sit on a pig Ep. 1

"Gorilla Librarian" Ep. 10

Grandstand ("Match Highlights") Ep. 39

"Gumby Brain Specialist" (and "Gumby Brain Surgeons") Ep. 32

"Gumby Crooner" ("Make Believe") Ep. 9

"Gumby Flower Arranging" Ep. 25

Gumbys introduce sketches ("Architect Sketch," "Chemist Sketch") (link) Ep. 17

"Hamlet" (and Ophelia, and "Curtain Call") Ep. 43

"Harold the Clever Sheep" Ep. 2

"Has anyone anything else to say?" (conclusion) Ep. 12

"Hell's Grannies" documentary Ep. 8

"Here is the news" ("Art Gallery Strike") Ep. 25

"Hermits" Ep. 8

"A Highland Spokesman Offers Corrections" Ep. 16

"Hijacked Bus to Cuba" Ep. 16

"Hijacked Plane (to Luton)" Ep. 16

"Historical Impersonations" Ep. 13

"History of Warfare" (intro) Ep. 8

"HM the Queen still watching *The Virginian*" (caption) Ep. 26

"Homicidal Barber" Ep. 9

"Horse of the Year Show" (Kelly's flat) Ep. 28

"Hospital Run by RSM" Ep. 26

"Housing Project Built by Characters from Nineteenth-Century English Literature" Ep. 35

"How Far Can a Minister Fall?" Ep. 12

"How Not to Be Seen" (Government Public Service film) Ep. 24

"How to Do It" Ep. 28

"How to Feed a Goldfish" Ep. 26

"How to Fling an Otter" Ep. 6

"How to Give Up Being a Mason" Ep. 17

"How to Recognize Different Parts of the Body" Ep. 22

"How to Rid the World of All Known Diseases" (*How to Do It*) Ep. 28

"Hunting Film" Ep. 9

"Icelandic Honey Week" Ep. 45

"Icelandic Saga" (Erik Njorl) Ep. 27

"Ideal Loon Exhibition" Ep. 37

"The Idiot in Society" Ep. 20

"If—A Film by Mr. Dibley" (and *2001, Midnight Cowboy, Rear Window, Finian's Rainbow*) Ep. 19

"If I Were Not in the CID" (song) Ep. 3

"I'm a Lumberjack" (song) Ep. 9

"In 1914 the Balance of Power Lay in Ruin . . ." (link) Ep. 25

"In 1970 the British Empire lay in ruins . . ." Ep. 25

"Industrial Relations Reorganization's Human Pyramid" Ep. 19

"Inspector Dim of the Yard" Ep. 3

"Inspector Flying Fox of the Yard" (and Baboon, Leopard, Panther, and Thomson's Gazelle) Ep. 29

"Insurance Sketch" (interrupted by the Queen tuning in) Ep. 26

"Interesting People" Ep. 11

"Interesting Sport: All-In Cricket" Ep. 11

"Intermission: A History of Irish Agriculture" Ep. 13

"International Wife-Swapping" Ep. 39

"Interruptions" Ep. 19

"Interruptions by Undertakers: The World of History—The Black Death" Ep. 11

"Interview (w/Ludwig Grayson) in Filing Cabinet" Ep. 24

"Is the Third Test in Here?" (interruptions) Ep. 20

"Is There? . . . Life after Death?" Ep. 36

"It All Happened on the 11:20 from Heinault . . ." Ep. 24

"It's" Show (with Ringo Starr and Lulu) Ep. 28

"It's a Living" Ep. 19

"It's a Man's Life in the British Dental Association" Ep. 4

"It's a Man's Life in the Modern Army" (and "It's a dog's life" and "It's a pig's life . . .") Ep. 4

"It's a Tree with Arthur Tree" Ep. 10

"It's" Man intro/link clips: Ep. 1—Ocean, Poole Harbour); Ep. 2—Dunes; Ep. 3—Fern forest; Ep. 4—Thrown from cliff; Ep. 5—Rowboat; Ep. 6—Ringing phone; Ep. 7—Running, falling; Ep. 8—Anarchist's bomb; Ep. 9—Exploding forest; Ep. 10—Abattoir; Ep. 11—Hit by cars; Ep. 12—Pinball; Ep. 13—Coffin; Ep. 14—Zoo cage; Eps. 15–18, 20—Seaside (head shot only); Ep. 22—Bikini; Eps. 23–25—Seaside, head shot; Ep. 27— Foliage background (head shot only); Ep. 28—Foliage, head shot (nighttime); Eps. 29–33—Foliage, head shot; Ep. 35—Jersey field; Ep. 36—Foliage, head shot; Ep. 37—Boxing ring; Eps. 38–39—Foliage, head shot; Ep. 42—Boxing ring

"It's the Arts" Eps. 1, 6

"It's the Mind: Déjà vu" Ep. 16

"It's Wolfgang Amadeus Mozart" Ep. 1

"I won't ruin this sketch for a pound" (link) Ep. 35

"Jack in a Box" (song) Ep. 34

"Jarrow—New Year's Eve 1911" ("Spanish Inquisition") Ep. 15

"Job Hunter" Ep. 24

"Jerusalem" (song: "And did those feet . . .") Ep. 8

"Johann Gambolputty . . . von Hautkopf of Ulm" Ep. 6

"Jokes and Novelties Salesman" Ep. 15

"Judging" (JP Beauty Pageant) Ep. 37

"Julius Caesar on an Aldis Lamp" Ep. 15

"Jungle Restaurant" Ep. 29

"Kami-kaze Advice Centre" Ep. 38

"Kamikaze Scotsmen" Ep. 38

"Karl Marx and Che Guevara, Kissing" (and in bed) Ep. 25

"Ken Buddha as His Inflatable Knees" Ep. 9
"Ken Russell's *Gardening Club*" Ep. 33
"Ken Russell's *Gardening Club* (1958)" Ep. 29
"Ken Shabby" (and "the story so far") Ep. 12
"Kilimanjaro Expedition (Double Vision)" Ep. 9
"Killer Sheep" Ep. 20
Knight-and-rubber-chicken (link) Eps. 2, 3, 5, 7, 9, 13

"Language Laboratory" Ep. 31
"The Larch" Ep. 3
"Last Five Miles of the M2" Ep. 42
"League for Fighting Chartered Accountancy" Ep. 10
"Leapy Lee" Ep. 21
"Leave Your Radio On during the Night" Ep. 7
"Legendary Batsmen of the Kalahari" Ep. 45
"Le Marche Futile" Ep. 14
"Lemming of the BDA" Ep. 4
"Let's Talk Ant" (University of the Air) Ep. 41
"Letters" (cannibalism) Ep. 26
"Letters" ("I object to . . .") Ep. 13
"Letters ('Lavatorial Humour'; 'Mary Bignall'; 'Cheap Laughs')" Ep. 11
"Letters" (self-destruction) Ep. 12
"Letters to *Daily Mirror*" Ep. 10
"Licence Fees" Eps. 7, 20
"Life and Death Struggles" Ep. 30
"Life of Sir Philip Sidney" Ep. 36
"*Life of Tschaikowsky*" Ep. 28
"Lifeboat" (cannibalism) Ep. 26
"Lifeboat" ("It's not a lifeboat . . .") Ep. 33
"*Light Entertainment Awards*" Ep. 39
"Linkman at the snack bar" (and on the bus) Ep. 18
"Literary Football Discussion" Ep. 11
"Live from Epsom" Ep. 43
"Live from the Grill-o-Mat Snack Bar, Paignton" Ep. 18
"Living Room on Pavement" Ep. 17
"Long John Silver Impersonators v. Bournemouth Gynaecologists" Ep. 23
"Lost World of Roiurama" Ep. 29
"Louis XIV" Ep. 40
"Lumberjack Song" Ep. 9
"Lupins" Ep. 37

"M1 Interchange Built by Characters from *Paradise Lost*" Ep. 35
"Man-Powered Flight" (intro) Ep. 15
"Man Turns into Scotsman!" Ep. 7
"Man Who Collects Birdwatcher's Eggs" Ep. 26
"Man Who Contradicts People" Ep. 22
"Man Who Finishes Other People's Sentences" Ep. 45
"Man Who Is Alternately Rude and Polite" Ep. 18
"Man Who Makes People Laugh Uncontrollably" Ep. 30
"Man Who Says Things in a Very Roundabout Way" Ep. 26

"The Man Who Says Words in the Wrong Order" ("Thripshaw's Disease") Ep. 36
"Man Who Speaks Only the Beginnings of Words" (and "Middles" and "Ends") Ep. 26
"Man Who Talks in Anagrams" Ep. 30
"Man with a Stoat through His Head" (link) Ep. 26
"Man with a Tape Recorder up His Nose" (and up "His Brother's Nose") Ep. 9
"Man with Three Buttocks" Ep. 2
"Man with Two Noses" Ep. 2
"Marriage Guidance Counsellor" (Deirdre and Arthur Pewtey) Ep. 2
"Mary Recruitment Office" Ep. 30
"*Match of the Day*: Erotic Film" Ep. 5; "Players Hugging/Kissing," Ep. 32
"Me Doctor" Ep. 13
"Merchant Banker" (at Slater-Nazi) Ep. 30
"*The Mill on the Floss*" (by balloon) Ep. 40
"Minehead By-Election" Ep. 12
"Minister for Not Listening to People" Ep. 32
"Ministry of Silly Walks" Ep. 14
"*Molluscs*—'Live' TV Documentary" Ep. 32
"Money Programme" Ep. 29
Monsters dance (animated link) to "Jack in a Box" (song) Ep. 34
"Montgolfier Brothers" Ep. 40
"Morning Teas on the Lifeboat" Ep. 33
"*Mortuary Hour*" Ep. 35
"Mosquito Hunters" Ep. 21
"*Most Awful Family in Britain*" Ep. 45
"Motor Insurance Sketch" (Mr. Devious) Ep. 17
"Mountaineering Sketch" Ep. 26
"The Mouse Problem" (and Vox Pops) Ep. 2
"Mr. and Mrs. Brian Norris' Ford Popular" Ep. 28
"Mr. and Mrs. Git" (and the "nice version") Ep. 21
"Mr. Attila the Hun" (Who is actually Alexander the Great) Ep. 13
"Mr. Bent Is in Our Durham Studios" Ep. 24
"Mr. Gulliver Becomes Clodagh Rogers Becomes Leon Trotsky Becomes Eartha Kitt" Ep. 34
"Mr. Hilter" (and Ron Vibbentrop, Bimmler) Ep. 12
"*Mr. Neutron*" ("Loves Mrs. S.C.U.M.") Ep. 44
"Mr. Neville Shunte" Ep. 24
"Mr. Pither" (*Cycling Tour*) Ep. 34
"Mrs. Nigger-Baiter Explodes" Ep. 28
"Mrs. Premise and Mrs. Conclusion Visit Jean-Paul Sartre" Ep. 27
"Mrs. Thing and Mrs. Entity" Ep. 21
"Music Critic and Famous Hairdresser" Ep. 28
"Must be one of them crackpot religions" (link) Ep. 24
"Mystico and Janet—Flats Built by Hypnosis" Ep. 35

"*Nationwide*" Ep. 43
"Naughty Bits" Ep. 22
"Neurotic Announcer" Ep. 30

"New Brain from Curry's" Ep. 39
"New Cooker Sketch" Ep. 14
"News for Parrots" (and Wombats, Gibbons) Ep. 20
"News on the Coal Strikes" Ep. 26
"The News with Richard Baker": Ep. 30—Vision Only; Ep. 33—"Lemon curry?"
"Newsflash" (Germans) Ep. 42
"Njorl's Saga" (and Parts II, III, and IV) Ep. 27
"Non-Illegal Robbery" Ep. 6
"North Malden Icelandic Society" Ep. 27
"No Time to Lose" (and Advice Centre) Ep. 38
"Notlob" Ep. 8
"Nude Organist" (intro/link) Ep. 27—Scottish highland; Eps. 28 and 29—Studio backstage; Ep. 30—Dungeonesque drawing room; Ep. 31—Church organ; Ep. 32—Battlefield; Ep. 33—Loses tux on stage; Ep. 35—Jersey field; Ep. 36—Animated and (live) Church organ; Ep. 37—Boxing ring; Ep. 38—Studio backstage; Ep. 39—Tilled field; Ep. 42—Boxing ring
"Nun KO" (link) Ep. 21

"The Office of Sir George Head, O.B.E." Ep. 9
"Old Lady Snoopers" Ep. 33
"Olympic Hide-and-Seek Finals" Ep. 35
"One More Minute of *Monty Python's Flying Circus*" Ep. 29
"Operating Theatre (Squatters)" Ep. 13
"Oscar Wilde Sketch" Ep. 39
"Other Religions" Ep. 24
"Our Eamonn" Ep. 31

"The Pantomime Horse Is a Secret Agent Film" Ep. 30
"Pantomime horses fight to the death" (and Goose, Princess Margaret) Ep. 30
"Part 2: Sheep" (Rustic, City Gent, and Flying Sheep) Ep. 2
"Part 2: The Llama" (Live from Golders Green) Ep. 9
"Party Hints with Veronica Smalls" Ep. 31
"Party Political Broadcast (Choreographed)" Ep. 38
"A Party Political Broadcast on Behalf of the Liberal Party" Ep. 45
"A Party Political Broadcast on Behalf of the Norwegian Party" Ep. 40
"A Party Political Broadcast on Behalf of the Wood Party" Ep. 12
"Pasolini's Film *The Third Test Match*" Ep. 39
"Penguins" (as BBC Programme Planners, and world domination) Ep. 38
"Pepperpots and French People" Ep. 2
"Pepperpots at War" Ep. 32
"Pepperpots in a Submarine" Ep. 26
"Personally I prefer more classical dishes" (link) Ep. 19
"Pet Conversions" Ep. 10
"Philip Jenkinson on Cheese Westerns" (and his death) Ep. 33

"Photos of Uncle Ted" Ep. 15
"Picasso/Cycling Race (Modern Artists at the Tolworth Roundabout)" Ep. 1
Pig head (link) Ep. 1
"Pigs 3 Nelson 1" Ep. 1
"Piranha Brothers" Ep. 14
"Playground Interview" Ep. 3
"The Poet McTeagle" Ep. 16
"Poet Reader, Wombat Harness" Ep. 17
"Poets" Ep. 17
"Police Constable Pan-Am" Eps. 17, 27
"Police Helmets" Ep. 43
"Police Raid" Ep. 5
"Police Station (Silly Voices)" Ep. 12
"Policeman Near Rottingdeans" ("Come back to my place") Ep. 13
"Policemen Make Wonderful Friends" Ep. 6
"Poofy Judges" Ep. 21
"Pornographic Bookshop" Ep. 36
"Post Box Ceremony" Ep. 44
"Praline's Current Affairs Show" (interrupted) Ep. 18
"Prejudice" Ep. 37
"Prices on the Planet Algon" Ep. 35
"Probe-Around on Crime" Ep. 13
"Prof. R. J. Gumby and Friends" Ep. 11
"Programme Titles Conference" Ep. 42
"Prime Minister" Ep. 44
"Psychiatrist Milkman" (and Complaints) Ep. 16
"Psychiatry—Silly Sketch" Ep. 13
"The Public Are Idiots" (link) Ep. 42
"Puss in Boots" Ep. 28

"Queen Victoria Handicap" Ep. 43
"Queen Victoria und Her Late Husband" Ep. 41
"The Queen Will Be Watching" Ep. 26

"RAF Banter" Ep. 42
"Racing Pigeon Fanciers" Ep. 26
"Radio 4 Explodes" Ep. 22
"Radio Times Man Narration" Ep. 44
Railway footage and Hove signal box (link) Ep. 12
"Ramsay MacDonald Striptease" Ep. 24
"Ratcatcher" (and "Chairman of the Test Selection Committee") Ep. 20
"Raymond Luxury Yacht" Ep. 19
"Red Indian in Theatre" Ep. 6
Redcoat and knight (link) Ep. 3
"Redgauntlet" ("A Book at Bedtime") Ep. 38
"Referee Interrupting" Ep. 21
Referee whistle (link) Eps. 1, 3, 4
"Refreshment Room at Bletchley" Ep. 9
"Registrar (Wife Swap)" Ep. 21
"Registry Office" (the five-man couple) Ep. 19
"Remains of Sir Alan Waddle" Ep. 39
"Repeating/Skipping Groove" Ep. 24

"Request Death" Ep. 1

"Restaurant Sketch (Abuse and Cannibalism)" Ep. 13

"Restaurant Sketch" Ep. 3

"Ricky Pule's Salon" (advert) Ep. 31

"Rival Documentaries" Ep. 38

"Rogue Cheddar (1967)" Ep. 33

"Ron Obvious" Ep. 10

"A Room in Polonius's House" (Sports Highlights) Ep. 43

"Royal Episode Thirteen" Ep. 26

"Royal Hospital for Overacting" Ep. 25

"Royal Philharmonic Goes to the Bathroom" Ep. 11

Royal Philharmonic (photo link) Ep. 11

"Rugby Commentary" ("And what about China?") Ep. 23

"Salad Days" Ep. 33

"Salvation Fuzz" (Church Police) Ep. 29

"Sandy Wilson's version of *The Devils*" Ep. 31

"School Prize-Giving" (by the Bishops of East Anglia) Ep. 19

"Schoolboys' Life Assurance Company" Ep. 28

"Schoolyard Interviews" ("More fairy stories about the police") Ep. 13

"Science Fiction Sketch" Ep. 7

"Scoreboard with Eddie Waring" Ep. 1

"Scott of the Antarctic" Ep. 23

"Scott of the Sahara" Ep. 23

"Scotsman on a Horse" Eps. 2, 6

"Seashore Interlude" (link) Ep. 33

"Secret Service Dentists" Ep. 4

"Secretary of State Striptease" (and the Social Security Register belly dance) Ep. 20

"Seduced Milkmen" Ep. 3

"Semaphore Version of *Wuthering Heights*" Ep. 15

"Sentencing a Naughty Judge" Ep. 15

"Seven Brides for Seven Brothers" (school version) Ep. 18

"Sexy Doctor's Examination" Ep. 20

"She's watching *News at Ten*" Ep. 26

"Sherry-Drinking Vicar" Ep. 36

Shoot the pig (link) Ep. 1

"Show Jumping (Musical)" Ep. 42

"The Show So Far" Ep. 33

"Signal Box Somewhere Near Hove" Ep. 12

"Silliest Interview We've Ever Done" ("Magna Carta") Ep. 32

"Silly Doctor Sketch (Immediately Abandoned)" Ep. 21

"Silly Disturbances (The Rev. Arthur Belling)" Ep. 36

"Silly Job Interview" (Management Training Course) Ep. 5

"Silly Noises" Ep. 36

"Silly walkers silent film" Ep. 14

"Similar Pet Shop in Bolton" Ep. 8

"Sinking Ocean Liner" Ep. 28

"Six More Minutes of *Monty Python's Flying Circus*" Ep. 29

"Slide No. 1: The Larch" Ep. 3

"Slide No. 3: The Larch and the Horse Chestnut" Ep. 3

"Smolensk" Ep. 34

"Smuggler" Ep. 5

"Soap Powder Commercial" Ep. 26

"Society for Putting Things on Top of Other Things" Ep. 18

"So much for pathos" Ep. 2

"Sotheby's Sells Empty Paintings" Ep. 25

"Spam" (and "Historian") Ep. 25

"Spanish Inquisition" Ep. 15

"Spectrum—Talking about Things" Ep. 12

Spiny Norman looks for Dinsdale (links) Eps. 14, 26

"Spot the Loony" Ep. 38

"St. John Limbo, Poetry Expert" Ep. 16

"Stock Exchange Report" Ep. 27

"Stolen Newsreader" Ep. 3

Stonehenge sacrifice (link) Ep. 13

"Storage Jars" Ep. 33

"Strangers in the Night" Ep. 10

"Sviatoslav Richter performs Tschaikowsky" Ep. 28

"Take Your Pick" Ep. 20

"A Tale of Two Cities for Parrots" Ep. 20

"Tape Recorded Love" Ep. 26

"Tax on Thingy" Ep. 15

"Tchaikovsky XXI Coverage" Ep. 28

"Teddy Salad (CIA Agent)" Ep. 44

"Ten Seconds of Sex" Ep. 35

"Tennis Scientists" Ep. 38

"Test Match" ("Well not-played") Ep. 20

"Thames TV Introduction" Ep. 39

"Theory on Brontosauruses by Anne Elk (Miss)" Ep. 31

"There Is Nothing Quite So Wonderful as Money" (song) Ep. 29

"There will now be a medium-sized intermission" (and "short" and "whopping-sized") Ep. 13

"There's Been a Murder" Ep. 22

"Thripshaw's Disease" (and film clips, t-shirts) Ep. 36

"Third-Tallest Mayor in Derby History" Ep. 23

"This Is satire" (Pepperpot link) Ep. 10

"The Time on BBC 1" Ep. 19

"Timmy Williams Coffee Time" Ep. 19

"Toad Elevating Moment" Ep. 26

"Tobacconists (Suggestive Notice Board)" Ep. 14

"Today in Britain" (groupies) Ep. 20

"Today in Parliament" Eps. 20, 32

"Tory Housewives Clean-Up Campaign" Ep. 32

Tough interviewers (link) Ep. 1

"Toupee Hall" Ep. 41

"Tourist Rant" ("Watney's Red Barrel") Ep. 31

"Towards the Russian bolder" Ep. 38

Tower flat striptease (intro) Ep. 16

"Travel Agent's Office" (The Tourist Rant) Ep. 31

"Trim Jeans Theatre" Ep. 28

"Tripod and Missile Float" Ep. 44

"Trivializing the War" Ep. 42

"Trotsky" Ep. 34

"Tudor Jobs Agency" Ep. 36

"Tunnelling from Godalming to Mercury" Ep. 10

"TV4 or Not TV4 Discussion" (*Great Debate*) Ep. 37

"Twentieth-Century Vole" Ep. 6

"Undertaker's Film(s)" Ep. 11

"Undertaker's Sketch" Ep. 26

"Undressing in Public" Ep. 4

"Unexploded Scotsman" Ep. 38

Uninteresting tales of the sea (link) Ep. 22

"Unoccupied Britain 1970" Ep. 8

"Unsuccessful Encyclopaedia Salesmen" Ep. 5

"Up Your Pavement" Ep. 42

"Upperclass Twit of the Year" Ep. 12

"Vicar Tied to Railroad Tracks" (link) Ep. 7

"Vicar Who Is Also a Salesman" Ep. 28

Victorian "Poetry Reading (Ants)" Ep. 41

"Visconti Career Review" Ep. 29

"Visitors" Ep. 9

"Visitors from Coventry" Ep. 12

"Vocational Guidance Counsellor (Chartered Accountant)" Ep. 10

"Vox Pops": "After-shave," Ep. 17; "Archbishops," Ep. 24; "Customs policies," Ep. 5; "Dear BBC," Ep. 5; "Full Frontal Nudity," Ep. 8; "I'd like to see . . .," Ep. 13; "Illegal things," Ep. 6; "National Bocialism," Ep. 12; "Politicians," Ep. 20; "Predictable," Ep. 10; "Realistic or Not?," Ep. 24; "Sex on the television," Ep. 9; "Silly voices," Ep. 12; "Taxation," Ep. 15

"Wacky Queen" film Ep. 2

"Wainscotting" ("A little Dorset village") Ep. 20

"Walk to Stonehenge" Ep. 45

"Walking Tree of Dahomey" Ep. 45

"Walk-On Part in Sketch" Ep. 10

"Weepy Judges" Ep. 37

"We'll be continuing with *Monty Python's Flying Circus* . . ." (link) Ep. 35

"What other ways are there of recognizing a Mason?" Ep. 17

"What the Stars Foretell" Ep. 37

What's on BBC 2" Ep. 5

"When Does a Dream Begin?" (song) Ep. 42

"'Where to Put Edward Heath's Statue' Contest" Ep. 22

"Whicker Island" Ep. 27

"Whicker's World" Ep. 27

"Whizzo Butter and a Dead Crab, On-the-Street Interview" Ep. 1

"Wink Wink, Nudge Nudge" Ep. 3

"Woody and Tinny Words" Ep. 42

Women's Institute footage (links) Eps. 2, 3, 5, 21

"Words that are not to be used again on this program" Ep. 17

"Working-Class Playwright" Ep. 2

The World around Us" Ep. 2

"World Domination T-Shirts" Ep. 44

"World's Deadliest Joke" Ep. 1

"Wrestling Epilogue: A Question of Belief" Ep. 2

"Writer/Dentist: *The Twelve Caesars"* Ep. 24

"Young Men's Anti-Christian Association" (YMACA) Ep. 34

"You're No Fun Anymore" (vignettes) Ep. 7

"Ypres—1914" (and "Abandoned") Ep. 25

"Yummy, Yummy" (song) Ep. 24

"Zeppelin" ("It's not a balloon!") Ep. 40

Bibliography

Abrams, Mark. "The Opinion Polls and the 1970 British General Election." *Public Opinion Quarterly* 34, no. 3 (1970): 317–24.

Abrams, M.H. *A Glossary of Literary Terms.* 4th ed. New York: Holt, Rinehart and Winston, 1981.

Ackroyd, Peter. *Albion.* London: Doubleday, 2003.

———. *J.M.W. Turner.* New York: Nan A. Talese, 2006.

———. *London: The Biography.* London: Doubleday, 2000.

Aldgate, Anthony. *Censorship and the Permissive Society: British Cinema and Theatre, 1955–1965.* London: Oxford University Press, 1995.

Aldous, Richard. *Macmillan, Eisenhower and the Cold War.* Dublin, Ireland: Four Courts Press, 2005.

Allen, Grant. *What's Bred in the Bone.* New York: Knight & Brown, 1898.

Altman, Rick. *The American Film Musical.* Bloomington: Indiana University Press, 1989.

Altman, Wilfred. "Harder Fight to Sell Air Time." *Times,* 2 July 1968: xi.

Anderson, Ronald, and Anne Koval. *James McNeill Whistler: Beyond the Myth.* London: John Murray, 1994.

Andors, Stephen. "Mao and Marx: A Comment." *Modern China* 3, no. 4 (1977): 427–33.

Araloff, Simon. "The Internal Corps—The Kremlin's Private Army." Global Challenges Research website: http://www.axisglobe.com/article.asp?article=178. Accessed 18 November 2006.

Argyle, John Michael. *Psychology and Social Problems.* London: Methuen, 1964.

Attfield, Judy. *Utility Reassessed: The Role of Ethics in the Practice of Design.* Manchester, NY: Manchester University Press, 1999.

"Attila" *World Encyclopedia.* Philip's, 2005. *Oxford Reference Online.* Oxford University Press. Brigham Young University (BYU). http://www.oxfordreference.com/views/ENTRY.html?subview=Main&entry=t142.e793. Accessed 1 May 2006.

Aylett, Glenn. "The Sporting Class." Transdiffusion Broadcasting System website: http://www.transdiffusion.org/emc/worldofsport/the_sporting_cl.php. Accessed 17 October 2006.

Bakhtin, Mikhail. *Rabelais and His World.* Trans. Helene Iswolsky. Bloomington: Indiana University Press, 1984.

Baldick, Chris. *Oxford Concise Dictionary of Literary Terms.* Oxford: Oxford University Press, 2001.

Baldwin, T.W. *Organisation and Personnel of the Shakespearean Company.* Princeton: Princeton University Press, 1927.

Barker, Ronnie. *Ooh-La-La: The Ladies of Paris.* London: Hodder & Stoughton, 1983.

———. *Ronnie Barker's Book of Bathing Beauties.* London: Hodder & Stoughton, 1974.

———. *Ronnie Barker's Book of Boudoir Beauties.* London: Coronet, 1975.

Barrie, J.M. *What Every Woman Knows.* New York: Scribner's, 1918.

Beck, Jerry. *Looney Tunes and Merrie Melodies: A Complete Illustrated Guide to the Warner Bros. Cartoons.* New York: Henry Holt, 1989.

Beerbohm, Max. *Zuleika Dobson.* New York: John Lane, 1911.

Benjamin, Walter. *Illuminations.* New York: Houghton Mifflin Harcourt, 1968.

———. "The Work of Art in the Age of Mechanical Reproduction." *Film Theory and Criticism,* 3rd ed. New York: Oxford UP, 1985.

Bennett, Alan, Peter Cook, Jonathan Miller, and Dudley Moore. *Beyond the Fringe.* New York: Random House, 1963.

Bergeron, David M. "Shakespeare Makes History: *2 Henry IV.*" *Studies in English Literature* 31, no. 2 (1991): 231–45.

Bergson, Henri. *The Creative Mind: An Introduction to Metaphysics.* 1946. New York: Dover, 2007.

———. "Laughter: An Essay on the Meaning of the Comic." Trans. Brereton and Rothwell. London: Macmillan, 1911.

Biao, Lin. "Advance Along the Road Opened up by the October Socialist Revolution." Foreign Languages Press, 1967.

Bird, Peter A. *First Food Empire: A History of J. Lyons & Co.* Chichester: Phillimore, 2000.

Bishop, Ellen. "Bakhtin, Carnival and Comedy: The New Grotesque in Monty Python and the Holy Grail." *Film Criticism* 15, no. 1 (1990): 49–64.

Blake, William. *Milton: A Poem*. France: Trianon Press, 1815.

Bogle, Donald. *Toms, Coons, Mulattoes, Mammies, & Bucks*. New York: Continuum International, 2003.

Bond, Maurice Francis. *The Gentleman Usher of the Black Rod*. London: HMSO, 1976.

Boose, Lynda. "Let It Be Hid: The Pornographic Aesthetic of Shakespeare's *Othello*." *Women, Violence, and English Renaissance Literature*. Ed. Linda Woodbridge and Sharon Beehler, *Medieval and Renaissance Texts and Studies*. Phoenix: Arizona State University Press, 2003, 34–58.

Bordwell, David, Janet Staiger, and Kristin Thompson. *The Classical Hollywood Cinema*. London, Melbourne, and Henley: Routledge and Kegan Paul, 1985.

Bordwell, David, and Kristin Thompson. *Narration in the Fiction Film*. University of Wisconsin Press, 1985.

"Boxing's Loss, Too." *Boxing Monthly* 10, no. 3 (July 1998).

Bradman, Sir Don. *The Art of Cricket*. London: Hodder & Stoughton, 1990.

Brettell, Richard R. *Modern Art 1851–1929*. London: Oxford University Press, 1999.

Brontë, Anne. *The Tenant of Wildfell Hall*. Whitefish, MT: Kessinger, 2004.

Brontë, Emily. *Wuthering Heights*. 1847. New York: Bantam, 1983.

Browning, Robert. *Home Thoughts, from Abroad*. 1845. http://www.emule.com/poetry/?page=poem&poem=297. Accessed 28 November 2007.

Bruce-Briggs, B. *Supergenius: The Mega-Worlds of Herman Khan*. North American Policy Press, 2000.

Bryk, William. "Defender of the Faith." *The New York Press*. 16 March 2000.

Buscombe, Edward. *British Television: A Reader*. Oxford: Oxford University Press, 2000.

Butler, David, and Michael Pinto-Duschinsky. *The British General Election of 1970*. London: Macmillan, 1971.

Caesar, Julius. *Commentarii De Bello Gallico*. http://www.gutenberg.org/etext/10657. Accessed 26 November 2007.

Cambridge History of English and American Literature, The. New York: Putnam, 1907–1921.

Campbell, John. *Edward Heath: A Biography*. London: Jonathan Cape, 1993.

Canetti, Elias, and Michael Hofmann. *Party in the Blitz: The English Years*. New York: New Directions, 2005.

Carpenter, Humphrey. *The Angry Young Men: A Literary Comedy of the 1950s*. London: Penguin, 2004.

———. *A Great Silly Grin: The British Satire Boom of the 1960s*. London: Da Capo Press, 2003.

———. *That Was Satire, That Was*. London: Victor Gollancz, 2000.

Catholic Encyclopedia, The. http://www.catholic.org/encyclopedia. Accessed 19 November 2007.

Chamberlain, Gethin. "Threatened Regiments Take Courage from Past." *The Scotsman*. 10 July 2004. http://thescotsman.scotsman.com/index.cfm?id=789542004. Accessed 25 January 2006.

Chandler, Raymond. "Smart Aleck Kill." *Black Mask* (July 1934): 64.

Chapman, George, Ben Jonson, and John Marston. *Eastward Ho*. Ed. Schelling. 1903. Complete digital reproduction at http://books.google.com/books?as_brr=1&id=qlL1LVR0xj8C&vid=OCLC05138166&jtp=1. Accessed 27 November 2007.

Chapman, Graham, John Cleese, Terry Gilliam, Eric Idle, Terry Jones, and Michael Palin. *The Complete Monty Python's Flying Circus: All the Words*, 2 vols. New York: Pantheon, 1989.

Chapman, Graham et al. *The Monty Python Song Book*. New York: Harper Trade, 1995.

———. *Monty Python's Big Red Book*. New York: Contemporary Books, 1980.

Chesneau, Roger. *Aircraft Carriers of the World, 1914 to the Present: An Illustrated Encyclopedia*. Annapolis: Naval Institute Press, 1984.

Christie, Ian. *Gilliam on Gilliam*. London: Faber and Faber, 1999.

Clark, Kenneth. *Civilization: A Personal View*. New York: Harper & Row, 1970.

Clarke, Peter. *Hope and Glory: Britain 1900–1990*. London: Penguin, 1996.

Cockerell, Michael. *Live from Number 10: The Inside Story of Prime Ministers and Television*. London: Faber, 1989.

Coleman, Alice. *Utopia on Trial: Vision and Reality in Planned Housing*. London: Hilary Shipman, 1985.

Colledge, J.J. *Ships of the Royal Navy*. London: Chatham, 1969.

The Complete Works of Shakespeare and Monty Python. Eds. Graham Chapman, et al. London: Methuen, 1981.

Cook, Chris, and John Stevenson, eds. *Modern British History: 1714–2001*. London: Longman, 2001.

Cook, Peter. *Tragically I Was an Only Twin*. New York: St. Martin's, 2003.

Corner, John. *Popular Television in Britain: Studies in Cultural History*. London: BFI, 1991.

Cox, John D., and David Scott Kastan, eds. *A New History of Early English Drama*. New York: Columbia University Press, 1997.

Crab, Roger. *The English Hermite, or, Wonder of This Age*. London, 1655. http://wwwlib.umi.com/eebo/image/42017 (Huntington Library reproduction).

Crawford, Robert. *The Savage and the City in the Work of T.S. Eliot*. Oxford: Oxford University Press, 1991.

Creaton, Heather. *Sources for the History of London 1939–45*. London: British Records Association, 1998.

Crisell, Andrew. *An Introductory History of British Broadcasting*. New York: Routledge, 2002.

———. "Filth, Sedition and Blasphemy: The Rise and Fall of Television Satire." *Popular Television in Britain: Studies in Cultural History*. Ed. John Corner. London: BFI, 1991.

Crisp, Quentin. *The Naked Civil Servant*. London: Penguin, 1997.

Crowe, Brian L. "British Entry into the Common Market: A British View." *Law and Contemporary Problems* 37, no. 2 (Spring 1972): 228–34.

Dale, Iain, ed., *Labour Party General Election Manifestos, 1900–1997*. London: Routledge, 2000.

Davis, John. "The London Drug Scene and the Making of Drug Policy, 1965–73." *Twentieth-Century British History* 17, no. 1 (2006): 26–49.

DeAndrea, William L. *Encyclopedia Mysteriosa: A Comprehensive Guide to the Art of Detection in Print, Film, Radio, and Television*. New York: Prentice Hall, 1994.

Deighton, Len. *Blood, Tears and Folly: An Objective Look at World War II*. New York: HarperCollins, 1993.

Dekker, Thomas. *The Shoemaker's Holiday. Drama of the English Renaissance: The Tudor Period*. Ed. Russell A. Fraser and Norman Rabkin. New York: Macmillan, 1976.

D'Emilio, John. *Sexual Politics, Sexual Communities*. Chicago: University of Chicago Press, 1983.

Denning, Lord Alfred Thompson. *Lord Denning's Report, Presented to Parliament by the Prime Minister by Command of Her Majesty*. London: HMSO, 1963.

De Syon, Guillaume. *Zeppelin!: Germany and the Airship, 1900–1939*. Baltimore: Johns Hopkins University Press, 2002.

Deutscher, Isaac. *The Prophet Outcast: Trotsky 1929–1940*. New York: Verso, 2003.

De Vries, Jan Vredeman. *Perspective*. New York: Dover, 1968.

Diamond, John. "Once I Was British." *Times*, 14 January 1995: 1.

Dictionary of National Biography. Oxford: Oxford University Press, 2004.

Dixon, T. J. "The Civil Service Syndrome." *Management Today* (May 1980): 74–79, 154, 158, 162.

Dodge, Mabel. "Speculations, or Post-Impressionism in Prose." *Arts and Decoration* (March 1913).

Dollimore, Jonathan, and Alan Sinfield, eds. *Political Shakespeare: Essays in Cultural Materialism*. Manchester: Manchester University Press, 1999.

Donald, David, ed. *Divided We Fought: A Pictorial History of the Civil War 1861–1865*. New York: Macmillan, 1952.

Dover, Harriet. *Home Front Furniture*. England: Scolar Press, 1991.

Doyle, Arthur Conan. *The Lost World*. New York: Tor Classics, 1997.

Drabble, Margaret. *For Queen and Country: Britain in the Victorian Age*. New York: Seabury Press, 1978.

———. *The Oxford Companion to English Literature*. 5th ed. Oxford: Oxford University Press, 1985.

Duberman, Martin. *Stonewall*. New York: Dutton, 1993.

Dynes, Wayne. *Homosexuality: A Research Guide*. New York: Taylor and Francis, 1987.

Ebert, Roger. *Julius Caesar*. 17 March 1971. http://rogerebert.suntimes.com/apps/pbcs.dll/article?AID=/19710317/REVIEWS/103170301/1023. Accessed 28 November 2007.

Eirik the Red and Other Icelandic Sagas. London: Oxford University Press, 1999.

Eliot, T.S. *Murder in the Cathedral*. 1935. San Diego: HBJ, 1988.

———. "The Waste Land." 1922. *The Norton Anthology of World Masterpieces*. Vol. 2, 5th ed. Ed. Maynard Mack et al. New York and London: Norton, 1985.

Ellsworth, Scott. "Interview with Amil Gargano." *Advertising and Society Review* 2, no. 4 (2001). Website: http://muse.jhu.edu/journals/asr/archives/archives.html. Accessed 18 January 2006.

Esher, Lionel. *A Broken Wave: The Rebuilding of England, 1940–1980*. London: Allen Lane, 1981.

Evans, G. Blakemore, ed. *The Riverside Shakespeare*. New York: Houghton Mifflin, 1974.

Evans, Peter. *Peter Sellers: The Mask behind the Mask*. New York: Signet, 1968.

Evelyn, John. *The Diary of John Evelyn*. Trans. E.S. de Beer. Oxford: Oxford, 1955.

Eyewitness: 1940–1979. Wr. Joanna Bourke, narr. Tim Pigott-Smith. CD. BBC Books, 2005.

Fielding, Henry. *Tom Thumb (The Tragedy of Tragedies)*. http://www.gutenberg.org/etext/6828. Accessed 28 November 2007.

Fraser, Rebecca. *The Story of Britain*. New York: W.W. Norton, 2003.

Fraser, Russell, and Norman Rabkin, eds. *Drama of the English Renaissance, I and II*. New York: Macmillan, 1976.

Freedman, Des. "Modernising the BBC: Wilson's Government and Television, 1964–66." *Contemporary British History* 15, no. 1 (Spring 2001): 21–40.

Fuller, Graham. "Winged Hope." *Kes* (1969) Criterion Collection DVD liner notes.

Gable, Jo. *The Tuppenny Punch and Judy Show—25 Years of TV Commercials*. London: Michael Joseph, 1980.

Gabler, Neal. *An Empire of Their Own: How the Jews Invented Hollywood*. New York: Random House, 1989.

Gage, John. "The Distinctness of Turner." *Journal of the Royal Society of Arts* 123 (1975): 448–57.

Gardner's Art through the Ages, 7th ed. Horst de la Croix and Richard Tansey, eds. New York: Harcourt Brace Jovanovich, 1980.

Genette, Gérard. *Narrative Discourse: An Essay in Method*. Ithaca, NY: Cornell University Press, 1980.

Geographers' A to Z Street Atlas of London. Kent, Seven Oaks: Geographers' Map Co., 1968.

"Germany's Heart: The Modern Taboo." Interview with Jurgen Syberberg in *NPQ* 10, no. 1 (Winter 1993).

Giddings, Robert, and Keith Selby. *The Classic Serial on Television and Radio*. New York: Palgrave-Macmillan, 2001.

Gilbert, Martin. *The First World War*. New York: Owl Books, 2004.

Gilbert, W.S., and Arthur Sullivan. *The Pirates of Penzance*. 1879.

Giles, Colum. *Yorkshire Textile Mills, 1770–1930*. London: HMSO, 1992.

Gilliam, Terry. *Gilliam on Gilliam*. Ed. Ian Christie. London: Faber and Faber, 1999.

Gillispie, Charles. *The Montgolfier Brothers and the Invention of Aviation, 1783–1784*. Princeton, NJ: Princeton University Press, 1983.

Glendinning, Miles, and Stefan Muthesius. *Tower Block: Modern Public Housing in England, Scotland, Wales and Northern Ireland*. New Haven: Yale University Press, 1994.

Goon Show, The. Starring Spike Milligan, Peter Sellers, and Harry Secombe, 1951–1960. "*The Goon Show* Old Time Radio MP3 Collection," 2007.

Gordon, David. "Shavian Comedy and the Shadow of Wilde." *The Cambridge Companion to George Bernard Shaw*. Ed. Christopher Innes. Cambridge: Cambridge University Press, 1998.

Grafton, Roger, and Roger Wilmut. *The Goon Show Companion: A History and Goonography*. London: Robson, 1976.

Gray, Andy, with Jim Drewett. *Flat Back Four: The Tactical Game*. London: Macmillan, 1998.

Greene, Robert. *Morando, the Tritameron of Love. The Life and Complete Works in Prose and Verse of Robert Greene*. New York: Russell & Russell, 1964.

Grimm's Teutonic Mythology. Trans. James Steven Stallybrass. London: Routledge, 1999.

Gurr, Andrew. *The Shakespearean Stage, 1574–1642*. Cambridge: Cambridge University Press, 1992.

Hamilton, A.C., ed. *The Faerie Queene*. London and New York: Longman, 1977.

———. *The Spenser Encyclopedia*. Toronto: Toronto University Press, 1997.

Hazewell, Charles Creighton. "The Indian Revolt." *The Atlantic Monthly* 1, no. 2 (December 1857): 217–22.

Henke, James. *Courtesans and Cuckolds*. New York: Garland, 1979.

Henri, Adrian, Roger McGough, and Brian Patten. *The Mersey Sound*. London: Penguin, 1967.

Hewison, Robert. *In Anger: British Culture in the Cold War 1945–60*. New York: Oxford University Press, 1981.

———. *Monty Python: The Case Against*. London: Eyre Methuen, 1981.

———. *Too Much: Art and Society in the Sixties, 1960–1975*. New York: Oxford UP, 1986.

Heyerdahl, Thor. *Kon Tiki: Across the Pacific By Raft*. Chicago: Rand McNally, 1950.

———. *The Ra Expeditions*. New York: Doubleday, 1971.

Hillier, Bevis. "Colour, Fizz and Bubble." *Times*, 21 September 1968: 17.

Holland, Steve. *The Mushroom Jungle: A History of Postwar Paperback Publishing*. Wiltshire, England: Zeon, 1993.

———. *The Trials of Hank Janson*. Richmond, KY: Books Are Everything, 1991.

Hopkins, Gerald M. "Felix Randal." http://www.bartleby.com/122/29.html. Accessed 28 November 2007.

Hopkins, James K. *A Woman to Deliver Her People: Joanna Southcott and English Millenarianism in an Era of Revolution*. Austin, TX: University of Texas Press, 1981.

Hoppenstand, Gary, Garyn G. Roberts, and Ray B. Browne, eds. *More Tales of the Defective Detective in the Pulps*. Bowling Green: Bowling Green University Press, 1985.

Howard, Philip. "How Britain Drifted to Tragedy of Munich." *Times*, 1 January 1969: 8.

Hughes, Merritt Y. *John Milton's Complete Poems and Major Prose*. Indianapolis: Odyssey, 1957.

Hughes, Robert. *The Shock of the New*. New York: Knopf, 1991.

Hughes, Ted. *Crow: From the Life and Songs of a Crow*. London: Faber, 1970.

Index to the Times. London: Times Publishing Co., 1969–1974.

Ingrams, Richard, ed. *The Life and Times of* Private Eye: *1961–1971*. New York: McGraw-Hill, 1971.

James, C.L.R. *World Revolution, 1917–1936: The Rise of the Communist International*. New Jersey: Humanities P, 1937.

James, Henry. *Portrait of a Lady*. London: Macmillan, 1881.

James, Lawrence. *The Illustrated Rise and Fall of the British Empire*. New York: St. Martin's Griffin, 1994.

———. *The Rise and Fall of the British Empire*. New York: St. Martin's Griffin, 1995.

Jardine, Doug. *In Quest of the Ashes*. London: Methuen, 2005.

Jenkins, Steven. *Cheese Primer*. New York: Workman, 1996.

Johnson, Kim. *The First 20 Years of Monty Python*. New York: St. Martin's Press, 1989.

———. *The First 28 Years of Monty Python*. New York: St. Martin's Press, 1998.

Jones, Robert K. *The Shudder Pulps*. New York: Dutton/Plume, 1978.

Jonson, Ben. *The Alchemist. Drama of the English Renaissance II: The Stuart Period*. Ed. Russell Fraser and Norman Rabkin. New York: Macmillan, 1976.

———. *Bartholomew Fair. Drama of the English Renaissance II: The Stuart Period*. Ed. Russell Fraser and Norman Rabkin. New York: Macmillan, 1976.

———. *Volpone. Drama of the English Renaissance II: The Stuart Period*. Ed. Russell Fraser and Norman Rabkin. New York: Macmillan, 1976.

Joyce, James. *Ulysses*. New York: Vintage Books, 1990.

Judt, Tony. *Postwar: A History of Europe Since 1945*. New York: Penguin, 2005.

Keynes, John Maynard. *The Economic Consequences of the Peace*. New York: Prometheus, 2004.

"KGB's 1967 Annual Report, The." Woodrow Wilson International Center for Scholars, Cold War International History Project (TsKhSD f. 89, op. 5, d. 3, ll. 1–14). Trans. Vladislav Zubok (6 May 1968).

Kierkegaard, Søren. *Either/Or: A Fragment of Life*. London: Penguin, 1992.

Klein, Rudolf, M.A. "The Troubled Transformation of Britain's National Health Service." *NEJM* 355, no. 4 (July 2006): 409–15.

Koszarski, Richard. *An Evening's Entertainment: The Age of the Silent Feature Picture, 1915–1928*. New York: Scribner, 1990.

"Kurt Schwitters Retrospective." *The Times*, 16 October 1958: 4.

Larsen, Darl. "'Is Not the Truth the Truth?' or Rude Frenchman in English Castles: Shakespeare's and Monty Python's (Ab)Uses of History." *Journal of the Utah Academy of Sciences, Arts, and Letters* 76 (1999): 201–12.

———. *Monty Python, Shakespeare, and English Renaissance Drama*. Jefferson, NC: McFarland, 2003.

Lawrence, D.H. *Lady Chatterley's Lover*. London: Penguin, 1960.

———. *The Rainbow*. London: Penguin, 1915.

———. *Sons and Lovers*. New York: Signet, 1953.

———. *Women in Love*. London: Penguin, 1921.

Laws of Cricket, 2003. 2nd edition. London: Lord's, 2003.

Laxdaela Saga. Trans. Magnus Magnusson. London: Penguin, 1969.

Lenin, V.I. *Lenin Collected Works, Volume 8*. Moscow: Foreign Languages Publishing House, 1962.

Loemker, Leroy E., ed. *G.W. Leibniz: Philosophical Papers and Letters*. 2nd ed. Dordrecht, 1969.

Machen, Arthur. *The Great God Pan*. http://www.gutenberg.org/etext/389. Accessed 28 November 2007.

Mack, Maynard et al., ed. *The Norton Anthology of World Masterpieces*, vols. 1 and 2. 5th ed. New York: W.W. Norton, 1985.

Mailik, Zaiba. "Watery Grave." *Guardian*, 15 December 2004.

Malik, Sarita. "The Black and White Minstrel Show." Museum of Broadcast Communication. http://www.museum .tv/archives/etv/B/htmlB/blackandwhim/blackand whim.htm. Accessed 29 April 2006.

The Maltese Falcon. Dir. John Huston, starring Humphrey Bogart. Warner Bros., 1941.

Man in the Frame. Dir. Fyodor Khitruk. Soyuzmultfilm, 1966.

Marwick, Arthur. *British Society Since 1945.* London: Penguin, 2003.

Marx, Karl, and Frederick Engels. *The Manifesto of the Communist Party.* Chicago: Kerr and Co., 1906.

Matyszak, Philip. *The Enemies of Rome.* London: Thames and Hudson, 2004.

McCabe, Bob. *The Pythons.* New York: St. Martin's, 2003.

Miller, Fredric. "The British Unemployment Crisis of 1935." *Journal of Contemporary History* 14, no. 2 (April 1979): 329–52.

Miller, Paul Allen. "Sidney, Petrarch, and Ovid, or Imitation as Subversion." *ELH* 58, no. 3 (Autumn 1991): 499–522.

Milligan, Spike. *The Goon Show Scripts.* New York: St. Martin's, 1972.

Mills, A.D. *A Dictionary of British Place Names.* Oxford: Oxford University Press, 2003.

Monty Python and the Holy Grail. Dir. Terry Gilliam and Terry Jones. EMI Films, 1975.

Monty Python's Fliegender Zirkus: Sämtliche deutschen Shows. Graham Chapman et al. Eds. Alfred Biolek and Tomas Woitkewitsch. Trans. Heiko Arntz. Zurich: Haffmans Verlag, 1998.

Monty Python's Flying Circus. Dir. John Howard Davies and Ian MacNaughton. BBC, 1969–1974.

Monty Python's Life of Brian. Dir. Terry Jones. HandMade Films, 1979.

Monty Python's The Meaning of Life. Dir. Terry Gilliam and Terry Jones. Universal Pictures, 1983.

Morgan, David. *Monty Python Speaks!* New York: Avon Books, 1999.

Morgan, Kenneth O. *Britain since 1945: The People's Peace.* Oxford: Oxford University Press, 2001.

———. *The Oxford History of Britain.* Oxford: Oxford University Press, 2001.

Motson, John, and John Rowlinson. *The European Cup 1955–1980.* London: Queen Anne Press, 1980.

Musser, Charles. *The Emergence of Cinema: The American Screen to 1907.* New York: Scribner, 1990.

Nelson, Russell. *English Wits.* London: Hutchinson, 1953.

Nettleton, George, and Arthur Case, eds. *British Dramatists from Dryden to Sheridan.* Boston: Houghton Mifflin, 1939.

Newman, Ray. "The Dialectic Aspect of Raymond Chandler's Novels." http://home.comcast.net/~mossrobert/ html/criticism/newman.htm. Accessed 24 December 2006.

Nietzsche, Frederick. *The Will to Power.* New York: Vintage, 1968.

Nixon, Richard. "Building for Peace: A Report by President Richard Nixon to the Congress, 25 February 1971." http:// www.state.gov/r/pa/ho/frus/nixon/e5/54812.htm. Accessed 28 November 2007.

Njal's Saga. Trans. Robert Cook. London: Penguin, 2002.

Nowell-Smith, Geoffrey. *The Oxford History of World Cinema.* Oxford: Oxford University Press, 1996.

Nuttgens, Patrick. "From Utopia to Slum." *Tablet,* 26 September 1998. www.the tablet.co.uk. Accessed 6 April 2006.

Orczy, Baroness. *The Scarlet Pimpernel.* 1905. First World Library, 2005.

Orlova, Alexandra. "Tchaikovsky: The Last Chapter." *Music & Letters* 62, no. 2 (1981): 125–45.

Ostrom, John. "*Archaeopteryx*: Notice of a 'New' Specimen." *Science* 170, no. 3957 (30 October 1970): 537–38.

Out of the Past. Jacques Tourneur, starring Robert Mitchum. RKO, 1947.

Oxenham, John. *Bees in Amber: A Little Book of Thoughtful Verse.* New York: American Tract Society, 1913.

Oxford Dictionary of Modern Quotations. Ed. Elizabeth Knowles. Oxford: Oxford University Press, 2003.

Oxford Dictionary of National Biography. Oxford: Oxford University Press, 2004. Online version at: http://www .oxforddnb.com.

Palin, Michael. *Michael Palin Diaries 1969–1979: The Python Years.* London: Weidenfeld & Nicholson, 2006.

Partridge, Eric. *Shakespeare's Bawdy.* London: Routledge, 1991.

Paxman, Jeremy. "The English." *Sunday Times,* 27 September 1998: 1–8.

Pearson, Cynthia, and Norbert Delatte, M.ASCE. "Ronan Point Apartment Tower Collapse and Its Effect on Building Codes." *Journal of Performance of Constructed Facilities* 19, no. 2 (May 2005): 172–77.

Pennell, E. R., and J., eds. *The Whistler Journal.* Philadelphia: Lippincott, 1921.

Pepys, Samuel. *Passages from the Diary of Samuel Pepys.* Ed. Richard Le Gallienne. New York: The Modern Library, 1964.

Perez, Joseph. *The Spanish Inquisition: A History.* New Haven, CT: Yale University Press, 2005.

Perry, Elizabeth J. *Patrolling the Revolution: Worker Militias, Citizenship, and the Modern Chinese State.* New York: Rowman & Littlefield, 2005.

Pickering, J.F. "The Abandonment of Major Mergers in the UK." *Journal of Industrial Economics* 27, no. 2: 123–131.

Pincus, Edward. *The Filmmaker's Handbook.* New York: New American Library, 1984.

Preble, Christopher A. "Review of E. Bruce Geelhoed and Anthony O. Edmonds, *Eisenhower, Macmillan and Allied Unity, 1957–1961*," H-Diplo, H-Net Reviews, February 2005. http://www.h-net.org/reviews/showrev .cgi?path=125481117220884. Accessed 29 November 2006.

Propp, Vladimir. *Morphology of the Folk Tale.* Austin: University of Texas Press, 1968.

Proust, Marcel. *In Search of Lost Time.* Trans. Lydia Davis. London: Penguin, 2004.

Quicherat, Jules. *Histoire du costume en France.* Paris, 1875.

Rainey, Laurence. "The Cultural Economy of Modernism." *The Cambridge Companion to Modernism.* Ed. Michael Levenson. Cambridge: Cambridge University Press, 1999.

Rampa, T. Lobsang. *The Third Eye.* 1956. New York: Ballantine, 1986.

Ratcliffe, Stephen. "MEMO/RE: Reading Stein." *Corner* 2 (Spring 1999). http://www.cornermag.org/corner02/ page07.htm#anchor76741. Accessed 2 February 2007.

Rattigan, Terence. *The Collected Plays of Terence Rattigan*. Ed. Elizabeth Knowles. Oxford University Press, 2002. Oxford Reference Online. Oxford University Press. Accessed 6 October 2003.

The Renaissance in Italy. New York: Modern Library, 1935.

Rigby, T.H. "The Soviet Leadership: Towards a Self-Stabilizing Oligarchy?" *Soviet Studies* 22, no. 2 (1970): 167–91.

Robertson, Jean. "Philip Sidney." *The Spenser Encyclopedia*. Ed. A.C. Hamilton et al. Toronto: University of Toronto Press, 1990.

Rosenbaum, Martin. *From Soapbox to Soundbite: Party Political Campaigning in Britain since 1945*. London: Macmillan, 1997.

Ross, Charles. *The Wars of the Roses: A Concise History*. London: Thames and Hudson, 1986.

Rundell, Michael. *The Dictionary of Cricket*. 2nd ed. Oxford: Oxford University Press, 1995.

Russell, Bertrand. *The Autobiography of Bertrand Russell*. London: Routledge, 2000.

———. *The Problems of Philosophy*. Oxford: Oxford University Press, 1997.

Rutherford, Jonathan. *Forever England: Reflections on Race, Masculinity and Empire*. London: Lawrence & Wishart, 1997.

R v. Inwood. (1973) 2 All ER 645. http://www.hrcr.org/safrica/arrested_rights/R_Inwood.htm.

Sachs, Albie. *Justice in South Africa*. London: Chatto & Heinemann, 1973.

Salmond, Dame Anne. *Two Worlds*. New Zealand: Penguin, 1991.

Santayana, George. *Soliloquies in England*. New York: Charles Scribner's Sons, 1922.

Sartre, Jean Paul. *Being and Nothingness*. Trans. Hazel Barnes. New York: Washington Square Press, 1966.

Schmidt, Steven C. "United Kingdom Entry into the European Economic Community: Issues and Implications." *Illinois Agricultural Economics* 12, no. 2 (July 1972): 1–11.

Schroth, Raymond A. "The One and Only." *National Catholic Reporter* 38, no. 14 (8 February 2002): 11.

Schur, Norman. *British English, A to Zed*. New York: Facts on File, 2007.

Scott, Walter, Sir. *Marmion: A Tale of Flodden Field*. London: John Murray, 1808.

———. *Redgauntlet*. Boston: Estes and Lauriat, c1894.

Shakespeare, William. *Cymbeline*. The Riverside Shakespeare. Ed. G. Blakemore Evans. Boston: Houghton Mifflin, 1974.

———. *Hamlet*. The Riverside Shakespeare. Ed. G. Blakemore Evans. Boston: Houghton Mifflin, 1974.

———. *1 Henry IV*. The Riverside Shakespeare. Ed. G. Blakemore Evans. Boston: Houghton Mifflin, 1974.

———. *2 Henry IV*. The Riverside Shakespeare. Ed. G. Blakemore Evans. Boston: Houghton Mifflin, 1974.

———. *Henry V*. The Riverside Shakespeare. Ed. G. Blakemore Evans. Boston: Houghton Mifflin, 1974.

———. *Henry VIII*. The Riverside Shakespeare. Ed. G. Blakemore Evans. Boston: Houghton Mifflin, 1974.

———. *Julius Caesar*. The Riverside Shakespeare. Ed. G. Blakemore Evans. Boston: Houghton Mifflin, 1974.

———. *King John*. The Riverside Shakespeare. Ed. G. Blakemore Evans. Boston: Houghton Mifflin, 1974.

———. *The Merchant of Venice*. The Riverside Shakespeare. Ed. G. Blakemore Evans. Boston: Houghton Mifflin, 1974.

———. *A Midsummer Night's Dream*. The Riverside Shakespeare. Ed. G. Blakemore Evans. Boston: Houghton Mifflin, 1974.

———. *Much Ado about Nothing*. The Riverside Shakespeare. Ed. G. Blakemore Evans. Boston: Houghton Mifflin, 1974.

———. *The Rape of Lucrece*. The Riverside Shakespeare. Ed. G. Blakemore Evans. Boston: Houghton Mifflin, 1974.

———. *Richard II*. The Riverside Shakespeare. Ed. G. Blakemore Evans. Boston: Houghton Mifflin, 1974.

———. *Richard III*. The Riverside Shakespeare. Ed. G. Blakemore Evans. Boston: Houghton Mifflin, 1974.

———. *Romeo and Juliet*. The Riverside Shakespeare. Ed. G. Blakemore Evans. Boston: Houghton Mifflin, 1974.

———. *The Tempest*. The Riverside Shakespeare. Ed. G. Blakemore Evans. Boston: Houghton Mifflin, 1974.

Shaughnessy, Robert. *The Shakespeare Effect*. London: Palgrave Macmillan, 2002.

Shaw, George Bernard. *Pygmalion*. 1916. http://www.bartleby.com/138/2.html. Accessed 28 November 2007.

Shaw, Harry E. *Critical Essays on Sir Walter Scott: The Waverley Novels*. London: Prentice Hall, 1996.

Shelley, Percy Bysshe. "Ozymandias." *Shelley's Poetry and Prose: Authoritative Texts, Criticism*. New York: Norton, 1977.

Shepherd, John. *Continuum Encyclopedia of Popular Music of the World*, Vol. 1. London: Continuum, 2003.

Sherrin, Ned. *I Wish I'd Said That*. Oxford: Oxford University Press, 2004.

Sidney, Sir Philip. *Astrophil and Stella*. Garden City, NY: Anchor Books, 1967.

Sickert, Walter P. "The Idealism News." In *A Free House! Or The Artist as Craftsman; Being the Writings of Walter Richard Sickert*, ed. Oscar Sitwell. London: Macmillan, 1947.

Smethurst, William. *The Archers—The True Story: The History of Radio's Most Famous Programme*. London: Michael O'Mara Books, 1996.

Smith, Alexander. *A Complete History of the Lives and Robberies of the Most Notorious Highwaymen* (1714). London: Routledge, 1926.

Smollett, Tobias. *Humphry Clinker*. Ed. James L. Thorson, Norton Critical Editions. London: W.W. Norton, 1983.

———. *The Letters of Tobias Smollett*, ed. L. M. Knapp. Oxford: Clarendon Press, 1970.

Somerville, Christopher. "Woodstock Oxfordshire Walk." *Weekend Telegraph*. http://www.woodstock-oxfordshire.co.uk/pages/sport_and_entertainment/walk/walk.htm. Accessed 31 January 2007.

Spraggs, Gillian. *Outlaws and Highwaymen: The Cult of the Robber in England from the Middle Ages to the Nineteenth Century*. London: Pimlico, 2002.

Springer, Steve. "The City Was Full of Fight." *Los Angeles Times*, 30 March 2006. Website accessed 24 November 2006.

Stam, Robert. *Reflexivity in Film and Literature: From Don Quixote to Jean-Luc Godard*. New York: Columbia University Press, 1992.

Stein, Gertrude. "Melanctha." *Three Lives*. New York: Vintage, 1909.

Stevenson, Robert Louis. *Treasure Island*. 1883. http://www.online-literature.com/stevenson/treasureisland. Accessed 29 November 2007.

Stewart, Gordon. "Tenzing's Two Wrist-Watches: The Conquest of Everest and Late Imperial Culture in Britain, 1921–1953." *Past & Present* 149 (November 1995): 170–97.

Swift, Jonathan. *Gulliver's Travels. The Writings of Jonathan Swift*. Robert A. Greenberg and William B. Piper, eds. London: Norton, 1973.

———. *The Lady's Dressing Room. The Writings of Jonathan Swift*. Eds. Robert A. Greenberg and William B. Piper. London: Norton, 1973.

Tansey, Richard, et al. *Gardner's Art through the Ages*. 7th ed. New York: HBJ, 1980.

Taylor, Basil. *Constable: Paintings, Drawings, and Watercolours*. London: Phaidon, 1973.

"Ten Years of TV Coverage." *Belfast Bulletin* 6 (Spring 1979): 20–25, published by the Belfast Workers Research Unit.

Tennyson, Alfred Lord. *A Dream of Fair Women*. 1832. http://whitewolf.newcastle.edu.au/words/authors/T/TennysonAlfred/verse/ladyshalott/dreamfairwomen.html.

———. *Mariana*. http://www.web-books.com/Classics/Poetry/anthology/Tennyson/Mariana.htm.

———. *The Princess: A Medley*. 1847, 1850. http://classiclit.about.com/library/bl-etexts/atennyson/bl-aten-princess.htm.

This Sceptred Isle: The Twentieth Century. Wr. Christopher Lee. CD. *BBC Radio 4 Series*, BBC Audiobooks, 1999.

Thompson, John O. *Monty Python: Complete and Utter Theory of the Grotesque*. London: BFI, 1982.

Tillyard, E.M.W. *Shakespeare's History Plays*. London: Chatto and Windus, 1944.

Took, Barry. *Laughter in the Air*. London: BBC, 1981.

Trevelyan, G.M. *History of England*. 2nd ed. New York: Longmans, Green and Co., 1926.

———. *History of England*. 3rd ed. New York: Longmans, Green and Co., 1952.

Trotsky, Leon, and Isaac Deutscher. *The Age of Permanent Revolution: A Trotsky Anthology*. New York: Dell Publishing 1964.

Unger, Roberto. *Passion: An Essay on Personality*. New York: Free Press, 1986.

Vague, Tom. *Bash the Rich: The Class War Radical History Tour of Notting Hill*. Notting Hill, London: Bash the Rich Press, 2007.

Vahimagi, Tise. *British Television*. Oxford: Oxford University Press, 1996.

Veblen, Thorstein. *The Theory of the Leisure Class*. 1899. New York: Dover, 1999.

Voltaire. *Candide*. London: Penguin, 1950.

Warburton, Nigel. *Philosophy: The Classics*. 3rd ed. London: Routledge, 2006.

Warwick, Charles, and John R. Neill. *Mirabeau and the French Revolution*. Whitefish, MT: Kessinger, 2005.

Watson, Peter. *The Modern Mind: An Intellectual History of the 20th Century*. New York: HarperCollins, 2002.

Waugh, Evelyn. *Labels: A Mediterranean Journal*. London: Duckworth, 1930.

———. *Waugh Abroad: Collected Travel Writing*. New York: Knopf, 2003.

Waugh, Thomas. *Hard to Imagine: Gay Male Eroticism in Photography and Film from Their Beginnings to Stonewall*. New York: Columbia University Press, 1996.

Webster, Charles. *The National Health Service: A Political History*. Oxford: Oxford University Press, 2002.

Weintraub, Stanley, ed. *Bernard Shaw on the London Art Scene, 1885–1950*. Penn State: University Park University Press, 1989.

Wells, Stanley, and Gary Taylor, eds. *The Oxford Shakespeare: Histories with the Poems and Sonnets*. Oxford: Oxford University Press, 1994.

Westman, Andrew, and Tony Dyson. *Archaeology in Greater London, 1965–1990*. London: Museum of London, 1998.

Weston, Richard. *Modernism*. London: Phaidon, 1996.

Westwood, J.N. *Railways of India*. Newton Abbot, UK: David & Charles, 1975.

"What Will the 1970's Bring?" *Awake!* 8 October 1969, 14–16.

Williams, Eric. *The Wooden Horse*. New York: Harper, 1949.

Wilmut, Roger. *From Fringe to Flying Circus*. London: Methuen, 1987.

Wilson, A.N. *After the Victorians: The Decline of Britain in the World*. London: Picador, 2005.

Wilson, J. Dover. *What Happens in Hamlet*. Cambridge: Cambridge University Press, 1935.

"Witnessing the End." *Time*. 18 July 1969. http://www.time.com/time/magazine/article/0,9171,901074-1,00.html. Accessed 28 October 2006.

Wodehouse, P. G. *The Luck of the Bodkins*. Boston: Little, Brown and Co., 1936.

Wolfe, Tom. *From Bauhaus to Our House*. New York: Farrar Straus & Giroux, 1981.

Wooden Horse, The. Dir. Jack Lee, 1950.

Woodward, Rachel. "'It's a Man's Life!': Soldiers, Masculinity and the Countryside." *Gender, Place and Culture: A Journal of Feminist Geography* 5, no. 3 (1 November 1998): 277–300.

Wynne-Thomas, Peter. *Hamlyn A–Z of Cricket Records*. London: Hamlyn, 1983.

SELECTED INTERNET RESOURCES

1970 General Election, review of the rebroadcast: http://www.offthetelly.co.uk/reviews/2003/election70.htm

Affected "gay" speech (by Caroline Bowen): http://www.speech-language-therapy.com/caroline.html. Accessed 16 August 2006

All Blacks Rugby: http://www.allblacks.com

"Anarcho-Syndicalism, History of." *Self-Ed Education Collective*, http://www.selfed.org.uk/units/2001/index.htm

Argyll Regiment: http://argylls.co.uk/today.html

At Last the 1948 Show information: http://orangecow.org/pythonet/1948show

Avengers, The, TV show: http://theavengers.tv/forever

Barr Soft Drinks: http://www.agbarr.co.uk

Baths, UK: http://www.localhistory.scit.wlv.ac.uk/interesting/htbaths/htbaths04.htm

BBC History: http://www.tvradiobits.co.uk

BBC Programme Catalogue: http://open.bbc.co.uk/catalogue/infax

BBC Radio (1967): http://www.radiorewind.co.uk/1967_page.htm. Accessed 1 January 2007.

BBC Radio (1971–1972): http://www.radiorewind.co.uk/1971_page.htm

BBC Television Centre history: http://www.martinkempton.com/TV%20Centre%20history.htm#stage%206

Best, George obituary: http://www.timesonline.co.uk/article/0,,2-1890892,00.html, and http://www.manutdzone.com/legends/GeorgeBest.htm

BFI Film and TV Database: http://www.bfi.org.uk/filmtvinfo/ftvdb

Board of Trade: http://dti.gov.uk/history/board.htm

British Broadcasting Corporation: http://www.bbc.co.uk

British Cartoon Archive: http://opal.kent.ac.uk/cartoonx-cgi/ccc.py

British Telephone Historical Archives (accessed through ancestry.com): http://content.ancestry.co.uk/iexec/?htx=List&dbid=1025&offerid=0%3a7858%3a0

British TV, anecdotal history: http://www.whirligig-tv.co.uk

British TV, history: http://www.teletronic.co.uk

Brown, Arthur, obituary: http://www.guardian.co.uk/obituaries/story/0,3604,969745,00.html (penned by Andrew Phillips).

Cambridge University prizes in Classics: http://www.admin.cam.ac.uk/reporter/2003-04/special/05/b5.html

"Catenaccio defense": http://naccio.cs.virginia.edu/catenaccio.html

Celtic FC: http://www.lonestarceltic.com/25_may_1967.php

Chichester Festival history: http://www.cft.org.uk/content.asp?CategoryID=1107.

Churchill Centre "darker days" speech: http://www.winstonchurchill.org/i4a/pages/index.cfm?pageid=423

Clergy Lists, UK: *Kelly's Clergy List, 1909*: http://midlandshistoricaldata.org

Commonwealth Immigration Act of 1968: http://britishcitizen.info/CIA1968.pdf

Corporal punishment in South Africa: http://www.corpun.com/jcpza9.htm

Courtauld Gallery collection search: http://www.courtauld.ac.uk/index.html

Cowdrey, Colin, obituary (by John Thicknesse): http://content-www.cricinfo.com/ci/content/player/10846.html

Cricket info.: http://content-usa.cricinfo.com/england/content/player/20159.html

Crystal Palace FC: http://www.cpfc.co.uk

"Desert Island Discs Archives: Harry Secombe." BBC Radio 4 podcast: http://www.bbc.co.uk/programmes/p00943sz

DeWolfe music: http://www.dewolfe.co.uk

Dorking Dramatic Society Archives: http://www.ddos.org.uk/archives.asp

Encyclopedia Britannica: http://www.ebo.com

Encyclopedia of Fantastic Film & Television: http://www.eofftv.com

Everest Climbing History: http://www.everestnews.com/everest1.htm

FBI files on Burgess, Maclean: http://foia.fbi.gov/filelink.html?file=/philby/philby1a.pdf

Forestry Commission UK: http://www.forestry.gov.uk

Freemasonry watchdog: http://freemasonrywatch.org

Gas Boards history: http://www.gasarchive.org/Nationalisation.htm and http://www.centrica.co.uk/index.asp?pageid=397

Gay characters on British TV: http://www.queertv.btinternet.co.uk

Gay men's magazines: http://www.planetout.com/news/history/archive/09271999.html

Guardian Century: http://century.guardian.co.uk

Highwayman Humphrey Kynaston: http://www.bbc.co.uk/shropshire/features/halloween/kynaston.shtml

Hitler's speeches: http://hitler.org/speeches

Homelessness in the UK in 1969: http://news.bbc.co.uk/onthisday/hi/dates/stories/september/11/newsid_3037000/3037650.stm

An Incomplete History of London's Television Studios: http://www.tvstudiohistory.co.uk/tv%20centre%20history.htm

Keele University General Elections Results, http://www.psr.keele.ac.uk.

"Kray Brothers" (by Thomas Jones): http://www.crimelibrary.com/gangsters_outlaws/mob_bosses/kray/index_1.html

Labour Manifesto, 1966: http://www.psr.keele.ac.uk/area/uk/man/lab66.htm

Labour Market Trends, Office for National Statistics, June 1999: http://www.statistics.gov.uk

London School of Economics riots (January 1969): http://news.bbc.co.uk/onthisday/hi/dates/stories/january/24/newsid_2506000/2506485.stm

Lord's (MCC) Laws of Cricket: http://www.lords.org/laws-and-spirit/laws-of-cricket

"Men of Harlech": http://www.data-wales.co.uk/harlech.htm

MPFC Scripts: http://www.ibras.dk/montypython/justthewords.htm

National Film Theatre: http://bfi.uk.org

National Gallery collection archive: http://www.nationalgallery.org.uk

National Portrait Gallery collection search: http://www.npg.org.uk/live/collect.asp

North Yorkshire photos (Unnetie Digitisation Project) http://www2.northyorks.gov.uk/unnetie

Man Alive: http://www.offthetelly.co.uk/features/bbc2/forty1.htm

McGonagall Online. http://www.mcgonagall-online.org.uk/articles/awful-poet-who-didnt-know-it.

McGuffie, Mary (McCheane) information, Farnon Society: http://www.rfsoc.org.uk/jim3.shtml

Mont Orgueil Castle: http://www.bbc.co.uk/jersey/content/image_galleries/mont_orgueil_one_gallery.shtml?5

"Northern Ireland Conflict and Politics (1968 to the Present)": http://cain.ulst.ac.uk/othelem/media/tv10yrs.htm

Notting Hill "pop" history (by Tom Vague): http://www.historytalk.org/Tom%20Vague%20Pop%20History/Tom%20Vague%20Pop%20History.htm

Nova (magazine) listserv: http://listserv.uel.ac.uk/pipermail/centrefornarrativeresearch/Week-of-Mon-20050411/000319.html

Online Medieval & Classical Library: http://omacl.org

Open University ("From Here to Modernity"): http://www .open2.net/modernity

"Overcrowding in London" (March 2004): http://www.lhu .org.uk

Oxford English Dictionary: http://dictionary.oed.com

Party Political (or Election) Broadcasts: http://www.psr .keele.ac.uk/area/uk/peb.htm

Peerage listings: http://www.thepeerage.com

Pinball machines, vintage: http://dguhlow.tripod.com/ pinballs/htmls/bankaball.html

Pontiac Firebirds in movies: http://www.imcdb.org/ vehicles_make-Pontiac_model-Firebird.html

Positivism: http://radicalacademy.com/philpositivists.htm

Postwar fireplaces (and fireplace inserts): http://www .c20fires.co.uk/fireplaces/original/postfires.htm

Pound devaluation, 1972: http://news.bbc.co.uk/onthis day/low/dates/stories/june/23/newsid_2518000/ 2518927.stm

"Poverty in England" (by Charles Booth): http://booth.lse .ac.uk

Proust, Marcel and *À la recherche du temps perdu*: http:// tempsperdu.com

Queen's itinerary and speeches, 1970: http://www.nla.gov .au/ms/findaids/9174.html#1970

Queen's Park Rangers FC: http://www.qpc.co.uk

"Radio Rewind." http://www.radiorewind.co.uk.

Radio Times official website: http://radiotimes.beeb.com

Radio Times (unofficial) cover art site: http://www.vintage times.org.uk

Railroad music: http://www.musicweb.uk.net/railways_ in_music.htm

Railway signal boxes: http://www.signalbox.org/gallery/ be.htm

Railway violence: http://btp.police.uk/History

Reith Lectures: http://www.bbc.co.uk/radio4/reith/reith_ history.shtml

Richter, Sviatoslav (chronology): http://www.trovar.com/ str/dates/index.html

Rijksmuseum Rembrandt collection: http://rijksmuseum .nl/index.jsp

Rock climbing jargon: http://www.myoan.net/climbing/ jargon.html

Roiurama Expedition: http://www.lastrefuge.co.uk/data/ adrian2.html

Royal Scottish Forestry Society: http://www.rsfs.org

Scott, Peter entry at WordIQ: http://www.wordiq.com/ definition/Peter_Scott

Scottish politics: http://www.alba.org.uk/nextwe/snp.html

Semaphore signals: http://www.cs.dartmouth.edu/ ~rockmore/semaphore.jpg

Shakespeare listserv: http://www.shaksper.net/www .shaksper.net

Julian Slade obituary (by Dennis Barker): http://arts .guardian.co.uk/news/obituary/0,,1801400,00.html

Society of Film and TV Arts (UK): http://www.bafta.org

"Squatting in London" (Andrew Friend): http://squat .freeserve.co.uk/story

St. Albans Operatic Society: http://www.saos.org.uk

Strike activity in the UK: http://www.eiro.eurofound .eu.int/1999/07/feature/uk9907215f.html

Tate Gallery Collection: http://www.tate.org.uk/britain

Tax Freedom Day in the UK: http://www.adamsmith.org/ tax/short-history.php

Tennis information: http://www.tennisfame.org/ enshrinees

Time Magazine online archives: http://www.time.com/ time/magazine/archives

The *Times* (London) Digital Archive, 1785–1985: http:// infotrac.galegroup.com/itw

UK Announcers archive: http://tvannouncers.thetvroom plus.com/channel-19.html

UK General Elections (including results since 1832): http:// www.psr.keele.ac.uk/area/uk/edates.htm

UK motorway exchanges: http://www.cbrd.co.uk/ reference/interchanges/fourlevelstack.shtml

UK Parliament: http://www.parliament.uk

UK postwar politics: http://politics.guardian.co.uk/politics past/story/0,9061,471383,00.html

UK postwar spending: "Long-Term Trends in British Taxa-tion and Spending" (Tom Clark and Andrew Dilnot) from the Institute for Fiscal Studies: http://www.ifs.org.uk/ bns/bn25.pdf

UK street maps: http://www.streetmap.co.uk

Victoria & Albert Museum collection: http://www.vam .ac.uk/collections

Vladimir Horowitz concert information: http://web.telia .com/~u85420275/index.htm

Western National bus number 350 EDV: http://www .bristolsu.co.uk/Su/operatordetails/westernnational/ 350edv.htm

Wimbledon archives: http://www.wimbledon.org

Wisden Cricketer, The: http://www.cricinfo.com/wisden cricketer

YMCA in Russia: http://www.ymca.ru/english/history

Index

Page numbers for both volumes are listed in each entry, with page numbers preceded by a Roman numeral to distinguish those in volume one from those in volume two (e.g., 10 Downing Street, **I**-xi, 17, 238, 368; **II**-xi, 53, 66, 67, 181, 200). For each entry, all the pertinent page numbers for volume one are listed first, followed immediately by those in volume two

"A" roadways: A3: I-3, 12, 21; A23: I-212, II-32; A25: I-10; A27: I-4, 6, 10; A29: I-10, 24; A38: I-8, 187; A39: I-187, 191, 198; A61: I-8; A231: I-212; A237: II-108; A272: I-3, 10, 21, 24; A283: I-24; A303: II-119; A308: II-29; A358: I-187, 198; A361: I-191; A372: I-187; A382: II-101; A630: I-8; A3022: I-278; A3205: I-4; A3210: I-21

"a fair cop," I-53, 95

"a priori," I-332; II-107

AA (British Automobile Association), I-3, 240; II-20, 202

AAQ Newsagent and Confectioners, I-273

Abagnale, Frank, II-188

Abanazar, II-170

ABC (Aerated Bread Company), I-276

"Abercrombie Plan," II-14

abattoir, I-264; II-20, 30, 178

ABC Cinema, New Zealand Avenue, Walton-on-Thames (location), I-268, 269, 273

ABC's Wide World of Sports, I-158

Aberdeen, I-264; II-27, 77

Aberfan mine disaster, I-394

Abicair, Shirley, II-34

"Abide-a-Wee," II-20

aboriginal/aborigines, I-214, 226, 278, 335, 339, 342

abortion, I-62, 90, 160–61, 302

Abraham, Abu, I-222

absurd/absurdities, I-42, 82, 110, 120, 131, 136, 152–53, 158, 164, 166, 169, 177, 192, 213, 216, 231, 232, 236, 238, 244, 255, 260, 298, 302, 305; II-37, 74, 78, 152, 205; "no safe ground," I-152; and Samuel Beckett, I-82

Abu Simbel, I-327, 330, 337

AC Bell Ltd., I-261

Academy Awards (and "Oscar"), I-309, 404; II-150, 152, 155, 156–57, 220

accents, I-6, 23, 27, 41, 43, 45, 46, 47, 48, 49, 51, 52, 60, 74, 80, 109, 111, 117, 119, 123, 130, 135, 181, 238, 247, 250, 255, 258, 260, 260, 268, 279, 308, 318, 323, 324, 332, 355; II-22, 44, 60, 76, 93, 103, 157, 163, 171, 175, 188, 208

acculturation, I-xiii, 36, 39, 64, 134, 279–80; II-xiii

Ackner, Desmond, I-57–58

acknowledging artifice and artificiality, I-19, 29, 36, 38, 70, 73, 88, 95, 117–18, 131, 134, 136, 137, 141–42, 169, 170, 175, 199, 202, 211, 227, 251, 270, 284, 287, 332, 339, 352, 374, 377, 379, 384; II-39, 44, 57, 60, 64, 114, 139, 168, 186, 205

Ackroyd, Peter, I-30, 72, 130, 133, 210, 213, 227, 236, 272, 321, 370, 388; II-30, 97, 115, 126; and *London: The Biography* I-30, 210, 213, 227, 272, 370

acquisitive culture, I-72, 76; II-52, 175, 176, 193

Action Comics, I-60

Acton, I-24, 35, 56, 139, 183, 253, 261; II-121; High Street (location), I-35, 56, 139; Town Hall, I-139

Adams, Douglas, I-212; II-152, 180, 202

Adams, John Quincy, I-53

adaptation, I-36, 39, 101, 113, 139, 187, 196, 238, 261, 353, 366; II-8, 20, 21, 34, 44, 46, 50, 56, 91, 107, 119, 134, 155, 184, 205

Ada's Snack Bar, I-143, 405; II-221

Addlestone (location), I-102, 121, 157

Aden, I-168, 386; II-120

"Admag" format, II-13, 21, 38

"Adopt, Adapt and Improve," I-156

"Adrian," II-377

A.E. Rodd, II-99

aeroplane, I-44, 153, 252

Africa, I-63, 91, 93, 97, 112, 115, 124, 125, 145, 148, 161, 171, 173, 179, 203, 212, 222, 231, 233, 242–44, 246, 248, 257, 259,

266, 294, 317, 318, 324, 330, 341, 347, 360, 368, 371, 402; II-9, 15, 29, 33, 40, 43, 115, 137, 157, 178, 179, 191, 196, 199, 202, 204; countries: Algeria, II-8, 34; Benin, II-204; Biafra, I-171, 347; Burundi, I-338; Dahomey, II-202, 204; Ethiopia, I-259; Kenya (*see* Kenya); Libya, I-70, 347; II-96; Morocco, II-24; Mozambique, II-8; Natal, II-191; Rhodesia, I-59, 168, 180, 188, 373, 389; II-36, 56, 66–67, 73, 137, 208, 209; Rwanda, I-338; South Africa, I-93, 124, 125, 161, 162, 173, 203, 231, 242–44, 246, 248, 257, 266, 294, 317, 318, 324, 330, 341, 347, 368, 371; II-9, 15, 34, 42, 157, 191, 202; "South West Africa," I-368

Africans, I-42, 59, 93, 97, 100, 131, 257, 347; II-34, 42, 43, 72, 196, 202, 208; Maasai and Watusi, I-338

"afters" II-40

A Green Tree in Gedde, Alan Sharp, I-166

Agnelli, Gino, II-177

A Hard Day's Night. See films

"A horse, a horse…," (*Richard III*) I-371

airlines, I-236, 253, 256, 262, 273, 339, 340; II-3, 12–14; Airbus, I-340; Air India, I-340; Alitalia II-3; Ariana Afghan, I-340; BEA, I-340; II-113; BOAC, I-253, 340; British United Airways, I-253; "East Scottish Airways," II-113; El Al II-117; Lufthansa, II-12; Monarch, I-236, 256; Pan Am (and PC Pan-Am), I-84, 264, 273, 307, 344, 411; II-352; TWA, I-340

"A-Level" and "O-Level." *See* exams

Albania, I-63, 201; II-102; and King Zog, I-63, 201

Albert, Prince Consort, I-9, 251; II-128, 155, 170, 174, 190

Alberti, Leon Battista, I-168

Aldbourne Road, Hammersmith and Fulham (location), II-153

"Aldebaran" in Taurus, II-110

"Aldermen," I-328, 349

Aldgate, Anthony, *Censorship and the Permissive Society*, I-35, 37, 49, 105, 111, 138; II-48, 85, 97

Aldis lamp, I-240

Aldridge, Arthur, I-26

Aldrin, Buzz, I-264, 272, 273

Aldwych Theatre, I-406; II-121, 127

Alexander the Great, I-206

Alexandra Palace Race Course (location), I-316, 317

Algy (Algernon Montgomery Lacey). *See* "Biggles"

Ali, Muhammad, I-158, 281

All Blacks, I-300, 349, 350, 351, 355, 389

All English Jumping Course, Hickstead (location), II-181, 184

"all-in," I-172, 173, 264, 286, 340, 405, 409; II-55, 84, 88, 221, 225; "All-In Cricket," I-172, 173, 264, 286, 340; II-84, 88

"All Kinds of Everything," Dana, I-341

All My Loving, Palmer, I-354

All Souls College, Oxford, I-392

"All Through the Night," I-386, 402; II-218

Allen, Sir George "Gubby" Oswald Browning, I-312; II-210

Allen, Woody I-46, 286, 353, 354; II-18, 119, 180

Allied Bomber Command, I-221

"Allied Breweries," I-368

allusions/allusiveness, I-xi, 7, 12, 16, 17, 19, 33, 34, 36, 40, 41, 48, 60, 61, 66, 79, 81, 90, 99, 101, 107, 110, 111, 125, 131, 132, 144, 146, 147, 153, 158, 166, 171, 173–74, 181, 193, 194, 195, 197, 200, 210, 229, 269, 320, 324, 326, 328, 332, 361; II-xi, 52, 65, 90, 92, 95, 96

The Alps/Alpine, I-14, 74, 101, 151; II-67

"Also Sprach Zarathustra," I-380, 402; II-218

Althusser, Louis, I-342

Altman, Wilfred, I-24

America (U.S.), I-6, 14, 35, 38, 39, 53, 58, 59, 63, 79, 89, 99, 112–13, 119, 124, 133–35, 137, 158, 160, 163, 165, 173, 179, 188, 193, 197, 203, 214, 230, 271, 286, 291, 297, 303, 312, 315, 321, 329, 333, 351, 365, 369, 387, 388, 394; II-13, 15, 18, 34, 39, 40, 48, 59, 64, 66, 83, 84, 88, 97, 102, 103, 105, 111, 114, 116, 117, 127, 131, 168, 178, 180–81, 188, 191, 196–99, 201, 206; "American," I-3, 4, 6, 7, 8, 13, 14, 16, 17, 20, 27, 31, 33–35, 37, 42–44, 46–48, 89, 93, 95, 99–107, 109, 110, 112, 113, 116, 118, 120, 122, 128, 129, 132, 135, 146, 152, 154, 156, 157–58, 163, 165, 166, 169, 170, 173, 176, 181, 188, 189, 194, 197, 198, 202, 204, 208, 209, 214, 221, 226, 228, 237, 241, 252, 257, 258, 259, 260, 263, 264–65, 267, 270, 271, 273, 281, 286, 292, 293, 297, 299, 302–4, 309, 315, 317, 318, 323, 325, 328, 330, 334, 335, 340, 351, 352, 354–55, 358, 361, 365, 367–69, 378–79, 386, 394; II-71, 72, 74, 75, 83, 87, 95, 97, 100, 102, 103, 105, 107, 113, 117, 120, 123–24, 125, 132, 133, 136, 140, 144, 145, 147, 152, 153, 157, 163, 164, 166, 168,

180, 182, 183, 184, 188, 190, 193, 195–202, 205, 206, 209; accent, 31, 33, 43, 47, 48, 51, 60, 74, 109, 111, 258; II-188; and "gunboat diplomacy" (Monroe Doctrine), I-165, 360; II-197

American International Pictures (AIP), I-302

Amery, Julian, I-346

Ames, Leslie 274

Amis, Kingsley and the "Angry Young Men," 27

Amontillado (sherry) II-128

"Amontillado," Tomlinson, I-82, 403; II-123, 127, 219

Amundsen, Roland, I-169

anagrams I-172, 191, 313, 405, 410; II-50, 51, 53, 56, 59, 125, 128, 221, 226

An Allegory with Venus and Cupid, Bronzino. *See* artworks *and* artists

"anarchosyndicalism," I-12, 372

Anatomical Chart, 1918 American Frohse, I-406; II-20, 39, 222

"ancien regime," I-131, 223, 340

"And did those feet…" ("Jerusalem" hymn), I-63, 66, 69–70, 127, 134, 140, 271, 399, 402, 405, 409; II-40, 218, 221, 225

"And Now" Man, I-22, 26, 27, 143, 221, 226, 240, 252, 264, 289, 311, 339, 349, 360, 371, 405; II-3, 10, 20, 21, 40, 50, 61, 77, 110, 116, 121, 130, 150, 221

"And now for something completely different," I-26, 27, 140, 143, 221, 226, 405; II-221

And Now For Something Completely Different (film), I-73; II-8, 10, 26

Anderson, Eddie, I-313

Anderson, Lindsay, I-103, 149, 206, 242, 283, 297, 305, 382, 387; II-36, 124, 171

Anderson, Marie, II-113, 114, 145

Andrews, Eamonn, I-; II-34, 71, 386

Andrews, Julie, I-139

"A new comedy series for the Switched On," I-10, 208

Angerstein, John Julius, I-379

Angliæ, I-291

Anglo-French, I-46, 221–22; Channel Tunnel, I-125, 163, 222; Concorde, 29, 46–47, 222, 303; II-132, 134, 138

Angry Young Men, I-27, 35, 37, 38, 105, 112–13, 149, 248, 306, 318, 333; II-28, 36, 87

Animal Kingdom Ltd., I-146, 229

animals/insects: agouti, II-174; albatross, I-201, 405; alligator, II-4; anemone, I-252; ant, I-169, 184, 193, 196, 251, ; II-170–71, 173–76, 178, 229; anteater, II-174; antelope, I-162, 347; "blind bat," I-199; bear, I-185, 189, 195, 198, 211, 305, 380, 397; II-31, 47, 56, 127; boar, I-252, 262; buffalo, I-36; bull, I-189, 407; II-31, 106, 110; camel (and dromedary), I-115, 123–24, 148, 168, 298, 318, 402; II-91, 102, 403; cassowary, I-195; cat, I-30, 32, 46, 56, 59, 67, 68, 77, 79, 81, 82, 90, 136, 147–48, 406, 407, 408; II-36, 44, 45, 46, 107, 127, 222, 223, 224; chicken, I-xii, 23, 26, 41, 50, 79, 110, 136, 143, 153, 166, 167, 201, 206, 222, 284, 318, 326, 387, 410; II-xii, 4,

50, 179, 206, 226, 264, 272; chigger, I-254; cobra, I-252, 262; coelacanth, I-159; coot, I-260; cow (and cattle), I-17, 29, 93, 96, 104, 262, 264, 292, 396, 407; II-31, 96, 106, 110, 170, 206, 207; crocodile, I-156; dog, I-7, 12, 21, 45, 52, 64, 77, 83–84, 98, 99, 119, 123, 129, 130, 152, 156, 161, 177, 250, 254, 262, 269, 279, 295, 296, 301, 313, 341, 362; II-21, 22, 23, 31, 38, 44, 47, 62, 86, 126, 170, 173; dragon, I-350, 387; II-11; duck, I-xi, 30, 63, 64, 82, 106, 128, 156, 204, 280, 376, 408; II-114, 132, 161, 193, 224; eel, II-93; elephant, I-16, 175, 327, 337, 381, 401, 402, 406; II-48, 127, 217, 218, 222; elk, I-262, 366; ferret, I-252, 262; fish, I-51, 57, 95, 98–99, 104, 118, 129, 130, 136, 152, 156, 159, 165, 177, 185–86, 188, 191, 231, 238, 245, 264, 337, 340, 343, 346, 349–50, 355, 362, 377, 385, 387, 406, 408, 409; II-13, 20, 23, 30, 44, 45, 47, 48, 55, 61, 64, 84, 88, 173, 188, 196, 222, 224, 225; flea, I-197; frog, I-xii, 24, 93, 96, 116, 157, 161, 221, 264, 364, 367–68, 379, 405, 407, 408; II-xii, 47, 130, 134, 139, 221, 223, 224; fruitbat, I-309; gannet, I-201; gibbon, I-311, 321, 411; II-227; goat, I-132, 146, 156, 189, 196, 229, 318; II-13; goldfish, I-51, 99, 245, 343, 385, 387, 409; II-185, 225; goose, I-201; gorilla, I-156, 163, 166, 185, 229, 409; II-43, 44, 46, 225; haddock, II-61; halibut, I-12, 188, 352; hartebeest, I-162; hedgehog, I-12, 136, 162, 236, 385, 392; horse, I-26, 44, 47, 57, 73, 100, 104, 105, 120, 123, 206, 241, 281–82, 317, 319, 328, 355, 371, 373, 409; II-10, 27, 36, 47, 51, 54, 56, 61, 71, 122, 125, 132, 138, 151, 153, 154, 177, 179, 181, 185, 186, 198, 225; iguana, II-205; koala, I-312, 402; II-55, 218; Komodo Dragon, II-134; leopard, I-176, 202, 206, 262; II-40, 46–47, 126, 191; limpet, I-396; II-50, 56, 84, 212; lion, I-108, 156, 164, 216, 252, 262, 343, 349, 351, 394, 395, 396; II-11, 56, 127, 150, 191, 194, 211, 212; lizard, I-30, 79, 82, 156; llama, I-136, 143, 148, 198, 407, 411; II-47, 223, 227; mandrill, II-227; molluscs, I-194, 386, 410; II-10, 56, 77, 81, 84, 85, 119, 226; monkey, I-78, 252, 262; II-168; moorhen, I-256; mosquito, I-21, 168, 327, 341, 410; II-77, 226; mouse/mice, I-26, 27, 33, 36–38, 40, 42, 49, 127, 182, 245, 255, 406; II-222, 226; ostrich, I-156; owl, I-45, 61, 63, 67, 86, 90, 207, 252, 262, 373; ox, I-318; pangolin, II-274; panther, I-46, 176, 408, 409; II-18, 34, 126, 224, 225; parrot, I-xi, 9, 19, 38, 43, 73, 93, 95, 104, 127, 128, 130, 134, 152, 154, 164, 166, 185, 234, 258, 274, 311, 315, 318, 321, 350, 356, 406, 407, 408, 411, 412; II-xi, 5, 44, 98, 127, 184, 222, 223, 227, 228; penguin, I-20, 44, 75, 87, 111, 118, 197, 248, 267, 325, 339, 343, 349, 352, 356, 406, 408, 411; II-134, 140, 145–46, 147–48, 222, 224, 227; pig, I-3, 9, 17, 23, 44, 63, 73, 93, 103, 156–57, 181, 266, 278, 292, 295, 339, 372, 386, 396, 405, 407, 408, 409, 411, 412; II-32, 51–52, 86, 127, 212, 221, 223, 224, 225, 227, 228; polecat, I-194,

274; "prawn," I-278, 301, 405; II-221;
rabbit, I-xi, 19, 29, 57, 64, 68, 74, 76, 106,
124, 136, 160, 167, 177, 206, 252–53, 262;
II-xi, 13, 36, 39, 44–45, 47, 72, 78, 114, 163;
"rabbit fish," I-57, 177, 257; II-13, 44–45,
47; raptor, I-197; rats, I-74, 177, 229, 311,
315, 323, 325, 327, 330, 335, 365, 372,
378, 392; II-4, 42, 45; robin, I-157, 337;
rooster, I-82; II-161; sea lion, I-396; II-50,
56, 212; sheep (and lamb), I-26–30, 40,
44–46, 47, 64, 69, 82, 90, 93, 115, 120, 136,
198, 234, 253, 279, 295, 311, 312, 318–21,
323, 326, 343, 347, 392, 405, 408, 409, 410,
411; II-91, 127, 131, 204, 221, 224, 225,
226, 227; shrew, I-23, 157, 197, 350; II-56;
stoat, I-89, 93, 106, 152, 236–37, 289, 306,
309, 333, 385, 406, 407, 410; II-52–53, 222,
223, 226; tapir, II-198; Thompson's [sic]
gazelle, I-13, 91, 176, 409; II-225; tiger,
I-13, 76, 163, 176, 180, 262, 289, 393, 406;
II-173, 222; toad, I-45, 116, 188, 229, 266,
318, 385, 412; II-43, 228; vole, I-47, 61, 91,
93, 107–8, 343, 405; II-95, 97, 99, 186, 210,
221, 229; walrus, I-31, 292; whale, I-110,
157, 159, 195, 197; wolf, I-64, 106, 129,
192, 198, 204, 326, 372, 396; II-7, 39, 50, 56,
86, 98, 212; wombat, I-31, 264, 271, 277,
311, 312, 321; II-227; Yeti (Yehti), I-110,
119, 126, 168, 254, 407; II-143, 223
animation: I-xii, 3, 4, 5, 11, 12, 17, 26, 27, 31,
32, 33, 45, 50, 51, 53, 62, 63, 66, 67–68,
74, 76, 79, 87, 93, 94, 96, 101, 102, 103,
106, 110, 111, 116, 127, 128, 129, 135, 143,
148, 156, 159, 162, 167, 169, 171, 172, 173,
184, 196, 197, 200, 201, 202, 206, 211, 217,
221, 222, 240–42, 245–46, 250–51, 252,
257, 264, 265, 273, 274, 278, 279, 280, 284,
289–92, 298, 301, 309, 311, 312, 314, 316,
322, 323, 327, 334, 339, 343, 349, 354, 355,
356, 360, 362, 364–65, 371–72, 383, 385,
386, 387, 393, 405–6, 407; II-xii, 3, 18, 20,
23, 26, 40, 44, 49, 50, 51, 61, 71, 77, 78,
83, 85, 91, 92, 101, 110, 111, 112, 118, 121,
122, 127, 130, 134, 140, 142, 145–46, 150,
161, 162, 164, 170, 175, 177, 187, 195, 202,
204, 221–22, 223; animators: Tex Avery,
I-6, 20, 29, 52, 71, 76, 104, 106, 127, 154,
178, 192, 204, 279, 363, 372, 387; II-39,
86, 98; Joseph Barbera, I-76, 314; Alison
De Vere, I-375; Walt Disney, I-20, 106,
178, 376; II-31, 48, 86, 145; Max Fleischer
(*see* Fleischer Bros.); Isadore Freleng, I-6;
William Hanna, I-76, 314; Chuck Jones,
I-7, 71, 104, 127, 154, 178, 248, 257; II-31,
39; Winsor McCay, I-6, 32, 94; II-44;
Norman McLaren, I-85, 87, 210; William
Nolan, I-6, 32; Stan Vanderbeek, I-66;
characters: Betty Boop, I-20; II-108; Bugs
Bunny, I-7, 20, 63, 104, 204, 257; II-74,
114: Daffy Duck, I-106, 128, 198; II-39,
114; Droopy, I-104; Elmer Fudd, I-63, 128;
II-74; Porky Pig, II-86; Screwy Squirrel,
I-20, 104; II-39; Tom and Jerry, I-76;
wolf and sheepdog, I-64, 129; Woody
Woodpecker, I-20; studios: Disney I-20,
86, 106, 178, 203, 376–78; II-31, 48, 60, 86,

127–28, 145; Famous II-106; Filmation,
I-314; Fleischer Bros., I-20, 32, 94; II-44,
108; Halas & Batchelor, I-242; II-112;
Hanna-Barbera I-76, 314; MGM, I-20, 29,
105, 106, 108, 127, 198; II-31, 39, 86; TV
Cartoons, I-375; United Productions of
America (UPA), I-106; Warner Bros., I-6,
9, 29, 63, 64, 76, 106, 127, 128, 129, 173,
198, 204, 257, 294, 326, 334, 363; II-31,
39, 74, 86; titles: *Ain't That Ducky*, I-128;
Animal Farm, I-242; *Bad Luck Blackie*, I-71,
76, 279; *Baseball Bugs*, II-114; *Blitz Wolf*,
I-106, 198, 204, 372; II-86, 98; *Bugsy and
Mugsy*, II-334; *Daffy the Commando*, I-198;
A Day at the Zoo, and *The Dover Boys of
Pimiento U*, I-154, 249; *Duck Amuck*, I-94;
II-39; *Duck! Rabbit, Duck!*, I-106; II-39,
114; *Duck Dodgers in the 24 ½ Century*,
I-63; *Dumb-Hounded*, II-39; *Grin and Bear
It*, I-376; *Huckleberry Hound*, I-20; *Inki and
the Minah Bird*, I-154; II-31, 39; *King Size
Canary*, I-279; *My Bunny Lies Over the Sea*,
I-257; *Prest-O Change-O*, I-204; *Rabbit Fire*,
I-106; II-39, 114; *Rabbit Seasoning*, I-106;
II-39, 114; *Rocky & Bullwinkle*, I-20, 122,
329; II-20, 168; *Screwball Squirrel*, I-20,
104; II-39; *Three Little Pigs*, II-86; *Victory
Through Air Power*, II-145; *Wackiki Rabbit*,
II-114; *What's Opera, Doc?*, I-63
Anka, Paul, I-333, 337, 350
Anne, Princess, I-19, 184; II-152, 178
Anne, Queen, I-136, 394
Anouk, Aimee, II-195
Anstey Cove, Torquay, Devon (location),
I-300
anthropomorphosis, I-46, 90; II-17
anti-Communism, I-50, 363, 365, 406; II-196,
198, 222
anti-establishment, I-43, 75, 162; II-51. *See
also* "establishment"
anti-theatricalists, I-151
anti-war demonstrations, I-38, 304; II-105,
156
Antonioni, Michelangelo, I-99, 133, 206, 297,
363, 406; II-41–44, 46, 100, 222
"Anything Goes," Cole Porter, I-404; II-183,
202, 220
Apollo space missions, I-39, 125, 164, 185,
189, 263, 264, 272, 286; II-21, 37, 110–11,
115, 188; and Buzz Aldrin, I-264, 272,
273, 407; II-223; and Mercury and Gemini
programs, I-164; and Saturn V, I-286;
II-37
apartheid/anti-apartheid, I-173, 203, 244,
266, 368
"apple boxes," I-357
Arab/Arabs, I-41, 115, 182, 269, 290, 292,
295, 298, 299, 322, 324, 349, 386, 389, 401,
408; II-40, 56, 185, 196, 198, 217
Arbuckle, Roscoe "Fatty," I-73; II-97
Arbuthnot, John, I-19
archaeology, I-235, 297, 302, 327, 328–31,
333–37, 389, 406; II-29, 79, 222, 224
The Archers, II-25, 187, 192, 193, 207
Archbishop of Canterbury, I-28, 361, 372;
II-22, 122

Architectural and Perspective Designs,
Giuseppe Galli Bibiena, I-42, 235, 290,
292, 349; II-91, 204; individual drawings:
"Charles VI" plate, I-42, 235; Part II, Plate
6, I-349; Part II, Plate 10, I-349; Part IV,
Plate 9, I-290; Part V, Plate 3, II-204; Part
V, Plate 7, II-91
architect/architecture, I-xii, 12, 13, 15, 42, 44,
96, 101, 117–18, 121, 168, 178, 224–25, 235,
259, 264, 265, 266–68, 272, 274, 275, 276,
280, 282, 290, 292, 305, 332, 336, 343, 349,
362–63, 384–86, 394, 406, 409; II-xii, 24, 50,
82, 91, 117, 134, 136–37, 144, 181, 183, 186,
204, 222, 225; Georgian, I-343, 351; II-181,
186; Gothic Revival, II-82; International
Style, I-121, 267; II-24; Le Corbusier,
I-267; "Mock Tudor," II-181, 183; "neo-
Georgian" 233; "New Barbarism," I-267;
terminology of, I-286
Arden, John, I-38
argument, I-39, 82, 132, 214, 258, 350, 368,
373, 385–86, 393, 406, 407; II-40, 41, 45, 53,
63, 68, 71, 114, 135, 174, 175, 197, 222, 223
Argyle, John Michael, I-139
Argylls, I-168, 386; II-120
Ariana Afghan Airlines accident, I-340
"Ariel," I-286
Ark Royal, I-396, 397; II-92, 126, 212, 213
Arkwright, I-27, 36, 250
Arlington Road, Chertsey Road, and St.
Margaret's Road, East Twickenham
(locations), I-233; II-12, 13, 20, 33
Arlington Television and Radio, I-324
Arlott, John, I-318
Armstrong, Herbert and Garner Ted, I-364;
II-120
Armstrong, Neil, I-272
Armstrong-Jones, Tony (Lord Snowdon),
I-184, 255, 305; II-52
Army School of Transport, Longmore
(location), I-328; II-77
Arni Magnusson Institute, II-10
Arnold, Malcolm, I-360
Arnold, P.P., I-328
"Arrivederci Roma," II-40
"Ars longa, vita brevis," I-376
art, I-xii, 3–4, 5, 6, 7, 8, 11, 13–14, 15, 16–17,
18–19, 21, 22, 32, 37, 42, 44, 54, 61, 63, 64,
66, 67–71, 74, 77–78, 80–81, 87, 93–94, 100,
101, 106, 108, 123, 125, 127, 144, 146, 153,
161, 164, 179, 181, 183, 186, 189, 196, 205,
209, 212, 217, 222–23, 230, 240–41, 243,
255–56, 261, 266, 280, 285–86, 304–5, 313–
14, 322–23, 339, 358, 362, 372, 374–84, 389,
405–6, 409, 411; II-33, 50, 51–52, 56, 71, 75,
77, 79, 85, 86, 99, 111, 119, 127–28, 130–31,
135, 136, 138, 157, 176, 204, 221–22, 225,
227; anamorphic perspective, II-71–72;
critics/criticism of, I-63, 68, 74, 77, 80,
127, 382–83, 406; II-75, 157, 222; Art Deco,
I-144, 150, 222; artists (*see* "artists");
consumption of, I-72, 76, 77, 127; (of the)
everyday, I-51, 54, 223, 247, 261, 262, 306;
galleries (*see* art galleries); movements/
periods/genre: abstract, I-3, 5, 6, 8, 13–16,
255; II-24; experimental, I-66; II-75, 155,

165, 185; Flemish, I-5, 68, 74, 101, 242, 373–75; Futurism, I-14, 82, 235; Gothic, I-68, 245; II-82, 122; High Art, I-64, 106, 161; Impressionism, I-9, 268, 373, 375, 377, 382; II-138; landscapes I-64, 70, 76, 137, 222, 373, 374, 376–77, 383; II-130, 134; Mannerism, I-68, 77, 94, 101; Modernism, I-6, 13, 14, 17, 25, 36, 42, 56, 72, 82, 101, 130, 133, 189, 191, 198, 212, 217, 247, 255, 266–68, 295, 297, 307, 350, 374, 379; II-8, 51, 72, 78, 79, 97, 115, 117, 176; Pop Art, I-230; Post-Impression, I-268, 373; II-147; Post-Modernist, I-13, 25, 35, 199, 254–55, 259, 298, 299, 374, 379; II-8, 44, 135; Realism, I-375; II-165; surrealism, I-10, 15, 20, 153; II-48, 85; and admission fees, II-77; and obscenity, I-66, 107; II-77, 79, 84; portraits, I-6, 15, 22, 33, 42, 51, 68, 77, 86, 98, 101, 103, 180, 193, 217, 222, 235, 241, 265, 305, 346, 374–76; II-33, 52, 112, 119, 162, 183; Renaissance, I-68, 74, 77, 242, 334, 378, 380; II-15, 33, 134, 183. *See also* museums

art galleries: Courtauld, I-66, 70, 77, 78; Ikon Gallery, II-135–36; London Arts Gallery, II-77; Museo del Prado, I-242, 382; National Gallery, I-5, 22, 42, 51, 64, 66, 68, 74, 76, 77, 78, 94, 101, 127, 143, 290, 306, 327, 375–76, 378–80, 382–83, 389, 393; II-33, 49, 56, 138; National Portrait Gallery, I-217, 235, 265; Tate Britain, I-66, 77, 377; II-77; Tate Modern, II-85; Victoria and Albert (V&A), I-42, 64, 66, 68, 100; II-81;

"Arthur," I-3, 8, 20, 21, 26, 27, 33, 36, 48, 63, 64, 77, 93, 98, 101, 140, 144–48, 153, 156, 221, 233, 302, 305, 311, 312, 316, 321, 327, 335, 352, 364, 406, 408, 409, 410, 412; II-114, 121, 222, 224, 225, 226, 228

Arthur, King. *See Monty Python and the Holy Grail* in films

"Arthur X," I-311, 312, 323, 406; II-127, 222

"arthropods," II-77

artists: John Alexander, II-153; Fra Angelico, I-380; Max Beckmann, I-376; Hieronymus Bosch, I-61, 256, 375; II-111, 121; Sandro Botticelli, I-94, 125, 128, 242, 376, 380, 383, 405; II-221; Constantin Brancusi, I-6, 13; Georges Braque, I-6; Pieter Brueghel, I-42, 242, 373–75; Agnolo di Bronzino, I-5, 68, 94; Bernard Buffet, I-6; Michelangelo Caravaggio, I-383; Paul Cezanne, I-77; II-147; Mark Chagall, I-6; John Constable, I-42, 64, 70, 137, 200, 375–79; Gustave Courbet, I-11, 375; Honoré Daumier, I-375; Leonardo Da Vinci, I-64, 101, 222, 376, 380, 383; II-33; Jacques Louis David, I-15, 383; Edgar Degas, I-77, 377; Willem De Kooning, I-8; Eugène Delacroix, I-382; Robert Delaunay, I-8; Jan Vredeman de Vries, I-5, 42, 143, 240–41, 245, 290, 292, 334, 349, 372, 386; II-83, 121; Lorenzo di Credi, I-386; Donatello, I-380; Gustave Doré, II-115; François-Hubert Drouais, I-327; Duccio, I-380; Marcel Duchamps, I-101, 362; II-119; Raoul Dufy, I-9, 14;

Albrecht Dürer (*see* "Dürer"); Franz Eichenberg, I-376; El Greco, I-68; Thomas Gainsborough, I-98, 222, 375–76; Paul Gauguin, I-77; II-147; Walter Gay, II-153; Gericault, I-11; II-56; Giotto, I-380; Spencer Gore, I-223; Francisco Goya, I-383; George Grosz, II-153; Frans Hals, I-375; J.T. Hart, I-376; David Hockney, I-137, 230, 232; II-85; William Hogarth, I-251, 306, 375; II-147, 153; Hans Holbein, I-127; Jacob Jordaens, I-5; Paul Klee, I-14; Franz Kline, I-3; Oscar Kokoschka, I-14, 17; Edwin Landseer, I-378, 394; Thomas Lawrence, I-375; Man Ray II-85; Édouard Manet, I-42, 374–75; Quentin Matsys, I-346; II-183; Michelangelo, I-11, 70, 100, 289, 301, 327, 334, 336, 375, 382, 405, 406; II-44, 207, 221, 222; Jean François Millet, I-375; Joan Miró II-85; Piet Mondrian, I-15, 16; II-24; Claude Monet, I-77, 375, 377; Henry Moore, I-3; Ben Nicholson, I-16, 17; Sidney Nolan, I-345; Roland Penrose, II-85; Francesco Pesellino, I-94; Camille Pissarro, I-377; Raphael, I-68, 74, 87, 382; II-33; John Robertson Reid, I-376; Rembrandt, I-42, 64, 180, 375–76, 378, 382; Renoir, I-77, 375, 377; Joshua Reynolds, I-375; Gerhard Richter, I-389; Hans Richter, I-66; William Rogers, I-235; George Romney, I-375; Dante Rossetti, I-196; Peter Paul Rubens, I-11, 64, 66, 70, 74, 127, 155, 375, 382; II-56; Walter Sickert, I-223; Tapies II-85; Tiepolo, I-66; Tintoretto, I-68; Titian, I-374, 380, 382; II-18; Henri Toulouse-Lautrec, I-14, 22, 376, 406; II-29, 147, 148; V.G. Tretchikoff, I-85, 119; J.M.W. Turner, I-64, 68, 70, 72, 76, 137, 377; Utrillo, I-70, 77, 217; Anthony Van Dyck, I-376, 383; Jan Van Eyck, I-68, 101, 375–76, 383; Velazquez, I-64, 376, 382–83; Vincent Van Gogh, I-70, 77, 373; II-147; Heinrich von Angeli, II-190; Johannes (Jan) Vermeer, I-42, 77, 127, 375, 383; Waterhouse, I-196; Watteau, I-78, 136

Arts Council, I-100, 214

artworks: *The Acrobats*, et al. (Léger), I-14; *Adoration of the Shepherds* (Poussin), I-5; *The Allegory of War and Peace* (Rubens), I-74; *An Allegory with Venus and Cupid* (Bronzino), I-5, 68, 94; *The Ambassadors* (Holbein), I-127; *Apocalypse of St. John, The Dragon with the Seven Heads* (Dürer), I-350; *Arabian Horses Fighting in a Stable* (Delacroix), II-56; *Ascent of the Blessed* (Bosch), I-256; *Bacchus*, et al. (Rubens), I-74; *The Baille Family* (Gainsborough), I-98; *The Battle of Trafalgar* (Stanfield), I-173, 175; *Bicycle* (Braque), I-6; *Big Julie*, et al. (Léger), I-14; *Birth of Venus* (Botticelli), I-94, 127, 128–29, 242, 376, 383, 405; *Black Spot I*, et al. (Kandinsky), I-5; "*Blue Boy*" (Gainsborough); I-375–76; *Bridge at Arles* (Van Gogh), I-373; *Bridge at Kew* (Turner), I-64; *Cardinal de Richelieu* (Champaigne), I-5; *Charles I Dismounted*

(Van Dyck), I-376, 383; "Charles VI" (Bibiena), I-42, 235; "Charles Cornwallis" (Smith), I-217; "*The Chinese Girl*" (Tretchikoff), II-85, 119; *Composition with Yellow, Blue and Red* (Mondrian), I-15; *Le Comte de Vaudreuil* (Drouais), I-327; *The Cornfield* (Constable), I-376; *A Country Cricket Match* (Reid), I-376–77; "The covered riding school…" (Bibiena), II-204; *Crossing the Brook* (Turner), I-64; *David* (Michelangelo), I-100, 375; II-81; *The Death of Marat* (David), I-15, 383; *Deauville, Drying the Sails* (Dufy), I-9; *Déjeuner Sur L'Herbe* (Manet), I-42, 375; *Les Demoiselles d'Avignon* (Picasso), I-12; *The Deposition* (Caravaggio), I-383; *Dido Building Carthage*, et al. (Turner), I-76; *Discus Thrower* (Myron), I-375; *The Doctor* (Fildes), I-96; *Early Dawn Attack* (Schreyvogel), II-204; "Elizabeth I" (Rogers), I-235; *Erasmus of Rotterdam* (Dürer), I-372; *Falconeers, Frontispiece* (Braque), I-6; *The Fighting Temeraire* (Turner), I-68, 76; *The Flight into Egypt* (Dürer), II-128; *The Gas Cooker* (Gore), I-223; *Giovanni Arnolfini and His Bride* (Van Eyck), I-68, 101, 375–76, 383; *Gloria* (Titian), I-382; *La Goulue Arriving at the Moulin Rouge with Two Women* (Toulouse-Lautrec), I-376; *Govaert van Surpele and His Wife* (Jordaens), I-5; *Guernica* (Picasso), I-7, 11–12; *Hampstead Heath With a Rainbow* (Constable), I-64; "Hanover Square" (Dayes), I-315; *The Hay Wain* (Constable), I-42, 70, 200, 325, 372, 376; II-18; *Head of a Bull* (Picasso), I-17; *The Immaculate Conception* (Gravelli), I-5; *John Before God and the Elders* (Dürer), II-121, 128, 130, 134; *The Kiss* (Rodin), I-26, 42, 290, 375; *The Knight and the Lansquenet* (Dürer), II-128; *Lady at the Window* (Vermeer), I-77; *Laocoön*, I-375, I-; *L.H.O.O.Q.* (Duchamps), I-101; II-119; *A Lion Hunt* (Rubens), II-56; *Man Taking Shower in Beverly Hills*, et al. (Hockney), I-230; *The Madonna and Child*, et al. (Raphael), I-74; *The Madonna of the Meadow* (Bellini), I-290, 372; *Marriage a la Mode* (Hogarth), I-306; II-147; *The Marsham Children* (Gainsborough), I-222; *Las Meninas* (Velazquez), I-375, 383; *Mona Lisa* (Da Vinci), I-101, 289, 376, 383, 406; II-119; *Moses* (Michelangelo), I-375; *Mr. and Mrs. Andrews* (Gainsborough), I-376; *Musician* (Da Vinci), II-33; *Numbering at Bethlehem* (Brueghel), I-373; *Olive Trees by the Golfe Juan* (Dufy), I-9; *Over London by Rail* (Doré), II-115; *Peace* (Picasso), I-12; *Place du Tertre* (Utrillo), I-77; "Part II, Plate 6" (Bibiena), I-349; "Part II, Plate 10" (Bibiena), I-292, 349; "Part IV, Plate 9" (Bibiena), I-42, 290; "Part V, Plate 7" (Bibiena), II-91; "Plate 7" (de Vries), I-245, 349, 372; "Plate 15" (de Vries), I-240, 290; "Plate 24" (de Vries), I-386; "Plate 28" (de Vries), I-245, 334; "Plate 39" (de Vries), I-245; "Plate 42" (de Vries), I-5; "Plate 47" (de Vries), I-5; *Portrait of an Elderly Man* (Matsys), I-346; II-183; *Portrait of a Gentleman*, et al. (Moroni), II-33; *Portrait of Willem Bartholsz. Ruyter* (Rembrandt), I-42, 180; *Portrait of the Artist* (Buffet), I-6; *Predella of the Pistoia Santa Trinità Altarpiece* (Pesellino), I-94; *Race of Riderless Horses* (Gericault), II-56; *The Rake's Progress* (Hogarth), I-251; *A Rustic Timepiece* (Hart), I-376; *Saint Vincent Ferrer* (del Cossa), I-143; *Self-Portrait*, et al. (Raphael), II-33; *Self-Portrait* (Rembrandt), I-376; *The Slave Ship* (Turner), I-68; *Stag at Bay* (Landseer), I-378; *Stage Curtain for the Ballet "Parade"* (Picasso), I-7; *St. Anthony Reading* (Dürer), I-350, 406; II-110, 111, 222; *Study for "The City,"* et al. (Delaunay), I-14; *Sunflowers*, et al. (Van Gogh), I-77; *Tarquin and Lucretia* (Crespi), I-75–76; *The Thinker* (Rodin), I-375; *The Third of May* (Goya), I-383; *Three Chairs with a Section of a Picasso Mural* (Hockney), I-230; *Triumph of Death* (Brueghel), I-242; *Two Greys Juxtaposed* (Richter), I-389; *Untitled*, et al. (Braque), I-6; *The Virgin and Child* (di Credi), I-386; *War* (Picasso), I-12; *Windows Open Simultaneously* (Delaunay), I-8; *Winter, Hunters in the Snow,* and *Winter Landscape with a Bird Trap* (Brueghel), I-373; *Women and Bird in the Moonlight* (Miro), I-15; *A Young Woman Seated at a Virginal*, and *A Young Woman Standing at a Virginal* (Vermeer), I-77, 383; *Young Woman with a Water Pitcher* (Vermeer), I-77

asceticism, I-129, 131, 132, 136
"Ascot water heaters," II-190
"asdic," I-391
Ashbrook, John, II-145
Ashburton and Newbridge, Dartmoor (location), I-261, 392
Ashmore, Jonathan, I-289, 290
Asia/Asian, I-39, 59, 85, 145, 184, 194, 217, 317, 331, 360, 365, 367, 371; II-19, 26, 48, 81, 103, 106, 117, 189, 197, 198; countries: Burma, I-287, 312; China, I-67–68, 71, 99, 165, 194, 284, 293–94, 296, 301, 334, 349, 352–53, 358, 360–61, 365, 367, 379, 406, 407, 412; II-16, 20, 23, 35, 67, 68, 75, 104, 105, 106, 117, 123, 180, 198, 201, 203, 222, 223, 228; Hong Kong, I-194, 253, 374; II-104; India, I-12, 23, 39, 71, 97, 101, 103, 111, 145, 210, 223, 282, 297, 315–16, 317, 321, 322, 329, 340, 342, 364, 371, 373, 387, 406; II-18, 35, 72, 89, 104, 154, 162, 166, 222; Japan, I-54, 101, 173, 174, 181, 185, 285, 304, 333, 364; II-46, 98, 102, 131, 188; Mongolia, I-13; II-198; Nepal, I-397; II-37, 64, 67, 72, 213; New Guinea, I-259, 278; New Zealand, I-125, 278, 317, 322, 335, 340, 349, 355, 358, 360, 368, 373; II-37, 93, 208; Pakistan, I-312, 316, 317, 322, 342, 371, 373; II-30, 68; Tasmania, I-278, 321; Thailand, I-285; Tibet, I-65, 126, 189; II-44;

Turkey, I-331, 350; regions: Australasia, I-278, 321, 360
Askey, Arthur, II-57
Asquith, H.H., I-17
"assignats," II-165–66
"Assizes," I-336, 372; II-119, 188
Associated Rediffusion TV, I-16, 49, 124, 139, 174, 237, 388, 398; II-10, 80, 214
Astaire, Fred, I-294
"Asteroid," Pete Moore, I-210
Aston Martin, I-265
astronauts, I-39, 158, 264, 273. *See also* Buzz Aldrin, Neil Armstrong *and* Apollo space missions; Gus Grissom and Alan Shepherd, I-158
Aswan Dam and Lake Nasser, I-327
"at a stroke," II-148
At Last the 1948 Show, I-3, 7, 26, 27, 31, 40, 45, 46, 47, 52, 65, 66, 77, 116, 134, 150, 154, 159, 189, 282, 292, 300, 315, 338, 388, 413; II-41, 76; and "I've Got a Parrot Up My Nose," I-154; and "Sheepdog Trials," I-45–46, 52; and "Top of the Form," I-66
"Atalanta," II-30
Atatürk, Kemal, I-12, 350
Atkins, Humphrey, I-247
"Atkins, Tommy," I-373
Atkinson, Prof. Richard, I-330, 336
"Atomic-Mutated Cat," I-211, 339, 343, 406; II-127, 222
Attenborough, David, I-40, 95, 280, 407; II-45, 88, 183, 202, 223
Attenborough, Richard, I-18, 230, 408; II-5, 17, 135, 150, 151, 154, 202, 224
Attila the Hun, I-201, 202, 311, 317, 320, 323, 396, 406
Attila the Hun (film stock), I-202, 323, 396; II-127, 212
Attlee, Clement, I-9, 119, 196, 357
"Audience Research Bulletin," I-204
"Aunt Edna," I-17, 43; II-58
"Auntie Beeb," I-31, 272, 276; II-4, 11, 155
austerity/rationing, I-34, 121, 133–34, 225, 244, 323, 381; II-25, 26, 40, 47, 87, 179
Austin 30, II-111, 115
Australia, I-22, 111, 118, 124, 125, 141, 144, 165, 183, 226, 257, 277, 278, 295, 312, 315, 317, 321, 322, 333, 335–36, 339–42, 344–48, 351, 355, 368, 372–73, 394; II-5, 34, 35, 49, 75, 76, 89, 103, 116, 119, 131, 132, 140, 145, 147, 151, 177, 203, 207, 210; aborigines, I-226, 278, 339, 342; Alice Springs, I-342; Sydney, I-96, 118, 342, 347, 348; II-72, 75; Woolloomooloo, I-339, 348; II-223
Australia Road, White City, Shepherd's Bush (location), I-104, 132, 134, 138, 149
"auteur theory," I-365–66
"authenticity," I-101; II-38, 124, 188, 189
authority figures, I-28, 39, 90, 103, 111, 112, 116, 118, 131, 136, 139, 176, 177, 196, 209, 233, 238, 258, 265, 291, 329, 366–67; II-9, 55, 115, 130, 206
avant garde, I-211, 235, 265, 362; II-127, 155, 157, 195

Avery, Tex, I-6, 20, 29, 52, 71, 76, 104, 106, 127, 154, 178, 192, 204, 279, 363, 372, 387; II-39, 86, 98
Avery, Charles, I-290
"Axis Café," I-185, 195, 197
Axis powers (WWII), I-173, 185; II-23, 134, 179
Ayres, Lew, I-204
"Ayrshire," I-262; II-115, 170
Aztec, I-157

"B" roadways: B2127, I-10; B3387, II-101
"BA hood," I-27
Babbacombe, I-278, 281
Babycham, I-386
Bach, Carl Philip Emanuel, I-98
Bach, J.S., I-94, 98, 355, 401, 402, 404; II-46, 181; and "Fantasia & Fugue in G minor," I-402; II-46, 218; and "Prelude & Fugue, D Major BWV 532," I-355, 401; II-217
Bacharach, Burt (and Hal David), I-205–6
"bachelor friend," II-187–88
back benches, I-312, 316, 319–20
"back marker," I-9, 14, 40, 280; II-207
back projection ("BP"), I-5, 174
Bacon, Francis, II-123
"bad faith," I-85, 201; II-189, 194
"Bad Ischl Dairy," II-50, 207
Baden-Powell, Robert, II-63, 102, 109
Badenov, Boris, II-20
Badger, Mr., I-36, 92; II-77, 111, 117, 119
Baez, Joan, I-317
BAFTA Awards, I-295; II-141, 150, 151, 154
"Bagot, Harry," II-62, 65, 72, 116
Bagshot, Surrey, I-80
Bailey, Jeff and *Out of the Past*, I-335
"Bailey, Betty," II-41
Bailey, Pearl, I-335
"baked beans," I-154, 372
Baker, Richard. *See MPFC* extras and walk-ons
Bakewell, Joan, I-80, 82, 299; II-75; and Michael Dean, I-299, II-75; on *Late Night Line-Up*, I-80, 82, 223, 299, 351, 366; II-75; and Newnham College, I-80; and Nicholas Tresilian and Denis Tuohy, I-82, 299; II-75
"Bakewell's tart," II-101
Bakhtin, Mikhail, I-82; II-125
"balance of payments," I-157, 167, 390; II-45
Balanchine, George, II-20
Balearic Islands, II-67, 69
Baldwin, Stanley, I-13, 222, 328, 361, 383; II-83 and "Mrs. Stanley Baldwin," I-328
Baldwin, T.W., *Organisation and Personnel of the Shakespearean Company*, I-66
Balfour, James, I-61, 352; II-149
"ballcock," II-161
Ballet Rambert, II-195
"Balleys [sic] of Bond Street," II-62
Balmoral, Scotland, I-40; II-132
BALPA (British Airline Pilots' Association), I-252–54, 258, 263, 364, 406; II-188, 193, 222
Bamberger, C.S., II-181

Band of the Grenadier Guards (BGG), I-15, 149, 190, 211, 212, 264, 321, 399–404; II-195, 208, 215–20

Bank-a-Ball pinball machine, I-191

bank holiday, I-29, 34, 364; II-118

banners and placards, I-33, 38, 59, 161; II-10, 11, 39, 56, 86, 139

Banning, James B., I-272

Bannister, Minnie. *See The Goon Show*

Banqueting House, Whitehall Palace, I-74, 272; II-134

Barber, Rt. Hon. Anthony, I-346, 393; II-35, 117, 141, 144, 147; as a "loony," II-35, 144

Barbican Estate, I-267, 276

Barclay, Humphrey, I-16, 197, 247, 291

"Barclaycard," II-41; Barclay's, I-261, 327; II-41, 49

Bardot, Brigitte, I-233

Barker, David and "North Flight," II-30

Barker, Ronnie, I-5, 75, 79, 107, 129, 163, 184, 202, 217; II-154, 162; as Arkwright, I-36

"barley cross fingers," I-128, 339–40; and "barley sugar," I-339–40

Barlow, William Henry and R.M. Ordish, I-393

Barnard, Christiaan, I-80, 342; II-42–43, 157

Barnes, I-9, 33, 60; II-29; and Barnes Police Station (location), I-33

Barnsley, I-27, 183; and Barnsley College, I-27

Barnstaple, I-191, 352

Baron and Baroness. *See* titles/honorifics

Baroque, I-5, 64, 74, 98, 268; II-138, 197

Barratt, Michael, I-187, 391; II-156, 189

Barré, Raoul, I-6

Barrie, J.M., I-44

Barron, Bebe and Louis, I-125

Barrow, Clyde and Bonnie Parker, I-321

Barrow-in-Furness, I-291

Barr's. *See* Tizer

Barry John, I-93, 98, 141, 399, 400; II-111, 215, 216

Barry, Maj. Gen. William Farquhar, I-290; II-71; and the "Barry Bigot doll," II-71

Barrymore, Lionel, I-204

Barthes, Roland, I-144

"Bartlett," I-50; II-161, 167

"Barwick Green," II-187

The Basil Brush Show, II-51, 172

"Basil Cassidy and the Sundance Sheep," I-321

Basing House, II-177

Basingstoke, Hampshire, I-253, 261, 364, 406; II-117, 177, 182, 222

Bassey, Shirley, II-111

Bates, Michael, I-176

Bath, I-159, 187, 223, 260, 344

"Bath and Wellsish," II-41–42

Batista, Fulgencio, I-255

Batley, West Yorkshire, (and the "Batley Townswomen's Guild") I-172, 173, 339; II-42, 77–78, 84, 88, 196, 222

Battersby, Roy, II-111

Battersea (and Power Station), I-4, 191

battles: Agincourt, I-46, 207; II-98; the Ardennes (and the Bulge), I-4; Borodino, I-393; Bosworth Field, I-18; Britain, I-23, 24, 77, 105, 137, 173; II-181; Cable Street, II-83; Maldon, II-13; Pearl Harbor, I-172, 173, 340, 392, 406; II-118, 222; the Somme, II-111, 112; "Spion Kop," I-223, 292; Stalingrad, I-189, 199–200; Trafalgar, I-16, 173, 175, 360, 393–94, 406; II-222; Ypres, I-371, 384, 413; II-182, 229

Bauhaus movement, I-266, 267, 362; II-24, 117

Bavaria (and Bavarian Television), I-xii, 14, 42, 75, 88, 108, 175, 196, 264, 290, 295, 332, 350, 372, 393; II-xii, 5, 6, 10, 50, 71, 74, 112

Baxter, Raymond, I-4, 313, 316, 338

BBC: BBC1, I-13, 40, 57, 86, 115, 204, 271, 278, 289, 291, 298, 314, 316, 327, 329, 338, 391, 406, 412; II-4, 12, 20, 22, 27, 32, 34, 40, 46, 50, 51, 74, 81, 88, 107, 112, 121, 130, 140, 151, 156, 161, 162, 183, 191, 202, 222, 228; BBC2, I-40, 49, 79, 80, 86, 95, 136, 138, 141, 213, 216, 223, 257, 263, 275, 283, 291, 328, 335, 336, 338, 388, 390, 413; Board of Governors, II-46; Booster Station, Gallanach (location), II-35; Broadcast House, I-81; II-99; canteen, I-374; Film Library, I-395, 397; II-65, 73, 153, 211; Home Service, I-21, 80, 86, 137, 146, 262; II-205; Light Entertainment, I-10, 32, 35, 50, 67, 82, 115, 131, 173, 275, 299, 307, 410; II-12, 15, 26, 33, 43, 45, 65, 73, 141, 142, 150, 151, 154, 171, 177, 182, 183, 196, 226; Managing Director for Television, II-39; microphone, I-19, 143; Publications Office I-361; II-22; Programme Planners, I-75, 84, 124, 248, 406, 411; II-140, 222, 227; puppet theatre, I-121; Radio, I-7, 21, 46, 81, 85, 112, 119, 136, 204, 207, 275, 313, 324, 345, 346, 361; II-16, 22, 80, 87, 93, 117, 132, 163, 187, 191, 202, 207, 208; Reith Lectures, I-167; and regional opt-outs, I-248, 365; II-26; Studios (at TC), I-58, 84, 149, 381; II-64, 69, 72, 73, 132, 142, 144, 185; Television Centre, I-10, 81, 84, 91, 97, 122, 134, 138, 149, 154, 182, 238, 243, 250, 280, 299, 371; II-25, 32, 53, 70, 72, 88, 95, 99, 121, 148, 172, 185, 197; "Variety Programmes Policy Guide for Writers and Producers," I-50, 59, 89, 276; Wardrobe, I-386

"the BBC is short of money," I-95, 328, 406; II-20, 22, 26, 179, 222

beach (location), I-xi, 4, 52, 64, 65, 75, 88, 157, 158, 240, 261, 361–62, 364–65, 370, 381, 405; II-xi, 10, 221

Beach, James, I-291

Beamish, Adrian, I-291

Beamon, Bob, I-166

Beat poets, I-145

The Beatles, I-32, 34, 53, 132, 141, 160, 162, 174, 210, 212–13, 225, 236, 256, 282, 285, 295, 303, 321; II-36, 119, 182; George Harrison, I-83, 162, 232, 309, 375, II-36; John Lennon, I-83, 167, 232, 346, 360, 366; II-36, 77; Paul McCartney, I-34, 167; Ringo Starr, I-333, 409; II-20, 36, 225; film (*see* films); songs: "Can't Buy Me Love," I-141; "Taxman," I-225; "When I'm Sixty-Four," I-34

Beatty, Warren, II-94

Beaumont, Hugh "Binkie," I-223

Beaverbrook, Lord, I-154; II-68

Beccles, Suffolk, I-86

Becket, Thomas, I-353, 361; II-20, 21, 22, 26, 27, 28, 34, 42

Beckett, Samuel. *See* novelists/prose writers

Bedfordshire, I-299–300, 354, 364; II-45

bed-sitter, I-185

Beecham, Sir Thomas, I-180

Beerbohm, Max, *Zuleika Dobson*, I-9, 70

Beethoven, Ludwig, I-5, 8, 15, 94, 327, 330, 331, 333–36, 399, 406; II-33–34, 215, 222

"Bell and Compasses," I-185

Bell Hotel, 5 Orford Hill, Norwich, II-21

"Belling, Rev. Arthur," I-327, 335; II-124, 228

Belloc, Hilaire. *See* novelists/prose writers

"The Bells of St. Mary's," I-28

Bell's Whisky, II-78, 178

Belmondo, Jean-Paul, I-354

"Belpit, Mr.," I-252, 253, 262, 313, 407

Belsize Park, I-241, 378

Belzoni, Giovanni, I-330

Bendix Laundrette, Uxbridge Road (location), I-56

Benjamin, Walter and "The Work of Art in the Age of Mechanical Reproduction," I-72

Benn, Tony (Anthony Neil Wedgwood Benn), I-87, 319

Bennett, Alan, I-16, 45, 105, 145, 286; II-61, 80, 103

Bennett, Derek, I-370

Bennett, Felix James, II-14, 15

Benny, Jack, I-313

The Benny Hill Show. See television shows

Benson Report, I-334

Bentaga, Abdallah, II-18

Bentham, Jeremy, I-344

Bentine, Michael, I-20, 212, 251

Berger, Helmut, II-47

Bergeron, David, I-212, 277; II-9, 62

Bergman, Ingmar. *See* film directors

Bergman, Ingrid and *The Bells of St. Mary's*, I-28

Bergson, Henri, I-40, 272, 313; II-111, 115

Berkeley, Busby, I-367; II-74

Berkshire, I-4, 18, 170, 175, 233, 285; II-12, 199, 203

Berlin, I-32, 80, 191, 198, 363; II-47, 51, 192; Air Lift, I-80

Berlin, Irving, I-179, 400, 403, 404; III-137, 180, 216, 219, 220: "A Pretty Girl is Like a Melody," II-137, 219; "Let's Face the Music," II-180; "There's No Business Like Show Business," I-179, 400

Bernadette of Lourdes, I-323

Berne, Eric, and *Games People Play*, I-27

Bernstein, Marcelle, II-14

Berwick-on-Tweed, I-112; II-209, 210

Bethmann-Hollweg, Theobald, II-164

Bethnal Green Road, I-224, 235

Bevan, Aneurin, I-102

"Bevis," I-80, 144

Beyond the Fringe, I-15, 16, 18, 35, 45, 57, 68, 80, 86, 105, 106, 137, 140, 144–45, 150,

162, 165, 202, 211, 265, 286, 313, 367, 390; II-61, 62, 80, 86, 103, 132, 139, 176, 199, 207; castmembers: Alan Bennett, I-16, 45, 105, 145, 286; II-61, 80, 103; Peter Cook, I-15, 16, 45, 105, 367; II-103; Jonathan Miller, I-16, 106, 140, 145, 165, 211, 390; II-103; Dudley Moore, I-15, 16, 45, 144, 150; II-103, 216; sketches: "A Piece Of My Mind (The Heat-Death Of The Universe)," I-106; "The Aftermyth of War," I-18, 80, 86, 137; "Bollard," II-176; "Civil War," I-68; "Home Thoughts From Abroad," I-165; "Man Bites God," I-140; "One Leg Too Few," I-150; "Porn Shop," I-211, 287, 390; "Royal Box," I-45; "Sitting on the Bench," I-367; "So That's the Way You Like It," I-57; II-132; "Steppes in the Right Direction" and "TV PM," I-68

Bexley, I-185, 297; II-12, 67, 156

Biao, Lin, I-296, 358; II-16

Bibiena, Giuseppe Galli, I-42, 235, 290, 349; II-91, 204

Bible, I-4, 159, 175, 207, 208, 210, 270, 323, 326, 368–69, 401; II-6, 17, 23, 74, 181, 203

Bible Belt, II-23

"biblical laments," I-4

Bicton, East Budleigh, Devon, II-209; College, II-180; Gardens (location), II-166, 180, 181

bicycling/bicycles, I-3, 6, 11, 14, 17, 21, 22, 50, 55, 59, 60, 94, 172, 185, 245, 289, 406

"bide-a-wee." *See* "Abide-a-Wee"

Bideford, I-185

"bidets," II-81

"Biff Boys," II-78

"big bad rabbit," II-78

Big Ben, I-238; II-82, 173

"Big Cheese," I-64, 67, 68, 74, 99, 247, 352

Big Country, Keith Papworth, II-142, 149, 203, 219, 220

"Big School," I-212, 345; II-22, 38

Biggles, Captain, I-7, 35, 58, 72, 83, 144, 151, 157, 160, 212, 223, 227, 237, 241, 253, 260, 366; II-10, 23, 59, 69, 91–95, 97, 98, 171, 195; Algy (Algernon Montgomery Lacey), I-7, 157, 160, 329, 366; II-91, 94, 95, 97, 98; and Ginger, I-10, 148, 151, 157, 160, 212; II-94–95, 97–98

"Biggles, Mary," II-92

Biggleswade, I-354

Biggs, Ronnie, I-233

"Bignall, Mary" (Mary Bignal-Rand), I-172, 174, 396, 410

Bilbow, Tony, I-351, 356

"Billy Bunter," I-380; II-63

Binder, Maurice, II-56

"Bing Tiddle Tiddle Bong," I-94, 182, 307, 339, 407

Bingley, II-63

"bingo boys," I-78, 83

"Binkie," I-223

"binomial theorem," I-386

Birmingham, I-90, 124, 187, 223, 271, 274, 279, 293, 295, 299, 320, 324, 340, 342, 365; II-27, 63, 64, 68, 69, 72, 89, 114, 135, 146, 204

"biro," II-21

birth control, I-80, 138, 160, 201, 208, 211, 250, 284; II-85

Birth of Venus, S. Botticelli, I-129, 383

"biscuitbarrel," I-192, 307

The Bishop film (and character), I-111, 141, 264, 265, 266, 268, 269–71, 273–75; II-23, 56, 223

"Bishop of Dulwich," I-361

"Bishop of East Anglia," I-289, 291

Bishop, Ellen, I-161

Bishop's crook and mitre, I-253, 266, 313

Bishop's Stortford, I-361

Bismarck, Chancellor, II-162

Bjornstrand, Gunnar, II-4

Black, C.W., I-166

The Black Death. *See* plague

Black Dyke Mills Band and John Foster, I-242, 400

Black Panthers, II-18, 34

Black Park, Fulmer, near Slough, Buckinghamshire (location), II-55

"Black Power," I-226, 312; II-4

Black Rod, I-313

"black spot," I-289, 290, 306, 406; II-78, 88, 222

"blackballing," I-267, 270

Blackburn, Tony, II-112, 118, 174; and David Gregory, I-112

Blackmon, Honor, I-24

Blackton, J. Stuart. *See* film directors *and* animators

blancmange, I-xii, 55, 62, 64, 73, 110, 111–12, 117, 124, 125, 153, 296, 320, 395, 407; II-xii, 116, 147, 170, 211, 223

The Black and White Minstrel Show. See television shows

"black cap," I-328

black (gallows) humor, I-68, 185, 189

"blacked up" (black face), I-313, 315, 324, 344; II-42, 46, 209

Blake, William, I-69, 134, 271, 399; II-40, 215

Blanchard, Jean-Pierre, II-161

"blank verse," I-340

blasphemy, I-20, 138, 245; II-11, 90

Blenheim Palace, I-195

Bletchley, Buckinghamshire, I-143, 144, 411

"Blind Pew," I-229; II-78

"blimey," I-5, 50, 128

Blofeld, I-67, 352

"Bloggs," I-291

"blood tragedies," I-380

Bloodnok, Major Denis. *See The Goon Show*

"bloody," I-5, 50, 54, 131, 157, 185, 217, 242, 245, 247, 250, 253, 261, 298, 323, 360, 371–72, 406, 407; II-177, 185, 222–23

"bloody daffodils," I-261, 275

Bloody Sunday, I-72

"bloody weather," I-5, 217, 245; II-177

Bloomfield, Robert, I-191

Blue Boy, Gainsborough. *See* artworks *and* artists

"Bluebottle." *See The Goon Show*

"blue cheese," I-28, 32

"The Blue Danube," J. Strauss, I-385, 386, 402, 404, 408; II-118, 140, 142, 218, 220, 224

The Blue Lamp. See "films"

The Blue Rider Group (Der Blaue Reiter), I-5, 8

Blue Streak missile system, I-63, 231

Blyth Agency. *See* talent (job) agencies

Board of Trade, I-231, 291, 340, 346

Boardman, Tom, I-299

Bodell, Jack, I-281, 407; II-130, 131, 133, 223

Bodleian Library, I-170, 306; II-61

"body stocking," I-328

"Bodyline Tour." *See* "cricket"

Bogarde, Dirk, I-53; II-47, 94, 150, 203

Bogart, Humphrey, I-354, 357

"bogie," II-366–67

Bognor Regis, I-10, 31; II-79, 118, 146; Bognor Regis Urban District Council, II-146

Bolan, Marc and T-Rex, II-99

"bollard," I-313; II-176

"bolour supplements," I-226; II-63

Bols, II-51, 56

Bolshevik, I-28; II-101, 105

Bolton, Lancashire, I-127, 128, 134, 135, 138, 209, 279, 340, 412; II-63, 228; as "Notlob," I-127, 135, 136, 209, 279, 411

Bonaparte, Napoleon, I-4, 28, 37, 38, 58, 86, 158, 163, 193, 208, 212, 353, 393, 396; II-94, 134, 205, 212; Napoleonic Wars, I-393; II-94

Bond, James, I-24, 30, 67, 68, 74, 77, 98, 105, 141, 273, 369; II-56, 111, 131, 136, 171, 197; cast/crew: John Barry, I-93, 98, 141, 399, 400; II-111, 215, 216; Nosher Powell, II-131, 133; Harry Saltzman, I-105; films: *Diamonds Are Forever*, II-111; *Dr. No*, I-77; *From Russia With Love*, I-93, 98, 273, 399; *Goldfinger*, I-77, 369, 396; *Live and Let Die*, II-136; *Thunderball*, I-141, 400; *You Only Live Twice*, I-67; II-189; Ian Fleming, I-30, 68

Bond Street, I-232; II-62, 68

"bong," I-84, 94, 307, 330, 339, 407; II-147

Bonham-Carter, Lady Violet, I-17

Bonhoeffer, Dietrich, I-28

"Mr. Boniface," I-257

Bonzo Dog Doo-Dah Band, I-199; II-163

"A Book at Bedtime," I-122, 407, 411; II-16, 140, 141, 223, 227

"Book of Maccabee," II-203

Book of the Month Club, I-160, 289, 290, 291, 295, 407

"books about belief," I-28, 33

"Boom Bang-a-Bang," Lulu, I-341; II-30

"boom boom," I-4; II-34, 51

Boose, Lynda, II-126

Booth, Albert, I-291

Booth, Charles, I-224

Booth, Connie. *See MPFC* extras and walk-ons

Booth, Webster and Anne Ziegler, I-310

Boothby, Lord, I-226

Boots (the Chemist), I-23, 74, 89

boredom (and dullness; ennui), I-29, 46, 58, 89–90, 93, 97, 115, 129, 139, 141, 158, 160,

175, 182, 188, 292, 298, 354, 379, 408; II-23, 130, 177–78, 186, 189, 193, 194, 223, 224

Borgias, II-33

Borlaug, Norman, I-284

Bormann, Martin, I-97; II-188, 192

Borthwick, Algernon, II-153

Bosanquet, Reginald, I-314, 320, 391; II-51, 162, 166; "Reginald Bo-sankway," II-162, 166

Bosch, Hieronymus, I-61, 256, 375; II-111, 121–22; *Ascent of the Blessed*, I-256

Boswell, James, I-112, 120, 123, 254; *Life of Samuel Johnson*, I-112, 120

Botany Bay, Australia, II-119

Botticelli, Sandro. *See* artists

"botty," I-29, 273, 370

Bough, Frank, I-313, 338, 391; II-113, 151, 152, 157, 189, 192

"boundaries" (between sketches/episodes), I-46, 69; II-152, 166

"Bounder," I-380; II-63

Bourke, Joanna (and Tim Pigott-Smith), I-88, 210; II-62

Bournemouth, I-12, 14, 29, 37, 52, 64, 69, 75, 78, 133, 149, 251, 337, 358, 370, 410; II-27, 63, 80; Bournemouth Pavilion (location), I-75

"bouzouki" and Alan Parker, II-92

Bovey Tracey, II-101

"bovver," I-128, 305

Bow Street Runner, I-238

Bowen, Caroline, II-24

Bowie, David, I-21, 148; II-104

"bowler hat and brolly," I-30, 280, 284; II-45

"box girder bridge," II-23

Boy Scouts, I-249; II-63, 73, 102

Boyce, William, I-190

Boyle, Katie, I-341; II-58, 144

Boys' Brigade, II-63

Braddon, Russell, II-131

Bradford, West Yorkshire (and as location), I-xii, 116, 120, 121, 131, 132, 137, 143, 153, 167, 176, 179, 182, 230, 239, 264, 265; II-xii, 58; Cemetery, I-176, 179, 182; City Stadium, I-xii, 116, 153; Harrogate Street, I-xii, 176, 179, 182; Otley Road, I-176, 179, 182; St. James Bolton church, I-176

Bradford FC, I-116, 143

Bradlaugh, Charles, II-171

Brady, Matthew, I-278

Brahms, Johannes, I-94

The Brains Trust. *See* television shows

Brainsample, Mr. and Mrs., I-114, 115, 117, 120

Brambell, Wilford, I-186; II-184

Bramble, Matthew, II-103, 104

The Brand New Monty Python Bok, I-350; II-134

Brando, Marlon, I-164–65, 170, 314, 317, 320; II-152

Brandon, Henry, I-105

Brandt, Willy, I-340

"Bratbys," I-51

Bray, Windsor and Maidenhead, Berkshire (location), I-70; II-88

Brazil, Gilliam. *See* films

"breach of promise," I-291

breakfast cereals; I-51; II-13, 89, 198, 202, 205

"bream," II-196

Breathless, Godard. *See* films

Brecht, Bertolt (and "Brechtian"), I-38, 153

Brentford, I-xii, 373; II-xii, 26

Breugel (or Brueghel). *See* artists

Brezhnev, Leonid, I-58, 103, 121, 199, 314; II-16, 45, 71, 105, 146

"Brian," I-14, 28, 29, 35, 49, 57, 65, 120, 131, 135, 143, 148, 171, 174, 236–37, 270, 291, 321, 325, 351–52, 405, 410; II-20, 146, 188, 191, 221, 226

Bridge at Arles, Van Gogh. *See* artworks *and* artists

Bridge at Kew, Turner. *See* artworks *and* artists

Bridge on the River Kwai, Lean. *See* films

Bridgwater, I-187, 198

Brighton, I-29, 44, 191, 192, 211; II-27, 91

Brighton (Royal) Pavilion (photo), II-91

Brighton Road and Liberty Lane, Addleston, Surrey (location), I-102, 157

Bristol, I-xi, 39, 133, 185, 189, 216, 223, 224, 291, 302, 319, 373, 386; II-xi, 63, 95, 113; Bristol Rovers, I-373; May Day rituals, I-224

Bristol 175s, I-236

Bristol Old Vic, I-224; II-95

"Bristols," I-291, 302

"British" accents, I-6, 23, 27, 41, 45, 46, 49, 52, 74, 80, 119, 123, 124, 130, 238, 247, 250, 260, 268, 279, 318, 323, 355; II-22, 76, 93, 157, 163, 175, 208

British Airline Pilots' Association (BALPA), I-252–54, 258, 263, 364, 406; II-188, 193, 222

British Automobile Association. *See* AA

British Board of Film Classification (BBFC), I-242; II-34, 48, 97

British Cartoon Archive, I-22, 55, 80, 88, 159, 173, 189, 203, 208, 215, 222, 237, 243, 245, 250, 253, 256, 262, 269, 271, 272, 274, 290, 293, 294, 296, 305, 311, 334, 343, 373, 379, 384, 388; II-22, 67, 68, 77, 86, 102, 116, 148, 153, 172, 200, 203

"British Common Market," II-79

British Dental Association (BDA), I-63, 66, 70, 77, 409

British Empire, I-31, 41, 39, 70, 71, 96, 150, 161, 165, 168, 180, 194, 216, 244, 250, 279, 321, 371, 373, 387, 409; II-36, 43, 54, 63, 68, 70, 78, 79, 149, 178, 225; "British Empire…in ruins," I-373

British Empire Exhibition, I-216

British Film Institute (BFI), I-69, 146, 294, 322; II-95, 189

British Footwear Ltd., I-66, 207

British landscape artists, I-64, 70, 76, 137, 375–77; II-294. *See also* Constable, Gainsborough and Turner

British Ministry of Supply and War Office, I-393

British Movietone News, I-135, 173, 369, 395, 396; II-152, 211, 212

British Museum, I-166, 297. *See also* museums

British National Party, I-190

British Pensioners and Trade Union Action Association, II-143

British New Wave, I-242

"British Psychiatric Association," I-253; II-193

British Rail. *See* trains

British Raj, India, I-145, 342

British satire movement, I-35, 37, 60, 105, 138, 145, 162, 232; II-63, 86, 97, 121, 123–24, 206

British School of Motoring (BSM), II-96

British Screen Awards: A Gala Night for Television and Film. *See* television shows (UK)

British Shoe Corporation, II-64

British space program, I-286

British Sugar, I-253

British Telephone archives (BT), I-35, 143, 226, 245, 316; II-15, 104

British Television, Vahimagi. *See* novels/prose literature

"British Tommy" ("Tommy Atkins"), I-373

British Union of Fascists, I-8, 197; II-73, 78, 87

Brixham Harbor (location), I-368, 381

Brixton, Lambeth, I-194; II-60

Brize Norton Theatre Club, II-21

Broadbent, Jim, I-379

"Broadcasting in the Seventies," I-346

Broadsands Beach, Paignton, Devon (location), I-361–62, 365, 381

The Broadway, Ealing (locations), I-130, 133; II-27

The Broadway, St. Margaret's Road, Twickenham (location), II-12

Brockenhurst County High/Grammar School, II-21

Broeder, Robert, I-31, 396; II-30, 212

Bromberg, Sheila, II-43, 48, 49

Bromley, Greater London, I-373; II-12

Bromley, Peter, II-191

Bromsgrove, I-187, 279, 288, 305; II-89

Brompton Road, Knightsbridge, I-162, 164, 276

Bromwich, John, I-111

Bronowski, Dr. Jacob, I-340; II-124, 201

Brontë, Anne, II-112, 114, 115, 119; and Charlotte, II-112, 115, 151; and Emily, I-251; II-105, 112, 114, 115

brontosaurus, II-61, 70, 74

Brooke, Rupert, II-121

Brooke-Taylor, Tim, I-45–46, 52, 85, 150, 189, 246, 300; II-41

Brook, Norman (1st Baron Normanbrook), II-46

Brookes, Norman, I-111

"Brooky," I-284

Broome, David and "Mr. Softee," I-328; II-36, 182

Brown, Arthur, I-144

"brown coats." *See* gas (natural)

Brown, George, II-163

Brown, Gen. George S., II-201

Brown, Jim, I-355

"Bruce," I-22, 31, 148, 339, 344, 370, 407, 408; II-107, 203, 223, 224

Bruce, Lenny, I-46

Brun, Herbert, II-201

Brunner, Alois, I-190

Bryk, William, I-28

"brylcreem," II-64

Buck, Pearl, I-295

Buckingham, Duke of, I-55; II-131, 133

Buckingham Palace, I-207, 208, 237; II-95

Buckinghamshire, I-4, 11, 144, 341; II-12, 55, 132

Budapest, Hungary I-59, 93, 94, 106, 152, 406; II-4, 222

"Buddy Holly and the Crickets," I-169, 350

Bude, II-101

"budgie," II-4, 5, 186

Budleigh Salterton, Devon, II-101

Buenos Aires, Argentina. *See* South America

buggery, I-186, 242, 243, 328, 345; II-178, 183

Bugs Bunny. *See* animation

building society, I-253

Bukharin, Nikolai, II-107

Bulganin, Nikolai, II-102

"Bulldog Drummond," I-94, 279; II-42

Bullock, Alan, I-12, 350

The Bullwinkle Show (or *Rocky and Bullwinkle and Friends*), I-20, 122, 329; II-20, 168; and Bill Scott and Jay Ward, I-122; II-168; and *The Dudley Do-Right Show*, I-122, 146

Bultmann, Rudolf, I-28

Bulwer-Long, Capt. W.M., I-308

Bumble, Mr., II-115

bungalow, II-64, 80, 116

"Bunn Wackett Buzzard Stubble & Boot," I-32, 45, 174, 197

Bunny Saunders Pop Singers & Orchestra, I-280, 303

Bunuel, Luis. *See* film directors

bureaucracy, I-234–35, 236

Burgess, Guy and Donald Maclean, II-102

Burke, James, I-297; II-37, 111, 115

burlesque, I-14, 42, 70, 238, 257; II-25

Burlington Arcade (and "Wallbanger"), II-114, 188

Burman, Maurice, I-308

Burnet, Alastair, I-320, 391

Burnett, Hugh, I-228

Burnley, Lancashire, I-340

Burns, Robert, I-38, 261, 262

Burns, Wilfred, I-4, 331, 391, 399, 401, 402

Burr, Raymond, I-271

Burroughs, Edgar Rice, I-183, 381; II-115

Burrows, Arthur, I-321

Burton, Richard, I-77; II-27

Bushido, I-54

"Busy Bee" airlines, I-256

Butler, David, I-294, 297, 300

Butler, Maj. Gen. Benjamin Franklin, I-278

Butler, Samuel, I-57; II-115, 118; *Erewhon* I-57; *The Way of All Flesh*, II-115, 118

Butley Down, I-113

Butlins Holiday Camps, I-29, 31, 52, 122, 145; II-79

Buxton, Derbyshire, II-145

"By George" ("The David Frost Theme"), I-163, 400

by-elections, I-11, 178, 184, 186, 296, 299, 302, 307, 319, 410; II-79, 144

Byers, Lord Charles, II-209

"C & A twin set," II-171, 181, 185, 196

caber, I-81, 113, 396

Cabinet (including cabinet offices), I-17, 41, 56, 88, 90, 107, 135, 188, 195, 214, 255, 256, 259, 265, 279, 285, 286, 289, 290, 293, 294, 303, 311, 314, 317, 322, 326, 334, 337, 345, 346, 347, 355, 375, 390, 408, 412; II-15, 19, 30, 35, 36, 46, 53, 54, 59, 82, 86, 126, 144, 147, 163, 165, 178, 190, 200, 224, 228

Cabot, Sebastian, II-123

"Cadaver Synod," II-88

Cadbury's Cocoa Essence, I-245–46

Caerphilly, Wales, I-32, 102, 353

Caesar, Julius, I-28, 37–38, 53, 158, 179, 208, 213–15, 240, 244–45, 361, 366, 370, 409, 413; II-118, 225

Caesar, Sid, I-7

Caesar's Palace, I-158

Cairn Avenue, Ealing (location), I-240, 243

Cairngorm, II-140

Calais, France, I-158, 161, 169

Caledon, Ireland, II-204

California, I-48, 70, 132, 146, 242, 351, 359, 364–65; II-17, 29, 37, 39, 97, 109

Callaghan, James, I-135, 237; II-181

Callan, Bob, II-112

Camber Sands, I-186

"Cambridge Apostles," I-276

"Cambridge Five," II-102

Cambridge Square (location), II-115

Cambridge University, I-xi, 19, 32, 35, 38, 46, 56, 61, 80, 82, 89, 104, 106, 158, 164, 170, 178, 179, 193, 205, 227, 246, 255, 257, 266, 271, 276, 291, 295, 297, 299, 300, 305, 306, 308, 309, 328, 342, 361, 364, 374, 377, 383, 386, 394, 400; II-xi, 164, 174, 208, 209, 216; "Cambridge Circus" ("A Clump of Plinths"), I-205, 300; colleges: Caius, I-305; Christ's, I-291; Downing, I-89; Jesus, I-305; Magdalene, I-255; Newnham, I-80, 82; Pembroke, I-246; II-15; Queens', I-377; St. Catharine's, I-257; Trinity, I-271, 276, 295, 297; II-75, 95, 164; "don," I-xi, 38, 170; Footlights, I-35, 227, 291, 295, 300, 308, 309

Camden, Greater London, I-35, 233, 241, 289, 364; II-12, 92

Cameo News Theatre, Charing Cross Road, I-20

Camerer Cuss & Co., I-81

"Cameron tartan," I-254

camp/campiness, I-52, 74, 81, 113, 131, 153, 158, 160, 166, 170, 238, 329, 339, 340, 345, 347, 407; II-24, 54–55, 74, 114, 131, 223

Camp, Sandy, I-81, 95, 277

"Campaign Against Moral Persecution," I-345

Campbell, Donald, I-158

Campbell, Gordon, I-256, 346

CAMRA (Campaign for Real Ale), II-76

Canada, I-3, 9, 45, 49, 57, 85, 87, 95, 132, 140, 144, 146, 149, 165, 167, 194, 199, 210, 322, 333, 342, 350, 373, 393; II-85, 196

Canada Way, White City, Shepherd's Bush (location), I-132

"canasta," II-99, 171

Candler, Capt. William L. *See* Civil War (US)

caning, I-242, 244; II-9

"canned laughter" (and music), I-314; II-150

cannelloni, I-325; II-196

Cannes Film Festival, I-206, 363

cannibalism, I-356, 385–86, 389, 392–93, 406, 410, 412; II-31, 80, 84, 222, 226, 228

Canning, Professor R.J., I-147, 172–76, 178–79, 183, 283, 406

"Cantab," I-342; II-164

Canterbury Tales (film; poem), I-89, 211, 273; II-31, 155

capital and corporal punishment, I-125, 180, 196, 198, 231, 242, 244, 246, 248, 250, 327, 330, 345, 347, 378, 388, 405; II-9, 17, 79, 93, 104, 106, 107, 110, 113–14. *See also* death penalty

"capitalist dog," II-23

Capone, Al, I-77

Capote, Truman, II-92, 97

Capra, Frank, I-359; II-102

Captain Action, I-107

Captain Marvel, II-35

captions, I-6, 17, 29, 31, 35, 36, 41, 65, 70, 73, 93, 95, 140, 154, 159, 177, 196, 207, 225, 243–44, 274, 345, 363, 385, 408, 409; II-86, 89, 90, 118, 178, 224, 225

Caractacus, I-361

Cardiff Arms Park, I-350–51

Cardiff, Wales, I-53, 70, 224, 225, 245, 350, 353, 355, 363; II-29, 38

Cardinal de Richelieu, Philippe de Champaigne. *See* artworks *and* artists

Cardinale, Claudia, II-46

Cargill, Patrick, II-145

Caribbean, I-23, 85, 322, 382; II-32, 124; Barbados, I-307, 322; Cuba, I-136, 252, 253, 255–56, 261, 409; II-97, 117, 198, 225; Port of Spain, II-32; Trinidad and Tobago, I-305, 312, 322; II-32; West Indies, I-59, 214, 301, 312, 316, 317, 318, 324; II-75, 209

Carlo, William, II-119

Carlson, Wallace, I-32

Carlton House Terrace (photo), I-103

Carlyle, Thomas, I-336

Carmarthen, Wales, I-386–87

"carnivalesque," I-161, 271

Carpenter, Humphrey, I-35, 60, 232, 307; II-61, 63, 68, 97–98; and Keble College, II-68; and *That Was Satire, That Was*, I-35, 60; II-97

Carr, Robert, I-346; II-82, 147

Carr, Vicki, I-6

Carrington, Lord, I-56, 346; II-147, 178

Carroll, Lewis, I-189, 255, 268, 307; II-132

Carry On films, I-52, 277, 280, 332; II-43, 44, 46, 58, 149, 150, 185

Carshalton, Sutton, I-365

Carson, Johnny, I-350

Carson, Violet, I-150

car-swapping, II-23

Carter, Howard, I-297

"Cartesian Dualism." *See* Descartes, Rene

cartoons (editorial; *see* "animations" for
moving pictures), I-10, 22, 29, 32, 33, 55,
60, 70, 71, 80, 88, 113, 118, 141, 159, 173,
180, 189, 193, 203, 208, 215, 221, 222, 231,
237, 244, 245, 250, 251, 253, 256, 258, 259,
261, 269, 271, 272, 274, 290, 293, 294, 296,
301–2, 305, 311, 322, 334, 342, 343, 347,
357, 358–59, 367, 373, 376, 378–79, 384,
388; II-21, 22, 67, 68, 77, 86, 102, 116, 132,
148, 153, 172, 200, 203; cartoonists: Abu
Abraham, I-22; Fritz Behrendt, II-102;
Margaret Belsky, I-237; Bernard Cookson,
II-86; Michael Cummings, I-203, 378–79;
II-86; "Gus," I-293; L.G. Illingworth,
I-269, 271; "Jak," I-231, 269, 274; "Jon,"
II-22; Osbert Lancaster, I-71, 262; David
Langdon, I-159, 294; David Low, I-243;
Sidney William Martin, I-173; William
Papas, I-55, 250; Gerald Scarfe, I-80, 251,
343; "Timothy," I-33, 359; Keith Waite,
I-10, 159, 215, 245, 256, 262; Victor Weisz
("Vicky"), I-22, 70

"cartoony," I-20, 104, 106, 136, 188, 195, 279;
II-39, 86, 114, 201; cartoony props: 16–ton
weight," I-75, 76, 195, 270, 279, 303, 349,
357; II-4, 149; "anarchist's bomb," I-106,
127, 279, 409; "flasher," I-127, 128, 408;
giant hammer, I-23, 76, 188, 270–71, 279,
313; II-4, 51, 114

Casino Royale. See films

"casting couch," I-366

Castle, Barbara, I-303

castration anxiety (and envy), I-149

Castro, Fidel, I-255; II-109

"cat detector van," I-170, 351, 357

"catamite," I-151; II-126

"catarrh," I-329

Caterham, Surrey, I-364

Cathay, II-123

Catholic Church (and Catholics,
Catholicism), I-28, 33, 49, 55, 89, 119, 132,
140, 149, 176, 180, 203, 210, 233, 245, 248–
49, 251, 268, 269, 306, 307, 320, 330, 345,
367–69, 392–94; II-21, 63, 65, 73, 93, 129,
165, 167, 175, 203; and the Inquisition,
I-233, 244, 245, 248, 249–50, 275

Catholic Encyclopedia, I-248, 249, 251, 320, 330;
II-165

"cat-o'-nine-tails," I-125, 242

"cauliflower ear," I-38, 264

Caversham, Reading, Berkshire, I-ix, 18, 52,
233 285; II-ix

CBE (Commander of the British Empire). *See*
Orders

"Cedron," II-203

"cell'd," II-131

Celts, I-125, 162; II-10

censorship, I-20, 35, 37, 53, 96, 105, 107, 138,
140, 160, 163, 193, 225, 242, 267, 306, 336;
II-70, 73, 78, 97, 107, 141, 156; and the
MPAA, I-130; rights issues, II-113, 142;
words: "bunt," I-193; II-70; "cancer," I-96,

290, 306; "masturbation," I-160; II-62, 70,
73; "sod," I-20, 267, 336, 343; II-73, 178

Central America, I-157; II-196; countries:
Costa Rica, I-107; Mexico/Mexican, I-104,
120, 166, 174, 291, 342, 365, 384; II-18,
36, 97, 101, 181, 184; Nicaragua, I-102;
Panama, I-233

Central Criminal Court, Old Bailey, I-228,
237, 240, 243, 247, 270, 328, 334

Central Intelligence Agency (CIA), II-196

Centre Point, II-203

Chabrol, Claude. *See* film directors

Chagall, Mark. *See* artists

Chaldea/Chaldean, I-4; II-188

Challenor, Det. Sgt. Harry, I-84

Chamberlain, Neville, I-17–18, 41, 392, 395;
II-54, 182, 211

Chamberlain, Richard, I-204, 225, 388; II-81

Champion and Trigger (horses), II-51

Chancellor of the Exchequer, I-237, 245, 250,
328, 346, 357, 393; II-35, 137, 144

Chandler, Raymond, I-64, 122; II-203

"Chandos" Shakespeare portrait, I-265

Chaney, Lon and *The Phantom of the Opera*,
I-95, 193

Chaney, Lon (Jnr.) and *Hawkeye and the Last
of the Mohicans*, I-105

Channel Tunnel. *See* Anglo-French

Chaplin, Charlie, I-48, 87, 399; II-154, 156–57,
215

Chapman, David Stephen, I-328

Chapman, George; and John Marston. *See*
playwrights

Chapman, Graham, I-3, 5, 7, 8, 10, 11, 14, 19,
20, 22, 26, 27, 29, 30, 32, 33, 34–38, 39, 43,
45, 47, 48, 51, 52, 53, 54, 55, 56, 59, 60, 66,
67, 73, 78, 79, 82, 84, 85, 88, 89, 92, 94, 95,
96, 98, 99, 100, 101, 103, 104, 105, 106, 107,
109, 111, 112, 114, 116, 117, 118, 120, 127,
128, 131, 134, 135, 136, 138, 139, 140, 146,
150, 152, 157, 159, 160, 161, 164, 166, 169,
170, 172, 173, 175, 176, 183, 186, 187, 188,
190, 192, 193, 195, 196, 197, 198, 200, 202,
204, 205, 206, 208, 209, 210, 211, 213, 214,
215, 216, 222, 226, 227, 228, 230, 234, 238,
240, 241, 243, 244, 247, 251, 252, 253, 254,
257, 260, 263, 265, 267, 270, 273, 274, 275,
277, 281, 282, 283, 284, 288, 296, 297, 298,
299, 300, 301, 302, 304, 305, 307, 308, 313,
314, 317, 318, 323, 325, 328, 329, 330, 331,
333, 335, 336, 337, 342, 347, 352, 354, 355,
361, 363, 364, 366, 370, 374, 377, 378, 379,
381, 383, 388, 391, 393; II-4, 9, 10, 12, 14,
16, 18, 20, 21, 27, 30, 32, 34, 35, 41, 44, 45,
49, 53, 59, 62, 64, 65, 69, 72, 76, 78, 83, 84,
86, 96, 103, 108, 112, 114, 116, 118, 119,
122, 124, 127, 131, 132, 136, 137, 142, 144,
145, 146, 152, 155, 161, 162, 163, 164, 166,
170, 174, 175, 177, 178, 179, 181, 183, 185,
187, 191, 195, 197, 199, 202, 206, 207, 209

Chappaquiddick scandal, I-39

Charing Cross Road, I-20, 210, 287, 298, 364,
390

Charles, King. *See* kings

Charles I Dismounted, Anthony Van Dyck. *See*
artworks *and* artists

Charles, Hughie and Ross Parker, "There'll
Always Be an England," I-382, 402

Charles, J.A.C., II-161

Charlton, Michael, I-185, 297; II-188, 193

Charles of Switzerland salon (location),
II-68

chartered accountancy, I-26, 29, 89, 95, 98,
105, 111, 115, 129, 156, 160, 161–62, 164,
188, 190, 243, 298, 410, 413; II-23, 194,
226, 229

Chataway, Christopher, II-37, 146, 148

Chaucer, Geoffrey, I-89, 211, 236, 273; II-31,
155; characters: The Monk, I-273; The
Pardoner, I-89, 273; II-31; The Summoner,
I-89; and the Tabard Inn, I-236. *See also*
Canterbury Tales

Cheapside, City of London, I-130

Cheese, Reginald Francis, I-301

"Cheese Westerns," I-21, 146, 411; II-91, 92,
227

Chekhov, Anton, II-21, 34, 35, 104

Chelsea, Greater London, I-83, 114, 192, 203,
271; II-12, 36, 134

Cheltenham, Gloucestershire, I-233, 297;
II-151

cherub, I-5, 374

Chessington Zoo, Epsom Road, Surrey
(location), I-226, 238

Chichester, West Sussex (and Cathedral),
I-6, 10, 76, 158, 159, 170, 307, 374, 395;
Festival, I-6, 374

Chichester, Sir Francis, I-150

"children of Marx and Coca-Cola," I-379

China (People's Republic of China), I-71, 99,
165, 194, 284, 294, 296, 301, 334, 349, 352–
53, 358, 361, 365, 366, 379, 412; II-16, 23,
35, 68, 75, 105, 117, 123, 180, 201, 203, 228;
and the Cultural Revolution, I-293, 296;
II-16; and Mao Tse-tung, I-284, 301, 334,
358, 379; II-16, 23, 107; and the Opium
War, I-194; and "purges," I-293, 358; and
the Red Guard, I-284, 293, 297

Chinese finger trap, I-359

Chippendale, I-159, 405

Chippenham, Wiltshire, I-159, 169

Chipperfield, Hertfordshire I-159

Chipstead, Surrey, I-364

"chiropodists," II-64, 68, 178, 181, 203

Chiswick, Hounslow, I-232; II-26

"chlorpromazine," II-80

Chobham Museum, I-315. *See also* museums

"chocky," I-95

cholera, I-361–62; II-73

Chopin, Frederick, I-94, 95, 183, 205, 400; "12
Etudien Op. 10," I-95, 399; "Music for
Vive L'Oompa," 183, 205, 400; "Funeral
March," I-8, 183, 205, 399, 400

choral societies, I-134, 399; II-63, 215

Christ, Jesus, I-6, 66, 70, 73, 74, 144, 166, 207,
208, 217, 222, 270, 353, 372, 383; II-21, 31,
63, 196

Christian/Christianity, I-20, 36, 136, 137,
138, 217, 245, 269, 347, 364, 413; II-5, 21,
63, 79, 89, 109, 208, 229

Christie, Agatha, I-172, 174, 175, 179, 199,
360, 370, 405; *Mousetrap*, I-172, 370; *The*

Secret Adversary, I-174; *The Spider's Web,* I-172

Christie, John, II-5, 9, 17, 110, 135

Christie, Julie, II-30, 34, 85

Christmas, I-55, 86, 112, 144, 158, 163, 164, 198, 204, 207, 213–14, 217, 229, 230, 246, 378, 390, 391, 397; II-33, 44, 57, 63, 78, 87, 97, 109

Christmas Night With the Stars. See television shows

"ChromaColour" and color processes, I-6, 280, 374

Chuckles Candy, I-159

Churchill, Diana, I-355, 357

Churchill, Lady (Clementine Hozier), II-46

Churchill, Lord Randolph, II-53

Churchill, Winston, I-9, 13, 17, 18, 24, 41, 80, 81, 88, 119, 187–88, 194, 216, 392; II-22, 46, 54, 134, 143, 182, 190

Church of England (C of E), I-134, 137, 141, 210, 266, 268, 269, 307, 323, 369; II-31, 34; dioceses: Bath and Wells, I-260; II-41–42; Canterbury, I-28, 361, 372; II-22, 23, 52, 122–23; Carlisle, II-123; Durham, II-42; "East Anglia," I-289, 291, 301, 412; Leicester, I-260; II-45, 69; Woolwich, I-28, 266, 368; Worcester, I-260

CID (Criminal Investigation Department), I-50, 51, 52, 70, 113, 305; "Special Branch," I-305

Cincinnati, Ohio, I-159, 165

cinema (and cinematic), I-20, 21, 37, 54, 76, 77, 87, 91, 99, 103, 111, 128, 139, 146, 150, 152, 201–4, 208, 210–11, 252, 268, 269, 272, 273, 277, 297, 326, 351–53, 365, 374, 407; II-31, 39, 41, 44, 61, 64, 66, 67, 72–73, 74, 100, 131, 188, 223: London-area cinemas: ABC Cinema, I-268, 269, 273; Academy Three, II-41; Cameo News Theatre, I-20; "civic cinemas," I-146; London Pavilion, I-170, 211, 344; Odeon, I-150, 286; The Other Cinema II-41; Paramount, I-211; Plaza, I-211, 351; Rank Organization, I-150, 204, 210

CinemaScope, II-71; Cinerama, II-72

city comedy, I-83, 99

"City Gent," I-23, 26, 30, 34, 42, 49, 80, 87, 97, 100, 105, 114, 129, 132, 152, 195, 205, 210, 226, 237, 250, 266, 267, 279, 280, 285, 298, 315, 321, 355, 360, 367, 396, 406, 411; II-49, 51, 52, 58, 59, 97, 112, 130, 134, 137, 186, 212, 222, 227

City of London. *See* London: City of London

civil servants, I-166, 193, 315

Civil War (US), I-xii, 222, 240, 241, 257, 278, 290, 292, 295, 298, 309, 387, 405; II-xii, 91, 166, 221; Matthew Brady, I-278; *Divided We Fought,* I-222, 241, 257, 290, 292, 298, 309, 344, 386, 387; II-40, 71, 91, 204; photos: Camp Northumberland, I-241; Capt. Candler, I-241; Capt. Hyde, I-222, 241; Capt. Tidball, I-241, 257; Dr. Letterman, I-241; Gen. Barry, I-290; II-71; Gen. Butler, I-278; James Gibson, I-241; Gen. Hooker, I-241; Gen. Logan, I-222, 241, 257, 290, 387; Gen. Lovell, I-309;

Gen. Robertson, I-222, 386; General T.W. Sherman, I-386; Gen. Stoneman, I-292, 298; Union mortar battery, II-91, 204; Union cannon battery, I-222, 240

Civilization. See Sir Kenneth Clark

Clapham, Lambeth, I-22, 84, 96; II-26

Clarendon House, Western Way, Exeter (location), II-178

Clark, Jim, I-316

Clark, Sir Kenneth, I-40, 173, 175, 345, 374, 407; II-130, 136, 223; *Civilization,* I-40, 173, 175, 374

Clark, Ossie and "Quorum," I-209

Clark, Petula, I-201, 203, 294, 309, 400; II-136, 216; "Don't Sleep in the Subway," I-203, 309, 400; II-216; and *Finian's Rainbow,* I-294

Clarke, George, I-161, 375; II-33

Clarke, Kenneth, I-374

Clarke, Peter and *Hope and Glory: Britain 1900–1990,* II-39

Classic Serial. See "radio" and television"

Claudius, I-361; II-192

Clay, Cassius, I-205, 281

Claygate, Surrey, II-63

Clayton, Jack. *See* film directors

Clean-Air System, Ken, I-84, 278, 297, 383, 408; II-114, 224

"clean bowled," II-203. *See also* cricket

Cleaver, Eldridge, II-34

Cleese, John, I-3, 5, 9, 12, 13, 15, 17, 19, 20, 21, 23, 26, 27, 29, 31, 32, 33, 35, 36, 38, 43, 44, 45, 46, 47, 49, 50, 51, 53, 55, 56, 57, 58, 60, 61, 63, 65, 66, 67, 70, 73, 74, 77, 78, 79, 82, 84, 85, 86, 88, 89, 93, 94, 95, 97, 98, 99, 102, 103, 104, 107, 108, 110, 111, 112, 115, 117, 121, 127, 128, 129, 130, 134, 136, 137, 138, 139, 143, 144, 146, 147, 148, 150, 151, 152, 154, 156, 158, 159, 161, 163, 164, 166, 167, 168, 169, 170, 171, 172, 173, 174, 176, 180, 182, 184, 185, 186, 187, 188, 189, 190, 192, 195, 197, 198, 199, 201, 202, 204, 205, 206, 207, 208, 209, 211, 212, 215, 216, 221, 222, 224, 225, 226, 230, 232, 236, 237, 238, 240, 241, 244, 246, 248, 251, 252, 253, 254, 255, 259, 260, 261, 264, 265, 266, 267, 269, 270, 272, 273, 274, 275, 278, 280, 281, 282, 283, 285, 286, 287, 295, 297, 298, 300, 301, 302, 305, 306, 308, 311, 313, 317, 318, 319, 322, 324, 327, 329, 330, 332, 333, 335, 336, 337, 338, 339, 341, 343, 349, 352, 354, 356, 361, 362, 364, 366, 368, 369, 371, 373, 374, 376, 377, 379, 380, 382, 383, 386, 388, 389, 394; II-3, 5, 8, 10, 11, 13, 15, 17, 18, 20, 21, 23, 24, 28, 31, 34, 35, 36, 38, 41, 45, 46, 50, 51, 52, 55, 56, 57, 58, 60, 61, 62, 64, 65, 67, 73, 74, 76, 80, 86, 88, 96, 97, 98, 99, 103, 107, 108, 110, 111, 112, 114, 116, 118, 119, 126, 127, 130, 131, 132, 135, 138, 143, 144, 146, 149, 150, 151, 152, 154, 161, 163, 167, 171, 175, 178, 180, 182, 191, 197, 198, 202, 203, 206, 209

Clement, John, I-341, 374

clergy. *See* religion/religious

Clerk of the Court, I-52

Clerkenwell, I-226; II-120

Cleveland, Carol, I-7, 22, 30, 34, 36, 44, 52, 81, 89, 120, 136, 147, 152, 180, 212, 213, 227, 247, 249, 257, 261, 273, 298, 306, 315, 330, 332, 337, 352, 358, 365, 367, 382, 396; II-32, 95, 127, 164, 177, 210, 212

"clever dick," I-66

Cliff Park Road, Brixham Harbour (location), I-368

Clifton College, Bristol , I-216, 308

clip joint, I-226, 237, 321; II-127

Clive, Colin, I-111

Clochemerle. See television shows

Clokey, Art, I-270

Close, Brian. *See* cricket

"cloth caps," II-64

coal and coal mining, I-12, 41, 47, 48, 49, 131, 149, 154, 183, 222, 223, 229, 250, 272, 283, 385, 387–94, 407, 411; II-29, 72, 81, 82, 83, 104, 148, 189, 190, 207, 223, 227; and the Aberfan disaster, I-394; and Barnsley, I-27, 183; and Black Dyke Mills, I-242, 400; and Jarrow, I-240, 246, 250, 397, 409; and Llanddarog, I-385, 386, 387, 392, 407; and Wardley, I-246; terminology: carbon monoxide, I-389; "coal face," I-47, 387, 392; colliery, I-115, 246, 387; "pit head," 387, 391; "pneumoconiosis," I-389; "tungsten carbide drills," I-47

"coat-and-kipper-tie," I-370; II-175

Coates, Eric: "633 Squadron," II-185, 220; and "Dambusters," II-185, 216; and "Knightsbridge March" from "London Suite," I-108, 259, 399, 401, 404; II-172, 215, 217, 220

Cobbley, John, II-23

Cobham, Oldcastle and "Falstaff," II-62

Coca, Imogene, I-7

Cockfosters, Greater London I-203

"Cockney," I-23, 118, 130, 160, 235, 247, 260, 279, 400; II-98, 118, 155, 216; rhyming slang, I-118, 160, 235; II-98; "Cockney Song," I-235, 400

Coffey, Denise, I-16

"Cogito ergo sum," I-31

Cohl, Emile, I-32, 94

Cohn, Nick, I-324

Cohn-Bendit, Daniel, I-355; II-88

Colchester, Essex, I-145; II-27

Cold War, I-41, 53, 58, 63, 68, 93, 103, 122, 231, 335; II-25, 196–99, 200, 201

Coldstream Guards, I-38; II-54

Coleman, David, I-313, 329, 331, 338, 352; II-152, 154, 157

Coleridge, Samuel Taylor, I-201, 277, 293

Collier's, I-74

Collins, Michael, I-272

Colmworth, Bedfordshire I-364

"The Colonel," I-63, 66, 91, 106, 127, 129, 131, 132, 136, 137, 138, 139, 141, 170, 183, 407; II-52

"Colonel Bogey March," I-73, 399

colonialism/colonialization, I-41, 63, 76, 94, 141, 144, 145, 153, 161, 168, 192, 210, 243, 250, 279, 343, 368, 387; II-8, 15, 16, 30, 36, 42, 43, 48, 62, 68, 72, 74, 78, 124, 126, 185, 191; and independence movements,

I-114, 347, 373; II-8, 36, 56, 67, 73, 93, 163, 208, 209
Colour Plate BBC Reference Library, I-173, 175, 396
"Colour Strike," I-376
"colour supplements," I-226, 232; II-63
Colwyn Bay, Wales, I-225, 374, 394; II-63, 72, 132, 194, 206
Comanche, II-202, 206, 209, 223
Come Dancing. See television shows
"comedic structures," I-61, 206; II-143
comic books, I-5, 52, 60, 93, 97, 106, 107, 139, 169, 405; II-99, 221; *Thrills and Adventure*, I-93, 107, 405
comic misunderstanding, I-12, 66, 99, 120, 130
commercial television (UK), I-162, 167, 197, 265, 369; II-4, 10, 11, 17, 80, 130, 132, 183, 208
commercials/adverts: Babycham, I-386; Barr's soft drinks, I-143; Bell Telephone, I-38; Blue Band margarine, I-38; Book of the Month Club, I-160, 289, 290, 291, 295, 407; Bovril, II-151, 178; BP, I-53; II-151; and the Church, I-259–60; II-38; and local cinemas, I-204, 208, 210–11, 213; II-64, 66, 67, 223; Coca-Cola, I-170, 379; II-65, 151; "Conquistador Coffee," I-9, 169, 360, 362, 379, 390, 407; II-99, 223; "Crelm," I-360, 361, 362, 369, 385, 387, 406; II-38, 222; Colgate, I-387; II-38; colour supplements, I-226, 232; II-63; Crest, I-362, 370, 387; dog food, I-177; Duff Gordon sherry, II-128; encyclopedias, I-143; Esso, I-387; "FibroVal," II-38; frozen peas, I-260; "Fun, Travel, Adventure" (US Army), I-140; Gibbs SR, I-387; Guinness, I-25, 161; II-151; Hertz, I-379; II-132; John Romain handbags, II-140; "La Gondola Restaurant," I-170, 201, 407; Lemon Hart, I-344; Lyons, I-203, 208; Madam Dowding corsets, I-5, 292, 298; Max Factor, I-344; "Mojave Run," I-361; New Pence, II-13, 154–55; Palmolive, II-38; Playtex, II-82, 87; and *Private Eye*, I-87, 108–9, 154, 205, 342; II-57, 63; Robertson's Jam (Golly), I-344; II-31; Salada Tea, I-131; Shell/ Shrill Oil (and Platformate), I-361, 362, 363, 369; "soap powders," I-385, 392, 412; II-38, 228; Stork Margarine, I-24; II-38; Surf, I-392; Texaco, II-38; Toffo Deluxe Toffees, I-91; "Trim-Jeans," II-13, 21, 24, 29, 38; "Vintage Model Monarchs," I-235; Wall's, I-69, 203, 393; White Tide, I-392; "Whizzo Butter," I-3, 12, 24, 108–9; II-38; Wrigley's, I-344
commissionaire, I-66; II-37
Common Market, I-294, 304, 315, 319, 329, 340; II-79, 82, 86, 93, 153, 201
Commonwealth nations, I-34, 39, 59, 73, 95, 111, 114, 122, 244, 276, 281, 311, 319, 321, 322, 346, 355, 371; II-19, 30, 32, 82, 84, 88, 89, 93, 124; Australia (*see* Australia); Barbados, I-307, 322; Botswana, I-322; Canada (*see* Canada); Cyprus, I-322, 373; II-54; Gambia, I-322; Ghana, I-165,

322; II-45, 218; Guyana, I-322; II-47; India (*see* Asia/Asian); Jamaica, I-322, 324; II-79; Kenya (*see* Kenya); Lesotho, I-322; Malawi, I-322; Malaysia, I-71, 96, 163, 174, 322, 373; Malta, I-322; II-13; Mauritius, I-322; New Zealand (*see* New Zealand); Nigeria, I-171, 322, 347; Pakistan, I-312, 316, 317, 322, 342, 371, 373; II-30, 68; Seychelles, I-373; Sierra Leone, I-322; Singapore, I-322; Sri Lanka, I-268, 312, 322; Swaziland, I-322; Tanzania, I-97, 145, 148, 322; Trinidad and Tobago, I-305, 312, 322; II-32; Uganda, I-322; Zambia, I-322, 373; Zimbabwe (Rhodesia), I-59, 168, 180, 188, 373, 389; II-36, 40, 56, 66–67, 73, 137, 208
Commonwealth Avenue and India Way, Hammersmith and Fulham (location), I-122
communication/miscommunication, I-41, 54–55, 85, 127, 130, 135, 147, 172, 191, 209, 212, 235, 245, 248, 250, 254, 256, 292, 299, 350, 379, 391, 406; II-11, 24, 55, 59, 100, 125, 141, 152, 170, 174, 182, 183, 222
Communism/Communist Party, I-7, 28, 50, 58, 71, 103, 121, 150, 165, 194, 198, 290, 296, 302, 304, 324, 344, 358, 359, 363, 365, 371, 372, 384, 406, 407; II-16, 23, 25, 45, 61, 62, 71, 101, 102, 104, 105, 109, 178, 180, 196, 198, 222, 223; British Communist Party, I-372
Como, Perry and "Arrivederci Roma," II-40
compère (host/presenter), I-31, 52, 94, 122, 129, 145, 199, 264, 282, 292, 405, 406; II-20, 98, 110, 166, 221, 222
complain/complaints, I-18, 35, 61, 82, 91, 92, 110, 119, 125, 127, 158, 185, 200, 206, 242, 251, 252, 255, 273, 275, 280, 299, 307, 330, 350, 354, 368, 372, 380, 388, 392, 407, 411; II-10, 13, 17, 29–31, 40, 41, 62, 75, 77, 80, 84, 86, 93, 97, 103, 104, 113, 136, 142, 144, 152, 155–56, 170, 173, 177, 193, 196–97, 206, 223, 227; by or about *MPFC*, I-35, 82, 158, 206, 242, 280, 299, 372, 392, 407; II-31, 84, 86, 113, 142, 144, 152, 155–56, 196–97, 206, 223, 242
The Complete and Utter History of Britain. See television shows
"Conchito," II-206
Concorde. *See* Anglo-French
concrete poetry, I-200
"conditional discharge," I-188
"conger," I-351
congresses: Communist Party, I-58; II-45; Nazi Party, I-10, 190, 195; Trade Union, I-289, 372; II-83; United States, I-135, 365; World Peace, I-7
Congreve, William, I-32, 60, 295
"Conrad Poohs' Dancing Teeth," I-164, 349, 362, 406
"conscientious objector," I-137, 230
Conservative Party (Tory/Tories)/ conservatism, I-9, 17, 27, 28, 30, 32, 33, 38, 42, 53, 54, 56, 59, 66, 87–91, 102, 105, 119, 124, 125, 138, 148, 154, 159, 162, 165, 168, 170, 180, 182, 186, 188, 190, 192,

194–95, 196, 197, 214, 221–22, 224, 225, 226–27, 229, 233, 237, 244, 247, 250, 255, 256, 259, 265, 279, 284–85, 287, 288, 289, 290, 293, 296–97, 300, 301, 304–309, 311, 316, 319–20, 321, 322, 326, 328, 329, 330, 333, 334, 336, 337, 345, 346, 347, 355, 357, 359, 361, 363, 367, 372–75, 384, 388, 390, 393, 412; II-19, 22, 25, 34, 35, 36, 41, 45, 46, 48, 51, 53, 54, 55, 56, 59, 59, 67, 68, 72, 73, 77, 78–82, 84, 85, 87, 89, 90, 104, 112, 113, 117, 126, 130, 132, 133, 135, 141, 142, 144, 147, 154, 163, 164, 178, 180, 181, 190, 199, 204–5, 206–210, 228
constable (PC; and police/policemen), I-4, 7, 10, 19, 33, 52, 53, 55, 62, 79, 81, 83–85, 90, 93, 95, 100, 103, 110, 111, 113, 116, 118, 119, 121, 125, 130, 131, 132, 135, 138, 140, 149, 153, 177, 178, 179, 180, 184, 191, 194, 201, 203, 207, 212, 214, 226, 228, 230, 232, 235, 236, 238, 243, 245, 260, 264, 273, 277, 283, 289, 298, 301, 307, 309, 314, 329, 339, 341, 342, 353, 354, 356, 377, 379, 387, 391, 406, 407, 408, 411, 412; II-3–4, 5, 9, 11, 12, 14, 15, 24, 40, 42, 43, 52, 73, 77, 98, 118, 123, 124–25, 126, 131, 137, 174, 179, 182, 184, 187, 188, 191, 193, 222, 223, 224, 227, 228
Constable, Det. Sgt. Robin, I-84, 277; and Mick Jagger arrest, I-84
Constable, John, I-42, 64, 70, 137, 180, 200, 375–77, 378; *The Cornfield*, I-376; *Hampstead Heath With a Rainbow*, I-64; *The Hay Wain*, I-42–43, 70, 200, 325, 371, 376
"consultation," I-371–72, 406
consumption/consumerism, I-72, 76, 156–57, 165, 177, 229, 236, 250, 298, 311, 319, 381; II-173, 175, 176, 193
Contagious Disease Acts, II-151
Contemporary Art Society, I-14
context, I-9, 10, 13–14, 15, 31, 37, 223, 230, 232, 254, 350, 356; II-11, 31, 42, 55, 146, 161; "context smashing," I-13, 14; decontextualizing/recontextualizing, I-9, 13
"continental version," I-26, 31
continuity, I-38, 91, 108, 133, 137, 153–54, 169, 188, 212, 275, 283, 352; II-70, 107, 150, 161
"cooey," I-226
Cook, James and *Endeavour*, I-392
Cook, Peter, I-15, 16, 32, 45, 64, 145, 232, 246, 312, 354, 367; II-63, 76, 103
"cooker," I-92, 223, 227, 294, 302; II-117
Cooper, D.B., II-117
Cooper, Henry, II-131
Cooper, Tommy, I-254
Cootes, Rev. John, I-368
Coover, Gary, II-24, 37
Copley, John Singleton , I-217
copyright issues, I-12, 18, 49, 87, 94, 103, 109, 117, 164, 237, 242, 307, 315, 341, 393; II-38, 113, 127, 180, 191, 195
Corday, Charlotte, I-15
"corn-plasters," II-203
Cornthwaite, Robert, I-110, 116

Cornwall, I-52, 55, 96, 173, 301, 304; II-27, 101, 103, 106, 122, 209, 210; "Cornish," I-96, 301

Cornwallis, Gen. Charles, I-216

Corona Stage School, II-112, 115

"Coronation Scot," I-341, 401

Corrigan, Douglas "Wrong Way," II-39

"cos lettuce." *See* Webb's Wonder

Costa-Gavras. *See* film directors

costume instructions/directions, I-14, 27, 30, 36, 39, 42, 44, 46, 72, 75, 84, 86, 91, 97, 104, 105, 155, 157, 161, 176, 178, 185, 186, 187, 188, 196, 202, 238, 253, 257, 257, 266, 279, 315, 329, 363, 377, 381; II-33, 49, 52, 66, 172, 173, 190, 197; and "type" (by costume), I-4, 14, 30, 31, 42, 43, 45, 75, 121, 122, 146–48, 152, 153, 159–60, 170, 187, 232–33, 265, 282, 285, 351, 370, 378; II-24, 30, 96–97, 115

"cottaging," II-36

Cotton, Bill, I-82, 151, 299; II-26, 151, 196

council estates (housing), I-90, 134, 149, 176, 214, 224, 239, 274, 276, 282, 292, 312, 319, 321; II-80, 204, 205

"Council on Prices, Productivity and Incomes," and Lord Cohen, II-141

Council Ratcatcher, I-315

counterculture, I-100, 163, 179, 208, 214; II-156

Courtauld Gallery. *See* museums

"courtesan," I-23, 34, 72, 213, 222; II-92, 95

Courtneidge, Cicely, I-96, 98, 172, 202; II-119

Cousteau, Jacques, II-18, 53, 60, 88, 142

Covehithe, Southwold (location), I-43, 48, 75, 157–59

Covent Garden (and Theatre), I-114, 123; II-23, 24, 134

Coventry, West Midlands, I-184, 187, 376, 413; II-27, 68, 149, 154, 229; Coventry City FC, I-376

Coward, Noël, I-92, 223; II-57, 112

Cowdenbeath, Scotland I-96

Cowdrey, Colin. *See* cricketers

Cowick Street, Exeter, Devon (location), I-xii; II-xii, 179, 206

Crab, Roger and *The English Hermite*. *See* novelists *and* novels

Crabbe, George, I-19

Crabtree Lane, Hammersmith and Fulham (location), I-185

"cradle to grave," I-119, 236; II-133

Crapper, Thomas, II-161

Crawford, Michael, I-343

"Crelm with Fraudulin." *See* commercials/adverts

creosote, I-76, 227; II-31

Crest toothpaste. *See* commercials/adverts

Crichton, Charles, I-98

cricket, I-4, 11, 51, 53, 62, 96, 110–11, 113, 114, 121, 141, 147, 172–73, 177, 192, 199, 206, 209, 216, 231, 242, 248, 264, 266, 286, 294, 299, 305, 311–13, 315–21, 324–26, 329, 330, 332–35, 337, 338, 340, 343–44, 350, 368, 376, 391, 396, 405, 407, 408, 409; II-3, 61–63, 75–76, 79, 84, 88, 102, 108, 116, 150, 151, 155, 157, 181, 192, 200, 202–4, 208–10, 212, 221, 223, 224, 225, 227; "Bodyline Tour," I-312; II-35, 210; broadcasting (media coverage), I-4, 62, 176–77, 313, 317, 318, 320, 321, 333, 337, 338; county cricket I-62, 319; II-157, 210; Lord's Cricket Ground, I-231, 312, 319, 324, 326, 396; II-212; MCC (Marylebone Cricket Club), I-11, 173, 213, 231, 312, 315, 317, 318, 324, 325, 326, 337; "one-day" cricket, I-110–11, 113; photos of, I-62, 96; and protests over apartheid, I-172–73, 248, 266, 294, 324; refreshments, I-216; "Rest of the World," I-315, 317, 324, 338; terminology, I-192, 216, 313, 315–16, 324, 326, 330, 334, 335; II-204; "Test" play, I-266, 311, 312, 313, 315, 317–18, 321, 324, 325, 329, 332, 333, 338, 344, 411, 412; II-75, 102, 116, 150, 151, 155, 204, 208, 227, 228; Wisden Cricketer of the Year, I-51, 266, 305, 312, 313, 315, 321, 325, 329, 332, 333, 344; II-62, 63, 75, 151

cricketers: Gubby Allen, I-312; II-210; Leslie Ames, I-312, 321; Alec and Eric Bedser, II-62; Richard Benaud, I-344; Don Bradman, I-344; II-210; Geoff Boycott, II-151, 157; Brian Close, I-317, 325, 327, 329; II-157; Denis Compton, I-329, 332; II-102, 108; Colin Cowdrey, I-313, 315; II-204, 208; Laurie Fishlock, II-62; W.G. Grace, I-201, 206, 240, 242, 332, 368; II-208; Z. Harris, II-208; Lindsay Hassett, I-344; Jack Hobbs, I-344; Len Hutton, I-313, 332; Ray Illingworth, II-151, 157; Douglas Jardine, II-210; Alan Jones, I-299; Alan Knott, I-321; Jim Laker, I-333; Ray Lindwall, I-344; Peter May, II-63; Keith Miller, I-344; Harold Newton and Harry Newton, I-321–22; Graeme Pollock, I-318; David Sheppard, I-266, 368; Thomas "Frank" Smailes, II-200; M.J.K. Smith, II-208; Sidney (or Sydney) Smith, I-305; Stewart Surridge, II-62; Herbert Sutcliffe, I-344; E.W. "Jim" Swanton, I-333, 337, 350; Fred Titmus, II-151; "Plum" Warner, I-325

Crimean War, I-205

The Crimson Permanent Assurance, I-29, 81, 160; II-23, 27, 30, 55, 81, 156

Crippen, Dr. Peter, I-45–46; II-92

Cripps, Richard Stafford, I-357

Crisp, Quentin. *See* novelists/prose writers

crochet, I-129–30

"crofter," I-114, 115, 120, 123, 254; II-132

Cromer, Norfolk, I-340

Crompton, Charles, I-314

Cronin, Archibald and *Dr. Finlay*, I-115

Crosland, Anthony, I-354

crossdressing, I-7, 55, 56, 78, 120, 147, 151, 192, 228, 235, 253, 269; II-117, 204

Crossroads. *See* television shows

crossword puzzle, I-28, 31

Crowcombe, Somerset, I-187, 197

Crowley, Alastair, II-75

Crown House, High Street, Walton-on-Thames, Surrey (location), I-261

Crowther, Leslie, I-24; II-180

Croydon, South London I-99, 178, 253, 365; II-3, 12, 78, 108, 172, 173, 200, 209

"Cruikshank," I-315

"Crun, Henry." *See The Goon Show*

"crunchie," II-103

Cryer, Barry, I-157, 161

Crystal Palace, I-20, 138, 150, 194, 241, 251, 384; II-40, 42, 48; Crystal Palace FC, I-151; II-170

"CS" gas, I-243

Cuba. *See* Caribbean

"Cuba Libres," II-65

Cubism, I-6, 8, 14, 376; II-24

Cudham, Bromley I-221

Cudworth, South Yorkshire I-144, 183

cultural lexicon, I-xiii, 134, 140, 254, 384

Cultural Revolution. *See* China

Cumberland, II-53, 98

Cumbrian Lake District, I-177

Cunningham, Sir John, II-80

Curran, Charles, II-156

currency restrictions, I-29, 34, 85

Curry's, II-150, 151, 155, 227

Curtis, Tony, II-132, 136

Cushing, Peter, I-262

"cut motor taxes," I-159, 301

"Cut-out, Mrs," II-3, 4, 13, 222

"Cutty Sark," II-189

czar/tsar, I-207; II-105, 193

Czechoslovakia. *See* Eastern Europe

"DIY," I-100, 343; II-78

Dada/Dadaist, I-10, 18, 153

Dad's Army and *Dad's Pooves*. *See* television shows

Dagenham (and Ford strike), I-387; II-86

Dance, James, I-279

Dane, Alec, I-323, 377

Daneford Street School, I-235

Daniel Street School, I-228

Daniels, Glyn, I-328

"Dark Ages," I-123, 380

"darkies," I-104, 131, 315; II-31; "Darkie" toothpaste, I-315; "Golliwog" jam, I-315, 344; II-31

Darlington, I-227, 377

Dartmoor, I-43, 55, 203, 249, 256, 261, 314, 390; II-106, 201

Dartmouth Road and Cliff Park Road (location), I-368

Darwin, Charles, I-313

Das Neue Kino, I-123, 146

David, Michelangelo. *See* artworks *and* artists

David Agency. *See* talent (job) agencies

David, Jacques-Louis. *See* artists

Davidson, Ian. *See* MPFC extras and walk-ons

Davies, John, I-346

Davies, John Howard, I-10, 31, 32, 35–36, 53, 67, 80, 96, 129, 161, 171, 182, 306, 375

Davies, Ray and the Kinks, I-333

Davies, Rita. *See* MPFC extras and walk-ons

Davis, Kingsley, I-203

Da Vinci, Leonardo. *See* artists

Davis, Joe, I-330

Day, Doris, I-104

Day, Robin, I-8, 12, 124, 136, 162, 187, 209, 212, 294, 297, 330; II-32, 180
Dayes, Edward and "Hanover Square," I-315
DBE (Dame Commander of the British Empire). *See* Orders
"dead bishop on the landing," I-202, 207; II-35, 42
"dead Indian," I-92, 289, 291, 293, 296, 302, 407, 408
"Dead March" ("Funeral March"), I-8, 182, 400
"dead parrot," I-xi, 9, 19, 38, 43, 73, 95, 104, 127, 128, 134, 152, 164, 166, 185, 234, 258, 274, 350, 356, 408; II-xi, 98, 174; in popular culture, I-134, 166–67; and Margaret Thatcher, I-134
Dean, Michael, I-82, 299; II-75
Dearden, Basil. *See* film directors
death, I-3, 8–11, 13, 14, 15, 17, 18–21, 40, 44, 54, 61, 67, 68, 73, 74, 75, 92, 93, 94, 96, 104, 106, 111, 130, 132–33, 140, 147, 158, 169, 172, 173–74, 182, 186, 189, 192, 194, 203, 206, 213, 228, 233, 242, 244, 246, 250, 256, 266, 267, 279, 280, 290, 293, 301, 312, 314, 325, 327, 328, 335, 339, 342, 358, 370, 378, 394, 407, 408, 409, 410, 411, 412; II-11, 14, 15, 18, 21, 23, 25, 26, 29, 34, 37, 39, 43, 47, 50, 53, 54, 65, 67, 94, 94, 97, 98, 101, 102, 110, 113–15, 119, 121, 122, 126, 127, 135, 138, 140, 143, 144, 152, 155, 172, 191, 194, 198, 206, 209, 223, 224, 225, 226, 227, 228
death penalty, I-242, 246, 327, 328, 378; II-113, 114; hanging, I-8, 42, 191, 193, 242, 257, 312, 327; II-9, 92, 110, 113, 114, 188; The Murder (Abolition of Death Penalty) Act, I-327. *See also* capital and corporal punishment
DeBakey, Michael Ellis, II-42, 157
The Debbie Reynolds Show. See television shows
De Beauvoir, Simone, II-16
"debs," I-187
Debussy, Claude, I-140, 400, 403; II-34, 96, 103, 216, 219
decimal coinage change, I-107, 287, 347; II-13, 154, 155
decontextualizing/recontextualizing. *See* context
"deed poll," I-330
"deerstalker and tweeds," I-388
De Gaulle, Charles, I-80, 222, 315, 329, 379; II-79, 88, 90, 93, 134
deinonychus, II-70
Déjeuner Sur L'Herbe, Manet. *See* artworks *and* artists
Dekker, Thomas. *See* playwrights
De Kooning, Willem. *See* artists
Delaney, Hugh, II-204
De la Fontaine, Jean, I-366
Delaunay, Robert. *See* artists
De Laurentis, Dino. *See* film directors
"De L'Hotel Des Dhuys" (photo), II-85
"deliberate ambiguity," I-362
De Manio, Jack, I-177
Denison, Michael and Dulcie Gray, I-96
Denning, Lord Alfred Thompson, I-41

Den's Café (location), I-185. *See also* Axis Café
Department of Trade and Industry, I-291, 340, 346
Deptford, Greater London I-227
DePugh, Robert, I-365
Der Spiegel, I-178
Derby, Derbyshire I-8, 296, 300, 349, 351, 354, 355, 389, 408, 412; II-224, 228; horse race ("The Derby"), I-316, 317; II-184, 189
Derbyshire, I-269; II-45, 133, 145; Light Infantry, I-339, 341
Derry and Toms, I-351; II-132, 171, 178
De Saussure, Ferdinand, I-342
Descartes, René, I-31, 32, 43, 225, 314
De Sica, Vittorio, I-100; II-46, 150; and *Boccaccio 70*, II-46; and *The Garden of the Finzi-Continis*, II-150; and *Marriage Italian Style*, I-100
De Stijl, I-15
De Torquemada, Tomas, I-249, 251
"Deutschland Über Alles," I-8, 190, 399, 400
"devaluation" (of the pound), I-188; II-45, 117, 148
De Vega, Lope. *See* playwrights
"Devil's Gallop," I-204, 244, 400, 401, 403, 404; II-55, 142, 145, 172, 216, 217, 219, 220
Devon (and Devonshire), I-43, 55, 154, 185, 191, 203, 249, 253, 257, 261, 275, 295, 301, 311, 321, 323, 351, 352, 362, 372; II-44, 64, 70, 101, 103, 105, 106, 108, 109, 122, 166, 179, 180, 184, 201, 209; and Cornwall, I-103, 122; II-55, 301
De Vries, Jan V. (and *Perspective*), I-5, 42, 143, 240–41, 245, 290, 292, 334, 349, 372, 386; II-83, 121, 150
DeWolfe Music, I-180, 265; II-113, 149
De Worms, Henry, II-153
Di Credi, Lorenzo, *The Virgin and Child*, I-386
Dial M for Murder. See plays
Diamantis, Alexandros, II-179; and "Alex Diamond," II-179, 184, 206
Diamond, John and "Once I Was British," I-134, 166, 282
"Dibley," I-9, 45, 268, 278, 286, 289, 292, 293, 294, 393, 409; II-14, 225; "Gwen Dibley," I-9, 45, 293; haircut, I-393
Dickens, Charles, I-191, 281, 293, 315, 324; II-80, 98, 115, 147: *Bleak House*, I-281; *A Tale of Two Cities*, I-311, 315, 324, 412; *Old Curiosity Shop* and *Oliver Twist*, II-115; *Our Mutual Friend*, I-191; *Pickwick Papers*, II-147
Didion, Joan, I-312
"Deirdre," I-31, 207
Dietrich, Marlene, II-5
Dim, Inspector, I-50, 51, 52, 60, 113, 409; II-164, 225
Dimbleby, David, I-297
Dimbleby, Richard, I-136, 152, 209, 293, 356, 389, 391; II-32, 42, 132
Dimmock, Peter, I-176
"Ding Dong Merrily On High," I-144, 400
"dinner-wagon," II-171
direct address, I-95, 100, 119; II-80
"dirty books," I-268; II-122, 125, 127
"dirty version," I-330

dismember (and re-membering), I-106, 136, 156, 171, 240; II-92; as "body horror," I-106, 240
Disney, Walt. *See* animation
Disraeli Road (location), I-240, 243; II-32
Divided We Fought. See Civil War (US)
"divvy," I-253, 254
Dixon of Dock Green, I-52, 53, 61, 79, 95, 100, 118, 119, 133, 145, 175, 176, 177, 228, 230, 231, 241, 268, 283, 378, 381; II-12, 15, 23, 25, 43, 55, 104, 113, 118, 123, 133, 142, 163, 179, 184, 189, 205; George Dixon, I-95, 283; II-43
Dixon, Reginald, I-73, 399
"DJ" (dinner jacket), I-143, 237, 244
Do Not Adjust Your Set. See television shows
Dobbe, Willy, I-341
Dobbin, I-86, 242, 257; II-54
Dobrogoszcz, Tomasz, II-ix, 124
The Doctor, Fildes. *See* artworks
"Doctor Doctor" jokes, I-257
Doctor in the House. See television shows
Doctor Who. See television shows
doctors (and medicine), I-16, 49, 73, 88, 89, 92, 96, 107, 114, 152, 162, 177, 181, 190, 192, 197–98, 201, 205–6, 209, 226, 232–33, 246, 256, 257, 258, 280–81, 286, 300, 311, 314, 325, 327, 339, 341, 342–43, 350, 382, 391–93, 406–8, 410, 412; II-30, 32, 64–65, 75, 80, 92, 103, 104, 123, 130, 132–33, 136–37, 140, 143, 144, 164, 180, 190, 202, 206–8, 222–24, 226, 228
Dodge, Mabel, I-268
"dog collar," I-262, 269, 296, 301, 313, 341
"dog kennels please," I-130, 254
Dogberry, I-13, 52, 140
"doing five years bird," II-122
Dollimore, Ralph, II-123
dominatrix, I-33
"Dominion status," I-373
"Domino Theory," I-344, 360, 363, 365, 406
Don John, I-30, 52
Don Quixote, Cervantes. *See* novels/literature
Doncaster, I-8, 44, 315; II-104, 151
"donkey jacket," II-113
Donovan, I-232
"Don't Sleep in the Subway," Petula Clark, I-203, 309, 400
"Doric," I-385, 386, 393
Dorking, Surrey I-10, 93, 96, 101, 102, 105, 175, 223, 224, 406
"dormice," I-255
Dorset, I-4, 13, 234, 311, 316, 325, 337, 358, 364, 413; II-63, 81, 115, 229
Douglas, Kirk, I-104, 245; II-94
Douglas-Home, Alec, I-104, 194, 255, 294, 307, 322, 346; II-54, 56, 66, 86, 94, 147, 200
Douglas-Home, William and *The Reluctant Debutante*, I-104
Dover, Kent I-158–59, 169, 235, 245; II-27, 96
Down Among the Z Men. See films
Down Your Way. See radio shows
Downs, Hugh, II-51
Doyle, Arthur Conan, I-153, 175, 257; II-47
Dr. Finlay. See television shows
Dr. Kildare. See television shows

"Dr. Scholl," I-207; II-64, 68

Dr. Strangelove. See films

Dr. Zhivago. See films

Drabble, Margaret, I-19, 27, 30, 36, 70, 79, 80, 81, 82, 181, 196, 199, 265, 275, 370; II-9

"drag," I-33, 131, 160, 207, 227, 231, 232; II-24, 118, 183

Drake, Sir Francis, I-150, 169, 176, 380, 381; II-70, 122

"dramatic irony," I-234

Drayton, Michael, I-90; II-30

"Dresden pottery," I-67

Dreyer, Carl Theodore. *See* film directors

Driffield, East Riding of Yorkshire I-293

Drobny, Jaroslav, I-114

Droitwich, Worcestershire I-187; II-204

drugs/drug use, I-30, 34, 39, 40, 57, 83–84, 96, 101, 136, 137–38, 162, 208, 215, 227, 236, 247, 276, 307, 312, 320, 366; II-48, 57, 80, 85, 144, 173, 196

Drummond-Hay, Annaley, I-328; II-179, 180, 184

Drury, Flying Squad Chief Kenneth, II-126

Dryden, John, I-xi, 46, 199, 234; II-xi, 112

Dublin, I-10, 100, 179; II-61, 65, 71, 107

Duchamps, Marcel. *See* artists

"Duchess of Normandy," II-138

Duck Amuck, I-94; II-39

"ducky," I-341; II-24; "duckety-poos" II-24

Dudley, Ambrose, 3rd Earl of Warwick, II-129

The Dudley Moore Trio. *See* Moore, Dudley

Duff Gordon Sherry, II-128

Dufy, Raoul. *See* artists

Duke and Duchess. *See* titles/honorifics

"Dull, John," II-189

Dullea, Keir, I-344

Dulwich, Greater London I-194, 293, 330, 361

"Dumaru," I-390

Dunaway, Faye, II-204

Dunbar, Scotland I-115, 254

Duncan, Trevor, I-279, 402, 403, 404; II-36, 66, 75, 218, 219, 220

"Dundee cakes," I-188

Dunfermline, Scotland I-388

"dung," I-92, 160, 223, 289, 291, 293, 307, 408; II-126, 224

"Dunkirk," I-82, 86

Dunkley, Chris, II-38

Dunraven, Earl of, II-153

Dunraven Road (location), I-226, 231

Durante, Jimmy, I-49, 330, 401

Duras, Marguerite, I-38

"duré" (Bergson), I-272

Dürer, Albrecht, I-83, 89, 115, 182, 350, 372, 376; II-111, 121, 128, 130, 134; works: *Apocalypse of St. John, The Dragon with the Seven Heads*, I-350; *Erasmus of Rotterdam*, I-372; *The Flight into Egypt*, II-128; *John Before God and the Elders*, II-121, 128, 130, 134; *The Knight and the Lansquenet*, II-128; *St. Anthony Reading*, I-350; II-111

Durbin, Deanna, II-200

Durham, County Durham I-182, 229, 246, 360, 365, 408, 410; II-42, 50, 54, 86, 89, 189, 204, 224, 226

Düsseldorf, Germany I-197

Dyall, Valentine, II-98

Dyer, G., I-381

Ealing: Fire Station, I-139; Lawn Tennis Club, Daniel Road (location), I-113; Studios, I-113, 122, 133, 147, 223; II-11; Technical College (location), I-51

Easington Terminal, I-234

East Acton, Greater London I-104, 134, 138, 149, 287

East Anglia, I-32, 289, 291, 301, 322, 324, 412

East End (London). *See* London

East Finchley, Greater London, I-116

East Germany (DDR), I-77, 80, 320, 340

East Grinstead, West Sussex I-82–83, 119, 161, 175

East India Company, I-315

East Lynne or *The Earl's Daughter. See* plays

East Midlands, I-46, 121, 234, 269, 302, 314, 351, 354; II-133, 204–5

Eastern Europe, I-58, 66, 267; II-102, 198; countries: Albania, I-63, 201; II-102; Czechoslovakia, I-17, 59, 114, 231; II-98, 154, 179; Hungary, I-59, 94, 354; II-102, 204; Poland, I-ix, 17, 57, 94, 184, 191, 349, 354; II-ix, 131; Romania, I-351; II-189

Eastgate House, High Street and Paris Street, Exeter (location), II-205–6

Easton Lodge, Easton (location), I-290

Eastward Ho. See plays

Eastwood, Nottinghamshire, I-36, 39

Ebert, Roger, I-244

"eccles cakes" (and Eccles, Salford), I-341

"Eccles, The Famous," I-104, 180; II-58, 75

"ecclesiastical accoutrements," II-43

economy: of Britain, I-34, 44, 47, 49, 56, 114, 167, 221, 237, 243, 244, 250, 259, 319, 371, 373, 390, 393; II-22, 30, 35, 45, 53, 54, 79–83, 104, 141, 144, 146, 148, 172, 173, 181, 193; of China, I-361; II-45; of the Commonwealth, I-165, 243, 244; of Europe, I-221, 378; II-79, 83, 137; and inflation, I-250, 373, 390; II-83, 132, 141, 144, 173, 204, 210; "stopped economy," I-237; of the USSR, II-45, 102; "wage spiral," I-250; II-81, 141

Edgware Road, I-207; II-191

Edinburgh (and Castle), I-14, 16, 18, 60, 96, 104, 112, 115, 122, 166, 179, 196, 238, 343; II-21, 141, 142, 148

Edinburgh, Duke of (Prince Philip), I-136, 150, 269, 305; II-145

Eddy, Duane, II-133

Eden, Barbara, I-352

Edenfield Gardens, Worcester Park, Surrey (location), I-59, 83

Edison, Thomas, I-5, 48, 71, 81

Edward, King. *See* kings

"Edwardian," I-xi, 5, 17, 28, 79, 107, 167, 222, 223, 243, 248, 272, 280, 288, 309, 322; II-122, 162

Edwards, Jimmy, I-394

Edwards, John, I-320

Edwards, Ralph, I-324

Edward Woods Estate, Hammersmith and Fulham (location), II-118

"Ee ecky thump," II-76

Eek Eek Club, I-32, 60

effeminization, I-7, 22, 33, 34, 37, 41, 49, 58, 59, 79, 81, 83, 96–97, 132, 135, 148, 151, 153, 166, 174, 179, 193, 207, 230–33, 284, 328–29, 332, 345, 346, 347, 393; II-122, 206, 24, 27, 54–55

"Egernon Road," I-227

Egg Nest, 24 New Broadway, Ealing (location), II-27

Eichmann, Adolf, I-178, 190

Eiffel Tower, II-17, 212

84 Acton High Street, Ealing (location), I-139

84 Alexandra Road, NW8, I-35

8mm cameras/film, I-211, 292

82 St. Marys Road, Ealing (photo location), II-11

Eisenhower, Dwight D., I-165, 193, 195; II-199–200, 201

Einstein, Albert, II-143

Ekberg, Anita, I-233

Election Night Special. See television shows

elections, I-9, 11, 54, 117, 168, 178, 185, 186, 188, 194–95, 211, 224, 229, 237, 244, 256, 279, 284, 287, 289, 291, 292, 293, 294, 296–97, 299, 300, 302, 303–4, 306, 307, 308, 318, 319, 334, 373, 390, 406–8, 410; II-15, 53, 66, 78, 79–80, 82, 85, 113, 116, 144, 145, 146, 148, 155, 163, 166, 180, 188, 200, 204, 205, 206–8, 209–10, 222, 224, 226; By-Elections, I-11, 178, 184, 186, 299, 302, 307, 319, 410; II-79–80, 144, 226; General Elections: 1931, II-78, 82; 1945, I-9, 188; II-15; 1951, I-279; II-85; 1955, I-196; 1959, I-188, 195; 1964, I-211, 224, 237, 279, 293; II-116, 188, 205; 1966, I-186, 195, 279, 284, 287, 303, 307, 308, 319; 1970, I-54, 185, 188, 229, 256, 279, 284, 291, 292, 293, 294, 296–97, 300, 302, 303–4, 306, 307, 318, 319; II-53, 66, 79–80, 82, 146, 148, 155, 163, 180; 1974, I-300, 319, 373; II-82, 163, 181, 200, 204, 206–7, 209–10

Elector of Hanover, II-131, 134

Electricity Council, 30 Millbank (location), II-119

electronic music, I-125; II-101, 197

elegiac/elegists, I-61, 90, 299, 306; II-135

Elegy Written in a Country Church-Yard, Thomas Gray, I-61, 90, 299; II-135

"elevenses," I-341

Elgar, Edward, I-96, 98, 321, 392–93, 399, 401–4; II-34, 48, 86, 105, 142, 157, 165, 168, 182, 185, 215, 217, 218, 219, 220

Eliot, T.S., I-xii, 6, 54–56, 62, 130, 191, 217, 247, 350, 362; II-xii, 21, 24, 30, 97, 176; *Murder in the Cathedral*, I-6; II-20, 21, 24, 34; Old *Possum's Book of Practical Cats*, I-56; *The Waste Land*, I-xii, 6, 54, 62, 130, 191, 362; II-xii, 24–25, 30

Elizabeth I (and Elizabethan), I-20, 30, 83, 132, 147, 190, 227, 235, 269, 350, 380, 408; II-3, 28, 31, 43, 44, 45, 49, 56, 70, 121, 122, 123, 124, 126, 127, 128, 129, 131, 190, 191, 224; Elizabethan world picture, I-147

Elizabeth II, I-6, 41, 305, 335, 356, 389; II-54, 57, 70, 94, 107, 203

Elizabeth R. See television shows

Ellington, Ray, I-22, 104, 104, 188; II-31

"Ellis, Michael," I-112, 136, 145, 169, 178, 259, 297; II-42, 170, 171

Elk, Miss Anne, II-61, 62, 74, 228

Elm Hill, Norwich (location), I-325, 337; II-8

Elmbridge Town Hall, New Zealand Avenue, Walton-on-Thames (location), I-268, 269, 270

"Elsan," II-205

Elsmore, Philip, I-188

Elstree (and studio), I-295, 396, 398; II-17, 171, 173, 212, 214

Emerson, Ralph Waldo, I-293, 309

emigration/emigrants, I-90, 244, 362, 408; II-20, 29, 37, 137, 224. *See also* immigration

"empire building," II-43, 70

Empire Pool, I-86; II-43

Empire Stores, II-155

empiricism, I-181; II-103, 107

Encyclopaedia Britannica (and *Online*), I-15, 41, 73, 77, 115, 116, 131, 146, 148, 151, 174, 202, 225, 311, 336; II-140, 162, 168, 169

Encyclopedia of Witchcraft and Demonology, R.H. Robbins, I-247

Enfield, Greater London I-407; II-12, 195, 198, 223

"England and the Rest of the World XI." *See* cricket

"England's Mountains Green," I-63, 69, 71, 405, 408

"English breakfast," I-372; II-32

English Channel, I-125, 156, 158–9, 161, 163, 169, 175, 215, 222, 302, 355, 408; II-68, 224; Channel Tunnel, I-125, 215, 222; swimmers, I-158–9, 169

English Civil War, II-177

English (colloquial), I-xi, 27, 38, 39, 72, 95, 98, 119, 138, 140, 160, 210, 213, 254, 261, 277, 290, 296, 315, 317, 329, 335, 341, 347, 352, 358, 394; II-xi, 5, 10, 31, 46, 64, 72, 73, 76, 108, 122, 128, 132, 146, 147, 163, 164, 182

English Renaissance, I-xi, 26, 38, 57, 65, 99, 120, 148, 151, 158, 307, 328; II-xi, 15, 43, 134

English Romantic period, I-27, 76, 261, 277; II-173, 176

"English Rose," I-186, 188, 195–96

English Stage Company, St. Martin's Lane, I-38

"Englishness," I-xiii, 13, 23, 47, 48, 64, 70, 134, 188; II-xiii, 62, 68, 69, 187

"Enlai, Zhou," I-358

Ensslin, Gudrun and Baader-Meinhof, I-324

"Enterovioform," I-102

The Entertainer. See plays *and* films

Entertaining Mr. Sloane. See plays

Environmental Theatre. *See* Schechner

Epilogue. See television shows

epistolary novel, II-119, 157

"Epsom Downs," and Epsom, Surrey, I-87, 316, 317, 393, 408; II-189, 224, 226

Epstein, Jacob, I-362

Erconwald Street, Shepherd's Bush (location), I-226

"erratum," II-133

Ernst, Max, I-10; II-85

"escalation" sketches, I-43, 168, 236, 267, 279, 282; "deflation" sketches, I-344, 366; II-8, 14

Esher, Greater London, I-83, 131, 135, 287, 375, 393; II-32, 129, 201

Esquire, I-40; II-92

Essex, I-124, 145, 367, 388, 405; II-12, 13, 35, 77, 221

Esso, II-387

"establishment," I-28, 38, 43, 75, 162, 168, 210, 231, 266, 332; II-9, 27, 51, 63, 121, 178, 206; "The Establishment" (club), I-232; II-63

"Et Tu Brute," I-244

Eton College, I-4, 188, 194, 196, 216, 255, 256, 279, 285, 316, 321, 384; II-52, 95, 178, 205, 209

eugenics, I-198, 367

euphemisms, I-26, 45, 54, 61, 77, 84, 130, 192, 205, 272; II-163, 185, 187

euphuism, I-177

Euripides, I-60, 212

Europe (and European), I-ix, xii, 4, 12, 14, 17, 23, 42, 46, 53, 70, 74, 79, 90, 94, 102, 106, 112, 123, 134, 146, 158, 171, 173, 174, 180, 181, 184, 190, 198, 216, 217, 221, 224, 229, 231, 253, 262, 264, 267, 271, 280, 281, 311, 315, 316, 317, 329, 331, 335, 336, 340, 341, 342, 362, 366, 378, 381, 393, 394, 405; II-ix, xii, 4, 7, 10, 25, 32, 37, 38, 40, 41, 71, 72, 74, 79, 86, 93, 94, 96, 98, 102, 105, 106, 107, 115, 133, 134, 137, 142, 153, 166, 172, 181, 182, 187, 189, 191, 192, 193, 194, 198, 201, 206, 221; Austria, I-14, 15, 94, 101, 180, 310, 332; II-47, 98, 118, 133; Belgium, I-329, 333, 340, 384; II-153; Denmark, I-36, 230, 237, 271; II-7, 10, 98, 127, 131, 153, 216; France, I-8, 12, 23, 28, 29, 37, 55, 94, 120, 146, 154, 158, 161, 181, 195, 206, 207, 211, 215, 297, 298, 302, 304, 306, 311, 315, 329, 331, 336, 353, 354, 355, 357, 358, 361, 365, 377, 378, 383–84, 394, 396, 408, 411; II-8, 13, 18, 33, 68, 72, 79, 88, 90, 98, 101, 112, 139, 148, 161, 162, 163, 165, 166, 168, 190, 198, 207; East Germany, I-77, 80, 320, 340; Germany, I-8, 10, 16, 17, 24, 42, 67, 77, 94, 97, 108, 137, 146–47, 154, 181, 185, 186, 189, 190, 191, 198, 262, 268, 324, 329, 354, 378; II-5, 26, 35, 51, 59, 74, 79, 83, 98, 102, 122, 162, 165, 179, 192, 197, 207; Greece/Greek, I-45, 61, 132, 141, 175, 180, 213, 266, 306, 340, 348, 381, 385, 386; II-94, 163; Holland (The Netherlands), I-29, 42, 169, 180, 181, 217, 242, 244, 268, 329, 333, 341, 394; II-58, 98, 126, 127, 162, 179, 196; Iceland, I-xii, 317, 333, 409, 411; II-xii, 3, 5–14, 17, 38, 57, 120, 173, 202, 225, 227; Italy, I-11, 63, 68, 70, 82, 100, 119, 131, 135, 146, 168, 168, 174, 181, 185, 213, 269, 275, 297, 309, 311, 329, 334, 344, 354, 361, 373, 378, 380; II-33, 37, 40, 46, 98, 106, 179; Luxembourg, I-329; Monaco, I-43, 345; II-14, 106; Norway, I-19, 136, 231, 383; II-7, 56, 94, 98, 101, 153, 161, 164, 168, 227; Portugal, I-93, 180, 394; II-8, 63, 65, 106, 139, 162; Spain, I-87, 103, 120, 130, 181, 206, 242, 311, 341, 347, 351, 367, 381–83, 394; II-xii, 10, 32, 33, 54, 63, 67, 69, 73, 90, 96, 99, 122, 123, 125, 126, 138, 195, 197, 228; Sweden, I-89, 123, 320, 326, 357–58; II-7, 131, 138, 198

European Cup, I-174, 180, 181, 216; II-189, 194

European Economic Community ("Common Market"), I-221, 294, 304, 315, 319, 329, 340; II-79, 82, 86, 93, 137, 153, 201

European Grand Prix, I-207, 316; II-28

Euroshow 71—May Day Special. See television shows

Eurovision Song Contest. See television shows

Evans, "Taff" and "Teddy," I-355

Evans, G. Blakemore, I-24; II-56, 112

Evelyn, John, I-114

Everything You Always Wanted to Know About Sex (book), I-47. *See also* films

Ewhurst, Surrey I-10

exams (academic), I-199, 368

Exchange Telegraph, II-8

"exeat form," II-25

Exeter, Devon, I-xii, 99, 352, 355, 372; II-xii, 103, 106, 178, 179, 200, 203, 205, 206, 207, 209; "Amateur Operatic Society," I-352; Cricket Club (location), II-203

existentialism, I-xi, 6, 12, 36, 43, 175, 180, 357, 386; II-xi, 8, 16, 23, 79, 135, 175, 176

explorers, I-14, 150, 157, 169, 330, 335, 362, 407; II-29, 37, 40, 42, 43, 47, 48, 80, 122, 123, 168, 223

expressionism, I-3, 6, 14, 77, 146

"eyes down," I-293

Eyre, Simon, I-54

Eyewitness (radio series); I-17, 71, 76, 88, 105, 113, 134, 147, 151, 187, 192, 198, 210, 216, 225, 237, 255, 274, 276, 293, 321, 356, 373, 380, 394; II-9, 36, 42, 47, 56, 57, 62, 63, 68, 73, 78, 80, 83, 89, 93, 104, 121, 125, 126, 155, 156, 182, 193, 204, 208

Fabian, Det. Inspector Robert, I-18

FA Cup, I-150, 216, 361, 375–76, 384; II-64, 177

Fairbanks, Douglas, I-48; II-75

Fairfax, John, I-362

"Fair-Isle Jersey," II-208

Fairlie, Henry, I-232

"fairly butch." *See* homosexuality

"fairy" (as an insult), I-10, 49, 83, 153, 160, 284; II-23, 95; (tale characters), I-32, 102, 103, 153, 163, 195, 201, 257, 329, 401, 406, 412; II-91, 92, 143, 184, 217, 222, 228

Falklands, I-389

Falstaff, John, I-66, 180, 277; II-5, 9, 22, 28, 62

The Family. See television shows

Fanny Hill, I-166; II-88

Fanshaw-Chumleigh, II-203

Fantoni, Barry, I-209

Farago, Ladislas, II-188, 192

Faroe Islands, II-11, 12

Farson, Daniel, II-123

Fascism and Fascists, I-8, 24, 63, 103, 190, 195, 197, 208, 374; II-42, 59, 67, 73, 78, 83, 87, 89, 98, 191

"fast bowler." *See* cricket: terminology

"fast-motion." *See* MPFC production elements

"faulty action" (Freudian slip), I-132, 140, 155, 205, 261

Fauvism, I-6, 9

"faux" elements, I-63, 76, 186, 217, 307, 381; II-141, 163, 166; "faux pas," I-186, 217

Faversham, Kent, II-8, 182

Fawlty Towers. See television shows

Feather, Vic, II-67

FBI (Federal Bureau of Investigation), I-41; II-23, 102

Federal Reserve Board, II-195

fee-paying schools, I-37; II-58

Felbrigg Hall, Norwich, Norfolk (location), II-43, 148

Feldman, Marty, I-65, 85, 94, 145, 150, 161, 300, 388; II-10, 12, 118, 131, 132. *See also* television shows

Felix, Julie, I-205, 216, 400

Fellini, Federico. *See* film directors

Feltham Marshalling Yards (location), I-112, 167

"female impersonator," I-55, 151, 228

Fen Ditton, Cambridgeshire I-364

Fenwick, Det. Chief Inspector George, II-126

Ferdinand and Isabella, I-244, 249, 251

fetish/fetishize, I-40, 207, 288; II-200

Ffitch, George, I-320, 391

Fielding, Henry, I-12, 54, 153, 366; II-96, 103

Fields, W.C., I-116

"Fifth Dynasty" and "Fourth Dynasty," I-331

50 Ellerby Street, Hammersmith and Fulham (location), I-197

55 Lincoln House, London SW3, I-164

"59 Club," I-141

52 Hill House, Market Square, Wickham Market (location), I-161

"Figgis," I-20, 33, 93, 94, 96, 98, 140, 316, 325, 406; as *Punch* librarian, I-33, 316

"*Fille Mal Gardée*," II-195

film directors: Lindsay Anderson (*see* Anderson, Lindsay); Michelangelo Antonioni (see Antonioni, Michelangelo); Edgar Antsey and Arthur Elton, I-224; Antonin Artaud, II-48; Richard Attenborough (see Attenborough, Richard); László Benedek, I-164; Compton Bennett, II-61; Ingmar Bergman, I-69, 83, 123, 129, 145, 256, 302; II-4; J. Stuart Blackton, I-32, 87, 94; II-44, 128; Mel Brooks, I-67; Richard Brooks, I-165; Luis Bunuel, I-213, 357; II-48; Stuart Burge, I-244; Claude Chabrol, I-357, 361; Rene Clair, II-48; Jack Clayton, I-37, 306; Jean Cocteau, II-48; Francis Ford Coppola, I-294; Costa-Gavras, II-150; Salvador Dali, II-48; Cecil B. DeMille, I-377; Guiseppe De Santis, I-375; Vittorio de Sica (*see* De

Sica, Vittorio); Basil Dearden, I-53, 124, 268; II-47; Jacques Demy, I-206; Stanley Donen, I-286; Clive Donner, I-133; Carl Theodor Dreyer, I-8; Sergei Eisenstein, II-124; Federico Fellini, I-213, 375; II-46, 48, 209; Robert Flaherty, I-110; II-195; Bryan Forbes (*see* Forbes); Aleksander Ford, II-124; John Ford, I-202, 373, 387; II-72, 92, 94, 97; Samuel Fuller, I-366; Pietro Germi, I-206; Jean-Luc Godard (*see* Godard); Robert Gordon, I-373; D.W. Griffith, I-122, 256, 351; Val Guest, I-110, 174; Henry Hathaway, II-72; Howard Hawks, I-245, 366; Cecil Hepworth, I-47; Alfred Hitchcock (*see* Hitchcock), Alfred; George Hoellering, II-34; John Huston, I-98; II-157; Humphrey Jennings, I-141, 389; Gene Kelly, I-343; Irvin Kershner, I-344; Stanley Kubrick (*see* Kubrick); Akira Kurosawa (*see* Kurosawa); Fritz Lang, I-146, 366; David Lean, I-18, 21, 313, 353; II-34, 62, 78; Claude Lelouch, I-206; John Lennon and Yoko Ono, II-185; Richard Lester, I-27, 91, 167, 206, 321; Ken Loach, I-27, 207, 387; Joseph Losey, II-47, 123; George Lucas, II-105; Sidney Lumet, II-29; Tony Mann, II-94; Chris Marker, II-99; George Marshall, II-72; Leo McCarey, I-28; Joseph McGrath, I-351, 353, 354; Georges Melies, I-85, 87, 91; Jean-Pierre Melville, I-265, 272; Arnold Miller, I-141; Peir Paolo Pasolini (*see* Pasolini); Sam Peckinpah, I-146, 240, 297, 350, 358; II-65, 91, 92, 96, 97, 100; Arthur Penn, II-350, 358; Edwin S. Porter, I-47; Michael Powell, I-18, 21, 153, 367; II-82; Emeric Pressburger, I-367; II-82; Alvin Rakoff, I-268; Man Ray, II-48, 85; Carol Reed, I-290; Karel Reisz, I-123, 367; Jean Renoir, I-154, 280, 367; Alain Resnais, I-83, 211, 272, 357, 384; Tony Richardson, I-34, 37, 366, 382; Leni Riefenstahl, I-146, 190, 195, 198; Martin Ritt, I-281; George Romero, I-240; Roberto Rossellini, I-13, 24; II-48; Ken Russell (*see* Russell, Ken); John Schlesinger, I-304; John Sturges, I-245; II-27; Preston Sturges, II-94; Jacques Tourneur, I-104; Francois Truffaut, I-211, 354, 363, 365–66; Luchino Visconti (*see* Visconti); Eric von Strohem, I-105, 213; II-85; Andrzej Wajda, I-357; Peter Watkins, I-102, 382; Orson Welles, I-353, 354, 366; II-124, 157, 171, 199; Bo Wideberg, I-326; Robert Wiene, I-146; Billy Wilder, II-5; Robert Wise, I-139; Ed Wood, I-113, 121; William Wyler, I-223

film festivals, I-15, 206, 363; II-42

Film Finders Limited, I-397

film genres, I-xiii, 68, 69, 100–1, 120, 240, 353, 366; II-xiii, 47, 74, 146: epic, I-112, 208, 223, 244, 313, 351; II-5, 34, 44, 62, 94, 183; "exploitation," I-113; II-75; gangster/noir, I-68, 74, 98, 111, 135, 226, 353; II-54, 94, 180; horror, I-111, 113, 120, 122, 123, 124, 147, 240, 316, 319; II-75, 146; melodrama, I-69, 247, 330; musical, I-51, 139, 170, 286,

294, 327, 328, 329, 343, 408, 412; II-40, 74, 76, 82, 94, 95, 177, 183, 224, 228; science fiction, I-110, 111, 113–17, 120, 123–25, 316, 319, 320, 323; II-49, 185; spy, I-68, 76, 77; II-128; war picture, II-62; western, I-20, 22, 37, 99, 146, 170, 202, 240, 296, 337, 373, 397, 411; II-51, 72, 87, 91, 92, 94, 96, 97, 100, 131, 213, 227

film noir, I-64, 76, 104, 226, 266; II-171

"film society," I-145

film stock, I-4, 106, 211, 242, 275, 311, 323, 326, 353, 356, 357, 395–98; II-54, 65, 72, 73, 82, 92, 105, 109, 118, 127, 150, 152, 153, 171, 184, 185, 211–14

films: Algeria: *Eldridge Cleaver, Black Panther*, II-34; Australia: *The Adventures of Barry McKenzie*, I-179; Belgium: *Lords of the Forest (Masters of the Congo Jungle)*, II-60; Canada: *Neighbours*, I-85, 87, 210; *Whispering City*, I-176; France: *400 Blows*, I-354, 366; *La Jetee*, II-99; *Le Ballon Rouge*, II-18; *Barbarella*, I-99, 138; II-18; *Les Biches*, I-361; *Le Cercle Rouge*, I-265; II-18; *Cinétracts*, I-353; *Clan des Siciliens*, I-264; *La Folie de Grandeurs*, II-18; "*Le Fromage Grand*," I-352; *The Grand Illusion*, I-280; *Jules and Jim*, I-211, 354; *Last Year at Marienbad*, I-83, 211, 272; *Les Mistons*, II-18; *M. Hulot's Holiday, Mon Oncle*, I-65; *The Passion of Joan of* Arc, I-8; *Le Petit Soldat*, II-18; *Rules of the Game*, I-154; *Le Salaire du péché*, II-18; *Le Samourai*, I-272; *Tout va Bien*, I-153; II-18; *Umbrellas of Cherbourg*, I-206; *Un homme et une femme*, I-206; *Le Vent d'est*, I-356; *Watering the Gardener*, I-48; *Week End*, I-213, 354, 356–57; II-185; *World Without Sun*, II-60; *Z*, II-150; Germany: *Das Blaue Licht*, I-146; *The Cabinet of Dr. Caligari*, I-146; *Lockende Wildnis*, II-60; *M*, I-146; *Metropolis*, I-115; *Triumph of the Will*, I-10, 190, 195, 197; *Die Weiße Hölle vom Piz Palü*, I-146; *Victory of the Faith*, I-197; Hong Kong: *Come Drink With Me*, I-253; Italy: *8 ½*, II-209; *Accatone*, II-124; *Adultery Italian Style*, I-100; *Bitter Rice*, I-375; *Blowup*, I-133, 206; *Boccaccio 70*, II-46; *The Canterbury Tales*, II-155; *Cronaca Di Un Amore*, I-42; *The Damned*, II-44, 47, 203; *Death in Venice*, II-47, 94, 150, 203; *The Decameron*, II-124, 155; *Divorce, Italian Style*, I-100; *Europa '51*, II-48; *Futurist Life*, I-82; *The Garden of the Finzi-Continis*, II-150; *Gente del Po*, II-42; *The Gospel According to St. Matthew*, I-207; *Hercules and the Captive Women*, I-351; *The Last Man on Earth*, I-116; *La Strada*, I-375; *L'Avventura*, II-41, 46; *La Dolce Vita*, II-181, 195, 220; *La Notte, L'Eclisse*, II-41, 46; *The Leopard*, I-206; II-46; *Love Italian Style, Marriage Italian Style*, I-100; *Oedipus Rex*, II-155; *Ossessione*, II-46; *Porcile*, II-155; *Red Desert*, II-41, 42; *La regina dei tartari*, I-323; *Rome: Open City*, I-13, 24; *Signore & Signori*, I-206; *Teorema*, II-209; *La Terra Trema*, II-46; *Tharus figlio di Attila*, I-323; "*The Third Test Match*,"

II-150, 155, 227; *Tiffany Memorandum*, I-231; *Waterloo*, I-375; *Zabriskie Point*, II-41, 100; Japan: *Branded To Kill*, I-135; *The Loyal 47 Ronin*, I-304; *Sanjuro*, I-304, 350; II-92, 96, 100; *Seppuku*, I-304; *Seven Samurai*, I-302; *Tokyo Drifter*, I-135; *Yojimbo*, I-304; II-92, 96; Mexico: *Los Olvidados*, I-357; Poland: *Ashes and Diamonds*, I-357; *Knights of the Teutonic Order*, II-124; Russia: *Alexander Nevsky*, II-124, 154, 220; Sweden: *Elvira Madigan*, I-326; *I Am Curious Yellow*, I-253; *The Seventh Seal*, I-83, 123, 129, 145, 256, 302; II-4; *Wild Strawberries*, I-83; UK: *10 Rillington Place* II-5, 17, 135, 150; *633 Squadron*, II-185; *Accident*, II-124; *A Clockwork Orange*, I-280; II-114, 124; ; *A Diary For Timothy*, I-280; *A Fish Called Wanda*, I-98; *A Kid for Two Farthings*, I-290; *Alfie*, I-242; II-85; *Alfred the Great*, I-133; *A Little of What You Fancy*, II-171, 179; *All You Need Is Cash*, II-136; *Asylum*, II-43; *A Taste of Honey*, I-34, 37; II-97; *The Barretts of Wimpole Street*, I-78; *Becket*, I-353; II-27; *The Best House in London*, I-99; *Billion Dollar Brain*, I-270, 280, 302; *Billy Liar*, II-97; *Blackmail*, I-155, 303; II-44; *The Blue Lamp*, I-118–19; II-43, 104, 184; *The Body*, II-111; *The Boy Friend*, II-65; *Bronco Bullfrog*, I-139; *Camp on Blood Island*, I-174; *Carry on Henry*, II-150; *Carry On…Up the Jungle*, I-280; II-43, 46, 149; *Carry On…Up the Khyber*, II-149; *Chelsea Bridge Boys*, I-134, 139; *Comedy Workshop: Love and Maud Carver*, I-160; *Cosh Boy*, I-139; *Dalek's Invasion Earth*, II-55; *The Day the Earth Caught Fire*, I-110, 116, 126; II-119, 195; *Dead of Night*, I-122, 146; *The Devils*, I-34, 44, 48, 49, 57, 61, 65, 228; *Devils of Darkness*, I-113; *Dick Barton at Bay*, I-204; *Dick Barton Strikes Back*, I-204; *Down Among the Z Men*, I-77, 92, 179; *Dr. Crippen*, II-92; *Eagle Squadron*, I-307; *The Elusive Pimpernel*, II-82; *The Entertainer*, I-105; II-97; *Far From the Madding Crowd*, II-34; *The Final Test*, I-333; *Goodbye, Mr. Chips*, I-108; II-58; *Growing Up*, II-84; *Gumshoe*, II-150; *Guns at Batasi*, I-230; *Hands of Orlac*, I-175; II-32; *Hands of the Ripper*, I-342; II-104; *Henry V*, I-187; II-216; *Hoffman*, I-268; *Housing Problems*, I-224; *If…*, I-103, 242, 283, 289, 297; II-124, 171; *I'm All Right Jack*, I-325; *Island of Terror*, I-113; *Julius Caesar*, I-244–45; *Kes*, I-27, 207, 387; *Kind Hearts and Coronets*, I-144; *The Knack…and How to Get It*, I-206; *The Lady Vanishes*, I-321; *The Ladykillers*, I-132; *The Lavender Hill Mob*, I-47, 91; *The League of Gentlemen*, I-124, 268; *Let's All Make Love in London Tonight*, II-85; *The Lion in Winter*, II-150; *Listen to Britain*, I-141; *Litter Defence Volunteers*, I-368; *Lloyd of the CID*, I-70; *Look Back in Anger*, I-37, 38, 105; II-97; *Love Among the Ruins*, II-179; *The Magic Christian*, I-38, 47, 187, 216, 251, 353, 354; II-18, 119, 127, 131, 145;

The Magnificent Seven Deadly Sins, II-10; *A Man for All Seasons*, II-34; *The Man in the White Suit*, I-121; II-104; *Mary, Queen of Scots*, I-345; *Meet the Rutles*, II-163; *The Mind Benders*, II-47; *Moll Flanders*, I-351; *Monty Python and the Holy Grail* (*HG*), I-5, 12, 19, 22, 27, 29, 30–32, 40, 43, 47, 53, 55, 57, 61, 63, 67–68, 76, 82–83, 102, 108, 113, 116, 123–24, 129, 130–31, 135–36, 138, 145–48, 152, 160–61, 167–68, 174, 176, 178, 182–83, 190, 192, 199, 200, 202, 206, 212, 217, 222, 245, 248, 253, 258, 262, 265, 297, 300, 309, 312, 317, 322, 326, 328, 354, 356, 358, 368, 372, 375, 386; II-5, 6, 8, 9, 13, 23, 28, 36, 41, 52, 65, 78, 98, 111, 113, 122, 124, 135, 149, 155, 162–64, 177, 200, 203, 205, 208; *Monty Python Live at the Hollywood Bowl*, I-40, 58, 62, 70, 95, 117, 172, 175, 180, 201, 222; II-55; *Monty Python's Life of Brian* (*LB*), I-29, 50, 52, 57, 71, 83, 91, 116, 130, 131, 135, 223, 245, 265, 270, 274, 306, 309, 356, 369, 419; II-11, 36, 90, 146; *Monty Python's The Meaning of Life* (*ML*), I-21, 49, 56, 72, 76, 77, 81, 92, 95, 116, 130, 160, 162–63, 168, 178, 191, 203, 210, 211, 222, 223, 234, 236, 239, 256, 340, 406, 419; II-14, 23, 31, 44, 48, 116, 203, 235; *Murder in the Cathedral*, II-34; *Night of the Big Heat*, I-113; *Not Tonight Darling*, II-93, 95; *The Office Party*, II-205; *Oh! What a Lovely War*, I-18; II-150; *Oliver!*, I-60, 225, 302, 380; *Passport to Pimlico*, I-121; *Peeping Tom*, I-18, 153; *Plague of the Zombies*, I-231; *Quatermass II*, I-269, 280; *Raging Moon*, I-326; *Recognition of the Zero Fighter*, I-343; *Rescued By Rover*, I-47; *The Rise and Rise of Michael Rimmer*, I-47, 176, 292; *Room at the Top*, I-37, 306; II-97; *Roundhay Garden Scene*, I-47; *Royal New Zealand Journey*, I-360; *The Running, Jumping and Standing Still Film*, I-91; II-34; *Saturday Night and Sunday Morning*, I-105, 123, 242; *Scent of Mystery*, I-47; *Scott of the Antarctic*, I-357; II-76; *Secrets of Sex*, I-297; "The Semaphore Version of Wuthering Heights," I-240–51, 412; *The Servant*, I-35; II-47, 123; *Shadowlands*, I-96; *The Slipper and the Rose*, II-142, 147; *The Spider's Web*, I-172; *The Statue*, II-154; *Strip*, I-322; *Sunday, Bloody Sunday*, II-150; *Sweeney Todd: The Demon Barber of Fleet Street*, I-146; *Teenagers Learn to Swim*, I-368; *This Sporting Life*, I-35, 37, 149, 387; II-28, 36; *Time Bandits*, I-129, 379; II-27, 85; *Tommy the Toreador*, II-106; *Twenty Questions Murder Mystery*, I-117; *Two Gentlemen Sharing*, II-79; *Up the Chastity Belt*, II-105, 171; *Up the Front*, I-182; *Up the Junction*, I-242; II-178; *Up Your Legs Forever*, II-185; *Wanted For Murder*, II-189, 197; *The Wooden Horse*, I-279, 280, 281, 282, 283, 285; *Victim*, I-53; *Village of the Damned*, I-114; *The War Game*, I-102, 382; *Young Winston*, II-150; *Zulu*, I-178; US (Hollywood): *40 Pounds of Trouble*, II-147; *42nd Street*, II-74; *55 Days at Peking*, I-351; *2001: A Space Odyssey*,

I-289, 297, 299, 320, 344, 371, 406, 409; II-140, 222, 225; *A Hard Day's Night*, I-27, 32, 47, 53, 80, 82, 162, 167, 186, 210, 256, 291, 321, 346, 380; II-119, 182, 184, 198, 202; *A Streetcar Named Desire*, I-164; *A Summer Place*, I-208, 212, 400; *The Alamo*, II-72; *Angel Unchained*, I-302; *Angry Red Planet*, I-110; *Annie Hall*, II-18; *Around the World in 80 Days*, II-150; *Asphalt Jungle*, I-76, 98, 111, 226; *Attila*, I-323; *Battle of Britain*, I-23, 77, 92, 105, 157, 176; *The Battle of the Century*, I-40; *Beginning of the End*, I-323; *Ben Hur*, I-223, 234, 404; II-183, 220; *Big Country*, II-203; *Birth of a Nation*, I-256, 351; "The Black Eagle," I-63, 82, 140, 249, 344, 371, 373; II-14, 19, 223; *Black Panther*, II-34; *The Black Swan*, I-373; *The Blob*, I-111, 115, 116; *The Blue Eagle*, I-373; *Bonnie and Clyde*, I-321, 350, 358; II-94, 100, 204, 210; *Brazil*, I-84, 193, 235, 236; II-171; *Bridge on the River Kwai*, I-73, 353, 360; *Bridge Over the River Trent*, I-353; *Bullitt*, I-264; *Butch Cassidy and the Sundance Kid*, I-108, 273, 274, 309, 321; *Capone*, I-132; *Captain Blood*, I-373; *Casablanca*, I-202; *Casino Royale*, I-251, 351, 353, 354, 380, 395; II-189, 211; *Cat on a Hot Tin Roof*, I-165; *C.C. and Company*, I-355; "The Cheese Who Shot Liberty Valance," II-94; *Cheyenne Autumn*, II-72; *Chinatown*, II-204; *Chisum*, I-358; *Colossus: The Forbin Project*, I-320; *Cops*, I-68; *Dr. No*, I-77; *Darby O'Gill*, II-119; *The Day the Earth Stood Still*, I-111, 115, 116; *Detour*, I-226; *Dial M For Murder*, I-96; II-152; *Double Indemnity*, I-266; *Dr. Strangelove*, I-26, 40, 80, 329, 370; II-55, 114, 127, 200, 201; *Dr. Zhivago*, I-18; II-30, 34, 62; *Duel in the Sun*, I-96; *Dumbo*, II-48; *The Egyptian*, I-390; *The Empire Strikes Back*, I-344; *Everything You've Always Wanted to Know About Sex…*, I-286; *Fantastic Voyage*, I-216; *Finian's Rainbow*, I-289, 294, 408, 409; *Foolish Wives*, II-85; *Forbidden Planet*, I-110, 111, 115, 125; *Frankenstein*, I-98, 111; *From Russia With Love*, I-93, 98, 273, 399; *Gentlemen Prefer Blondes*, I-240, 245; II-87; *The Giant Gila Monster*, I-320, 323; *Glenroy Brothers Comic Boxing*, I-81; *The Golddiggers of 1933*, II-74; *Goldfinger*, I-77, 369, 396; *Gone With the Wind*, II-74, 126; *Goodbye, Mr. Chips*, I-108; II-58; *The Great Escape*, I-32, 281, 285, 402; II-20, 27, 218; *The Great Train Robbery*, I-47; *The Great White Hope*, I-281; *The Greatest Story Ever Told*, I-207; "Gunfight at Gruyère Corral," II-94; *Gunfight at the OK Corral*, I-240, 245; II-94; *The Guns of Navarone*, I-325; *The Haunted Hotel*, I-87; *Haunted Spooks*, I-61; *Hello, Dolly!*, I-108, 170, 339, 343, 358; *Help!*, I-118; II-34, 99; *High Noon*, I-37, 96; *HMS Defiant*, II-94; *The Hoodlum Priest*, I-344; *How Green Was My Valley*, I-120, 387; *How the West Was Won*, II-72, 75; *Humorous Phases of Funny Faces*, I-94; *The Hustler*, I-165; *I Am a Fugitive From a*

Chain Gang, II-128; *I Married a Communist, I Married a Heathen,* and *I Married a Witch*, I-178; *Ice Station Zebra*, I-101, 108, 351, 354–56; "Ilchester '73," II-94; *In Like Flint*, II-197; *The Incredible Shrinking Man*, I-320; *Invaders From Mars*, I-114; II-49; *Invasion of the Body Snatchers*, I-114, 120; *It Came From Beneath the Sea*, I-323; *It's a Wonderful Life*, I-359; *Juarez*, I-353; *The Killers*, I-98, 132; *The Killing*, I-98; *The King of Kings*, I-207; *King Rat*, I-325; *The Kiss*, I-5; "Krakatoa, East of Leamington," *Krakatoa, East of Java*, I-354; *The Last Rebel*, I-355; *Lawrence of Arabia*, I-269, 313, 351, 353; "Lawrence of Glamorgan," I-353; "The Life and Loves of Toulouse-Lautrec," II-29; *The Life of Emile Zola*, I-353; II-128; *The Life of Moses*, II-128; *Little Big Man*, II-150; *Little Caesar*, I-74; *Little Nemo*, I-94; *Little Shop of Horrors*, II-75; *Live and Let Die*, II-136; *Lolita*, I-26, 213, 299; *London in the Raw*, I-31, 145; II-188; *The London Nobody Knows*, II-73; *The Lonedale Operator*, I-122; *Long Day's Journey Into Night*, II-29, 33; *The Lost World*, II-47; "The Mad Woman of Biggleswade," *The Mad Woman of Chaillot*, I-354; *Major Dundee*, II-96; *The Maltese Falcon*, I-74; *The Man Who Shot Liberty Valance*, I-94; *M*A*S*H*, II-144; *Memphis Belle*, II-145; *Midnight Cowboy*, I-289, 297, 304, 409; *My Darling Clementine*, I-202, 390; II-92; *Myra Breckenridge*, I-358; *Nanook of the North*, I-110; II-195; *Nice and Friendly*, II-154; *Night of the Lepus*, II-131; *Night of the Living Dead*, I-240; *North By Northwest*, I-79; *Norwood*, I-355; *The Omega Man*, I-116; *One Million Years B.C.*, I-216; *Our Man Flint*, II-197; *Out of the Inkwell*, I-32, 94; *The Outlaw*, II-87; *Out of the Past*, I-74, 104; "The Pantomime Horse is a Secret Agent," II-50, 87, 94, 145, 227; *Patton*, I-176; *Phantom of the Opera*, I-95, 193; *Pickup on South Street*, I-266; *Pillow Talk*, I-104; *Plan 9 From Outer Space*, I-111, 113, 121; *Planet of the Apes*, I-110, 115; *Primitive London*, I-31, 141, 145, 157, 362; *Prisoner of Zenda*, II-126; *The Producers*, I-67, 99; *Psycho*, I-147, 149; *The Public Enemy*, I-74, 98; *Rear Window*, I-289, 303, 409; *Rio Lobo*, I-358; *Road to Bali*, II-83; "Rogue Cheddar," II-91, 98, 228; *The Royal Hunt of the Sun*, I-157; *Ryan's Daughter*, I-351; II-34; "Sam Peckinpah's Salad Days," I-146; II-65, 91–92; *The Sands of Iwo Jima*, II-62; *Saturday Night Fever*, I-324; *Scarface*, I-74, 111; "Scott of the Antarctic," I-65, 284, 349, 351, 353, 357, 381, 412; II-76, 100, 147, 228; "Scott of the Sahara," I-xii, 349, 351, 357, 412; II-xiii, 118, 228; *The Sea Hawk*, I-373; *The Searchers*, I-105; II-72; *Seven Hills of Rome*, II-40; *Shane*, I-33, 37, 357; II-92; *Seven Brides for Seven Brothers*, I-51, 209, 278, 283, 284, 286, 287, 293, 296, 345, 412; *Shock Corridor*, I-266; *The Sound of Music*, I-139, 404; *Spellbound*, II-74; *Stagecoach*, I-202; *Stalag 17*, I-280;

Star Wars, I-228, 241, 280, 293, 303, 378, 381; II-49, 131, 171, 189; *The Story of Louis Pasteur*, I-353; *Straw Dogs*, II-96, 100; *Strawberries Need Rain*, I-302; *Sweet Bird of Youth*, I-165; *Take the Money and Run*, I-286; II-119; *Tarantula*, I-123, 320, 323; *Tassels in the Air, Their Purple Moment*, I-40; *Them!*, I-110, 114, 115, 123, 124, 320, 323; *The Thing From Another World*, I-110, 111, 116, 126; *The Third Man*, II-171; *THX-1138*, II-105; *T-Men*, I-266; *To Sir, With Love*, I-333; II-30; *Tora! Tora! Tora!*, I-358; *Towed in the Hole*, I-40; *The Towering Inferno*, II-204; *Treasure Island*, I-86, 373, 378; *True Grit*, I-358; *The Undefeated*, I-355, 358; *Victory At Sea*, II-185, 216, 217; *Victory Through Air Power*, II-145; *Viva Villa!*, II-126; *Viva Zapata!*, I-164; *Voyage to the Bottom of the Sea*, I-352; *War of the Worlds*, I-111, 113; *What's Up Tiger Lily?*, II-180; *Where Eagles Dare*, I-101, 108; *Why We Fight*, II-145; *The Wild Bunch*, I-350, 358; II-96, 100, 210; *The Wild One*, I-131, 164; *Winchester 73*, II-94; *Witness for the Prosecution*, II-5; *The Yellow Submarine*, I-22, 89, 134, 193, 297, 375; *Yellowstone Cubs*, II-60; *Zorba the Greek*, II-90

Finch, Peter, II-150
Finchley, Greater London, I-116, 146, 337
Finian's Rainbow. See films
Finney, Albert, I-123; II-150
"fire balloon," II-163
Firearms Act of 1968, II-196
"The Firm," I-232
Fischer, Bobby, I-364
"fish and chips," I-188, 377
A Fish Called Wanda. See films
"Fison's Fertilizers," II-75
"fisties," I-375
Fittipaldi, Emerson, II-28, 207
Fitzjones, Brian, I-294
"five frog curse," I-116, 264, 405
5 Orford Hill, Norwich, II-21
F.J. Wallis Store (location), I-24, 35, 130, 139
flagellants, I-129, 145
Flaherty, Robert. *See* film directors
Flanagan, Bud, *Together Again*, I-283
Flanagan, Maureen ("Flanagan"). *See* MPFC extras and walk-ons
"flannel," II-163
"Flashman," I-394
Fleet Street, I-146, 228, 233, 300; II-123
Fleischer, Max (and Dave), I-20, 32, 94; II-44, 108
Fleming, Alexander, I-353; II-143
Fleming, Ian. *See* "Bond, James"
Flemish, I-5, 30, 68, 74, 101, 196, 242, 373–75; II-33
Flick Colby Dancers, I-331, 335; II-120
Flintstones, The. See "television shows"
"floating the pound," II-144
Floor Manager, I-161, 269, 352, 375; II-123
"Flopsy," I-68
Florentine, I-68–69, 128; II-33
Flutter, Sir Fopling, I-199

"Fly Me to the Moon," Bart Howard, I-255
"flying philosopher" and "Flying Doctor Service," I-342
Flynn, Errol, II-61
"foamite," I-359
folk music/singers, I-69, 75, 205, 206, 216, 228, 299; II-34
Fonteyn, Margot, II-197–98, 200
Fontwell, West Sussex, I-352
Foot, Michael, I-18, 134
football clubs: Aberdeen, II-77; AC Milan, I-181; Arsenal, I-310, 361, 363, 374, 376; II-64, 84, 102, 177; Bologna, I-174, 180, 181; Bradford, I-xii, 116, 143, 153; Brentford, I-xii, 373; II-xii, 26; Brighton & Hove Albion, II-170; Bristol Rovers, I-373; Celtic, I-180, 181, 307; Chelsea, I-361, 363; Chippenham, I-169; Coventry City, I-376; II-154; Crystal Palace, I-150; II-170; East Jarrow United, I-176; Fenerbahçe SK, I-370; Fulham, I-150, 195, 197; II-91; Galatasaray SK, I-370; Inter Milan, I-180–81; Leeds United, I-177, 225, 361; II-189; Leicester, I-374; Liverpool, I-361, 374; II-84; Manchester United, I-174, 177, 186, 376; II-154; Newcastle, I-180; II-87; Queens Park (QPR), I-138, 381; Raith, II-77; Real Madrid, I-181; II-191–92; Sheffield Wednesday, I-144; Southampton, I-228; II-154; Sunderland, I-180; Thames Ironworks, Tottenham Hotspur, I-376; West Ham United, I-147, 150, 185, 376; II-87; Wolverhampton, I-171, 310, 373, 374, 376; Wrexham, II-191, 194
football players: Malcolm Allison, II-170; George Best, I-174; Ernie Blenkinsop, I-144; Peter Bonetti, I-361; Billy Bremner, I-225; Bobby Charlton, I-186; Jack Charlton, I-361; Brian Clough, II-170, 188; Charlie George, II-64; Jimmy Greaves, I-33, 147; Jimmy Hill, II-170, 189; Geoff Hurst, I-147; Rodney Marsh, I-138; Martin Peters, I-186; Bryan "Pop" Robson, II-87; Joe Shaw, I-304; Bill Wright, I-310
"Football Special," I-363
"fop," I-78, 199; II-133, 134
"For free repetition of doubtful words…," II-121, 123, 224
"For He's Going to Marry Yum Yum," Gilbert and Sullivan, II-184
Forbes, Bryan, I-268, 294, 325–26, 354; II-124
Ford, Aleksander. *See* film directors
Ford Motors, I-264, 289, 387, 388, 410; II-20, 23, 24, 26, 86, 157, 196, 226
Foreign Office, I-243; II-66
Foreign Secretary, I-289, 293, 294, 347, 408; II-163, 224
Formby, George, II-57, 180
Formula 1 and/or 2 racing, I-342; II-177, 192
Forster, Air Chief Marshal, I-221, 230; II-55
48 Ullswater Road, Barnes (location), I-9, 33, 60
49 Elers Road, Ealing (location), I-108, 240, 243, 245, 251, 287, and "M. Korobko" 245

46–50 Uxbridge Road, London, (location) I-139
Foster, Jill, I-95, 280
Foucault, Michel, I-342
424 Hornsey Road, Greater London, I-323
4 Simpson House, New Zealand Avenue, Walton-on-Thames (location), I-273
14 Arlington Road, Twickenham (location), II-34
"Four Yorkshire Gentlemen" sketch, I-150, 210, 338
"fourth wall," I-134, 312
Fox, Paul, II-26, 39, 92, 183
"Frampton Cottrell," I-189
France. *See* "Europe"
Francis, Anne, I-110
Francis, Kevin, II-26
Franco, Gen. Francisco, I-367; II-67, 73, 90
Frankenstein monster, I-60, 98, 123, 205
frankincense, I-270, 274
Franklin, Sir John, I-392
Fraser & Dunlop Scripts Ltd., I-280
Frazier, Joe, I-281
The Fred Tomlinson Singers, I-82, 145, 149, 154, 342, 402, 403; II-43, 48, 67, 123, 128, 133, 137, 218, 219
Frederick William and the Seven Years' War, I-25; II-133
Free French, II-134
"free" health care, I-390–91, 393
"freedom," I-12, 35–36, 43, 53, 201; II-8, 12, 16, 17, 23, 175, 188–89. *See also* Sartre, Jean-Paul
"Freeman, Hardy and Willis" (and "Freedom, Hardy and Willis"), I-207
Freeman, John, I-228
Freemasonry (and Masonry), I-84, 101, 264, 265, 267, 270, 271, 274, 276, 279, 281, 405, 409, 413; II-114, 137, 184, 221, 225, 229
Freemasons Estate, I-267
"Frelimo," II-8
French (language), I-ix, 23, 26, 41–42, 51, 55, 100, 136, 198, 237, 308; II-ix, 69, 108, 164, 167, 171, 224
The French Lieutenant's Woman, John Fowles, I-293, 295
French New History, I-336
French New Wave. *See* "New Wave"
French, Philip, I-356
French Revolution, I-15, 315, 316; II-134, 165
Fresno, California, II-97
Freud, Sigmund (and "Freudian"), I-79, 132, 140, 149, 155, 205, 265; II-79, 190
Frischauer, Willi and *David Frost*, I-310
Froberger, Johann, I-98
"Frog Trampling Institute," I-116
From Russia With Love. See films
"Le Fromage Grand." See films
"front bench," I-316, 337
Frost, David, I-35–36, 85, 95, 156, 158–160, 163, 170, 205, 211, 216, 233, 246, 268, 292, 294–95, 297, 299, 303, 304, 305, 306, 309, 310, 378–79; II-57, 130, 134, 152, 199; TV shows, I-15, 35, 61, 77, 85, 94, 134, 156, 159, 163, 202, 211, 216, 268, 282, 292, 294–

95, 297, 299, 302, 309; II-15, 46, 130, 134, 152, 199. *See also* television shows
Frost, Edward Purkis, I-246
The Frost Report. See television shows *and* David Frost
"fruit machine," I-225, 232; II-198
"F'tang," I-72, 192, 270, 307
Fuchs, Klaus, II-116
"Führer," I-189
Fulham, Hammersmith and Fulham, I-84, 85, 185, 191, 195, 347, 363; II-26, 118, 184; Stadium, I-197; II-91
"full employment," I-197, 390; II-143
"Full frontal nudity," I-127, 129, 130, 140, 147, 207, 242, 413; "Full Frontal Radio," I-130
Fuller, Graham, I-207
"fumetti," II-99
"furlong," I-358

"Gabriel, Archangel," I-261; II-111
Gabriel, Roman, I-355, 358
"gaffer," I-39, 389
Gainsborough, Thomas. *See* artists
"gaiters," II-179
"Gala Evening Franco-Britannique," II-58
Galileo, I-353; II-143
Gall, Sandy, I-320
Gallieni, Gen. Joseph, II-111
Galsworthy, John, I-194, 327, 331, 335
Galtymore Ballroom, 184 Cricklewood Broadway (location), II-151
"Gandulf," I-392
Gardner, John E., and *Madrigal*, I-65
Gardening Club. See television shows
Gardner, Andrew, I-320, 391
Gardner's *Art Through the Ages*, I-15, 68, 375, 374–75; II-138
Gargantua and Pantagruel, Rabelais. *See* novels/literature
Gargoyle Club, I-123
"The Garibaldis," I-154, 302; II-204, 205
Garnett, Alf, I-297
Garrick, David, I-190
Garson, Greer, I-240; II-61
gas (natural): "brown coats," I-231, 236, 319; II-154; Gas Act of 1948, I-234; "gas cooker," I-92, 159, 221, 223, 226, 236, 289, 294, 302, 411; II-117; gas men, I-228, 229, 231, 236, 260; problems/accidents, I-273–74, 294; II-116, 117. *See also* "brown coats" *and* North Sea Gas
Gascoigne, Bamber, II-202
"gastroenteritis," I-295
The Gathering Storm, Churchill. *See* novels/literature
Gatwick Airport, I-285, 340
"gavotte," I-86
Gay, John, I-19, 74, 194
Gaynor, Janet, I-373
Gaynor, Mitzi, I-102, 332
"Gedderbong," I-84, 281
Gee, Dr. David, II-32
"gelignite," I-69
Geller, Uri, I-177; II-96

General Hospital, Gloucester Street, St. Helier, Jersey (location), II-104
General Register Office, II-46
General Strike of 1926, I-383
Genet, Jean, I-208; II-9, 18, 79, 83, 127
Genette, Gérard, II-64, 105
Genghis Khan, I-3, 4, 12, 13, 19, 408
Genn, Leo, I-279
Genovese crime family, I-135
Gentlemen Prefer Blondes. See films
The Gentleman Usher of the Black Rod, I-313
geologic references: "alluvial deposits," "fel(d)spar," II-172; Gobi Desert, II-198; "granite," II-171–72; Jurassic, II-145; *"Limestone, Dear Limestone,"* II-145; massif, I-148; II-47, 68; Old Man of Hoy, I-327, 334; II-72, 92, 94; Pleistocene, II-145; "shale," I-75, 158; II-171–72; syncline, I-337, 352; tepui, I-47. *See also* mountains/ranges
George, King. *See* kings
The George on the Green, Holyport (*May Day* location), I-86
George, Charlie, II-84
George, David Lloyd, II-182, 205
George-Brown, Lord, II-163
Georgian, I-272, 343, 351; II-181, 186
Gericault, Theodore, I-11; II-56
"German Baroque," I-98
German, Edward, II-28
Germany/German. *See* Europe
"germoline," I-281
Gerrard, Det. Chief Superintendent Frederick (CID), I-52
Gerrard Street, Soho, I-268
Gerrards Cross, Buckinghamshire I-11, 369
Gerry and the Pacemakers, I-169
Gestapo, I-9, 19, 99, 100
Gethin, Peter, II-28
Gandhi, Indira, I-364, 392; II-18
Gibbs, James, I-393
Gibbs toothpaste, I-387
Gibson, James. *See* Civil War (US)
Gielgud, John, I-38, 244; II-27, 33, 36
Gilbert and Sullivan, I-256, 299, 330; II-184
Gilbert, Humphrey, II-123
Gilbert, James, I-295
Gilbert, John, I-48
"Gildor," II-9, 11
Gilliam, Terry, I-xii, 3, 4, 5, 10, 11, 12, 13, 18, 23, 24, 31, 32, 33, 34, 39, 42, 45, 51, 53, 55, 56, 61, 62, 66, 67, 68, 69, 72, 75, 76, 79, 81, 83, 84, 87, 94, 95, 96, 101, 102, 103, 104, 106, 107, 108, 111, 116, 118, 129, 130, 136, 140, 143, 146, 148, 151, 153, 154, 156, 158, 159, 160, 161, 162, 167, 170, 173, 183, 184, 185, 193, 196, 197, 207, 210, 211, 212, 217, 222, 223, 228, 229, 230, 235, 236, 237, 239, 240, 241, 242, 245, 247, 250, 253, 257, 265, 269, 270, 272, 273, 275, 278, 280, 284, 290, 291, 292, 295, 299, 301, 309, 312, 313, 314, 315, 316, 322, 323, 327, 329, 333, 337, 343, 344, 346, 349, 354, 360, 362, 364, 365, 372, 374, 375, 379, 380, 383, 386, 387, 393, 395; II-xii, 3, 10, 12, 13, 18, 23, 40, 44, 49, 51,

52, 53, 56, 62, 64, 67, 69, 71, 78, 85, 91, 92, 99, 109, 111, 113, 121, 122, 128, 130, 134, 140, 145, 161, 162, 164, 165, 167, 171, 175, 177, 182, 185, 187, 191, 204, 211

Gillingham, I-364

"Ginger." *See* Biggles

"Ginger beer." *See* Biggles

"Gingham Auto Diner Restaurant," I-285, 382

Giovanni Arnolfini and His Bride, Jan van Eyck, I-68, 101, 376, 383

"The Girl From Ipanema," II-9

"giveaway," I-131, 205–6, 229, 391

Gladstone, William. *See* Prime Ministers

Glaisher and Coxwell, II-163

"Glam Rock," I-148, 157, 329, 391; II-97, 99

Glamorgan, Wales, I-32, 53, 58, 60, 62, 299, 324, 353

Glasgow, Scotland, I-166, 196, 258, 307, 354, 403; II-30, 67, 142, 163, 168, 170, 201, 219; "Glasgow kiss," II-167

"glen," I-115, 256

Glencoe, Scotland, I-12, 43, 157; II-9, 11, 12, 18, 56, 80–82, 99

Glenfield, Old Torwood Road, Torquay (location), I-281, 282

Globe Theatre, I-186, 404; II-125, 192, 220

glockenspiel, I-13

Gloucester, I-233; Duke of II-89, 123, 229

Glitter, Gary, I-148

God, I-5, 17, 20, 28, 33, 36, 45, 50, 53, 69, 81, 111, 117, 129, 134, 140, 172, 178, 189, 202, 206, 225, 226, 276, 278, 301, 334, 364, 405; II-17, 22, 28, 38, 46, 82, 102, 109, 116, 119, 120, 121, 128, 130, 134, 173, 178, 187, 192, 208, 221

Godalming, Surrey, I-156, 161–62, 393, 413

Godard, Jean-Luc, I-83, 211, 213, 298, 353, 354, 356–57, 363, 365, 379; II-18, 44, 48, 185

Goebbels, Joseph, I-191, 271

Golden Egg, II-27

"golden hour," I-256

Golden Palm, I-206

Golden Rose. *See* Montreux

Golders Green, Barnet (and Hippodrome; location), I-10, 97, 143, 146–47, 149, 186, 271, 411; II-70, 191, 197, 227

Goldhawk Road and Bamborough Gardens (location), II-184

Goldie, Grace Wyndham, I-271

"Golly," I-315, 344; II-31

Gomme, Donald and E. Gomme Ltd., I-229–30

Gomshall, Surrey, I-10

"Gone, and never called me mother," I-69, 72, 247; II-46

"gonk," I-281, 285

Goodhall Street (location), I-222

The Goon Show, I-4, 7, 19, 20, 21, 22, 23, 29, 34, 38, 40, 46, 51, 55, 57, 58, 60, 64, 67, 69, 71, 72, 74, 80, 84, 85, 86, 93–94, 96, 103, 104, 106, 112, 116, 119, 122, 123, 128, 136, 137, 138, 148, 158, 162, 163, 170, 178, 180, 186, 188, 190, 197, 202, 203, 204, 207, 212, 221, 223, 230, 238, 241, 244, 251, 254–55, 260, 262, 268, 270, 272, 281, 292, 304, 307, 310, 313–14, 322, 329, 354, 356, 361, 364–65, 381, 390; II-8, 22, 29, 31, 39, 41, 42, 47, 51, 58, 60, 70, 75, 80, 86, 92, 98, 107, 112, 114, 121, 126, 132, 139, 163, 185, 207–8; (major) characters: Minnie Bannister, I-72, 96, 180, 238, 308; Major Bloodnok, I-58–59, 112, 203, 221, 268, 322; Bluebottle, I-55, 60, 112, 116, 197, 207; II-58, 75; Henry Crun, I-72, 96, 180, 238, 307–8, 381; Hercules Grytpype-Thynne, I-29, 112, 186, 197, 255, 365; II-126; Jim Moriarty, I-23, 29, 55, 112, 136, 197, 364–65; II-29; Neddie Seagoon, I-21, 22, 69, 112, 114, 136, 170, 221, 238, 272, 307, 313, 365, 381; II-22, 29, 42, 70, 121, 207; episodes: "The £50 Cure," I-22; "1985," I-313; II-163; "The Affair of the Lone Banana," I-64; "Around the World in Eighty Days," I-119; "The Ascent of Mount Everest," II-70; "The Battle of Spion Kop," I-223, 292; "The Call of the West," I-72, 104, 106, 122, 270, 307; "The Choking Horror," I-137; "The Crystal Palace Project," I-241, 251; "The Curse of Frankenstein," I-123; "Dishonoured," I-69; "The Dreaded Batter Pudding Hurler," I-112; "Drums Along the Mersey," II-29; "Emperor of the Universe," I-93–94, 123; II-42; "The End: Confessions of a Secret Senna-Pod Drinker," II-207–8; "The Fireball of Milton Street," II-47; "The First Albert Memorial to the Moon," II-126; "The Flea," I-85; II-58; "The Giant Bombardon," II-98; "The Great Bank of England Robbery," I-230; "The Great Bank Robbery," I-7; "The Great Spon Plague," I-203, 260; "The Great Tuscan Salami Scandal," I-21; "The International Christmas Pudding," I-55, 112, 390; "The Jet-Propelled Guided NAAFI," I-71, 270; "The Junk Affair," I-190; "King Solomon's Mines," I-55, 390; "The Last Goon Show," I-20; "The Last Smoking Seagoon," I-238, 272; "The Last Tram (From Clapham)," I-22, 84, 96, 356; "Lurgi," II-92; "The Man Who Never Was," I-58, 313–14; "The Missing Boa Constrictor," II-121; "The Missing Scroll," I-128; "Moriarty Murder Mystery," I-364–65; "The Mountain Eaters," I-221; II-70; "The Mystery of the Fake Neddie Seagoon," I-307; "The Mystery of the Marie Celeste (Solved)," I-313–14; "Napoleon's Piano," I-4, 58, 158; "The Pevensey Bay Disaster," I-20, 55, 197, 390; "The Plasticine Man," I-204; "Queen Anne's Rain," I-136; "The Sale of Manhattan," I-186; "Scradje" and "Shifting Sands," I-72; "The Silent Bugler," I-188; "The Silver Doubloons," I-86, 238; "Six Charlies in Search of an Author," I-254–55; "The Sleeping Prince," II-75; "The Starlings," I-38, 356; "The Tales of Old Dartmoor," I-55, 313–14; "The Tay Bridge Disaster," I-262; II-22; "The Telephone," I-38; "The Thing on the Mountain," I-381; "The Treasure of Loch Lomond," I-123; "The Whistling Spy Enigma," I-204; "The White Box of Bardfield," I-57; "The White Neddie Trade," II-207; "Who Is Pink Oboe?," I-51, 104; "The Yehti," I-119; film projects: *Down Among the Z Men*, I-77, 92. *See also* Spike Milligan, Harry Secombe, *and* Peter Sellers

"gorn," II-179, 186

Gorton, Rt. Hon. John Grey, I-346

Goschen, David and Florian Studios, I-295

Gosse, Edmund, I-295

Gottenberg, Sweden, II-7

"Götterdämmerung epic," II-44

government (UK), I-8, 17, 18, 20, 34, 38, 41, 53, 56, 60, 71, 75, 80, 88, 93, 99, 112, 114, 119, 134–37, 145, 157, 159, 162, 167, 186, 188, 192, 196, 197, 203, 214, 221, 224–26, 229–32, 235–37, 244, 245–46, 248, 250, 255, 256, 259, 272, 274, 285, 289, 291, 301, 303, 305, 311, 314, 315, 318, 319, 328, 337, 346, 347, 349, 353, 354, 360, 361, 368, 371, 372, 374, 376, 380, 384, 387, 388, 390, 393, 409; II-9, 13, 19, 21–22, 25, 29, 36, 37, 47, 53, 59, 66–68, 70, 78, 79, 80, 81–84, 86–88, 103, 104, 111, 117, 124, 130, 141, 144, 146, 147, 148, 152, 155, 163, 164, 173, 181, 182, 190, 193, 196, 200, 204, 209, 225

Gowers, Michael, I-295

G-Plan, I-222, 229, 230, 238

GPO (General Post Office), I-34, 56, 256; II-198, 200

Grable, Betty and Playtex adverts, II-82, 87

Grace, W.G. *See* cricketers

Grade, Leslie and Lew, II-107

"gradient signs," I-363

Graham, Archie, II-38

Graham, Billy, I-40, 89

Graham, Martha, II-120

gramophone, I-11, 190, 206, 360, 368

Grand National, I-265

Grand Prix. *See* European Grand Prix

Grandstand. *See* television shows

Grantley, Baron (William Norton), II-133, 134, 182

Grants Department Store, High Street, Croydon (location), I-178; II-172

Granville Cup, Bishop Vesey's Grammar School, I-295

Gravelli, Carlo and *The Immaculate Conception*. *See* artists or artworks

Gray, Thomas. *See* poets

Gray's Inn, I-371, 374, 376

Grayson, Rupert and Frank Spencer, I-204

The Great Escape. *See* films

Great Exhibition, I-18, 138, 150; II-42

The Great (Indian) Revolt, I-101

The Great Fire of London, II-73

"Great Man" history, I-332, 336

Great Northern War, II-131

Great Swan Alley and Copthall Avenue, I-164

The Great Train Robbery, I-18, 100, 177, 233

"great white hope," I-281; II-114
Great Yarmouth, Norfolk, II-27
Greater London. *See* London
Greater London Council (GLC), I-363; II-113
"Greater London Development Plan," I-199; II-14
Greaves, Jimmy, I-33, 147
Greek national costume, II-172
"green baize apron," I-281
Green, Hughie, I-179
green paper, I-391; II-103; and white papers, I-303, 391; II-107
Greenblatt, Stephen J., I-246, 336; II-15
Greene, Hugh, I-59, 162, 177; II-21, 79, 90
Greene, Robert, I-66
"greengrocer," II-67
Greenpeace, I-215
Greenslade, Wallace, I-80, 85, 260; II-51
Greenwood Act (1930 Housing Act), I-225
Gregory, Alfred, II-64, 72, 213
Gregg, Hubert, I-283; II-69
Grenadier Guards, I-15, 149, 190, 211, 212, 264, 321, 399–404; II-195, 208, 215–20
Grenville, Lord, II-82
Greswell Street, Hammersmith and Fulham (location), I-195, 197
Griffith, D.W. *See* film directors
Grim, Edward, II-20
Grimond, Jo, II-205–6
Grimwade, Peter, I-296
Grisewood, Harman, I-84
"The Grocer." *See* Edward Heath
Gropius, Walter, I-362
Grosvenor Square Marriott, I-272
Grosz, George. *See* artists
grotesque, I-83, 95, 158, 161–62, 171, 240, 271–72, 372; II-125, 169, 200
The Group, McCarthy. *See* novels/literature
Groupie, Fabian and Byrne. *See* novels/ literature
"groupies," I-163, 215, 317, 318, 412
The Growth of Industrial Art, Benjamin Butterworth, I-222
"Gruyère," II-94
Grytpype-Thynne, Hercules. *See The Goon Show*
"Guardia," I-73
"The Guards," I-194, 316; II-178
"Gudmund," II-6, 9
"Gudreed," II-7
Guernica, Picasso. *See* artworks
Guevara, Che, I-371, 379, 409; II-79, 225
Guildford, Surrey, I-12, 45, 104, 162, 216, 297, 370, 393
Guinness, Alec, I-91; II-94
Guinness Book of World Records, I-25, 161; II-34; Guinness Stout, I-161; II-151
Gumby/Gumbies, I-74, 78, 84, 88, 91, 143, 144, 147, 172, 174, 176, 179, 181, 192, 195, 198, 206, 215, 264, 268–71, 275, 360, 369, 371, 406, 409, 411; II-61, 77, 110, 121, 130, 140, 205, 222, 225, 227
"gunboat diplomacy," I-165, 194, 360; II-89, 197
Gunfight at the O.K. Corral. See films
"gunga," II-198

Gunpowder Plot of 1605, I-93
Gurney, Goldsworthy, I-344
Guthrie, Tyrone, I-332
"guttering," II-94
Gwen Dibley's Flying Circus, I-9, 45, 293

HMS (ships): Ark Royal, II-92, 126, 212, 213; Bacchante, II-49; Barham, I-397; II-213; Belfast, Symons Wharf (location), II-183; Defiant, II-94; Eagle, II-95; Erebus, II-80; Hopeful, I-389; Terror, II-80
Haakon, King. *See* kings
Hackforth, Norman and *The Twenty Questions Murder Mystery*, I-117
Hackney Empire Theatre, I-104
The Hague, I-180, 378
Haig, General Douglas, II-112
Haig, Kenneth, I-162
Haight-Ashbury, I-208
Hailsham, Lord, I-346
Hainault, Greater London, I-233, 364, 365
Hal, Prince (Henry V), II-22, 28
HAL 9000, I-320
Halas and Batchelor Studio, I-242; II-112–13
"Half-a-Bee," I-82, 403
"Half-troll," II-7
Ham House (location), I-12, 40
Hambledon Place, Dulwich Common, I-293
Hamer, Neil, II-164, 167
Hamilton, A.C., I-71, 148
Hamilton, David, II-152
Hamlet. See plays
Hammer Studios, I-174
The "Hammers," I-376
Hammersmith (and Fulham), I-84, 85, 122, 132, 182, 197, 363; II-12, 32, 95, 118, 153, 184, 194, 198
Hammersmith Hospital (location), I-281, 383
Hammett, Dashiell, I-72
Hammond organ, I-331, 337
Hampshire, I-4, 261, 328, 364; II-77
Hampstead, I-26, 64, 146; II-47
Hampton Wick, I-292
Hancock, Tony, I-258–59; II-207
Handel, G.F., I-12, 98, 200, 399, 400; II-162
"Hanover Square," Dayes. *See* artworks
Hansen, Fleur, I-187
Hanworth Road, Houslow, Middlesex, I-189
"Happenings" theatre, I-101
Hardacre, Paul H., I-190
Hardy, Thomas. *See* novelists/prose writers
Hardy, Thomas (RN flag captain), I-14
Harlech Castle, I-178
Harley-Davidson motorcycles, I-159
Harley Street, I-206, 232, 343; II-77, 82, 123, 190
Harlow New Town, Essex, I-367
Harold the Flying Sheep, I-26, 27, 33, 318, 405, 409; II-91, 204, 221, 225
Harpenden, I-256, 293, 296
Harris, Sir Arthur "Bomber," I-221
Harris, Colin "Bomber," I-172, 273
Harris, Julie, II-132
Harris, Reg, I-296
Harris, Richard (Footlights member), I-309
Harris, Richard, I-35, 149; II-42

Harris, Rolf, I-217, 243; II-111
"Harris, Simon," I-197
Harris, Dr. Thomas, I-27
Harris, Z. *See* cricketers
Harrison, George. *See* The Beatles
Harrison, Linda, I-110
Harrods, I-162, 164, 276, 318, 331; II-172
Harrogate Street, Bradford (location), I-xii, 176, 179, 182; II-xii
Harrow, I-38; II-12, 78, 151, 191, 198
Harrow School, I-81, 194, 216, 279, 285, 384, 394; II-58, 76
Hart, Alan, I-320
Hart, Derek, I-264, 271, 295, 408; II-86, 224
Harvard University, I-39; II-15, 137, 174
Harvey, Ian, I-38
Harvey, Laurence, I-37
Hatch, Tony, I-203
Hawkins, Jack, I-231
Hawks, Howard. *See* film directors
"The Hay Wain," Constable. *See* artworks
Haydn, Franz Joseph, I-4, 8; II-33
Hayden, Sterling, I-76; II-200
Haydon-Jones, Ann, I-73, 118, 124, 125, 267, 296, 343
Hazewell, Charles Creighton, I-101
Headingley, West Yorkshire, I-317, 368
Headland Warren (location), I-249
Hearst, William Randolph, I-48
heart transplant, I-339, 341–42, 406; II-42, 157, 222
"Hearts and Flowers," Czibulka and Warren, I-61, 72, 402, 404; II-46, 59, 142, 148, 218, 220
"Hearts of Oak," I-190
Heath, Edward (Ted), I-41, 54, 88, 90, 124, 162, 185, 186, 194, 225, 240, 250, 256, 259, 289, 294, 306, 309, 319, 326, 329, 331, 337, 339, 346, 347, 367, 371, 375, 388, 390, 396, 397, 413; II-35, 53, 54, 66, 67–68, 79, 81, 82, 83, 104, 117, 130, 132, 133, 141, 142, 144–48, 153, 164, 171, 173, 181, 186, 190, 199, 209, 212, 213, 229
heavy water, I-6, 23
hedgehog, I-12, 136, 162, 236, 385, 393
"He Do the Police in Different Voices," I-191
Heflin, Van, I-357
Hefner, Hugh, I-40
Hegel, G.W.F., I-343; II-82
Heidegger, Martin, I-298, 340
Hellman, Marcel, I-351
Heim, Aribert, I-190
"Hello, hello!" I-238
"Hello Sailor," I-34, 162, 230, II-27, 54
Hell's Angels, I-132–33, 138
"helping police with their inquiries," I-84
Hemingway, Ernest, I-295
Hemmings, David, I-99, 100, 129, 133, 194, 206; II-41
"hen," I-331; II-164
"hen teaser," II-198
Hendon, Greater London, I-146, 271; II-79, 180, 209
Hendrix, Jimi, I-317
Henke, James, *Courtesans and Cuckolds*, I-34, 45, 65, 71, 222

Henley, South Oxfordhsire, I-190

Henri, Adrian, I-262

Henry, King. *See* kings

Henry V. See plays

Hepburn, Kate, I-354

Hepburn, Katherine, I-354

Hepworth, Cecil. *See* film directors

Her Majesty's Treasury Building (photo), I-327

Herbert, George, I-297

Hereford, Herefordshire, I-8, 186

"heresy," I-44, 242, 243, 245, 251, 256, 372

hermits, I-106, 127, 129, 131, 132, 133, 135, 136, 137, 139, 140, 148, 284, 409

Herrera, Helenio, I-180–81

Herrick, Robert, II-30

Heston, Charlton, I-115, 207, 223, 244; II-96, 183

Hewison, Robert, I-20, 138, 225, 265, 274, 341

Heydon Village, Norwich (location), I-308, 313, 314, 315, 316, 325

Heyerdahl, Thor, I-333, 335, 362; II-24, 26, 27, 29, 33, 35, 37, 94

Higgs, John, I-279

High Art. *See* art

High Chaparral. See television shows

High Street, Croydon (location), II-172

High Street and Paris Street, Exeter (location), I-205–6

high streets, I-35, 56, 99, 128, 133, 139, 207, 227, 229, 233, 241, 261, 289, 351; II-11, 12, 13, 22, 27, 71, 108, 132, 172, 179, 196, 205

highwaymen, I-134, 137, 138

hijackings, I-39, 252, 253, 255, 256, 260, 290, 340, 409; II-17, 77, 116, 117, 225

Hill, Benny, I-106, 154, 248, 329, 393. *See also The Benny Hill Show* in televisions shows

Hill, Graham, I-201, 207, 316

Hill, Lord Charles, I-162, 177–78, 198, 231, 241, 258, 282–83, 300, 304; II-22

Hillary, Edmund, I-125, 150–51; II-37, 64, 67, 70, 73, 94

Hillier, Bevis, I-144

Hillman, II-172

"The Hills Are Alive," II-179

Himmler, Heinrich, I-178, 185, 188, 191, 193, 196, 197, 199, 310; II-188, 192

Hinckley, Leicestershire, I-114

Hindhead, I-3

hippies/flower children, I-67, 75, 85, 99, 100, 179, 205, 207, 208, 231, 317, 318; II-4, 84

Hippocratic Oath, II-206

"hire purchase agreements," I-54, 62, 167, 263; II-25

"history of Irish agriculture," I-201, 207, 409; II-65, 225

Hitchcock, Alfred, I-xiii, 18, 21, 79, 96, 147, 149, 155, 303, 321, 390; II-xiii, 44, 95

Hitchhiker's Guide to the Galaxy, Douglas Adams, II-202

Hitchin and Harpenden, I-256, 293, 296

Hitler, Adolf, I-9, 10, 17–18, 24, 99, 137, 178, 181, 184, 185, 189, 191–94, 195, 197–99, 270, 350, 379, 392, 395, 399, 406; II-40–41, 45, 87, 110, 112, 192, 211, 215, 222

Hittites, I-331

hoarding, I-271; II-109

Hobbes, Thomas, I-344

hobbies, I-22, 44, 113, 124, 129, 197, 366, 390; II-61, 62, 65, 73, 79, 113, 116, 119, 183. *See also* trainspotting

Hochhuth, Rolf and *The Soldiers*, I-221

Hockney, David. *See* artists

Hoddesdon, Hertfordshire, II-67

Hoffman, Dustin, I-304; II-150

Hogarth, William. *See* artists

Hogg, Ima, I-328

Hogg, Quintin, II-147

Hoggart, Richard, II-57, 112

Holbein, Hans. *See* artists

Holborn, Greater London, I-233, 297, 308, 309, 310, 363

"Hole in the Wall Gang," I-321

holiday money, I-29, 34

"holidaymaker" and "Holidaymaker Special." *See* trains

holidays (including holiday camps), I-29, 31, 34, 44, 46, 51, 52, 65, 87, 89, 103, 122, 145, 158, 187, 340, 363–64; II-63, 69, 79, 118, 126, 149, 215

Holinshed, Raphael, I-381

Holland. *See* Europe

Hollowood, Bernard, I-343

Holly, Buddy, I-169, 350

Hollywood (for films *see* films; for TV *see* television shows), I-20, 21, 22, 23, 29, 43, 47, 48, 73, 74, 91, 96, 99, 100, 103, 104, 105, 107, 108, 111, 123, 132, 139, 147, 152, 172, 183, 211, 216, 245, 263, 275, 286, 290, 296, 308, 312, 314, 329, 350, 351, 353, 354, 357, 358, 363, 377, 381, 387, 390, 401; II-126, 128, 132, 146, 152, 204, 210, 217; studios: Columbia, I-102; Disney (*see* animation: studios); Goldwyn Studios, I-108; MGM, I-20, 29, 105, 106, 108, 127, 198, 204, 286, 377; 31, 39, 86; Metro Pictures, I-108; Twentieth-Century Fox, I-39, 107, 358, 381; "Twentieth-Century Vole," I-47, 91, 93, 107–8, 343, 405, 413; II-210, 221, 229; Universal, I-98, 105; Warner Bros. (excepting animation), I-294; II-74, 94; WB-Seven Arts, I-294

"The Hollywood Ten," I-103

The Holocaust, I-181

Holy Ghost, I-381

"Holy Hand Grenade," I-202, 206, 262, 317, 326; II-78, 203

Holy Roman Empire, I-122, 213, 236, 370, 393, 394; II-7

Holy Trinity Church, Lyne Lane, Chertsey, Surrey (location), I-108, 158, 159, 170

Holyport, Windsor and Maidenhead, Berkshire (location), I-70, 86; II-88

Holyport Road, Hammersmith and Fulham (location), I-185

Home, Storey. *See* plays

Home Affairs (ministry). *See* Home Secretary

Home Charms store (location), I-45

"home rule," I-113, 168

Home Secretary, I-135, 204, 214, 259, 265, 317, 326, 334, 345, 346, 390; II-82, 126, 144

"Homes Before Roads," II-113

homosexuality, I-7, 10, 22, 34–35, 37, 38, 40, 41, 49, 58, 73, 81, 90, 96–97, 103, 105, 111, 116, 125, 131, 146, 151, 153, 160, 166, 193, 203, 207, 209, 224, 230, 238, 258, 266, 284, 289, 291, 329, 346, 350; II-9, 25, 27, 31, 36, 47, 55, 58, 79, 82, 83, 85, 89, 94, 97, 114, 126, 153, 154, 183, 206, 209; "butch," I-97, 132, 160, 328, 341, 387, 388; II-55, 187; "fairy" (*see* fairy; homoeroticism), I-3, 33, 35, 103, 111, 135, 230; II-128; homosociality, I-3, 7, 10, 34, 35, 81, 111, 135, 160, 258, 366; II-94

Hong Kong. *See* Asia/Asian

Hood, Robin, I-267, 285, 403; II-8, 134, 137, 163, 219

Hookney Tor, Dartmoor, Devon (location), I-249; II-201, 209

Hoover, J. Edgar, II-23

Hope, Bob, I-275; II-83

Hope-Mason, John, I-309

Hornchurch, Greater London, I-364

Hornsby-Smith, Pat, II-36

"horse" (vaulting), I-281–82, 285

Horse of the Year Show. See television shows

Horsham, West Sussex, I-365

"Hosanna in Excelsis," I-144

Hospital Loch, Glencoe Hospital (location), II-11–12

Hotel Des Dhuits ("De L'Hotel Des Dhuys"), II-85

Hotel El Bousten, Hammamet, Tangiers, I-102

Houdini, Harry, II-25

Houghton, Lord, II-153

Hounslow, Middlesex, I-14, 35, 36, 92, 160, 167, 189, 233, 252, 300, 301, 362, 406, 408; II-12, 20, 26, 27, 35, 36–37, 222, 224

House Un-American Activities Committee (HUAC), I-103

Houses of Parliament, I-xii, 8, 37, 75, 87, 135, 186, 238, 253, 258, 311, 315, 316, 318, 324, 325, 353, 367, 380, 396; II-xii, 13, 17, 36, 37, 48, 52, 53, 77, 82, 89, 93, 173, 183, 193, 198, 203, 212; Commons, I-xii, 13, 17, 28, 36, 37, 41, 52, 53, 72, 73, 87, 106, 107, 180, 186, 196, 202, 205, 206, 243, 244, 246, 258, 285, 305, 312, 319, 322, 323, 337, 365; II-36, 54, 67, 72, 73, 82, 86, 163, 181, 182, 204, 205, 206, 225; Lords, I-56, 226, 258, 295, 303, 313, 322; II-15, 36, 82, 93, 116, 178, 209

Household Cavalry, I-38, 194, 224, 316

Housewive's Choice. See radio shows

housing, I-122, 132, 159, 176, 177, 203, 204, 214, 224–25, 238–39, 271–76, 319, 346, 354, 367, 388, 409; II-12, 21, 64, 80, 82, 89, 110, 116, 117, 119, 194, 203–4, 205, 225; 1956 Housing Act, II-117; council housing, I-90, 134, 149, 159, 214, 224, 239, 282, 292–93, 319, 321; II-80, 204; razing 511; semi-detached, I-286, 293; II-35, 64, 116, 203; terraced houses, I-12, 49, 222, 224, 239, 312, 387; II-64, 89, 116–17; tower blocks, I-22, 44, 111, 162, 239, 252, 267, 274, 293, 294; II-64, 117–18, 203

"Housey Housey," I-293; II-104, 106

Hove, I-184, 185, 191–92, 211, 324, 411, 412; II-170, 227, 228

Hovey, Richard, I-295, 297

Howard, Trevor, I-39, 46; II-163

Howerd, Frankie, I-163, 214, 303, 320; II-105, 145, 149

Howorth, Nicki. *See MPFC* extras and walk-ons

"howzat," II-206

Hoxha, Enver, II-102

Hoxton, Hackney, Greater London, I-224

Hudson, Rock, I-100, 104, 146, 354, 355, 358

Hughes, Geoffrey, I-297

Hughes, Prof. Norman, I-377

Hughes, Robert. *See* novelists/prose writers

Hughes, Ted, I-246

Hughman, John. *See MPFC* extras and walk-ons

Huguenots, I-55

Hull, Yorkshire, I-xi, 12, 215, 293, 370; II-xi, 153

Human Sexual Response, Masters and Johnson, I-47

"Humber to the Mersey," II-10

humor (types/analyses), I-6, 13, 21, 25, 29, 30, 31, 49, 54, 68, 69, 81, 82, 105, 119, 120, 132, 156, 160, 161, 167, 172, 177, 186, 189, 197, 212, 234, 243, 244, 271, 305, 313, 339, 373, 382, 405; II-4, 30, 51, 52, 54, 87, 88, 89, 98, 99, 143, 144, 183, 206, 221

Humperdinck, Englebert, I-179, 282

Humphrey, Hubert H., II-145, 154

Humphries, Barry, I-345

Huns, I-202, 206, 311, 317, 323; II-127, 212, 221, 222, 226

Hundred Years War, I-8

"Hungarian Rhapsody," Franz Liszt, I-242, 400

hunger marches, I-246; II-82; and the "means test," I-246

Hunkin, Oliver, I-372

Hunter, Meredith, I-132

Huntingdon, Arthur, I-114, 118, 119

Hurlingham Park (location), I-191, 199, 205, 207, 294; Road, I-199, 207

Hurst, Geoff, I-147

Hurt, John, II-150

Husserl, Edmund, II-16–17

Hyde, Lt. Col. William B. *See* Civil War (US)

Hyde Park, II-34

Ibiza (Ibeezer/Ibitha), I-236; II-10, 69, 96

Iceland, I-xii, 92, 317, 333, 409, 411; II-xii, 3, 5, 6–14, 57, 120, 173, 202, 225, 227; Icelandic sagas, I-; II-3, 5–14, 17, 20, 38, 82, 135, 225, 227

ICI (Imperial Chemical Industries), I-297, 317; II-11

I Wandered Lonely As a Cloud, Wordsworth. *See* poems *and* poets

Ideal Home Exhibition, I-133, 135, 213

Ideal Toy Company, I-107

Iddesleigh, West Devon, II-105

"idiots," I-32, 42, 200, 291, 302, 311, 315, 325, 341; II-11, 210

Idle, Eric, I-4, 5, 8, 14, 16, 24, 27, 30, 31, 32, 36, 39, 40, 45, 47, 50, 51, 52, 53, 55, 57, 61, 65, 66, 67, 73, 75, 78, 81, 83, 85, 87, 88, 91, 92, 97, 99, 102, 103, 104, 105, 114, 116, 117, 118, 120, 121, 122, 127, 131, 136, 137, 139, 140, 141, 142, 143, 144, 145, 146, 147, 148, 151, 152, 154, 159, 160, 161, 163, 164, 166, 171, 176, 177, 178, 181, 184, 186, 187, 192, 193, 195, 199, 201, 202, 205, 206, 207, 208, 210, 211, 212, 216, 217, 223, 227, 229, 230, 233, 234, 238, 241, 246, 247, 249, 254, 257, 258, 259, 260, 262, 267, 268, 269, 271, 272, 273, 275, 277, 279, 287, 288, 290, 291, 292, 294, 295, 298, 300, 303, 307, 310, 319, 320, 323, 324, 331, 332, 333, 336, 337, 340, 341, 351, 352, 353, 356, 360, 361, 362, 364, 366, 367, 368, 370, 373, 374, 375, 376, 377, 379, 381, 384, 385, 389, 402, 403; II-5, 8, 10, 15, 16, 17, 18, 26, 28, 31, 33, 34, 36, 38, 41, 42, 45, 46, 48, 50, 51, 52, 53, 59, 62, 63, 65, 66, 67, 68, 69, 70, 72, 73, 76, 77, 78, 80, 81, 84, 85, 86, 89, 90, 94, 97, 100, 195, 106, 108, 109, 111, 117, 118, 125, 132, 136, 137, 141, 143, 144, 148, 149, 150, 157, 161, 162, 163, 164, 166, 168, 169, 170, 173, 174, 179, 181, 185, 191, 193, 195, 197, 198, 199, 202, 204, 206, 207, 209, 218, 219

Idle, Lyn (Ashley), I-287, 290, 353; II-5, 8, 81, 85

"I know what I like," I-9, 70

Ilfracombe, North Devon, I-105

Ilkley Moor, West Yorkshire, (location), I-121

"I'll Never Fall in Love Again," I-206

I'm Sorry I'll Read That Again (*ISIRTA*), I-23, 27, 112, 130, 138, 160, 202, 204, 205, 206, 215, 250, 306, 317, 322, 362, 380; II-41, 51, 55, 76, 157; episodes: "Billy Bunter of Greyfriars School," I-380; "Cambridge Circus" (pilot episode), I-205, 300, 317; "The Desert Song," I-112; "Incompetence: The Story of the Arkwright Family," I-27, 250, 362; "Inimitable Grimbling," I-216; "Jack the Ripper," II-55; "John and Mary," I-205; "Macbeth," I-306; "Radio Prune," I-130; "The Return of the Son of the Bride of Frankenstein," I-160; "The Six Wives of Henry VIII," I-138; "The Taming of the Shrew," I-23; "The Telephone," I-23; "Tim Brown's Schooldays," I-205, 394

immigration/immigrants , I-59, 87–88, 90, 180, 197, 227, 276, 290, 304, 309, 375; II-4, 19, 81, 82, 124, 127. *See also* emigration

Imperial War Museum (IWM), II-123, 180, 214. *See also* museums

Impressionism. *See* art: movements

"In Place of Strife: A Policy for Industrial Relations," I-303

incidental music, I-117, 120, 265, 279; II-25, 95, 109, 113

incongruities, I-112, 117, 121, 129, 131, 133, 136, 140, 148, 173, 196, 234, 243, 286, 303, 318, 323, 325, 332, 339, 341, 379, 387; II-xi, 4, 8, 18, 25, 42, 51, 56, 67, 104, 126, 133, 140, 144, 156, 194

Independent Television (ITV), I-31, 105, 136, 156, 257, 295, 308, 312, 369, 376, 391; II-8, 25, 17, 22, 31, 80, 86, 135, 136, 148, 151, 153, 156, 162, 166, 180, 183, 191; News (ITN), I-8, 31; II-148, 166

Independent Television Authority (ITA), I-162, 167, 214; II-38, 138

India. *See* Asia/Asian

Indianapolis 500, I-207

Indians (and "Red Indians"), I-30, 81, 92, 93, 98–100, 103–05, 152, 157, 172, 175, 185, 211, 223, 229, 289, 291, 293, 296, 302, 407, 408, 411; II-20, 27, 33, 152, 181, 204, 222, 223, 224. *See also* Asia/Asians

"The Industrial Proletariat," I-377, 384

"industrial relations," I-289, 303, 374, 409; II-53, 67–68, 104, 225

Industrial Revolution, I-49, 316, 362; II-86, 111

"Ingbare the Brave," II-7

"ingle," I-151; II-126

Inglis, Brian, I-325

Ingrams, Richard, I-19, 30, 32, 33, 34, 35, 38, 109, 154, 160, 184, 191, 202, 251, 274, 300, 303, 309, 316, 343, 354, 359; II-4, 132, 144, 164, 205

in-jokes/references, I-36, 148–49, 155, 166, 263, 287, 292, 339; II-96, 98. *See also* reflexivity

Inner London Education Authority (ILEA), II-113

Innes, Neil. *See MPFC* extras and walk-ons

"innings." *See* cricket (terminology)

"Inniskillin Fusiliers and Anglian Regiment," II-56

Inns of the Court, I-376

"Inspector," I-13, 50, 51, 52, 55, 91, 93, 99, 100, 113, 121, 171, 172, 176–78, 180, 199, 229, 232, 273, 277, 291, 307, 329, 343, 361, 406, 407, 408, 409; II-3, 40, 44, 47, 126, 164, 191, 222, 223, 224, 225

Institute of Chartered Accountants in England and Wales, I-164, 190

International Court of Justice. *See* The Hague

International Federation of Airline Pilots, I-256

International Style, I-121, 267; II-24

Interregnum, I-158; II-127

interruptions, I-4, 36, 38, 73, 85, 100, 107, 119, 141, 154, 172, 176, 179, 182, 252, 278, 283, 289, 298, 306, 307, 325, 327, 329, 335, 406, 409, 411; II-3, 20, 39, 65, 77, 105, 110, 222, 225, 227

intertextuality, I-xi, 56, 124, 166, 209, 211, 286, 294, 329, 338; II-xi, 170, 202

Inverness, Scotland, I-257

"Investiture of the Prince of Wales," II-48, 149

"investment grants," I-237

Ionesco, Eugene. *See* playwrights

Ipswich, Suffolk, I-134

Ireland, I-123, 256, 324, 341. *See also* Northern Ireland

Irish Republican Army (IRA), I-10; II-54, 65, 72, 93

"the Irish situation," I-325; II-11, 65, 78, 83

Iron Age, I-331

Iron Cross, I-191

Ironmonger Row baths, I-308

Ironside, Edmund, I-271

Irving Davies Dancers, II-119

"Is the Queen Sane?," II-50, 56

Isaacs, Jeremy, II-180

"Isenbert," II-7

Islam, I-148, 299, 405

Isle of Wight, I-34, 40, 133, 194, 203, 304, 317, 389; II-126, 195, 199, 209, 210

Isleworth, II-33

Islington, I-226, 272, 308, 312; II-12, 58

Italian Grand Prix at Monza, II-28

It's a Knockout. See television shows

"It's a Man's Life…" I-63, 69, 164, 408, 409

"It's" Man, I-4, 15, 43, 63, 66, 75, 106, 115, 128, 158, 163, 175, 226, 292, 299, 308, 333; II-116, 187

"It's my only line," I-63, 127, 130, 407

"It's Not Unusual," Tom Jones, II-56

It's That Man Again (ITMA). *See* radio shows

Ivan IV, I-207

Ivanov, Capt. Eugene, I-41

"Jabberwock" languages, I-ix, 8, 51, 57, 100, 198, 206, 237, 268; II-ix, 26, 69, 164, 166

"Jack and the Beanstalk." See pantomimes

"Jack in the Box," Clodagh Rogers, II-105, 107, 108

"Jack the Stripper," I-388

Jackanory. See television shows

Jacklin, Tony, I-266–67, 327, 332; II-144

The Jackson 5, II-205

Jackson, Glenda, I-345; II-28, 43

Jaclyn Model Agency, I-341

Jacob, Ian, II-156

"Jacobean," I-83, 301, 380; II-3, 43

Jacobs, David, I-163

Jagger, Mick, I-84–84, 232

"Jak," I-231, 269, 274

James, King. *See* kings

James, Henry. *See* novelists/prose writers

Jampton, Hugh, I-51, 292

Janson, Hank (aka Stephen Frances). *See* novelists/prose writers

"Japanese businessmen," I-343; II-190

Jarrow, I-176, 180, 181, 240, 246, 250, 397, 409; II-82–83, 213, 225

Jason, David, I-16

Jasper, Ann, I-308

Java, I-156, 163

Jehovah's Witnesses, II-173

Jellicoe, Earl, I-346

jelly babies, I-207

Jenkins, Clive, II-67, 68

Jenkins, Roy, I-34, 245, 250; II-137

Jenkinson, Philip, I-174, 248, 323, 356, 397, 411; II-54, 91, 94, 95, 97, 99, 127, 213, 227

Jensen (car), II-68

Jersey, Channel Islands (location), I-43, 409, 411; II-66, 68, 70, 102, 103, 104, 106, 108, 112, 116, 118, 119, 127, 132, 138, 225, 227

"Jerusalem." *See* "And did those feet"

Jerusalem (city), I-4, 70, 364; II-203

Jeux Sans Frontieres. See television shows

"jewelled line," I-271

Jews/Jewish, I-6, 55, 105, 117, 119, 123, 178, 249, 286, 304, 332, 334, 390; II-11, 31, 74, 83, 88, 96, 107, 115, 139, 181, 201

Joan of Arc, I-8, 323

"Jocasta," I-117

"Joe Public," II-11

"Joey Boy," I-318

"John and Mary" skits. *See I'm Sorry I'll Read That Again*

John Holt Carpets, II-179

"Johnners," II-203

Johnnie Spence Orchestra, I-388, 400, 402, 404; II-180, 216, 218, 220

John of Gaunt, I-215; II-96, 98

John Sanders Department Store (location), I-130

John the Baptist, I-129, 207, 353, 365

Johns, Mervyn, I-146

Johns, W.E., I-157; II-91, 92, 94, 95

Johnson, J.B., I-159

Johnson, Lyndon B., I-89, 307, 379; II-71

Johnson, Dr. Samuel, I-112, 120, 123, 254, 265, 304; II-10, 112

Johnson, Teddy and Pearl Carr, I-378

Johnston, Brian, I-338; II-157, 203

Johnstone, Paul, I-336

"joiners and craftsmen," II-125

Jonah and the whale, I-159

Jones, Alan. *See* cricket: players

Jones, Alan (driver), II-177

Jones, Brian, I-28

Jones, Chuck. *See* animation: animators

Jones, Freddie, I-370

Jones, Inigo, I-114, 117–18; II-134, 136

Jones, Nigel. *See MPFC* extras and walk-ons

Jones, P.F. *See* Ann Haydon-Jones

Jones, Robert K. and *The Shudder Pulps*, I-74

Jones, Terry, I-3, 5, 6, 7, 8, 16, 20, 22, 23, 28, 30, 32, 33, 34, 39, 45, 48, 50, 53, 57, 58, 61, 65, 67, 72, 75, 76, 78, 79, 88, 94, 95, 98, 101, 102, 108, 111, 112, 116, 117, 119, 120, 121, 122, 127, 128, 130, 131, 132, 134, 135, 136, 139, 145, 148, 150, 157, 158, 160, 161, 165, 167, 170, 177, 178, 179, 182, 184, 185, 186, 187, 189, 191, 195, 198, 199, 200, 202, 205, 207, 208, 211, 212, 215, 216, 223, 224, 225, 226, 228, 229, 233, 234, 235, 236, 237, 239, 240, 246, 249, 250, 252, 253, 254, 256, 257, 260, 261, 263, 265, 266, 267, 269, 271, 273, 275, 276, 277, 282, 283, 294, 298, 299, 302, 311, 312, 313, 317, 321, 322, 323, 325, 330, 332, 333, 344, 346, 350, 357, 361, 364, 374, 378, 384, 388, 393, 394, 396, 403, 404; II-5, 8, 11, 17, 25, 26, 30, 31, 36, 41, 43, 46, 47, 48, 50, 53, 55, 58, 61, 63, 68, 70, 71, 72, 86, 89, 93, 95, 96, 104, 106, 107, 115, 116, 118, 119, 131, 132, 133, 136, 138, 142, 145, 153, 161, 162, 163, 164, 169, 170, 172, 174, 178, 181, 182, 184, 185, 186, 191, 193, 194, 196, 197, 199, 202, 206, 207, 209, 212, 219, 220

Jones, Thomas and *The Kray Brothers. See* novelists/prose writers

Jones, Tom, I-243, 350, 366; II-56

Jonson, Ben. *See* playwrights

Joseph, Keith, I-319, 346; II-180, 190

Joyce, James. *See* novelists/prose writers

Joyce, William ("Lord Haw-Haw"), I-8

"JP" (Justice of the Peace), I-332, 409

judges/judiciary, I-3, 41, 96–97, 122, 153, 205, 228, 233, 240, 244, 247, 327, 328, 330, 372, 375, 378, 411, 412, 413; II-9, 14, 30, 84, 130, 137, 188, 227, 228, 229

Judt, Tony. *See* novelists/prose writers

jug band, I-148, 400

"jugged," I-177; II-13, 45

Juliana, Queen, II-58

"Jupp, Mrs," II-115, 118

"jurisprude," I-378

"Just an Old-Fashioned Girl," II-106, 219

juvenile delinquency, I-107, 139, 144, 244

KGB, I-55; II-101, 102

Kadar, Janos, II-102

Kafka, Franz, I-43

Kaiser, I-307; II-23

Kandinsky, Wassily. *See* artists

Kane, Gil, I-107

Kant, Emmanuel, I-176–77, 181, 332, 333, 343

Katchen, Julius, I-182, 400

Katherine (from *Henry V*), I-23

Kaye, Danny, I-279

Kazan, Elia. *See* film directors

Keaton, Buster, I-68, 381

Keats, John. *See* poets

Keeler, Christine, I-41

Keighley, II-153

Kelly, Grace, I-96, 303; II-14

Kelly's Clergy List, I-307

Kempton, David, I-291

Kempton, Martin, I-149

Kendal, Westmorland, I-177

Kendall, Jo, I-205

Kennedy, Edward, I-39

Kennedy, John F., I-39, 80, 303, 363

Kennedy, Ludovic, I-255; II-110, 135

Kennington Oval, I-324, 344

Kensington, Greater London, I-191–92, 195, 271, 301, 351; II-4, 12, 81, 132, 166

Kent, Duke of, I-19, 184; II-54

Kentucky Fried Chicken (KFC), II-179, 206

Kenya, I-145, 148, 150, 322; II-19, 62, 81, 191, 208; Mau Mau uprising, I-150; II-62, 191; Nairobi, I-149

Kerensky, Alexander, II-105, 108

Kerr, Malcolm, I-299; II-15

Kershner, Irvin. *See* film directors

Kettering, II-68

"Kettle-trout," II-7

Keynes, John Maynard, I-377

Keystone Cops (and Studio), I-40, 154, 290, 397; II-97, 132, 213

Khan, Prof. Herman, II-114, 115

Khitruk, Fyodor and *Man in the Frame*, I-66, 129

"kiddy-winkies," II-164

Kierkegaard, Søren, I-27, 36, 97, 230, 298; II-17, 28, 177–78, 186

Kilimanjaro. *See* mountains/ranges

"killer rabbit," I-19, 124, 136, 168, 206, 262; II-78

The Killers. See films

Kilmarnock, Scotland, II-115

kilts, I-122, 123–24, 257

Kimberley, Lord(s) and Lady, II-15

Kind Hearts and Coronets. See films

Kinemacolor, I-9

King, Clive. *See* novelists/prose writers

King, Dr. Horace, I-323

King Edward VII Grammar School, Melton Mowbray, I-216

"King Edwards" potato, II-199

kings: Æthelstan, I-57; Arthur, I-206, 248; II-5, 162; Asa, II-203; Charles I, I-29, 376, 383; II-58, 127; VI, I-42, 235; XII, II-131; Constantine II, II-94; David, II-203; Edmund, I-271; Edward I, I-178, 183; IV, I-196; II, I-257; VII, I-9, 17, 40, 156, 216, 280, 389; II-18, 46, 54, 56; VIII, I-156; II-18; Ferdinand, I-244, 249, 251; George, III, I-117, 175; II-134, 161, 163, 166, 170, 220, 224; IV, II-97, 163; V, I-9, 150, 361; II-155; VI, II-18; Haakon, II-56, 94; Hafdan and Harald Fairhair, II-7; Henry II, II-22, 26, 27, 28; IV, II-112, 167; V, I-23, 46, 55, 60, 66, 192, 187, 206, 211, 400, 404; II-98, 128, 187, 192, 216, 220; VI, II-123, 167, 205; VII, I-18, 196; VIII, II-41, 43, 167; Hrothgar, II-6, 7; Hussein, I-294; James I, II-43, 93, 127, 128; V, I-345; VI, I-272; John, II-7, 84; Louis XIII, I-55; XIV, I-50, 71, 188, 394, 410; II-161–68, 226; XV and XVI, I-50, 71; II-165–66; Philip II, I-382; II-126; Philip V, I-394; Rainier III, II-14; Ramses II, I-327; Richard I, II-41; II, I-257; III, I-6, 18, 22, 58, 66, 113, 371–72, 380, 381; Tut, I-297, 337; II-77; Xerxes, II-186; Zog, I-63, 201

"King Rats," I-378

King's College, Hampstead, I-26–27

King's Cross, Greater London, I-364

"King George bitch," II-170

Kings House Hotel, Glencoe, Ballachulish, Argyll (location), II-9

The King's Men, I-21

"Kingston by-pass," I-14; II-29

Kingston upon Thames, Greater London, I-14; II-15

Kinsey, Dr. Alfred, I-47

Kirby, Kathy and "I Belong," I-258

"kirk," I-100, 105

The Kiss. See films

The Kiss. See artworks

Kiss Me Kate, Cole Porter. *See* plays

Kissinger, Henry, II-180, 214

Kit Cat Club, I-32, 60

Kitchen Front. See radio shows

"Kitchen sink" dramas, I-37, 223; II-178

Kitchen Sink School (painting), I-51

Kitt, Eartha, II-101, 105, 107, 109, 224, 226

Klee, Paul. *See* artists

"Kleenex," I-100

Kline, Franz. *See* artists

"Knacker of the Yard, Inspector," I-100, 229

Knievel, Evel, I-158–59

"knight and chicken," I-xii, 23, 26, 41, 79, 110, 143, 153–54, 201, 206, 410; II-xii, 4

Knight, G. Wilson, and L.C. Knights, I-147

Knightsbridge, I-95, 108, 162, 318, 331; II-42, 172

Knights of the Teutonic Order, A. Ford. *See* films

"Knights Who Say 'Ni'," I-85, 129, 131, 322

"knobkerrie," I-257; II-188

Knox-Johnston, Robin, I-169

Kodak cameras, I-227; II-68

Kokoschka, Oskar. *See* artists

Kon-Tiki, II-29, 94; Ra I and Ra II, II-24, 33

Korobro [sic], Mrs. (location owner), I-245

"kosher," I-55, 304, 390

Kozeluh, Karel, I-114

Krakatoa, East of Java. See films

Kray brothers (Reggie and Ronnie), I-52, 84–85, 88, 115, 129, 135, 141, 170, 215, 223–29, 232–37, 273; II-126, 137, 198

The Kremlin, I-290, 396, 397; II-71, 108, 148, 212, 213

Krull, Maria, I-11

Khrushchev, Nikita, I-70, 121, 165, 236, 314; II-16, 71, 102, 109, 198

Kubrick, Stanley, I-26, 40, 80, 98, 120, 213. 299, 370; II-124, 140, 200, 201

Kuleshov, Lev, II-53

kung fu films, I-253, 374

Kup Kakes, II-95, 103, 106

Kurosawa, Akira, I-91, 123, 302, 304, 350, 357; II-92, 96, 100

Kuznets, Simon, II-137

Kyle, Keith, I-297

Kyoto, Japan, I-285

L'Amour, Louis. *See* novelists/prose writers

La Dolce Vita soundtrack, Nino Rota, II-181, 220

La Gondola Restaurant, I-170, 201, 407

La Jetée, Marker. *See* films: France

Labienus, Titus, I-366

Labour Party (and government), I-9, 28, 34, 53, 63, 87, 114, 119, 134, 159, 168, 177, 186, 188, 192–94, 196, 214, 224–26, 229, 233, 237, 243–45, 250, 256, 279, 284–85, 289, 291, 293, 296–97, 300, 303–8, 318–20, 333, 347, 357, 361, 365, 367, 369, 373–74, 384, 388; II-15, 19, 21, 22, 25, 36, 41, 68, 78, 79, 80, 81, 82, 83, 84, 87, 104, 111, 113, 117, 124, 125, 130, 137, 141, 143, 146, 148, 155, 163–64, 166, 173, 178, 181, 182, 190, 200, 204, 206–7, 208, 209, 210

Lacan, Jacques, I-342

Ladd, Alan, I-37, 357

The Ladykillers. See films: UK

Lambs Green, I-364

Lammas Park and Road, Ealing (locations), I-51, 108, 131, 133, 134, 243, 265, 287; II-99, 201; and Park Gardens (location), I-113, 131, 134, 241, 243, 245; II-99, 201

Lambert, Verity, I-141

Lambeth Conference, C of E, I-210

Lambeth Palace, I-372

Lambrianou, Tony and Chris, I-141

Lamour, Dorothy, II-82–84

Lampton, Joe, I-37

Lana, Francesco, I-197, 349

Lancashire, I-49, 102, 115, 128, 135, 261, 284, 291, 314, 320, 324, 340; II-57, 76, 89, 93

Lancaster bomber (location), II-180

Lancaster, Burt, I-245; II-46, 94

The Lancet. See magazines

Landnámabók. See novels/prose literature

Landseer, Edwin. *See* artists

Langdon, David. *See* cartoonists

Langdon, Harry, I-102

Langdon, Lord, I-366

Lantz, Walter (and Gracie), I-20

Laocoön. See artworks

Lardner, Ring, I-103, 352

"Large chest for sale," I-226

"Lassie the Wonderdog," I-295

Last, Roger. *See* MPFC extras and walk-ons

Last Exit to Brooklyn, Selby. *See* novels/prose literature

The Last Man on Earth. See films

Last Year at Marienbad. See films

Late Night Line-Up. See television shows

"latently homosexual professional lacrosse player," I-34

Lauderdale, P.C., I-230–31

Laughton, Charles, II-5

Laurel and Hardy, I-40

Law, Bonar, I-328

Lawley, Sue, II-189

Lawrence, D.H., I-9–10, 34, 36, 39, 41, 46, 48, 49, 115, 163, 229, 247, 387; II-78, 207

Lawsbridge Refuse Depot (location), I-357

"lbw." *See* cricket: terminology

Le Carré, John. *See* novelists/prose writers

"laying off the ball," I-313. *See also* cricket: terminology

Le Comte de Vaudreuil, François-Hubert Drouais. *See* artworks *and* artists

Le Corbusier, I-267

"lead piping," I-366

Leamington, Warwickshire, I-36, 354; II-73

Lean, David, I-18, 21, 313, 353; II-34, 62, 78

Leapy, Lee, I-327, 333, 410

Leary, Timothy, I-39–40, 208

Leatherhead, Surrey, I-34, 81, 86, 100, 102, 104, 105, 175, 212, 393

Lederhosen Teutonic figure, I-14

Lee, Jennie, I-296

Leeds, I-47, 192, 215, 317, 324; II-58, 113

"leg-before-wicket." *See* cricket: terminology

Leger, Ferdinand. *See* artists

Leibniz, Gottfried, I-xii, 340; II-xii, 82

Leicester, Leicestershire, I-56, 96, 164, 260, 282, 291, 292, 296, 297, 299–300, 303–4; II-45, 69, 84, 145, 206

Leicester Square, I-150; II-24

Leigh, Janet, I-147

Leigh, Mike, I-100

Leighton Buzzard, Bedfordshire, I-187

"Lemming of the BDA," I-63, 70, 77, 410

"Lemon curry?" I-12, 411; II-99, 155, 227

Lend-Lease, I-323

Lenin, V.I. (and Leninism), I-314, 377, 379, 384, 397; II-16, 71, 101, 105, 108, 109, 207, 213

Lennon, John, I-34, 83, 167, 232, 346, 360, 366; II-36, 77
Le Prince, Louis, I-47
Leroux, Maurice, II-18
Le Roy Funeral, Cowick Street, II-179
"*Les Sylphides,*" II-198
Lester, Frank. *See MPFC* extras and walk-ons
Lester, Richard. *See* film directors
Letterman, Dr. Jonathan. *See* Civil War (US)
letters, I-70, 75, 79, 80, 86, 91, 95, 97, 103, 110, 119, 137, 143, 146, 148, 153, 156, 161, 162, 164, 167, 168, 172, 175, 184, 191, 200–1, 205, 207, 210, 214, 221, 241, 242, 244, 253, 254, 280, 202, 207, 318, 349, 364, 365, 380, 385, 392, 406, 407, 408, 410; II-11, 38, 40, 59, 80, 81, 91, 97, 102, 103, 104, 112–13, 121, 142, 148, 165, 171, 180, 196, 209, 222, 223, 224, 226
Levi-Strauss, Claude, I-342
"Leviticus 3–14," I-272
Lewis, C.S., I-147, 178
"Lewis, Mrs. Fiona," I-51, 59, 407
Lewis, Sinclair, I-295
Lewisham, Greater London, I-227, 233; II-12
Leytonstone, Greater London, II-200
Lhotse Face, II-73
"Liar, Mr. K.V.B.," II-118
Liberal Party, I-8, 17, 28, 92, 103, 173, 186, 194, 225, 255, 285, 296, 302, 320, 373, 390, 411; II-82, 164, 187, 204, 205–7, 208, 209–210, 227; and 1974 General Election gains, II-210
"Liberty Bell," I-13, 15, 114, 149, 338, 399; II-195, 208, 215
Libya. *See* Africa
licence fee, I-110, 311, 318, 410; II-37, 226
Liddell, Alvar, I-85–86, 137
Life of Samuel Johnson. See novels/prose literature
lifeboat, I-178, 211, 254, 346, 385, 390, 410; II-54, 91, 83, 95, 96, 99, 226
Light Entertainment Awards, I-231, 410; II-150, 151, 153, 202, 226
"light music," I-107, 279, 352; II-8, 66, 119, . *See also* Appendix B for all music cues and composers/performers
"like a dead pope," II-88
Lime Grove Studios, I-168; II-193
Limebank House (photo), I-327; II-49
Limington, Roger, I-17
Lincoln, Abraham, I-14, 89
Lincoln Cathedral, I-121
Lincolnshire, I-39, 44, 165, 195, 269, 270
Lindley, Richard, I-320
Lindsay, Vachel, I-362
Lingfield Racecourse, Lingfield, Surrey (location), II-189, 201
linking/links, I-xii, 3, 4, 5, 9, 11, 15, 16, 17, 23, 26–29, 31, 33, 35, 36, 39, 40, 41, 42, 43, 45–47, 50–52, 55, 56, 58, 63, 65, 66, 69, 71, 73, 74, 75, 79, 81, 82, 83, 85, 87, 88, 90–96, 98–104, 106–110, 111, 113–120, 122, 124, 127–32, 135, 136, 139–41, 143, 144, 147–49, 151–54, 158–64, 167, 168, 170, 176–78, 181, 182, 184, 185, 188–98, 200, 202, 203, 205, 207, 209–11, 213, 214, 217, 221–23, 226,

230, 231, 232, 235, 237, 238, 240, 242–46, 248, 250, 251, 252, 257, 259, 261, 262, 264–66, 269–71, 278–85, 288, 290, 292, 294, 298, 299, 301, 304, 306, 308, 309, 312, 317, 318, 319, 325, 334, 336–37, 339, 342–44, 346, 350, 352, 355, 357–64, 365, 367, 369–73, 385–87, 389–94, 402, 405–13; II-xii, 3, 10, 12, 18, 21, 23, 26, 30, 32, 35, 37, 39, 45, 49, 51, 57, 67, 71, 74, 76, 81, 85, 88, 91, 92, 107, 112, 116, 118, 119, 122, 125, 132, 133, 134, 136, 140, 145, 149, 151–154, 157, 162, 163, 165, 167, 168, 173, 174, 177, 178, 180, 184, 185, 187–192, 194–196, 198, 202, 203, 207–9, 218, 221–29
Lionel Blair Troupe, II-119, 198
Lister, Moira, II-34
literality, I-147, 178, 209, 238, 299; II-59, 179
"Little Arrows," I-333
Little Dutch Masters, I-77
Little Golden Books, I-175
"Little Nell," II-115
The Little Oxford Dictionary, II-208
"Little Tich," I-221
"Little White Bull," II-106, 108
Littlewick Green, Windsor and Maidenhead, Berkshire (location), I-70; II-88
Liverpool, Merseyside, I-5, 216, 225, 261, 262, 266, 342, 361, 374, 402, 403, 404; II-93, 96, 131, 136, 172, 194, 218, 219, 220; Liverpool-Manchester Railway, I-5; "Liverpool Poets," I-261, 262; II-136
Livy, I-286
"Ljosa water," II-6, 10, 12
Llanddarog, Carmarthen, Wales, I-385, 386, 387, 392, 407
Llanofer, Lady, II-49
Llewellyn, Richard and *How Green Was My Valley. See* novelists/prose writers
Lloyd, Harold, I-61
Lloyd, Rt. Hon. J. Selwyn, I-323; II-205
Lloyd, Marie, II-247
Loach, Ken. *See* film directors
lobotomy, I-177
Local Government Act, I-349
"loch," I-31, 123, 227, 236, 256; II-9, 11, 18, 59, 83
Loch Ness Monster, I-31, 113, 227, 236; II-59, 83
Locke, John, I-344; II-103, 107
Lockheed Starfighter, I-333
"Locus of Control Scale," II-16
Logan, Maj. Gen. John A. *See* Civil War (US)
"logical positivism," I-344
Lollabrigida, Gina, I-310
London: City of London, I-30, 114, 130, 164, 236, 243, 279, 285, 297; II-13, 32, 52, 79, 156; East London (East End), I-83, 115, 137, 215, 224, 227, 238; II-93; Greater London, I-11, 12, 56, 62, 83, 85, 128, 164, 173, 191, 192, 194, 199, 203, 207, 216, 224, 225, 226, 227, 233, 234, 239, 241, 247, 253, 271, 275, 282, 293, 300, 316, 323, 326, 330, 363, 364, 365, 368, 373, 375, 388, 393; II-5, 11, 12, 13, 14, 15, 17, 27, 29, 30, 37, 64, 67, 70, 72, 74, 79, 103, 104, 108, 113, 121, 133, 153, 156, 197, 200, 209; North London,

135, 146, 391; South London, I-28, 152, 393; West End, I-84, 95, 172, 213, 215, 223, 283, 287, 315, 321, 343, 370; II-41, 87, 95, 127, 193, 199, 387
London Arts Gallery, II-77
London, Brian, I-201, 205, 343; II-131
London Brick Company, II-45
London Docklands, I-227
London Electricity Board, II-29
London in the Raw, Miller. *See* films
The London Nobody Knows, Cohen. *See* films
London School of Economics (LSE), II-9
Long Day's Journey into Night, O'Neill. *See* plays
Long Cellar (Crypt Chapel), Mont Orgueil Castle, Jersey (location), II-112
"longeurs," I-272
"loony" (and "looney"), I-179, 307, 341, 355, 412; II-35, 56, 69, 81, 127, 140, 144, 145, 147–48, 154, 168, 190, 228
Lopez-Cortero, Miguel (guitarist), I-18, 399
Lord and Lady. *See* titles/honorifics
Lord, Thomas, I-326
Lord Chamberlain, I-187; II-97
Lord Denning's Report, I-41
"Lord Mayor." *See* titles/honorifics
Lord's Cricket Ground, St. John's Wood, I-231, 312, 324
Loren, Sophia, I-100, 323
Lorentz, Hendrik, II-143
Lorre, Peter, I-146
lorry, I-56, 81, 102, 129, 275, 294; II-17, 109, 142, 145
Losey, Joseph. *See* film directors
"The Lost Chord," I-327, 330, 401, 406
"lost deposit," I-302; II-207
Lotterby, Sydney, I-295, 300
Louis, King. *See* kings
Lovell, Maj. Gen. Mansfield. *See* Civil War (US)
Lowestoft, Suffolk, II-33
LSD, I-39, 67, 208, 247
Lucas-Tooth, Sir Hugh, I-107
Ludgate Hill (photo and location), I-237, 276; II-137
Lulu, I-327, 333, 341, 409; II-20, 30, 109, 225
Lumière brothers, I-48
"lunar module," I-272; II-37
"Lunar Orbiter 5," II-57
"lurex," I-258
Luton, Bedfordshire, I-162, 177, 231, 236, 241, 252, 255, 256, 258, 261, 287, 297, 299–300, 304, 409; II-67, 69, 117, 225
Luxury Yacht, Raymond ("Throatwobbler Mangrove"), I-22, 155, 289, 300, 346, 411
Lynn, Johnny, I-300
Lyons shops (and Joe Lyons), II-27, 95, 106; Lyons Maid, I-203, 208

"M" motorways: M1, I-320, 410; II-110, 226; M2, II-177, 182, 226; M4, I-289, 301, 407; II-113, 223; M5, I-187; II-113; M25, II-13, 14, 17
MGM. *See* Hollywood: studios
Mac Fisheries, II-173
MacDonald, Aimee, I-27

MacDonald, Ramsay. *See* Prime Ministers
Machen, Arthur and *The Great God Pan*. *See*
    novelists/prose writers
Machiavelli, I-344
Mack Trucks, I-159
Mackintosh ("mac"), I-143, 152, 185–86, 211,
    274, 319, 407; and Charles Mackintosh,
    I-274
Maclean, Alistair, I-68
MacLean, Donald. *See* Burgess, Guy
Macleod, Iain, I-346
Macmillan, Harold, I-8, 41, 56, 63, 70, 88, 105,
    114, 119, 162, 188, 194, 196, 221, 222, 255,
    285, 388; II-46, 86, 132, 141, 199–200
MacNaughton, Ian, I-31, 35, 36, 51, 57, 115,
    186, 306, 354, 375; II-26, 92, 149, 178
MacPherson, Sandy, I-21
Mad. *See* magazines
Madagascar, I-159
"Madame Dowding," I-5, 292, 298
"madeleine cookie," I-356
Madison Square Garden, II-188, 192
The Madonna of the Meadow, Bellini. *See*
    artworks
The Mad Woman of Chaillot. *See* films
"mafia," I-128, 132, 135, 140, 168, 374
magazines: *Atlantic Monthly*, I-80, 101;
    Black and White, I-246; *Black Mask*,
    I-64; *Collier's*, I-74; *Country Life*, I-199;
    Cricketer International, I-325; *Esquire*,
    I-40; II-92; *Exchange & Mart*, I-363; *Fang*,
    I-242; *Focus*, I-268; *Health & Efficiency*,
    II-164; *Help!*, II-99; *The British Journal of
    Psychiatry*, II-193; *Kamera*, I-268; *Lancet*,
    I-192; II-83; *LIFE*, II-75, 201; *Lilliput*,
    I-343; *Listener*, I-208, 367; II-97; *Mad*, I-52;
    II-60; *Management Today*, I-237; *Mayfair*,
    I-5, 145, 167; *New Left Review*, II-194;
    A New Society, I-363; *Newsweek*, I-138;
    Nova, I-209; *Oz*, I-124–25, 126; *Physique*,
    I-156, 167, 407; *Playboy*, I-167; *Popular
    Flying*, II-95; *Private Eye* (see *Private Eye*);
    "Psychiatry Today," II-193; *Psychological
    Monographs*, II-16; *Punch*, I-33, 87, 94, 251,
    316, 343; *Radio Times*, I-19, 80, 115, 151,
    207, 257, 333, 356, 380, 388, 394, 411; II-34,
    63, 65, 81, 85, 89, 112, 162, 189, 195, 199,
    227; *Sight and Sound*, I-367; *Solo*, I-268;
    The Spectator, I-41; II-119; *Spontan*, I-5;
    II-125; *Stern*, I-226; *The Cricketer*, I-325;
    The Tatler, I-199; *Time*, I-40, 53, 305; II-31,
    42, 75, 93, 201; *Tip Top*, I-5; II-125; *TV
    Times*, I-308; *Vanity Fair*, I-74; *Which?*,
    II-29; *Woman & Home*, II-125; *The Young
    Physique*, I-167
The Magic Christian. *See* films
magic lantern, I-56
Magna Carta, II-77, 84, 228
Magnusson, Magnus, I-328, 329, 333, 336;
    II-44
Maharishi Mahesh Yogi and TM, I-132
Majorca (also Mallorca), I-236; II-10, 64, 69
"Make Believe," Hammerstein and Kern,
    I-143, 150, 409; II-225
malapropisms, I-34, 52, 127, 140, 172, 261
Malenkov, Georgy, I-105

Malik, Sarita, I-313
Malaya, I-71, 73, 76, 387
Mallory, George, II-64, 70
Malmesbury, Wiltshire, I-365
Malone, Edmund, I-271
"Maltese Claret," II-13
Man Alive. *See* television shows
Man of Mode. *See* plays
"mandies," II-173
"man-trap," II-84
The Man Who Shot Liberty Valance. *See* films
Manchester, I-5, 12, 14, 49, 113, 128, 174, 177,
    185, 215, 225, 243, 287, 304, 309, 320, 324,
    367, 376; II-25, 136, 154, 194, 199
Manchester Harriers, I-12
Manchester University student elections,
    I-304–5
Manet, Édouard. *See* artists
mango, I-71, 355
Manhattan Project, I-6
Mannerism. *See* art
Mansell Collection, I-32, 111, 212, 213
Mansfield, Keith, I-331
Mantovani (and orchestra), I-55, 129, 212–13,
    262, 399, 400, 401, 403; II-88, 215–16, 217,
    219
Marat, Jean-Paul, I-15, 383
Marceau, Marcel, I-201, 208, 328; II-18
Marconi, II-92, 143
Marcus, Frank, I-380
Margaret, Princess, I-19, 184, 185, 305, 411;
    II-52, 57, 97, 98, 152, 171; The Dummy
    HRH Princess Margaret, I-17, 86, 257,
    258, 378; II-30, 50, 52, 57, 97, 112, 142, 152,
    171, 227
Margaret's Post Office, The Broadway,
    Twickenham (location), II-12
marginalization, I-110, 152, 178, 183, 254
Marinetti, F.T., I-14, 82, 235
Market Square, Wickham Market, Suffolk
    (location), I-161
Market Street Methodist Hall, Torquay
    (location), I-356
marketing boards, I-289, 301; II-32
Marks & Spencer stores, I-130
Marks, Harrison, I-268
Marks, Ginger, I-137
Marlowe, Christopher. *See* playwrights
"Marlowe, Philip," II-203
Marquesas Islands, II-26
"marquetry," II-181
"Mars bar," I-103
"Le Marseillaise," I-211, 400
Marsh, Alec, II-154
Marsh, Rodney, I-138
Marshall, Alan John "Jock," I-336, 348
Marshall, Jack Wilton, I-316
Marshall Plan, I-80
Marshall's Roundabout, Walton Bridge
    Road, Shepperton (location), I-21–22
Marston, John. *See* playwrights
Martin, Reuben. *See* MPFC extras and walk-
    ons
Martin, Sidney William. *See* cartoonists
Marty Feldman Comedy Machine. *See*
    television shows

Mauri, Carlo, II-24
"Marvin Martian," I-7, 63
Marwood, Reginald, I-301
Marx Brothers, I-40; II-132, 164
Marx, Karl (and Marxism), I-43, 213, 304,
    314, 371, 377–79, 384, 409; II-12, 16, 45, 79,
    88, 106, 107, 124, 125, 196, 207, 225
Mary, Queen of Scots, I-119, 339, 344–45,
    408; II-28, 224
Mason, James, II-73
Mason, Roy, II-200
Mason, Stanley. *See* MPFC extras and walk-
    ons
Masonic. *See* Freemasonry
Masters and Johnson. *See* *Human Sexual
    Response*
Mastroianni, Marcello, I-100; II-46
masturbation, I-47, 160, 209, 340; II-62, 65,
    70, 73, 79, 84
Match of the Day. *See* television shows
"Mater" and "Pater," I-258–59
Mathieu, Mirielle, II-58
matron, I-33, 149
Matsys, Quentin. *See* artists
Matthau, Walter, I-343
"mattress," I-22, 69, 127, 132, 133, 135, 196,
    249, 254, 407
Mature, Victor, I-390; II-75
Mau Mau uprising. *See* Kenya
Maudling, Reginald, I-88, 195, 259, 265, 294,
    309, 326, 334, 336, 345, 346, 367, 390;
    II-11, 54, 57, 82, 86, 126, 144, 147, 155;
    "Maudling, Mrs. Reginald," I-334
Mawer, Anthony, II-28, 35, 218
"May 1968" student riots, I-243, 275, 355,
    356; II-72, 88, 90, 117
"Maybe It's Because I'm a Londoner,"
    Hubert Gregg, I-283; II-69
May Day Special. *See* *Euroshow 71*
Mayfair, Greater London, I-35, 232, 272, 315;
    II-74
Mayfair. *See* magazines
Mazarin, Cardinal, I-71
MCC (Marylebone Cricket Club). *See*
    "cricket"
McCabe, Stan, II-34–35
McCarey, Leo. *See* film directors
McCartney, Paul, I-34, 167
McCay, Winsor. *See* animation: animators
McCheane, Mary, I-352, 390
McCloskey, Pete, II-145
McClure, Doug, I-394
McDowell, Malcolm, I-297; II-114
McGonagall, William, I-262–63
McGoohan, Patrick, I-354, 356
McGough, Roger, I-262; II-136
McGovern, Des. *See* MPFC extras and walk-
    ons
McGovern, George, II-145, 156
McGuffie, Bill, I-58, 60, 273, 330, 331, 337,
    352, 390, 399, 401, 404; II-48, 186, 215,
    217, 220
McGrath, Joseph. *See* film directors
McKellen, Ian, I-252, 257, 259
"McKenzie, Barry," I-258, 345
McKenzie, Robert, I-294, 297, 306

McKern, Leo, I-110; II-34

McKinley, Chuck, I-125

McLaren, Norman. *See* animation: animators

McLuhan, Marshall, II-18

McQueen, Steve, I-116, 264; II-27

"McRettin, Jimmy," I-353, 354

McShane, Ian, I-251

McWhirter, Norris and Ross, I-161; II-34

Meard's Street, Soho, II-123

Medici, I-129; II-33, 36

medieval, I-19, 61, 83, 101, 124, 129, 183, 300, 325; II-xi, 5, 11, 17, 33, 50, 124, 145

Mediterranean, I-325; II-10, 64, 69, 71, 96, 195

Méliès, Georges, I-85, 87, 91

Mellitus Street, Shepherd's Bush, I-226

melodrama, I-69, 72, 247, 330, 380; II-46

Melton Mowbray, I-164, 216, 269

Melville, Herman, I-381

"memorial baths," II-69–70

memorialization, I-24, 25, 31, 134, 187, 374; II-121, 166

"Men of Harlech," I-178

Mendelssohn, Felix, I-94, 332, 334, 361, 402; II-166, 218

Mengele, Dr. Josef, I-190, 198

Menuhin, Yehudi, I-3; II-63

Mercer, David. *See* playwrights

"merchant banker," I-110, 186, 368, 410; II-50, 52, 55, 57, 59, 112, 226

"merde," II-167

Merino sheep, I-316, 319

"Merseybeat," I-160

The Mersey Sound, I-261, 262, 285

Merton and Morden, Greater London, I-62, 247; II-12

"metope," I-385–86,

Metropolitan Museum of Art, I-77, 375

Metropolitan Police, I-19, 52, 62, 177; II-43, 124, 126

Meusnier de La Place, Jean-Baptiste Marie, II-161

Mexico. *See* Central America

Mexico City 1968 Olympics. *See* Olympic Games

MI6, II-79

Michael Joseph Publishing, I-310

Michael X, I-226, 312

Michelangelo. *See* artists

Michelmore, Cliff, I-185, 292, 293, 294, 297

Mickey Mouse, I-23, 192; II-127

Middle Ages, I-12, 161; II-135. *See also* medieval

middle class. *See* working class

Middle East, I-33, 41, 83, 122, 182, 185, 222, 321, 328; II-116, 198; countries: Egypt, I-296, 327, 330, 331, 337; II-62, 89, 139, 162, 175; Israel, I-73, 296, 299, 322, 390; II-79, 89, 198; Jordan, I-290, 294, 296; Persia (Iran), I-41, 321; II-186; Syria, I-256; II-198; regions: Gulf of Amman, I-296; Palestine, II-117; Suez, I-136, 188; II-89, 95, 162; "The Crater," I-386

Middlesex, I-35, 92, 177, 189, 227, 285, 329, 391; II-128, 199, 200

Middleton, Thomas and William Rowley. *See* playwrights

Midgley, Bob. *See MPFC* extras and walk-ons

Midland Bank (and photo), I-253, 312, 323

Midlands, I-12, 20, 93, 111, 222, 287, 335, 353, 365, 367, 388; II-80, 89, 178; East Midlands, I-46, 121, 234, 269, 302, 314, 351, 354; II-133, 204–5; West Midlands, I-90, 146, 287, 367; II-63, 68, 69, 73

"mighty lines." *See* Marlowe *in* playwrights

Mike Sammes Singers, II-136

Miles, Michael, I-324, 373, 376, 377, 379, 384; II-31

military, I-4, 9, 18, 24, 54, 63, 64, 67, 68, 69, 71, 74, 75, 77, 80, 82, 86, 91, 111, 122, 125, 127, 131, 135, 136, 137, 139, 140, 141, 164, 168, 170, 186, 189, 190, 192, 193, 194, 196, 203, 205, 210, 231, 232, 245, 262, 286, 290, 296, 307, 316, 320, 328–29, 340, 344, 347, 353, 358, 367, 373, 374, 383, 389, 393, 395, 406, 409; II-23, 44, 50, 54, 58, 60, 63, 67, 73, 77, 84, 87, 89, 94, 98, 102, 105, 106, 109, 111, 112, 114, 123, 126, 133, 136, 141, 143, 149, 156, 162, 167, 168, 178, 179, 180, 182, 184, 186, 191, 193, 195, 197–201, 206, 211, 222, 225

"milk-float," I-259, 267

Milk Marketing Board. *See* marketing boards

Mill, John Stuart, I-313

"Millais, George," I-316

Millar, Gavin, I-360, 362, 367, 408

Miller, Jonathan. *See Beyond the Fringe*

Milletts stores (location), I-12

Millichope, Ray, I-301; II-136

Milligan, Spike, I-20, 29, 55, 72, 91, 94, 96, 104, 115, 136, 190, 238, 254, 268, 304, 305–7, 345; II-29, 32, 37, 45, 80. *See also The Goon Show*

mills/milltowns, I-20, 27, 37, 49, 70, 99, 239, 241, 242, 247–48, 250

Mills, George Holroyd, I-313

Mills, John, I-355, 357; II-27

Mills, Michael, I-10, 32, 61, 67, 97, 145, 161, 375; II-12

Milo, II-70

Milton, John. *See* poets

Minehead, Somerset, I-11, 178, 184, 185, 187, 190, 192–93, 197–98, 410

miners/mining, I-12, 27, 37, 41, 46–49, 149, 154, 159, 165, 183, 229, 246, 289, 336, 368, 384, 385–89, 391–92, 394; II-29, 72, 81–83, 104, 132, 189, 190, 207

Ministerial positions: Minister (MP), I-17, 32, 41, 56, 87, 134, 184, 188, 190–92, 204, 225, 228, 231–32, 236–37, 246, 274, 279, 293, 311, 314, 319, 322, 331, 346, 355, 409, 410; II-25, 30, 37, 53, 65, 77, 86, 87, 117, 118, 147, 225, 226; Prime Minister (PM), I-17–18, 33, 56, 103, 104, 114, 134, 162, 222, 238, 246, 255, 279, 294, 346, 369, 411; II-54, 82, 83, 86, 98, 133, 145, 164, 166, 173, 179, 195, 200, 205, 227; Minister without Portfolio, I-319; II-56; Shadow Minister, I-319; II-86, 87–88

"minority rule," I-59, 168, 180; II-36, 209. *See also* Rhodesia *and* South Africa

minstrels, I-; II-42, 123, 125, 180, 209, 220

Mirabeau, Honoré, II-165

Miro, Jean, I-15; II-85

"*Mirror View*," I-164

"misspeaking," I-40, 135, 172; II-78

Mitchum, Robert, I-104

"m'lud," I-56, 247

mnemonic device, II-119

mock epic, I-68, 112

"mock Tudor," I-181, 183

modern art. *See* art

Modernism/Modernist. *See* art

"Mods," I-141, 144, 160

Mohs Hardness Scale, I-47

Molineux Stadium, I-373

mollusca, II-81

Mona Lisa, Leonardo Da Vinci. *See* artworks

Monarch Airlines. *See* airlines

monasticism, I-129, 131; II-88

Mondrian, Piet. *See* artists

"Money, Money, Money," Fred Tomlinson and John Gould, I-48, 218

Mongolia. *See* Asia/Asian

The Monkees, II-205

Monkhouse and Goodwin, I-238

monochrome broadcast, I-67, 275, 396

"Monopolies and Mergers Act of 1965," I-303

monosodium glutamate (MSG), I-101

Monroe, Marilyn, I-233, 245

monsignors, I-28, 38, 172

Mont Orgueil Castle, Jersey (location), II-112

Montand, Yves, II-18

Montesquieu, I-122

Montgolfier brothers, I-50, 82, 246, 410; II-161–68

Montreux (and "Mon-trerx"), I-94, 95, 147, 152, 202, 212, 235, 245, 272, 287, 396, 397; II-118, 131, 133, 205, 212, 213

Monty Python and the Holy Grail (HG). *See* films

Monty Python Live at the Hollywood Bowl. *See* films

Monty Python record albums, I-16, 31, 82, 89, 118, 260; II-115

Monty Python, Shakespeare and English Renaissance Drama (MPSERD), Larsen. *See* novels/prose literature

Monty Python's Big Red Book, I-xii, 5, 222, 341; II-xi, 123, 134, 145

Monty Python's Fliegender Zirkus (FZ). *See* television shows

Monty Python's Flying Circus extras and walk-ons (as scheduled). *See MPFC* extras and walk-ons

Monty Python's Life of Brian (LB). *See* films

Monty Python's The Meaning of Life (ML). *See* films

Moore, Brian, I-174

Moore, Dudley, I-15, 16, 45, 64, 144, 150, 354; II-103; and The Dudley Moore Trio, I-144, 400

Moore, Henry. *See* artists

Moore, Marianne. *See* poets

Moore, Roger, II-132

Moore Street beauty salon, Jersey (location), II-68

Moorer, Gen. Thomas H., II-201

moors, I-119, 123, 149, 185, 321; II-137; Dartmoor, I-43, 55, 203, 249, 256, 261, 314, 390, 392; II-106, 201; Ilkley Moor, I-121

moped, I-149

Morecambe and Wise, I-194, 238, 243, 320; II-154, 179. *See also* television shows

Moran, Bugs, I-77

More, Thomas, I-381

Morgan, Cliff, I-355

Morgan, David, and *Monty Python Speaks!* *See* novelists/prose writers

Morgan, Kenneth, *Britain Since 1945*, I-29, 34, 44, 119, 165, 224, 271, 373, 387; II-17, 104

Moross, Jerome, II-203, 220

Morpeth Arms, 58 Millbank, London (photo location), II-49

Morris (car), II-111, 145

Morris, Desmond. *See* novelists/prose writers

Morris, William, II-50

Morrison, Herbert, II-182

Morse code, I-240, 245

Moses, Michelangelo. *See* artworks *and* artists

Mosley, Oswald and the British Union of Fascists, I-103, 190, 195, 374; II-78

Moss, Stirling, I-7

"Most Favored Nation," I-311

"Mother Goose," I-204. *See also* pantomimes

Motor Tax. *See* cut motor taxes

Motspur Park (location), I-164; II-162, 209

Mould, Marion Coakes. *See* MPFC extras and walk-ons

Mount, Peggy, I-225

Mount Everest. *See* mountains/ranges

"mountains [sic] film," I-146

mountains/ranges: Alpine/Alps, I-14, 101, 152; II-67, 74; "Andes," II-172; Annapurna, II-68; Ben Machdui, II-140; Cairngorms, II-140; Carpathians, II-172; Everest, I-125, 151, 408; II-37, 61, 63, 64, 65, 67, 68, 70, 72, 74, 91, 140, 178, 203, 224; Himalayas, I-126; II-63, 68, 140; K2, I-65, 68, 73, 83, 213; Karakorum Range, II-68; Kilimanjaro, I-143, 148–50, 187, 410; Pennines, I-49, 62, 276, 311, 321; Roiurama, II-40, 47, 213, 226; Sierra Nevadas, I-146; II-83; "Urals," II-172. *See also* geologic references

Mountbatten, Lord, I-19; II-154

Mounties (Royal Canadian Mounted Police), I-146, 149

Mr. Mousebender, I-29; II-96, 106

mouth-organ, I-38

Mozart, Wolfgang Amadeus, I-3, 5, 6, 9, 13, 15, 21, 23, 94, 163, 179, 206, 332, 334, 336, 399, 401, 403, 404, 409; II-128, 165, 207, 215, 217, 219, 220, 225

MPAA (Motion Picture Association of America), I-130

MPFC extras and walk-ons (as scheduled): Hilary Abbot, II-189; Tony Adams, II-43, 180, 220; Troy Adams, I-330, 388; Omo Ade (or Aide), II-43, 46, 142; David Aldridge, I-318, 319; Gerry Alexander, II-55; Lewis Alexander, I-363; David

Allen, II-147; Derek Allen, II-133; Tony Allen, II-5; Marie Anderson, II-113, 114, 145; Reid Anderson, II-133; Andrew Andreaus, I-381; Johnathon Andrew, II-197; Scott Andrews, I-231; Desi Angus, II-81; Sally Anne, II-43, 68; Cliff Anning, II-179; Ajibade Arimoro, II-43, 46; Jane von Arrensdorff, II-197; Keith Ashley, II-25; Lyn (or Lynn) Ashley (Idle) (see Lyn Ashley Idle); Barry Ashton, I-330; II-152; Eve Aubrey, II-171, 175; Rosalind Bailey, II-123; Richard Baker, I-411; II-31, 50, 85, 91, 93, 152, 155, 227; Dennis Balcombe, I-175, 179; II-81; Barbara Ball, I-280; Brian Ball, I-302; David Ballantyne, I-202, 211, 228, 229, 300; II-118; George Ballantyne (or Ballantine), I-268; II-81; Douglas Barlow, II-205; Bill Barnsley, II-189; Kay Baron, I-175; Paul Barton, II-110, 113; Bernadette Barry, I-61, 105, 175; Mike Barrymore, II-163, 179; John Beardmore, II-104, 123; Annetta Bell, II-152; Fernando Benito, II-205; Maurice Berenice, I-388; Fred Berman, I-61; David Billa, I-105; Sue Bishop, II-179; Peter Blackburn, I-53, 56; Ernest Blythe, II-205; Neill Bolland, II-5; Connie Booth, I-53, 80, 85, 145, 146, 186, 188, 193, 246, 258, 280, 281, 285, 287, 300, 332; II-5, 8, 95, 189; Neville Bourne, I-388; Willy (or Willi) Bowman, I-231, 363, 388; Marc Boyle, II-189; Mrs. Bradwell, II-197; Julia Breck, I-261; II-5, 25, 32, 95; Roy Brent, I-378; II-5, 12, 43, 81; Sylvia Brent, II-179; Peter Brett, I-50; II-104, 161, 205, 207; Geoffrey Brighty, II-25, 81; Jackie Bristow, II-189; Mike Briton (or Bridon, Britton or Brydon), I-145; II-167, 190, 191; Sheila Bromberg, II-43, 48, 49; Arthur Brooks, II-5; Elizabeth Broom, I-53, 61, 228, 268; II-23; Laurel Brown, II-110, 113, 152; John Brunton, II-5; Les (or Leslie) Bryant, I-378; II-118, 163; Michael Buck, II-5; Betty Budd, II-197; Karen Burch, I-52, 68, 142; Richard Burke, II-133; Ishaq Bux, I-381; Milton Cadnam, II-81; John Caesar, I-231; Cecil Calston, II-205; Donald Campbell, I-5, 118; Jack Campbell, II-81; Fanny Carby, I-145; Constance Carling, I-330; Elaine Carr, II-93; Jonas Carr (or Card), II-5, 43; Richard Cash, II-163; Barry Casley, II-197; John Casley, II-179; Stephen Cass, II-81; Maxine Casson, I-145; Hazel Cave, I-302; Derek Chafer, I-231; II-118; Johnny Champs, II-81; David Chandler, II-197; Jean Channon, II-179; Michael Channon, I-228; Victor Charrington, II-189; Tony Christopher, II-5, 12, 43; Kock Chuan, II-142; The Cittie Waites, II-123, 125; Hunter Clark, II-145; George Clarke, I-161, 345; II-33; Jean Clarke, I-130, 247, 249; II-93, 133; Norton Clarke, I-231; Helena Clayton, I-287; II-118, 133; John Clement, I-341; Fred Clemson, I-381; Pat Cleveland, II-104; Brian Codd, II-55; June Collinson,

I-175; Tim Condren, II-171, 189; Eddie Connor, I-388; Terence Conoley, II-5; Les Conrad, II-163; Leslie Conroy, II-197; Stella Conway, II-163, 179; Nicholas Coppin, II-81; Alf Coster, II-113; Harold Coward, II-205; Ken Cranham, II-191; Neil Crowder, I-378; Edith Crump, II-189; Barry Cryer, I-157, 161; William Curran, I-61; II-118; Alexander Curry, I-341; Freda Curtis, II-189, 197; Jane Cussons, II-55; Michael Dalton, II-189, 190, 192; Aubrey Danvers-Walker, I-378; Daphne Davey, I-228, 230, 232; II-118; Ian Davidson, I-71, 157, 160, 179, 223, 280, 292, 293, 296, 313, 314, 385, 388; II-179; Aldwyn Francis Davies, II-104; John Howard Davies (see John Howard Davies); Rita Davies, I-130; II-5, 8, 95; Fred Davies (or Davis), II-55, 179; Harry Davis (or Davies), II-163, 179, 189, 190; Adam Day, II-133; Giovanna de Domenici, II-152; Denton De Gray, I-269, 280; Gary Deans (or Dean), I-330; II-5; Jim Delany (or Delaney), I-61, 241; Vi Delmer, II-171; Richard de Meath, II-93; Jean Dempsey, I-145; Terence Denville II-81; Julie Desmond, I-269, 273; II-5, 43, 68; Mrs. G. Dewhurst, I-280; Keith Dewhurst, I-302; Roy De Wynters, II-152; David Docherty, I-302; Mrs. I. Docherty, I-280; Ralph Dollimore, II-123; Carolae Donaghue, I-160, 161; Pat Dooley, I-363; Jack Dow, II-81; Michael Earl, I-231; II-118; Bill Earle, II-163, 197; Bernard Egan, I-231; David Ellen, II-142; Ian Elliott, I-88; II-23, 81; Marcelle Elliott, I-88; Katie Evans, II-113, 189; Muriel Evans, II-197; David Ewing, II-5; W.F. Fairburn, I-88; Stenson Falke, II-210; Barbara Faye, II-171; George Feasey, I-363; Cyma Feldwick, II-113, 115; Alan Fields, I-175; Michael Finbar, II-179, 189, 190, 191; Helen Fishlock, II-197; Michael Fitzpatrick, II-133; Flanagan, I-115, 175, 185, 205, 215, 236, 342; Al Fleming, I-51, 53; Susanne Fleuret, II-171; Ciona Forbes, I-187; Sally Foulger, II-179; Eden Fox, I-241, 379; II-179, 197; Neil Fraser, I-205; Paul Fraser, I-388; David Freed, II-81; John Freeman, I-341; Joyce Freeman, I-268; Eric French, II-171; Jack Fulton, II-152; Brian Gardner, I-270, 302; Caron Gardner, II-123; Isobel Gardner, II-81; Jonathan Gardner, I-228; Raymond George, II-143; David Gilchrist, I-318, 319; Leslie Glenroy, II-163; Sue Glover, II-167; Derek Glynne, I-241; Matthew Gray, I-205; Laurie Goode, I-105; Stuart Gordon, I-161; Bill Gosling, I-61; Alan Granville, I-61; Beatrice Greek, II-171; Charlotte Green, I-104; Richard Gregory, II-104; Ron Gregory, I-231; II-104; Mr. D. Grice, I-280; Nigel Grice, I-302; David Grinaux, I-231; Donald Groves, I-378; II-189; Bruce Guest, II-81; Roy Gunson, I-341; Anne Hall, II-142; Ken Halliwell,

II-93, 95; Michael Hamilton, II-5; Tony (or Anthony) Hamilton, II-5, 55; Laura Hannington, II-179; Pippa Hardman, II-81, 93; Jim (or James) Haswell, I-318, 319, 378; II-171, 179, 189, 190, 193; Joan Hayford-Hobbs, I-53, 78; Dennis Hayward, II-171, 172, 173; Kathleen Heath, II-171, 179; Emmett Hennessy, II-113, 118, 152; Walter Henry, I-231; Margo Henson, II-5; Bill Hewitt, II-81; Jeremy Higgins, II-25; Rosetta Hightower, II-167; Jimmy Hill, II-170, 189; Edgar Hing, II-189; Chris Hodge, II-25; Malcolm Holbrooks, I-341; Cathy Holland, II-152; Martine Holland, II-189; Chris Holmes, II-81; Peter Holmes, II-171, 172, 173; Diane Holt, II-179, 205; Alex Hood, I-231; Billy Horrigan, II-189; Lyn Howard, II-171, 175, 179; Philip Howard, I-228, 241; Len Howe, I-88; Nicki Howorth, I-58; II-10, 93, 95; Beulah Hughes, I-175, 187, 205, 342; II-32, 93, 104; Bill Hughes, II-179, 197; John Hughman, I-48, 169, 228, 273, 276, 291, 388, 391; II-23, 25, 26, 27, 81, 118, 141, 142, 171, 179, 205; Derek (or Derrick) Hunt, I-330; II-171; Alan Hutchinson, II-93; Douglas Hutchinson, II-25; Neil Innes, I-280, 404; II-163, 178, 179, 186, 192, 220; Steve Ismay, II-93, 95; George Janson, I-318, 319; Anne Jay, I-241; Freda Jeffries, II-25; Bill Johnston, I-241; Daniel Jones, II-43; Deborah Jones, II-179; Matthew Jones, II-179; Nigel Jones, I-302; II-5, 11; Simon Joseph, II-163, 171, 173; David Joyce, I-231; Ade Jumal, II-205; Nicholas Kane, II-163; Vi Kane, II-171; Peter Kaukus, I-51, 53, 61, 161; Kyesi Kay, II-43, 46; Steve Kelly, I-381; II-171; Alison Kemp, II-197, 205; David Kempton, I-291; Barry Kennington, I-388; II-55; Eric Kent, I-231; II-25, 118; Karen Kerr, I-341; John Kimberlake, II-163; Sabu Kimura, II-142; Les King, II-5; Richard Kirk, II-118, 152; Mrs. Kitty, II-189; Peter Kodak, II-5, 12, 43, 123, 133, 142; Len Kingston, I-363; Jill Lamas, II-43; Brian Lancaster, I-38; Sylvia Lane (or Laine), II-163, 179; Roger Last, I-161, 352; II-123; George Laughing-Sam, II-104, 106; Arnold Lee, II-104, 106; Belinda Lee, II-179, 197; Peter Leeway, II-179; Terry Leigh, II-81, 118; Bill Leonard, I-270, 280, 302; II-81; Frank Lester, II-55, 69, 123, 133, 154, 162; Perrin Lewis, I-175; Barbara Lindley, I-280, 329, 330, 342; Paul Lindley, I-52, 53, 228; II-23, 113, 133; Eric Lindsay, I-228; Frank Littlewood, I-67; Cecil Lloyd, II-163; Bill Lodge, II-163; Rosemary Lord, I-205; II-81; John Lord, I-264; Peter Lovell, I-55, 67; George Lowdell, II-163; Lulu, I-327, 333, 341, 409; II-20, 30, 109, 225; Tony Maddison, I-231; Tobin Mahon-Brown, I-105; Suzy Mandel, II-171, 173; Susan Marchbanks, I-175, 187; Stephanie Marrian, I-280; Tony Marshall, II-197;

Betty Martin, I-161; Reuben Martin, I-47, 280; II-43, 44, 46, 68; Dilys Marvin, I-363; Stanley Mason, I-228, 272; II-118; Marie, I-342; Eileen Matthews, II-171; Mary Maxted, I-268, 273; II-171, 175; Anthony Mayne, I-231; Antonia McCarthy, II-152, 153; Des McGovern, I-161; Alison McGuire, II-152; Horace McKenzie, Louie McKenzie, II-205; Paul McNeill, I-228; Dennis McTighe, I-95, 97; Terry Medlicote, I-38; David Melbourne, I-241, 302, 381; II-118; Frank Menzies, II-25; Bob Midgley, II-123, 186; Deborah Millar, I-228; Bernard Mistovski, II-142; Everett Mitchell, II-205; P.R. Monument, II-5; Nick Moody, I-341; Peter Moore, Kevan Morgan, II-142; Anton Morrell, I-175; Clinton Morris, II-93, 95; Francis Mortimer, II-133; Marion Mould, II-179, 181; James Muir, II-171, 173; Kurt Muller, I-175; Ronald Musgrove, II-163, 179, 197; Philip Mutton, I-53, 78; Stuart Myers, I-378; II-179, 189, 192; Ken Nazarin, II-104, 106, 189, 190; Jay Neill (or J. Neil), I-115, 378; II-5, 12, 43, 81; Maureen Nelson, II-5; Robert Ng, II-189; Jenifer Nicholas, II-152; Brian Nolan, I-231; Keith Norrish, II-171, 173; Leslie Noyes, I-314; Garry O'Brien, I-302, 308; Mrs. P. O'Brien, I-280; Rory O'Connor, II-163, 179, 197; Bill Olaf, II-179, 184; Tom O'Leary, I-270, 302; Bola Omoniyi, II-205; Jim O'Neill, II-163; Marion Park, II-81, 93; Alan Parker, II-92, 93, 219; Lesley Parker, I-231; Sharon Parmee, II-179; Rosemary Parrot, II-189, 197; Jennifer Partridge, I-145, 342; Ann Payot, II-179; Roy Pearce, II-43, 49, 93, 95, 142; Moyra (or Moira) Pearson, I-53, 61, 228; David Peece, II-81; Annet Peters, II-163, 171, 179, 189, 190, 197; Steve Peters, II-55; Tricia Peters, I-145; Gillian Phelps, I-187, 197, 381; II-152; Paul Phillips, II-179; Frances (or Francis) Pidgeon, II-43, 93, 133; David Pike, II-113, 118; Pip, II-205; Dominic Plant, II-179; Mrs. Please, II-197; Alec Pleon, II-171, 172; Noel Pointing, II-163, 197; Anthony Powell, I-264; Nosher Powell, II-131, 133; Pat (or Patricia) Prior, I-205, 241, 329, 330; II-171, 173; Pat Quayle, II-5; Maurice Quick, I-61, 241; Charles Rayford, II-163; Bob Raymond, II-118, 162, 171, 174, 179, 187, 189, 191, 197, 205; Henry Raynor, II-113; Donna Reading, I-115; Constance Reason, II-171, 173, 174; Tony Regar, II-205; Mike Reynell, II-55, 81; Eileen Rice, II-189; Mrs. Richards, II-197; Sandra Richards, I-275, 342; Colin Richmond, II-142; Hattie Riemer, II-163; Araby Rio, Jasmine Rio, II-197; Joanna Robins (or Robbins), I-145, 268; Christopher Robinson, II-142; Peter Robinson, I-175; II-178; Judy Roger, II-163, 179; Clive Rogers, I-145; II-55, 152; Laurence Rose, II-81; Evan Ross, I-105, 300, 302; Peter Roy, I-179; II-133; Jean

Sadgrove, I-330; Pam Saire, I-241; Naomi Sandford, II-23; Sheila Sands, I-161, 175, 205; Lionel Sansby, I-51; II-171, 173, 189, 190; Joe Santo, I-175; Terence (or Terry) Sartain, II-25, 93, 95; Bunny Saunders, I-280, 303; Charles Saynor, II-104; Sandra Setchworth, I-115; Roy Scammell, I-280; John Scott-Martin, II-81; Eddy (or Eddie) May Scrandrett, I-105, 280, 300, 302, 314; Peggy Scrimshaw, I-302; Audrey Searle, II-163; Mike Seddon, I-161; Bill Shani, II-205; Les Shannon, II-179; Balfour Sharp, II-112, 113, 115; Willie (or William) Shearer, II-171, 174; Richard Sheekey, II-189; Jill Shirley, II-152; Micki Shorn, II-133; Tina (or Tania) Simmons, I-145; II-179; Neville Simons, I-231; Danny Sinclair, II-81; Sally Sinclair, II-179; Peggy Sirr, II-171; Colin Skeaping, I-280, 303; Graham Skidmore, II-5, 12, 25, 43, 123, 142; Tony Smart, II-189; Steve Smart, I-318, 319; Barbara Smith, II-280; Elsa Smith, II-171, 175, 179; Richard Smith, II-55; Tony Snell, II-189, 190, 192; Derrick Southern, II-203, 205; Constance Starling, I-115; Ringo Starr, I-22, 118, 210, 333, 409; II-20, 36, 225; Michael Stayner, I-270, 280, 302; Raymond St. Claire (or Clair), I-228; II-163; Louis St. Just, II-205; David Stevenson, II-5; Donald Stratford, II-179; Jackie Street, II-171, 179; Alistair Stuart-Meldrum, I-378; Kelwin Sue-a-Quan, II-104, 106; Arthur Sweet, II-142, 147; Angela Taylor, II-179; Thelma Taylor, I-52, 53; Tony Taylor, I-82; Morris Terry, I-228; Colin Thomas, II-152, 179; Reg Thomason, II-189, 190; Harry Tierney, I-231; II-25, 81, 118; Ron Tingley, II-43, 49, 93, 95, 142; Rita Tobin, II-171; E. Toller, I-280; Robert Toller, I-302; Fred Tolliday, I-268; Fred Tomlinson and Singers, I-92, 145, 149, 154, 342, 402, 403; II-43, 48, 65, 67, 74, 123, 128, 133, 137, 218, 219; Jack Tong, II-104, 106; Barry Took, I-67, 89, 160, 166; Cy Town, I-16, 61, 228, 241, 381; II-43, 49, 81; Chet Townsend, II-43; Ken Tracey, II-203, 205; Nigel Tramer, I-175; Alan Troy, I-175, 179; Gordon Turnbull, I-161; Reg Turner, II-55, 163, 171, 172, 179, 188, 189, 190, 193, 197; Desmond Verini, II-55, 81, 104; Wolfgang von Jurgen, II-81; Dick Vosburgh, I-77, 85; George Wade, II-5; Peter Walker, II-142, 147; Albert Ward, I-67, 247, 249; Nicholas Ward, II-43; Vi Ward, II-171; Pam (or Pamela) Wardell, II-171, 174, 175, 189, 190, 197; David Waterman, II-93, 95, 142; Garth Watkins, I-231; II-179; Dorothy Watson, I-363; John Watters, I-53, 60; Dot and Len Webb, II-179, 199; Philip Webb, I-363; Leslie (or Lesley) Weekes, I-16, 175, 179; Adrien Wells, II-133; Babs Westcott, II-189; Michael White, II-81; Jeanette Wild, I-255, 261; David Wilde, II-93, 167; Marjorie Wilde, I-241, 251; II-95; Fred Wilkinson,

II-5; Bowle Williams, II-205; Elaine Williams, I-105, 268; Frank Williams, II-5; Joanna Williams, II-167; Robyn (Robin) Williams, II-43, 81, 142; Terry Williams, I-280, 303; Peter Willis, I-161; Carey Wilson, II-104; Gordon Winter, I-302; Jeff Witherick, II-142; Vincent Wong, I-343; II-189, 190; Edna Wood, II-189, 197; Ralph Wood, I-341; Teresa Wood, II-205; Henry (or Harry) Woodley, I-44, 105; II-125; Peter Woods, II-179; Katya Wyeth, I-66, 72, 130; II-124; C.H. Yang, II-104, 106; Christine Young, I-53, 69

MPFC production elements (costumes/ props/lighting/FX, etc.), I-xii, 6, 12, 17, 19, 23, 27, 29, 36, 44–46, 61, 63–64, 69, 75–76, 81, 95, 97, 101, 112, 113, 117, 127, 130, 135, 149, 154, 157, 174, 183, 195–97, 199–200, 208, 214, 222, 229–30, 237, 238, 241, 243, 247–48, 251, 257, 269, 270–71, 279–80, 286, 292, 301, 303, 304, 312, 351–52, 356, 357–58, 377, 391; II-xii, 11, 22, 27, 33, 39, 52, 54, 66, 72, 92, 96, 99, 112, 114–16, 118, 123, 135, 138, 147, 155, 180–81, 192, 197–98, 208–9. *See also* costume instructions/directions *and* prop and set instructions/directions

"MP Repertory Company," II-189

Mr. and Mrs. Andrews, Thomas Gainsborough. *See* artworks *and* artists

"Mr. and Mrs. Brian Equator," I-127, 147, 148

"Mr. Softee" and David Broome, I-328; II-36, 184

"Mrs. S.C.U.M.," I-3, 240; II-20, 196, 197, 199, 200, 202

"Mrs. Wilson's Diary," I-34

"Muffin the Mule," I-345; II-34

Muggeridge, Malcolm, I-181

Muller, Karl-Heinz, II-15

Munich Agreement, I-17; II-41

Munro, Janet, I-110; II-119

Murder in the Cathedral, T.S. Eliot. *See* plays

Murdoch, Rupert, I-362, 369, 372, 380; II-132, 210

Murray, Don, I-344

Murrow, Edward R., II-182

Museum of Modern Art (MoMA), I-372. *See also* museums

museums, I-6, 11–12, 42, 64, 66, 69, 72, 77, 84, 100, 115, 120, 123, 159, 166, 180, 246, 254, 297, 313, 315, 327, 372, 375, 398; II-71, 77, 79, 81, 84, 86, 123, 131, 136, 180, 184, 214

Musial, Stan, II-34

music cues (by episode). *See* Appendix B

music hall/vaudeville, I-9, 10, 14, 23, 40, 48, 108, 113, 116, 118, 138, 146, 203, 221, 247, 254, 257, 271, 299, 303, 313, 320, 329, 330; II-4, 41, 55, 57, 58, 60, 95, 106, 127, 180, 185

Muskie, Edmund, II-145, 154, 156

Muslims, I-249, 347

Mussolini, Benito, I-185, 191, 392; II-87

"Mutual Assured Destruction" (MAD), II-114

Mutton, Philip. *See MPFC* extras and walk-ons

Muybridge, Eadweard, I-81; II-121, 122, 127, 165, 168

"My Old Man," I-247

Myron and *Discus Thrower*. *See* artworks

Nabarro, Sir Gerald, I-12, 27, 159, 180, 214, 240, 250, 301–2, 304, 334, 355, 357, 367; II-40–41, 46, 63

Nader, Ralph, II-75

"Nae Trews," I-113, 256, 336; II-136

Nairobi. *See* Kenya

The Naked Ape, Morris. *See* novels/prose literature

The Naked Civil Servant, Crisp. *See* novels/prose literature

"naked sailor" photo, I-31; II-30

Namath, Joe, I-355

"namby-pamby," I-265

naming/power of names, I-9, 12, 13, 22, 25, 27–28, 30, 31, 34, 47, 52, 57, 66, 81, 113, 143–44, 146, 148, 150, 153–55, 190, 195, 197, 227, 230, 233–34, 236, 252, 256–57, 268, 270, 273, 287, 289, 291–92, 293, 300, 301, 303, 307–8, 321, 328, 333, 344–45, 352, 354, 356, 364, 367–68, 384; II-6–7, 8, 11, 13–14, 17, 18, 20, 24, 27, 31–32, 38, 42, 48, 50, 53, 54, 62, 71, 74–75, 89, 92, 95–96, 98, 106, 111, 115, 118, 126, 132, 134, 136, 141, 144–45, 157, 161, 167, 168, 181, 188–89, 195, 205, 207, 208–9

Napoleon, I-28, 37–38, 86, 163, 193, 208, 212, 353, 393, 396; II-94, 134, 205, 212

narrative disruption/transgression, I-14, 22, 25, 28, 36, 38, 40, 47, 66, 73, 76, 91, 104, 120, 131, 133, 135–37, 152, 154, 166, 167, 176, 183, 193, 202, 212, 248, 254, 260, 298; II-3, 13–14, 17, 34, 39, 44, 56, 62, 93, 105, 107, 114, 135, 137, 152, 168, 174

Nash, John, I-394

Nash, Ogden and "The Camel." *See* poets *and* poems

"nasty continental," II-82, 84

Nathan, L.H., II-150

National Action Party, I-190

National Archives (UK), I-84, 393

National Archives and Records Administration (US), I-241

"National Bocialists," I-117, 184, 193, 413

National Bus Company, I-253

National Economic Development Council (NEDC), I-56–57, 371

National Farmers Union, I-293, 311

National Film Theatre, I-15; II-42

National Front, I-59, 304; II-207

National Gallery (NG). *See* art galleries

National Health Service (NHS), I-102, 390–91; II-35, 103, 133, 136, 149, 207

National Light Orchestra, I-4, 399

National Picasso Museum, I-12

National Portrait Gallery (NPG). *See* art galleries

National Savings, I-56

National Service, I-71, 74, 75, 137, 230, 232; II-84

National Theatre, I-27, 38

National Trust, I-334, 337

National Viewers and Listeners Association (NVLA), I-138, 169, 214, 309; II-4, 84, 88, 89, 99

nationalized industries, I-119, 234, 253, 387; II-29

Nationwide. See television shows

NATO (North Atlantic Treaty Organization), I-41, 53, 63, 230; II-197

"naughty bits," I-195, 205, 250, 339, 341, 346, 410

"naughty dentists," I-65, 72

"Naughty Humphrey," I-246, 247

Nazi/Nazism (National Socialist Party), I-4, 6, 8, 9, 10, 11, 13, 16, 17, 19, 20, 22–24, 97, 124, 154, 175–76, 178, 179, 184–87, 189–91, 193–98, 199, 204, 304, 310, 347, 392, 406, 410; II-20, 30, 41, 50, 59, 79, 98, 109, 188, 192, 198, 222, 226

"NBG," I-247

"Neaps End," I-165

Necker, Jacques, I-15; II-165–66

"Neddy" and "Teddy," I-278, 405

Negus, Arthur, I-302, 335

Neighbours, dir. Norman McLaren. *See* films

Nelson (town), I-102

Nelson, Admiral Horatio, I-3, 10, 13, 14, 16, 17, 44, 169, 173 252, 343, 393–94, 408, 411; II-31, 70, 115, 224, 227; pillar destruction, I-10; Nelson's Column, I-10, 393; II-31

"nem. con.," I-246–47

"neo-Georgian," I-272

Neo-Plasticism, I-15

neo-realism, I-145, 253; II-42, 46, 49

"Nesbitt, Mrs," I-367; II-136

"never called me mother," I-69, 72, 247; II-46

"New Age Labourite," I-256, 285

"New Barbarism" architecture, I-267

New Criticism, I-336

Newhaven, East Sussex (and lifeboat), I-178, 211, 254, 302, 346, 410; II-54, 91, 93, 95, 96, 99, 226

"New Historicism," I-336; II-15

New Left, I-81, 93; II-68, 194. *See also* politics

"new pence," I-107, 123; II-13, 154–55

New Pudsey, West Yorkshire train station (location), I-114, 120

"New Towns," I-24, 224, 276, 367; II-115, 117, 203; and the New Towns Act of 1946, I-203

New Wave (film), I-83, 123, 146, 211, 213, 242, 253, 272, 297, 352–54, 356–57, 361–63, 365; II-41, 44, 94, 123–24, 155, 185

"new" universities, I-32, 192, 291, 322, 324

New York School, I-8, 17

New Zealand, I-125, 278, 317, 322, 335, 340, 349, 355, 358, 360, 368, 373; II-37, 93, 208

New Zealand Avenue, Walton-on-Thames, Surrey (location), I-268, 269, 270, 271, 273, 277

Newman, Nanette, I-326

Newman, Paul, I-165, 170

Newport, Wales, II-70, 200

News at Nine. See television shows

News At Ten. See television shows

"*News in Welsh*," I-53, 321

newsagents, I-102, 165, 226, 231, 273; II-118

newspapers, I-xii, 5, 7, 10, 18, 38–39, 45, 53, 63, 68, 71, 80, 84, 93, 102, 103, 104, 111, 112, 113, 116, 119, 120, 121–22, 126, 135, 148, 150, 152, 154, 157, 159, 164–66, 177, 189–90, 191, 208, 209, 210, 226, 228, 230, 233–34, 237, 244, 250, 258, 259, 265, 271, 272, 275, 289–90, 294, 296, 300, 301, 305, 306, 316, 326, 327, 334, 342, 345, 347, 354, 365, 367, 377–80, 384; II-xii, 4, 11, 14, 16, 22, 29, 41, 57, 59, 62, 63, 68, 70–71, 79, 86, 100, 102, 103, 132, 135–38, 148, 149, 153, 154, 165, 184, 188, 191, 192, 202, 209, 210: *Bath Chronicle, Bristol Evening Post*, I-223; *Daily Courier, Daily Echo*, I-316; *Daily Express*, I-39, 71, 154, 203, 244, 262; II-68, 82, 132, 135, 137, 192; *Daily Gazette*, I-120; *Daily Mail*, I-22, 102, 145, 250, 269, 271, 295, 300; II-22, 135; *Daily Mirror*, I-91, 119, 156, 164, 166, 305, 362, 372, 380, 386, 410; II-21, 74, 226; *Daily Sketch*, I-102, 208, 300; *Daily Standard*, I-102; *Daily Telegraph*, I-337, 391; II-85, 131; "*The Daily Torygraph*," II-85; *Daltons Weekly*, I-51; *Darlington and Stockton Times*, I-377; *Essex Gazette*, II-35; *Evening News*, I-293, 300; II-86, 136; *Evening Standard*, I-18, 22, 231, 269, 274; *The Financial Times*, I-368; II-45; *The Guardian*, I-8, 55, 80, 84, 139, 157, 177, 180, 250, 318; II-79, 112, 136; *The Manchester Guardian*, I-243; *The New Statesman*, I-22, 356; II-52; *The New York Times*, II-191; *News of the World*, I-39; *Newcastle Daily Chronicle*, I-246; *The Observer*, I-90, 177, 222, 333, 356, 374; II-14, 52, 102; *Pall Mall Gazette*, II-156, 157; *Richmond & Twickenham Times*, II-96; *The Stage*, I-250; "*The Scun*," II-209–210; *The Sun*, I-159, 215, 237, 245, 256, 262, 273, 362, 369, 372, 380, 382; II-210; *Sunday Express*, I-173, 226; *Sunday Mirror*, I-159, 226, 294; II-74; *The Sunday Times*, I-19, 184, 295; II-78, 144–45; *The Times (of London)*, I-7, 9, 24, 28, 39, 58–59, 80, 84, 85, 86, 87, 88, 93, 99, 101, 102, 107, 118, 121, 123, 124, 133, 135, 137, 144, 145, 157, 158, 162, 164, 165, 166, 168, 171, 173, 177, 180, 181, 189–90, 191, 204, 208, 209, 213, 214, 216, 221, 226, 228, 229, 232, 234, 237, 243, 244, 284, 286, 294, 295, 305, 336, 338, 342, 345, 351, 363, 365, 369, 371, 379; II-14, 15, 25, 29, 32, 37, 38, 46, 65, 80, 93, 109, 125, 128, 130, 131, 132, 133, 135, 141, 145, 148, 153, 165, 184, 188, 190, 194, 196, 209; *Western Daily News*, I-223; *The World*, II-157

newsreaders, I-50, 55, 56, 58, 79, 83–85, 136, 142, 277, 314, 320, 391, 406, 412; II-22, 35, 51, 118, 135, 162, 166, 186, 222, 228

Newsweek. *See* magazines

Nicaragua. *See* Central America

Nicholson, Ben. *See* artists

Nielsen, Leslie, I-111

Nietzsche, Friedrich, I-334

Nightingale, Florence, I-205

Nile River, I-390

Nimmo, Derek, I-380; II-208

Nine O'Clock News. *See* television shows

19 Southmere Terrace, Bradford (location), I-xii, 121, 137; II-xii

"nirvana," I-136

"Nissen hut," I-182

Niven, David, II-150, 154, 223

Nixon, Richard M., I-68, 80, 103, 165, 193, 195, 303, 361, 365, 396; II-35, 51, 52, 117, 145, 154, 156, 181, 212

"No time to lose," I-72, 102, 254, 411; II-140, 146, 227

Nobel Prize (and Alfred Nobel), I-43, 69, 167, 284, 313, 331, 353; II-16, 108, 137, 143, 156, 180

Noble, Michael, I-291

Nolan, Sydney, I-345

Nolan, William, I-6, 32

Noonan, Robert (aka Robert Tressell), II-15

Norbiton, Greater London, II-29

Norfolk County Cricket Ground (location), I-319

"Norfolk jacket and plus fours," II-46, 54

Norgay, Tenzing, II-37, 64, 67, 73

Norman, Barry, II-32

Normandy, I-15, 385, 408; II-156, 224

North, Lord, II-164

North By Northwest. *See* "films"

North Col, II-70

"North Malden," I-233, 298, 411; II-3, 8, 10, 11–13, 17, 38

"North Minehead," I-178, 190

North Sea (gas and oil), I-114, 159, 234, 273, 367. *See also* gas (natural)

North Walsham, Norfolk, I-367–68

"Northern" elements, I-10, 27, 36, 39, 41, 43, 46, 49, 70, 102, 112, 124, 150, 166, 197, 238, 246, 247, 248, 250, 284, 299, 304, 307, 315, 331, 343; II-20, 44, 53, 64, 76, 112, 115, 145

Northern Ireland, I-33, 49, 68, 69, 85, 103, 123, 134, 174, 185, 256, 294, 304, 328; II-11, 54, 65, 67, 71, 72, 82, 83, 88, 89, 93, 141, 174, 196

Northwest Territories, I-392

Norwich, Norfolk, I-32, 43, 156, 216, 238, 251, 275, 291, 308, 314, 316, 322, 324, 325, 337, 340, 365, 368, 379, 405; II-4, 5, 8, 21, 27, 34, 43, 53, 141, 142, 145, 200, 221

"nostalgia," I-70, 105, 164, 223, 298, 356; II-63, 74, 80

"not at all well," I-57, 102; II-13

Not Only…But Also. *See* television shows

"Notlob," I-127, 135, 136, 209, 279, 411

Notting Hill, I-85, 195, 225, 301, 312; II-4, 78, 79, 193

Nottingham, I-121, 321, 324, 353, 380

Nottinghamshire, I-36, 39, 269, 320; II-115, 151, 168; as "Notts," I-320

Nova (Barbara Harrison), I-110

Nova. *See* magazines

novelists/prose writers: Douglas Adams, I-212; II-152, 180, 202; Joseph Addison, I-32, 41; Grant Allen, I-309; F.G. Ashbrook, I-329; S. Baring-Gould, I-193, 396; Samuel Beckett, I-38, 82; II-127;

Robert Leslie Bellem, I-74; Saul Bellow, I-202; Hilaire Belloc, I-28, 33, 40, 213; Stephen Vincent Benet, I-286, 287; Henri Bergson (*see* Bergson); Dirk Bogarde, I-53; II-47, 94, 150, 203; Russell Braddon, II-131; Anne Brontë, II-112, 114, 115, 119; Charlotte Brontë, II-112, 115, 151; Emily Brontë, I-251; II-105, 114, 115; Pearl Buck, I-295, 335; Edgar Rice Burroughs, I-183, 381; II-115; Samuel Butler, II-115, 118; Truman Capote, II-92, 97; William Carlo, II-119; Lewis Carroll, I-189, 255, 268, 307; II-132; Willa Cather, I-295; Miguel Cervantes, I-58; II-90, 103; Raymond Chandler, I-64, 122; II-203; Agatha Christie, I-172, 174–75, 179, 182, 199, 360, 370, 405; John Cleland, II-88; Nick Cohn, I-324; Joseph Conrad, I-281; II-105; Roger Crab, I-132; Crew, Soper and Wilson, II-94; Quentin Crisp, I-166, 193; Dante, I-389; II-34, 39; Charles Dickens (*see* Dickens); Tim Dinsdale, I-227; Mabel Dodge, I-268; Fyodor Dostoevsky, II-35, 46; Arthur Conan Doyle, I-153, 175, 257; II-47; George Eliot, II-165; Frederick Engels, I-377; II-16; H.E. Evans, II-76; Jenny Fabian, I-163; Ladislas Farago, II-188, 192; Henry Fielding, I-12, 54, 153, 366; II-96, 103; R. Fiske, II-22; John Fowles, I-293, 295; Willi Frischauer, I-310; John Galsworthy, I-194, 327, 331, 335; II-61; Jean Genet, I-208; II-9, 18, 79, 83, 127; Gérard Genette, II-64, 105; Ivan Goncharov, II-108; Stephen Gosson, I-151; Ernest Gowers, I-65; Kenneth Grahame, I-229; Robert Greene, I-66, 266; Edward Grim, I-20; Thomas Hardy, I-10, 271, 316; II-81, 115, 151; Martin Heidegger, I-298, 340; Frederick Hegel, I-343; II-82; Ernest Hemingway, I-295; O. Henry, I-373; David Hoggan, I-181; Caroline Holland, II-175; Bernard Hollowood, I-343; Richard Hooper, II-22; Robert Hughes, I-13, 42; II-51, 75, 79; Victor Hugo, I-295; C.L.R. James, II-108; Henry James, I-70; Hank Janson, I-163; W.E. Johns (*see* Johns, W.E.); Thomas Jones, I-224, 227, 228, 229, 232, 234, 235, 238; James Joyce, I-25, 217, 350, 379; II-12, 96, 97, 176; Tony Judt, I-112, 223, 244, 271; II-124; Soren Kierkegaard (*see* Kierkegaard); Clive King, I-89; Rudyard Kipling, II-170, 198; Louis L'Amour, I-65; D.H. Lawrence (*see* Lawrence); John Le Carré, I-68, 77; Anna Austen Lefroy, I-303; David Stuart Leslie, II-79; Sinclair Lewis, I-295; Arthur Machen, I-152; Herman Melville, I-381; Gavin Millar (*see* Millar); Margaret Mitchell, I-295; Montesquieu, II-165; David Morgan, I-9, 11, 34, 45, 67, 88, 96, 104, 115, 116, 124, 138, 158, 160, 162, 166, 167, 174, 184, 267, 282, 303, 305, 419; II-73, 149, 235; Kenneth Morgan (*see* Morgan, Kenneth); II-17; Desmond Morris, I-65, 193; II-171; Vladimir Nabokov, I-120; Marcel Proust,

I-3, 12, 31, 55, 175, 179, 181, 356, 403, 405;
II-61, 64–65, 69, 70, 72, 116, 201, 219, 221;
Edna O'Brien, II-85, 88; Baroness Orczy,
II-134; George Orwell, I-49, 193; II-76;
E.R. and J. Pennell, II-153; Kim Philby,
II-79; David Pollard, I-361; J.B. Priestley,
II-76; William Prynne, I-151; Thomas
Pynchon, II-4; François Rabelais, I-190;
II-88, 114; Arthur Ransome, II-168; David
Reuben, I-47; Frank Richards (Charles
Hamilton), I-380; J.P.F. Richter, I-90;
Bertrand Russell, I-314; II-73, 79, 82–83,
156; Rafael Sabatini, I-373; J.D. Salinger,
I-351; William Saroyan, I-295; Jean-Paul
Sartre (see Sartre); Richard Savage, I-304;
Walter Scott, I-60, 119, 122, 256, 309; II-20,
112, 140, 147; Hubert Selby, I-163; Anna
Sewell, II-140; Nevil Shute, I-369, 370;
Alexander Smith, II-137; Tobias Smollett,
I-176; II-102, 103, 104; Aleksandr
Solzhenitsyn, II-108; Mickey Spillane,
I-65; John Stabb, II-122; Gertrude Stein,
I-25, 189, 217, 268, 307, 350; II-97; John
Steinbeck, I-38; Laurence Sterne, I-73;
II-56, 59, 103, 135; Bram Stoker, I-381;
David Storey, I-35, 37, 38, 370, 387; II-27,
33, 36; Harriet Beecher Stowe, I-324;
Philip Stubbes, I-151; A.J.P. Taylor, I-147,
174–75, 178, 179, 181–82, 186, 368; II-205;
Lowell Thomas, I-390; J.R.R. Tolkien,
II-5, 9–11; Leo Tolstoy, I-381; Thorstein
Veblen, II-175; Andreas Vesalius, II-187;
Paul Villiard, I-329; Voltaire, I-42–43,
47–48, 64–65, 87, 89–90, 105, 249, 272;
II-151; Lew Wallace, I-223; Horace and
Hugh Walpole, I-25, 99; II-98, 106, 112;
Sylvia Townsend Warner, I-295; Evelyn
Waugh, I-43–44, 145, 167; II-66, 71; H.G.
Wells, I-113, 178, 297; II-199, 200; Patrick
White, I-145; Whitting and Bryer, II-22;
E.O. Wilson, II-174; J. Dover Wilson,
II-190; P.G. Wodehouse, I-41, 152, 197,
198–99, 232, 238, 293, 338; Virginia Woolf,
I-25, 289, 268, 281, 350
Novello, Ivor, I-98, 212, 278, 399, 401, 402
novels/prose literature: 1984, II-76;
  Aftermath: Martin Bormann and the Fourth
  Reich, II-192; Alice's Adventures in
  Wonderland, I-255; The Anatomie of Abuses,
  I-151; The Angry Young Men: A Literary
  Comedy of the 1950s, I-35, 37; Anecdotes of
  Painting in England, II-98; Answered
  Prayers, II-92; The Antiquary, I-122; Around
  the World in 80 Days, II-150; Arrow of Gold,
  I-281; Awopbopaloobop Alopbamboom, I-324;
  "Barbering for Fun and Profit," I-329; The
  Bastard, I-304; Being and Nothingness,
  I-201; II-8, 14, 130, 189; Ben Hur, I-223;
  II-183; Beyond the Tenth, I-65; II-45; The Big
  Sleep, I-122; Biggles Flies Again, Biggles
  Flies East, and Biggles Looks Back, II-92;
  Biggles Sorts It Out, I-366; The Black Cliff:
  Clogwyn du'r Arddu, II-94; Black Beauty,
  II-140; Bleak House (see Dickens); "A Book
  at Bedtime," I-122, 407, 411; II-140, 141,
  223, 227; Book of Settlements and Book of the

Icelanders, II-7; British Society Since 1945
  (see Morgan, Kenneth); British Television,
  I-49, 82, 163, 248, 283, 299, 313, 320, 386,
  390; II-13, 22, 27, 44, 60, 63, 75, 124, 207,
  208; Bulldog Drummond, II-42; Byzantium,
  II-22; The Cambridge History of English and
  American Literature, II-7; The Camels Are
  Coming, II-92; Candide, I-29, 42, 43, 48, 64,
  65, 89, 90, 105, 123, 249; Captain Blood,
  I-373; The Castle of Otranto, A Catalogue of
  Engravers, and Catalogue of Royal and Noble
  Authors of England, II-98; Catcher in the
  Rye, I-351; Chamber Music, II-22; "Chinese
  for Advertising Men," I-361; The Class
  Struggles in France, 1848–1850, I-384; Code
  of the Woosters, I-197, 232, 238, 338; Colour
  in Britain, II-22; Comentarii De Bello Gallico,
  I-215; The Complete Plain Words, I-65; The
  Condition of the Working Class in England,
  I-377; Cricket on the Brain, I-343; David
  Frost, I-310; Das Kapital, I-379; II-79; De
  humani corporis fabrica, II-187; The Delta
  Factor, The Detective, I-65; "Devonshire
  Country Churches," II-122; The
  Disappearance of Mr. Davenheim, I-199; The
  Divine Comedy, I-389; II-39; Don Quixote,
  I-229; II-90, 103; Dracula, I-115; East Lynne,
  I-247; The Economic Consequences of Peace,
  I-377; Egil's Saga, II-7; Either/Or, I-36, 97,
  298; II-28, 177; End Play, II-131; The
  Enforced War, I-181; The English Hermite,
  I-132; English History 1914–1945, I-181;
  Englishmen and Others, I-182, 186; Europe
  and the Indies: The Era of the Companies,
  II-166; Eyrbyggja Saga, II-7; The Expedition
  of Humphry Clinker, I-176; II-103, 104;
  Fanny Hill, I-166; II-88; Farewell My Lovely,
  II-203; Figures III, II-64; Frankenstein, I-98;
  The French Lieutenant's Woman, I-293, 295;
  Gargantua and Pantagruel, I-190; The
  Garrick Year, I-82; The Gathering Storm,
  II-134, 143; La Gitanilla, I-58; The Godfather,
  I-168; Gone With the Wind, I-295; The Great
  God Pan, I-152; A Green Tree in Gedde,
  I-166; Grimm's Teutonic Mythology, II-12;
  The Group, I-166; Groupie, I-163; Gulliver's
  Travels, I-57, 89, 112, 286; II-104; Guy
  Mannering, I-309; II-144; Heart of
  Midlothian, II-144; Herzog, I-202; High
  Adventure, II-94; Hillbilly Nympho, II-122;
  Histriomatrix, I-151; The Hobbit, II-9;
  Honest to God, I-28; How Green Was My
  Valley, I-120; I Am Legend, I-116; I Am Still
  the Greatest Says Johnny Angelo, I-324; "An
  Illustrated History of False Teeth," I-77; In
  Cold Blood, II-92; The Insect Societies, II-174;
  Introduction to Chinese: A BBC Radio
  Course in Spoken Mandarin, I-361; Invisible
  Man, I-182; The Invisible Man (Wells),
  I-178; Ivanhoe, II-144; Jane Eyre, II-112;
  Jerusalem the Golden, I-82; Joseph Andrews,
  I-103; Jude the Obscure, II-151; "Kemal
  Ataturk, the Man," I-350; Kon-Tiki, II-29;
  Königin der Lust (Great Balls of Fire), II-122;
  Labels, I-43, 145; II-71; Lady Chatterley's
  Lover, I-34, 163, 229; II-146; "The Lady With

the Naked Skin," II-92; Landnámabók, II-6, 7;
  À la recherche du temps perdu (Remembrance
  of Things Past), I-179, 356; II-61, 72; Last
  Exit to Brooklyn, I-163; Laughter, I-163;
  Laughter in the Air, I-89; Laxdaela Saga, I-6,
  7; Les Miserables, I-295; Leviathan, I-344;
  The Life of Napoleon Bonaparte, I-193; A
  Literary Comedy of the 1950s, I-37; The Lives
  of the English Poets, I-304; Loch Ness
  Monster, I-227; Lolita, I-120, 166; Lord Jim,
  II-105; Lord of the Rings, II-9; The Lost
  World, II-47; The Lost World of the Kalahari,
  II-143, 203; Love Lottery, II-122; The Luck of
  the Bodkins, I-42; Lucky Jim, I-27; Madrigal,
  I-65; The Man With Two Left Feet, I-199;
  Manifesto of the Communist Party, I-384;
  Manon Lescaut, II-105; Market, I-324;
  Marriage and Morals, II-83; Mein Kampf,
  I-193, 204; The Midwich Cuckoos, I-114;
  Mill on the Floss, II-161, 165, 226; The
  Millstone, I-82; Monty Python, Shakespeare
  and English Renaissance Drama (MPSERD),
  I-xi, 12, 22, 23, 24, 36, 66, 83, 99, 113, 120,
  125, 134, 151, 153, 157, 161, 188, 212, 231,
  271, 272, 299, 328; II-xi, 3, 5, 78, 106, 112,
  125, 126, 170, 186; My Silent War, II-79;
  The Myth of the Six Million, I-181; The
  Naked Ape: A Zoologist's Study of the
  Human Animal, I-65, 193, 291; II-171; The
  Naked Civil Servant, I-166, 193; The Naked
  Island, II-131; Njal's Saga (Burnt Njal), I-6,
  7, 10, 13; No Highway, I-369; Notebooks of a
  Spinster Lady, I-251; II-175; Of Mice and
  Men, I-38; Morando, the Tritameron of Love,
  I-266; Oblomov, II-108; Old Curiosity Shop
  (see Dickens); Old Mortality, II-20, 144;
  Oliver Twist (see Dickens); On the Structure
  of the Human Body, II-187; One Day in the
  Life of Ivan Denisovich, II-108; The Origins
  of the Second World War, I-175, 179, 181;
  Our Mutual Friend (see Dickens); The
  Oxford Book English Mystical Verse, I-309;
  Permanent Revolution, II-107; Persian
  Letters, II-165; The Pickwick Papers (see
  Dickens); "Plato," II-79; Plum Pie, I-152;
  Pop, I-324; Portrait of a Lady, I-70; A
  Postillion Struck by Lightning, II-203; The
  Proletariat and the Peasantry, I-384;
  "Protestants Remember!," II-175; The
  Quotations of Mao Tse-Tung (The Red Book),
  II-107; The Ra Expeditions, II-94; Ragged-
  Trousered Philanthropists, I-15; "Raising
  Gangsters For Fun & Profit," I-327, 329,
  406; Raising Small Animals for Fun & Profit,
  Raising Small Animals for Pleasure and
  Profit, I-329; "Rape of the Sabine
  Women," I-286; Redgauntlet, I-60, 122, 256,
  407, 411; II-140, 147, 148, 223, 227; The Red
  Mask, and The Red Owl, I-373; Reflections
  on the Causes of the Rise and Fall of the
  Roman Empire, I-122; "The Rise and Fall of
  the Roman Empire," I-122; The Rise and Fall
  of the Third Reich, I-291; Road to Wigan,
  I-49; Roads to Freedom, II-8, 16, 175, 218;
  Rob Roy, I-20; Roderick Random, II-102, 103;

Rogue Herries, I-25; II-98; *Ronnie Barker's Book of Bathing Beauties*, I-5, 75, 107, 129, 184; *Ronnie Barker's Book of Boudoir Beauties*, I-5, 75; *Russia and History's Turning Point*, II-105; *Scaramouche*, I-373; *The Scarlet Pimpernel*, II-134; *Schoole of Abuse*, I-151; *The Sea Hawk*, I-373; *The Secret Adversary*, I-174; *The Secret Agent*, I-281; *Selected Works* (of Mao Tse-tung), II-23; *Selina: Or, Above Immortality*, I-90; *Die Sexfarm* (*Meanwhile, Back at the Sex Farm*), II-122; *The Shock of the New*, I-13, 42; II-75, 79; *Slaves of the Lamp*, II-170; *Sleep-In Maid*, II-122; *The Sobbin' Women*, I-286; *Social Learning and Clinical Psychology*, II-16; *The Solid Mandala*, I-144; *Some Old Devon Churches*, II-122; *Sons and Lovers*, I-11, 39, 41, 46, 48, 115, 229, 247, 387; II-207; *Soul on Ice*, II-34; *The Spectator*, I-41; II-119; "Speculations, or Post-Impressionism in Prose," I-268; *Spicy Detective*, I-74; *Stranger's Meeting*, I-304; *The Spy Who Came in from the Cold*, I-68, 77; *Stig of the Dump*, I-89; *A Summer Bird Cage*, I-82; *A Tale of Two Cities* (*see* Dickens); *That Uncertain Feeling*, I-27; *Technique of Film Editing*, I-367; *The Tenant of Wildfell Hall*, II-112, 114, 118, 119; *Tess of the D'Urbervilles*, II-115; *Theory of the Leisure Class*, II-175; *Three Lives*, I-217; *Three Men in New Suits*, II-76; *The Third Eye*, II-44; *This Sporting Life*, I-387; II-36; *Titan*, I-306; *Tom Jones*, I-12, 366; II-103; *Treasure Island*, I-86, 229, 230, 378; II-78, 88; "Tribal Rites of the New Saturday Night," I-324; *Tristram Shandy*, I-73; II-56, 105, 135; *The Tropic of Capricorn*, I-166; *Two Gentlemen Sharing*, II-79; *The Ultimate Reducibility of Essence to Existence in Existential Metaphysics*, II-119; *Ulysses*, II-12, 96–97; *Uncle Tom's Cabin*, I-324; *V*, II-4; *Vita S. Thomae, Cantuariensis Archepiscopi et Martyris*, II-20; *The Wanderer*, I-304; *War of the Worlds*, I-113, 297; II-199–200; *Wasp Farm*, II-76; *The Waterfall*, I-82; *Waugh Abroad: Collected Travel Writing*, II-66, 71; *The Waves*, I-281; *The Way of All Flesh*, II-115, 118; *Whatever Happened to Baby Jane?*, I-78; *What Happens in Hamlet*, II-190; *What is Metaphysics?*, I-298; *What's Bred in the Bone*, I-309; *The Whistler Journal*, II-153; *White Nights*, II-46; *Why I Am Not a Christian: And Other Essays on Religion and Related Subjects*, II-79; *The Wind in the Willows*, I-229; *Women in Love*, II-78; *World Revolution 1917–1936*, II-108; The *Wreck of the Dumaru*, I-390; *Wuthering Heights*, I-xii, 240, 251; *Zuleika Dobson*, I-9, 70

nuclear power/weapons, I-3, 6, 16, 23, 63, 67–68, 89, 124, 138, 211, 234, 258, 300, 339, 367, 382, 392, 406; II-20, 35, 69, 79, 86, 114, 156, 196, 197, 199, 200, 201, 222

nude/nudity, I-5, 8, 30, 31, 42, 51, 65, 79, 89, 94, 100, 104, 107, 111, 120, 127, 129, 130, 138, 140, 147, 155, 167, 172, 184, 193, 240, 242, 261, 264, 265, 273, 280, 287, 289, 303, 328, 369, 375, 405, 406, 408, 411; II-30, 37, 40, 44, 50, 52, 61, 77, 81, 86, 92, 96, 110, 116, 121, 130, 150, 168, 171, 177, 221, 222, 224, 229

"nudie" (clubs, posters, etc.), I-238, 303, 321, 342

Nureyev, Rudolf, II-25

Oakdene school, I-391

Oban, Scotland (location), I-xi, 43, 157; II-xi, 10, 12, 27, 140, 145; Oban Bay, II-10

OBE (Order of the British Empire). *See* orders

O'Brien, Denis, II-36

O'Brien, Edna, II-85, 88

O'Brien, George, I-373

Obscene Publications Acts, I-107, 163; II-77, 122, 129, 146

"O/C," II-191

Occidental College, I-242, 299

October Revolution, I-314, 379, 384; II-16, 109

Odeon cinemas, I-150, 286

Odinga, Jaramongi Oginga , II-208

Oedipal moments, I-36–37

off-licence, I-289, 302, 408; II-13, 130, 174

"off-spin bowling," I-231, 327, 334. *See also* cricket: terminology

"off stump," I-320. *See also* cricket: terminology

O'Hara, Maureen, I-373

Okehampton, West Devon, II-106, 184

"Old 666" bus, I-95, 122

Old Age Pensioners (OAP), I-86, 112, 137

Old Bailey. *See* Central Criminal Court

Old Curiosity Shop, Dickens. *See* Dickens

Old Man of Hoy. *See* geologic references

"Old Queen," I-166, 205, 335. *See also* slang/slurs/idioms

Old Oak Club, Acton, I-253

Old Oak Common, Acton (location), I-253, 256

The Old Place, Boveney, Windsor (location), I-44; II-126

Old Possum's Book of Practical Cats. See Eliot

"Old Sketch Written Before Decimalisation," II-154–55

Old Vic (Royal Victorian Theatre). *See* theaters (live)

Oldham, Greater Manchester, II-199

Olivier, Laurence, I-38, 50, 57, 75, 207, 210, 307, 374, 407; II-132, 223

Olsen, Merlin, I-355, 358

Olympia Press, II-122, 127

Olympic Games, I-65, 174, 216, 234, 248, 280, 296, 320, 328, 338, 355, 394, 411; II-30, 36, 110, 116, 151, 178, 181, 184, 189, 192, 227

O'Malley, II-32

Omnibus. See television shows

"on film," I-4, 73, 91, 106, 120, 137, 149, 251, 280, 282, 283, 284, 288; II-40, 67, 118, 168

"onanism," II-116

Onassis, Aristotle, I-80, 321

"Once more unto the breach," II-98

one-day cricket. *See* cricket: terminology

186–188 Uxbridge Road, Ealing (photograph location), I-81

111–115 New Zealand Avenue, Walton-on-Thames, Surrey (location), I-268, 269, 273

102 Thorpebank Road, Hammersmith (location), I-235

107 Thorpebank Road, Hammersmith (location), I-226, 231, 235

177 South Ealing Road, Ealing (location), II-99

123 New Zealand Avenue, Walton-on-Thames, Surrey (location), I-271, 273

Ono, Yoko, I-366; II-77, 185

onomatopoeia, I-106, 268

"open shelves," I-166

Ophelia, I-298, 409; II-187, 190, 192, 225

Opium War, I-194

Oppenheimer, Robert, I-116

"orangery," II-166

"oranges," I-355

Orders (of the British Empire): CBE, I-150, 360; DBE, II-36; OBE, I-149, 150, 199, 295, 296, 330

"ordinary suburban living room," I-85, 119

organized labor. *See* trade unions

Oriental Casting, I-388

ornithopter, I-246

Orkney Islands, I-334; II-205, 208

"Orpheus in the Underworld," Jacques Offenbach, I-240, 399, 401; II-146, 215, 217

Orphism. *See* art

Orton, Joe, I-121

Orwell, George. *See* novelists/prose writers

Osborne House, I-12, 40, 389

Osborne, John. *See* playwrights

Osborne, Sir Cyril, I-214

"Ostende" postcards, I-184

Ostrogoths and Theodoric, I-311

"othering/others," I-28, 39, 83, 80, 88, 90, 103, 105, 208, 249, 275, 341

Otley, Sir Roger, I-54

Otley Road, Bradford (location), I-176, 179, 182

O'Toole, Peter, I-38, 353; II-27, 196

Ottery St. Mary, II-106

Oude Kerk (image), I-183

"outside loo," I-321

"over." *See* cricket: terminology

Over London by Rail, Doré. *See* artworks

"over the top," I-23, 77, 105, 308, 323, 329, 365, 371, 380; II-46, 96, 110, 174

"Overland to Oregon Part 1," I-337, 401

Ovid/Ovidian, I-71, 160, 299; II-125

"O.W.A. Giveaway," I-391

Owl-Stretching Time, I-45, 63, 67

Owen, Alun, I-27

"Owzat," I-327, 335

"Oxbridge," I-44, 57, 70, 123, 159, 260, 289, 295, 306, 310, 317, 392; II-125

Oxenham, John. *See* poets

Oxfam, I-194

Oxford Dictionary of National Biography (*ODNB*), I-3, 8, 9, 16, 28, 33, 46, 51, 59, 70, 72, 76, 82, 84, 90, 114, 132, 141, 144, 159, 182, 216, 224, 225, 232, 233, 242, 265, 269, 275, 276, 282, 295, 315, 321, 323, 325, 329,

330, 333, 337, 344, 346, 386, 389, 392; II-45, 49, 63, 72, 78, 80, 82, 93, 95, 102, 119, 123, 124, 126, 128, 141, 154, 157, 163, 166, 171, 176, 177

Oxford English Dictionary (*OED*), I-xiii, 3, 5, 9, 28, 29, 34, 39, 45, 46, 50, 53, 54, 55, 56, 58, 59, 65, 66, 69, 73, 74, 81, 88, 90, 93, 95, 100, 106, 107, 108, 113, 114, 118, 120, 121, 123, 124, 125, 127, 128, 131, 133, 134, 136, 137, 141, 144, 145, 147, 148, 149, 151, 153, 157, 159, 160, 166, 168, 170, 176, 182, 185, 187, 188, 189, 190, 194, 195, 196, 202, 203, 204, 209, 212, 213, 214, 221, 226, 227, 228, 232, 235, 242, 243, 245, 247, 248, 251, 253, 255, 256, 257, 258, 259, 260, 263, 264, 266, 267, 269, 270, 271, 272, 273, 274, 275, 284, 285, 287, 296, 304, 305, 307, 309, 313, 315, 318, 328, 329, 330, 331, 335, 338, 339, 347, 352, 358, 366, 368, 369, 373, 385, 386, 396; II-xiii, 5, 6, 12, 13, 40, 41, 44, 45, 46, 48, 49, 56, 59, 71, 78, 84, 87, 99, 122, 127, 137, 138, 147, 155, 163, 167, 184, 185, 186, 199

Oxford University, I-38, 46, 70, 106, 119, 139, 144, 158, 170, 178, 179, 181, 193, 222, 227, 236, 255, 275, 299, 306, 315, 321, 325, 333, 342, 350, 376, 382–83, 392, 394; II-18, 23, 46, 48, 58, 59, 61, 68, 76, 119, 131, 135, 136, 174, 193, 204, 208, 209; colleges: All Souls, I-392; Brasenose, II-68; Exeter, I-382; II-61; Keble, II-68; Magdalen, I-222, 255, 333; Oriel, II-76; St. Catherine's, I-350; St. Edmunds, II-68; Trinity, II-58, 75, 95; University, I-275, 290; Wadham, II-46

Oxfordshire, I-4, 190, 195, 341; II-21

Oxley, Mel, I-166, 170

"Oxon," I-142

Pachelbel, Johann, I-98

"package tours," I-236, 258, 287; II-69, 71

"padre," I-209, 268, 286, 296, 341, 345, 371, 383; II-182

"Page Three Girls," I-115, 273, 369, 371, 384; II-210

Paige, Satchel, I-37

Paignton, Devon, I-xi, 29, 43, 154, 228, 278, 282, 284, 311, 349, 353, 355, 358, 405, 410; II-xi, 63, 119, 221, 226; Police Station (location), I-228

paisley, II-174

Paisley, Reverend Ian, I-80; II-65, 83, 170, 174, 175

Palace Court Hotel, London, (location), I-69

Palance, Jack, I-7, 357

Palestinian Liberation Organization (PLO), I-290, 294

Palethorpe, Dawn, I-12, 355, 357

Palin, Michael, I-4–5, 7, 9, 12–16, 19, 21, 27, 29, 30–32, 34–38, 41–42, 45, 47, 49–53, 55, 60, 62, 67, 72, 75, 77–78, 82–85, 88, 94–95, 98–99, 102, 104–8, 111, 114, 119–22, 124–25, 128–31, 134–36, 139, 143, 145, 146, 148, 150–52, 155, 156, 159–61, 163–64, 169–70, 180, 182, 186, 189, 192, 195–98, 201–3, 205–7, 209, 216, 217, 223–26, 231, 233–38, 241, 246, 253–54, 257–60, 262, 264, 266–68, 270–72, 275, 277, 282–84, 286, 288,

295, 298–99, 304–5, 308–9, 313–15, 317–18, 326–28, 330–31, 333, 335, 338, 341, 343, 350, 352, 355, 360, 364, 366, 369–70, 372, 379, 382–83, 388–90; II-3–5, 10–11, 14, 20–21, 23–24, 27, 29–30, 38, 40, 41, 44–46, 48, 51, 53–56, 59, 61, 65, 67–68, 75–77, 86, 89, 92, 96, 98–100, 103–4, 106–7, 110, 116–18, 121, 124, 130–31, 133, 135, 140–41, 144, 146–47, 149, 151, 153, 161–66, 169–70, 174–75, 182, 184–87, 191, 193–94, 196–97, 201–3, 206–7

palindrome, I-135, 136, 234

Pall Mall, I-173, 238, 379; II-42, 156, 157

Palladio, II-136

"palm court set," II-116, 166

Panama Canal, I-233

Panorama. *See* television shows

"Pan's People," I-331

pantomime, I-30, 69, 79, 86, 136, 163, 164, 173, 185, 221, 229, 230, 242, 257–58, 260, 261, 263, 330, 345, 372, 378, 386, 391, 406, 407, 411; II-30, 32, 36, 39, 50, 52, 54, 55, 57, 58, 78, 87, 94, 97, 112, 127, 145, 152, 170, 222, 223, 227: characters: Blind Pew, I-229; II-78; Goose, I-86, 173, 185, 257–58, 378, 391, 411; II-30, 50, 55, 227; Horse, I-86, 136, 185, 242, 257–58, 378, 411; II-30, 50, 54–55, 57, 87, 94, 127, 145, 227; Jim Hawkins, I-230; Princess Margaret, I-17, 86, 257–58, 378, 411; II-30, 50, 52, 57, 97, 112, 142, 152, 171, 227; Puss in Boots, I-86, 242, 257, 261, 378, 411; II-20, 36, 179, 227; Long John Silver, I-86, 164, 242, 257, 300, 349, 372, 378–79, 410; II-37, 83, 226; Dick Whittington, I-263, 378; II-36; titles: *A Wish for Jamie*, I-258; *Aladdin*, I-86, 258; II-30, 57, 170; *Babes in the Woods*, I-86, 386; *Cinderella*, I-86; *Dick Whittington*, I-86, 263, 378; II-30, 36; *Give a Dog a Bone, Humpty Dumpty*, I-86; *Jack and the Beanstalk*, I-86, 163, 264, 405; *Mother Goose*, I-86, 391; II-30; *The Owl and the Pussycat*, I-86; *Puss in Boots*, I-86, 261, 411; II-20, 36, 179, 227; *Queen Passionella, Robinson Crusoe*, I-86; *Sleeping Beauty*, I-86; II-30; *Treasure Island*, I-86, 164, 229, 260, 345, 379; II-37, 78

Panza, Sancho, I-229

Papadopolous, Col. George, II-94

Papas, William, I-55, 250

Papworth, Keith, I-108, 213, 279, 228, 400–3; II-51, 55, 56, 109, 142, 149, 216–19

Paradine Productions, I-35

Paradise Lost, Milton. *See* poems *and* poets

Park, Reg, I-351

Park Hill estate, I-267

Parkinson, Michael, I-194

Parliament. *See* Houses of Parliament

Parnell, Thomas, I-19

Parsons Green, Hammersmith, II-32

"party feeling," II-137

Party Political Broadcasts, I-136, 170, 184, 194–96, 319, 407, 411; II-77, 85, 135, 140, 144, 146, 148, 161, 166, 187, 202, 208, 223, 227

Pascal, Blaise, I-40, 43; II-80

Pasolini, Pier, I-207, 411; II-124, 150–51, 155, 156, 209, 227

Pasteur, Louis, I-353; II-32

"pastoral" (poetry/music), I-10, 74, 265, 375, 391, 401, 402, 403; II-135, 137, 142, 217, 218, 219

"Pat-a-cake," I-260

Paterson, Andrew "Banjo," I-348

Pathé, I-10, 24, 395–98; II-184, 211–14

Patten, Brian. *See* poets

Patterson, Floyd, I-205

Pawnee Indians. *See* Indians

Paxman, Jeremy, I-282; II-78

"P.B.T.R.," II-208

Peacock, Michael, II-88

"Peanuts" comic strip, I-123

Pearl & Dean, I-210

Pearl Bailey Sings the Cole Porter Songbook, I-335

"Pearls for Swine," I-210

Pearson, Lester, I-167

Peaslake, Surrey, I-10

Peckham, Greater London, I-233

Peckinpah, Sam. *See* film directors

"puckish," I-73

"pederast," I-288; II-95, 97, 99

Peel, Sir Robert, I-19, 194

Peele University Election Results, I-279, 302–3, 304

Peenemünde, I-16, 23; II-198

peerage, I-39, 84, 119, 180, 192–93, 196, 210, 226, 230, 258, 276, 303, 319; II-36, 63, 116, 118

"PEG" (Price Earnings to Growth ratio), II-59

The Peirson, Royal Square, St. Helier, Jersey (location), II-108

Pelican Books, I-65

Pembroke, Wales, II-194

Penguin Books, I-44, 65, 87, 163, 229; II-146

Penguin Pool, Children's Zoo, Hotham Park (location), II-146

penicillin, I-353; II-143

Pennine sheep, I-321

The Pennines. *See* mountains/ranges

Penrose, Roland. *See* artists

Penshurst Place, II-126

Penycate, John, I-302

Pepperpots, I-12, 13, 16–19, 26, 30–31, 35, 42–44, 49, 68, 70, 72, 74, 75, 78, 87, 91, 100, 105, 113, 114, 125, 151, 152, 156, 170, 179, 195, 198, 227, 298, 306, 347, 367, 374, 385, 386, 411, 412; II-12, 16, 49, 58, 61, 64, 77, 81, 85, 96, 97, 135, 136, 139, 156, 172, 185, 196, 204, 207, 227, 228

Pepys, Samuel, I-114

peripatetic, I-43, 349; II-103, 116

Perkins, Anthony, I-147, 149

"permanent revolution," II-107

permissions, I-24, 82, 130, 161, 210, 226, 242, 245, 252, 308, 316; II-30, 68, 113, 119, 127, 146

"permissive society," I-35, 37, 59, 137–38, 147, 156–57, 160, 162, 166, 167, 169, 181, 208, 214, 244, 333, 405; II-48, 79, 85, 90, 180, 221

Perrin, Commander Harold, I-33–34

Perry, Elizabeth, I-365

"Persian radio," I-41, 321

Perspective, Jan Vredeman de Vries. *See* artworks *and* De Vries

Pesellino, Francesco and *Predella of the Pistoia Santa Trinità Altarpiece. See* artists *and* artworks

"The Peter Gunn Theme," Henry Mancini, I-141, 273, 401

Peterborough, Cambridgeshire, I-194; II-115–17

"*Petrouchka*," Igor Stravinsky, II-195

"Pewtey" (and "Pudey"), I-21, 26, 27, 36, 42, 43, 44, 74, 123, 128, 156, 206, 231, 238, 389, 410

The Phantom of the Opera. See films

pharaoh, I-337

Phelps, Brian, I-248

Philby, Kim, II-79

Philip of Spain. *See* kings

Philips, Ambrose, I-265

Phillips, Captain Mark, II-178

"Phillips-Bong, Kevin," I-307; II-147

"philistine," I-266, 272

"Philosophers' Football Match," I-175, 180, 298, 340

philosophy / philosophers, I-xi, 13, 25, 31, 35, 36, 40, 68, 89, 97, 99, 148, 175, 176, 180–81, 235, 293, 298, 313, 314, 332, 334, 339, 340, 342–44, 386, 407; II-xi, 8, 13, 16, 28, 34, 73–74, 79, 80, 103–4, 107, 124, 130, 143, 156, 223

PHS (*The Times Diary*), I-190, 208, 213, 305

"PIB" (Price and Incomes Board), I-247

Piccadilly Circus, I-170, 188, 210–11, 253, 276, 343; II-87, 151, 155, 188

picaresque, II-102, 103

Picasso, Pablo. *See* artists

Pickford, Mary, I-48; II-75

Pickfords (location), I-226, 235

Pidgeon, Walter, I-110

Pierce, Edward, I-112

pigs. *See* animals

"pikelet," I-335

Pilcher, Sgt. Norman, I-83–84, 232, 236

"the pill." *See* birth control

pillar box, I-260, 349; II-200

Pink Floyd, II-104

Pioneer 10 spacecraft, II-110

pince nez, I-163, 167

Pinner, Middlesex, II-128, 151, 191

Mrs. Pinnet, Mrs. (also Crump-Pinnet), I-75, 228, 231, 235, 236, 238, 294, 302, 381; II-96, 116, 207

Pinter, Harold. *See* playwrights

Pirbright and Pirbright Army Camp (location), I-24

Pisarro, I-157

pitch (playing field), I-121, 173, 175, 248, 319, 324, 351

Pitzhanger Manor House (and former Library), Mattock Lane, (location), I-128, 240, 241, 243; II-11

pixilation, I-85–87, 210

placards and banners. *See* banners

plague, I-57, 102, 147, 172, 174, 297, 409; II-13, 73, 200, 225

Plantagenets, I-18, 345, 381, 389

"plastic arts," I-13, 15, 179, 223, 332; II-86

plastic surgery, I-73, 97, 300, 346

"plate glass" universities. *See* new universities

Plato, I-209, 340; II-79

plays (and live theatrical events) *A Day By the Sea*, II-57; *A Trip to Scarborough*, I-199; *The Alchemist*, I-67, 89, 98, 233; *The Beaux' Stratagem*, I-257; *Beyond the Fringe* (see *Beyond the Fringe*); *The Browning Version*, II-87; *Call Me Madam*, I-96; *The Careless Husband*, I-199; *The Changeling*, I-34, 65; *The Cherry Orchard*, II-34; *The Coxcomb*, II-96; *Double Cross*, I-96; *Dial M for Murder*, I-96, 99; *East Lynne*, I-69, 72, 247; II-46; *Emma's Time*, I-259; *The Entertainer*, I-49, 53; *Entertaining Mr. Sloane*, II-121; *Every Man in His Humour*, I-83, 263; *Every Man Out of His Humour*, I-98; *Gay's the Word*, I-98; *Hair*, II-81; *Hamlet*, I-15, 36, 38, 52, 54, 60, 61, 62, 152, 187, 215, 265, 298, 350, 372, 400, 409; II-50, 56, 123, 166, 187–94, 216, 225; *Hansel and Gretel*, I-282; *Henry IV*, I-113, 277, 350; II-112, 167; *Henry V*, I-23, 46, 55, 60, 92, 187, 206, 211, 400, 404; II-98, 192, 216, 220; *Henry VI*, II-123, 167, 205; *Home*, II-27, 33, 36; *The Importance of Being Earnest*, II-153, 156; *In Two Minds*, I-259; "*It All Happened on the 11:20 From Hainault…*," I-360, 365, 409; II-37, 225; *Julius Caesar*, I-15, 28, 37–38, 214, 240, 244–45, 350; *Long Day's Journey into Night*, I-29, 33; *Love's Labours Lost*, I-263; *King John*, I-59; *Kiss Me, Kate*, II-183; *The Madwoman of Chaillot*, I-354; *Major Barbara*, I-325; *The Man of Mode*, I-199; II-133; *Marat/Sade*, II-121; *The Merchant of Venice*, I-59, 350; II-50, 56, 207; *Merry Wives of Windsor*, II-167; *The Mikado*, II-184; *Morgan: A Suitable Case for Treatment*, I-259; *Mousetrap*, I-172, 370; *Mrs. Warren's Profession*, II-154; *Murder in the Cathedral*, I-6; II-20, 21, 24; *My Girl Herbert*, I-309; *Oedipus the King*, I-118; *Oklahoma!*, II-177, 179, 180, 220; *On the Eve of Publication*, I-259; *The Parachute*, I-259; *Pieces of Eight*, II-76; *The Pirates of Penzance*, I-299; *Pork*, II-32; *Promises, Promises*, I-206; *Pygmalion*, I-41, 174, 175, 196; *Pyjama Tops*, I-238, 303; *Radcliffe*, I-35; II-36; *Ralph's Roister Doister*, I-286; *The Rebel Maid*, I-146; *Red Peppers* (from *Tonight at 8:30*), I-92; *The Relapse*, I-199; *The Reluctant Debutante*, I-104; *Richard III*, I-6, 22, 24, 57, 66, 113, 350, 371–72, 374, 380, 381, 400; II-56, 106; *The Rivals*, I-12; *Salad Days*, II-95; *Salome*, II-156; *The Seagull*, II-35; *The Shadow of Mart*, I-358; *The Shoemaker's Holiday*, I-12, 54; *Showboat*, I-150; *Six Characters in Search of an Author*, I-255; *The Soldiers*, I-221; *Spider's Web*, I-172; *The Taming of the Shrew*, I-350; II-56; *The Tempest*, I-53; *The Temple Beau*, II-96; *This Way Out*, I-309; *Tom Thumb: The Tragedy of Tragedies*, I-54, 153; *Twelfth Night*, I-263; II-56; *Two Gentlemen of Verona*, II-38, 56; *Veterans*, II-27; *Volpone*, I-89, 225; *What Every Woman Knows*, I-44; *What d'ye call it*, I-194; *The Winslow Boy*, II-87

playwrights: J.M. Barrie, I-44; Beaumont and Fletcher, II-96; Russell Braddon, II-131; George Chapman, I-4848; Anton Chekhov, II-21, 34, 35, 104; Colley Cibber, I-199; Noël Coward, I-92, 223, II-57, 112; Stig Dagerman, I-357–58; Thomas Dekker, I-xi, 12, 54, 65, 83, 157, 299, 301, 328; William Douglas-Home, I-104; T.S. Eliot (*see* Eliot, T.S.); George Etherege, I-199; II-133; George Farquhar, I-257; Jean Giradoux, I-354; Henry Fielding (*see* Fielding); John Galsworthy, I-194, 327, 331, 335; II-61; John Gay, I-19, 74, 194; Jean Genet, I-208; II-9, 18; Rolf Hochhuth, I-221; Richard Hovey, I-295, 297; Engelbert Humperdinck, I-282; N.C. Hunter, II-57; Eugene Ionesco, I-208; Ben Jonson, I-7, 30, 34, 45, 67, 83, 89, 98, 99, 225, 233, 263, 272, 299, 307, 328; II-3, 59; Nigel Kneale, I-309; Frederick Knott, I-96; John Lyly, I-83; Christopher Marlowe, I-57; II-131; John Marston, I-23, 26, 48; Phillip Massinger, I-301; David Mercer, I-259; Thomas Middleton, I-34, 65, 83, 301;Eugene O'Neill, II-29; Joe Orton, II-121; John Osborne, I-35, 37, 38, 49, 53; Harold Pinter, I-35, 37, 169, 363, 370; II-47, 124; Luigi Pirandello, I-255; Terence Rattigan, I-16, 17, 43, 173, 209, 223, 257, 333, 370; II-50, 54, 58, 70, 87, 142; Rachel Reynolds, I-263; Richard Savage, I-304; William Shakespeare (*see* Shakespeare); G.B. Shaw, I-41, 174–75, 196–97, 260, 284, 325; II-153–56; R.B. Sheridan, I-12, 194, 199; Julian Slade, II-95; Sophocles, I-118; David Storey, I-35, 37, 38, 370, 387; II-27, 33, 36; Nicholas Udall, I-286; John Vanbrugh, I-32, 199; Lope de Vega, II-122; Andy Warhol, I-230; II-32; Peter Weiss, II-121; Oscar Wilde, I-196, 411; II-150–57, 167, 227; Thornton Wilder, I-384

Plaza Cinema, Piccadilly, I-211, 351

Pleasance, Donald, II-92

"plumage," 128

Plummer, Christopher, I-139, 157

Plutarch, I-286

Plymouth, Devon, I-203; II-64, 199

Pococurante, I-87

"Podgorny, Angus," I-110, 115, 119–21, 123, 254, 314

Podgorny, Nikolay, I-121, 314

Poe, Edgar Allan. *See* poets

poems/poetry: *Albert and the Red Devils* (Bilsborough), II-87; *Arcadia* (Sidney), II-138; *The Arctic Ox (Or Goat)* (Moore), I-318; *The Bard* (Gray), I-183; *The Bastard* (Savage), I-304; *Bees in Amber: A Little Book of Thoughtful Verse*, I-309; *Beowulf*,

II-6–8; *Cake* (McGough), I-262; II-136; *The Camel* (Nash), I-115; *Celestial Love* (Emerson), I-309; "*Charge of the Ant Brigade*," *Charge of the Light Brigade*, *Charge of the Heavy Brigade* (Tennyson), II-172; *Crow* (Hughes), I-246; *Elegy Written in a Country Church-Yard* (Gray), I-61, 90, 183, 295, 299; *Erik the Red's Saga*, II-6–7; *Dream of Fair Women* (Tennyson), I-169; *The Faerie Queene* (Spenser), I-71; *Felix Randal* (G.M. Hopkins), I-138; *Gunga Din* (Kipling), II-198; *The Hand that Signed the Paper* (Thomas), I-203; *Home Thoughts, From Abroad* (Browning), I-169; *Hyperion* (Keats), I-261; *I Wandered Lonely as a Cloud* (Wordsworth), I-261; II-173; *Jabberwocky* (Carroll), I-268; *The Lady's Dressing Room* (Swift), I-95; *The Lake Isle of Innisfree* (Yeats), I-133; *El Libro de buen amor*, I-213; *Lyrical Ballads*, I-277; *Marcel Proust* (Bennett), II-61; *Mariana* (Tennyson), I-169; *Milton: A Poem* (Blake), I-69–70; *Ode to a Nightingale* (Keats), II-173; *Ozymandias* (Shelley), II-172; *Paradise Lost* (Milton), II-110, 111, 115, 226; II-261, 410; *Poem* (Adams), I-53; *The Princess: A Medley* (Tennyson), I-276; *Profit and Loss* (Oxenham), I-309; *Rape of the Lock* (Pope), I-54, 57, 112, 195; *The Rape of Lucrece* (Shakespeare), I-76; *The Rime of the Ancient Mariner* (Coleridge), I-201; *The Seasons* (Thomson), I-135; *Sir Gawain and the Green Knight*, I-176; *Sunlight Soap* (McGonagall), I-262; *The Tale of Eirek the Traveller*, II-17; *The Tale of Ragnar's Son*, II-6; *Tam o'Shanter* (Burns), I-263; *Testaments* (Swinburne), I-320; *To a Mouse* (Burns), I-38; *To Autumn* (Keats), I-261; *To Mother* (Lowell), I-202; *Tristram and Iseult* (Arnold), *Tristram and Isoud* (Malory), and "*Tristram of Lyonesse*" (Swinburne), I-125; *The Wanderer* (Savage), I-304; *The Waste Land* (Eliot), I-xii, 6, 54, 62, 130, 191, 362; II-xii, 24–25, 30
Poet Laureate, I-46, 48, 276, 277; II-28, 176
poets: John Quincy Adams, I-53; Matthew Arnold, I-125; Alan Bennett (*see* Bennett, Alan); John Bilsborough, II-87; William Blake, I-69, 134, 271, 399; II-40; Robert Browning, I-169, 235; Robert Burns, I-38, 261–63; Lord Byron, I-194; Thomas Carlyle, I-106, 336; Samuel Coleridge, I-201, 277, 293; William Cowper, I-309; Walter De La Mare, II-54; T.S. Eliot (*see* Eliot); Ralph Waldo Emerson, I-293, 309; Allen Ginsburg, I-145; Thomas Gray, I-61, 90, 183, 295, 299; Adrian Henri, I-262; G.M. Hopkins, I-138; Ted Hughes, I-246; John Keats, I-257, 261; II-170, 173, 176; Rudyard Kipling, II-170, 198; Vachel Lindsay, I-362; Henry Wadsworth Longfellow, I-169; Robert Lowell, I-202; William McGonagall, I-262–63; Malory, I-125; Roger McGough, I-262; II-136; John Milton, I-xi, 69, 87, 169, 261; II-xi, 115; Marianne Moore, I-318; Ogden Nash,

I-115; John Oxenham, I-293, 309; Brian Patten, I-262; Ambrose Philips, I-265; Edgar Allen Poe, II-144; Alexander Pope, I-19, 54, 57, 74, 112, 195, 265; II-30, 59; Ezra Pound, I-362; William Shakespeare (*see* Shakespeare); Percy Bysshe Shelley, I-275; II-170, 172, 176; Osbert Sitwell, II-174; Edmund Spenser, I-xi, 71; II-xi, 30; "Dame Irene Stoat," I-289, 407; Jonathan Swift, I-19, 57, 89, 95, 112, 272, 286; II-104, 151; A.G. Swinburne, I-125, 275, 320; Alfred, Lord Tennyson, I-46–48, 169, 177, 270, 275–76, 370; II-21, 28, 170, 172, 176; Dylan Thomas, I-203; II-123; William Thomson, II-135; William Wordsworth, I-261, 275, 277, 293, 325; II-170, 173, 176; W.B. Yeats, I-133, 148
pogostick, I-87
"pogrom," II-107
"Polar Express," I-231
Polari language, I-160
political parties (minor or fringe), I-136, 184, 194, 296, 302, 304–5, 372, 411; II-147, 161, 166, 174
politics: Left/leftist, I-22, 28, 58, 81, 93, 112, 134, 165, 168, 186, 195, 203, 255, 265, 296, 301, 334, 355–56, 360, 372; II-22, 36, 52, 55, 59, 68, 79, 82, 99, 101, 117, 194; Right/far-right, I-28, 168, 199, 244, 304, 360; II-22, 36, 41, 45, 51, 99. *See also* Liberal *and* Conservative
"Polynesia/Polynesian," I-257, 335; II-29
polystyrene, I-303, 321
"Poisonville," I-72
police/policemen. *See* "constable"
Pollock, Jackson. *See* artists
Polonius, II-187, 192, 194
"pommie," "pommy," I-345–46
Pontiac Firebird, I-264
"pooftah." *See* slang/slurs/idioms
Poole Harbour, Dorset (location), I-4, 13, 409
pop festivals, I-317
Pope, Alexander, and *Rape of the Lock. See* poets *and* poems
Popes and popery, I-xi, 6, 80, 81, 210, 236, 244, 249, 346, 395; II-xi, 22, 33, 41, 88, 175, 205, 211
Popeye, I-252; II-27
Popular Front for the Liberation of Palestine, I-290; II-117
pornography, I-28, 71, 138, 166–67, 170, 180, 211, 213, 230, 237, 253, 268, 408, 411; II-89, 93, 121–27, 224, 227
Porter, Cole, I-335, 404; II-177, 202, 220
Porter, Edwin S. *See* film directors
Porter, Nyree Dawn, I-331
Porthcawl, Wales, I-53, 58
Portland, Duke of, II-166
Portland House (photo), I-121
Portman, Lord(s), I-303
Portree, Scotland, I-123, 254
Portsmouth, Hampshire, I-6, 64, 143, 173
positivism, I-181
"Post-Impressionists." *See* art: movements
Post-Modernism. *See* art: movements
Post Office Telegram, II-123

postal codes (Greater London), I-32, 35, 69, 75, 81, 91, 109, 138, 147, 164, 182, 185, 191, 194, 199, 226, 227, 228, 231, 253, 276, 294, 301, 323, 368, 369, 388; II-194, 367; II-11, 32, 74, 78, 79, 99, 112, 119, 127, 151, 193, 200
"postilion," II-137
postwar Britain, I-21, 29–31, 34, 37, 44, 71, 80, 88, 112, 119, 121, 122–23, 134, 140, 152, 165, 194, 203, 214, 223–25, 229–30, 234, 236, 238, 244, 271, 293, 310, 322, 329, 373, 380–81, 384, 387, 390, 394; II-17, 22, 25, 26, 47, 85, 102, 104, 134, 136, 187, 193, 203
"pouffe," I-261
Poulson, John, I-265
Pound, Ezra. *See* poets
Pounder, Rafton, I-188
Powell, Enoch, I-xii, 58–59, 80, 87–88, 90, 180, 195, 197, 289, 290, 309, 375, 405; II-xii, 19, 72–73, 221; and "Rivers of Blood" speech, I-88, 90, 195, 290
Powell Duffryn Coal Company, I-392
Powell, Michael. *See* film directors
Power, Tyrone, I-373; II-5
"PPS" (Parliamentary Private Secretary), I-247; II-36
"Prague Spring," I-58, 114
"Mr. Praline," I-12, 95, 104, 128, 130, 134, 135, 136, 141–42, 152, 170, 179, 180, 185, 206, 209, 211, 274, 278, 283, 284, 319, 349, 350, 352, 356, 407, 408, 411; II-61, 223, 224, 227
"prefabricated concrete slabs," II-117
"Mrs. Premise and Mrs. Conclusion," I-35, 43, 161, 333; II-3, 11–13, 16, 96, 175, 226
"Pre-Raphaelite," I-275
Presley, Elvis, I-347; II-133
Preston, Lancashire, I-115, 279, 284; II-89
Price, Vincent, I-116
Pride and Prejudice, Jane Austen. *See* novels *and* novelists
Prime Ministers: Anthony Asquith, I-17; Stanley Baldwin, I-13, 222–23, 328, 361, 383; II-83; William Henry Cavendish-Bentinck (Duke of Portland), II-166; Neville Chamberlain (*see* Neville Chamberlain); Winston Churchill (*see* Winston Churchill); Alec Douglas-Home (*see* Alec Douglas-Home); William Gladstone, I-33, 41, 47, 48, 103, 255; John Grey Gorton, I-346; Ted Heath (*see* Edward Heath); David Lloyd George, II-182, 205; Bonar Law, I-328; Ramsay Macdonald, I-13, 328, 360, 361, 366, 369, 384, 411; II-82, 83–84, 118, 227; Harold Macmillan (*see* Harold Macmillan); Lord North, II-164; Lord Palmerston, I-194; Margaret Thatcher (*see* Margaret Thatcher); Robert Walpole, II-98; Harold Wilson (*see* Harold Wilson)
Primitive London. See films
Prince of Wales, I-156, 389; II-46, 148–49, 153, 155, 166
"principal boy," I-378, II-32, 39
printed script asides, I-xii, 21, 36, 150, 154–55, 157, 173, 186, 198–200, 207, 275,

287, 292, 319, 339; II-xii, 3, 10, 53, 70, 90, 96, 181, 205

Prior, James, I-346; II-30

prisons/imprisonment, I-84, 178, 183, 194, 203, 215, 224, 226, 228, 229, 232, 236, 247, 272, 286, 327, 328; II-9, 11, 34, 102, 126, 154, 156, 157, 188; Brixton, I-194; Clerkenwell, I-226; Dartmoor, I-203; Durham, I-229; Holloway, I-272; Leyhill, I-203; Parkhurst, I-194, 203, 229; II-126, 129, 132, 154; Wormwood Scrubs, I-203

"private dick," II-194

Private Eye, I-19, 27, 30, 32, 33, 34, 35, 37, 38, 40, 41, 54, 56, 57, 58, 63, 80, 83, 87, 88, 89, 91, 94, 100, 108, 114, 119, 124, 148, 154, 160, 162, 165, 166, 168, 175, 177, 184, 191, 202, 205, 209, 210, 214, 224, 225, 228, 229, 233, 251, 258, 259, 265, 267, 274, 277, 287, 294, 295, 300, 301, 303, 307, 309, 316, 318, 325, 333, 342, 343, 345, 346, 354, 358, 367, 368, 380, 382, 384, 390, 394; II-4, 11, 25, 30, 37, 42, 52, 53, 54, 56, 57, 59, 63, 66, 67, 69, 70, 80, 92, 111, 132, 144, 163, 164, 170, 173, 174, 194, 199, 203, 205, 208, 210

"privateers," I-380

The Producers. See films

Production Code Administration (PCA), I-350

Profumo, John, I-26, 38, 41, 88, 188, 285, 288

Prokofiev, Sergei, II-33, 34, 124, 154, 219, 220

prologues, I-153, 202, 206, 211, 229

prop and set directions/instructions: 16–ton weight, I-75, 76, 195, 270, 279, 303, 349, 357; II-4, 149; Catering department, I-76; Construction Organiser memo, I-75; "edible" Turner, I-76; giant hammer, I-23, 76, 188, 270–71, 279, 313; II-4, 51, 114; giant penguin, I-75, 352, 356; II-147; hole in the studio floor, I-186; Mrs. Pinnet's front door, I-222; pig's head, I-17; Visual Effects department, I-76

Propp, Vladimir, II-143

proscenium, I-73, 88, 374; II-121

prostitutes/prostitution, I-41, 60, 71, 88, 140, 207, 213, 215, 216, 221, 225–26, 231, 237, 250, 283, 351, 388; II-9, 88, 92, 115, 127; and Street Offences Act of 1959, I-226

Proust, Marcel. *See* novelists

Provost of Edinburgh, I-60, 122

Prøysen, Alf, I-16

Prussia, I-184, 191, 333, 394; II-168

psephology, I-300

pub (public house), I-54, 62, 94, 96, 114, 152, 185, 213, 276, 302, 331, 350, 406; II-49, 109, 121, 127, 221

The Public Enemy. See films

public schools. *See* fee-paying schools

"pule," II-72

Pulitzer Prize, II-74

"pulp," I-xiii, 68, 72, 74, 110, 128, 132, 163, 192, 266, 350, ; II-xiii, 128

pun, I-4, 10, 72, 76, 78, 135, 136, 138, 141, 179, 234, 249, 282, 317, 361, 367; II-176

Punch. See magazines

"punchline," I-10, 22, 23, 28, 58, 61, 70, 73, 84, 113, 118, 131, 138, 167, 186, 202, 206,

211, 238, 240, 248, 257, 271, 280–81; II-14, 59; and set-up/payoff structure, I-4, 10, 128, 138, 147, 192, 238, 257, 286, 305, 320, 341; II-143

Puritans, I-89, 98, 151, 190

Purley, Greater London, I-54, 58, 212, 393; II-32

"purulent," I-95, 267

Puss in Boots. See pantomimes

Putney, Greater London, I-122, 207; II-32; High Street, I-207; Public Library, II-32

"Putrid Peter doll," I-290, 406; II-61, 71, 222

Pyatt, Graham, I-292

Pythagoras, I-235, 266

"Pythonesque," I-xi, xiii, 57, 167, 213, 250, 265, 289, 305, 308, 314, 339; II-xi, xiii, 3, 7, 34, 182

"Python's Playhouse," II-189

Pythonland, I-4, 60; II-100

Q Division, I-18

QE2 (ship), I-17; II-111

Quadrangle, Sussex Gardens and Norfolk Crescent, Haringey (location), II-114, 115

Quakers, I-372

Quantity Surveyor, I-58

Quarry, Gerry, II-190

Quatermass and the Pit. See films

Queen Anne's War, I-394

Queen's Counsel (QC), I-58, 104, 335, 380; II-127

"Queen's evidence," I-335

Queens Park Rangers (QPR), I-138, 381

Queensbury, West Yorkshire, I-242

"Queer theory," II-16

"Quickie Duel," I-36–37

"R101 Disaster," I-208

R v. Inwood 1973, II-4

Rabelais, François. *See* novelists/prose writers

Rabbi Buddha Whitman/Ginsburg, I-144

Rachman, Peter, I-201, 208, 211

Rachmaninov, Sergei, "Symphony No. 1 in D Minor Op. 13," I-209

racialism/racialist, I-xii, 85, 87–88, 90, 103, 104, 117–18, 131, 136, 173, 186–87, 195, 198, 203, 309, 312, 318, 375; II-xii, 4, 31, 42, 48, 66, 72, 88, 106, 201, 209

"the rack," I-248

Radio 4, I-80, 339, 346, 411; II-89, 227

radio shows: *The Archers*, II-25, 187, 192, 193, 207; *At Your Request*, I-21; *A Book at Bedtime*, II-116, 140, 141, 223, 227; *Byzantium*, II-22; *Children's Favourites*, I-21; *Children's Hour*, I-321; *Classic Serial*, II-77, 80, 164, 223; "The Death of Mary Queen of Scots," I-339, 344–45, 408; *Dick Barton*, I-204, 244; II-172; *Down Your Way*, II-132; *The Golden Disc*, I-163; *The Goon Show* (see *The Goon Show*); *The Great McGonagall…*, I-262–63; *Hitchhiker's Guide to the Galaxy*, I-202; *Housewives' Choice*, I-21; *I'm Sorry I'll Read That Again* (see *I'm Sorry…*); *It's That Man Again*, I-163; *The Jack Benny Show*, I-313; *Juke Box Jury*,

I-163; *Kitchen Front*, I-162; *Memories For You*, I-21; *Music For You*, I-168; *Paul Temple*, I-341; *PC 49*, I-119; *Semprini Serenade*, I-274–75; *This Is Your Life*, I-324; *Today in Parliament*, I-311, 324, 412; II-77, 89, 228; *Two-Way Family Favourites*, I-21; *War of the Worlds*, I-113

Radio Times. See magazines

RAF, I-23, 116, 157, 168, 186, 190, 221, 253, 356, 357, 397, 400, 411; II-46, 54, 58, 87, 95, 177, 180, 183–84, 185, 213, 216, 227; Museum, Hendon (location), II-180

RSM (Regimental Sergeant Major), I-64, 68, 71, 74, 76, 122, 180, 230, 254, 260, 385, 409; II-9, 58, 142, 225

Raft, George, II-122

"Rag Week," II-174

The Ragged-Trousered Philanthropists. See novels/prose literature

railway timetables. *See* "British Rail"

"Raindrops Keep Falling on My Head," B.J. Thomas, I-273–74, 309

Rainier, Prince, II-14. *See also* Grace Kelly

Rains, Claude, I-120

Raleigh, Sir Walter, I-90; II-123, 126

Rampa, Lobsang (Cyril Hoskins), I-65, 126; II-44–45

Rampling, Charlotte, II-47

Ramsgate, Kent, I-254

RAND Corporation, II-114

Ranevsky, Madame, II-34

Rank Organization, I-204

The Rape of the Lock. See poems

The Rape of Lucrece. See poems

Raphael, I-68, 74, 87, 382; II-33; "Raphael's Baby Jesus," I-74

rationing. *See* austerity

"rat's bane," I-392

"rating" (Royal Navy), II-84, 87

ratings (television), I-83, 249, 285; II-5, 104, 147, 162

Rattigan, Terence. *See* playwrights

"Ratty" (Water Rat), I-229, 372, 378

Ray, Robin, I-202

Raymond, Paul, I-303

Raymond of Mayfair ("Teasy Weasy"), I-303; II-74

Raynor, Henry, I-351

RCA, I-125, 384, 401; the Electronic Music Synthesizer, I-125

Read, Inspector Leonard "Nipper," I-226, 229, 232, 273, 329

Reader, Ralph, II-75

Reading, Berkshire, I-233, 285, 364; II-25, 203, 205

Reading, Donna. *See* MPFC extras and walk-ons

reality/unreality, I-19, 71, 86, 102, 127, 139, 141, 148, 152–53, 175, 178, 211, 388; II-39, 93, 135, 194, 205

Rear Window. See films

"rebel maid," I-146, 188, 281

recovery/recuperation, I-37, 105, 125, 188

Rector of Stiffkey, Harold Davidson, I-216

recurring characters, I-15, 206, 268, 299, 356

"red card," II-192

Redcar, II-155
"red" (Communist), I-58, 88, 103
"Red Arrows," II-87, 213
"redcoat," I-26, 31, 50, 94, 122, 145, 407, 411; II-110, 118, 223. *See also* Butlins
"Red Devils," II-87
Redgauntlet, Sir Walter Scott. *See* novels *and* novelists
Redgrave: Michael, I-38; Vanessa, I-82, 345; II-48
Redhill, Surrey, I-365
"Red Indians." *See* Indians
Red Rover coach, II-138
Red Square, II-147
Redundancy Payments Act of 1965, II-58
Reed, Carol. *See* film directors
Reed, Oliver, II-48, 65
Reeves, George, I-55, 60, 107
reflexivity and self-consciousness, I-xiii, 6, 12, 20, 38, 84, 170, 255, 269, 275, 277, 282, 286, 294, 309, 323, 329, 347, 367, 374, 382; II-xiii, 4, 39, 51, 60, 92, 96, 135, 144, 152
"reformism," I-371
"Regency," I-351
Regent Street, London, I-280; II-87
"Reggie." *See* Maudling, Reginald
regional television: ABC Television, I-166, 366, 386, 388; II-8, 13, 80, 152; ATV, I-154, 156, 166, 171, 174, 237, 254; II-10, 12, 13, 15, 107, 130, 132, 152, 178; Associated Rediffusion TV, I-16, 49, 124, 139, 174, 237, 388; II-10, 80; Granada Television, I-20, 49, 75, 122, 156, 248, 260, 370, 384; II-4, 10, 15, 80, 202; London Weekend TV, I-282; II-15, 131, 146, 152, 170; South Wales TV, I-20; Southern TV, I-20; II-27; Telefis Eireann, I-271; Thames TV, I-188, 237, 248, 324, 393, 412; II-4, 15, 123, 145, 150, 151, 152, 156, 180, 228; West of England TV, I-20; Yorkshire TV, I-160; II-15
Regius Professor, I-179
Reich Labor Service, I-10
Reigate, Surrey, I-285, 365, 393
Reiniger, Lotte, I-66
religion/religious (depictions/clergy), I-28, 29, 33, 47, 60, 85, 89, 90, 108, 110, 111–12, 129, 131, 133, 138, 139–40, 141, 145, 148, 149, 167, 210, 211, 213, 217, 242, 244, 245, 259, 266, 269, 274, 275, 277, 323, 327, 360, 361–70, 372, 406, 407, 408, 410, 411, 412; II-20, 31, 34, 38, 43, 49, 73, 79, 87, 121, 128, 150, 151, 173, 184, 203, 222, 223, 224, 226, 227, 228, 229
Reith, Lord John, I-167, 237, 244; II-156
Relph, Harry. *See* "Little Tich"
"*The Reluctant Debutante*," William Douglas-Home. *See* plays
"remaindered," II-33
Rembrandt. *See* artists
Renaissance. *See* art *and* English Renaissance
Reno, Peter, II-142, 162, 216, 218, 220
repatriation, I-59, 90
repeat fees, I-61, 95, 205, 303; II-13, 18, 58, 142, 180, 196
"Report on Industrial Reorganization," I-303

Representation of the People Act, I-293, 318
Resnais, Alain. *See* film directors
"respray jobs," I-370
Returning Officer, I-304
Reuben, David. *See* novelists/prose writers
revels, I-xi, 158, 242
revisionism/revisionist, I-47, 179, 181; II-15, 16, 23, 35
"revolutionnaire," I-356; II-108
Reynolds, Rachel. *See* playwrights
Rhineland, I-198
Rhodesia. *See* Africa
Rhondda, Wales, I-392
Rhyl, Wales, II-72
rhyming slang, I-160, 235, 291; II-72, 98, 122
"rhythm method." *See* birth control
Ribena, II-174
Rich, Buddy, II-107, 109
Rich, John, I-114
Richard, King. *See* kings
Richard, Cliff, I-303; II-58
Richards, I-179
Richards, Sandra. *See MPFC* extras and walk-ons
Richardson, Charlie, I-232
Richardson, Ralph, II-27, 29, 33, 36
Richardson, Tony. *See* film directors
"The Richardsons." *See* Charlie Richardson
Richelieu, Cardinal, I-5, 42, 50–52, 55, 60, 71, 167, 203, 213, 407; II-5, 49, 57, 65, 164, 223
Richmond & Twickenham Times. See newspapers
Richmond-upon-Thames (and Richmond), Surrey, I-12, 40, 60, 86, 282, 284, 286, 377; II-12, 26, 29, 32, 33, 40, 96
Richter, Gerhard. *See* artists
Richter, Hans. *See* artists
Richter, J.P.F. *See* novelists/prose writers
Richter, Sviatoslav, I-20, 25, 33, 228
Rickman, John, II-153
"Right Honourable." *See* titles/honorifics
"right on my uppers." *See* slang/slurs/idioms
Rijksmuseum, I-42, 180
"ringways," II-113
Rio de Janeiro, Brazil. *See* South America
Rio Tinto, I-368
riots/rioting, I-7, 59, 85, 103, 172–73, 195, 243, 312, 353, 355, 373, 374; II-4, 83, 107, 130, 195
"ripple effect," I-304, 332; II-33–34
Rippon, Geoffrey, I-319, 346
The Rise and Fall of the Roman Empire. See novels/prose literature
The Rise and Rise of Michael Rimmer. See films: UK
"Risorgimento," II-46
The Rivals, Richard Sheridan. *See* plays *and* playwrights
rivers: Avon, I-223; II-121; Clyde, II-111, 163; Coe, II-18; Danube, I-95, 108; Dart, I-154; Exe, II-109; Fleet, I-388; II-123; Lea, I-227; Loughor, I-53; Lowman, II-109; Nile, I-390; Ribble, I-284; Rhymney, I-53; Snake, I-158; Tawe, I-60; Thames, I-4, 18, 38, 80, 190, 233, 236, 260, 282, 285,

287, 316, 361, 388; II-7, 12, 13, 17, 30, 33, 82, 193; Tiber, I-90; II-88; Trent, I-353; Tyburn, I-388; Wey, I-12; White, II-201; Yellow, II-201; Zambezi, II-157
"Rivers of Blood" speech. *See* Enoch Powell
Roach, Harold, I-48, 61
Road to Wigan. See novels/prose literature *and* George Orwell
Roads to Freedom. See novels/prose literature *and* Jean-Paul Sartre
Robards, Jason, I-244
Robbins Report, I-291, 322, 324
Robert Browning Youth Club, I-235
Roberts, Garyn, I-74
Roberts, Rachel, I-35
Robertson, Brig. Gen. Beverly Holcombe. *See* Civil War (US)
Robertson, Fyffe, I-295
Robey, George, II-57
"Robin Hood," Fred Tomlinson, II-137, 219
Robin Hood Gardens, I-267
Robinson, Eric, I-168
Robinson, Bishop John, I-28, 33
Robinson, Kenneth, I-87, 225
Robinson, Peter, I-175; II-178
Robinson, Robert, I-91; II-79, 87
Robinson, Roger, II-118
"The Robinsons," II-192
Roche, Tony, I-111, 124
"Rochester," I-313, 324; II-42, 209
"rock buns," II-98
"Rockers," I-141
Rodin, Auguste: *The Thinker. See* artists *and* artworks
Rodway, Norman, I-380
"Roiurama." *See* mountains/ranges
Rolls Royce, I-347
"Rolo Nice Sweeties," II-75
Roman Britain, I-387, 389, 393, 394
Romano House, The Strand, II-73–74
Romanticism. *See* English Romantic
Rome, Open City. See films: Italy
Ronan Point disaster, I-88, 224–25, 244, 267–68, 271–75; II-99, 116, 117
The Ronettes, I-317; II-167
Rongbuk Monastery, II-72
"roof garden," II-171
Room at the Top. See films: UK
Rorschach test, I-259
Rose, David and his Orchestra, I-75, 182, 399, 400
Rose Theatre. *See* theaters (live)
rosettes, I-305
Rossellini, Roberto. *See* film directors
Rossiter, Leonard, I-380
"rota," I-285; II-118
"Rotarian," I-59
Rothwell, Talbot, II-58
Rotter, Julian, II-16
Rottingdean, East Sussex, I-201, 209, 211–12, 411
The Round Table, II-34
Rouen Cathedral, I-377
Rowan & Martin's Laugh-In. See television shows
Royal Academy of Dramatic Art, II-5

Royal Albert Hall, I-3, 173, 180; II-34, 58, 151
Royal Army Medical Corps, II-144
Royal Borough of Kensington and Chelsea,
    I-271. *See also* Kensington *and* Chelsea
Royal Borough of Windsor and Maidenhead,
    I-285
Royal Charters, I-81; II-37, 126
Royal College of Surgeons, I-342; II-126
Royal Command Performance, I-6, 45
Royal Court Theatre. *See* theaters (live)
Royal Festival Hall, II-33
Royal Grammar School, Guildford, I-216
Royal Mail, I-285; II-200
Royal Military Academy at Sandhurst, I-316,
    403
Royal National Life-Boat Institution, I-254;
    II-54
Royal Navy, I-68, 71, 111, 125, 169, 383, 385,
    388, 392, 396, 406; II-49, 59, 77, 80, 83, 84,
    92, 94–95, 178, 212, 222
Royal Opera House, Covent Garden, I-343;
    II-23–24
Royal Philharmonic Orchestra, I-3, 172–73,
    180, 412
Royal Scottish Forest Society, II-141
Royal Shakespeare Company (RSC), I-82,
    380; II-121
Royal Societies, I-281, 283, 285–86, 341, 387;
    II-141
Royal Square, St. Helier, Jersey, II-106, 108
Royal Victorian Theatre ("Old Vic"). *See*
    theaters (live)
Royal Wolverhampton School, I-216, 279,
    374; II-63
RSPCA, I-387
rubber chicken (and knight). *See* knight and
    chicken
"rubber mac." *See* Mackintosh
"rubbish" (criticism), I-31, 32, 41, 67, 129,
    171, 204, 213, 237, 307–8, 357; II-15, 44,
    45, 198
"rubbish tip," I-213, 357
Rubens, Peter Paul. *See* artists
Rubinstein, Nikolai, II-38
Rudd, Lewis, II-15
"*Rues à Liberté.*" *See* Roads to Freedom
rugby football, I-48, 149, 169, 172–73, 215–16,
    300, 349–358, 368, 389, 408, 412; II-157,
    189, 224, 228
Ruislip, Greater London, I-233–34; II-151,
    200
"Rule Britannia," II-150, 186, 199, 215, 220
The Rules of the Game. See films
"running-in," I-168
Russell, Bertrand, I-314; II-73–74, 79, 82–83,
    156
Russell, Jane, II-82, 87
Russell, Ken, I-354, 410; II-28, 34, 40, 44, 48,
    49, 57, 65, 95, 144, 226. *See also* films
Russell, Richard, I-29
Russia (USSR; Soviet Union), I-6, 13, 16, 41,
    53, 55, 57–59, 63, 66, 68, 70, 77, 80, 88,
    93, 99, 103, 114, 120–21, 129, 134, 165,
    189, 191, 207, 209, 231, 236, 267, 286, 293,
    296, 301, 314, 320, 379, 384, 393, 400, 402,
    413; II-12, 16, 25, 26, 27, 33, 35, 38, 40–41,

45–46, 67, 71, 79, 86, 101, 102, 104–9, 114,
    116–17, 120, 131, 140, 146, 164–66, 168,
    172, 186, 188, 198–200, 216, 218, 229
"Rustic" (type/accent), I-23, 26, 30, 31,
    41–42, 46, 52, 63, 73, 74, 83, 100, 105, 107,
    110, 115, 120, 125, 190, 195, 200, 254, 263,
    314, 318, 323, 325, 374, 376, 378, 408, 411;
    II-97, 186, 224, 227
Rutherford, Ernest, II-143
Ryan, Robert, I-207

Sabatini, Raphael, I-373
Sabine School for Girls, I-286
Sadler's Wells, II-120, 197–98
Saint Vincent Ferrer, Francisco del Cossa. *See*
    artworks *and* artists
St. Albans, Hertfordshire, I-146, 364;
    Operatic Society, I-146
St. Bartholomew's Hospital, I-226, 336, 348,
    391, 392; II-152
St. Brelade's Rectory, La Route des Camps,
    Jersey (location), II-127
St. Catherine's College, Oxford. *See* Oxford:
    colleges
St. Helier, Jersey (location), II-102, 104, 106,
    108, 127
St. Hubert's School, Shepherd's Bush
    (location), I-226
St. James Bolton church, I-176
St. James Palace, I-117; II-167
St. John, Kenneth Oliver Musgrave, I-192
St. John the Evangelist (St. John's), Bradford,
    I-131, 137
St. Margaret's Road, The Broadway,
    Twickenham (location), I-233; II-12, 13,
    33
St. Martin-in-the-Fields, I-33, 116, 327, 393;
    II-91, 130
St. Martin's Theatre. *See* theaters (live)
St. Mary's Road, Ealing, I-51
St. Peter's Square, I-140, 308
"St Stephen," I-20
St. Thomas Aquinas, II-119
St. Tikhon, II-102
St. Valentine's Day Massacre, I-77
Sabini, Charles "Darby," I-141
Sainsbury's, II-200
Salad Days. See plays *and* Peckinpah
Salisbury, Wiltshire, I-18; II-21, 71:
    Cathedral, II-71; Plain, I-4, 18
"salle à manger," II-166–67
Salon des Refusés, I-42
Salt Hill Park, Slough (location), II-148
"salt of the earth," I-212; II-96, 98
"Saltzberg," I-96, 104–5; II-204
Samuel, Lord Herbert, I-196; II-85
samurai (and samurai films), I-54, 289, 302,
    304, 350, 405; II-100, 221
sandalwood, I-274
Sandhurst. *See* Royal Military Academy at
    Sandhurst
Santayana, George, I-44
"Sapper," II-147
sarcasm, I-88, 226, 234
Sardinia, II-118
Sarris, Andrew, I-366

Sartre, Jean-Paul (and "Sartrean"), I-12, 27,
    35, 38, 43, 85, 146, 161, 201, 208, 333, 386,
    410; II-3–5, 8–18, 34, 53, 79, 83, 96, 130,
    135, 175–76, 188–89, 194, 226
Sassoon, Vidal, II-68, 74
satire/satirize, I-15–16, 18, 29, 32, 35, 37, 38,
    40, 41, 43, 47, 49, 54, 56, 57, 60, 66, 67, 75,
    80, 83, 84, 87, 88, 92, 95, 101, 105, 119, 122,
    138, 141, 145–47, 156–59, 163–64, 174, 184,
    188, 195, 199, 214, 225, 229, 230, 232–34,
    236, 244, 249, 259, 262, 267, 269, 274, 286,
    294, 298, 299, 301, 306–7, 318, 329, 342,
    343, 363, 369, 373, 384, 412; II-6, 24, 30, 52,
    57, 59, 61, 62, 63, 67, 70–71, 86, 87, 88, 97,
    99, 103, 104, 114, 123–24, 141, 155, 157, 73,
    178, 199, 205, 210, 228
Saturday Night and Sunday Morning. See
    films
Sauna Belt, Inc. (and Trim-Jeans), II-13,
    20–21, 24–27, 29–30, 34, 37–38, 104, 229
Savage, Richard. *See* novelists/prose writers
"Save the Argylls," I-168, 386
Savundra, Emil, I-267–68, 275
Saxby and Farmer, I-196
"Saxe-Coburg," II-98, 128, 134, 171
Saxmundham, Suffolk, (location), I-4, 48,
    157, 162, 295
"Saxones," I-207; II-72–73
Sayes Court Fields, Addlestone, Surrey
    (location), I-157
"scar," I-256
Scarfe, Gerald, I-80, 251, 343
The Scarlet Pimpernel. See novels
Schechner, Richard, I-101
Schell, Maxmilian, I-354
Schenck, Joseph M., I-381
Schlesinger, John, I-304
"Schnapps With Everything," I-332
Schreyvogel, Charles and *Early Dawn Attack.*
    See artists *and* artworks
Schubert, Franz, and Robert Schumann, I-94;
    II-33
Schwitters, Kurt. *See* artists
science fiction genre. *See* film genres
Science Museum of London, I-246
scorn/ridicule/derision, I-19, 30, 58, 76, 87,
    105, 175, 178, 183, 193, 196, 198–99, 225,
    233–34, 255, 260, 267, 286, 296, 316, 318,
    322, 332, 334, 337, 353, 366; II-55, 59, 70,
    85, 97, 103, 153, 172, 182, 206, 207,
Scotland/Scotsmen, I-xii, 12, 17, 18, 23, 26,
    38, 43, 44, 73, 81, 85, 92, 93, 96, 104, 105,
    107, 110, 112–117, 119, 120–23, 134, 135,
    137, 141, 157, 166, 168, 193, 210, 225, 233,
    254, 256–58, 261, 262, 270, 272, 314, 328,
    331, 333, 336, 345–46, 353, 354, 388, 389,
    400–4, 408–10, 412–13; II-xii, 9, 12, 18, 22,
    23, 27, 28, 35, 44, 46, 53, 58, 65, 69–70, 77,
    78, 80, 82, 92, 114, 115, 116, 125, 139, 140,
    141, 143, 144, 145, 147, 149, 161, 163, 167,
    170, 174, 197, 208, 217, 224, 225, 226, 228,
    229
Scotland Yard, I-18, 19, 52, 62, 176, 233, 291;
    II-44, 114, 125
"Scots Guards," I-58, 137, 219, 220
"scots pine." *See* trees

Scott, Bill and Jay Ward. *See Rocky and Bullwinkle*

Scott, Peter, I-177; II-50, 58, 59, 142, 201

Scott, Robert Falcon, I-169, 353, 355, 357; II-59

Scott, Robin, II-88

Scott, Sir Walter. *See* novelists/prose writers

Scottish National Party, I-194, 296, 302, 307

Scoular, Angela, I-251

Scowcroft, Philip, I-370

Screen. See magazines

Scriblerus Club, I-19, 153

"scudding clouds," I-381

sculptures. *See* artworks

"scuppers," II-35

Seaford Cliffs, Seaford (location), I-246, 345

Seagoon, Neddie. *See The Goon Show*

The Seagull, Anton Chekhov. *See* plays *and* playwrights

Seberg, Jean, I-354

Secombe, Harry, I-4, 20, 21, 58, 69, 72, 84, 94, 106, 114, 128, 170, 179, 221, 238, 255, 268, 313, 365, 381; II-22, 29, 86, 207

Second Armoured Division, I-347

"Second Cuppa," I-216

"second form," I-212

Securicor, II-134

Seeger, Pete, I-75

Selfridges, I-322

Sellers, Peter, I-4, 7, 20, 29, 34, 38, 55, 57, 58, 60, 67, 72, 91, 96, 116, 128, 136, 163, 186, 207, 213, 216, 221, 238, 255, 260, 268, 270, 307, 313, 322, 353, 354, 356, 365, 381; II-18, 29, 58, 60, 75, 108, 126

Selznick, David O., II-74, 126

semaphore code, I-xii, 240, 248–49, 251, 412; II-xii, 114, 164, 201, 228

"semi-detached." *See* housing

Semprini, A.F.R., I-272, 274–75

Sennett, Mack. *See* Keystone Cops

"Sensible Party," I-289, 296, 305, 408

"sent off," II-192

serializations, I-7, 70, 73, 117–19, 204, 238; II-4, 75, 77, 80, 92, 151, 164, 166, 168, 197, 223

Seuss, Doctor (Theodor Geisel), I-147–48, 175; II-6

Seven Brides for Seven Brothers. See films

The Seven Years' War, I-25; II-133

The Seventh Seal. See films

79 Stebbing House, Hammersmith and Fulham (location), II-118

sex/sexuality, I-7, 10, 22, 26–29, 32–35, 37–38, 40, 45, 47, 49, 53, 58, 59, 60, 62, 65–66, 71, 73, 79–81, 88–90, 92, 96–97, 99, 103, 105, 107, 108, 110–13, 115–16, 120, 125, 127–28, 131, 132, 138–40, 143–44, 145, 147–51, 153, 160–63, 166–67, 178, 181, 186, 192–93, 198, 203, 207, 209–11, 213, 222–27, 229–30, 232–33, 238, 242–43, 250, 252, 258–59, 261, 265–66, 272, 276, 284–89, 291, 297–98, 306, 309, 318, 321–22, 323, 328–29, 331–33, 338, 340–41, 345–46, 350, 353, 357–58, 361–62, 364–67, 369, 375, 378, 406, 412; II-

"sex kitten," I-233

Sexual Offences Act of 1967, I-203, 289

Seymour, Gerald, I-320

"Shabby, Ken," I-150, 184, 186, 189, 192, 196–98, 246, 274, 282, 331, 360, 410; II-184, 226

Shackleton, Sir Earnest, I-150

Shadow Cabinet. *See* ministerial positions

"shadow minister." *See* ministerial positions

Shaftesbury Avenue, I-343

Shaindlin, Jack, I-60, 107, 108, 223, 265, 391, 399–404; II-66, 88, 215–20

Shakespeare, William (and Shakespearean), I-xi, xiii, 6, 13, 15, 18, 21, 23–24, 26, 36, 38, 43, 46, 53–54, 55, 57, 59–61, 63, 66, 70, 76, 82, 92, 99, 113, 124, 140, 169, 175, 187, 206, 211–12, 215, 229, 244, 265, 271, 277, 286, 299, 327, 328, 332, 336, 345, 350, 371, 374, 380, 381, 400, 405, 406; II-xi, xiii, 5, 9, 22, 28, 38, 50, 56, 62, 70, 74, 106, 112, 121, 122–23, 126, 131, 151, 166, 167, 170, 187–90, 192–93, 207, 216, 221, 222. *See also* plays

Shaoqi, Liu, I-358

Shand, Neil, I-304

Shane. See films

"Shangri-La Style," II-74

Shanklin, Isle of Wight, II-195, 199

Sharif, Omar, II-30, 62

Shaw, George Bernard. *See* playwrights

Shaw, Joe, I-304

Shaw, Robert, I-157

Shawn, Dick, I-67

"Shazam," II-35

Shearman, Russell, I-359

"sheepdip," I-347

Sheffield, South Yorkshire, I-49, 62, 82, 267, 274, 304; II-25, 206

"Sheila," I-347

Shell Oil. *See* commercials/adverts

Shelley, Percy, I-275; II-172, 176

Shepherd's Bush, Hammersmith and Fulham, I-60, 81, 84, 132, 226, 374, 383; II-32, 99, 121, 148

Sheppard, David, I-266, 368

Shepperton (Film Library and Studio), I-395; II-211

Sheridan, Richard Brinsley. *See* playwrights

Sheridan's grocery, II-11

Sherlock, David, I-212; II-64, 152

Sherman, Bobby, II-205

Sherman, Brig. Gen. Thomas W., I-386

Sherrin, Ned, I-88, 211, 271; II-46, 105

sherry, I-30, 89, 145, 213, 275, 347, 412; II-121, 127, 128, 131, 228

Sherwood, Sheila, I-174

shibboleth, I-135

"shit." *See* slang/slurs/idioms

"shock" (in comedy), I-22, 68, 124, 140, 150, 153, 158, 162, 164, 167, 178, 350; II-163, 178

Shock, Joan, I-116

"the shops," I-102, 213, 276, 336; II-66, 146, 199

Shoreham, I-254, 285

Showboat. See plays

Shrewsbury School, Liverpool, I-216, 305

"Shrill Petrol." *See* commercials/adverts

Shuster, Joseph, I-60

Shute, Nevil. *See* novelists/prose writers

Sicily, I-168; II-46

Sickert, W.P. *See* artists

Sidcup, II-156

Sidney, Sir Philip, I-71, 113, 410; II-99, 121, 123–29, 138, 226

Siegel, "Bugsy," I-334

Siegel, Jerry, I-60

Sielmann, Heinz, II-42, 59, 60

"sight gags," I-47; II-137

signalboxes, I-184–85, 192, 196–97, 211, 411, 412

Silbury Dig (and Hill), I-328, 330–31, 336–37

"silliness," I-6, 19, 29, 40, 52, 53, 57, 79, 82, 85, 87, 91, 105, 115, 118, 120, 127, 131–32, 136–37, 139, 148, 151, 154–56, 161, 164–65, 172, 175–76, 184, 187, 190–93, 197, 201, 221, 225–26, 234, 235, 252, 268, 280, 286–87, 289, 292, 295, 298, 300, 304–9, 327, 352, 362, 377, 381–82, 384, 388–90, 408, 410–13; II-16, 18, 26, 34, 38, 40, 51, 53, 56, 58, 70, 78, 115–16, 121, 124, 140, 143, 144, 147, 149, 157, 164, 168, 180, 182, 192, 196, 224, 226–29

"silly bunt." *See* slang/slurs/idioms

"Silly Party." *See* political parties

Silver, Long John. *See* pantomime: characters

Silver Rose. *See* Montreux

Silwood Park, I-285

Simpson, Dorothy Raynes, II-62

Simpson, O.J., I-355

Simpson, Wallis, II-18

Sinatra, Frank, I-65, 255, 333; II-123, 188, 192

sinecure, I-279, 361, 369; II-88

"Sir Ambrose Fleming Memorial Award," I-302

"Sir Gerald." *See* Gerald Nabarro

Sistine Chapel, I-301; II-44

Six Characters in Search of an Author. See plays

16 Maddox Street, London, I-215

16mm cameras/film, I-153, 251, 275, 284, 292; II-24, 52

60 Uxbridge Road, London (Ealing Fire Station), I-139

60b Victoria Road South, Southsea, Portsmouth (location), I-143

64–65 Princes Square, London (location), I-69

67 Broughton Avenue, Ham, Richmond, Surrey (location), I-286

"slit up a treat" ("slit your face"). *See* slang/slurs/idioms

skinheads, I-99, 128, 136, 138, 139, 144, 305

Skybolt, I-63

Skye Cottage Museum, I-115, 120, 123, 254. *See also* museums

Slade (band), I-148

Slade House (location), I-92, 189, 233, 252

Slade Professor of Fine Art, Oxford, II-136

Slade, Julian. *See* playwrights

slang/slurs/idioms: "a bit flash," II-195; "Abbos," I-339; "bag," I-127; "bally," I-157, 253; II-185; "bang," I-143; "bashing," I-339, 340, 407; "bent," I-328; II-96; "bird," I-144; II-122; "bird lime," II-122; "bit crook," I-340; "a bit of tail,"

I-223; II-95; "Blighty," I-373; "blimey," I-5, 50, 128; "bog," II-63; "botty," I-29, 273, 370; "bother," I-128; "botherkins," I-202; "briny," II-183; "Bristols," I-291, 302; "Bubbles," I-139; "bugger," I-242–43, 328; II-178; "bum," I-29, 379, 393; "bunt," I-193; I-70; "butch" (*see* homosexuality); "cake hole," I-186; "camp" (*see* camp/ campiness); "cave," I-387; "cheek(y)," I-34, 50, 53, 279, 280, 329; II-95; "cheesed off," II-5; "Chinks," II-139; "chuffed," II-5; "clap," I-362; II-151; "clever dick," I-66; "codgers," I-166, 386; "coon," I-186; II-31; "cottaging," II-36; "crumb bum," I-351; "crumpet," I-316; "dagos," I-131; II-65, 139; "darkies," I-104, 131, 315; II-31; "dead butch" (*see* homosexuality); "dicky birdie," II-185; "dinna," I-115; "divvy," I-253, 254; "dolly bird," I-160; "done over," I-130; "eyeties," I-131; II-139; "fairy" (*see* fairy); "festering gob," II-44; "fag," I-255; "finger out," I-352, 359; "fiver," I-189, 228; II-38; "flog back," I-294; "foul the foot," I-98; "Froggy," I-157, 161; II-139; "fruit," I-160; II-95; "gammy," I-162, 389; "get knotted," I-363; "Gippos," II-139; "git," I-331, 410; "gob," I-186, 189, 331; II-44; "grotty," I-162; "han," I-132; "hairy blighter," II-185; "How's your father?," II-185; "innit," I-85, 128, 134; "jacksey," II-208; "Jerry," II-26, 185; "Jocks," II-139; "ken," I-118; "kipping," I-19, 134, 207; "kit(ted)," I-100, 141, 177, 262, 317; "kite," II-185; "knockers," I-271; II-68; "Krauts," II-138, 183; "ligging around," II-45; "lolly," I-69, 386; II-45; "loo," I-168; II-12; "merde," II-12; "mince," I-160, 284, 341, 345; II-95, 112; "m'lud," I-56, 247; "muggins," I-208; "mush," I-259, 272; II-55; "nicked," II-46; "Nigs," II-138; "nip," I-120; II-46; "No fear!," I-232; "Paddies," II-139; "parky," II-174; "piddles," I-103; " pillock," I-284, 288; II-167; "pinch," I-112, 121, 124; "pinko," I-103; "pinny," I-210; "pluck," I-80, 110, 121, 122, 195, 254, 314, 389; "plumped," I-273; "Polacks," II-139; "ponce," I-34, 41, 131, 148, 151, 183, 193, 341; II-26, 72, 74, 206; "poof(tah)," I-10, 49, 148, 151, 157, 237, 284, 327, 329, 345–46, 411; II-9, 27, 31, 32, 47, 95, 130, 140–41, 222; "prang," II-185; "pule," II-72; "pulling the birds," I-167; "queen," I-58, 166, 205, 335; II-24; "quid," I-273, 346, 357; "rat-bag," I-151, 260, 335; II-135; "ratty," I-346; II-13; "safe as houses," I-347; "sap," I-196; "scrofulous," I-89; II-88; "semitic," I-304; "Semprini," I-272, 274–75; "shagged out," I-139; "shirty," I-180; "shit," I-160, 344; II-12, 43, 167, 175, 178; "shtoom," I-235; II-118; "skint," I-262; "skivers," II-137; "smartarse," II-167; "smegma," I-369; "snogging," I-105–6, 372; II-188; "spotty sassenach pillock," II-167; "sod," I-20, 267, 336, 343; II-73, 178; "sodding," II-73, 178; "spotted prancer," I-284;

"square-bashing," I-339, 340; "sticky beak," I-347; "Strewth," I-20, 45; II-209; "stroppy," I-170; "swag," I-107; II-130, 138; "swanning about," I-329, 339, 341, 347, 407; "swish," I-102, 153, 230, 238, 356; II-41, 46, 55; "tadger," II-198; "tart," I-140; "tatty," II-88; "tit," I-46; II-44, 186; "toffee-nosed," II-44; "top-hole," II-185; "trollope," I-288; "tuck in," I-394; "tuts," I-182; "tweedy," I-38, 170; "wee wee," I-276, 284; "weedy," I-108, 333; "winkle," I-246; "wop," I-104, 131, 309; II-31, 46, 138; "yah boo," I-380; "Yidds," II-139

Slater, Lt. Comm. Jock, I-388
"Slater Nazi," II-50, 59, 109, 226
Slim Inn, I-215
Slipper, Jack, I-18, 100, 177
Sloan, Tom, I-35
Slough, Berkshire, I-369; II-55, 148
"slow-motion." *See MPFC* production elements
"Smith, Arthur J." I-305
Smith, Benjamin, I-217
Smith, Cyril, II-209
Smith, Harvey, II-31–32, 36
Smith, Herbert Vernon "Bounder," II-63
Smith, Ian, I-59, 168, 389; II-36, 56, 66–67, 72–73, 208–9,
"Smith Major," I-287, 294
"Smith, Sidney," I-305
Smithson, Alison and Peter, I-267
Smollett. Tobias. *See* novelists/prose writers
The Smothers Brothers, I-75
Snagge, John, II-51
Snoopy. *See* "Peanuts"
Snowdon, Lord (Antony Armstrong-Jones), I-184–85, 255, 305; II-52
"soap powder." *See* commercials/adverts
"Sochnadale" and *Thorstein Staff-Struck*, II-7
Society of Film and Television Arts, II-151–52
Socrate, Mario, I-207
"sod." *See* slang/slurs/idioms
"sodomitical," I-111, 128, 151, 242, 288; II-127, 182–83. *See also* sex/sexuality
"soft sell," I-369
Soho, I-32, 157, 210, 213, 216, 225–26, 232, 237, 268, 321–22; II-63, 66, 123–27, 188; "walk-ups," I-65–66, 213
Solomon, I-55, 381, 390; II-18
Solti, George, II-23
Solzhenitsyn, Aleksandr. *See* novelists/prose writers
"Someone Else I'd Like to Be," I-60, 273, 399
Somerset, I-186, 193, 197–98, 325; II-41, 108, 119, 138
Somerset House, the Strand, I-66, 197; II-46–47
Sons and Lovers. See films
Sopwith, Sir Thomas, and the Sopwith Camel, I-123
Sotheby's, I-371, 381, 412
Sound of Music. See films (US)
Sousa, John Philip, I-13, 15, 154, 338, 399, 400, 402–3; II-138, 195, 215, 216, 218–19. *See also* "Liberty Bell March"

South Africa. *See* Africa
"South African Test," I-317
South America, I-63, 97, 104, 148, 165, 233, 362, 382, 387, 397; II-29, 36, 47, 172, 178, 213; states: Argentina, I-93, 113; II-192; Bolivia, I-379; II-36, 99; Brazil, I-104, 191, 233, 279, 384; II-29, 36, 47; Chile, II-36, 83, 192; Ecuador, II-36; Guyana, I-322; II-47; Paraguay, II-36, 116; Peru, II-27, 29; Uruguay, II-36, 99; Venezuela, I-382; II-32, 36, 47, 98
"South Col," II-73
South East Gas Holders (location), II-162
South Shields, Tyne and Wear, II-206
Southall, Greater London, I-233; II-151
Southampton, Hampshire, I-158, 228, 397; II-87, 138, 154, 182, 213
Southcott, Joanna, I-323
Southern Television. *See* regional television
Southern, Terry, I-38, 40, 329; II-55, 127, 200
Southey, Robert and *Life of Nelson*, I-14
Southmere Terrace, Bradford (location), I-xii, 121, 137
"southpaw," I-287
Southwark, Greater London, I-235–36, 293, 361; II-12, 125
Southwold, Suffolk, I-43, 55, 157
Soviet Bloc. *See* Russia
Soviet Union. *See* Russia
Spade, Sam and *The Maltese Falcon*, I-335
"Spam," I-323, 325, 371, 381, 412; II-132, 168, 228
Spaniel, Mugsy, I-327, 334, 406
The Spanish Armada (and Main), I-169, 176, 381–82; II-43, 44, 122
The Spanish Inquisition, I-xii, 240, 244–45, 248, 249–50, 251, 275
"Spanish practices," I-249
"Spanish tummy," II-73
Spartacus International Gay Guide, I-306
"Special Branch," I-305
"Special Operations Fraud Squad," II-44
The Spectator. See magazines
Speech Day, I-305
Speer, Albert, I-178
Spencer, Herbert, I-313
Spenser, Edmund. *See* poets
The Spider's Web, Christie. *See* plays *and* playwrights
Spim, Roy and Hank, I-336, 348
Spinetti, Victor, I-32
"Spiny Norman," I-12, 221, 236, 237, 300, 392–93, 412; II-152, 228
Spitz, Mark, II-192
"Spode," I-232
spontaneous human combustion, II-32
"Spoonerism," II-59
Sportpalast, I-191, 198
Sportsview. See television shows
"Springbok," I-173, 318, 347
"sprocket holes," II-39
Spycatcher. See television shows
squatting, I-201, 203–4, 208, 211, 214, 224–25, 411; II-203, 204, 227
"Squiffy," II-184
Squire Records shop, I-128

Staffordshire, I-146, 287
Stag at Bay, Landseer. *See* artworks
Staines Recreation Ground (location), I-122;
    II-200
Stalag-Luft III, I-281–82; II-27; "Tom, Dick
    and Harry" tunnels, I-282
Stalin, Josef, I-379, 392; II-16, 71, 101, 105–9
Stalingrad, I-189, 199
Stamford, John, I-297, 306
"Stan the Bat," II-34–35
"Stand and Deliver!" II-137
Stanfield, W.C. and "1805 Trafalga." *See*
    artists *and* artworks
Stanford Training Area, West Tofts Camp,
    Norfolk (location), I-341, 392
Stanmore, Greater London, II-200
Stanshall, Vivian Anthony, I-199
"star prize," I-324, 268, 372–73, 379
"Star Spangled Banner," I-264, 401; II-138,
    217
Starewicz, Ladislaw, I-87
Starr, Hattie, I-303, 306
Starr, Ringo. *See* MPFC extras and walk-ons
Starrett, Joey, I-33
"Stars and Stripes Forever," II-138, 195, 215
"starter for ten," I-382
Stebbing House, Edward Woods Estate,
    Hammersmith and Fulham (location),
    II-118
Steele, Tommy, I-106
Stein, Gertrude. *See* novelists/prose writers
Stein, Jock, I-180
Steinbeck, John. *See* authors
Steiner, Max, I-212, 400
Stephens, Rev. Ronald, II-38
Stepney, Greater London, II-198
Steptoe and Son. See television shows
stereotypes/types, I-xi, 4, 9, 13–14, 27, 30–31,
    35, 38, 42–44, 47, 49, 74–75, 77, 89–90, 100,
    103, 105, 107, 118, 119, 120, 122, 123, 128,
    145–46, 148, 156–57, 159, 167, 168, 170,
    172, 177, 183, 187, 194, 209, 231–33, 237,
    243, 248, 250, 257, 258, 263, 265, 279, 282,
    285, 288, 295, 304, 306, 317, 320, 322, 324,
    329, 345, 346, 352, 367, 370–72, 378–79,
    381, 384, 386; II-xi, 23–24, 27, 31, 42, 45,
    49, 51, 65, 79, 87, 96, 97, 102, 112, 115, 121,
    136, 148–49, 153, 155, 178, 189, 190, 201,
    207, 209
"Stetson," I-89
Stevenson, Justice Melford, I-229
Stevenson, Robert Louis. *See* novelists
Stewart, Avril (and Ian), I-386
Stewart, James (Jimmy), I-303; II-72, 94
Stewart, Michael, I-347
"Stig," I-89, 155, 161, 357–58
stoat. *See* animals
"Stoat, Dame Irene." *See* poets
stock film (film clips), I-xii, 4, 20, 45, 49, 59,
    123, 170, 173, 192, 287, 312, 315, 323, 354,
    357, 369, 377, 382, 395–98; II-22, 48, 65, 73,
    83, 84, 87, 95, 108, 127, 148, 184, 185, 201,
    211–14. *See also* Appendix A
stock music (live and recorded music cues),
    I-265, 399–404; II-22, 215–20. *See also* light
    music *and* Appendix B

Stockwell, Dean, I-39
Stogumber, Somerset, I-187
Stoker, Bram, I-381
"stone," I-213, 280; II-197
Stone, F.J., II-15
Stonehenge, I-201, 234, 412, 413; II-202, 205,
    207, 209, 228, 229
Stoneman, Brig Gen. George, I-292, 298
Stonewall Riots, I-7
"stopped economy," I-237
Storey, David. *See* novelists *and* playwrights
Stork margarine, I-24; II-38
Stott, Wally (Angela Morley), II-8, 218
"straight fight," I-306
The Strand, I-66, 311, 343; II-47
Stratford-on-Avon, I-286; II-121
Stravinsky, Igor, II-195
"stream-of-consciousness," I-xii, 25, 73, 189;
    II-xii, 80, 93, 181
Street Offences Act of 1959, I-226
Streisand, Barbra, I-343
"stretching owls," I-45, 67
"Strewth!" *See* slang/slurs/idioms
strike actions, I-15, 70, 77, 165, 253, 256, 289,
    394, 371–76, 383–84, 386, 388–90, 391–92,
    394, 406, 409, 411; II-21, 26, 29, 44, 67–68,
    72, 81–83, 86, 88, 104, 141, 190, 199, 222,
    225, 227. *See also* organized labor *and*
    trade unions
"string remained confident," II-17
"string vest," I-393; II-27
structuralists, I-342
Stuart, Gloria, I-120
Stuarts, I-151, 345; II-127, 128, 167
Studio Theatre Club, II-21
"sub-aqua," II-88
"suburban fin-de-siecle ennui," I-46, 89
Sudetenland, I-198; II-41
Sues, Alan, II-24
Suez (Canal and Crisis), I-136, 188; II-89, 95,
    162
Suffolk, I-4, 55, 75, 86, 134, 157, 161, 291, 295;
    II-15
"Suffragan or diocesan?" II-48
suffragettes, I-17, 185, 318
sumptuary laws, I-151
Sunleys (London) Ltd., I-209
Sunlight Soap, I-262
"Super Shell with Platformate." *See*
    commercials/adverts
Superboy, I-60
Superman, I-50, 53, 55, 60, 107, 406
"Support Rhodesia," I-168
Surbiton, Kingston upon Thames, I-14, 393,
    406, 408; II-20, 29, 36–37, 67, 117, 222, 224
"surgical garment," I-385, 390, 406
Surrealism. *See* art: movements
Surrey, I-4, 10, 12, 15, 21, 24, 58, 59, 62, 80,
    83, 96, 100, 102, 108, 157, 159, 162, 175,
    178 192, 226, 261, 285, 286, 287, 294, 316,
    333, 340, 364, 370, 393, 394; II-12, 13, 32,
    62, 63, 96, 174, 189, 199, 201, 209
Sutton, Greater London, I-364; II-189, 201
Swadlincote, Derbyshire, II-133
Swahili, I-153
Swanage, Dorset, I-337

Swanborough, I-364
Swansea, Wales, I-53, 60, 113, 324, 353; II-69,
    70
Swanton, E.W. "Jim." *See* cricket
"sward," II-138
"Swedish businessmen," II-190
"Sweet Thames, run softly…," II-30
swearing/invectives. *See* slang/slurs/idioms
Sweeney Todd, I-146
"Swell's Goody," I-69, 393
Swift, Jonathan. *See* poets
Swinburne, Algernon. *See* poets
Swindon, Wiltshire, I-146, 159, 364, 390
"swing" (political), I-279, 296–97, 306; II-180,
    206; "swingometer," I-297, 306
"Switched On," I-10, 208
"Sydney Harbour Bridge," I-347
symphony (and orchestras), I-5, 16, 182, 209,
    237, 327, 331, 334, 393, 399–403; II-25–26,
    35, 55, 86, 108, 124, 138 154, 157, 165, 168,
    182, 196, 215–19

tableaux vivants, I-8, 44, 144
Take Your Pick. See televisions shows
A Tale of Two Cities. See Dickens *and* novels
talent (job) agencies, I-xii, 38, 72, 268, 270,
    341, 363, 413; II-98, 106
"tam-o'-shanter," II-167
Tangiers, I-102
tannoy, II-37
Tanzania. *See* Commonwealth nations
"tarn," I-256
"tassles," II-37
Tate Galleries. *See* art: galleries
Tati, Jacques, I-65
Tatum, Michael George, II-188
Taunton, I-187, 198; II-108
Tavistock, I-206, 253; II-108, 193
taxes/taxation, I-86, 88, 90, 91, 95, 104, 122,
    159, 160, 188, 225, 237, 240, 243–45, 259,
    265, 294, 301, 319, 341, 376, 393, 412, 413;
    II-4, 7, 11, 55, 58, 83, 137, 148, 194, 228,
    229; "tax freedom day," I-250
"Taxman," The Beatles, I-225
Taylor, A.J.P., I-147, 174–75, 178, 179, 181–82,
    186, 368; II-205
Taylor, Dan, II-83
Taylor, Dr. John, I-336
Taylor, John Russell, I-354
Taylor, Tony, I-82
Tchaikovsky, Peter Ilyich, I-182, 272, 400,
    402, 404, 413; II-24, 25–35, 37, 38, 216, 218,
    220, 229
"tea boy," I-21
"Teasy Weasy" Butler, I-232; II-68, 74
Technicolor, I-123, 374, 395
Teddington Lock, Richmond upon Thames
    (location), I-32
Teddy Boys, I-103, 134, 136
Telefunken, I-182
television shows: France/Italy: *Jeux Sans
    Frontieres*, I-23; *World Without Sun*, II-60;
    Germany: *Beat Club*, I-333; UK (Britain):
    About Homes and Gardens, II-13; *The
    Adventures of Long John Silver*, *The
    Adventures of Robin Hood*, *The Adventures*

of the Scarlet Pimpernel, and *The Adventures of Sir Lancelot*, II-8; *Aladdin*, I-86; *Alice in Wonderland*, II-34; *All Gas and Gaiters*, I-380; *An Age of Kings*, I-345; *And Mother Makes Three*, II-178; *Animal, Vegetable, Mineral?*, I-329; *Apollo 11—Man on the Moon*, II-37; *Are You Being Served?*, II-95, 179, 197; *The Ascent of Man*, I-340; II-201; *At Last the 1948 Show* (*see At Last the 1948 Show*); *Babes in the Wood*, I-386; *Barlow at Large*, I-381; II-171, 179; *The Basil Brush Show*, II-51; *BBC-3*, II-87; *BBC Election 70*, I-293, 300; *The Bedsit Girl*, I-380; *Before the Fringe*, I-202; *The Benny Hill Show*, I-52, 106, 115, 154, 175–76, 202, 203, 210, 238, 248, 275, 280, 329, 330, 342, 382, 393; II-85, 97, 125, 139, 151, 154, 171, 173, 183; *Beryl Reid Says Good Evening*, I-202; *The Black and White Minstrel Show*, I-24, 104, 313; II-42, 180, 209; *The Black Arrow*, II-8; *The Blackpool Show*, II-179; *Blakes 7*, II-163, 179, 189; *Blandings Castle*, I-380; *Blue Peter*, I-99, 168; II-22, 27; *The Borderers*, II-43, 133; *Boy Meets Girl*, I-297; *The Brains Trust*, I-156, 340; II-124; *Brett*, I-241, 378; *The Brontes of Haworth*, II-133; "The British Screen Awards: A Gala Night for Television and Film," II-5, 151–52, 156, 178; *The Bruce Forsythe Show*, I-283; *The Buccaneers*, II-8; *The Caesars*, I-370; *Call My Bluff*, II-122; *Casanova*, I-269; II-43, 68; *The Children of the New Forest*, II-8; *A Christmas Night With the Stars*, I-207, 217; *Chronicle*, I-328–29, 333, 336; II-44; *Cinderella*, I-86; *Cinema*, I-194; *Civilization* (*see* Sir Kenneth Clark); *Classic Serial*, II-76, 80, 164, 273; *Clochemerle*, II-4, 112; *Cluff*, I-176; *Colditz*, II-43, 49, 104, 142, 197; *Come Dancing*, I-320–21; II-151; *Complete and Utter History of Britain*, I-291; II-32, 131; *Coronation Street*, I-150, 297; *The Count of Monte Cristo*, II-8; *Crackerjack*, II-71; *Crossroads*, II-178, 207; *Crown Court*, II-4; *Culloden*, I-102; *Dad's Army*, I-5, 86, 151, 192, 228, 297, 302, 314, 318; II-141, 143, 154, 178, 179, 180, 182, 184; "Dad's Doctors," II-140, 143, 222, 223; "Dad's Navy," II-178; "Dad's Pooves," I-97, 151, 406, 407; II-140, 141, 154, 222, 223; *Dante's Inferno* (*Omnibus*), II-34; *Dateline*, I-314; *David Copperfield*, II-201; *The David Frost Show*, I-292, 299, 309; *Department S*, II-139; *The Des O'Connor Show*, I-243, 388; *Dick Barton*, I-204, 244; II-172; *The Dick Emery Show*, I-102, 141; *Dick Whittington*, I-86; *Dixon of Dock Green* (*see* Dixon of Dock Green); "Doctor at Bee" and "Doctor at Cake," II-178; *Doctor at Large*, II-147, 178; "Doctor at Three," II-178; *Doctor in Charge*, II-25, 144, 146, 152, 178; *Doctor in Love*, II-202; *Doctor in the House*, I-161, 197, 198, 231, 241, 291, 379; II-25, 64, 113, 118, 152, 178, 179; *Do Not Adjust Your Set*, I-7, 16, 102, 148, 160, 199, 275, 280, 291; II-86, 163, 197; *Double Your Money*, I-179; *Dr. Finlay's Casebook*, I-115, 388; *Doctor*

Who, I-16, 51, 61, 88, 105, 115, 141, 145, 161, 168, 175, 176, 227, 231, 241, 264, 272, 296, 297, 314, 318, 330, 343, 363, 378, 379, 381, 388; II-5, 12, 23, 25, 43, 49, 55, 81, 93, 95, 104, 106, 113, 118, 123, 142, 152, 163, 166, 171, 173, 179, 189; *The Eamonn Andrews Show*, I-386; II-34, 71; *Edward II*, I-257; *The Edwardians*, I-248; *Elizabeth R*, II-43; *The Elusive Pimpernel*, II-82; *Emma*, I-105, 145, 241, 259, 268, 302; II-25, 81, 95, 171; *The Engelbert Humperdinck Show*, I-282, 297; *Engelbert with the Young Generation*, II-133, 171; *Engines Must Not Enter the Potato Siding*, I-197; *Epilogue*, I-32, 38; *Euroshow 71—May Day Special*, I-xii, 70, 86, 128, 139, 173, 186, 224, 261, 264, 286, 340; II-xii, 32–33, 52, 84, 88, 166; *Eurovision Song Contest*, I-94, 147, 152, 258, 285, 378; II-30, 34, 107, 144, 201; *The Fabulous Frump*, I-270, 302; *Face the Music*, II-202; *Face to Face*, I-228; *The Fall and Rise of Reginald Perrin*, II-163, 179, 189, 197; *The Family*, II-203, 205; "Fate of the Armada" (*Chronicle*), II-44; *Father, Dear Father*, II-145; *Fawlty Towers*, I-146, 188, 246; II-5, 8, 161; *Film; Film Night*, I-356; II-95; *The Forsyte Saga*, I-331, 335; II-61; *The Frankie Howerd Show*, II-145; *The Frighteners*, II-4; *Frontiers of Science*, II-143; *The Frost Programme*, I-; 268, 292, 295, 297, 302; II-134; *The Frost Report*, I-15, 61, 77, 94, 134, 159, 202, 282, 292, 295; *The Gang Show Gala*, II-75; *Gardening Club* and *Gardening World*, II-44; "George I," II-136; *Girl Talk*, I-335; *Going For a Song*, I-302; *The Goodies*, I-67, 269; II-35, 55, 76, ; *Goodies Rule—OK?*, I-55; *Grandstand*, II-113; *The Great Store Robbery*, I-322; *The Guardians*, I-227, 231; *Guess My Story*, I-321; *Halesapoppin!*, I-117; *Half Hour Story*, I-388; *Hancock's Half Hour*, I-258; II-207; *The Happiest Days of Your Life*, I-388–89; *Hawkeye and the Last of the Mohicans* (Canada/UK), I-105; *Hearts and Flowers*, I-61; *H.G. Wells' Invisible Man*, I-178; *Hitchhiker's Guide to the Galaxy*, II-202; *Horne A'Plenty*, II-95; *Horse of the Year Show*, II-20, 27, 186, 198, 225; *How*, II-27; *How to Irritate People*, I-77, 85, 189; *Humpty Dumpty*, I-86; *Ian McKellen as John Keats*, I-257; *Idle at Work*, I-295; *It's a Knockout*, I-13, 19, 23, 163, 299, 313; II-28, 35, 144; *It's a Long Way to Transylvania*, and *It's a Man's World*, I-163; *It's a Square World*, II-28; *It's a Woman's World* and *It's Dark Outside*, I-163; *It's Marty*, I-161; *It's Only Us*, I-163; II-28; *It's Sad About Eddie*, and *It's Sunday Night*, I-163; *It's the Bachelors*, II-55; *It's the Mind*, I-252, 257, 258, 409; *ITV News*, II-148; *ITV Seven*, II-151, 153; *Ivor the Engine*, I-174; *Jackanory*, II-80, 81, 113, 123, 133, 142, 162, 189; *Jason King*, II-139; *The Jimmy Logan Show*, I-335; *Jim's Inn*, II-13; *Joint Account*, I-161; *Jude the Obscure*, II-151; *Juke Box Jury*, I-163; *Just a Minute*, I-183; II-208;

"Ken Russell's Gardening Club," II-40, 44, 57, 65, 226; *The Kenneth Williams Show*, I-160; *Late Night Line-Up*, I-80, 82, 223, 299, 351, 366; II-75; *Law and Order*, II-81; *Lights of London: Part 1*, II-113, 118; "Limestone, Dear Limestone," II-145; *Liver Birds*, I-300; II-179; *London: A New Look*, I-294; *Lord Peter Whimsey*, II-4; *The Lost World of the Kalahari*, II-143, 203; *Love Thy Neighbour*, II-4; *Magpie*, II-15; *Man About the House*, II-43; *Man Alive*, I-136, 137, 138, 183, 283, 290, 316; II-50; *Man on the Moon*, II-37; *Marty*, I-189, 248, 356, 388; II-95; *Marty Amok*, II-10; *Marty Feldman Comedy Machine*, I-94; II-10, 12, 118, 131, 132; *Masters of the Congo Jungle*, II-59; *Match of the Day*, I-79, 86, 338, 340, 352, 396, 408, 410; II-12, 77, 84, 154, 157, 170, 189, 190, 212, 224, 226; *Me Mammy*, I-295; *Microbes and Men*, I-381; II-152, 163, 179, 189, 197; *Mind Your Own Business*, I-351; *The Money Programme*, II-45; *Monty Python's Fliegender Zirkus*, I-xii, 14, 16, 21, 31, 75, 83, 88, 89, 102, 115, 175, 180, 182, 186, 233, 264, 295, 298, 322, 332, 340, 350, 372, 376, 393; II-xii, 8, 10, 26, 50, 71, 74, 88, 107, 111, 112, 128, 134, 184, 196, 207; *The Morecambe and Wise Show*, I-194, 320; II-154, 179; *Mother Goose*, I-86; *Music For You*, I-168; *Mystery and Imagination*, I-318; *Not So Much a Programme, More a Way of Life*, I-211; II-46; *Nationwide*, I-168, 187, 280, 391, 410; II-50, 113, 151, 187, 189, 191, 193, 226; *New Faces*, I-168; *News at Ten*, I-174, 314, 320, 385, 391, 412; II-31, 93, 146, 166, 228; *Newsroom*, I-283; *Nine O'Clock News*, I-174; II-51, 85; *Nine Tailors*, II-55; *Not Only—But Also…*, I-15, 64, 68, 295, 301, 354; II-125, 139; *Oh Brother!*, I-380; *Omega Factor*, II-81; *Omnibus*, I-363, 397; II-82, 213; *On the Braden Beat*, I-312; *On the Bright Side*, II-205; "On the Dad's Liver Bachelors at Large," II-146; *Opportunity Knocks*, I-179; *Panorama*, I-49, 116, 136, 137, 139, 168, 185, 187, 209, 228, 269, 327, 330, 335, 356, 384; II-32, 37, 74, 117, 148, 188; *Pantomania*, I-86, 386; *Paul Temple*, I-88, 231, 341; II-23, 81, 104; *PC 49*, I-119; *The Persuaders*, II-132, 136; *Play For Today*, I-228, 231, 268, 363; II-81, 95, 171, 173, 205; *Playschool*, II-88; "Plunder," II-75; *Points of View*, I-91; *Pride and Prejudice*, II-81; *Public Eye*, I-231; II-118; *Puss in Boots*, I-86; *Q5*, I-115, 304; II-5, 25, 80; *Quatermass and the Pit*, I-84; *A Question of Sport*, I-281; *Ragged-Trousered Philanthropists*, I-15; "The Ratings Game," II-147; *Record Breakers*, II-34; "Religion Today," II-87; *Review*, I-137; *Roads to Freedom*, II-8; *Robin Hood*, II-8; *Robinson Crusoe*, I-86; *The Rolf Harris Show*, I-217, 243; II-111; *Rolf's Amazing World of Animals*, I-243; *The Ronnie Barker Yearbook* and *Ronnie Corbett in Bed*, II-10; *Rugby Special*, I-355; *Rutland Weekend Television*, II-351, 356; II-15, 95; *The Saint*, I-77;

II-123, 163; *Seven of One*, I-36; *The Shadow of Mart*, I-358; *Sherlock Holmes*, I-254, 262; *The Shock of the New*, I-13, 42; II-75, 79; *Sid Caesar Invites You*, I-7; *Signal Man*, I-197; *Slater's Bazaar*, II-13; *Society of Film and Television Awards*, II-151, 152; *Softly Softly*, I-115, 176, 231, 241, 264, 302, 330, 381; II-5, 25, 43, 81, 93, 95, 104, 113, 118, 123, 152, 163, 171, 189; *Some Mothers Do 'Ave 'Em*, I-55, 61, 105, 378; II-12, 81, 189; *Songs of Praise*, II-87; *Sorry I'm Single*, I-380; *Sportsnight*, II-113, 151; *Sportsview*, I-4, 176, 310, 325, 338, 396; "*Spot the Loony*," II-140, 141, 147–48, 168, 228; *Spycatcher*, I-13; *Steptoe and Son*, I-168; II-184; *Sunday Night at the Palladium*, I-213, 324, 400; *Sutherland's Law*, II-81; *Take Your Pick*, I-112, 253, 311, 323–24, 326, 354, 369, 373, 376, 377, 379, 412; *Talkback*, II-156; *Telegoons*, II-70; *The Tenant of Wildfell Hall*, II-112, 114, 119; *That Was the Week That Was*, I-211, 303; II-22, 97, 199; *This Is Tom Jones*, I-243, 366; *This Is Your Life*, I-324, 332, 362, 386; II-71, 134; *This Week*, I-49, 237; II-135; *Till Death Us Do Part*, I-52; II-113; *Timeslip*, I-175; II-81; "*Timmy Williams' 'Coffee Time'*," I-289, 292, 412; *To the South Pole with Peter Scott*, II-58, 201; *Toad of Toad Hall*, I-229; *Toast of the Town*, I-58, 119; *Tomorrow's World*, I-4, 183, 313; II-111, 115; *Tonight*, I-271, 295, 333; II-18; *Top of the Pops*, I-331, 352, 369; II-18, 112, 152; *The Three Musketeers*, II-8; *The Troubleshooters*, I-161, 175, 228, 230, 251, 329, 363; II-118; *Tuesday Documentary*, II-77, 223; *Two in Clover*, I-188; *The Two Ronnies*, I-160, 295, 301; II-10, 154, 178; *UFO*, I-231; *University Challenge*, I-4, 382, 383; II-12, 41, 202; *Up Pompeii!*, I-214, 255, 297, 300; II-58, 178, 185; *Up the Junction*, I-242; II-178; "*Up the Palace*," II-149; "*Up Your Pavement*," I-xii, 157, 196, 413; II-185, 206, 229; *Upstairs, Downstairs*, I-61, 301, 330, 388; II-163–64; *Van der Valk*, II-55; *The Very Merry Widow*, II-34; *Warship*, I-228; *The Wednesday Play*, I-100, 105, 175, 231, 259, 309, 363, 378, 388; II-81, 118, 163, 171; *Whack-O!*, I-394; *What's in Store*, II-13; *What's My Line?*, I-386; II-71, 138; *Whicker Down Mexico Way, Whicker Down Under*, and *Whicker On Top of the World*, II-18; *Whicker's World*, II-3, 8, 18, 212, 229; *Whoops, Baghdad!*, I-182; II-27, 81, 179; *The World About Us*, I-49, 223, 404; II-47, 74, 202, 210, 220; *The World At One*, I-280; *World At War*, II-123, 180; *World in Action*, I-49, 194, 384; *The World of Beachcomber*, I-52, 304; *W. Somerset Maugham*, I-141; *Wuthering Heights*, I-251; *Year of the Sex Olympics*, I-309; *Yes, It's the Cathode Ray Tube Show*, I-163, 299; "*Yes It's the Sewage Farm Attendants*," I-157; *Youth Sportsview*, I-310; *Z Cars*, I-16, 60, 61, 118, 145, 175, 176, 231, 251, 255, 296, 302, 314, 318, 330, 363, 381, 388; II-5, 15, 25, 49, 55, 65, 81, 93, 95, 104, 113, 118, 142, 152, 163, 171, 173,

179, 189, 197; US: *The Adventures of Ozzie and Harriet*, I-318; *The Adventures of Superman*, I-60, 107; *All in the Family*, II-210; *Amahl and the Night Visitors*, II-147; *An American Family*, II-205; *Beat the Clock*, II-50, 51, 222; *Ben Casey*, I-146; *Big Valley* and *Bonanza*, I-31, 257; *The Cisco Kid*, I-260; *The Dating Game*, II-147; *David Frost Presents…Frankie Howerd*, I-163, 292; *The Debbie Reynolds Show*, I-312, 314, 316; II-33; *The Dick Powell Show*, I-146; *The Doctors*, I-197; *Dr. Kildare*, I-204, 206, 225, 388, 400, 402–4; II-81, 180, 216, 218–20; *Dragnet 1967*, I-355; *The Dudley Do-Right Show*, I-146; *The Ed Sullivan Show*, I-243, 333; *The Golden Age of Comedy* and *Greece: The Golden Age*, II-163; *The Gumby Show*, I-270; *Gunsmoke*, I-31; *Here's Lucy*, I-355; II-180; *The High Chaparral*, I-31, 257–58; *The Honeymooners*, I-312; *The Howdy Doody Show*, I-270; *I Love Lucy*, I-312, 314, 316, 318; II-27, 38, 180; *I Married Lucy*, II-180; *Ironside*, I-271; *The Jack Benny Show*, I-313; *Leave it to Beaver*, I-318; *The Lone Ranger*, I-31; *Love American Style*, I-100; *Marcus Welby, M.D.*, II-83; *Maude*, II-210; *Maverick*, I-31; *Medical Center*, I-355; *Meet the Press*, I-228; *The Monkees*, I-154, 176; II-205; *Mystery of Animal Behavior*, II-59; *Perry Mason*, I-57, 271; *Petula*, II-136; *Rawhide*, I-31; II-199; *Rowan & Martin's Laugh-In*, I-7, 176, 263, 292; II-24, 51, 55, 125; *Sanford and Son*, II-184; *This is Your Life*, I-324, 332, 362, 386; II-71, 134; *The Tonight Show*, I-350; *Twenty-One*, I-237; *The Twisted Cross*, I-197; *The Undersea World of Jacques Cousteau*, II-18; *The Untouchables*, I-266; *Victoria Regina*, II-132; *The Virginian*, I-385, 394, 409; *Yellowstone Cubs*, II-60; *You Bet Your Life*, I-132; *Your Show of Shows*, I-7
Television Act of 1964, II-38
Temple of Abu Simbel, I-327
10 Downing Street, I-xi, 17, 238, 368; II-xi, 53, 66, 67, 181, 200
"10 Rillington Place" murders, II-110
"ten woods," II-108
The Tenant of Wildfell Hall, Anne Brontë. *See* novels *and* novelists
tennis, I-62, 73, 106, 110, 111, 113, 116–18, 121, 124, 125, 205, 260, 294, 296, 316, 336, 343, 407, 412; II-35, 128, 140, 147, 148, 157, 173, 181, 207, 223, 228; players: Peaches Bartkowicz, I-124; II-147; Cliff Drysdale, I-124; Pancho Gonzales, I-116–17, 260; Ann Haydon-Jones, I-73, 118, 124–25, 267, 296, 343; Lew Hoad, II-140, 147; Billie Jean King, I-118; Jack Kramer, I-118; II-147; Rod Laver, I-118, 125; II-147; Chuck McKinley, I-125; Angela Mortimer, I-125; Charlie Pasarell, I-124; II-147; Tony Roche, I-124; Ken Rosewall, I-118; II-140, 147; Fred Stolle, I-118, 124, 336; Virginia Wade, II-207
Tennyson, Alfred. *See* poets
Tennyson-d'Eyncourt, Eustace Gervais, I-192

"terpsichorean," II-99, 136
terrorism, I-226–27, 253, 290, 386; II-62, 117, 196, 198. *See also* hijackings
Tesler, Brian, I-382
Tess of the D'Urbervilles, Thomas Hardy. *See* novels *and* novelists
test card, I-214–15
"Test Selection Committee," I-311, 324, 325, 411. *See also* cricket
Thalberg, Irving, I-105
thalidomide, I-57–58
Thames. *See* rivers
Thames Ditton, I-287
Thames TV. *See* regional television
Thant, U, I-217
Thatcher, Margaret, I-90, 134, 293, 305, 316, 330, 337, 346, 347, 361, 367, 371, 393; II-52–53, 147, 173, 180, 206
That Was the Week That Was (TW3). *See* television shows
theaters (live), I-7, 14, 16, 17, 22, 27, 32, 38, 38, 42, 75, 86, 93, 96–97, 100, 101, 104–5, 114, 117, 121, 133, 146, 152, 158, 164–65, 170, 172, 175, 186, 214–15, 223–24, 238, 250, 257–58, 285, 296, 303, 332, 337, 343–45, 360, 370, 374, 380, 397, 402, 404, 406, 411, 413; II-15, 20, 21, 27, 28, 33, 35, 36, 38, 42, 50, 91, 95, 97, 104, 107, 112, 120, 121, 125, 127, 130, 148, 150, 167, 190, 193, 197, 213, 218, 220, 222, 227, 229: Aldwych, II-121, 127, 222; Ambassadors, I-172; Apollo, II-33; Dorking Halls ("Dorking Civic Theatre"), I-93, 96, 101, 223, 224, 406; Empire, I-133, 146, 257; II-41; Fortune, I-16, 345; Globe, I-186; II-125, 192, 220; Hackney Empire, II-104; Her Majesty's Theatre (photos), I-343–44; II-50, 91, 130; King's (Glasgow), I-257–58; "Leatherhead Rep," I-81, 100, 104; Mermaid, I-86, 164, 345; "Old Vic," I-38; Palladium, I-86, 213, 324, 352, 400, 401; Pier Theatre (Bournemouth), I-75; Richmond, I-86; The Rose, I-186; Roundhouse, II-32; Royal Court, I-27, 38; II-27, 36; Rugby, I-96; Saville, I-86; St. Martin's, I-172; The Theatre, II-125; Thorndike (Leatherhead), I-86; Wembley Empire Pool, I-86; II-133; Westminster, I-86; Whitehall, I-238; Windmill, I-7, 104
"thesaurus sketch," I-3, 43, 67, 89, 130, 138, 139, 204, 215, 237; II-139
"thing-in-itself," I-334
The Thinker, Rodin. *See* artworks *and* artists
"Third Dynasty," I-337
Third Programme, I-84, 358
Third Reich. *See* Nazi/Nazism
Thirty Years War, I-55, 393–94; II-138
This Is Your Life. *See* radio *and* television shows
"this realm, this England," I-215; II-98
This Sporting Life. *See* films
This Week. *See* television shows
Thomas, Dylan. *See* poets
Thomas, Peter, I-346
Thompson, Kristin, I-153, 362
Thompson, Llewellyn, I-120

"Thorkel," I-6

Thorne House, Ham Common, Richmond (location), I-284

Thorp, Roderick and *The Detective. See* novelists *and* novels

Thorpe, Jeremy, I-186, 255; II-206, 209–10

Thorpebank Road (location), I-102, 222, 226, 227–28, 231–32, 235, 381

347–351 High Street North, Newham, Greater London (photo location), II-13

3 Pierson Road, St. Helier, Jersey (location), II-102

The Three Stooges, I-40

38 and 40 Ludgate Hill (location), I-237, 276; II-137

39 Elers Road, Ealing (location), I-243

33 Wardour Street, Soho (location), I-32

"three-cornered fight," I-307

"three-stage model," I-272; II-37

Thrills and Adventure. See comic books

"Throatwobbler Mangrove," I-22, 155

Thunderball. See films

Thurtle, Ernest, I-365

Tibbenham, Philip, II-189

Tidball, Capt. John C. *See* Civil War (US)

Tiepolo, Giambattista. *See* artists

Tilbury, Essex, II-49

Tillich, Paul, I-28

Tillyard. E.M.W., I-147, 368

Tilsley, Reg, II-55, 66, 216, 218–20

"Tim the Enchanter," I-31, 146, 167

Time. See magazines

Time-Life, II-58, 75, 201

The Times of London. See newspapers

"Timothy." *See* cartoons

Timothy Whites, II-74, 89

"Tinea Pedis," I-362, 382

"tinny and woody" words, II-177, 183, 185, 186, 229

Tio Pepe sherry, I-145

Tiomkin, Dimitri, I-96

Titian. *See* artists

title cards, I-29, 31, 95, 100, 128, 148, 151, 159, 233, 243–44, 303, 343; II-67, 130, 163, 167

titles/honorifics: Baron/Baroness, I-188, 258, 308, 337; II-15, 46, 54, 84, 134; Duke/ Duchess, I-12, 19, 32, 55, 78, 88, 136, 150, 184, 215, 269, 305; II-11, 18, 34, 54, 116, 132, 142, 145, 162, 166, 204; Earl, I-346, 356; Lord/Lady, I-8, 10, 13, 19, 41, 46, 56, 104, 153, 154, 162, 173–74, 177–78, 181, 184, 187, 190, 194, 196, 198, 199, 226, 231, 237, 241, 247, 248, 255, 258, 263, 282–83, 295, 300, 303, 304, 305, 313, 322, 346, 347, 366, 393, 408; II-15, 22, 36, 46, 49, 52, 65, 68, 82, 85, 93, 107, 116, 122, 131, 141, 146, 147, 153, 154, 163, 164, 178, 209, 224; Lord Mayor, I-54, 196, 263, 300, 354, 355; II-199; His/Your Grace, I-180; II-116; His/Her/Your Majesty, I-xi, 34, 75, 135, 245, 250, 319, 324, 343, 344, 347, 356, 389; II-xi, 50, 91, 130, 204; The Right Honourable, I-196; II-15, 30, 35

"Titty," II-168

Tiverton, Devon, II-109

Tizer, I-143; II-101, 109; Barr's and Irn-Bru, I-143

"The Toad Elevating Moment," I-45, 116, 385, 412

Toad the Wet Sprocket, I-116

"toad in the hole," I-188

Toad of Toad Hall. See television shows

"toadie," I-266, 318; II-143

tobacconist, I-76, 77, 213, 221, 229, 231

"Today (I Hear the Robin Sing)," Bill McGuffie, I-337

Today in Parliament. See radio *and* television shows

Todd-AO, I-381

"toff," I-34

Tolkien, J.R.R. *See* novelists

The Tolkien Society, II-10

Tolstoy, Leo. *See* novelists

Tolworth, Greater London, I-3, 14, 21, 411; II-37, 227

Tom Thumb, Fielding. *See* plays *and* playwrights

Tomorrow's World. See television shows

Took, Barry. *See MPFC* extras and walk-ons

toothpaste: Colgate, I-387; II-38; "Crelm," I-360, 361–62, 369, 385, 387, 406; II-38, 222; Crest, I-362, 370, 387; "Darkie," I-315; Euthymol, II-81; Gibbs SR, I-387. *See also* commercials/adverts

Tooting, Greater London, I-365; II-37

Top of the Pops. See television shows

Topcliff, Richard, I-269

Torbay Airport Museum (location), II-184. *See also* museums

Torbay Road (Avon Guest House; South Sands Hotel—locations), I-282

"Torn Jersey," II-53

Torquay, I-44, 172, 191, 230, 257, 261, 278–82, 284–85, 300, 311, 349–51, 353, 355–57, 381, 383–84; II-119

Torquay Rugby (team and location), I-349, 350

Torremolinos, Spain, I-87, 103, 206

Torrey Canyon, II-54, 59, 212

"Tory." *See* Conservative Party

Totnes, Devon, I-154

Tough Guys Agency. *See* talent (job) agencies

Toulouse-Lautrec, Henri de. *See* artists

"Tour de France riders," II-190

tourism/tourists, I-46, 73, 87, 90, 102–3, 188, 193, 198, 210, 223, 228, 231, 236, 258, 287, 302, 315, 413; II-10, 61, 63–66, 68–70, 73–74, 76, 81, 89, 90, 96, 190, 195, 204, 228–29

tower blocks. *See* housing

Tower Bridge, I-227

Tower Hamlets, I-227; II-12

Town and Country Planning Act of 1947, I-203

Town Centre of Walton-on-Thames, I-24, 45

Townsend, Group Captain Peter, I-52

Trade Union Congress (TUC), I-289, 373; II-83

trade unions, I-249–50, 253, 289–90, 293, 303, 311, 372–74, 381, 384, 387–89, 394; II-15,

22, 53, 67–68, 72, 83, 86, 137, 141, 143, 156, 190, 196

Trafalgar Square (and area), I-172, 237–38, 343, 379, 387, 392–93; II-113, 119, 134, 31, 149

trains, I-5, 18, 22, 44, 47, 53, 79, 82, 100, 110, 113, 114, 120, 124, 129, 174, 177, 182, 185, 192, 196, 210, 233, 289, 344, 347, 363–64, 366–70, 390, 393, 396, 397, 400, 406, 407; II-26, 29, 54, 75, 109, 118, 119, 124, 165, 182, 183, 187, 201, 212, 213, 216, 222, 223; "bogies," I-366, 367; British Rail, I-106, 127, 129, 134, 197, 369, 407; II-30, 223; Civil War Union train, I-344; Goldsworthy Gurney, I-344; "Holidaymaker Special," I-363–64; II-149; Inter-City Rail, I-134; "level crossing," I-366; "shunt," I-366, 369; "stopping train," I-369; timetables, I-26, 221; II-360, 364, 370, 405; trainspotting, I-22, 44, 110, 113, 124, 196, 367, 390; stations, I-114, 120, 125, 198, 222, 233–34, 287–88, 363, 368, 369, 382, 393; II-26, 30, 187, 201

trainspotting. *See* trains

transactions (successful/failed), I-30, 50, 72, 73, 87, 101, 127, 161, 165–66, 235, 254, 262, 350, 366, 369, 379; II-98, 152, 174, 176

"transatlantic," I-273; II-182

transitions, I-xii, 5, 15, 23, 42, 81, 90, 129, 131, 139, 144, 154, 156, 159, 167, 185, 190, 199, 206, 209, 212, 241, 245, 253–54, 263, 275, 281–82, 302, 304, 314, 316, 320, 325, 328, 331, 332, 337, 350, 367, 379, 393; II-xii, 3, 8, 27, 34, 36, 60, 108, 125, 137, 147, 165, 168, 191. *See also* links/linking

"transport café," II-109

Transport House, I-237

Transworld International, I-74

Traveller's Companion press, II-127

"travelogue music," I-360

"treacle," I-337, 387

Treasure Island, Stevenson. *See* novels *and* novelists

Treaty of Utrecht, I-25, 217, 394

Treaty of Westphalia, I-393–94; II-138

trees, I-9, 13, 26, 50, 55, 56, 71, 146, 156–57, 159, 163, 166, 169, 193–94, 204, 217, 282, 312, 343, 348, 396, 406, 408–9, 413; II-35, 104, 110, 112–13, 128, 134, 135, 166, 173, 202, 210, 212, 222, 224, 225, 229

Trelawney, Squire, II-78

"trencherman," II-138

Tretchikoff, V.G., and *Chinese Girl. See* artists *and* artworks

Trevelyan, G.M. and *The History of England,* I-25, 55, 378, 394; II-41, 133, 137, 168, 182

Trevor-Roper, Hugh, I-179

Trident, I-262–63

Trigorin, II-37–38

Trinity College, Cambridge. *See* Cambridge University

Tristram Shandy, Sterne. *See* novels *and* novelists

Triumph Herald, I-347

Triumph of the Will. See films

troll dolls, I-246, 247

trolley, I-262, 276; II-174
"trollope." *See* slang/slurs/idoms
Trondheim, Norway. *See* Europe: Norway
The Tropic of Capricorn, Miller. *See* novels *and* novelists
Trotsky, Leon (and Trotskyism), I-377, 379, 410, 413; II-71, 101, 104–9, 226, 229
"The Troubles." *See* Northern Ireland
Trubshaw, Captain Brian, I-29, 46
Trubshawe, Michael, I-47, 237
Truman's beer and pubs, I-331
"Trumpington," II-14
"try," I-358. *See also* rugby football
Tse-tung, Mao, I-284, 293, 296, 301, 334, 358, 367, 377, 379; II-16, 23, 75, 102, 104, 106–7, 109
"tuck shop," I-394
Tuck-Away, II-184
Tudor/Tudors, I-xii, 18, 72, 151, 230, 268, 287, 337, 345, 413; II-xii, 43, 45, 98, 121, 123–28, 134, 181, 183, 229
Tuesday Documentary, II-77, 89, 223
Tunbridge Wells, II-109
Tuohy, Denis. *See* Joan Bakewell
Turkish bath, I-308
Turner, J.M.W. *See* artists
Turner, Tina, I-328
Tussolini, K., I-185
Tuvey, Roy, I-182
TV Times. See magazines
12 Whitehall (location), I-238
12, 14 and 19–20 King Street, Richmond, Surrey (locations), I-377; II-96
20 Edenfield Gardens, Worcester Park, Surrey (location), I-59, 83
25 Goldhawk Road, Hammersmith and Fulham (location), II-184
24 and/or 28 New Broadway, Ealing (location), I-128; II-27
"22a Wimpole Street," I-78
Twickenham, I-xii, 233; II-xii, 12, 13, 20, 30, 33, 96; Rail Bridge (location), I-233; II-33; Rail Station (location), II-30
"twin set and pearls," II-171, 181, 185, 196
Twiss, Frank Roddam, I-313
Two Gentlemen Sharing. See novels/prose literature
"two hundred cigarettes," I-348
"2LO" broadcasting, I-321
278–280 Uxbridge Road, Hammersmith and Fulham (location), II-xii, 127
261 High Street, Ealing (Bendix Laundrette, location), I-56
232 High Street, Exeter (location), II-179
Tynan, Kenneth, I-332–33, 382; II-87
"tyranny of the punchline," I-202
Tzou, Chang, I-342

Ulster, II-63, 175
Ulster Unionist Party, I-188
Uncle Toby, I-73; II-59, 103, 135. *See also Tristram Shandy*
"Uncle Tom," I-324
"The Underground," II-4, 30, 79, 124, 128
undertakers, I-73, 143, 171–72, 176, 182, 201, 205, 207, 239, 294, 366, 385; II-

Unger, Roberto, I-13
Unit 9 Shopping Precinct, Acton High Street (location), I-35
"unit-trust" scheme, II-38
United Nations, I-365, 378
United Service Club, Pall Mall, I-173
United States. *See* America *and* California, etc
universities, I-4, 11, 16, 19, 22, 32, 32, 44, 59, 64, 82, 93, 122–23, 144, 164, 179, 181, 185, 192, 236, 248, 255, 275, 279, 290, 291, 297, 302, 304–5, 313, 315, 317, 322–25, 333, 339, 342, 343, 348, 355, 364, 368, 374, 382–83, 391, 394, 407, 410; II-xi, 12, 14, 15, 17, 32, 41, 69, 72, 76, 79–80, 84–85, 88, 107, 117, 146, 148, 170, 172, 174, 175, 181, 191, 193, 202, 204, 207–8, 223, 226
University Challenge. See television shows
University of the Air (Open University), I-322, 410; II-117, 172, 175
"university wits," I-xi, 16, 144, 181
"unknown joke," I-22, 170
"unseen translation," I-308
"Up, Up and Away," Fifth Dimension, I-79
uranium mining, I-368
Uris, Leon. *See* novelists/prose writers
usher, I-61, 313
USSR. *See* Russia
"Utility Scheme." *See* G-Plan
Utrillo, Maurice. *See* artists
Uxbridge, I-11, 132, 229
Uxbridge Road, Ealing, I-xii, 56, 81, 85, 139, 151, 231, 407; II-

Valachi, Joseph, I-135
Valentino, Rudolph, I-377
Valenzuela, Laurita, I-341
Vallauris, France, I-11–12
Van Damm, Sheila, I-7
Vanderbeek, Stan, I-66
Van der Post, Laurens, II-143
Van Doren, Charles, I-237
Van Dyck, Anthony. *See* artists
Van Eyck, Jan. *See* artists
Van Gogh, Vincent. *See* artists
Vandals and Genseric, I-311
Vanguard, I-262–63
Vanity Fair. See magazines
Vass, Baillie. *See* Alec Douglas-Home
vaudeville/music hall, I-9–10, 14, 23, 40, 48, 108, 113, 116, 138, 146, 203, 209, 221, 247, 254, 257, 271, 299, 303, 313, 320, 329–30; 4, 41–42, 55, 57–58, 60, 95, 106, 127, 180, 185
"VC" (Victoria Cross), I-383
Veblen, Thorstein. *See* novelists/prose writers
vegetarianism, I-215
Velázquez, Diego. *See* artists
The Velvet Underground, II-104
"Veni, Vidi, Vici," I-37
Venus de Milo. See artworks
Vercotti, Dino and Luigi, I-127, 131, 139, 141, 156, 158, 170, 201, 203, 213, 215, 231, 233–35, 237–38, 268, 283, 407; II-118, 194, 223
Verity, Frank, I-211
Vermeer, Jan. *See* artists

Verne, Jules, II-150
Vernon, Richard, I-82
Versailles, I-71, 377; II-164, 207
Vespasian, I-370
vicar/vicarage. *See* religion
Victoria (and Victorian), I-9, 28, 33, 38, 40, 46–48, 64, 66, 80–82, 88, 112, 114, 167, 206, 216, 223, 239, 241, 242, 246, 251, 271, 275–76, 280, 281, 287–88, 335, 347, 351, 373, 383, 389, 393, 411, 413; II-40, 42, 50, 54, 78, 81, 83, 115, 128, 132–33, 147, 151, 154–55, 168, 170–71, 173–76, 180, 187, 188–90, 201, 203, 227, 229
Victoria and Albert Museum (V&A). *See* art
Vienna Circle, I-344
Vietnam War, I-38, 89, 95, 103, 106, 137, 138, 140, 165, 179, 240, 271, 293, 354, 363, 366; II-79, 83, 84, 89, 120, 182, 197, 198
Viking, I-22–23, 28, 108, 160, 325, 333, 371, 381, 383; II-5, 7, 10, 11, 13, 50, 168
"village idiot." *See* idiots
"*vin ordinaire*," I-170; II-13, 18
Vine, David, I-23
The Virginian. See "television shows"
Visconti, Luchino, I-206, 297, 413; II-40, 94, 44, 46, 48–49, 229
Visigoths and Alaric, I-311
VisNews, I-18, 135, 357, 369, 395–97; II-93, 105, 211–13
Vitti, Monica, II-42, 46
vittler, I-128
"V-joke," I-3, 23, 408
"Volare," Dean Martin, II-49
Voltaire. *See* novelists/prose writers
Von Braun, Werner, I-16
Von Bülow, Bernhard, II-168
Von Goethe, J.W., I-333–34
Von Ribbentrop, Joachim, I-178, 185, 191, 193, 194, 197, 199
Von Stroheim, Erich. *See* film directors
Von Tirpitz, Alfred, II-167–68
Von Zeppelin, Ferdinand, II-161, 164, 166–69, 229
Vox Pops, I-12, 24, 26, 48, 79, 81, 93, 102, 127, 130, 141, 143, 156, 167, 184, 190, 195, 201, 208, 240, 250, 264, 275, 308, 311, 348, 355, 360, 382, 410, 413; II-36, 51, 72, 81, 141, 146, 208, 226, 229
voyeurism, I-42, 147, 171; II-181
Vrancic, Faust and *Machinae Novae*, II-187
V-rockets, I-23; II-69
"V-sign," I-392; II-89
vulgarity, I-22, 28, 85, 127, 134, 272, 292, 299; II-63, 66, 151, 165, 167

"W12." *See* postal codes
WAC (Written Archives Collection, by file): T12/1,082: I-4, 6, 8–10, 12, 14–15, 17–18, 21, 25, 31, 32, 67, 78, 168, 171, 208, 214, 187, 395; II-13, 211; T12/1,083: I-4, 9, 10, 12–16, 21, 29, 31–33, 36, 38–39, 43–44, 48, 51, 55, 56, 59–60, 64, 75, 83, 91, 105, 157, 161, 285, 395; T12/1,084: I-xii, 24, 35, 51–53, 55, 58–60, 67, 395; II-xii, 211; T12/1,085: I-67, 73, 75–76, 108, 395; T12/1,086: I-65, 82, 88, 92, 122, 141, 159,

167, 395; II-200, 211; T12/1,087: I-96, 97, 108, 395; T12/1,088: I-93, 95, 97–98, 105, 107, 109, 112, 115, 122–23, 125, 395; T12/1,089: I-129–30, 134–35, 140, 395; T12/1,090: I-144–46, 148–49, 153–54, 395; T12/1,091: I-157, 160, 163–64, 168, 395; T12/1,092: I-173–76, 179, 182–83, 396; T12/1,093: I-75, 185, 187, 190, 193, 200, 253, 396; T12/1,094: I-67, 185, 199, 202–6, 208–9, 211–13, 215–16, 300, 396; T12/1,242: I-32, 35, 51–52, 56, 60, 69, 75, 95, 97, 102, 104–5, 108, 131, 134, 138, 145–46, 153, 157, 164, 188, 226, 228, 231, 245, 247, 251, 258, 273, 280, 286, 293–94, 300, 302, 308, 314–15, 323, 325–26, 337, 342, 357, 378, 381, 396; II-171, 212; T12/1,413: I-147, 242, 245, 287, 291, 328, 331, 337, 392, 396; II-113, 118, 212; T12/1,414: I-361, 369–70, 396; T12/1,415: I-386, 388, 390–93, 396; II-32, 212; T12/1,416: I-222, 226, 228, 230, 243, 246–47, 252, 257, 261, 278, 281–82, 284–85, 287, 300, 345, 349, 350, 356–57, 361–62, 365, 371, 381–83, 391, 396; II-191, 212; T12/1,417: I-223, 228, 229, 235, 237, 248, 396; T12/1,418: I-264, 268, 270, 314, 396; II-26, 212; T12/1,426: II-5, 8, 17, 212; T12/1,427: II-22, 26–28, 30, 32–33, 36, 212; T12/1,428: I-233, 242, 357, 375, 396; II-10, 12, 15, 23, 25–26, 32–33, 35, 38–39, 40, 43, 45, 46, 48–49, 54–56, 59, 66, 79, 82, 92, 114, 118–19, 123, 125, 127, 142, 146, 148, 153, 212–13; T12/1,429: I-328–31, 335, 337, 397; T12/1,430: I-279, 282, 284, 287, 313, 316, 319, 341, 397; II-77, 213; T12/1,431: I-268–69, 273, 397; T12/1,432: I-341, 347–48, 397; T12/1,433: I-312, 316, 318, 319, 323, 324, 397; T12/1,434: I-291, 301–2, 397; T12/1,435: I-351–53, 357–58, 397; T12/1,436: I-257–59, 262, 397; T12/1,437: I-240–42, 244, 246, 248–49, 397; T12/1,440: II-104–6, 108–9, 213; T12/1,441: II-64–66, 69–70, 72–73, 76, 213; T12/1,442: II-51, 54–55, 57, 213; T12/1,443: II-111–13, 213; T12/1,444: II-92–93, 95–99, 145, 213; T12/1,445: I-251, 397; II-43–46, 48–49, 52, 68, 92, 147, 213; T12/1,446: II-77, 81–88, 213; T12/1,447: I-82, 397; II-122, 124–25, 128, 213; T12/1,460: II-110, 112, 114–15, 132–33, 136–38, 151, 213; T12/1,461: II-150, 152–57, 213; T12/1,462: II-140–43, 145–49, 156, 214; T12/1,467: II-171–75, 214; T12/1,468: II-188–93, 214; T12/1,469: II-161–63, 165–67, 172, 178, 180–82, 184–86, 189, 195–97, 199, 200–3, 209, 214. *See also* Appendix A
Wade, Virginia. *See* tennis: players
"waggled," I-338
Wagner, Richard ("Dickie"), I-332–33, 404; II-44, 75, 209, 220
Waite, Keith. *See* cartoons: cartoonists
Waiting for Godot, Beckett, I-82
Wales (and Welsh), I-14, 17, 20, 32, 53, 58, 60, 67, 92–93, 102, 120, 154, 156, 164, 174, 178, 190, 194, 221, 224–25, 238, 243, 253, 299, 301–2, 309, 321, 336, 346, 350, 353, 355, 366, 368, 372–74, 384, 386–87, 389, 390,

392, 394, 402, 404; II-29, 49, 60, 65, 68–69, 72, 82, 111, 119, 132, 141–42, 148–49, 153, 155, 164, 166, 182, 194, 203, 206, 213, 220
walk-ons/extras, I-10, 16, 23, 52–53, 56, 61, 67, 69, 97, 130, 145, 156–57, 162, 169, 170–71, 176, 178, 223, 240–41, 244, 251, 255, 259, 287, 296–97, 308–9, 318–19, 329–30, 333, 341, 351, 357, 378, 381–82, 391, 406, 413; II-5, 8, 15, 22, 25, 66, 81, 93, 104, 106, 113, 118, 127, 152, 171–72, 185, 189, 197, 205, 207, 209, 222, 229. *See also* MPFC extras and walk-ons
"walk-out," I-383
Walker, Peter, I-346; II-59, 86
Wallace, George, II-145
Wallace, Lew, *Ben Hur*. *See* novelists *and* novels
Wallington, Sutton, I-364
Wall's, I-69, 203, 393
Walpole, Horace and Hugh, I-25; II-98, 106, 112
Walpole Park, I-131, 133, 243, 245; II-11
Walsingham, Frances and Francis, II-123, 128–29
Walton Bridge, Walton Bridge Road, Shepperton, Middlesex (location), I-285, 382
Walton Carpets, I-262
Walton-on-Thames, I-15, 21, 22, 24, 45, 99, 252, 261, 268–70, 273, 275–76, 285, 393
"Walton Street," I-276
Walton, William, I-43, 187, 400, 402–4; II-54–55, 93, 192–93, 213, 216, 218–20
"Waltz from Faust," Gounod, II-108, 219
Wandsworth, I-4; II-12, 108, 198
War of the Roses, I-18
War of the Worlds, H.G. Wells. *See* novels *and* novelists
Warbeck, Perkin, I-196
Ward, Dame Irene, I-306
Ward, Jay and Bill Scott. *See Rocky and Bullwinkle*
Ward, Vernon, I-64
Warhol. Andy, I-230; II-32
Waring, Eddie, I-3, 4, 9, 19, 23, 48, 163, 187, 201, 208, 313, 370, 412; II-35, 157, 228
Warner, Jack, I-79; II-43
Warner, Plum, I-325
Warner, Sylvia Townsend, I-295
Warsaw Pact, I-63
Warwick (Ambrose Dudley), II-129
Warwickshire, I-36, 187, 223, 354; II-208, 210
"Washington Post March," J.P. Sousa, I-144, 154, 338, 400
The Waste Land, T.S. Eliot. *See* poems *and* poets
waterbutt, I-370
Wates Ltd., II-112, 114
Watford, Hertfordshire, I-159, 271, 349, 358
Watkins, Peter. *See* film directors
Watney's Red Barrel, I-73, 413; II-61, 63, 76, 109, 228
Watson, Alan, I-297
Watt, James, II-143
Watteau, Antoine. *See* artists
wattles, I-133, 141, 348

"Watutsi," I-338
Waugh, Evelyn. *See* novelists
The Way of All Flesh, Butler. *See* novels *and* novelists
Wayne, Naunton and Basil Radford, I-321
Wayne, John, I-146, 355, 358; II-62, 72, 94,
"We are not amused," I-240–41, 250–51; II-175
Webb, Captain Matthew, I-159, 169
Webb, Len and Dot, II-197, 199
"Webb's Wonder(ful)," I-351, 358
The Wednesday Play. *See* television shows
Weetabix, II-89, 202
Weimar period, I-146, 186
Weisz, Victor ("Vicky"). *See* cartoons: cartoonists
Welch, Raquel, I-174, 216, 233, 251
"Welcome All Sexual Athletes," I-309, 406
Weldon, Huw, II-39
Weldon, Joan, I-110
welfare state, I-87, 119, 134, 208, 234, 236, 244–45, 393; II-10, 19, 83
"well hung," I-338
"We'll Keep a Welcome," I-309
Welles, Orson. *See* film directors
Wellings, Bob, II-189
Wellington boots ("wellies"), I-78, 84, 91
Wellington Close, Walton-on-Thames (location), I-22, 252, 261
Wellington, Duke of, I-78
Welsh harp, I-14, 154
"Welsh national costume," I-154
"weltbild," I-230
Wembley Stadium, I-215–16, 281, 327, 338, 376, 384, 396, 406; II-24, 133, 212, 222
"Wensleydale, Mr.," I-29; II-65
Wesker, Arnold, I-38
"Wessex," I-316; II-115
West, Mae, I-5; II-65
West, Peter, I-338; II-157
West Country, I-276
West End (London). *See* London
West Hartlepool, I-182
West London Radio, II-127
West Yorkshire, I-242, 246; II-63, 78
Westminster Bank Limited, I-312, 323
Westminster Bridge, II-187–88, 193
Western Electric, I-384
Western films. *See* film genres *and* films
"Western Front," I-4; II-186
Western National bus, I-253
Westminster, Greater London, I-xi, 19, 22, 40, 62, 75, 164, 181, 287, 293, 307, 318, 324, 325, 330, 356, 393; II-xi, 11, 12, 24, 82, 187, 188, 193
Westminster Abbey, I-22, 325, 356, 393
Weston, Maggie, I-140
Weston-Super-Mare, I-56, 185, 186, 225
West Park Pharmacy and Cheapside Post Office (locations), II-102
West Sussex, I-6, 10, 161, 364; II-12, 145, 209
"wet things," II-193
Weybridge, Surrey, I-192, 393; II-199
What Do People Do All Day? Richard Scarry, I-51, 148
"What the Butler Saw" mutoscope, I-71

"*Whatever Happened to Baby Jane? See* novels *and* films

"What's all this then?" I-238, 277, 309; II-52

What's My Line? See television shows

Wheatcroft, Geoffrey, I-80

Wheeler, Mortimer, I-329, 336

"When Does a Dream Begin?" Innes and McGuffie, II-177, 186, 220, 229

"When the Roses Bloom Again," II-200

Which? See magazines

Whicker, Alan, I-187, 212, 271, 295, 413; II-18, 141

"Whiskey in the Jar," I-394–95

Whisky a Go Go, I-32

Whistler, James McNeill. *See* artists

Whitby and "The Whitby Lad," II-119

White City, I-84, 122, 132; II-184

White City Stadium, I-122; II-184

"white flannels and boater," I-370

White House, I-103, 365, 392; II-52, 105

Whitehouse, Mary, I-20, 42, 71, 138, 147, 169, 181, 214, 309, 333; II-4, 37, 43, 48, 79, 81, 83–90, 99, 148 156, 180

Whitehall, I-19, 74, 118, 237, 238, 303; II-134, 186

Whitehall Theatre, I-238, 303

White Hart Hotel car park (location), I-161

white paper. *See* green papers

"white rule." *See* minority rule

Whittington Hospital, St. Mary's Wing, Highgate Hill, London (location), I-294

Whiz Comics, II-35

"Whizzo": butter, I-3, 11, 24, 35, 45, 52, 108, 405, 413; II-38, 80, 221, 229; chocolate, I-24, 101. *See also* commercials/adverts

wickets. *See* cricket: terminology

Wide Angle. See magazines

"wide-boy type," I-30, 370

Wideberg, Bo. *See* film directors

Wigan, Greater Manchester, I-49, 215

Wiggin, Maurice, I-144–45

Wilcox, Desmond, I-138, 297

The Wild Bunch. See films

The Wild One. See films

"wild slogging," I-326

Wilde, Marjorie. *See* MPFC extras and walk-ons

Wilde, Oscar. *See* playwrights

Wilder, Thornton, I-384

Wilkie, Bernard, I-61

Wilkie, Thomas A., II-32, 212

Williams, Dorian, II-39

Williams, George Walton. *See* playwrights

Williams, Joan, II-32

Williams, Rt. Rev. Ronald R., II-45

Williams, Shirley, I-296

Willis, Peter, I-161

Williton, West Somerset, I-187

Wilmut, Roger, I-11, 45, 160, 163, 167, 168, 197, 212, 279

Wilson, A.N. and *After the Victorians*, I-80, 82, 88, 112, 206, 271; II-154, 205

"Wilson, Arthur," I-147, 152, 154–55

Wilson, Harold (PM), I-34, 53, 55, 114, 159, 162, 177, 180, 188, 193–94, 203, 221, 225,

237, 249–50, 255, 256, 285, 289, 303, 319, 347, 388, 390; II-19, 21, 22, 37, 59, 66–67, 80–82, 104, 117, 130, 137, 142, 146, 163–64, 173, 181, 199, 200

Wilson, Robert, I-31

Wilson, Sandy, I-81, 95, 412; II-61, 65, 76, 228

Wiltshire, I-4, 18, 159, 336, 364–65; II-138

Wimbledon, I-14, 62, 110–11, 113–14, 117–18, 124–25, 194, 296, 316, 320; II-37, 63, 95, 116, 147

"Wimbleton fortnight," I-125

"Wimpy, J. Wellington," II-27; and Wimpy's, I-252, 309–10; II-27

Winchester Assizes. *See* assizes

Winchester, Hampshire, I-389; II-188, 199

Winchester '73. See films

Windmill Theatre, I-7, 104

Windsor, Berkshire, I-44, 285, 316, 369; II-69, 126, 145

Windsor Castle, I-4; II-43, 57, 95, 145, 203

Windsor (family name), II-18, 98, 128, 134, 171, 181

"Wingco," II-186

"Wink, wink, nudge, nudge," I-50, 53, 61, 85, 147, 192, 199, 229, 238, 360, 413; II-152, 170, 202, 229

Winn, Anona, I-183

Winters, Mike and Bernie, I-36

"Wintrex," I-354, 359

Wisborough Green, West Sussex, I-24, 364

Wisden Cricketer of the Year. *See* cricket

"Wislon," II-66

Withers, Googie, I-122

Wittgenstein, Ludwig, I-340, 377; II-82

Wodehouse, P.J. *See* novelists/prose writers

Woking, Surrey, I-24, 113; II-199

Wolfenden Report, I-111, 203, 207; II-183

Wollongong, New South Wales, I-348

Wolstenholme, Ken, I-176, 313, 329, 338; II-84

Wolverhampton, West Midlands, I-57, 87, 90, 145–46, 216, 290, 297; II-63, 72, 90, 204; Grammar School, I-46

"Wombat, Harness," I-31, 264, 271, 277, 411

women (depictions/treatments of), I-20, 22, 27–28, 30, 34, 44–45, 49, 55, 64, 66, 70–72, 76, 79, 81–82, 87–88, 90, 103, 105, 111, 118, 120, 124, 127–30, 133, 135, 139, 140, 144, 147, 150, 160, 163, 167, 178, 187–88, 202, 205, 207, 213, 227–28, 231, 233, 249, 269, 288, 291, 303, 332, 353, 395–96, 406; II-8, 24, 39, 52, 89, 95, 114, 125, 171, 209

Women's Auxiliary Air Force (WAAF), II-44, 185

Women's Institute, I-26, 39, 49, 50, 109, 153, 327, 338, 379, 384, 395–96, 413; II-118, 211–12, 229. *See also* Appendix A

Women's Royal Army Corps, II-60

The Wooden Horse, Williams. *See* novels/prose literature

Wood, Duncan, I-375; II-26, 38, 43, 70, 73, 92

Wood, Ed. *See* film directors

Wood, Rt. Hon. Richard, I-346; II-30

"wooden spoon," I-306

Woodlawn Road, Hammersmith and Fulham (location), I-185

Woodley, Harry. *See* MPFC extras and walk-ons

Woods, Peter, II-186

Woods Close School, I-235

Woody Woodpecker. *See* animation: characters

Woolf, Virginia. *See* novelists/prose writers

"Woolton Pie" and "Brown Windsor Soup," II-47

Woolwich, Bishop of, I-28, 266, 368

"Woppi's," I-308–10

Worcester Park, Surrey, (location), I-59, 83

words (power/shifting meaning), I-22, 28, 37, 55, 113, 135, 189, 191, 217, 238, 268, 342–43; II-24, 103, 121, 123, 125, 144, 177, 181, 186, 224, 226, 229. *See also* naming/power of names

Wordsworth, William. *See* poets

working-class (and middle class), I-17, 26, 29, 34, 36, 37, 41, 51, 78, 131, 144, 149, 167, 180, 193, 198, 229, 231, 238, 245, 260, 277, 318, 345, 352, 367, 374–75, 387, 413; II-36, 58, 64, 69, 78–79, 84–85, 112, 175, 127, 207, 229

The World About Us. See television shows

The World Around Us. See television shows

The World at One. See television shows

The World at War. See television shows

World Cup, I-33, 147, 152, 185, 216, 329, 338, 361, 384; II-24

World in Action. See television shows

World Peace Congress, I-7

World War I, I-49, 94, 97, 123, 130, 141, 157, 179, 185, 191, 194, 196, 278, 309, 362, 372–73, 377, 384, 387, 389, 390, 405–6; II-22–23, 26, 42, 51, 54, 93, 98, 110–12, 128, 134, 143, 164, 168, 171, 176, 183, 186, 207, 221, 228. *See also* battles

World War II, I-6–7, 9–10, 17, 20, 22–23, 38, 62–63, 67, 74, 80, 82, 86, 91, 93, 100, 107, 125, 137, 145–46, 173, 175–76, 178, 179, 181, 185–86, 188, 192, 196, 198, 204–5, 209–10, 214, 221, 224, 227, 230, 233, 263, 281, 283, 287, 318, 322, 343, 346–47, 353–54, 367, 373, 378, 380, 382, 395, 400; II-18, 23, 26, 31, 40–41, 46, 47, 58, 92, 102, 115, 134, 143–44, 149, 156, 179, 182, 184–88, 198, 200–1, 211, 216. *See also* battles

World's End, I-241, 289–90

Wormwood Scrubs, I-203, 281, 383

The Wren Church of St. Martin Within Ludgate (location), I-276; II-137

Wren, Christopher, II-75, 136

Wrexham, Wales, II-191, 194

"writerly" text. *See* printed script asides

Written Archives Collection. *See* WAC

Wuthering Heights. See novels *and* television shows

Wyeth, Katya. *See* MPFC extras and walk-ons

Wyler, William. *See* film directors

Wyman, Bill and Charlie Watts, I-328

Wyndham, John (architect), II-43

Wyndham, John and *The Midwich Cuckoos*, I-114

Wyngarde, Peter, I-30; II-139

xenophobia, I-90, 329, II-18–19, 84
Xiaoping, Deng, I-293
"Xmas," I-207

"yah boo" (and "yarooh"), I-380
Yates, Edmund, II-153
Yeats, W.B. and *The Lake Isle of Innisfree*. *See* poets *and* poems
The Yellow Submarine. *See* films
Yeovil, Somerset, II-119
"Yes/No Interlude," I-326, 376–77, 379
Yiddish, I-58, 105, 235, 304, 381; II-139

YMCA, I-12; II-109
yokel, I-42, 200
York, North Yorkshire, I-113, 182, 196, 222, 293; II-119
York, Duke of, I-215; II-142
Yorkshire, I-20, 23, 27, 45 49, 52, 62, 91, 96, 128, 132, 144, 150, 153, 159–60, 173, 177, 183, 192, 210, 215, 239, 242, 246, 248, 250, 293, 317–18, 325, 332–33, 338, 370, 389; II-15, 36, 63, 76, 78, 112, 119, 151, 153, 157, 179, 198, 200, 210
The Young Generation, I-179; II-109, 133, 171
Young, Victor, II-150
Young's Bakeries, II-99
You Only Live Twice. *See* films

Your Show of Shows. *See* television shows
The Yukon, II-201
"Yummy, Yummy, Yummy," Resnick and Levine, I-360, 370, 401, 413

"Zanie," I-253, 263
"Zatapathique," I-49, 171, 237, 307, 343, 352
Zeiss Ikon cameras, II-135
"zero population," I-203
Ziegler, Anne and Webster Booth, I-310
Ziggy Stardust, I-148; II-104
zinc, I-49, 93, 106, 152, 197, 406
"zodiacal signs," II-139
Zog, King. *See* kings
"Zulu," I-21, 94, 100, 162–63, 168, 178
"Zulu knobkerrie," I-257; II-188

About the Author

Darl Larsen was born in California in 1963 and has been part of the film faculty at Brigham Young University since 1998. He took degrees at UC Santa Barbara, Brigham Young University, and Northern Illinois University. At BYU he is professor of media arts and animation and teaches film and popular culture studies. He lives in beautiful Provo, Utah, with his family.